# 3D MODELING
# IN AUTOCAD

## Second Edition

## Creating and Using 3D Models in AutoCAD 2000, 2000i, 2002, 2004

John E. Wilson

CRC Press
Taylor & Francis Group
Boca Raton  London  New York

CRC Press is an imprint of the
Taylor & Francis Group, an **informa** business

First published 2002 by CMP Books

This edition published 2015 by Focal Press

Published 2021 by CRC Press
Taylor & Francis Group
6000 Broken Sound Parkway NW, Suite 300
Boca Raton, FL 33487-2742

CRC Press is an imprint of Taylor & Francis Group, an Informa business

No claim to original U.S. Government works

ISBN 13: 978-1-57820-091-7 (pbk)

**Visit the Taylor & Francis Web site at**
**http://www.taylorandfrancis.com**

**and the CRC Press Web site at**
**http://www.crcpress.com**

Cover art:          Damien Castaneda

# Table of Contents

## Chapter 14    Visualizing and Using 3D Solid Models . . . . . . 347

# Preface

With mechanical engineering degree in hand, John Wilson cut his CAD teeth in Idaho beginning with AutoCAD 2.5. Joining project teams that numbered 8,000-plus, he designed nuclear reactors for the Department of Energy back in the days before nuclear power developed a less than stellar reputation. Wilson was a member of project teams in charge of designing fuel rods and constructing experiments that would place these rods under severe conditions to determine their meltdown threshold. Talk about the vital application of design principles and the need for high quality — and accurate — design tools!

His Idaho days also saw Wilson designing fuel rods for use in nuclear submarines, but a yearning for city life and independence drew him to Minneapolis where he set up shop as an independent designer. He submitted his first feature to an upstart CAD publication in 1991. His article on fonts that ran in the September issue of CADENCE turned into a four-part series. And that became the mark of John Wilson. He soon earned the reputation as a writer who was a master of his material, and one who preferred covering subjects comprehensively.

When AutoCAD with Release 10 introduced 3D capabilities, Wilson went to work mastering them in short order. By Release 11, he had proposed a series of articles on how to plumb AutoCAD's 3D depths. The June 1993 issue of CADENCE debuted Wilson's 3D tips for AutoCAD, and he hasn't missed turning in a column since.

With the current tome, I'll go on record saying that Wilson has written the book on AutoCAD and 3D. This book has everything you could possibly want to know about how to take advantage of AutoCAD's 3D features, including the latest changes introduced with AutoCAD 2002. Wilson jokingly says that the book probably even sports a thing or two about 3D that you'd rather not know. But that's a mark of his infectious self-deprecating humor. You do want to know everything you can about AutoCAD's 3D capabilities, if it's your software of choice. And John Wilson takes you through each 3D feature step-by-step in his usual clear, concise and insightful manner.

If you're an architect, Wilson will show you how to render simple models for your client proposals. And for those of you who belong to the MCAD discipline, Wilson can show you how to achieve about 80 percent of all the solid modeling capabilities you'll ever need for modeling parts and machinery. And you'll find using AutoCAD in this way to be easier in many cases than work-ing with a parametric modeler.

Today John Wilson continues his very successful independent one-person business designing waste-water treatment facilities and working on other environmental projects. A team of one is a bit smaller than one of 8,000, and water treatment doesn't necessarily have the adrenaline-boost-ing affect of fuel-rod experiments, but Wilson nevertheless sees a challenge in continually working to hone his design skills. In his columns, as in this book, he generously shares insights into 3D gained over years and years of perfecting his craft.

We at CADENCE find him to be one of our top columnists and authors. And we're sure you'll find him to be without parallel in helping you mine the 3D riches of AutoCAD.

—Arnie Williams, Editor in Chief, CADENCE

# Introduction

Hard to use, impractical, difficult to learn, crude, slow. All these expressions have been used to describe 3D modeling in AutoCAD. At one time there was some validity in each of them, but as AutoCAD and the computers that run AutoCAD become more and more powerful and sophisticated, the reasons for not using the 3D features of AutoCAD become less and less valid. AutoCAD has good 3D modeling capabilities, most objects in the real world are 3D, and most designs should be done in 3D.

The advantages of designing in 3D are almost self evident. Because you actually construct (in a computer) the object you are designing, rather than draw views of it that are as you imagine it looks, the design is more likely to be correct and accurate. From that model, realistic shaded pictures (renderings) can be produced to show what the design will look like, and dimensioned, multi-view 2D drawings can be made for manufacturing it.

## What's in This Book

This book guides you through all the AutoCAD commands and techniques for building 3D models. You will discover that most 3D work involves the same commands, and uses the same tools that 2D drafting does. To be successful in 3D, you should have a good basic knowledge of AutoCAD's commands, along with skill and experience in using those commands.

Although this book assumes that you have a working knowledge of AutoCAD, it makes no assumptions about your knowledge and experience in using its 3D features. Therefore, all the concepts and principles of AutoCAD's 3D features are explained completely, and you can gain experience in using them through hands-on exercises. Furthermore, detailed descriptions of every AutoCAD command related to 3D are included to serve as a reference. These descriptions go beyond those of AutoCAD's on-screen help, and even beyond the AutoCAD manuals.

AutoCAD, a computer to run AutoCAD, this book, and the files availible via FTP that come with the book are all you need. You do not need to acquire or learn any extra cost external pro-

grams. Also, you do not need to know anything about AutoCAD customization or about programming. Although a few AutoLISP programs are used to enhance some AutoCAD functions, they are included on the CD-ROM, and instructions for using them are given in the book.
The book is divided into five sections, as follows:

**Section 1**   Working with 3D Wireframe Models in 3D Space. This section introduces you to 3D space and to the tools for working in it. Chapters in this section teach you, among other things, how to specify 3D points, how to view objects in 3D space, and how to control AutoCAD's moveable coordinate system. Although the section's emphasis is on wireframes, its information is valuable even if your primary interest is in surface modeling or solid modeling.

**Section 2**   Building Surface Models. This section of the book explains how to build models that represent building and rooms, as well as models that have sculpted free-form shapes, such as those in automobile body parts. It also shows you how to set up perspective views, and how to remove obstructing objects from views.

**Section 3**   Solid Modeling. Chapters in this section tell you how to use the powerful solid modeling capabilities that are built into AutoCAD. You learn how to build solids from profiles, as well as from primitives, and how to use Boolean operations to make complex solid models.

**Section 4**   2D Output and Paper Space. Even though the objects you design are 3D, most manufacturing and construction operations depend on 2D documentation. Chapters in this section show you how to make conventional 2D drawings from 3D models.

**Section 5**   Renderings from 3D Models. In this section, you find out how to make realistic shaded images from 3D models. You learn how to install lights, how to make shiny surfaces (and even transparent and reflective surfaces), how to attach images of building materials (such as bricks and shingles) to surfaces, and how to add landscape objects to renderings.

Subjects are arranged in an order that builds upon previous information to systematically lead you through all of AutoCAD's 3D features; beginning with an elementary explanation of coordinate systems and ending with advanced techniques in rendering.

Ideally, therefore, you should read each chapter in order. However, depending upon your level of 3D experience and your areas of interest, you might choose to concentrate on specific sections and chapters. If, for example, if your interests are largely architectural, the subjects you might want to concentrate on are in Sections 1, 2, and 5. On the other hand, if your interests are principally related to mechanical parts, you might want to concentrate on the subjects in Sections 1, 3, and 4.

## About this Book's Electronic Files

Practice and experimentation is the best way — perhaps the only way — to become adept in building 3D models. Therefore, this book contains numerous exercises to give you experience in using the AutoCAD 3D related commands and features. To fully use this book, you should do the exercises. Finished versions of the 3D models of most exercises are in AutoCAD drawing files are availible via FTP. You can then compare the model you built with the corresponding model from the FTP site. Also, some exercises start with a model that is in a file on the FTP Site.

The FTP site also contains the script files and the AutoLISP programs that are referred to in the book. As a bonus, numerous bitmap image files suitable for use in rendering materials are included. See Appendix A for details on the FTP site contents.

# Working with Wireframe Models in 3D Space

# CHAPTER 1

# The World Coordinate System and 3D Space

*This chapter will help you establish a foundation for working in 3D space. Even though the principles and techniques explained in this chapter are in the book section emphasizing wireframes, they apply equally well to surface models and solid models.*

*This chapter*

- *describes AutoCAD's 3D World Coordinate System;*
- *explains how to interpret and manage AutoCAD's coordinate system icon;*
- *discusses the proper orientation of models in 3D space;*
- *shows you how to establish viewpoints in 3D space;*
- *describes techniques for specifying points in 3D space.*

## AutoCAD's 3D World Coordinate System

AutoCAD uses three mutually perpendicular lines, which intersect at a point called the *origin*, to identify point locations in 3D space. These three lines are named the *X axis*, the *Y axis*, and the *Z axis*. With them, the location of any point in 3D space can be specified by the point's distance from the origin in the X direction, in the Y direction, and in the Z direction. These three distances, which are called *coordinates*, are usually written together, separated by commas.

A point, for example, having the coordinates of 2.25, 1.75, 2.50 is 2.25 units from the origin in the X direction, 1.75 units from the origin in the Y direction, and 2.50 units from the origin in the Z direction. The coordinates of the origin are 0,0,0. The units used for distance can be inches, millimeters, miles, light-years, or any other measurement system you choose.

AutoCAD displays the current coordinates of the screen cursor in the drawing editor status bar on your computer screen. Beginning with Release 14, all three coordinate values are displayed (the Z coordinate will generally be 0). Previous releases of AutoCAD displayed only the X and Y coordinates.

The X, Y, and Z axes extend an infinite distance in both directions from the origin, with each axis having a positive and a negative direction. A minus sign preceding a coordinate value means that the distance is in the negative direction from the origin. The accompanying figure shows the point coordinates for selected corners on a 3D solid model. Notice that some of the coordinate values have negative numbers, indicating they are on the negative side of the origin.

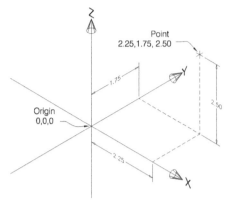

The coordinates of a point represent its distance from the origin in the X, Y, and Z directions.

AutoCAD refers to this setup for designating point locations as the *World Coordinate System* (WCS). AutoCAD has a secondary coordinate system, called the *User Coordinate System* (UCS), which can be moved about within the WCS to make it easier for you to draw objects in 3D space. Because this movable coordinate system is extremely important in building 3D models, considerable space is devoted to the UCS in the next chapter.

Two other terms regarding coordinate systems that you will encounter as you work with AutoCAD are *model space* and *paper space*. Model space is the fully 3D environment just described. It is the space

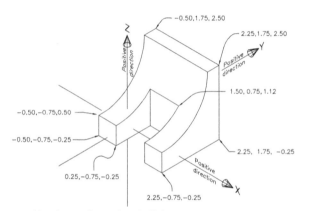

Negative coordinate values signify that the direction is in the negative direction from the origin.

you work in as you build 3D models. Paper space, on the other hand, is a 2D world that has only X and Y axes and is used for making 2D drawings of 3D objects. AutoCAD's **tilemode** system variable determines whether model space or paper space is in effect. Section 4 of this book describes paper space fully and explains how you use it.

## The X-Y Plane

Although the WCS contains an infinite number of planes, the one defined by the X and Y axes is especially important in AutoCAD, because

- A pointing device, whether it is a mouse or a digitizer, can specify points off the X-Y plane only through the use of object snaps on existing objects. (There is one exception that is covered later in this chapter when AutoCAD's ELEVATION command is discussed.)

- Virtually all 2D drafting is done on the X-Y plane.

- Many AutoCAD objects — including circles, arcs, and 2D polylines — are always drawn either on or parallel to the X-Y plane.

- When AutoCAD's grid is displayed, it is placed on the X-Y plane. (Again, one exception will be covered soon.)

- Most AutoCAD prototype and template drawings start out with a viewpoint that looks straight down on the X-Y plane. This particular viewpoint is often referred to as the *plan view*.

- The X-Y plane is generally considered to be a level, or horizontal, plane. Therefore, most 3D models are based on the X-Y plane. A 3D model house, for instance, is almost always drawn with its floor on, or parallel to, the X-Y plane.

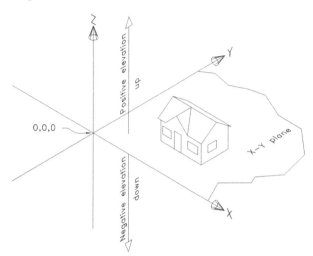

The plane defined by the X and Y axes is especially important in AutoCAD.

Because the X-Y plane represents a horizontal plane, distance from the X-Y plane in the Z axis direction represents height, or *elevation*. Consequently, the term elevation is often used in AutoCAD prompts and messages when referring to distance in the Z direction from the X-Y plane, as well as to the value of the Z coordinate. Also, the terms *up*, *down*, *above*, and *below* are commonly relative to the X-Y plane; with up and above referring to the positive side of the X-Y plane, and down and below referring to the negative side.

## The Right-Hand Rule

Because the positive end of the Z axis can physically point in either of two directions from the X-Y plane, a convention is needed to consistently establish its positive and negative directions. Autodesk, along with everyone else involved in 3D geometry, follows the *right-hand rule*. Although the right-hand rule can be defined by vector mathematics, it is more easily defined and visualized by using your right hand. One method is to mentally extend your right arm along the Y axis toward the origin, with your fingers curled toward the X axis. Your extended thumb will then point in the positive direction of the Z axis.

Another technique commonly used in visualizing the right-hand rule is to point the thumb of your right hand in

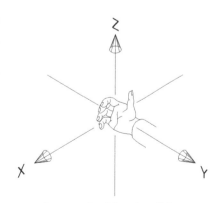

One method for visualizing the right-hand rule.

the positive X direction and extend your index finger in the positive Y direction. Then, curl your middle finger 90 degrees from your index finger — it will point in the positive direction of the Z axis.

See if you can spot the right-hand coordinate systems in the figure below.

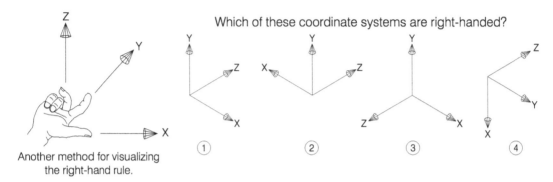

Another method for visualizing the right-hand rule.

## The UCS Icon

The coordinate systems numbered 2 and 3 in the previous figure are right-handed, while the other two are not. To assist you in keeping directions straight as you work in 3D space, AutoCAD has an icon that shows the directions of the X, Y, and Z axes. It is called the *UCS icon* because it indicates the current location and orientation of AutoCAD's supplementary, movable UCS. (The UCS is discussed in the next chapter.) When no UCS is being used, which will be the case throughout this chapter, the icon shows the direction of the WCS axes.

Beginning in AutoCAD 2000i, you can choose between 2D and 3D styles of the UCS icon. Previously, only the 2D UCS icon was available. The 2D icon has just X and Y axes, while the 3D icon has X, Y, and Z axes.

Even though the 2D icon is missing the Z axis, it is packed with information:

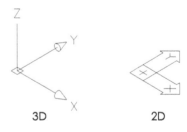

3D          2D

- The icon lies on the X-Y plane and has two wide arrows indicating the directions of the X and Y axes.

- When the icon is located on the coordinate system origin, the icon will have a plus-sign-shaped cross at the junction of the X and Y axes.

- When the 3D space viewpoint looks toward the X-Y plane from the positive Z direction, a box is drawn at the junction of the X and Y axes.

- When no UCS is being used, a W is shown on the Y axis.

The UCS icon is managed through AutoCAD's UCSICON command. This command has options for turning the display of the icon on or off, for selecting the icon style and relative size, and for causing it to be positioned either on the coordinate system origin or in the lower-left corner of the current viewport. When the option to position the icon on the origin is in effect and the origin is either outside the current viewport or very close to the viewport's edge, the icon automatically moves to the lower-left corner of the viewport.

The following figures show a 3D solid model and the 2D UCS icon when various UCS icon settings, viewpoints, and coordinate systems are used. Notice the differences in the appearance of the UCS icon.

Similar to AutoCAD's dot grid, the UCS icon is transparent to screen picks and cannot be printed. Although you might prefer to keep the UCS icon turned off while working in 2D, you will want it on as you work in 3D space. Most of the time you will also want it positioned on the coordinate system origin. Occasionally, however, especially if you are working close to the origin, it might obscure objects. Then, you might want to temporarily move it to the lower-left corner of the viewport, or perhaps even turn it off for a while.

When your viewpoint in 3D space is 1 degree or less from the X-Y plane, the 2D UCS icon is replaced by an icon showing a broken pencil. The broken pencil represents a warning that you should not rely on your pointing device to specify points. You can, however, continue to use object snaps with your pointing device to specify points. The next figure shows the

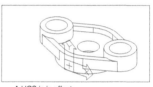

This arrow points in the Y axis direction.

If no UCS is being used, this W will be shown.

If the UCS icon is positioned at the origin, this cross will be shown.

If you are looking down on the X-Y plane, these lines will be shown.

This arrow points in the X axis direction.

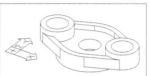

No UCS is in effect.
UCS icon is located at the origin.
The viewpoint looks at the X-Y plane from the positive Z direction.

No UCS is in effect.
UCS icon is located at the origin.
The viewpoint looks at the X-Y plane from the negative Z direction.

No UCS is in effect.
UCS icon is not located at the origin.
The viewpoint looks at the X-Y plane from the positive Z direction.

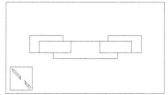

A UCS is in effect.
UCS icon is located at the origin.
The viewpoint looks at the X-Y plane from the positive Z direction.

The broken pencil version of the 2D UCS icon indicates that the viewpoint is within 1 degree of the X-Y plane.

same solid model shown in the previous figures as it is seen when the viewpoint is parallel to the X-Y plane.

Variations in the appearance of the 3D UCS icon

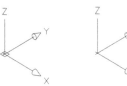   

| Icon is at the origin. No UCS is in effect. | Icon is at the origin. A UCS is in effect. | Icon is not at the origin. No UCS is in effect. | The viewpoint looks at the X-Y plane from the negative Z direction. | The viewpoint is edge-on to the X-Y plane. |

The 3D style icon also varies in form to indicate its relationship with the coordinate system and to help you visualize viewing directions:

- When the icon is located on the coordinate system origin, the X and Y axes extend across one another to form a small cross.
- When the 3D space viewpoint looks up toward the X-Y plane from the negative Z axis direction, the Z axis of the icon becomes a dashed line.
- When no UCS is in effect, a small box is drawn at the junction of the X and Y axes.

| | |
|---|---|
| Command: | UCSICON |
| Purpose: | This command controls whether or not the UCS icon is displayed and whether or not it is positioned at the coordinate system origin. |
| Initiate with: | • On the command line, enter UCSICON. |
| | • From the View pull-down menu, select Display. Then select UCS Icon. |
| Options: | The following options are offered in a command line menu: |

- ON          This option causes the UCS icon to be displayed.
- OFF         The display of the UCS icon is turned off by this option.
- All          By default, the ON, OFF, Noorigin, and ORigin options affect only the current viewport. This option, however, causes their settings to affect all viewports. When this option is selected, AutoCAD reoffers the ON, OFF, Noorigin, and ORigin options on the command line.
- Noorigin    When this option is in effect, the UCS icon always is positioned in the lower-left corner of the viewport, regardless of the location of the UCS origin.
- ORigin      This option causes the UCS icon to be positioned on the UCS origin. When the view is such that the UCS origin is either not in the current viewport or is close to its edge, the UCS icon is positioned in the viewport's lower-left corner.
- Properties  This option displays a dialog box for setting the icon's style, relative size, line width, and color.

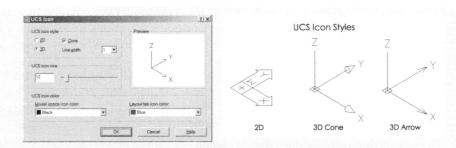

UCS Icon Styles

2D          3D Cone          3D Arrow

Notes:

• In paper space, the UCS icon is shaped like a 30- to 60-degree triangle with the short side indicating the direction of the X axis.

• Beginning with AutoCAD 2000, the UCS icon is displayed as three mutually perpendicular cone-shaped, colored arrows when the 3D wireframe viewing mode of the SHADEMODE command is in effect. You might prefer this form of the UCS icon, even though it does not give as much information as the standard icon. See the description of the SHADEMODE command in Chapter 7 for more information about the 3D wireframe viewing mode and this alternate UCS icon form.

UCS icon in paper space

Related system variable:

• ucsicon

The integer within this system variable controls the UCS icon display in the current viewport. Its value, which can range from 0 to 3, is the sum of the following:

| | |
|---|---|
| 0 | The UCS icon is not displayed. |
| 1 | The UCS icon is displayed. |
| 2 | The UCS icon will be positioned at the UCS origin. |

Thus, when **ucsicon** equals 3, the UCS icon is displayed and positioned at the UCS origin, provided the origin is in the viewport. When **ucsicon** equals 2, the UCS icon is not displayed. (If it were displayed, however, it would be at the UCS origin.) You must use the SETVAR command to access this system variable because its name duplicates a command name.

## Directions and Model Orientation in 3D Space

As you construct a 3D model, you should orient it so that as many of its straight edges and flat sides as possible are parallel with the X, Y, and Z axes. One reason for this is that eventually you are likely to make an orthographic, multiview drawing of your model,

Orienting your model with the coordinate system axes

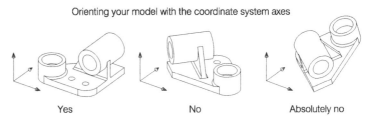

Yes          No          Absolutely no

and it will be much easier to set up the views when the model's orientation matches the three principal axes. A second reason is that because viewpoint directions in 3D space are relative to the principal axes, it will be easier to keep your directions straight when you orient your model with the axes.

Although your choices of sides to represent the top and front of your model are often rather arbitrary, especially for mechanical items, AutoCAD has some conventions for directions in its menus, toolbars, and dialog boxes that are based upon model orientation. You should keep these conventions in mind as you construct your model:

- The top of the model is the side seen when you are looking straight down on the X-Y plane from the positive end of the Z axis.

- The front of the model is the side seen when you are looking from the negative Y direction toward the positive Y direction.

- The right side of the model is the side seen when you are looking from the positive X direction toward the negative X direction.

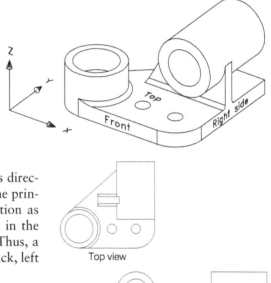

Occasionally, AutoCAD menus for view directions use compass directions rather than axes directions. The relationship of compass directions to the principal axes is that north points in the same direction as the positive end of the Y axis, while east points in the same direction as the positive end of the X axis. Thus, a NW isometric view is one that looks at the top, back, left side of the model.

Top view

Front view        Right side view

Orthographic views

## Setting Viewpoints in 3D Space

Just as you walk around a large physical object, such as an automobile or a chair, to examine features on its various sides, you move around in 3D space to see, and work on, features on various sides of your 3D model. AutoCAD has three different commands for setting general viewpoints in 3D space — VPOINT, 3DORBIT, and DVIEW. 3DORBIT, which was introduced in AutoCAD 2000, and DVIEW are

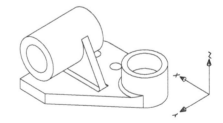

more complex than VPOINT, being able to set up perspective views and clip away portions of your 3D model to obtain unobstructed views of a particular section, in addition to setting viewpoints. Because these uses are particularly applicable to surface models, 3DORBIT and DVIEW are not discussed until Section 2 of this book.

Although 3DORBIT will probably become your favorite command for setting viewpoints, you will still find VPOINT useful for quickly setting exact viewpoints with minimum effort, and you will often use it even though it is an old 3D command.

AutoCAD also has a dialog box version of the VPOINT command — DDVPOINT — that you might find useful at times. And, because views looking straight down from the Z axis toward the X-Y plane (and the top of your model) are common, AutoCAD has a specialized command — PLAN — for setting that particular viewpoint.

## Using the VPOINT Command

The most important thing to remember as you use VPOINT is that in spite of the command's name and this book's (as well as AutoCAD's) frequent use of the word *viewpoint*, it sets a viewing direction rather than an observation point in space. Consequently, in using the command you specify just a view direction, rather than establish camera and target points. The command automatically displays your entire 3D model regardless of where it is located in 3D space, doing the equivalent of a Zoom-Extents. Then you can use the ZOOM command to move in closer to your model, or farther away from it.

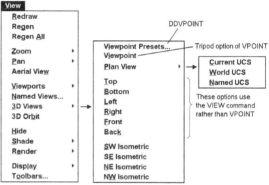

Screen pull-down menus for 3D viewpoints

VPOINT offers three different methods for setting a view direction — vector direction coordinates, rotation angles, and a rotating tripod. Of the three methods, you are not likely to find the rotating tripod (which represents the principal axes) with its companion bull's-eye target useful. This method is neither faster nor more convenient to use than the other methods, and you cannot set precise, repeatable view directions with it. You cannot, for instance, set up a viewpoint that looks exactly at the right side of your model. You can come close by carefully positioning the bull's-eye cursor in a certain spot, or by rotating the axes tripod until the X axis is pointing directly out of the screen, but it is unlikely that the resulting view direction will be exactly perpendicular to the X-Y plane.

Although direction vector coordinates can be used to set any view direction angle, they are especially convenient for quickly and precisely setting one of the principal orthographic and isometric views. A principal orthographic view looks straight at one of the principal coordinate system planes, while an isometric view has the same angle with each principal plane. Table 1-1 shows the viewpoint direction coordinates for the six principal orthographic views and the eight isometric views.

Although at times you might want to set a viewpoint that looks precisely head on at one side of your model, most of the time you are better off working from an isometric-type view, because it is hard to visualize depth in your model when you look at it head on. Furthermore, head-on views generally have objects stacked on top of other objects, which make point selections by object snaps uncertain.

Consider, for example, the wireframe model of a cube. It will be made of 12 equal-length lines. If you have a view looking straight at one side of this cube, it will look like a square, with the lines of the back edges exactly behind the lines making up the front edges. Moreover, the lines for the side edges will not even be noticeable because only their ends are shown.

An isometric view is better for working in 3D, but it has visualization problems, too. Although you can generally see all of objects in the model, lines that are parallel to one another sometimes appear to run into each other. This causes an isometric view of the 3D cube to look like a 2D hexagon that has been divided into triangles. True isometric views are a carry-over from 2D drafting, where they are fairly easy to draw because their scale in the three cardinal

**Table 1-1**

| View | View Coordinates | | |
|------|---|---|---|
| Top (Plan) | 0, | 0, | 1 |
| Bottom | 0, | 0, | -1 |
| Front | 0, | -1, | 0 |
| Back | 0, | 1, | 0 |
| Left | -1, | 0, | 0 |
| Right | 1, | 0, | 0 |
| Top/Front/Left Isometric | -1, | -1, | 1 |
| Top/Front/Right Isometric | 1, | -1, | 1 |
| Top/Back/Right Isometric | 1, | 1, | 1 |
| Top/Back/Left Isometric | -1, | 1, | 1 |
| Bottom/Front/Left Isometric | -1, | -1, | -1 |
| Bottom/Front/Right Isometric | 1, | -1, | -1 |
| Bottom/Back/Right Isometric | 1, | 1, | -1 |
| Bottom/Back/Left Isometric | -1, | 1, | -1 |

Same wireframe cube seen from three viewpoints

View coordinates:
0,-1,0

View coordinates:
1,-1,1

View coordinates:
0.4967,-0.7094,0.5000

directions is equal (hence the name, isometric). They are seldom useful viewpoints in 3D modeling, however.

The best viewpoints for working in 3D space are those that have a different angle to each of the three principal axes, such as the one of the cube shown on the right in the previous figure. The view angles you select will depend upon the shape of your model and upon the orientation of the section of the model you are working on. Although the correct name for views having unequal viewing angles is *trimetric*, that name is seldom recognized or used. Therefore, I refer to them in this book as *isometric-type views*.

Although some people are comfortable using VPOINT's direction vector coordinates in setting isometric-type views, most prefer to use rotation angles. The method is easy to implement, and after some practice, you will have no trouble visualizing the results. You simply enter the value of two angles — one for the horizontal angle from the X axis, and one for the vertical angle from the X-Y plane. You can input the angles by pointing, but it is generally easier to type them in.

AutoCAD has no limit on the sizes of angles in VPOINT, although there is no reason for you to specify angles greater than 360 degrees since angles greater than 360 degrees wrap around. Thus, a 385-degree angle is the same as a 25-degree angle. Also, vertical angles (those from the X-Y plane) wrap around after 90 degrees and add 180 degrees to the horizontal angle at the same time. For example: A viewing angle 30 degrees from the X axis and 110 degrees from the X-Y plane is equivalent to one 210 degrees from the X axis and 70 degrees from the X-Y plane.

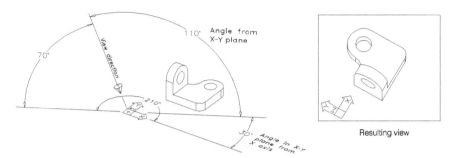

Resulting view

Positive and negative angle-rotation directions are controlled by AutoCAD's **angdir** system variable. The default value of 0 for this variable sets the positive angle-rotation direction to be counterclockwise. VPOINT accepts negative angle input to rotate the view direction angle in the opposite direction, and you might prefer to do this for angles that exceed 180 degrees. If, for instance, you wanted to set up a view looking up toward the underside of the X-Y plane while making the model of a boat hull, you could specify the angle from the X-Y plane as -35 degrees rather than 325 degrees. Even though these two angles are the same, the negative rotation angle may be easier for you to visualize.

| | |
|---|---|
| Command: | VPOINT |
| Purpose: | VPOINT sets a general view direction in 3D space.<br>Initiate with: |
| | • On the command line enter VPOINT. |
| | • From the View pull-down menu select 3D Views, and then select Viewpoint. |
| Options: | VPOINT displays the current view direction coordinates on the command line and offers the following options: |

• Rotate          This option is initiated by entering the letter r (you also can enter the entire word rotate) when you are prompted to choose an option after starting VPOINT from the command line. AutoCAD prompts you to enter two angles:

```
Enter angle in XY plane from X axis <current>: Specify an angle.
Enter angle from XY plane <current>: Specify an angle.
```

The angles of the present viewpoint are offered as defaults. VPOINT has no maximum angle limit, with horizontal angles greater than 360 degrees and vertical angles greater than 90 degrees wrapping around. The command also accepts either positive or negative values for angles. Positive angles indicate counterclockwise view angle rotation, and negative angles indicate clockwise rotations, unless you have set AutoCAD's **angdir** system variable to measure positive angles clockwise.

The following figure shows the viewpoint resulting from a 30-degree angle in the X-Y plane from the X axis, and a 35-degree angle from the X-Y plane. Notice that even though the vertex of each angle is at the WCS origin, the resulting view centers on the 3D model: VPOINT establishes a view direction rather than a specific viewing point in space.

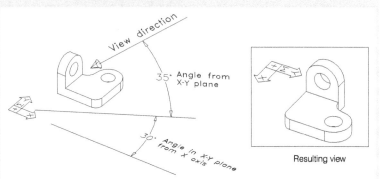

Resulting view

- Vector
You initiate this option by entering the coordinates of a 3D point when you are prompted for an option after starting VPOINT from the command line. Although the command displays the coordinates of the current viewpoint (regardless of the option used to specify the viewpoint), you cannot press the Enter key to accept them — you must type in three new coordinate values, separated by commas, and then press Enter. The resulting view direction will be the same as the direction of a line drawn from the specified point to the origin.

Thus, you could set a viewing direction by entering the vector coordinates 0.7094, 0.4096, 0.5736 when AutoCAD prompts for a viewpoint option. You also could enter the coordinates 7.0941, 4.0958, 5.7358, or even the coordinates 70.9406, 40.9576, 57.3576, to obtain the same viewpoint because the coordinates establish a viewing direction rather than a viewing point.

Vector option of VPOINT

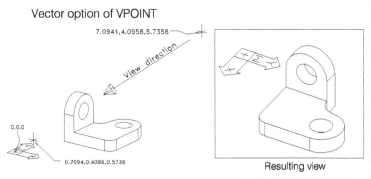

Resulting view

- Tripod

This option is initiated by selecting VPOINT (in AutoCAD 2000 and 2000i) or Viewpoint (in AutoCAD 2002) from the View/3D Views pull-down menu or by pressing Enter when you are prompted to select an option after starting VPOINT from the command line.

Your model will disappear as AutoCAD switches to a special screen showing three mutually perpendicular lines labeled X, Y, and Z, which meet at a point to form a tripod-like object, and a bull's-eye-type target. Beginning with Release 14, AutoCAD also shows the UCS icon in its existing position on the screen. The UCS icon, however, is static, and plays no role in selecting a viewpoint.

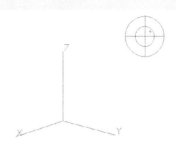

The VPOINT axes tripod and bulls-eye target.

A small cross will be in, or near, the bull's-eye target, and as you move your pointing device, the small cross moves and the axes rotate about their common point. The position of the small cross within the bull's-eye determines the view direction, while the tripod helps you see how the view direction relates to the coordinate system.

The bull's-eye target consists of two concentric circles, a horizontal line, and a vertical line. The position of the small movable cross within the target is related to the viewpoint as follows:

- When the cross is in the exact center of the circles, the viewpoint is perpendicular to the X-Y plane from the positive Z direction. In other words, it results in a plan view.

- When the cross is in the inner circle, the viewpoint looks down from the positive Z direction toward the X-Y plane.

- When the cross is on the perimeter of the inner circle, the viewpoint looks at the edge of the X-Y plane.

- When the cross is in the outer circle, the viewpoint looks up from the negative Z direction toward the underside of the X-Y plane.

- When the cross is below the horizontal line, the viewpoint looks toward the positive Y direction. When the cross is above the horizontal line, the viewpoint looks toward the negative Y direction.

• When the cross is to the right of the vertical line, the viewpoint looks toward the negative X direction. When the cross is to the left of the vertical line, the viewpoint looks toward the positive X direction.

When you have a viewpoint to your satisfaction, press the Pick button on your pointing device. AutoCAD restores the graphics screen, using the newly specified viewpoint.

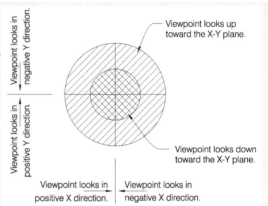

Viewpoint looks up toward the X-Y plane.

Viewpoint looks down toward the X-Y plane.

Viewpoint looks in positive Y direction.

Viewpoint looks in negative Y direction.

Viewpoint looks in positive X direction.

Viewpoint looks in negative X direction.

Notes:

• It is important that you recognize that VPOINT, despite its name, sets a viewing direction rather than a point in space from which you are viewing your model.

• Even though VPOINT bases viewpoints — whether they are specified as rotation angles or as vector coordinates — on the coordinate system origin, the model always is centered in the resulting view, even if it is located a considerable distance from the origin. Also, the zoom level of the resulting view is always the equivalent of a Zoom-Extents.

• Unless the system variable **worldview** has been changed from its default value of 1 to 0, the view direction is based upon the WCS even if a UCS is being used. AutoCAD automatically switches from the current UCS to the WCS when VPOINT is started and switches back to the UCS when the command is finished.

• When multiple viewports exist, VPOINT affects only the current viewport.

Related system variables:

• **angdir**   This system variable controls the rotation direction and the measurement direction of positive angles. Its default setting is 0.
0   Positive angles are measured counterclockwise.
1   Positive angles are measured clockwise.

• **viewdir**   This read-only system variable contains the coordinates of a 3D point. The view direction is equivalent to that of a line drawn from this 3D point to coordinate system origin (0,0,0).

• **worldview**   This system variable controls whether viewpoints set by VPOINT and DVIEW based upon the WCS or the UCS. It will have an integer value of 0 or 1.
0   View directions are based upon the UCS.
1   View directions are based upon the WCS. This is the default setting.

## Setting Viewpoints through a Dialog Box

DDVPOINT is a dialog box version of VPOINT's Rotate option, in which you can use your pointing device in image tiles to set both the horizontal and vertical viewing angles. Although this dialog box is neither faster nor easier to use than the command line version of VPOINT, you might like the protractor-like display of angles that the dialog box uses. Also, its up-front ability to switch the view direction angles from the WCS to the UCS is occasionally useful, and it gives you another way to set plan views.

| Command: | DDVPOINT |
|---|---|
| Purpose: | This command enables you to set viewpoint rotation angles graphically through a dialog box. |
| Initiate with: | • On the command line, enter DDVPOINT. |
| | • From the View pull-down menu, pick 3D Views and then Viewpoint Presets. |

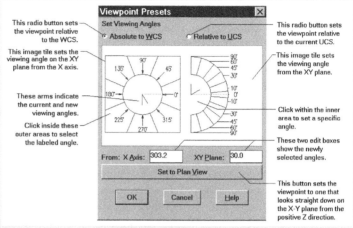

| Dialog box description: | • Set Viewing Angles | This section of the dialog box contains two radio buttons. When the button labeled Absolute to WCS is set, the viewpoint will be relative to the WCS. When the button labeled Relative to UCS is set, the viewpoint will be relative to the UCS. |
|---|---|---|
| | • Image Tiles | The image tile on the left sets the horizontal view direction, in units of degrees, from the X axis, while the image tile on the right sets the vertical view direction angle from the X-Y plane. You can use your pointing device within these image tiles to set a view direction angle. A red arm indicates the current view direction angle, and a black (or white, depending on your screen color) arm indicates the new angle. If you pick a point in one of the outer bounded areas, the angle snaps to the labeled degree value. Picking a point within the inner areas sets a precise angle. |
| | • From | These two edit boxes, labeled X Axis and XY Plane, show the angles selected within the image tiles. They also can be used to directly type in view direction angles. |
| | • Set to Plan View | This button sets a viewpoint looking straight down on the X-Y plane. It is equivalent to setting the horizontal angle from the X axis to 270 degrees, and the vertical angle from the X-Y plane to 90 degrees. |
| Notes: | | • This command and dialog box is based upon an AutoLISP program named DDVPOINT.LSP and a Dialog Control Language file named DDVPOINT.DCL. |
| | | • The two radio buttons in the cluster labeled Set Viewing Angle turn the system variable **worldview** on and off. |

## Setting Plan Views

Virtually all 2D drafting with AutoCAD is done using a viewpoint that looks straight down from the positive end of the Z axis toward the X-Y plane. Because it is such an often-used viewpoint, AutoCAD has a special command — PLAN — for setting it. Even though you will generally do your 3D work from a viewpoint that is askew to the principal axes, you will occasionally want to work in a plan view. And, the PLAN command is more convenient than VPOINT in establishing plan views. By default, PLAN sets the plan view according to the current UCS, but you can set it according to WCS, and even to a UCS orientation that has been named and saved by AutoCAD's UCS command. UCS is discussed in detail in the next chapter.

| Command: | PLAN |
|---|---|
| Purpose: | This command sets a view direction that looks straight down on the X-Y plane from the positive Z direction. |
| Initiate with: | • On the command line, enter PLAN. |
| | • From the View pull-down menu, pick 3D Views, pick Plan View, and then pick one of the three options. |
| Options: | The options for the PLAN command are presented in a command line menu. |
| | • Current UCS — This option sets the view direction perpendicular to the positive side of the X-Y plane of the current UCS. It is the default option. |
| | • UCS — This option sets the plan view relative to a UCS position and orientation that has been given a name and saved through an option in the UCS command. See the description of AutoCAD's UCS command for details on named UCSs. When you select this option of PLAN, AutoCAD issues a command line prompt for you to specify a UCS name and gives you an opportunity to see a list of all named UCSs. |

Original viewpoint      Current UCS option of PLAN      World option of PLAN

| | • World — When you select this option, the plan view will be relative to the WCS, regardless of whether a UCS does or does not exist. |
| Notes: | • All options of the PLAN command display the model with a zoom level that is the equivalent of Zoom-Extents. |
| | • When multiple viewports exist, PLAN affects only the current viewport. |
| | • The World option of PLAN is equivalent to the VPOINT command's direction coordinates of 0,0,1 when the system variable **worldview** is set to 1. |
| | • The Current UCS option of PLAN is equivalent to the VPOINT command's direction coordinates of 0,0,1 when the system variable **worldview** is set to 0. |

# Setting Orthographic Views

In AutoCAD 2000, options were added to the VIEW command for setting orthographic and isometric viewpoints. In the dialog box displayed by this command, select the Orthographic & Isometric Views tab. The names of the six principal orthographic views plus the four isometric views that look down on the X-Y plane are shown in a list box. You can click on one of these names, and then click the Set Current button to set the viewpoint to the selected view. If the check box labeled Restore Orthographic UCS with View is checked and an orthographic view is to be the current view,

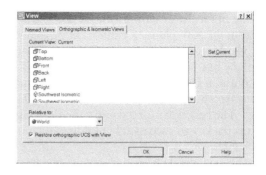

the UCS rotates so that its X-Y plane is perpendicular to the view direction. This check box controls the **ucsortho** system variable. When the box is checked, **ucsortho** is set to a value of 1, and when it is cleared **ucsortho** will have a value of 0. Autodesk intended for this action to be a convenience, but you will probably prefer to set the UCS yourself and you will clear this check box so that the UCS does not change when you use the VIEW command to set a viewpoint.

The **ucsortho** system variable also controls the behavior of the UCS when the View/3D Views pull-down menu and the View toolbar are used to set orthographic viewpoints, because the VIEW command is used to initiate those viewpoints. Therefore, you need to manually change the value of **ucsortho** from its default value of 1 to 0 if you do not want the UCS to change when you set an orthographic viewpoint. The relationship between the UCS and orthographic viewpoints is discussed in more detail in the next chapter.

# Specifying Points in 3D Space

### Pointing

All wireframe objects are drawn by specifying points in 3D space — lines begin and end at points, circles are based on a center point, and polylines are a based on a series of vertex points. Your pointing device is the most efficient method for specifying points; however, it is confined to the X-Y plane unless you use object snaps on existing objects.

To circumvent this problem, AutoCAD long ago (in 1985 with Version 2.1) introduced a command named ELEV that allows you to move the drawing plane to a position that is either above or below the X-Y plane. The command prompts you to enter a distance value, and then moves the drawing plane to the specified elevation. The current elevation of the drawing plane is stored in AutoCAD's **elevation** system variable. The ELEV command also sets the extrusion thickness of certain wireframe objects. Extrusion thickness is an object property that is completely unrelated to drawing plane elevation. It is a surfacelike property that is discussed extensively in Section 2 of this book.

Although AutoCAD still supports the ELEV command, along with its associated system variable **elevation**, it is an obsolete command representing an early attempt by Autodesk to incorporate 3D features within AutoCAD. It is limited to simply moving the drawing plane up or down from the X-Y plane. It cannot tilt or rotate the drawing plane, or move its origin away from the Z axis. Moreover, it is a potentially confusing command because the only evidence that the drawing plane has been moved is that AutoCAD's grid moves along with the drawing plane (provided, of course, it is turned on), and beginning with Release 14 the cursor location coordinates on the status bar show a Z coordinate other than 0.

The best way to reposition the drawing plane is to move the X-Y plane with the UCS. Because it is the key to successfully building 3D models, the UCS command is discussed in detail in the next chapter.

| | |
|---|---|
| Command: | ELEV |
| Purpose: | This command controls two unrelated parameters. It sets the elevation of the drawing plane, and it sets the extrusion thickness of wireframe objects. |
| Initiate with: | On the command line, enter ELEV. |
| Options: | ELEV issues two options in the form of prompts on the command line. |

Specify new default elevation <current elevation>: Specify a distance, or press Enter to accept the current elevation.

The drawing plane — the plane on which you can freely use your pointing device to specify point locations — will be moved to the elevation specified. Positive values move the drawing plane above the X-Y plane, while negative values move it below the X-Y plane. The Z coordinate in the cursor location displayed on the editing screen status bar will reflect the new elevation. If AutoCAD's grid is displayed, it will move to match the current elevation. The UCS icon, however, will remain on the X-Y plane of the current UCS.

Specify new default thickness <current extrusion thickness>: Specify a distance, or press Enter to accept the current thickness.

This option gives wireframe objects (such as lines, 2D polylines, circles, and arcs) height in the Z direction. Thus, a line will be drawn as a wall, and a circle will be drawn as a cylinder. This property is called *extrusion thickness* because the objects appear to have been stretched, or extruded, in a direction that is perpendicular to the drawing plane. Positive values extrude objects in the positive Z direction, while negative values extrude objects in the negative Z direction.

|   |   |
|---|---|
| Notes: | • The ELEV command is obsolete, even though it is still present in AutoCAD 2002. You should use the UCS command, rather than ELEV, for positioning the drawing plane. |
| | • Although the command can be used to set extrusion thickness, it is easier to set that property directly through the **thickness** system variable. |
| | • The extrusion thickness of existing objects, even if they were drawn with no extrusion thickness, can be changed through the CHANGE, CHPROP, and PROPERTIES commands. The CHANGE command also can change the elevation of existing objects, but the CHPROP and PROPERTIES commands cannot. |

| Related system variables: | • **elevation** | The current elevation of the drawing plane — its distance from the X-Y plane — is stored in this system variable. |
| | • **thickness** | This system variable stores the extrusion thickness that is currently in effect. |

# Entering 3D Coordinates

Entering point coordinates from the keyboard is relatively commonplace when working in 3D. Consequently, AutoCAD provides several methods for you to enter point coordinates.

## X, Y, Z Coordinates

The most common method for specifying the location of a point with the keyboard is to enter the point's X, Y, and Z coordinates. You also can precede the coordinates with the @ symbol to signify that the coordinates represent a point relative to the previous point. When entering relative coordinates, you can skip the Z coordinate if you intend to remain in the elevation of the last specified point. Moreover, you can use relative polar coordinates to indicate a point's location in the last elevation specified. Absolute polar coordinates, however, will place the point on the current drawing plane.

For example, you could draw a series of lines at an elevation of 1.5000 with the following command line input:

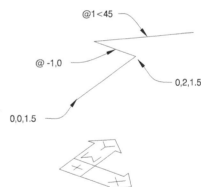

```
Command: LINE (Enter)
Specify first point: 0,0,1.5 (Enter)
(Absolute input with three coordinates.)
Specify next point or [Undo]: 0,2,1.5 (Enter)
(Absolute input with three coordinates.)
Specify next point or [Undo]: @-1,0 (Enter)
(Relative input with two coordinates.)
Specify next point or [Close/Undo]: @1<45 (Enter)
(Relative input with polar coordinates.)
```

## XYZ Point Filters

Although you will generally specify all three coordinates of a point at once by (1) picking a location with your pointing device, (2) using an object snap, or (3) typing in coordinates, AutoCAD has filters that permit you to enter each of the three coordinates independently. You can implement these filters anytime AutoCAD is looking for a point by entering a period followed by the coordinate you want to filter: .x for the X coordinate, .y for the Y coordinate, and .z for the Z coordinate. After you specify a coordinate to be filtered, AutoCAD will ask you to identity a point that can supply that coordinate. Often, you will use an object snap to do this. AutoCAD will then prompt for the missing coordinates, and you can use filters for them also.

Suppose, for example, that you have a partially constructed 3D room that has two walls and a rectangular-topped table. In preparation for a rendering, you want to place a point light over the middle of the table, at a height equal to the top of the walls. (Rendering, and lights for rendering, are discussed in Section 5. For now, all you need to know is that a point light is positioned at a point in space, and that it radiates light in all directions from that point.) You do not know the coordinates of any of these positions. When the LIGHT command prompts you to specify the location of the light, you could use the following input:

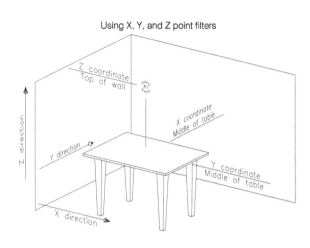

Using X, Y, and Z point filters

```
Enter light location <current>: .x (Enter)
of (use a midpoint snap on the long side of the table top)
(need YZ): .y (Enter)
of (use a midpoint snap on the short side of the table)
(need Z): (use an endpoint snap to pick the top of the wall)
```

Notice that AutoCAD uses the word *of* as it prompts you to specify the filtered coordinate. No filter was needed for the Z coordinate because that was the only one remaining. If, in this same example, you wanted the light to be placed over the center of the table as before, but 6 feet from the floor rather than at the top of the wall, you could have entered 6' (or 72) for the Z coordinate.

Sometimes a single point can supply two coordinates. In those situations, you can filter a pair of coordinates by typing in a period followed by the two coordinates you want to filter: .xy for the X and Y coordinates, .xz for the X and Z coordinates, and .yz for the Y and Z coordinates.

For an example of this type of filter, consider the same 3D room, but with a round-topped table instead of a rectangular-topped. You could position a light over the center of the table at a height equal to the wall with the following command line input:

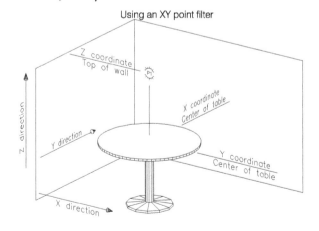

Using an XY point filter

```
Enter light location <current>: .xy (Enter)
of (use a center object snap on the top of the
    table)
need Z: (use an endpoint snap to pick the top of
    the wall)
```

You can initiate point filters by pressing the second button on your pointing device (usually the right-hand button on a two-button mouse) as you hold down the Shift key. A menu pops up on the computer screen. Select Point Filters from this menu, and then select a specific filter from the resulting flyout menu. You also can, of course, specify point filters from the command line, as in the previous examples.

## Cylindrical Coordinates

Even though the locations of 3D points are stored as XYZ coordinates, AutoCAD has two alternate methods for specifying them. One of these two input methods is to use cylindrical coordinates. The format for cylindrical coordinates is

**distance<angle, height**

where    *distance* represents the point's horizontal distance from the origin for absolute entry or from the last point specified for relative entry.

*<angle* represents the angle on the X-Y plane from the X axis to the point. The angle's direction depends upon the setting of AutoCAD's **angdir** system variable. By default, angle directions are counterclockwise.

*height* represents the point's elevation relative to the X-Y plane for absolute entry, or from the last point specified for relative entry.

You probably noticed that this format is the same as that for 2D polar coordinates, with the addition of a height value. The following command line input draws a line from the origin to a point 45 degrees from the X axis on the X-Y plane, 0.5 units above the X-Y plane, and 3.0 units from the origin on the X-Y plane:

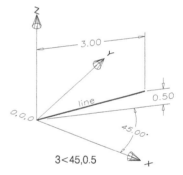

```
Command: LINE (Enter)
Specify first point: 0,0,0 (Enter)
Specify next point or [Undo]: 3<45,.5 (Enter)
Specify next point or [Undo]: (Enter)
```

The actual length of this line will be longer than 3.0 units. Further examples of cylindrical coordinates are in Chapter 5, where they are used for drawing 3D helical curves.

## Spherical Coordinates

The second alternate format for specifying a 3D point is spherical coordinates. Its format is

**distance<hor_angle<ver_angle**

where    *distance* represents the point's distance from the origin for absolute entry, or from the last point specified for relative entry.

*<hor_angle* represents the angle on the X-Y plane from the X axis to the point.

*<ver_angle* represents the angle from the X-Y plane.

Positive directions of the angles depend upon the setting of AutoCAD's **angdir** system variable. By default, this system variable is set to 0, which means that angles are measured counter-clockwise. The following command line input with spherical coordinates draws a line from the origin to a point 3.0 units away on the X-Y plane, 45 degrees from the X axis on the X-Y plane, and 30 degrees from the X-Y plane:

```
Command: LINE (Enter)
Specify first point: 0,0,0 (Enter)
Specify next point or [Undo]: 3<45<30 (Enter)
Specify next point or [Undo]: (Enter)
```

The actual length of this line will be 3.0 units.

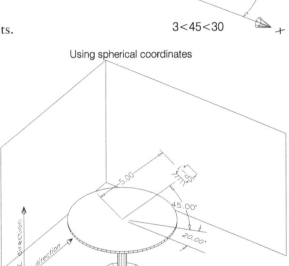

3<45<30

Using spherical coordinates

For an example application of spherical coordinates, suppose you wanted to install a spotlight in a rendering of the 3D room with a circular table that was used a few paragraphs ago in an example of coordinate filters. (Lights for renderings are discussed extensively in Section 5 of this book. For now all you need to know is that spotlights have a location, and they are pointed toward a target. Both the light location and its target are 3D points.) You want the light pointing 45 degrees toward the center of the table top, to be rotated 20 degrees in the X-Y plane, and to be 5.0 units away. To achieve this, you could use the following command line input when AutoCAD prompts for light target and light location points:

```
Enter light target <current>: (Use a center object snap to pick the center of the round table top.)
Enter light location <current>: @5<20<45 (Enter)
```

## Exercises

The following two exercises in making simple wireframe models give you an opportunity to experiment with the principles and commands covered in this chapter. Start a new drawing with the default English settings. That you don't need to keep these models, so your AutoCAD setup of layers, text, and so forth is not important. To make point specification easier, however, you should activate AutoCAD's snap mode, with a snap spacing of 0.5. Also, you should turn on the grid and set it to 0.5 to help you visualize the X-Y plane. Use the following command line input to position the UCS icon in the lower-left corner of the AutoCAD graphics area:

```
Command: UCSICON (Enter)
Enter an option [ON/OFF/Noorigin/ORigin/Properties] <ON>: N (Enter)
```

## Exercise One

In this first exercise, you will use the ELEV command to help draw a wireframe model. Start by drawing a rectangle that is 3 units long in the X direction and 2 units long in the Y direction. Base the lower-left corner of the rectangle at the 0,0,0 point of the WCS. Your rectangle should look similar to the one shown in Figure 1-1, except your drawing will not display the coordinates shown in the figure. So far, your wireframe is strictly a 2D drawing of a rectangle.

Next, move the drawing plane up 2 units in elevation using the following command line input:

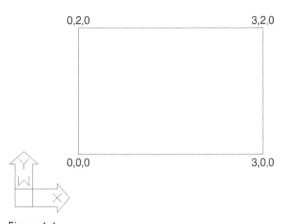

Figure 1-1

```
Command: ELEV (Enter)
Specify new default elevation <0.0000>: 2 (Enter)
Specify new default thickness <0.0000>: (Enter)
```

Because your viewpoint looks straight down on the X-Y plane, nothing in the graphics area of your computer screen will be changed. Nevertheless, the drawing plane has been moved up 2 units, and the Z coordinate on the AutoCAD status bar will read 2.0000.

Use your pointing device to draw another rectangle — 1.5 units in the X direction and 1.0 units in the Y direction — using the coordinates and directions shown in Figure 1-2. Drawing this rectangle is also exactly like drawing in 2D.

This rectangle is 2 units higher than the previous one, even though that is not apparent from your current viewpoint. To obtain a better look, use the following command line input to set up an isometric viewpoint:

```
Command: VPOINT (Enter)
Current view direction: VIEWDIR=0.0000,0.0000,1.0000
Specify a view point or [Rotate] display compass and
    tripod: 1,-1,1 (Enter)
```

Figure 1-2

You can obtain this same viewpoint by selecting an SE Isometric view from AutoCAD's View/3D Views pull-down menu, as well as from AutoCAD's Viewpoint toolbar. After stepping back with a zoom level of approximately 0.5X, your model should look similar to the one in Figure 1-3. Even though the smaller rectangle appears to be on the same plane as the larger rectangle, it is actually 2 units higher.

Finish the wireframe by drawing a line from each corner of one rectangle to the corresponding corner of the other rectangle. The easiest way to do this is to turn the snap-to-grid off and turn the object endpoint-snap on. Then simply draw a line from each corner on one rectangle to the matching corner on the other. Your completed wireframe model should look similar to the one shown in Figure 1-4.

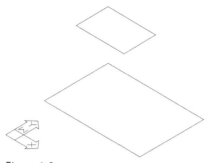

Figure 1-3

You should now return the drawing plane back to the X-Y plane. This time, move the drawing plane by changing the value of the **elevation** system variable rather than by using the ELEV command. The command line input to do this is

```
Command: elevation (Enter)
New value for ELEVATION <2.0000>: 0 (Enter)
```

The Z coordinate for the cursor location in the status bar will change to 0 and the grid will shift, indicating that the drawing plane has moved back to the X-Y plane. In the next chapter, you will see how the UCS command does a much better job than ELEV in establishing a drawing plane. You do not need to save the drawing, although you may want to use its setup for Exercise Two.

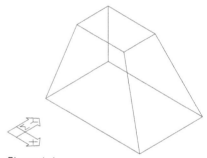

Figure 1-4

### Exercise Two

In this exercise, you will use the keyboard to input point locations while drawing a wireframe with two rectangles and one triangle that are slanted to the X-Y plane. Start the exercise by either beginning a new drawing having the grid and UCS icon options listed earlier, or by erasing all the objects used for the previous exercise.

If your viewpoint is an isometric type, switch to a plan view by using the following command line input:

```
Command: PLAN (Enter)
Enter an option [Current ucs/Ucs/World] Current: (Enter)
```

Because the current UCS is equivalent to the WCS, both the Current UCS and World options of PLAN result in the same viewpoint.

Now, use the point coordinates shown in Figure 2-1 to draw four connected lines. You can conveniently use your pointing device, with snap set to 0.5 or 1.0, to draw these lines, because they are on the WCS's X-Y plane.

Next, use the following command line input to set up an isometric-type viewpoint:

```
Command: VPOINT (Enter)
Current view direction: VIEWDIR=0.0000,0.0000,1.0000
Specify a viewpoint or [Rotate/display compass and tripod]: r
  (Enter)
Enter angle in XY plane from X axis <270>: 305 (Enter)
Enter angle from XY plane <90>: 35 (Enter)
```

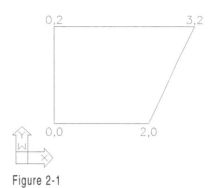

Figure 2-1

This results in a viewpoint that looks toward the top-front-right side of the model. Because the viewpoint is 305 degrees in the XY plane from the X axis, rather than the 315 degrees of a true isometric view, it is less likely that lines will hide one another.

AutoCAD does the equivalent of a Zoom/Extents as it changes viewpoints, so use a method of your own choosing to create some drawing space by zooming out. When you are satisfied with your zoom level, use the following command line input to draw a rectangle that is above, and tilted to, the X-Y plane:

```
Command:  LINE (Enter)
Specify first point:  0,.5,1 (Enter)
Specify next point or [Undo]:  @1.5<0 (Enter)
Specify next point or [Undo]:  @1.5<90,.5 (Enter)
Specify next point or [Close/Undo]:  @1.5<180 (Enter)
Specify next point or [Close/Undo]:  c (Enter)
```

Notice that the end of the first line was established by 2D polar coordinates. If you do not specify a Z coordinate when you use relative input (which is signified by the @ character), AutoCAD stays at the last elevation specified (which, in this case, is 1.0). The third line also was drawn using polar coordinates.

The end of the second line was established by cylindrical coordinates. Their format is the same as for 2D polar coordinates, with an elevation tacked onto the end. The input signified that the end of the line was to be 1.5 units in the Y direction (90 degrees) and 0.5 units in the Z direction. The actual length of the line is longer than 1.5 units. If you had wanted it to be exactly 1.5 units long, you would have used spherical coordinates, similar to the following:

@1.5<90<20

The first angle in this input means that the line will be 90 degrees counterclockwise from the X axis, while the second angle tilts the line 20 degrees from the X-Y plane.

Your wireframe model should now look similar to the one shown in Figure 2-2, except of course, yours will not have the text.

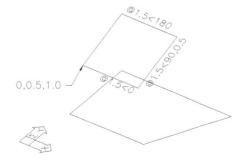

Figure 2-2

Finish the model by connecting the line endpoints as shown in Figure 2-3. This is best accomplished by first turning on a running-endpoint–object snap. I won't show the command line input to do this or draw the lines, because you are undoubtedly well acquainted with those steps.

Before you abandon this wireframe model, you should use it in setting some viewpoints. Figure 2-4 shows the top, front, and side views of the model. You can set each of these viewpoints by typing in view direction coordinates on the command line with the VPOINT command, by selecting them from the View/3D Viewpoints pull-down menu, or by selecting them from the Viewpoint toolbar. You will not be able to see all three views at one time, as shown in the fig-

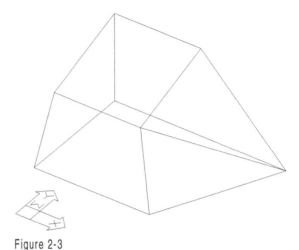

Figure 2-3

ure. Multiple viewports are discussed in Chapter 3. Until then you will work with just a single viewport.

This finishes Exercise Two. You will not use this model in any future exercises, so you do not need to save or retain it.

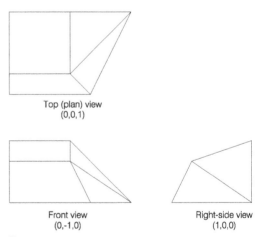

Top (plan) view
(0,0,1)

Front view
(0,-1,0)

Right-side view
(1,0,0)

Figure 2-4

# CHAPTER 2

# Managing AutoCAD's User Coordinate System

*AutoCAD's movable local coordinate system — the User Coordinate System — is explored exten-sively in this chapter. The UCS is one of AutoCAD's most important 3D features because it allows you to use the same techniques in making 3D models that you have always used in making 2D drawings. The UCS makes working in 3D practical.*

*This chapter*

- *describes the characteristics of the UCS;*

- *describes the commands for controlling the UCS;*

- *explains how to choose the best option for setting up a UCS.*

The key to working successfully in 3D space — whether you are making wireframe, surface, or solid models — is AutoCAD's User Coordinate System. It enables you to efficiently use your point-ing device in 3D space, and it allows you to use the same techniques in making 3D models that you have long used in making 2D drawings. The snap and ortho modes, as well as the commands asso-ciated with 2D, such as ARRAY, MIRROR, BREAK, and ROTATE, work just as well on the X-Y plane of the UCS as they do on the X-Y plane of the World Coordinate System (WCS) discussed in Chapter 1. The UCS X-Y plane, however, can be positioned anyplace in the WCS you want.

Conceptually, the UCS is easy to understand. It is a 3D coordinate system identical to the WCS, but it is a movable coordinate system whose origin can be placed in any location within the WCS, and its principal axes can be rotated into any orientation. It is a local coordinate system for work-ing in a specific area.

In your everyday life, you often use local coordinate systems without even thinking about them. For example, if you were to measure the length, width, and height of a box that is located somewhere in a room, you would undoubtedly base those measurements on one corner of the box. Although the room could be considered a global coordinate system (similar to the WCS) and you could base all of the box measurements on one corner of the room, you are not likely to do so. Even if the position of the box within the room was important, you would probably specify its location relative to one key point on the box — not to every corner of it.

In AutoCAD versions 10 through 14, only one UCS can exist at any given time, but beginning in AutoCAD 2000, individual viewports can simultaneously have their own UCS. Multiple viewports and multiple UCSs are discussed in the next chapter.

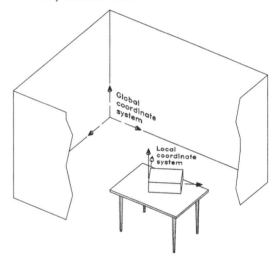

## The UCS Command

AutoCAD's appropriately named UCS command manages the UCS. Because it is such an important command, you need to become very familiar with it so that you will be able to quickly and precisely set UCSs.

Typically, you work in one plane at a time as you build 3D models. You set up a UCS, draw the portion of the model that is on the X-Y of the UCS, and then set up another UCS so that you can work in another section of the model.

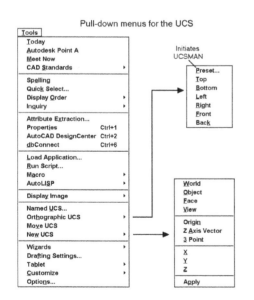

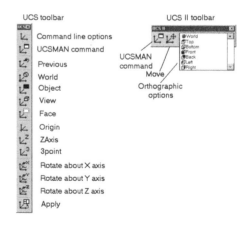

You can initiate the UCS command and access its more than 20 options through any one of four different ways — from AutoCAD's command line, through the UCS and UCS II toolbars, through the UCS flyout on the Standard toolbar, and by choosing one of the UCS selections in AutoCAD's pull-down menu labeled Tools. The UCS toolbar is an especially convenient method of selecting UCS options, and you will probably want it somewhere on your screen so that you have ready access to the most useful UCS options.

| | |
|---|---|
| Command: | UCS |
| Purpose: | The UCS command sets the location and orientation of the UCS and allows you to name, save, restore, and manage specific UCS orientations. |
| Initiate with: | • At the command line prompt, enter UCS. |
| | • Choose the UCS flyout from the Standard toolbar or select an option from the UCS or UCS II toolbars. |
| | • From the Tools pull-down menu, select one of the four UCS option groups. |
| Options: | New/Move/orthoGraphic/Prev/Restore/Save/Del/Apply/?/World. |

• New          When you select New from the list of options, the command line prompt is

          `Specify origin of new UCS or [ZAxis/3point/Object/Face/View/X/Y/Z]<0,0,0>:`

    • Origin      This is the default option in the New category. It moves the UCS to a new location in 3D space without changing the orientation of the X, Y, and Z axes. AutoCAD prompts you for a point in 3D space at which to locate the origin.

          `Specify origin of new UCS <0,0,0>: Specify a point.`

          You can use any of the standard methods in specifying this point. Typed-in coordinates are relative to the current UCS origin rather than to the WCS origin.

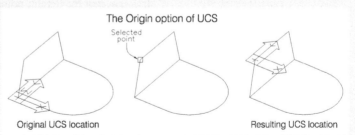

The Origin option of UCS

Selected point

Original UCS location                        Resulting UCS location

    • ZAxis      Two point locations are required for this option. The first point specifies the origin of the new UCS, while the second point establishes the positive direction of the Z axis. The X-Y plane will be located on the first point selected and will be perpendicular to a line from the first point to the second point.

          `Specify new origin point <0,0,0>: Specify a point.`

          `Specify point on positive portion of Z-axis <current direction>: Specify a point.`

AutoCAD sets the direction of the X axis to be parallel with the WCS X-Y plane. If you accept the current location of the origin and specify a new Z-axis direction, AutoCAD tilts the X-Y plane. If you specify a new origin while accepting the current Z-axis direction, the X-Y plane of the new UCS remains parallel to that of the old UCS (similar to the Origin option).

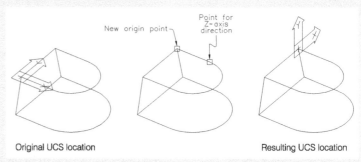

Original UCS location    Resulting UCS location

• 3point

This option asks for three points. The first point sets the origin of the new UCS, the second point establishes the direction of the X axis relative to the new origin, and the third point determines how the X-Y plane is to be rotated in space. The third point does not have to be on the Y axis. It can be anywhere off the line between the first two points.

```
Specify new origin point <0,0,0>: Specify a point.
Specify point on the positive portion of the X-axis <current
   direction>: Specify a point.
Specify point on the positive-Y portion of the UCS XY plane
   <current direction>: Specify a point.
```

If you accept the default point for the first point, the origin of the new UCS will be the same as that of the old UCS. If you accept the default for the second point, the X axis direction of the new UCS will be the same as the current X axis. And, if you accept the default for the third point, the X-Y plane of the new UCS will be parallel to the X-Y plane of the old UCS.

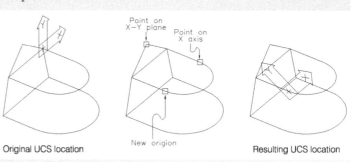

Original UCS location    New origin    Resulting UCS location

- Object

This option moves and orients the UCS according to an existing object. The Z-axis direction of the new UCS is the same as the object's extrusion direction. The location of the UCS origin depends on the type of object selected, and the directions of the X and Y axes are dependent on the location of the object-selection point, as shown in Table 2-1 on page 37. The option's follow-up prompt is

Select object to align UCS: Select an object.

You must select an object by picking a point on it — window and crossing selection methods are not allowed. Any object type can be selected, except for the following: 3D solid, 3D polyline, spline, polygon mesh, viewport, mline, region, ellipse, ray, xline, leader, and mtext.

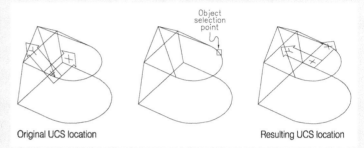

Original UCS location                    Resulting UCS location

- Face

This option places the UCS on the flat face, or surface, of a 3D solid. The option's prompts are

Select face of solid object: Select an object.
Enter an option [Next/Xflip/Yflip] <accept>: Enter an option or press
    Enter.

You select the face by picking a point on its surface or on one of its edges. The edges of the selected face are highlighted, and the UCS X-Y plane moves to the face with its origin in a corner nearest the pick point. If you choose the Next option, the next suitable face becomes the selected face. Its edges are highlighted, and the UCS X-Y plane moves to it. The Xflip option rotates the UCS X-Y plane 180 degrees about the X axis, while the Yflip option rotates the X-Y plane 180 degrees about the Y axis.

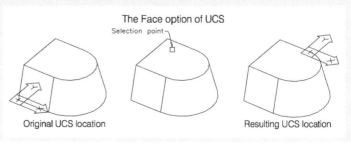

The Face option of UCS

Original UCS location                    Resulting UCS location

• View

The View option reorients the UCS so that the X-Y plane is perpendicular to the current view direction. The X axis is parallel to the bottom of the viewport, the Y axis is pointed vertically, and the Z axis is pointed out of the screen toward the viewer. The origin of the UCS is not changed. No follow-up prompts are issued.

The View option of UCS

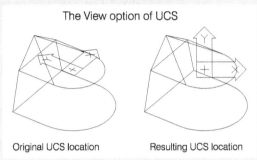

Original UCS location          Resulting UCS location

• X/Y/Z

Each of these three options rotate the other two principal axes about the specified axis. The location of the origin is unchanged. AutoCAD issues the follow-up prompt:

`Specify rotation angle about N axis <90>: Specify an angle.`

The letter N is replaced by X, Y, or Z in the actual prompt. You can respond to the prompt by either typing in an angle value or by picking two points representing an angle from the current X axis.

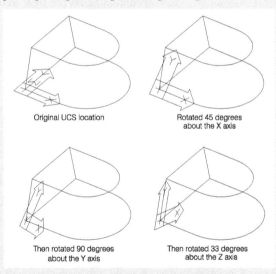

Original UCS location          Rotated 45 degrees
                               about the X axis

Then rotated 90 degrees        Then rotated 33 degrees
about the Y axis               about the Z axis

• Move

This option of the main UCS command line menu controls the UCS origin. It issues the following command line prompt:

`Specify new origin point or [Zdepth] <0,0,0>: Enter a z, or specify a point.`

When you select a point, the UCS origin moves to that point. The Zdepth option moves the origin to a new location along the Z axis. This option prompts you to specify a distance. Positive values move the X-Y plane in the positive Z-axis direction, while negative values move it in the minus Z-axis direction. If you pick two points to specify a distance, the direction is always positive.

When an orthographic UCS is in effect, the Move option not only sets the origin of the current orthographic UCS, it also sets the origin for subsequent calls to that particular orthographic UCS. Suppose, for example, the Front orthographic UCS is in effect and the Move option is used to relocate the origin. Then, suppose you restored the WCS, and next you selected the Front orthographic UCS option again. The origin of the UCS would be on the point established by the last Move option — not on the origin of the base UCS for orthographic UCSs.

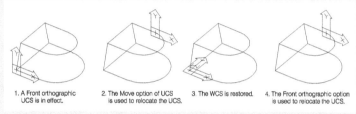

1. A Front orthographic UCS is in effect.   2. The Move option of UCS is used to relocate the UCS.   3. The WCS is restored.   4. The Front orthographic option is used to relocate the UCS.

- orthoGraphic

This option moves the UCS origin to the origin of a named UCS stored in the **ucsbase** system variable and rotates the Z axis so that it points in one of the six principal directions of that UCS. It issues the prompt:

```
Enter an option [Top/Bottom/Front/Back/Left/Right] <current>: Enter an
    option or press Enter.
```

The results of the options are shown in the following table:

| Option | Z Direction Relative to Named UCS |
| --- | --- |
| Top | Positive Z direction |
| Bottom | Negative Z direction |
| Front | Negative Y direction |
| Back | Positive Y direction |
| Left | Negative X direction |
| Right | Positive X direction |

- Prev

This option, which uses no additional prompts, returns the UCS to the previous location and orientation. Prev can be repeated to step back through the last 10 UCS settings in model space and through the last 10 settings in paper space.

• Restore

The Restore option brings back a UCS location and orientation that has been saved by the Save option of UCS. AutoCAD issues the follow-up prompt:

```
Enter name of UCS to restore or [?]: Enter a name or ?.
```

The question mark option brings up a prompt that you can use to obtain a list of the names of all UCSs that have been saved.

• Save

The current UCS location and orientation can be saved by this option. AutoCAD asks for a name to be assigned to the UCS:

```
Enter name to save current UCS or [?]: Enter a name or ?.
```

The question mark option brings up a prompt that can be used to obtain a list of existing UCS names. Names can be up to 255 characters long and can contain letters, digits, dollar signs ($), hyphens (-), underscores (_), and even spaces.

• Del

This option allows you to delete one or more named UCSs.

```
Enter UCS name(s) to delete <none>: Enter a name list.
```

You can delete more than one UCS by using the question mark (?) and asterisk (*) wild card characters, or by entering several UCS names, separated by commas.

• Apply

When multiple viewports exist, you can use this option to set the UCS of a selected viewport to be the same as that of the current viewport. It issues the command line prompt:

```
Pick viewport to apply current UCS or [All] <current>: Specify a view-
    port, enter A, or press Enter.
```

You specify a viewport by moving the screen cursor to within it and pressing the pick button of your pointing device. If you select the All option, the UCS of the current viewport is applied to all viewports. No changes occur if you press the Enter key.

• ?

The question mark option allows you to see information about all named UCSs. AutoCAD prompts for a name list.

```
Enter UCS name(s) to list <*>: Enter a name list.
```

A list of all saved UCSs, including their names, their origin locations, and the directions of their X, Y, and Z axes relative to the current UCS, is displayed. Also, the name of the current UCS is displayed. If the WCS is currently being used, it will be listed as *WORLD*. If the current UCS is not a named UCS and is not the WCS, it will be listed as *NO NAME*. You also can use wild card characters to obtain a filtered list of named UCSs.

• World

This, default option restores the WCS.

Notes:

• Beginning with AutoCAD 2000, the UCS can vary between viewports. When multiple viewports exist, the UCS command affects only the current viewport (except for the Apply option, which applies the UCS of the current viewport to another viewport).

• You can initiate the suboptions of New from the main UCS prompt, even though they are not listed in the main prompt. With the Face option, however, you must enter its entire name or its first two letters — entering just the letter F does not work.

- Unless the system variable **ucsfollow** has been set to a value of 1, changing a UCS location or orientation will not change the viewpoint, or the zoom level. This is true even when named UCSs are restored.

- Although the UCS command has no provisions for renaming a saved UCS, you can use the RENAME or the UCSMAN commands to do so.

- Prior to Release 13, the Object option was named "Entity," and AutoCAD still accepts that name, or even just the letter E.

| System variables: | | |
|---|---|---|
| | • **angdir** | The direction of positive rotation is controlled by this toggle-type system variable. When **angdir** is set to 0, which is the default setting, rotation direction follows the right-hand rule. Thus, positive rotation is counterclockwise when viewed from the positive direction of the rotation axis. |
| | • **ucsaxisang** | This system variable stores the default angle of revolution offered in the X, Y, and Z axes options of UCS. Its initial value is 90 degrees. |
| | • **ucsbase** | The name of the UCS used for the origin and axes orientation of the Orthographic options of UCS is stored in this system variable. Initially, the name in **ucsbase** is World. |
| | • **ucsfollow** | This is a toggle-type system variable having a value of either 0 (off) or 1 (on). When it is set to 1, AutoCAD automatically switches to a plan view whenever you change from one UCS to another. As in the PLAN command, AutoCAD performs the equivalent of a Zoom/Extents when setting up the plan view. |
| | • **ucsname** | The name of the current UCS is stored in this read-only system variable. If the current UCS is unnamed or is the WCS, **ucsname** will contain just a pair of quotation marks. |
| | • **ucsorg** | This read-only system variable holds the origin of the current UCS as a 3D point relative to the WCS. |
| | • **ucsxdir** | The direction of the current UCS X axis as a point offset from the WCS origin is stored in this read-only system variable. |
| | • **ucsydir** | This read-only system variable contains the direction of the current UCS Y axis. It is stored as a 3D point representing a direction from the WCS origin. |
| | • **worlducs** | If this system variable contains a value of 1, the current UCS is the same as the WCS. If the UCS is different from the WCS in origin, axes orientation, or both, then **worlducs** will have the value of 0. It is a read-only system variable. |

## Table 2-1 The Object Option's Choice of Origin and X Axis Direction

| Object Type | Origin Location | Direction of X-Axis |
|---|---|---|
| Arc | Center of arc | The X axis passes through the arc endpoint closest to the object pick point. |
| Circle | Center of circle | The X axis passes through the object pick point. |

## Table 2-1 The Object Option's Choice of Origin and X Axis Direction (Continued)

| Object Type | Origin Location | Direction of X-Axis |
|---|---|---|
| Dimension | Midpoint of dimension text | The X axis is parallel to the X axis of the UCS in effect when the dimension was placed. |
| Line | Endpoint nearest the object pick point | The X axis is on the selected line. |
| Point | The location of the point | The direction of the X axis is controlled by AutoCAD's Arbitrary Axis Algorithm. |
| 2D polyline | Start point of the polyline | The X axis passes through the polyline's second vertex. |
| Solid | Start point of the solid | The X axis passes through the solid's second point. |
| Trace | Start point of the trace | The X axis passes through the second point of the trace, ignoring the trace's width. |
| 3D face | Start point of the 3D face | The X axis is on the edge between the first and second point of the 3D face. The positive direction of the Y axis is from the first and fourth point of the 3D face, or from the first and third point if the 3D face has only three edges. |
| Text, blocks, and shapes | Insert point of the object | The X axis is in the direction of the rotation angle of the object. Therefore, the selected object will have a rotation angle of 0 in the new UCS. |

# Choosing the Right UCS Option

Over 20 options are available with the UCS command. This abundance of options does not mean that the command is complicated to use; it means that you have a variety of tools and methods for setting up a UCS.

The command line options of UCS are

```
New/Move/orthoGraphic/Prev/Restore/Save/Del/Apply/?/World
```

These options are also available in a right-click shortcut menu. When you select the New option, a secondary prompt containing the following options appears:

```
Origin/ZAxis/3point/OBject/Face/View/X/Y/Z
```

As with all AutoCAD command line menus, you can select an option by typing in the entire option name or just the uppercase letters in the option name. You can use this method to start the Origin, ZAxis, 3point, Object, View, X, Y, and Z options, even though those options are not listed in the main prompt. You also can start the Face option from the main prompt by entering its first two letters or its entire name.

Your choice of an option is governed by the desired position and orientation of the new UCS X-Y plane and on the availability of objects that can be used for point selections. Often, two or more steps are needed before the UCS is positioned as you want it, and there is more than one way, and more than one choice of options, for setting the UCS in the position and orientation you need.

The options of the UCS command can be conveniently divided into five categories.

- Options that move the UCS origin while leaving the orientation of the principal axis as it is. The Move and Origin options are in this category.

- Options that move the UCS origin and, at the same time, position the principal axes in a specific orientation. The options that can do this are ZAxis, 3point, Face, and Object.

- Options that change the orientation of the UCS axes without moving the UCS origin. Four options are within this category: View, X, Y, and Z.

- Options that return the UCS to a previously established origin location and axes orientation. The Prev, World, and Restore options do this directly, while the Save, Del, and question mark (?) options manage previous UCS configurations.

- Options that point the Z axis perpendicular to the principal planes of a base coordinate system. These are the orthographic options.

An option that does not fit in any of these categories is Apply. When multiple viewports exist, you can use this option to set the UCS of a selected viewport to be the same as that of the current viewport. In the next few pages, you'll see how the options within the five categories work and how you can put them to use.

## Options that Move the UCS Origin without Changing the Axes Orientation

The Move and Origin options fall within this category. The Move option is for relocating the origin of the orthographic views, while the Origin option is for general use in positioning the UCS origin. Often, you will use these options to move the UCS to a plane that is higher or lower than the current X-Y plane without changing the orientation of the principal axes. You might,

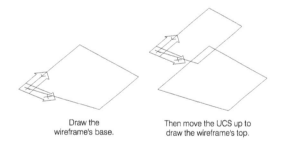

Draw the wireframe's base.

Then move the UCS up to draw the wireframe's top.

for example, after drawing the base of a wireframe, use the Origin option to raise the drawing plane in preparation for drawing the top of the wireframe.

Also, you will sometimes use the Origin option as the first of two or more steps in positioning the UCS. For instance, you might first move the origin to a specific point, and then use another UCS option to rotate the axes into a new orientation.

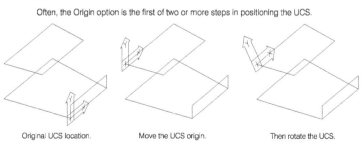

Often, the Origin option is the first of two or more steps in positioning the UCS.

Original UCS location.          Move the UCS origin.          Then rotate the UCS.

## Options That Move the UCS Origin and Change the Axes Orientation

Four UCS options can move the UCS origin and, at the same time, rotate the principal axes. They are ZAxis, 3point, Object, and Face. The first two are especially flexible, allowing you to move the origin or leave it in its current location, as well as to selectively rotate certain axes. Object, on the other hand, moves the origin and points the axes according to rules that depend on the type of object selected. The Face option

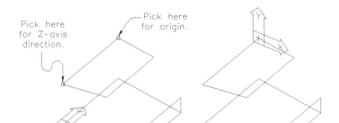

Using the ZAxis option to move and tilt the UCS X-Y plane

Pick here for Z-axis direction.

Pick here for origin.

Original UCS location          Reslting UCS location

can be used only on 3D solid objects, which are discussed in Section 3.

The ZAxis option is more versatile than it first appears to be. You can use it to relocate the UCS origin and also tilt the X-Y plane, or you can use it to simply tilt the X-Y plane. The option issues a follow-up prompt for two points. The first point establishes the origin, while the second point establishes the positive direction of the Z axis. The X-Y plane is perpendicular to a line drawn between the two points, and the X axis is parallel with the X-Y plane of the WCS.

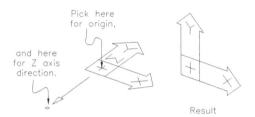

Pick here for origin,

and here for Z axis direction.

Result

For example: if, from the WCS, you keep the UCS origin at 0,0,0 and point in the minus Y direction for the new Z axis direction, AutoCAD simply tilts the X-Y plane. The result is the same as rotating the UCS 90 degrees about the X axis.

On the other hand, if from the WCS you keep the UCS origin at 0,0,0 and point in the positive X direction for the new Z-axis direction, AutoCAD both tilts and rotates the X-Y plane. The result is the same as rotating the UCS 90 degrees about the Z axis, and then rotating it 90 degrees about the X axis.

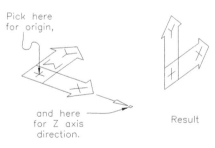

Pick here for origin,

and here for Z axis direction.

Result

When you become used to it, the ZAxis option can be handy for quickly setting the UCS with minimum input. With one step, you can attain the same results as several steps used to rotate the X-Y plane about an axis.

The 3point option is useful for precisely setting a UCS that matches existing objects. Typically, you use object snaps to specify the three points. The first point sets the origin location, and the second point sets the direction of the X axis. The third point establishes the orientation of the X-Y plane — not the direction of the Y axis. Consequently, the third point can be anywhere off the line between the first two points. It does not have to be 90 degrees from the line establishing the X axis.

The Object option of UCS moves and orients the coordinate system according to an existing object. In AutoCAD Releases 10 through 12, this option was named "Entity," and even in later releases, AutoCAD accepts that name, or just a typed-in letter E. This option requires that you select the object

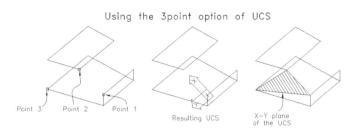

Using the 3point option of UCS

Point 3    Point 2    Point 1

Resulting UCS

X-Y plane of the UCS

by picking a point on it because the UCS origin, as well as the directions of the X and Y axes, are sometimes dependent upon the selection point. See Table 2-1 on page 37 for details.

Often the Object option is used to change the UCS for editing an existing object. Prior to Release 13, when the orientation of the UCS was critical for operations such as fillets, trims, and breaks, this option was needed more than it is now. But it is still useful in preparing to change an object, for locating text relative to

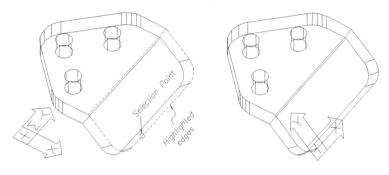

Selection Point

Highlighted edges

an existing object, and for making sure the UCS is located on a particular object.

The Face option places the UCS X-Y plane on the flat face, or surface, of a 3D solid object. (See Section 3 of this book for information about 3D solids.) You are prompted to select a face. You can do this by picking a point on an edge or on the surface of the face (even in wireframe viewing modes, when the surface is transparent). Usually, however, you have better control if you pick a point on an edge. AutoCAD highlights the edges of the selected face, moves the UCS origin to the corner on the face nearest the pick point, and issues the prompt:

```
Enter an option [Next/Xflip/Yflip] <accept>: (Enter an option or press Enter)
```

Select the Next option to switch to the other possible face. That face becomes highlighted, the UCS origin moves to it, and the prompt is repeated. The Xflip option rotates the X-Y plane of the UCS 180 degrees about the X axis, while the Yflip option rotates it 180 degrees about the Y axis. When the UCS is on the face you want, and oriented as you want, press the Enter key.

### Using the Face option's Xflip and Yflip options

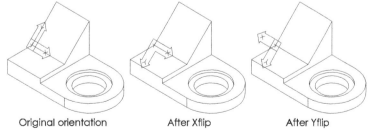

Original orientation          After Xflip          After Yflip

## Options That Rotate the Principal Axes without Moving the Origin

Four options of the UCS command leave the UCS origin location unchanged as they rotate the UCS principal axes about the origin. Of these, the View option is the most straightforward. No additional input is needed — the axes are simply rotated so that the X axis is parallel to the horizontal sides of the current viewport, while the Y axis is parallel to the vertical sides. The Z axis points straight out of the computer screen. The result is similar to the PLAN command, but the operations themselves are opposite. PLAN rotates the viewpoint so that the line of sight is directly down on the X-Y plane, while the View option of UCS rotates the X-Y plane so that it is perpendicular to the line of sight.

The View option is useful for ensuring that text placed in 3D space for an illustration or presentation is seen head-on. In fact, much of the text in the figures of this book was added after using the View option of UCS. The View option is also good when used with paper space viewports for properly orienting the UCS to add dimensions to a 3D model. I will discuss that use of the View option when I explain how to make dimensioned 2D drawings from 3D models in Section 4 of this book.

Each of the three options designated by the letters X, Y, and Z rotate the other two principal axes about the specified axis. The Y option, for instance, rotates the X and Z axes about the Y axis. AutoCAD prompts for a rotation angle when you choose one of these options, and you can respond by typing in an angle or by picking two points to show the angle to AutoCAD. The default angle of revolution is stored in the **ucsaxisang** system variable.

The positive rotation direction is counterclockwise when you look down the rotation axis toward the origin. An easy way to visualize rotation direction is to mentally grasp the rotation axis with your right hand so that your thumb is pointed away from the origin. Positive rotation will be in the direction of your curled fingers.

You might prefer to use negative rotation angles in specifying clockwise rotation, even though you do not have to use them. For example, if you want to revolve the UCS clockwise around the Z axis, it might be easier for you to think in terms of −45-degree rotation rather than 315-degree rotation, even though they are equivalent.

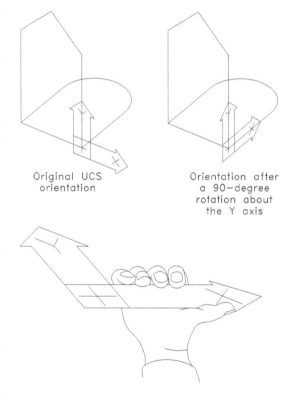

Original UCS
orientation

Orientation after
a 90−degree
rotation about
the Y axis

One final note about rotation direction: If you have AutoCAD's **angdir** system variable set to 1, positive rotation will be in the opposite direction from what was just described.

### Options for Restoring a Previous UCS

The fourth category of UCS options restores a previous UCS. One of the choices, the Prev option, allows you to step back through as many as 10 UCS configurations. (You also can step back through up to 10 UCS configurations in paper space. Paper space is discussed in Section Four.) This option uses no additional prompts. The process is similar to stepping back through Zooms, although the Prev option affects only the UCS, not zooms or views.

You will often go from one UCS to another as you build 3D models, but occasionally you will find it beneficial to return to the WCS before you move on. Also, it is a good idea to develop the habit of restoring the WCS when you complete a 3D model. World, the default option of the UCS command, restores the WCS. You also could describe the result by saying the UCS is configured exactly like the WCS, because in some subtle ways, AutoCAD considers a UCS to exist at all times, even though it is sometimes equivalent to the WCS.

### Named UCS

The remaining four options for restoring a previous UCS are for saving, recalling, and managing named UCSs. You use named UCSs when making complicated 3D models that have planes to which you will return, especially when you have a critical UCS that is difficult to set up and you want to ensure that you can return to it with minimal effort.

Save is the first of these options that you will use. AutoCAD asks you for a name and saves the current UCS origin and axes orientation in the drawing file's database. The Restore option changes the current UCS to one that has been saved. If you forget the name of a saved UCS, you can use the question mark option (?) to bring up a list of UCSs, along with their origins and axes directions relative to the current UCS. Whenever you want to get rid a saved UCS, you can delete it with the Del option.

If you have more than one named UCS, you will probably prefer to use AutoCAD's UCSMAN command for managing and restoring them, rather than the UCS command, because UCSMAN displays a dialog box showing all of the names.

## The Orthographic Options

The six options in this category place the UCS origin on the origin of a base coordinate system and point its Z axis perpendicular to one of the principal planes of the base coordinate system. The name of the base coordinate system is stored in the **ucsbase** system variable. By default it is the WCS, but it can be any named UCS. The Move option also affects the location of the UCS origin. The names of the orthographic options and the direction their Z axis points relative to the base coordinate system are shown in the following table.

| Option | Direction of Z Axis Relative to the Base Coordinate System |
|--------|-----------------------------------------------------------|
| Top | Positive Z direction |
| Bottom | Negative Z direction |
| Front | Negative Y direction |

| Back | Positive Y direction |
|------|----------------------|
| Left | Negative X direction |
| Right | Positive X direction |

Although you are not often likely to often use the orthographic options of the UCS command, they can be useful when you are starting a 3D model, and also when you have a complex model, on which you have established some named UCSs that are suitable for the base coordinate systems for orthographic views. You might also find them useful in creating orthographic views for a multiview 2D drawing of a 3D model. (Multiview 2D drawings are discussed in Section 4 of this book.)

| | |
|---|---|
| Command: | UCSMAN |
| Purpose: | This command restores and manages named and preset UCS configurations, controls the UCS icon setting, and controls the relationship of the UCS with view-ports and view directions. |
| | Initiate with: |
| | • On the command line, enter UCSMAN. |
| | • From the Tools pull-down menu, select Named UCS. |
| | • From the UCS and UCSII toolbars, select Display UCS Dialog. |
| | UCSMAN dislays a dialog box with three tabs. Each tab opens one of the following secondary dialog boxes. |
| Named UCSs: | The names of all the UCS configurations currently in the drawing are displayed in a list box, with the current UCS shown above the list box. The names of all saved UCSs are listed, and if more than one UCS has been used during the current AutoCAD editing session, a UCS named Previous is included. When the current UCS does not have a name, it is shown as Unnamed. You can highlight any of these UCSs by clicking its name. |

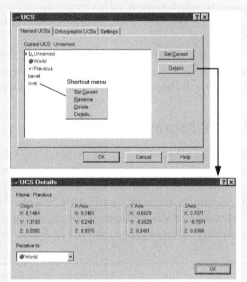

A shortcut menu (displayed by pressing the return button of your pointing device) allows you to make the highlighted UCS the current one, to rename it, and to delete it. This shortcut menu is a convenient way to name the current UCS if it is unnamed. You cannot rename or delete the World and Previous UCSs. The Details option in this shortcut menu brings up a secondary dialog box that shows the origin and the directions of the principal axes of the highlighted UCS. The information is in the form of 3D points relative to any of the other UCSs, except Prevous. The Set Current and Details dialog box buttons duplicate the results of the same options in the shorcut menus.

- Orthographic UCSs:

The dialog box opened by this tab is similar to the one for the Named UCSs tab. The six listed UCSs, however, are preset by AutoCAD. The Z axis of each preset UCS points in one of six principal directions relative to the UCS shown in the dropdown list box in the lower-left corner of the dialog box. The name of the reference UCS for the orthographic UCSs is stored in the **ucsbase** system variable.

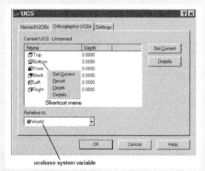

ucsbase system variable

By default, the origin of the preset UCS is the same as the origin of the reference UCS. When you override the default by specifying a depth, the origin is moved in the Z axis direction by the specified depth. Thus, if you specified a depth of 2.0 for a Right UCS, the Z-axis of the UCS would point in the WCS X-axis direction and its origin would be on the WCS point having the coordinates of 2,0,0. This example assumes that the WCS is the reference coordinate system for orthographic UCSs. You can set the Depth through a shortcut menu, or by double-clicking the Depth value in the list box.

The Details and Set Current options produce the same results as those in the Named UCSs dialog box. The Reset option restores the original origin of the orthographic UCS.

- Settings:

The dialog box for this tab has three check boxes for setting the same UCS icon parameters controlled by the UCSICON command. The check box labeled On controls whether or not the UCS icon is displayed, and the check box labeled Display at UCS Origin Point controls whether the UCS icon is located on the UCS origin (provided the origin is within the viewport) or is always located in the lower-left corner of the viewport. When the check box labeled Apply to All Active Viewports is checked, the settings for the other two check boxes affect all viewports; otherwise, they apply only to the current viewport.

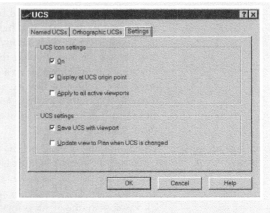

The check box labeled Save UCS with Viewport controls the relationship of the UCS of the current viewport to other viewports. When it is checked, the UCS of the viewport is independent of the UCS in other viewports. When it is cleared, the UCS of the viewport changes as needed to match the UCS of the current viewport. This check box controls the value of the **ucsvp** system variable for the current viewport. When it is checked, **ucsvp** is set to 1, and when it is cleared, **ucsvp** is set to 0.

## Exercises

Practice and use are the best ways to become skillful in manipulating the UCS. The following two exercises lead you through the steps of moving and orienting the UCS in building two wireframe models. The first is a simple warm-up exercise; the second is more involved.

### Exercise One

In this exercise, you will remake the wireframe you made during Exercise Two in Chapter 1. In that exercise, you had to type in the coordinates to draw the lines that were off the WCS X-Y plane. In this exercise, you will move and orient the UCS so that you can use your pointing device to draw all of the wireframe's lines.

You will not want to keep this wireframe, so your drawing setup is not important. However, because the lengths of the lines will be in increments of 0.5 units, you might find it convenient to turn on AutoCAD's snap mode with a snap spacing of 0.5.

Draw four lines on the WCS X-Y plane using the dimensions given in Figure 1-1. Their actual location on the X-Y plane is not important.

Next, switch to an isometric-type view by using VPOINT with rotation angles of 305 degrees in the X-Y plane from the X axis, and 35 degrees from the X-Y plane. Zoom back and pan as necessary to give yourself room to work.

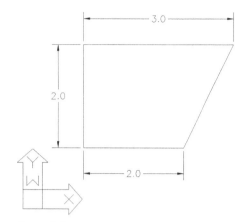

Figure 1-1

In preparation for drawing the left side of the wireframe, use the ZAxis option of the UCS command to place the UCS origin on the left end of the 2.0-unit-long horizontal line and rotate the UCS X-Y plane so that it is perpendicular to this line. The command line input to do this is

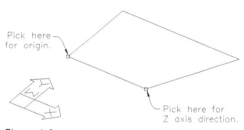

Figure 1-2

```
Command:  UCS (Enter)
Current UCS name: *WORLD*
Enter an option [New/Move/orthoGraphic/Prev/Restore/Save/
    Del/Apply/?/World]<World>: ZA (Enter)
Specify new origin point <0,0,0>: (Use an endpoint object
    snap to pick the point shown in Figure 1-2.)
Specify point on positive portion of Z-axis <0.0000,0.0000,1.0000>: (Use an endpoint object snap to pick the
    point shown in Figure 1-2.)
```

Notice that you can start the ZAxis option from the main UCS menu, even though it does not appear in the menu. Now draw the left side of the wireframe model, using the dimensions shown in Figure 1-3.

Use the 3point option of the UCS command to set the UCS X-Y plane in a position that enables you to draw the slanted rectangular face on the front of the model.

```
Command:  UCS (Enter)
Current UCS name: *NO NAME*
Enter an option [New/Move/orthoGraphic/Prev/Restore/Save/Del/
    Apply/?/World]<World>: 3 (Enter)
Specify new origin point <0,0,0>: (Press the Enter
key to accept the present location.)
```

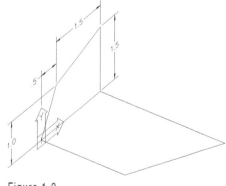

Figure 1-3

```
Specify point on positive portion of X-axis
    <1.0000,0.0000,0.0000>: (Use an endpoint object snap to pick the point shown in Figure 1-4.)
Specify point on positive-Y portion of the UCS X-Y plane <0.0000,1.0000,0.0000>: (Use an endpoint object snap
    to pick the point shown in Figure 1-4.)
```

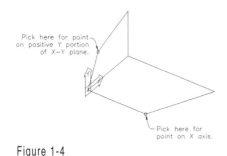

Figure 1-4

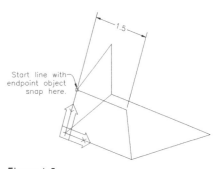

Figure 1-5

After the UCS is in position, draw the 1.5-unit line representing the top of the face and the slanted line that ties into the line previously drawn on the WCS X-Y plane, as shown in Figure 1-5. You have to start the 1.5-unit line with an endpoint object snap and draw the line using AutoCAD's ortho mode because its location does not match your snap setting.

Next, you set the UCS in a position for completing the wireframe's back side. You use the 3point option again, even though the ZAxis option would work equally well. Although the ZAxis option often permits you to use less input in placing a UCS in the same location and orientation as the 3point option, the 3point option is usually the surer way.

```
Command:  UCS (Enter)
Current UCS name: *NO NAME*
Enter an option [New/Move/orthoGraphic/Prev/Restore/Save/Del/
   Apply/?/ World]<World>: 3 (Enter)
Specify new origin point <0,0,0>: (Use an endpoint
object snap to pick the point shown in Figure 1-6.)
Specify point on positive portion of X-axis
   <1.0000,0.8944,-1.7889>: (Use an endpoint object snap to pick
   the point shown in Figure 1-6.)
Specify Point on positive-Y portion of the UCS XY plane
   <0.0000,1.8944,-7.7889>: (Use an endpoint object snap to pick
   the point shown in Figure 1-6.)
```

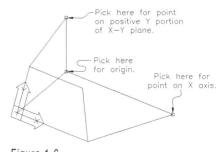

Figure 1-6

Draw the remaining two lines of the wireframe's back using the dimensions shown in Figure 1-7.

All the vertex points have now been established on the wireframe, so you can use object end-point snaps to draw the remaining three lines. Your completed wireframe model should be similar to the one shown in Figure 1-8.

This finishes the exercise. On the CD-ROM that comes with this book, you will find the finished wireframe model in file f0232.dwg.

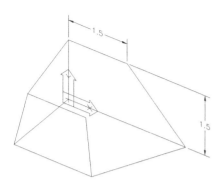

Figure 1-7

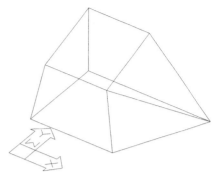

Figure 1-8

Exercise Two

In this exercise, you construct a wireframe model of a sheet-metal part. Such a 3D model can be used by some sheet-metal unfolding programs to make a flat pattern of the part. Their flat patterns account for metal deformation through bends so that the part can be cut to shape and the holes punched on a flat piece of sheet metal and still meet the 3D dimensions when the metal is folded.

Building this wireframe will reinforce your knowledge of AutoCAD's UCS and will also introduce some techniques that are useful in building 3D models of any type.

Start the part by drawing the three lines and two circles shown in Figure 2-1 on the WCS X-Y plane. The dimensions in this figure are for your use and should not be added to your model. Be certain that you draw the two lines that are parallel to the Y axis exactly 0.56 units long. The lines represent outside edges on the sheet-metal part, while the two circles represent holes in its surface.

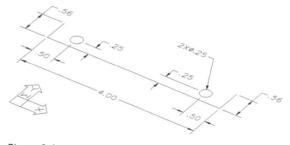

Figure 2-1

Use the ZAxis option of the UCS command with the points shown in Figure 2-2 to move and reposition the X-Y plane of the UCS. The command line input to do this isn't shown because you used this option of the UCS command in Exercise One.

Draw five lines using the dimensions shown in Figure 2-3. In this figure, the previously drawn lines and circles are shown in dashed line types.

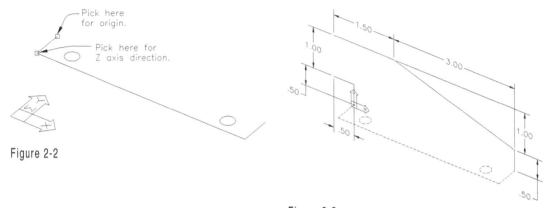

Figure 2-2

Figure 2-3

When you have drawn the five lines, use the ZAxis option of the UCS command to move the UCS once more. Use endpoint object snaps to pick points for the new origin and Z-axis direction, as shown in Figure 2-4.

When the UCS is positioned, draw three lines and two circles in accordance with the dimensions given in Figure 2-5.

This finishes all the edges and holes on the outside surface (which is the side that has the outside, or larger, bend radius) of the sheet-metal part. You use copies of them to make the inside surface. Your sheet-metal part is to be made of 16-gauge (0.060 inches thick) carbon steel, therefore, the copy displacement distance is 0.06 units.

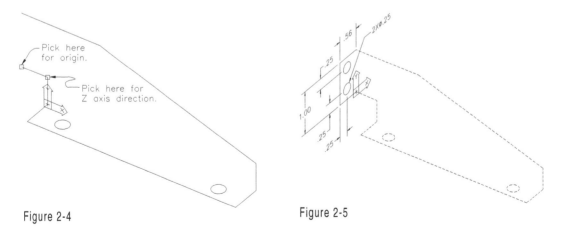

Figure 2-4

Figure 2-5

Before making the copies, use the World
option of AutoCAD's UCS command to return
the UCS to the WCS position and orientation.
Then copy the three lines and two circles that are
on the X-Y plane 0.06 units in the Z direction as
shown in Figure 2-6. Probably the easiest way to
do this is to use command line input to specify
the displacement distance of the copies.

Command: COPY (Enter)

Select objects: Select the three lines and two circles
    shown in Figure 2-6.

Specify base point or displacement, or [Multiple]:
    0,0,.06 (Enter)

Specify second point of displacement or <use first point
    as displacement>: (Enter)

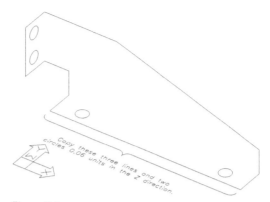

Figure 2-6

Then copy the five lines shown in Figure 2-7
that are in a plane parallel to the WCS Z-X plane
0.06 units in the minus -Y direction.

Command: COPY (Enter)

Select objects: Select the five lines shown in Figure
    2-7.

Specify base point or displacement, or [Multiple]: 0,-.06
    (Enter)

Specify second point of displacement or <use first point
    as displacement>: (Enter)

Lastly, copy the three lines and two circles shown
in Figure 2-8 that are in a plane parallel to the
WCS Y-Z plane 0.06 units in the X direction.

Command: COPY (Enter)

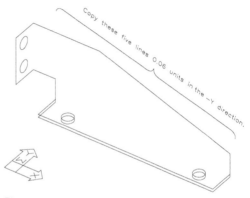

Figure 2-7

Select objects: Select the three lines and two circles
    shown in Figure 2-8.

Specify base point or displacement, or [Multiple]: .06,0
    (Enter)

Specify second point of displacement or <use first point as displacement>: (Enter)

Fillet the lines representing the inside surface of the sheet-metal part 0.06 units, as shown in Figure 2-9. You can make these fillets regardless of how the UCS is oriented.

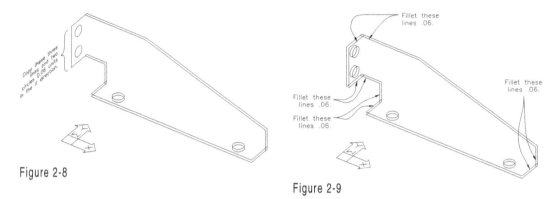

Figure 2-8

Figure 2-9

Next, fillet the lines on the outside corners of the bends 0.12 units, as shown in Figure 2-10. Your wireframe model should now look similar to the one shown in Figure 2-11.

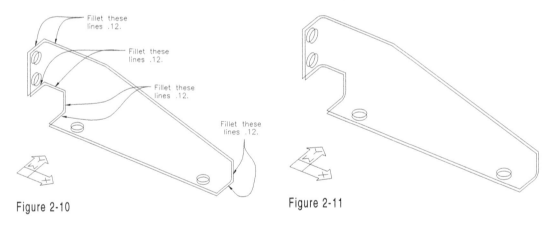

Figure 2-10

Figure 2-11

To finish the wireframe, use object endpoint snaps to draw lines across the sharp corners between the front and back surfaces of the sheet-metal part as in Figure 2-12.

Although many would consider the wireframe model finished, other people would draw lines across the wireframe connecting the points of tangency between the fillets and the straight edges as shown in Figure 2-13. This is easily done by using object endpoint snaps to draw the lines.

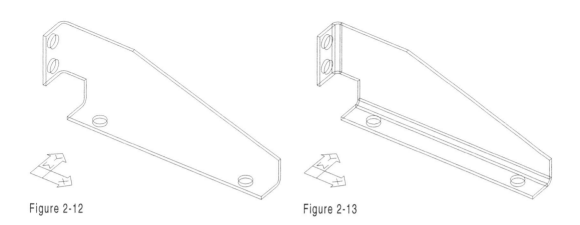

Figure 2-12                              Figure 2-13

In Section 4 of this book, I will show you how to make 2D multiview drawings from 3D models such as this. Such a drawing of this wireframe, without the tangency lines, would be similar to the one in Figure 2-14.

The completed wireframe model is in file f0245.dwg on the CD-ROM that comes with this book.

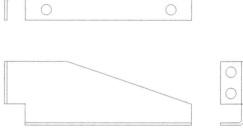

Figure 2-14

# CHAPTER 3

# Using Multiple Viewports

*In this chapter, you learn how AutoCAD's screen graphics area can be divided into multiple sections, called viewports, that allow you to simultaneously view and work with your 3D model from different viewpoints and under different conditions.*

*This chapter*

- *describes the properties and characteristics of model space viewports;*

- *explains how to create and work with multiple viewports;*

- *offers suggestions for fully utilizing multiple viewports;*

- *describes the relationships between multiple viewports, the User Coordinate System (UCS), and views.*

The flat, 2D computer screen you work with will always be a major problem as you build 3D models because it gives you no depth perception. Everything you draw appears to be in the same plane. To help alleviate this problem, AutoCAD can divide its screen graphics area into multiple sections, called *viewports*, which allow you to simultaneously see your model from different view directions. You can then compare the different views of your model to gain a better idea of its shape and the relationships of its components and points.

The accompanying figure shows an AutoCAD graphics area divided into three viewports. Although you can see three circles in the upper-left viewport, you cannot tell whether the circles represent holes or cylinders from that viewport alone. By looking in the other viewports, however, you can see that the two smaller circles are really holes, and moreover, one of them does not go completely through the model.

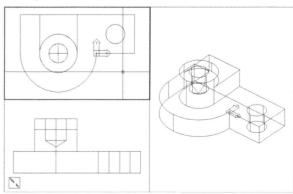

AutoCAD refers to these viewports as *tiled viewports* because, like ceramic tiles on a floor or wall, they always abut one another — there can be no space between adjacent viewports. Unlike operating-system windows, these tiled viewports have no title bars, and they cannot overlap, be dragged to other locations, or be stretched to another size. AutoCAD has more Windows-like viewports, called *floating viewports*; however, they are for making 2D drawings from models and are restricted to AutoCAD's paper space mode. Paper space and floating viewports are discussed in Section 4 of this book.

## Characteristics of Tiled Viewports

In addition to fitting tightly next to one another, tiled viewports are always rectangular in shape, and they always completely fill the AutoCAD graphics area. Each viewport can have its own view direction and zoom level, as well as its own snap and grid settings. Each viewport also can have a different setting for the UCS icon, and its own UCS origin location and axes orientation.

Although multiple viewports might exist, you are confined to working in just one of them in any instance in time. This viewport, called the *current viewport*, has a slightly thicker border than the others and contains the cursor crosshairs. All additions and changes made in the current viewport, however, are instantly shown in the other viewports (provided the changes are in a location covered by the viewport). Also, only the contents of the current viewport can be printed.

Screen redraws (with AutoCAD's REDRAW command) and regenerations (with REGEN) normally affect only the current viewport. You can, however, issue the REDRAWALL command to redraw all viewports, and you can use the REGENALL command to regenerate all viewports.

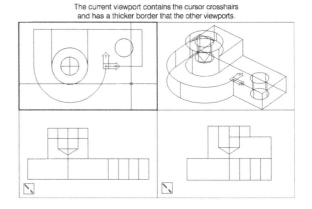

The current viewport contains the cursor crosshairs and has a thicker border that the other viewports.

Internally, AutoCAD assigns an identification number to the viewports and stores their lower-left and upper-right corner locations as decimal fractions of the sides of the full graphics area. The lower-left corner of the graphics area is represented as 0,0, and the upper-right corner of the graphics area is represented as 1,1. In the command line versions of VPORTS, you can use the question mark option to see this information for the current set of viewports.

For example, the viewport configuration shown in the next figure would be listed as
id # 3
corners: 0.0000,0.0000 0.5000,1.0000
id # 2
corners: 0.5000,0.5000 1.0000,1.0000
id # 4
corners: 0.5000,0.0000 1.0000,0.5000

The current viewport — the one containing the crosshair cursor — is always listed first. Furthermore, because AutoCAD reserves identification number 1 for the main paper space viewport, the lowest identification number that a model space viewport can have is 2. AutoCAD sometimes changes viewport identification numbers when a new drawing editing session begins. Thus, if you exited and then re-opened the drawing used for the previous figure, the large viewport might be number 2, rather than number 3.

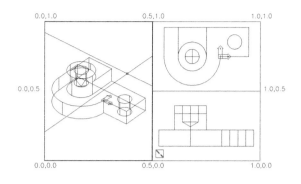

Most of the time, you do not need to know the viewport identification numbers and the coordinates of the viewports, but they are useful (as is demonstrated later in this chapter) in application programs related to viewports.

## Creating Tiled Viewports

By default, AutoCAD starts with a single viewport that fills the entire graphics area. Additional tiled viewports are created and managed by AutoCAD's VPORTS command, which also goes by the name VIEWPORTS. Both a dialog box and a command line version of VPORTS exists. Most of the time, you will use the dialog box version. However, the command line version, which is started by preceding the command's name with a hyphen (-VPORTS), has an option for joining viewports and another for obtaining information about viewports that are not available in the dialog box version.

Both versions of the command allow you to make up to four viewports at a time, but because you can divide the current viewport, more than four viewports can be created by repeating the command. The total number of viewports allowed, as well as the minimum viewport size, depends upon your computer's video system. Not having enough viewports, however, is not likely to ever be a problem. Generally, three or four viewports are enough.

By joining and subdividing viewports, you can create viewport arrangements that go beyond the standard options of the VPORTS command. For instance, suppose you want to have one large viewport covering the bottom two-thirds of the graphics area, and have three side-by-side viewports in the remaining one-third of the graphics area.

Create three horizontal viewports.

Join the two lower viewports.

Create three vertical viewports in the top viewport.

side-by-side viewports in the remaining one-third of the graphics area. You could make such an arrangement by first creating three horizontal viewports, then joining the two lower viewports, and lastly dividing the top viewport into three vertical viewports.

The dialog box version of VPORTS, which is the default version of the command, is an especially convenient way to create viewports. Select its New Viewports tab, and then select the name of a viewport arrangement from the list on the left side of the dialog box. The selected arrangement will be displayed in the image tile on the right. The Apply To drop-down list box allows you to specify whether the current viewport or the entire graphic area is to be divided. When 2D is selected from the Setup drop-down list box, the viewpoint in all the new viewports is the current viewport; when 3D is selected, the viewpoints are as shown in the accompanying figure.

You can, however, change the viewpoint of selected viewports by selecting an orthographic or isometric view from the drop-down list box labeled Change View To. Suppose, for example, you wanted to create two horizontal viewports, with the upper viewport showing the top of your model and the lower viewport showing its front, rather than the default SE isometric view. You would select Two Horizontal for the viewport arrangement and 3D as the Setup; click in the lower viewport shown in the image tile to make it the current one, and select Front as the view type.

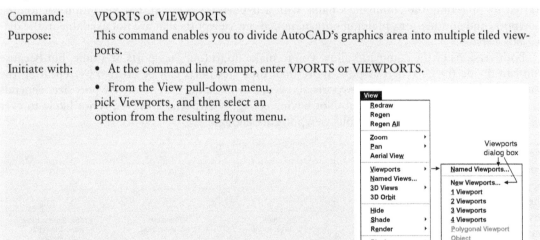

| Command: | VPORTS or VIEWPORTS |
| Purpose: | This command enables you to divide AutoCAD's graphics area into multiple tiled viewports. |
| Initiate with: | • At the command line prompt, enter VPORTS or VIEWPORTS. |
| | • From the View pull-down menu, pick Viewports, and then select an option from the resulting flyout menu. |

New Viewports tab of the Viewports dialog box options:

- New
  Name

Enter a name in this edit box to save the current viewport configuration. The rules for the length of the name and the characters that are allowed are the same as for other AutoCAD named objects — such as layers, views, and UCSs. Entering a name is optional.

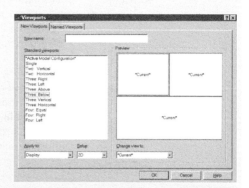

- Standard
  Viewports

The names of the 12 standard viewport arrangements, plus the current viewport arrangement, are shown in this list box. Click a name to select it.

- Preview

The viewport arrangement of the selected viewport name is displayed in this image tile. The type of viewpoint in each viewport is listed.

- Apply To

The two choices in this drop-down list box — Display and Current Viewport — control whether the selected viewport arrangement is to apply to the entire graphics area or to just the current viewport. This option has no effect when Single has been selected as the viewport arrangement.

- Setup

When 2D is selected from this drop-down list box, the view directions in the viewports will be the same as that of the current viewport. When 3D is selected, each viewport initially will have an orthographic or isometric viewpoint, as indicated in the Preview image tile.

- Change
  View To

This drop-down list box, which is enabled only when 3D has been selected as the Setup type, enables you to change the viewpoint in selected viewports. First, select a viewport from the Preview image tile, and then select a view direction for that viewport from this list box.

Named Viewports tab of the Viewports dialog box options:

- **Named Viewports** — The names of all saved viewport configurations are displayed in this list box. To choose a configuration, click on its name. You can rename or delete a saved configuration through a right-click shortcut menu.

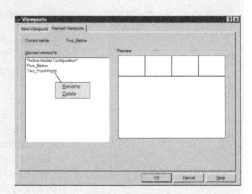

- **Preview** — The viewport arrangement of the selected named viewport is displayed in this image tile.

Command line options:

When you precede VPORTS with a hyphen, the following command line options are displayed:

```
Save/Restore/Delete/Join/Single/?/2/3/4/
```

The Save, Restore, Delete, Single, 2, 3, and 4 options correspond to options that are available in the New Viewports and Named Viewports tabs of the Viewports dialog boxes. The Join and question mark (?) options, however, are available only from the command line.

- **Join** — This option combines two viewports. The viewports must share a common edge, and the resulting viewport must be rectangular. A follow-up prompt asks you

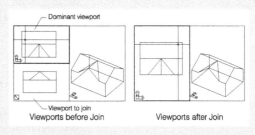

Viewports before Join          Viewports after Join

to select the dominant viewport, offering the current viewport as a default. The properties and viewpoint of the resulting viewport are of the dominant viewport. Next, AutoCAD asks for the viewport that is to be joined to the dominant viewport. Viewports are selected by picking a point inside their borders. The resulting viewport must be rectangular — you cannot create L-shaped or T-shaped viewports. Therefore, in the accompanying figure, you only can join the two left-hand viewports.

- ? The question mark option displays each viewport's identification number along with its lower-left and upper-right corners, expressed as a decimal fraction of the sides of the graphics area. The current viewport is listed first. This list is followed by the names of saved viewport configurations and the lower-left and upper-right corners of their viewports.

Notes:

- The smallest allowable viewport size depends upon your computer's video system. If you continue to make viewports within a viewport, AutoCAD will eventually issue the message "The current viewport is too small to divide" and will not allow further division of that viewport.

- Viewports created when the 2D option of the New Viewports dialog box is in effect will have the UCS of the current viewport. When the 3D option is selected, the behavior of the UCS in each viewport with an orthographic view is affected by the **ucsortho** system variable. When **ucsortho** is set to 0, the UCS will not change; when **ucsortho** is set to 1, the UCS will be oriented so that its Z axis points out of the computer screen.

- Beginning with AutoCAD 2000, VPORTS works in paper space to make floating viewports, as well as in model space to make tiled viewports. The paper space version of VPORTS, however, is very similar to the MVIEW command that is discussed in Section 4.

Related system variables:

- **vport** The identification number of the current viewport is stored within this system variable. Because the main paper space viewport is always viewport number 1, no model space viewport has an ID number less than 2.

- **tilemode** When **tilemode** equals 1, tiled viewports are made. When **tilemode** equals 0, floating viewports are created.

- **ucsvp** This system variable is set on a viewport-by-viewport basis. When **ucsvp** equals 0, the UCS of the viewport will change to match the UCS of the current viewport. When **ucsvp** equals 1, the UCS of the viewport will not change.

- **ucsortho** When the 3D setup of VPORTS is in effect, the UCS of viewports having orthographic views is controlled by this system variable. When **ucsortho** equals 1, the UCS of viewports having orthographic views will have their Z axis pointed directly out of the viewport. When **ucsortho** equals 0, the UCS of viewports for orthographic views will not change.

# Using Multiple Viewports

Although you can work in only one viewport at a time, you can freely move from one viewport to another, even in the middle of most commands. You can, for instance, start a line in one viewport and finish it in another. You also can start picking objects for a selection set in one viewport, continue building the selection set in other viewports, and switch to still other viewports to specify such things as displacement locations.

The current viewport — the one that you can work in — is indicated by a viewport border that is slightly thicker than those of the other viewports. It is the only viewport that has the crosshair cursor. When you move your pointing device to another viewport, the crosshair cursor remains in the current viewport while movement of your pointing device is indicated by a small arrow.

The most common method for selecting a new current viewport is to move your pointing device to the desired viewport and press the pick button on your pointing device. AutoCAD identifies the first pick in a new viewport as a viewport selection pick, even if it is looking for point input. After a new current viewport has been established, you can continue picking points or selecting objects.

You also can change viewports by simultaneously pressing your computer's Ctrl and R keys until you get to the viewport you want. Yet another way to change viewports is by setting the system variable **cvport** to the value of the identification number of the viewport that you want to become the current viewport. Although this is not a practical method while manually using the VPORTS command, it is a useful method for setting the current viewport in AutoLISP programs.

Most likely, you will have a different view direction and zoom level in each viewport. Although there are no rules or standard conventions, for setting view directions, some people find it helpful to establish viewports that show the principal views of the model plus one with an isometric-type viewpoint.

## Viewports and the UCS

Beginning with AutoCAD 2000, each viewport can have its own UCS. This useful property can save you steps as you work with 3D models because you do not need to move and reorient the UCS as often as you did when only one UCS could be used at a time. It is also a potentially confusing property because you cannot determine the UCS location in a viewport by observing its location in other viewports. Consider, for example, the UCS and the viewports shown in the accompanying figure. By merely looking at the computer screen, you cannot be certain where the UCS is located in the

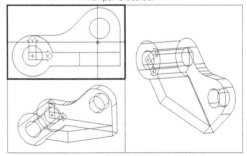

You cannot be certain where the UCS in the upper left-hand viewport is located.

upper-left viewport. It could be in the same location as the UCS in the lower-left viewport, in the same location as the UCS in the right-hand viewport, or anywhere along the axis of the round hole.

You must know exactly where the UCS is placed in every viewport. Therefore, you might prefer not to use the 3D setup of VPORTS New Viewports dialog box, so that you can set both the UCS and the viewpoint as you want in each viewport.

AutoCAD has two tools for ensuring that the UCS in one viewport is the same at that of another viewport. One of these tools is the Apply option of the UCS command. In effect, the Apply option places the copy of a UCS from one viewport into another viewport. To use this option, make the viewport that has the UCS you want to copy to be the current viewport. Then, invoke UCS and choose its Apply option. Make the viewport you want to receive the copy be the current viewport, and press the Enter key. This option also allows you  to apply the UCS of a viewport to all viewports.

The other tool for ensuring that the UCS in one viewport is the same as that of another viewport it the **ucsvp** system variable. This system variable, which accepts a value of either 0 or 1, is viewport specific; **ucsvp** can be set to 0 in some viewports and to 1 in other viewports. When **ucsvp** is set to 0, the viewport's UCS always matches that of the current viewport. In the three following figures, **ucsvp** has been set to 0 in the right-hand viewport. Notice in the second and third figures that the UCS of this viewport is automatically moved and oriented to match that of the current viewport.

ucsvp is set to 0 in
the right-hand viewport

As you make other viewports current, the UCS in the
right-hand viewport changes to match the current viewport.

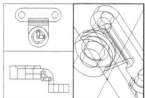 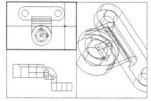 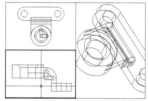

You can effectively turn off the capability of AutoCAD to support different UCSs in different viewports by setting the system variables **ucsvp** and **ucsortho** to a value of 0, rather than leave them at their default value of 1. This also prevents the 3D view options in the Viewports dialog box and the orthographic views in the View dialog box from affecting the UCS. Using the same UCS in viewports is actually a good practice; one that can prevent you from mistakenly drawing on the wrong X-Y plane.

## Using Saved Viewport Configurations

The Save option of the VPORTS command, and New Name in the New Viewports tab of the Viewports dialog box, does more than simply save the current number and arrangement of viewports — it also saves

*   The grid and snap settings in each viewport
*   The UCS and the UCS icon setting in each viewport
*   The view direction and zoom level in each viewport

A convenient way to keep a particular arrangement of viewports, along with the settings within them that you often work with, is to save it as a named viewport configuration in a prototype, or template, drawing. You can have AutoCAD start with the viewport configuration, or you can start with a conventional single viewport and restore your named set of viewports whenever it is convenient.

Saved viewport configurations also can be useful in setting up paper space floating viewports. The command that creates paper space floating viewports, MVIEW, has an option to translate saved model space viewport configurations into floating viewports. This option is discussed in detail in Section 4 of this book.

## Using AutoLISP to Create Viewports

A minor disadvantage to using named and saved viewport configurations in prototype and template drawings is that the zoom level in the viewports might not be appropriate for the size of the model you are constructing. Say, for example, you are building a 3D model house, but the zoom level in the saved viewport configuration is more suitable for working with small mechanical objects. You have to go into each viewport and zoom out so that you can see the entire house.

Even though this is only a slight inconvenience, you can use AutoLISP to create viewports with zoom levels that fit the model you are currently working on. The AutoLISP program 4_LgR.LSP is an example. It divides the AutoCAD graphics area into four viewports — one large one on the right side of the area and three small ones arranged vertically on the left side. The large viewport on the right shows an isometric-type view, the topmost small viewport on the left shows a plan view, the middle viewport shows a front view, and the lower small viewport shows the right side of the model.

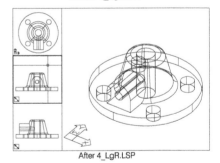

Before 4_LgR.LSP

After 4_LgR.LSP

The resulting viewport configuration is comparable to that of the Four Left configuration of VPORTS New Viewports dialog box when 3D has been selected as the Setup style. This AutoLISP program has some advantages over the VPORTS configuration, though: It does not set the UCS in any of the viewports, it zooms back a little in each viewport to give you some working room, and it sets a slightly off-center isometric-type view direction in the large viewport (which is better to work with than a true isometric viewpoint).

The program, which is on the CD-ROM that accompanies this book, is heavily commented to help you understand how it works. If you look through the program, you will notice that it starts by making sure that `tilemode` is set to 1, then it creates and joins viewports until a large viewport, taking up three-fourths of the graphics area, is on the right. The left-hand one-fourth of the graphics area is then divided vertically into three viewports.

After creating the four viewports, the program steps through each one of them, setting the viewing direction and the zoom level to the equivalent of 0.9 Zoom/All. The three small viewports show the top, front, and right-side views of the model, while the large viewport shows an isometric-type view of it.

Direction coordinates are used with the VPOINT command within the program to set viewing directions. The coordinates used for setting the isometric-type view (0.8112, -1.1585, 1.0) are equivalent to the VPOINT rotation angles of 305 degrees in the X-Y plane from the X axis, and 35 degrees from the X-Y plane.

The program uses AutoCAD's cvport system variable when it needs to go to a viewport. It also makes use of AutoLISP's `vports` function. This function, which takes no arguments, returns a list for the current viewport configuration showing the identification number of each viewport and its corner coordinates. The corner coordinates are shown as decimal fractions of the sides of the graphics area, just as they are by the question mark option of the VPORTS command.

For example, the vports function might return the following for the viewport configuration 4_LgR.LSP creates:

```
( (4 (0.0 0.666667) (0.25 1.0))
  (3 (0.25 0.0) (1.0 1.0))
    (2 (0.0 0.0) (0.25 0.333333))
    (5 (0.0 0.333333) (0.25 0.666667) )
```

The corner coordinates for this viewport arrangement are always as shown here, but the viewport identification numbers and the order they are in can vary from one AutoCAD session to another, and the order also depends on which viewport is the current one.

## Views and UCSs

The VIEW command's orthographic and isometric view options

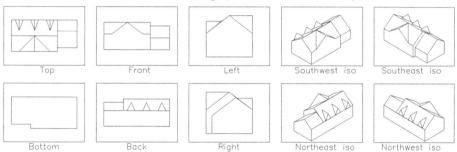

Beginning with AutoCAD 2000, the VIEW command has options for restoring one of 10 preestablished views; 6 are orthographic, while the other 4 are isometric. To restore one of the views, open the Orthographic & Isometric Views tab of the VIEW command's View dialog box, and select the view you want from the list box. You can use any of three following methods to make the selected view become the current view:

The VIEW command's orthographic and isometric view options

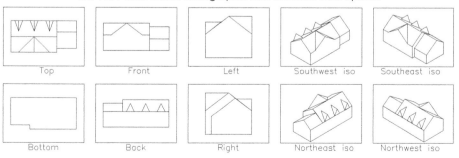

- Click the Set Current button.

- Double-click the highlighted view name.

- Right-click the highlighted view name, and select Set Current from the menu.

After you have selected a view, click the OK button of the dialog box to restore it. You also can set one of these 10 views by selecting a view button in the Views toolbar, or by selecting an orthographic or isometric option in the View/3D Views pull-down menu.

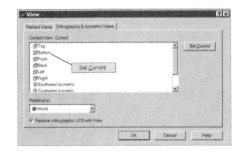

If the check box labeled Restore Orthographic UCS with View is checked, the X-Y plane of the UCS revolves so that the Z axis points directly out of the computer screen when an orthographic view is restored. If the check box is cleared, the UCS doesn't change as the orthographic view is created. This check box controls the value of the **ucsortho** system variable. When **ucsortho** is set to a value of 0, the UCS is not changed when an orthographic view is created. When **ucsortho** is set to 1, the UCS rotates so that its X-Y plane is perpendicular to the view's line of sight. This system variable only affects orthographic views established by the VIEW command, and by the 3D option of the VPORTS command. It has no affect when isometric views are restored, or when another command (such as VPOINT) is used to set an orthographic viewpoint.

The origin and orientation of the UCS is relative to the coordinate system stored in the **ucsbase** system variable. By default this base coordinate system is the WCS. You can, however, store the name of any UCS that has been named and saved by the UCS or UCSMAN commands. The drop-down list box labeled Relative To in the Orthographic & Isometric Views tab is a convenient way to store a named UCS in the **ucsbase** system variable.

# CHAPTER 4

# 2D Wireframe Objects in 3D Space

*Most of the components of 3D wireframe models are the same objects — principally lines, arcs, and circles — you have long used in creating 2D drawings. In this chapter, you learn how creating and editing those objects in 3D space differs from using them to make 2D drawings. You also learn to use some specialized AutoCAD commands for editing and duplicating objects in 3D space.*

*This chapter*

- *describes the properties of 2D wireframe objects in 3D space;*
- *explains how 2D editing commands are used in 3D space;*
- *introduces you to four special AutoCAD commands for manipulating objects in 3D space — ROTATE3D, MIRROR3D, 3DARRAY, and ALIGN.*

Most objects in 3D wireframe models are 2D objects — they can be defined completely by using just X and Y coordinates. Even a line is a 2D object, because the entire length of any one line lies in a single plane, even though all three coordinates are often used to define its endpoints. The only AutoCAD wireframe objects that are truly 3D are splines (those made by the SPLINE command, rather than 2D polylines converted to spline curves) and 3D polylines. Although you do not often need those two object types, they are able to create geometries that no 2D object can create. Because of their uniqueness, 3D polylines and splines are discussed separately in the next chapter.

## Relationships of 2D Wireframe Objects to 3D Space

Although wireframe objects share the common characteristic of having no width or thickness, their relationship to 3D space varies among object types. Therefore, this chapter describes how each 2D AutoCAD wireframe database object type relates to three dimensions. Most of these objects can also be given a thickness, and some can be given a width as well, but they cease to be wireframe objects when they have either of those properties. They become surface objects, which are discussed in Section 2 of this book.

## Arc

An arc always lies in a plane that is either on the current X-Y plane or is parallel to it. The first point specified for the arc sets its elevation. If you use object snaps to locate the other two points of the arc, AutoCAD projects (in a direction that is parallel with the Z axis) the object snap locations to the elevation of the first point. If you enter the subsequent coordinates from the keyboard, AutoCAD rejects points entered with a Z coordinate — you can specify only the X and Y coordinates.

## Circle

A circle always lies on a plane that is on the current X-Y plane or is parallel to it. The first point specified sets the circle's elevation. If this point represents the center of the circle, the second point selected will be the circle's radius or diameter (depending upon the option selected), and if an object snap is used to specify the radius (or diameter), AutoCAD will give the circle a radius (or diameter) that is equal to the 3D distance from the circle's center point to the object snap point. In other words, AutoCAD does not project the object snap point onto the plane of the center point.

If, on the other hand, the 2P or 3P options for defining a circle are selected, the first point specified sets the elevation

When points are used to specify a circle's radius, the 3D distance between the points is used as the radius value.

Line

Circle's center is at −0.5,0,1.

Plan view

−0.5,0,1  Pick point for circle's center

Line

0,0,0

Pick point for circle's radius

Circle's radius

Inclined view

The specified radius.

The resulting circle.

of the circle, and subsequent points selected by object snaps are projected to that elevation. If the Tangent-Tangent-Radius option is selected, both of the arcs or circles used for specifying a tangent must be on a plane that is parallel to the current X-Y plane. The subsequent circle is drawn on the X-Y plane, even if the circles or arcs are in other planes.

## Dimension

AutoCAD always draws dimensions on the current X-Y plane, even if the object or the points selected are in other planes. With linear dimensions, horizontal dimensions parallel to the X axis, while vertical dimensions are parallel to the Y axis. If a linear feature that is not parallel to the X-Y plane is being dimensioned, the resulting dimension will not equal the feature's true length. AutoCAD is, however, able to properly determine the true radius and diameter of arcs and circles, even if they are not parallel to the current X-Y plane.

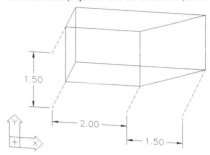

Dimensions are projected onto the current X-Y plane.

## Ellipse

Ellipses, whether they are made as splines or as polylines, are always drawn on a plane parallel to the current X-Y plane. The ellipse is drawn on a plane having the same elevation as the first point selected for the ellipse. If object snaps are used to specify subsequent points, they are projected onto the ellipse's plane.

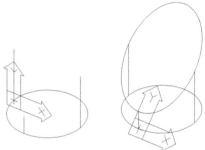

## Leader

Leaders are always drawn on a plane parallel to the current X-Y plane. The first point specified for the leader determines the elevation of the leader's plane.

Circles, arcs, and ellipses are drawn on the X-Y plane, or on a plane parallel to it.

## Line

A line can be drawn from any point in 3D space to any other point in 3D space, although this hasn't always been true. Prior to Release 10, the LINE command was restricted to drawing lines on, or parallel to, the X-Y plane.

## Mline

Multilines are always drawn on a plane parallel to the current X-Y plane, at the elevation of the first point specified. If object snaps are used to specify subsequent points, the points are projected to the multiline's elevation, even if the specified points have other elevations.

## Mtext

AutoCAD always places multitext on a plane parallel to the current X-Y plane. The elevation of the first corner of the text box is used as the elevation for the multitext.

### Point

You can place a point in any location in 3D space. If a point has a supplementary object (such as a cross or bull's-eye, as determined by the **pdmode** system variable) attached to it, the supplementary object is drawn on a plane parallel to the current X-Y plane.

### 2D Polyline

Polylines, along with polyline-based objects such as polygons and donuts, are always drawn on a plane that is parallel to the current X-Y plane at an elevation equal to the first point specified. If object snaps in other elevations are used to specify points, they are projected to the elevation of the polyline.

### Ray

Rays, which are generally used for construction lines, are line-like objects that extend an infinite distance from their starting points. The starting point can be located anywhere in 3D space, and the ray can extend in any direction from that starting point.

### Shape

Shapes are objects that are defined by an external file having a file extension of .SHX, similar to ordinary AutoCAD text. Often, they are used as symbols in electronic diagrams. They can be positioned in any elevation in 3D space, and they are always drawn in a plane parallel to the current X-Y plane.

### Text

Text is always placed in a plane parallel to the current X-Y plane at an elevation equal to the insert point of the text.

### Xline

Xlines, which are commonly used for construction lines, extend an infinite distance in both directions from a point. AutoCAD imposes no 3D restrictions in specifying the base point or the direction of an xline.

## Editing Wireframe Objects in 3D Space

Editing is an important phase in creating both 2D drawings and 3D models, and you will use a variety of AutoCAD's editing commands as you work in 3D space. You will, for example, modify the shape of 3D wireframe models by changing the length of their objects (with the STRETCH, LENGTHEN, TRIM, and EXTEND commands); you will add to models by making copies of existing objects (with the COPY, ARRAY, and MIRROR commands); and you will use the interaction between two objects to create new objects (with the FILLET and CHAMFER commands).

For the most part, AutoCAD's editing commands work just the same in 3D space as they do on 2D drawings, but there are some subtle differences, and some of the commands have 3D extensions that you have no reason to use while making 2D drawings. Therefore, I will review AutoCAD's editing functions and commands, taking a special look at their 3D capabilities.

## Object Snaps

AutoCAD recognizes most object snaps in 3D space. It has no problem, for instance, recognizing the endpoints and the midpoints of lines regardless of how they are oriented in 3D space. AutoCAD also has no problem performing perpendicular snaps or finding centerpoints of circles and arcs, even if the objects are not parallel to the current X-Y plane. However, quadrant and tangent snaps can be used only on circles, arcs, and ellipses that are parallel to the current X-Y plane.

Intersection object snaps also have no 3D restrictions, but the two objects must either a) actually intersect or b) intersect if they were to be extended. AutoCAD is also able to snap to apparent intersections of objects that are actually in different planes. Apparent intersection snaps can be initiated from the command line by entering APPINT or APP, from the Object Snap toolbar, or from the cursor menu (which is activated by holding down the Shift key as you press the Return button on your pointing device), whenever AutoCAD is expecting a point. If there is no intersection (real or apparent) at the point you select, AutoCAD begins an apparent extended intersection object snap and expects you to select a second object. Then, AutoCAD snaps to a point at which the two objects would appear to meet if they were extended.

Because this object snap is view-related, the apparent intersection varies as the viewpoint varies. For example, two lines that are in different planes, and therefore, do not actually intersect, could apparently intersect at the coordinates of 1,1,1 from the plan view. From an isometric-type view, however, the

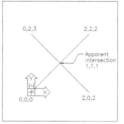

Plan view

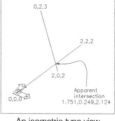

An isometric-type view

Another Isometric-type view

apparent intersection point could be 1.751,0.249,2.123, and from yet another viewpoint their extended apparent intersection point could be -0.436,2.436,3.218.

As an example of how you can use apparent intersections, suppose you are drawing a wireframe model of a house that is to have a dormer on its roof. Three corners of the dormer, points A, B, and C, on the roof surface, but locating these points is not straightforward because the roof is empty space — there is nothing for you to attach anything to. You do know, however, the elevations of points A, B, and C, as well as their locations along the roof.

To establish point A, you could move the UCS origin to a location corresponding to point A's WCS X coordinate, and then rotate the UCS so that the X axis points into the house and the Y axis points in the WCS Z-axis direction. (The UCS ZAxis option is a good way to set this UCS in a single step.) Then, you could draw a horizontal construction line at the elevation of point A into the roof of the house. Point A will be somewhere on this line. You would probably use the VPORTS command to divide AutoCAD's graphics area into two viewports; one viewport would have an isometric-type viewpoint, and the other would have a plan view of the current UCS.

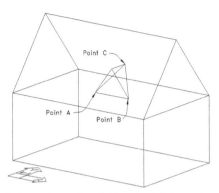

Finding points A, B, and C is not straightforward.

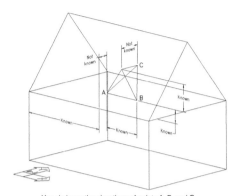

You do know the elevations of points A, B, and C,
as well as their location along the length of the roof.

Next, using the viewport that has the plan view, you would invoke AutoCAD's BREAK command, select the construction line as the object to break, use an apparent intersection to pick the first break point, and pick the second point beyond an endpoint of the construction line to delete the line beyond the first pick point. It doesn't make any difference which end of the construction line you keep.

The end of the broken line is point A. You would then move the UCS origin to that point and rotate the UCS about the Y axis so that the X-Y plane is parallel with the front of the house, and would you would draw the triangular-shaped front face of the dormer.

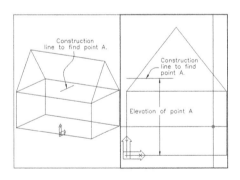

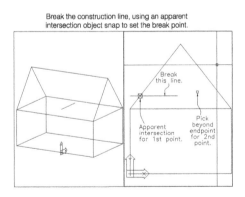

Break the construction line, using an apparent intersection object snap to set the break point.

After drawing the front of the dormer, you would draw a line from its apex in the minus Z direction through the roof. You would then break that line at its apparent intersection with the roof in the side view of the house to find point C on the dormer.

Lastly, you would use object endpoint snaps to draw lines along the edge of the dormer's roof from point A to C and from C to B, as shown in the figure at the beginning of this example.

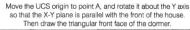

Move the UCS origin to point A, and rotate it about the Y axis so that the X-Y plane is parallel with the front of the house. Then draw the triangular front face of the dormer.

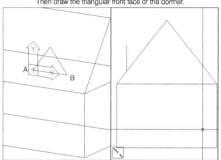

Draw a construction line into the house roof, and use an apparent intersection to break it at point C.

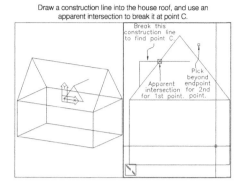

## 2D Editing Commands in 3D Space

### COPY and MOVE

Although the COPY and MOVE commands have different objectives, they both are implemented in the same way. After building a selection set of objects to be moved or copied, you specify a base point and then a displacement point. These points are fully 3D, and you can use any of the methods described in Chapter 1 to specify them.

### OFFSET

The OFFSET command gives you one more way to make copies of existing objects. For lines and straight segments of polylines, the copy is placed parallel to the original object by a specified distance. For arcs, circles, and arc segments of polylines, the radius of the copy is also increased or decreased, depending upon whether the offset is outside or inside the original arc or circle. The copy is always offset in a direction that is parallel to the current X-Y plane. The objects, however, even if they are 2D polylines, do not have to be parallel to the current X-Y plane.

### FILLET and CHAMFER

AutoCAD's FILLET command works on any two wireframe objects that are in the same plane, regardless of how their plane is oriented relative to the UCS. You can also fillet two lines that are parallel — a 180-degree arc is drawn between the two selected lines.

In the accompanying figure, you can fillet the following pairs of objects:

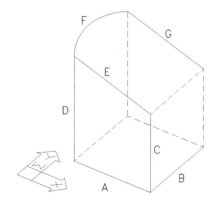

| A and B | A and C | A and D | A and E | B and C |
|---------|---------|---------|---------|---------|
| C and D | C and E | D and E | E and F | E and G |
| F and G |         |         |         |         |

You cannot, however, fillet the following pairs of objects:

| A and F | A and G | B and D | B and E | B and F |
|---------|---------|---------|---------|---------|
| B and G | C and F | C and G | D and F | D and G |

The CHAMFER command makes a beveled corner, rather than rounded corner, between two line objects. It does not work with arcs or with parallel lines, but the command is not affected by the current orientation of the UCS X-Y plane.

## BREAK

The BREAK command is fully 3D beginning with AutoCAD Release 13. It breaks a wireframe object, such as a line, arc, or circle, at the point (or points) specified, regardless of how the object is oriented within the UCS. In releases previous to Release 13, however, AutoCAD reflected the specified points off the current X-Y plane back onto the object. As a result, the breakpoints did not match the specified points unless the current X-Y plane was parallel to the plane of the object.

## TRIM and EXTEND

Because the operation of AutoCAD's TRIM and EXTEND commands are similar (TRIM trims an object back to a boundary object, while EXTEND lengthens an object to a boundary object), I will discuss the 3D characteristics of just the TRIM command. For a description of how EXTEND works in 3D space, simply replace the word TRIM with EXTEND in the following discussion.

On the command line, the TRIM command issues the following messages and prompts:

```
Command: TRIM (Enter)
Current Settings: Projection=UCS Edge=None
Select cutting edges ...
Select objects: Select one or more objects to serve as cutting edges.
Select object to trim or [Project/Edge/Undo]: Select an object or choose an option.
```

Notice that when the command starts, AutoCAD issues a message on the current settings of two modes: *Projection* and *Edge*. The contents of this message vary to reflect the current status of these two modes. *Projection* determines how the cutting edge object is projected toward the object to be trimmed. It has three possible settings, which are discussed shortly.

*Edge* controls whether the ends of the cutting edges can, or cannot, be extended. It has two possible settings: Extend or No extend. When *Edge* is set to No Extend, the boundary object and the object to be trimmed must intersect for the trim to occur. When *Edge* is set to Extend, the two objects do not have to intersect. If they do not intersect, the cutting boundary

When Edge is set to Extend, the cutting edge object does not have to intersect the object that is to be trimmed.

Pick point

Cutting edge object

Object to be trimmed

No extend

Extend

is extended to the point where it would intersect the object that is to be trimmed, and the length of the trim object is adjusted to that point.

Both *Edge* and *Projection* are set through options in the TRIM command's main menu. The Edge option in the main menu brings up the submenu of:

`Enter an implied edge extension mode [Extend/No extend] <current mode>:`

Select the Extend option to set the *Edge* mode to Extend, or select the No Extend option to set the Edge mode to No Extend.

The Project option in the TRIM command's main brings up the submenu:

`Enter a projection option [None/Ucs/View] <current mode>:`

When *Projection* is set to None, the cutting-edge object and the object to be trimmed must be in the same plane. On the other hand, when *Projection* is set to UCS, the cutting-edge object and the object to be trimmed do not have to be in the same plane.

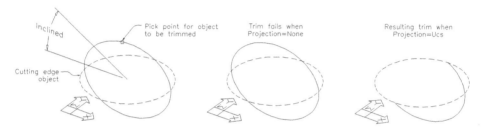

The Ucs trim mode projects the cutting-plane object perpendicularly, relative to the X-Y plane of the UCS, to the object that is to be trimmed. As a result, the two objects do not even have to intersect. The next figure shows the same two circles shown in the previous figure, but the inclined circle that is to be trimmed has been moved above the WCS X-Y plane and does not even touch the circle that serves as the cutting-edge object. Nevertheless, it is still trimmed.

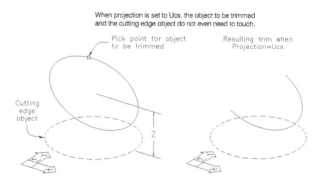

To visualize the trim points on an object, look at the objects from a plan view of the current UCS. The point, or points, at which the object to be trimmed appears to intersect the cutting edge object will be the points at which it will be trimmed. The next figure shows plan views of the same circles shown in the previous figures.

The third setting of *Projection* is View. When this mode is in effect, the cutting object is projected in the view direction and trims the object at the point, or points, where they visually intersect.

It is even possible, when *Projection* is set to View and *Edge* is set to Extend, to trim an object that does not intersect the cutting plane from the current viewpoint, but would if the cutting plane were extended.

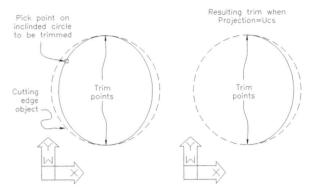

To visualize trim points when projection is set to Ucs, look at the objects from the plan view of the current UCS.

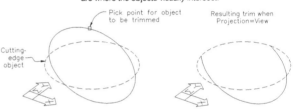

When projection is set to View, the trim points are where the objects visually intersect.

The default setting for *Projection* when either the TRIM or EXTEND command is started is controlled by AutoCAD's **projmode** system variable. This system variable can have three possible values. These values and their results are:

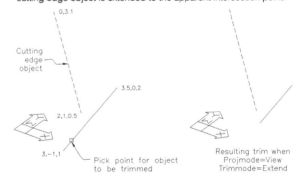

When Projection is set to View, and Edge is set to Extend, the cutting edge object is extended to the apparent intersection point.

| Projmode Setting | Result |
|---|---|
| 0 | No projection |
| 1 | UCS projection |
| 2 | View projection |

Changing the value of the **projmode** system variable causes the TRIM and EXTEND commands to offer different default *Projection* settings, but because it is so convenient to choose a projection mode from within the TRIM and EXTEND command, there is little reason to access the **projmode** system variable directly.

You also can change the *Edge* mode default for extending or not extending the cutting edge through a system variable. When AutoCAD's **edgemode** system variable is set to a value of 0, No Extend is offered as a default. When it is set to a value of 1, the default offered is Extend.

## ROTATE

AutoCAD's ROTATE command rotates objects about an axis that is perpendicular to the current X-Y plane. The rotation base point you select establishes the location of the rotation axis on the X-Y plane. Objects selected to be rotated are then revolved about this axis regardless of their orientation to the current X-Y plane.

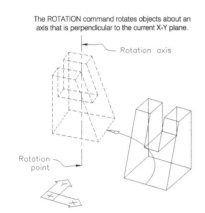

The ROTATION command rotates objects about an axis that is perpendicular to the current X-Y plane.

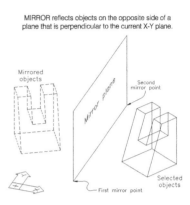

MIRROR reflects objects on the opposite side of a plane that is perpendicular to the current X-Y plane.

## MIRROR

MIRROR makes copies of objects by reflecting them on the opposite side of a plane that is perpendicular to the current X-Y plane. The two points you specify for the mirror line determine the angle of the mirroring plane relative to the X-Z and Y-Z planes. The distance between these two points is not important because objects selected to be mirrored are reflected across the plane regardless of their spatial position.

## ARRAY

AutoCAD's ARRAY command makes multiple copies of objects. The copies are arranged either in rows and columns — a rectangular array — or in a circle — a polar array. Rows are in the current Y-axis direction, while columns are in the current X-axis direction. Therefore, you can make rectangular and polar arrays in any orientation to the WCS by first orienting the UCS X-Y plane.

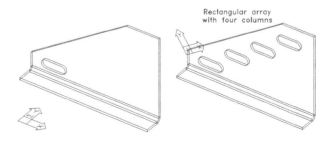

Rectangular array with four columns

## STRETCH

AutoCAD's STRETCH command works
well on 3D wireframe objects. Although
the crossing selection window appears to
be a simple rectangle, it is actually a 3D
fence extending in the view direction,
having a depth that takes in all objects,
regardless of the plane they are in.
Because crossing windows are always
drawn as rectangles with their sides parallel to the viewport sides, you often will
use a polygon crossing window when
using the STRETCH command in isomet-
ric-type views. You even can stretch objects in the Z direction, although you have to type in coordinates for the displacement.

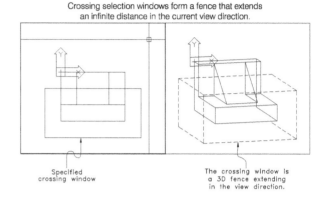

Crossing selection windows form a fence that extends
an infinite distance in the current view direction.

Specified
crossing window

The crossing window is
a 3D fence extending
in the view direction.

### Exercise One

In this exercise, you will create and manipulate wireframe objects to make a 3D skeleton of a
house. This exercise will give you experience in using 2D editing commands in building 3D models. Keep this model, because in Section Two of this book you will add surfaces to it, and in Section
5 you will make a rendering of the house.

You should set up the drawing to use architectural units (feet and inches). Make a new layer,
with a name such as OBJ01 or WF01, to be used for drawing the house wireframe. This layer
should have a continuous linetype and a color appropriate for your computer's display. Most
lengths on this model are in increments of 6 inches, so you might want to activate AutoCAD's snap
mode with a snap spacing of 6 inches.

Begin the house by drawing an outline of its floor plan on the WCS X-Y
plane using the dimensions given in Figure 1-1. Its location on the X-Y plane is
not important, but be certain that the
long side of the house is parallel to the
X axis.

When you have drawn the eight lines
making up the floor outline, switch to
an isometric-type view and draw a line
in the Z direction that is 10 feet long
from any of the floor's corners. You can
either type in relative coordinates to
specify the end of this line, or move and
rotate the UCS to draw it by pointing.
Then make seven copies of this vertical
line so that one is at each corner of the house.

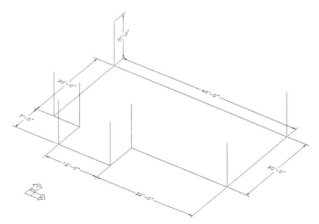

Figure 1-1

Now, zoom in on the left side of the house so that you can draw one-half of one end of the house's roof as shown in Figure 1-2. Notice that the roof extends 1 foot beyond all sides of the floor plan. The easiest way to set up the UCS for drawing the five lines of the overhang part of the roof is to use the ZAxis option of the UCS command, and pick a point 1 foot to the left of the floor outline as the UCS origin and a point in the WCS X axis direction for the Z-axis orientation.

After the UCS is set, use the dimensions shown in Figure 1-2 to draw the end of the roof. In this figure, the objects you have already drawn are shown as dashed lines. After drawing the five lines, copy two of them 1 foot in the WCS X direction, as shown in Figure 1-2, to delineate where the roof meets the house wall.

Then use the MIRROR command, using a mirror plane through the midpoint of the left end of the floor plan, to make the other half of this end of the roof. This end of your house should now look similar to the the one in Figure 1-3. Fillet the two pairs of lines that overlap, using a fillet radius of 0, to square them up.

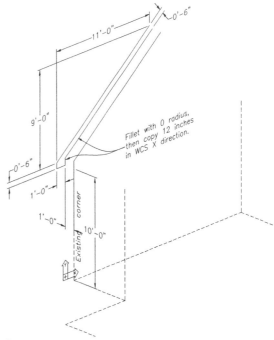

Figure 1-2

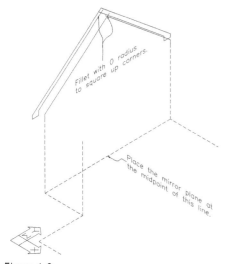

Figure 1-3

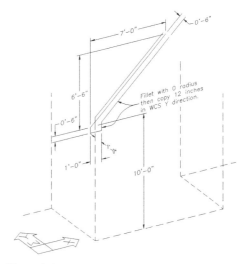

Figure 1-4

Next, draw the gable on the front of the house. Use the dimensions shown in Figure 1-4 to draw one-half of the gable. Notice that it, too, overhangs the floor plan by 1 foot and that its dimensions are the same as those of the main roof's end, except for the pitch of the roof.

After drawing one half of the gable, use AutoCAD's MIRROR command to make the other half, and fillet the two pairs of lines (with a 0 fillet radius) that overlap. Then, zoom back so that you can see the entire house, and mirror the roof end on the left side of the house to the right side. All these uses of the MIRROR command can be done from the WCS by using midpoint object snaps on the house floor plan. Your house should now look like the one shown in Figure 1-5.

The ends of the roof are complete, so you can now draw the eaves of the roof. Zoom in to the upper-left front corner of the house and position the UCS on the end of the roof as shown in Figure 1-6. Because this UCS X-Y plane is parallel with the WCS X-Y plane, the easiest way to position the UCS is to make certain that the WCS is in effect, and then use the Origin option of the UCS command with an object endpoint snap on the bottom of one of the vertical lines of the roof end. When you have positioned the UCS, draw four lines from the endpoints of existing lines, as shown in Figure 1-6. In this figure, previously drawn objects are shown in dashed lines.

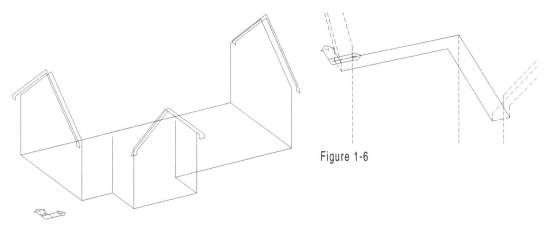

Figure 1-6

Figure 1-5

Next, make a copy of the outside two lines. The location of these copies is 6 inches above the original lines, as shown in Figure 1-7.

Move the UCS to the other side of the front gable and use the same techniques to draw the eaves for the remaining front of the roof. Your house should now look like the one in Figure 1-8 (although previously drawn objects are shown in dashed lines in this figure).

Drawing the peak of the gable roof is best done by using two viewports — one viewport having an isometric-type viewpoint, and the other having a viewpoint that looks straight toward the end of the house (such as that from the VPOINT coordinates of 1,0,0). See Figure 1-9. Draw a line from the peak of the gable roof in the WCS Y direction. You won't know exactly where to stop this line. After drawing this line, go to the viewport showing the end of the house and use the

TRIM command (or EXTEND, if your line doesn't reach the main roofline) with *Projection* set to View to clip the line at the point where the gable peak intersects the main roof.

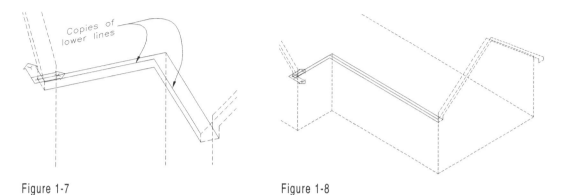

Figure 1-7                                        Figure 1-8

Finish the house wireframe by drawing lines from the end of the gable peak to its eaves, the back eaves, and the main roof peak. You can use object endpoint snaps to draw all these lines. Your 3D wireframe house should look like the one shown in Figure 1-10. On the CD-ROM that comes with this book, the model is in file f0431.dwg. In the next section of this book, you will add surfaces to this wireframe model.

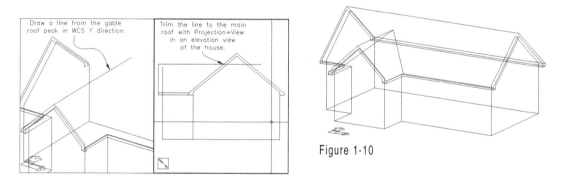

Figure 1-10

Figure 1-9

## 3D Editing Commands

AutoCAD has four editing commands intended specifically for 3D work. Three of these commands — ROTATE3D, MIRROR3D, and 3DARRAY — are enhanced versions of 2D commands, while the fourth — ALIGN — has no 2D counterpart. Align performs a move-and-rotate type of operation, and can be useful in 2D drawings as well as in 3D models. Although you can use standard AutoCAD commands to duplicate the results of these 3D commands, they are often much more convenient to use because they can perform some tasks that would take several steps with standard commands in just a single step. These commands are based on external programs, but they are automatically loaded, ready for use at any time, and operate just like built-in AutoCAD commands. They are listed under the Modify/3D Operation pull-down menu.

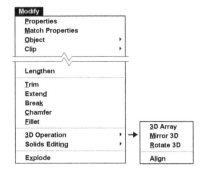

| Command: | 3DARRAY |
|---|---|
| Purpose: | This is an enhanced version of AutoCAD's ARRAY command. It is able to make rectangular arrays that have copies in the Z direction as well as in the X and Y directions. Also, polar arrays are not restricted to axes that are pointed in just the Z direction. |
| Initiate with: | • At the command line prompt, enter 3DARRAY. |
| | • From the Modify pull-down menu, pick 3D Operation, and then select 3D Array. |
| Options: | After selecting the objects to be copied, the command offers you the choice of arranging the copies in a rectangular or polar array. |

> • Rectangular   This option makes copies arranged in rows (the Y direction), columns (the X direction), and levels (the Z direction). You are first prompted to specify the number of copies to be made in each direction:
>
> ```
> Enter number of rows (--) <1>: Enter a positive integer.
> Enter number of columns (|||) <1>: Enter a positive integer.
> Enter number of levels (...) <1>: Enter a positive integer.
> ```
>
> If you specify a quantity of 1 for any direction, no copies are made in that direction. If you specify a quantity of 1 for all three directions, no copies are made, so the command reissues the three prompts. Specifying a quantity of 1 for level is equivalent to a 2D rectangular array.

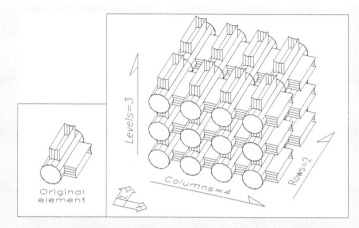

After you specify the number of rows, columns, and levels, the command prompts you for a distance in each direction in which more than one copy was specified:

```
Specify the distance between rows (--): Specify a distance.
Specify the distance between columns (|||): Specify a distance.
Specify the distance between levels (...): Specify a distance.
```

Positive distance values generate the copies in the positive axis direction, while negative values generate the copies in the negative axis direction. The figure above shows a rectangular array having four columns, two rows, and three levels.

- Polar

Although this option makes copies arranged in a circle similar to the polar option of the ARRAY command, you can specify an axis that is oriented in any direction in space, rather than in just the Z direction. Its first three prompts are

```
Enter the number of items in the array: Enter a positive integer.
Specify the angle to fill (+=ccw, -=cw) <360>: Enter an angle or press
    Enter.
Rotate arrayed objects? [Yes/No] <Y>: Enter Y, N, or press Enter.
```

Enter a negative angle to reverse the normal rotation direction of the copies. Usually, you want the copies to be rotated as they are copied.

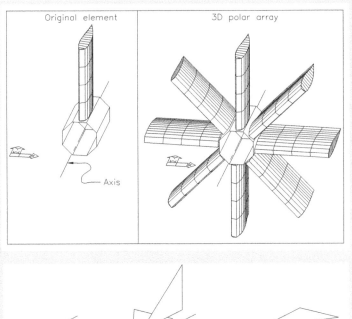

Original element        3D polar array

Axis

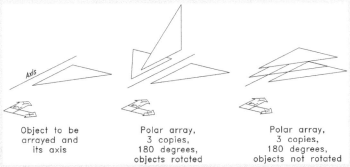

Axis

Object to be          Polar array,          Polar array,
arrayed and           3 copies,             3 copies,
its axis              180 degrees,          180 degrees,
                      objects rotated       objects not rotated

After you have established the paramaters of the polar array, the command asks you to define the rotational axis by specifying two points:

```
Specify center point of array: Specify a point.
Specify second point on axis of rotation: Specify a point.
```

The order in which you pick these points is important, because the positive direction of the axis is from the first point to the second point. You can visualize the rotation direction by mentally grasping the axis with your right hand so that your thumb is pointed in the positive direction of the axis. The copies are placed in the direction in which your curled fingers are pointing.

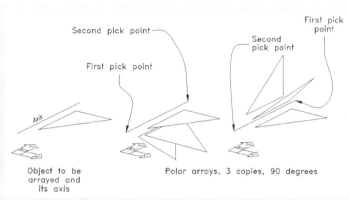

Object to be
arrayed and
its axis

Polar arrays, 3 copies, 90 degrees

Notes:

- This command is based on an AutoLISP program named 3DARRARY.LSP.

| Command: | MIRROR3D |
|---|---|
| Purpose: | This command creates a mirror-image copy of selected objects on the opposite side of a user-specified plane. Options for the command provide a wide variety of methods for specifying the mirror plane. |
| Initiate with: | • At the command line prompt, enter MIRROR3D. |
| | • From the Modify pull-down menu, pick 3D Operation, and then select Mirror 3D. |
| Options: | After selecting the objects to be copied, MIRROR3D offers eight options for defining a mirror plane. After a mirror plane is defined, you are given the option of retaining or deleting the original objects that were selected to be copied. |

- 3points    This option, which is the default option and can be started by selecting a point in response to the main MIRROR3D menu, allows you to define the mirror plane by specifying three points. You are prompted to specify three points on the mirror plane. They can be specified in either a clockwise or counterclockwise order.

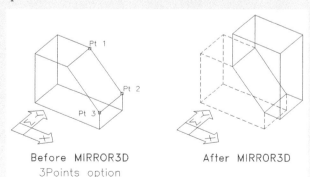

Before  MIRROR3D
3Points  option

After  MIRROR3D

• Object

This option uses an existing object to define the mirror plane. It issues the follow-up prompt:

`Select a circle, arc, or 2D-polyline segment: Select an object.`

Notice that you cannot use a line to define a mirror plane, although you can use the straight segment of a 2D polyline, even if the entire polyline consists of only a single straight-line segment.

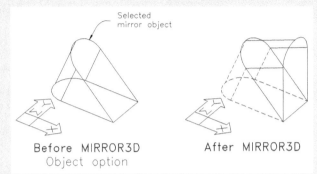

Before MIRROR3D
Object option

After MIRROR3D

The size of the mirror object is not important and it can be located away from the objects to be mirrored because its plane is extended for an infinite distance. In the accompanying figure, for instance, the circle used to define the mirror plane is away from the objects that are to be mirrored.

The mirror plane extends for an infinite distance.

MIRROR3D, Object option

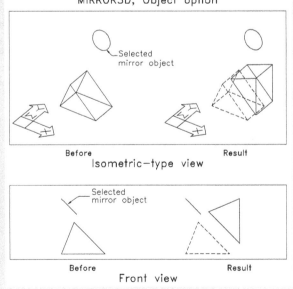

Before                        Result
Isometric—type view

Before                        Result
Front view

- Last

The Last option uses the previous mirror plane as the current mirror plane. If there is no previous mirror plane, the main MIRROR3D options menu is repeated.

- Zaxis

With this option, you define a mirror plane by picking a point on the plane and a second point away from the plane. The mirror plane is oriented perpendicular to a line drawn between the two points. The option's prompts are

```
Specify point on mirror plane: Specify a point.
Specify point on Z-axis (normal) of mirror plane: Specify a point.
```

In geometry, the word "normal" is often used to represent a direction that is perpendicular to a plane. The wording used in this option is as if the mirror plane is the X-Y plane of a coordinate system, and the normal of the mirror plane is its Z-axis direction.

Before MIRROR3D        After MIRROR3D
Zaxis option

Point on
Z axis

Point
on plane

- View

This option orients the mirror plane perpendicular to the current view direction. A follow-up prompt asks for the location of the plane:

```
Specify point on view plane <0,0,0>: Specify a point.
```

In the current viewport, you can't see the results of the operation because the new objects are aligned exactly with the old objects. In a viewport that has a different viewpoint, however, the mirrored objects are visible.

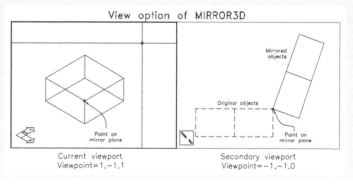

View option of MIRROR3D

Mirrored
objects

Original objects

Point on
mirror plane

Point on
mirror plane

Current viewport
Viewpoint=1,-1,1

Secondary viewport
Viewpoint=-1,-1,0

- XY/YZ/ZX    Each of these three options orients the mirror plane so that it is parallel to one of the principal planes. A follow-up prompt asks you to specify a point that the mirror plane is to pass through.

  `Specify point on MN plane <0,0,0>: Specify a point.`

  In the actual prompt, the letters MN will be XY, YZ, or ZX, depending upon which option was selected. The YZ and ZX options are equivalent to AutoCAD's MIRROR command when the two points selected for the mirror plane are parallel with the X or Y axes.

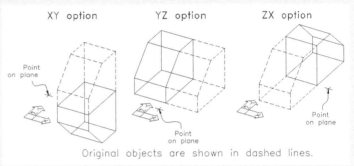

- Delete old objects    After a mirror plane has been defined using any of the options just described, the MIRROR3D command issues the following prompt:

  `Delete source objects? [Yes/No] <N>: Enter Y, N, or press Enter.`

  If you respond by entering N or by pressing the Enter key, the original objects selected to be mirrored are retained. If you enter Y, they are deleted.

Notes:    - This command is based on an external Autodesk program named GEOM3D.ARX.

| Command: | ROTATE3D |
|---|---|
| Purpose: | This command rotates objects about a user-specified axis. |
| Initiate with: | - At the command line prompt, enter ROTATE3D. |
| | - From the Modify pull-down menu, pick 3D Operation, and then select Rotate 3D. |
| Options: | After selecting the objects to be rotated, this command gives you seven different options for defining the rotational axis. Each axis has a direction that determines the positive direction of rotation. You can visualize the positive rotation direction by mentally grasping the axis with your right hand so that your thumb is pointed in the positive direction of the axis. The positive direction of rotation then is in the direction of your fingers when they are curled about the axis. |
| | After defining the axis, you are given the choice of specifying the rotation angle by entering its value directly or by supplying an old angle and a new angle. |

- 2points    This option, which can be started by picking a point or by entering a 2 in response to the main ROTATE3D prompt, uses two points to define the rotation axis. The positive direction of the axis is from the first point to the second.

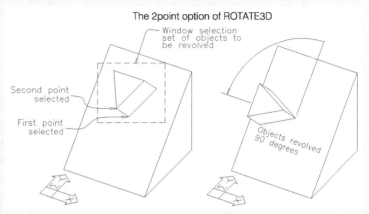

The 2point option of ROTATE3D

- Object    This option uses an existing object to define the rotation axis. It issues the follow-up prompt:

Select a line, circle, arc, or 2D polyline segment: Select an object.

The axis location and direction are shown in the accompanying table.

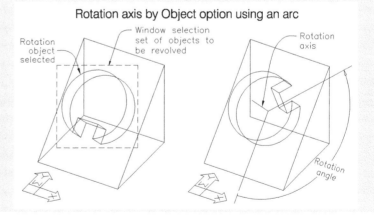

Rotation axis by Object option using an arc

| Object Type | Axis Location and Direction |
| --- | --- |
| Line | Along the line |
| Arc | Through the center of the arc and perpendicular to the plane of the arc |
| Circle | Through the center of the circle and perpendicular to the plane of the circle |
| Polyline line segment | Along the line segment |
| Polyline arc segment | Through the center of the arc segment and perpendicular to the plane of the arc |

- Last          This option uses the last defined rotation axis as the current rotation axis.

- View          This option aligns the rotation axis to be parallel to the current view direction. The positive direction of the axis is out of the screen, toward the viewer. A follow-up prompt asks you to specify a point that the axis is to pass through.

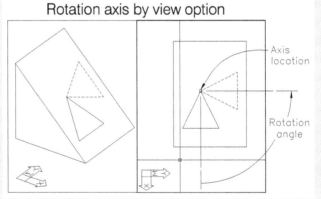

Rotation axis by view option

- Xaxis/
  Yaxis/
  Zaxis          Each of these three options uses a rotation axis that is parallel to one of the principal axes. A follow-up prompt asks you to specify a point that the axis is to pass through. The Zaxis option is equivalent to AutoCAD's standard ROTATE command.

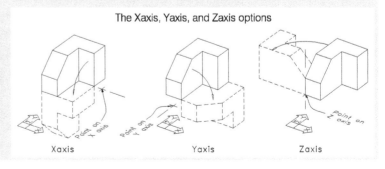

The Xaxis, Yaxis, and Zaxis options

- Rotation Angle/Reference

  After you specify a rotation axis, the ROTATE3D command displays the prompt:

  `Specify Rotation angle or [Reference]: Enter an angle or enter R.`

  When an angle is specified, the objects in the selection set are rotated around the axis by that angle. You can enter negative values to reverse the normal rotation direction.

  The Reference option uses two pairs of points to establish a rotation angle by pointing. The first pair of points represents a base point and a point away from it for the current (or reference) angle, while the second pair represents a base point and a point away from it for the new angle.

  Its prompts are:

  `Specify the reference angle <0>: Specify a point.`
  `Specify second point: Specify a point.`
  `Specify the new angle: Specify a point.`
  **Specify second point:** *Specify a point.*

  You also can type in a reference angle and a new angle. When you do, the prompts for a second point are skipped. Unfortunately, specifying reference rotation angles by pointing works properly only when the current X-Y plane is perpendicular to the rotation axis. The points for specifying the angles are projected onto the X-Y plane, and the resulting rotation angles might not match the 3D angles.

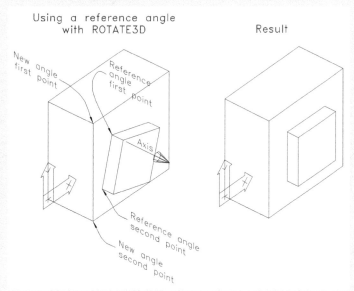

Notes:          • This command is based on an external Autodesk program named GEOM3D.ARX.

| | |
|---|---|
| Command: | ALIGN |
| Purpose: | This command moves and rotates objects in 3D space. It is especially useful for aligning one object, or a set of objects, with another. |
| Initiate with: | • At the command line prompt, enter ALIGN.<br>• From the Modify pull-down menu, pick 3D Operation, and then select Align. |
| Options: | The ALIGN command first asks you to select the object (or objects) to be moved and aligned. It then asks you to specify up to three pairs of source and destination points. The first pair of source and destination points moves the selected object, the second pair rotates the object in one 3D direction, and the third pair rotates the object in another 3D direction. AutoCAD draws a temporary line between each source and destination point. You can stop the command anytime after the first pair of points has been entered by pressing the Enter key during a prompt for a source point. |

• Specifying One Pair of Points

> When just one pair of points is used, the object (or objects) is simply moved by the distance and direction from the source point to the destination point. It is equivalent to AutoCAD's MOVE command.

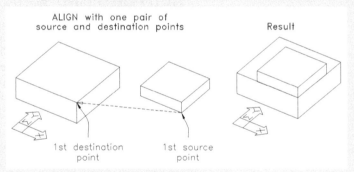

ALIGN with one pair of source and destination points          Result

1st destination point          1st source point

```
Select objects: Select one or more objects.
Specify first source point: Select an origin point.
Specify first destination point: Select a destination point.
Specify second source point: Press Enter.
```

• Specifying Two Pairs of Points

> By specifying two pairs of source and destination points, you are able to move the object (or objects), and then tilt it in one direction.

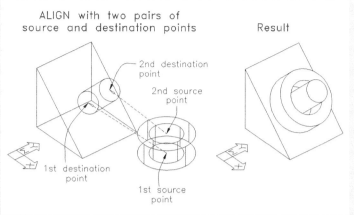

ALIGN with two pairs of source and destination points

Result

2nd destination point
2nd source point
1st destination point
1st source point

```
Select objects: Select one or more objects.
Specify first source point: Select an origin point.
Specify first destination point: Select a destination point.
Specify second source point: Select a second origin point.
Specify second destination point: Select a second destination point.
Specify third source point: Press Enter.
Scale objects based on alignment points? [Yes/No] <No>: Press Enter.
```

The option to scale the objects as they are moved and rotated is useful when the size of the object (or objects) to be moved and rotated does not match the stationary object. The option is presented whenever you stop ALIGN after specifying two sets of source and destination points. If you respond to it with a yes, the aligned objects are scaled by a ratio based on the distances between the two source points and between the two destination points.

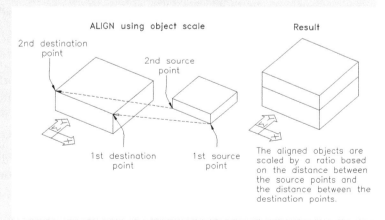

ALIGN using object scale

Result

2nd destination point
2nd source point
1st destination point
1st source point

The aligned objects are scaled by a ratio based on the distance between the source points and the distance between the destination points.

- Specifying Three Pairs of Points

    When three pairs of source and destination points are used, the first pair represents the move displacement, the second represents a rotation in one direction, and the third represents a rotation in a second direction.

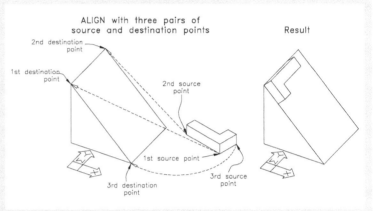

```
Select objects: Select one or more objects.
Specify first source point: Select an origin point.
Specify first destination point: Select a destination point.
Specify second source point: Select a second origin point.
Specify second destination point: Select a second destination point.
Specify third source point: Select a third origin point.
Specify third destination point: Select a third destination point.
```

    Notice that the second and third destination points represent directions from the first destination point rather than distances from it.

Notes:
- This command is based on an external Autodesk program named GEOM3D.ARX.

## Exercise Two

In this exercise, you will build a wireframe for a surface model of an oil pan, similar to one that an automobile might have. This surface model will have just one surface — it won't try to simulate the thickness of the metal. Such a surface model could be used to make a mold or die for manufacturing the oil pan. Keep this wireframe because you will add to it in the next chapter, and you will add surfaces to it in Section 2.

Set the drawing up to use inches, and make a new layer that has a name such as WF01 to be used for drawing the wireframe objects. Much of the wireframe's dimensions will be in increments of 0.25 inches, so you might want to use AutoCAD's snap mode much of the time, with the snap spacing set to 0.25.

Start the wireframe by drawing the top flange of the oil pan, using the dimensions given in Figure 2-1. Draw these wireframe objects on the WCS X-Y plane, with one edge of the flange on the X axis, and another edge on the Y axis. Do not draw the lines shown in dashed linetypes. You will add those lines in the next chapter.

Because these lines and arcs are going to be used as surface boundaries, they

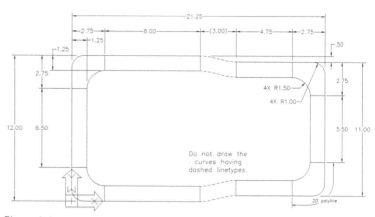

Figure 2-1

require a slightly different treatment than if they were part of a 2D drawing. That is why the flange is divided into rectangles. Also, the four outside corners should be drawn as 2D polylines, having a line segment 1.75 inches long, a 1.0-inch-radius arc, and another 1.75-inch-long line segment.

When you have finished drawing the flange, move the UCS to the center of the lower-left inside arc and rotate the UCS 90 degrees about the X-axis. Then, use the dimensions shown in Figure 2-2 to draw two arcs and one line that represent the tapered vertical side of the oil pan. You should also draw the vertical center-line along the current Y direction. Use a layer that has a CENTERLINE linetype for this line. Its length is not critical.

Use a polar array to make a copy of the two arcs and the line that is tangent to them. As shown in Figure 2-3, rotate the copy 90 degrees from the original objects. This is a convenient occasion to use the 3DARRAY command, because you can use the just-drawn centerline as a rotation axis. Then, copy the rotated copy eight units in the X-axis direction. This copy is on the opposite end of the flange segment (next to the missing section on the flange).

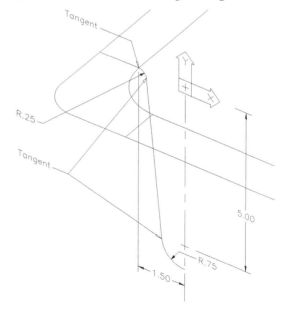

Figure 2-2

Now, move the UCS to the center of the lower-right corner flange inside arc and point the UCS Y axis in the WCS Z direction. Draw two arcs and a line representing the tapered vertical side of the oil pan on this end, using the dimensions shown in Figure 2-4. These dimensions have the same values as those used for the other end, except the center of the 0.75 radius arc is 3.50 inches from the flange top, rather than 5.00 inches. You also should draw a vertical centerline in the center of the flange arc.

Make a 90-degree polar array copy of the two arcs and one line, and then copy the copy 4.75 inches in the minus X direction, as shown in Figure 2-5. These operations are similar to those you performed at the other end of the oil pan.

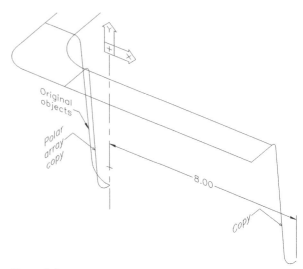

Figure 2-3

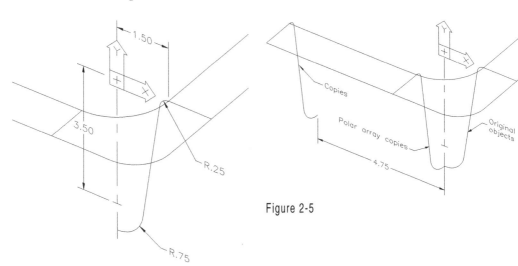

Figure 2-4

Figure 2-5

Restore the WCS and use AutoCAD's MIRROR command to make mirror-image copies of the six sets of lines and arcs on the opposite side of the oil pan. You do not need to make copies of the center-lines. Your wireframe model should look similar to the one shown in Figure 2-6. The viewing directions for this figure are 305 degrees from the X axis and 35 degrees from the X-Y plane. Your viewpoint, of course, might be different.

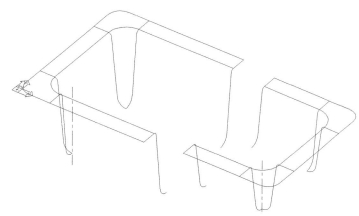

Figure 2-6

Finish this stage of the wireframe model by connecting the lower end of the large arcs with lines to form two rectangles that are parallel with the WCS X-Y plane. A running endpoint snap is convenient when drawing these eight lines. Your model should be similar to the one shown in Figure 2-7. On the CD-ROM that accompanies this book, the wireframe model is in file f045.dwg. You will connect the two sections as an exercise in the next chapter.

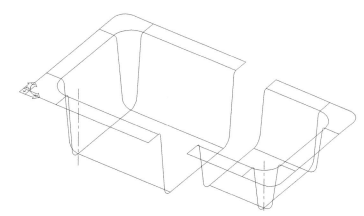

Figure 2-7

# CHAPTER 5

# 3D Curves

*Curves that twist and turn through 3D space are discussed in this chapter. These curves enable you to create geometric shapes that cannot be made by any of the 2D objects discussed in the previous chapter.*

*This chapter*

- *describes the characteristics and uses of 3D polylines;*
- *explains how to use the 3DPOLY command;*
- *shows you how to make 3D helix and spiral curves;*
- *describes how to use PEDIT in modifying 3D polylines;*
- *describes the properties of NURBS curves;*
- *shows you how to use the SPLINE command;*
- *explains how to modify splines with SPLINEDIT.*

Most of the curves on your wireframe models lie on a plane, even though that plane may be skewed to the principal planes of the WCS. After you locate and align the plane for such a curve, the curve itself can be defined by using only X and Y coordinates. Occasionally, however, your models will need a curve, or some wireframe geometry, that does not fit on a plane. These are 3D curves, and all three coordinates

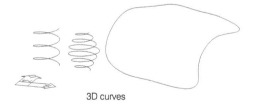

3D curves

— X, Y, and Z — are needed to define their shape. Examples of such curves are the edges of screw threads, the wire centerline of coil springs, the edge of a propeller blade, and even the edge of automobile trunk lids.

AutoCAD has two commands that can make 3D wireframe geometry: 3DPOLY and SPLINE. This chapter explores both of these commands and what they can do, what they are good for, how to implement them, and how to modify them.

# 3D Polylines

Although 3D polylines, which are made by the 3DPOLY command, are similar to the 2D polylines made with the PLINE command, in that they are multi-segmented, 3D polylines are not confined to a single plane. However, they cannot have arc segments or width. Furthermore, 3D polylines can be drawn only in the continuous linetype. You can assign a noncontinuous linetype, such as HIDDEN, to them, but AutoCAD still draws them with solid, continuous lines. 3D polylines do, however, accept an overall line thicknesses.

## Using 3D Polylines

Although 3D polylines are often referred to as 3D curves, they are actually composed of line segments. On your computer screen, a 3D polyline might look exactly like a set of ordinary lines that are connected end to end. It is, however, a single object that can be moved, copied, erased, and rotated the same as any other single object. The command for making 3D polylines, 3DPOLY, also works in the same way as AutoCAD's LINE command, offering the same options after the first segment has been drawn. These options are (1) to specify an endpoint, (2) to close the polyline back to the first point, and (3) to undo the last segment and return to the previous point.

You use 3D polylines in a wireframe model anytime you want a set of lines to behave as a single object. In surface models, you sometimes use 3D polylines as surface boundaries. This use is described in Section 2. 3D polylines also can serve as an extrusion path while making a solid model. Solid models are discussed in Section 3.

Using 3D polylines for surface boundaries

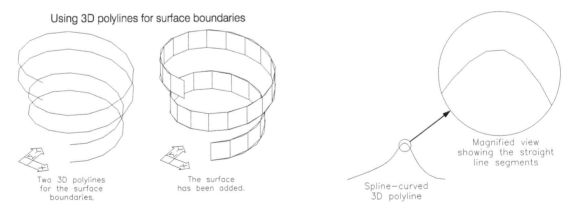

Two 3D polylines for the surface boundaries.

The surface has been added.

Spline-curved 3D polyline

Magnified view showing the straight line segments

Even though 3D polylines are made of straight line-like segments, you can create curves that appear to be reasonably smooth by keeping the segments relatively short. You also can use an option in the command for editing 3D polylines — PEDIT — to transform the 3D polyline into a B-spline curve. The resulting curve, however, still is made of line-like segments — it isn't a true

B-spline curve. You have to look very closely to discern the individual lines, but they are there. Also, splines made from polylines require a relatively large amount of data, which tends to increase both file size and computation time. Moreover, because the edges of AutoCAD surfaces are always made of straight lines, there is seldom any advantage in using spline-curved 3D polylines for surface boundaries. A final drawback is that AutoCAD's solid modeler does not allow spline curves to be used as extrusion paths.

If you need a B-spline curve, you usually are better off using the SPLINE command to make them. I discuss this command later in this chapter. Incidentally, 3D polyline spline curves can be transformed into true splines through the SPLINE command.

| | |
|---|---|
| Command: | 3DPOLY |
| Purpose: | This command makes polylines composed of straight-line segments of width 0. Unlike 2D polylines, the vertices in 3D polylines can have different Z coordinates. |
| Initiate with: | • On the command line, enter 3DPOLY. |
| | • From the Draw pull-down menu, select 3D Polyline. |
| Options: | The 3DPOLY command prompts you to draw two segments of the 3D polyline, and then displays the following command line prompt: |

`Specify endpoint of line or [Close/Undo]:`

| | | |
|---|---|---|
| | • Endpoint of Line | You can respond to this option by specifying a point or by pressing the Enter key. When a point is specified, AutoCAD draws a line to it from the previous point, and then repeats the command line prompt. |
| | • Close | This option draws a line segment from the last specified point to the starting point of the 3D polyline and ends the command. |
| | • Undo | The last segment is removed when this option is selected, and the command line prompt is redisplayed. You can step back to the first point. |
| Notes: | • This command operates very much like AutoCAD's ordinary LINE command, and the resulting 3D polyline looks exactly like ordinary lines. The lines making a 3D polyline, however, are connected to make a single object. |
| | • AutoCAD considers polylines that were finished by specifying a vertex on the same point as the polyline's first point and then ending the 3DPOLY command to be open. It considers those that were ended by using the Close option to be closed. |
| | • 3D polylines, unlike 2D polylines, cannot have width, and they are always drawn in a continuous linetype. They can, however, have a line thickness. |

## Drawing Helixes and 3D Spirals

You will not have any trouble using the 3DPOLY command because it works so much like the LINE command that you have long used. Nevertheless, some forethought and planning is required to fully use the command's capability to make 3D objects. It also often reqires you to use input methods that you would not use in drawing lines.

One use of 3DPOLY is in drawing helixes and 3D spirals. A helix is a curve form you can obtain by wrapping a string around a cylinder, and a spiral is a curve you can obtain by wrapping a string around a cone. Generally, the word **pitch** is used to signify the distance between adjacent coils along the cylinder or cone. Screw threads, coil springs, barber poles, spiral staircases, and some parking and freeway ramps are examples of objects based on helixes and spirals.

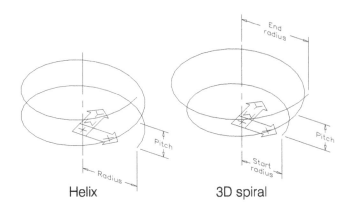

Helix            3D spiral

AutoCAD's cylindrical coordinates, which were discussed in Chapter 1, are especially useful for drawing helixes and 3D spirals. Recall that cylindrical coordinates for specifying a point location have the form:

`distance<angle, height`

In this case, **distance** is the point's distance from the origin for absolute input, or from the last point for relative input; **angle** is the horizontal angle to the point from the X axis; and **height** is the point's distance in the Z direction from the X-Y plane for absolute input or from the last point for relative input.

The process for making a wireframe helix involves moving around and along a cylinder, using cylindrical coordinates to set 3D polyline endpoints. Distance remains the same, angle is used to step around the cylinder, and the height component is used to move up the cylinder. Notice that this method restricts you to drawing helixes and spirals around a centerline pointed in the Z direction. Also, the method works best if the helix centerline passes through the UCS origin. Otherwise, you have to use relative input, which can be cumbersome.

Cylindrical horizontal coordinate angles increase 45 degrees per step if the helix is to have 8 steps per revolution.

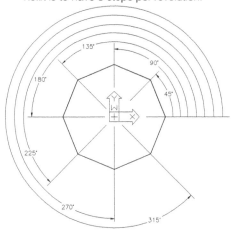

A 3D spiral can be made in the same way, but distance changes as the spiral follows a cone shape. Pitch usually stays constant, but there is no reason (other than the complexity it will cause) it, too, cannot change as the helix or spiral grows.

Before you start drawing your helix or spiral, you need to do some planning and arithmetic. First, you need to decide how many steps around the cylinder you want to take with each revolution. This determines the relative coarseness of the resulting curve. More steps make a smoother curve, but they also require more work. Then, you divide the number of degrees for each revolution (360 degrees) by the number of steps per revolution. The angle in each cylindrical coordinate input increases by this angle for each step around the cylinder.

Suppose, for example, you decide to make a helix that has eight steps per revolution. Because 360 divided by 8 equals 45, the cylindrical coordinate angle increases 45 degrees with each step around the cylinder. The angle for the first point is 0, for the second step it is 45, for the third it is 90, and so forth, until the first revolution is completed. Then, the angle drops back to 0.

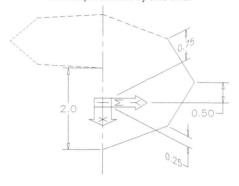

In drawing a helix having a pitch of 2 and 8 steps per revolution, the elevation of each step increases by 0.25 units.

Next, you need to decide what pitch your helix is to have. Divide that pitch by the number of steps per revolution to determine the height increment for the cylindrical coordinates. If, to continue the example, you chose a pitch of 2.0, the increment for each height is 0.25 (2.0 divided by 8). The helix starts with an elevation of 0, the next point has an elevation of 0.25, the elevation of the third point is 0.50, for the fourth point it is 0.75, and so forth. Unlike angle, height continues to increase through each revolution.

The command line input to draw one revolution of the example helix, with a radius of 2.0 units, is

```
Command: 3DPOLY (Enter)
Specify start point of polyline: 2,0,0 (Enter)
Specify endpoint of line or [Undo]: 2<45,.25 (Enter)
Specify endpoint of line or [Undo]: 2<90,.50 (Enter)
Specify endpoint of line or [Close/Undo]: 2<135,.75 (Enter)
Specify endpoint of line or [Close/Undo]: 2<180,1.00 (Enter)
Specify endpoint of line or [Close/Undo]: 2<225,1.25 (Enter)
Specify endpoint of line or [Close/Undo]: 2<270,1.50 (Enter)
Specify endpoint of line or [Close/Undo]: 2<315,1.75 (Enter)
Specify endpoint of line or [Close/Undo]: 2<360,2.00 (Enter)
Specify endpoint of line or [Close/Undo]: (Enter)
```

The resulting helix is shown in the accompanying figure. It is admittedly not very impressive. You can use the PEDIT command to transform it into a spline curve, however. As shown on the right in the figure, this improves its looks greatly. Actually, a smooth helix can be obtained by using only four points per revolution if it is transformed into a B-spline with PEDIT.

Nevertheless, because AutoCAD approximates the edges of curved surfaces with short straight segments, there is no point in smoothing 3D polylines that are to be used for surface boundaries. Moreover, AutoCAD does not allow splines to be used as extrusion paths for 3D solids.

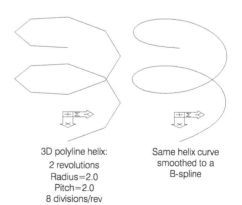

3D polyline helix:
2 revolutions
Radius=2.0
Pitch=2.0
8 divisions/rev

Same helix curve smoothed to a B-spline

A major disadvantage in using such command line input to draw a 3D helix is that it is tedious and error prone. Script files are a good alternative to command line input. Recall that script files are external text files that can initiate a command and provide all of its command line input, just as if you were typing it in. A script file to draw the example helix consists of 11 lines. The first line is simply the word **3DPOLY**, the next 9 lines are the point inputs, and the 11th line is just a line break (made by pressing the Enter key). In other words, the script file contains the human side of the command line interface.

You can make script files with any word processor or text editor that can save files in text format (which is sometimes referred to as ASCII format). Notepad, the editor that comes with the Windows operating systems, is such a text editor. The extension name used for the script file must be .SCR.

A script file for drawing the previous example is included on the CD-ROM that comes with this book. It is named HELIX_01.SCR. To use this script file, invoke AutoCAD's SCRIPT command. A dialog box titled Select Script File appears. This dialog box has the capability to search through various directories and drives to find files with an extension of .SCR. When you find the HELIX_01.SCR script file, click on it to highlight it, and click the Open button. The helix is automatically drawn in the positive Z direction at the UCS origin.

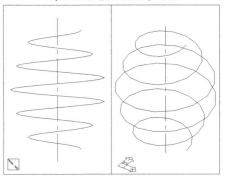

This helix-spiral curve was drawn by the HELIX_02.SCR script file.

The CD-ROM contains another script file, which has the name HELIX_02.SCR, for a more complex example. As shown in the nearby figure, this script file draws a combination helix-spiral curve. It increases in diameter through two revolutions, maintains a constant diameter through the third revolution, and reduces in diameter through the final two revolutions. It makes 16 steps per revolution. The script file has more than 80 lines of cylindrical coordinate input. Making the script file, however, was not especially difficult, because a spreadsheet program was used to do the arithmetic. Three spreadsheet columns were used — the first was for the cylindrical coordinate's distance, the second was for the rotation angle, and the third was for height. Each spreadsheet row represented a cylindrical coordinate point. The spreadsheet was saved in a text format, and the word 3DPOLY, along with the characters needed for AutoCAD's cylindrical coordinate input, were added with a text editor.

Although script files can be useful for drawing helixes and 3D spirals that have unusual, and perhaps varying, shapes, an AutoLISP program is more convenient for drawing the majority of the helix and 3D spiral forms you will encounter. The data in script files is absolute, and any change — such as in diameter, pitch, or the number of revolutions — requires a new script file. With AutoLISP, on the other hand, many parameters can be in the form of variables that are assigned a value when the program is executed.

Although it is not difficult to write an AutoLISP program for drawing helixes and 3D spirals, Autodesk already has such a program named 3DSPIRAL.LSP. Originally, it was written to draw

2D spirals, but it was modified for Release 12 to draw 3D spirals as well. Although this program is not included with subsequent AutoCAD releases, it works well in them. This AutoLISP program is included on the CD-ROM that accompanies this book. You are free to use, copy, modify, and distribute the program, as long you retain the program's Autodesk copyright notice.

AutoCAD's APPLOAD command is a good way to locate and load this, or any other, AutoLISP program. After you have loaded this program, you can create either a helix or a 3D spiral by entering 3DSPIRAL on the command line. The program asks you for the following input from the command line:

| Prompt | User Input |
| --- | --- |
| Center point | Specify a center point. It does not have to be on the X-Y plane. |
| Number of rotations | Enter a number. It cannot be 0, negative, or null (that is, you cannot just press the Enter key). |
| Starting radius | Specify a number. It cannot be 0, negative, or null. You can, however, specify it by pointing. |
| Horizontal growth | Enter a number. It can be 0 or negative. You cannot, however, give a null response. A 0 value creates a straight helix coil. |
| Vertical growth per rotation | Enter a number. A negative number causes the coil to grow in the minus Z direction. You cannot enter 0 or give a null response. |
| Points per rotation <30> | Enter a number or press Enter to accept the default of 30 points per rotation. |

## Modifying 3D Polylines

After a 3D polyline has been created, it can be modified by any of AutoCAD's standard editing commands. It can be moved, stretched, rotated, lengthened, trimmed, extended, and broken into two 3D polylines. This hasn't always been true. The BREAK and TRIM commands do not work on 3D polylines in versions of AutoCAD earlier than Release 13.

For more specialized editing, use the PEDIT command. Even though this is the same command that is used for editing 2D polylines, AutoCAD recognizes a 3D polyline when it is picked to be edited, and it issues a command line menu of editing functions that are appropriate for 3D polylines. Missing in this menu are the Join, Width, Fit, and Ltype gen options found in the menu for 2D polylines.

One of the main reasons you use PEDIT with a 3D polyline is to edit its vertices. You can add or remove vertices from 3D polylines through the Edit vertex option of PEDIT. You also can move vertices with PEDIT, but you will probably find grips or the STRETCH command to be just as convenient for this task.

Prior to Release 13, the Spline curve option was another good reason for using the PEDIT command. However, because spline curves made with the SPLINE command (which was introduced in Release 13) are true B-splines, and are just as easy to make as splines from polylines, you seldom now have any reason to smooth 3D polylines to B-splines.

You also can edit 3D polylines through the PROPERTIES command that was indroduced in AutoCAD 2000. This command displays a dialog box for you to use in changing the same properties of a selected 3D polyline that the PEDIT command changes, plus its general properties, such as color and layer. Unlike the PEDIT command, PROPERTIES allows you to select on-the-fly whether the equation for transforming a 3D polyline into a spline curve is to be quadratic or cubic.

Occasionally, you will want to join two 3D polylines. For example, you might want to increase the number of coils in a helix-shaped 3D polyline or you might want to add a hook, or some other curve, to its endpoints. However, AutoCAD has no provision for joining 3D polylines as it does for 2D polylines. Nevertheless, it can be done by the AutoLISP program named JOIN3DPL.LSP that is on the CD-ROM that accompanies this book.

The Properties dialog box for 3D polylines

After you have loaded the program, enter JOIN3DPL on the command line and select the two 3D polylines you want combined. The 3D polylines must be open, and the endpoint of one must touch an endpoint of the other. Also, they cannot have been spline-fit.

| | |
|---|---|
| Command: | PEDIT |
| Purpose: | This command performs editing operations on 3D polylines. It allows you to open a closed 3D polyline or to close one that is open, to smooth the polyline's segments into a relatively smooth curve, and to edit individual vertices. You cannot, however, use it to join 3D polylines. |

| | |
|---|---|
| Initiate with: | • From the command line, enter PEDIT. |
| | • From the Modify II toolbar, select Edit Polyline. |
| | • From the Modify pull-down menu, select Object, and then Polyline. |
| Options: | When you pick a 3D polyline in response to the PEDIT command's prompt to select an object, AutoCAD offers the following command line menu of options appropriate for 3D polylines: |

`Close/Edit vertex/Spline curve/Decurve/Undo.`

- Close

This option is offered only if the 3D polyline is open. AutoCAD draws

Before Close

After Close

a line segment from the 3D polyline's last point to its first point and changes the status of the polyline from Open to Closed. If the 3D polyline was finished by drawing a segment back to the start point, no segment is added, but the status of the polyline changes from Open to Closed. When this option is completed, AutoCAD redisplays the main PEDIT option menu.

- Open

This option is offered only if the 3D polyline is closed. The segment of the polyline that was

Before Open

After Open

drawn by the Close option of the 3DPOLY or PEDIT commands is removed, and the status of the polyline changes to open. AutoCAD returns to the main PEDIT option menu when this option is finished.

- Edit Vertex

You can edit a 3D polyline on a vertex-by-vertex basis with this option. It allows you to break a 3D polyline into two 3D polylines, replace several segments with a single segment, insert new vertices, and remove existing vertices. The option displays the following secondary command line menu:

```
Next/Previous/Break/Insert/Move/Regen/Straighten/eXit <N>:
```

An X marker is positioned on the first visible polyline vertex that is closest to the initial point.

- Next

This option, the original default option, moves the X marker to the next vertex away from the beginning point of the polyline. If you continue to specify this option, the marker stalls on the last vertex of the polyline, even if the polyline is closed. It also stalls if the next vertex is not visible.

- Previous

This option moves the X marker to the previous vertex — the one closer to the beginning of the polyline — and changes the default option of the Edit vertex menu to Previous. If the previous vertex is currently not visible, the X marker will not move.

- Break

This option allows you to break a 3D polyline into two separate 3D polylines at one or more vertices. The current location of the X marker is used as one break point, and the following submenu is displayed for you to use in specifying the other break vertices:

`Next/Previous/Go/eXit <N>:`

Next and Previous move the X marker to another vertex. The Go option performs the break and returns to the Edit vertex menu. If Go is selected without having moved the X marker, the polyline is broken without the removal of a segment. If one of the selected vertices is an end vertex, the polyline is shortened. At least one of the selected vertices must be an interior vertex. The eXit option is an escape that allows you to return to the Edit vertex menu without performing a break.

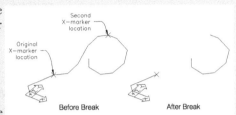

- Insert

This option inserts a new vertex after the vertex that has the X marker. AutoCAD prompts for the point location of the new vertex.

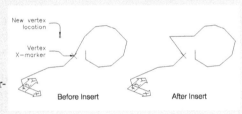

- Move

The position of the vertex with the X marker can be moved with this option. AutoCAD asks for the new location of the vertex.

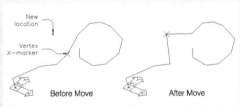

- Regen

This option regenerates the 3D polyline.

- Straighten

This option removes the vertices and line segments between two vertices and replaces them with a single line segment. The current location of the X marker establishes the first vertex. AutoCAD displays the following submenu for you to use in specifying the other vertex:

`Next/Previous/Go/eXit <N>:`

The Next and Previous options in this menu move the X marker to a vertex marking the other end of the section to be straightened.

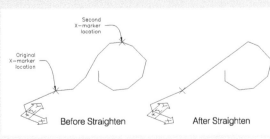

The Go option performs the straightening operation and returns to the main Edit vertex menu. The eXit option can be used to return to the main Edit vertex menu without straightening the 3D polyline.

- eXit    Exit returns to the main PEDIT menu.

- Spline Curve

This option in the main PEDIT menu smooths the 3D polyline to a shape that approximates a B-spline curve. The curve will still be made of line segments, but the lines will generally be so short that the curve appears to be smooth. The relative length of the line segments is controlled by AutoCAD's **splinesegs** system variable. Its default value is 8. Individual segments of spline-curved 2D polylines are made of arcs, rather than straight lines. When **splinesegs** is given a negative number, however, the negative sign is ignored when 3D polylines are smoothed.

The degree of the equation used to make the spline curve is controlled by AutoCAD's **splinetype** system variable. When **splinetype** is set to 5, a quadratic equation is used, and a cubic equation is used when **spline-type** is set to 6 (its

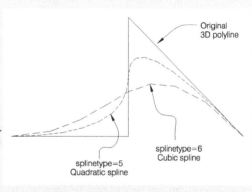

default setting). The vertex points of the polyline are used as control points for the spline. Consequently, except for the endpoints, the spline will not pass through the polyline's original vertex points. Quadratic splines usually come closer to the original vertex points than cubic splines.

- Decurve

This option restores the original shape and condition of a spline-curved 3D polyline. Spline-curved polylines that have been edited with AutoCAD's BREAK or TRIM commands cannot be decurved. Those edited by the LENGTHEN, EXTEND, and STRETCH commands, however, can be decurved.

Notes:

- Spline-curved 3D polylines can be converted to true spline objects through the SPLINE command's Object option.

- You seldom need to use PEDIT's Spline curve option because you can make reasonably smooth-looking 3D polyline curves by using closely spaced vertex points.

- PEDIT does not have any provisions for joining 3D polylines as it does with 2D polylines.

Related system variables:

- **splframe**

This system variable can have a value of either 0 or 1. When it is set to 1, the original shape of a spline-curved polyline is displayed along with its spline-curved form. A screen regen is required for this to take effect. The default setting of **splframe** is 0.

- **splinesegs**   This system variable controls the relative size of the line segments used to draw spline-curved polylines. Its default setting is 8, and you will seldom have any reason to change it.

- **splinetype**   The degree of the equation used for making polyline spline curves is controlled by this system variable. When **splinetype** is set to a value of 5, the shape of spline curve is based on a quadratic (second degree) equation. When **splinetype** is set to a value of 6, spline-curved polylines are based on a cubic (third degree) equation. The default setting of **splinetype** is 6.

# Splines

Splines are natural curves. Your garden hose is a good example of a spline (as long as it isn't kinked), as it twists through your lawn and garden. Its curves gradually blend into each other so that it is impossible to determine exactly where one curve ends and another curve starts. Also, changing the curvature, location, or direction of any section of the hose affects the neighboring sections as well. Those sections closest to the change are affected the most, with the effects gradually diminishing so that sections some distance away are not affected at all. The new curves still smoothly blend together.

Curves in splines blend smoothly into each other. When a section is moved, the spline's curves adjust to maintain the smooth curve transitions.

Thin, flexible strips of metal, wood, and plastic also form spline curves. In fact, such strips have long been used by drafters to draw profiles for ships and airplanes. Weights, which are often called **ducks**, are attached to the strips to hold them in position. In some cases the shape of the spline is fine-tuned by using some weights that are heavier than the others. These strips are called *drafting splines*, which is where the name for the computer-based curves comes from.

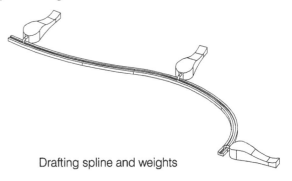

Drafting spline and weights

## NURBS

The shape of AutoCAD B-splines is controlled by equations rather than metal strips. For computational purposes, a spline is divided into segments. The spline's shape for one segment is computed, then the shape for the next segment is computed, and so forth, through the total length of the spline. The ends of these segments are generally referred to as *knots*. Although some computer graphic programs show the knots along B-splines, AutoCAD does not. Some spline algorithms use segments of equal length, while others, including the one AutoCAD uses, use segments of unequal length. Therefore, you occasionally see references to *uniform B-splines* and to *non-uniform B-splines*.

The equation used to calculate the shape of a spline segment has a property called *degree*, which represents the value of the largest exponent in the equation. For example, an equation whose greatest component is squared is a second-degree (quadratic) equation, and one whose greatest component is raised to the third power (cubed) is a third-degree equation. You have already encountered these terms during the discussion of the spline fit options for 3D polylines within PEDIT.

Sometimes the word *order* is used rather than degree. The order of an equation is its degree plus 1. Thus, a third-degree equation is an order 4 equation. From a graphical standpoint, the degree (and order) of an equa-

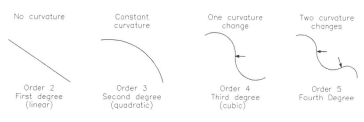

tion determines how many curvature changes can occur within one segment of a spline. The number of curvature changes is equal to the degree of theequation minus 2. Therefore, a third-degree equation has one curvature change, and a fourth-degree equation has two curvature changes.

The computer version of spline weights, or ducks, are **control points**. These points, which are invariably off the curve (except for the spline endpoints), pull the spline into position. The number of control points used for shaping a spline is determined by the degree of the spline's equations. Most of the time, all the control points for a spline have an equal effect, but you can give some control points more weight, and conse-quently a greater effect in shaping the curve, than oth-

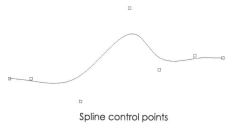

Spline control points

ers. B-splines with unequally weighted control points are called **rational B-splines**.

A B-spline curve that has non-uniform segment lengths and unequally weighted control points is called a *Non-Uniform Rational B-Spline*. This name is almost always shortened to the acronym of NURBS. (The acronym sounds as if it is a plural word, but it isn't.) Splines made by smoothing 2D and 3D polylines are not NURBS, but AutoCAD can create true NURBS curves through the SPLINE command, which was introduced in Release 13.

Although a spline made with the SPLINE command does not have unequally weighted control points when it is created, and is therefore not a rational spline (and therefore not actually a NURBS), through editing, some control points can be given a weight that is different from the oth-ers, which make it a rational B-spline (and, thus, a true NURBS). Usually, however, unequally weighted control points are needed only in special situations to fine-tune the shape of a curve.

| Command: | SPLINE |
| --- | --- |
| Purpose: | This command creates true 3D wireframe B-spline curves. The spline can be based on user-specified points or on an existing 2D or 3D polyline that has been spline-fit. |
| Initiate with: | • On the command line, enter SPLINE. |
| | • From the Draw pull-down menu, select Spline. |
| | • Select the Spline button from the Draw toolbar. |
| Options: | AutoCAD begins the SPLINE command with a command line menu containing two options: |

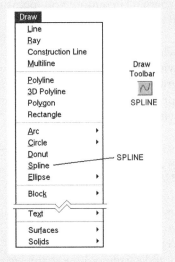

```
Specify first point or [Object]:
```

| | |
| --- | --- |
| • Object | This option brings up a prompt for you to select one or more objects to be converted into a spline. The objects selected must be 2D or 3D polylines that have already been fit to a spline through the PEDIT command. The shape of the spline is not changed during the conversion. If the system variable **delobj** is set to 1, the old spline is automatically deleted as the new one is created. |
| • Enter first point | The default option of the SPLINE command is to enter the starting point of the spline. As soon as the starting point is selected, AutoCAD prompts for a second point. When you have entered two points, the following secondary menu is displayed: |

```
Specify next point or [Close/Fit tolerance]<start tangent>:
```

| | |
| --- | --- |
| • Next Point | Specify another point location to continue drawing the spline. A rubber-band line, anchored on the previous point, is displayed, along with the extension to the spline itself. Moreover, the spline dynamically changes shape as you move the screen cursor. AutoCAD refers to each of these user-specified points as a fit point. The secondary menu is repeated after each point is specified. |
| • Undo | This option exists, even though it is not listed in the secondary menu. Entering the letter U, or the entire word undo, removes the last point. You can undo back to the first point. |
| • Start Tangent | When you press Enter in response to the secondary menu, AutoCA stop drawing the spline and issues prompts for its start and end tangents. If you respond to these prompts by pressing the Enter key, AutoCAD allows the spline to swivel about the start point or end point as it assumes its shape. If you respond by specifying a point, AutoCAD aims the spline end toward the specified point. |

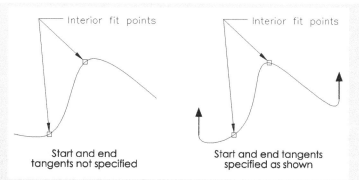

Start and end
tangents not specified

Start and end tangents
specified as shown

- Close

When you select this option, AutoCAD draws a segment back to the start point of the spline and prompts for a tangent direction. Both the start and end segments of the spline use this single tangent, and the spline adjusts its shape to accommodate the tangent direction.

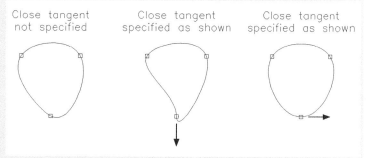

Close tangent
not specified

Close tangent
specified as shown

Close tangent
specified as shown

- Fit Tolerance

By default, splines pass through each fit point. When you apply a fit tolerance, however, the spline bypasses the interior fit points. (It always passes through the first and last fit points.) When this option is selected, which can be done by entering either F or T, AutoCAD issues the command line prompt:

`Enter Fit tolerance <Default>:`

The initial default fit tolerance value is 0. The value entered controls the relative distance by which the spline deviates from the fit points. Although you can change the fit tolerance at any point as you draw a spline, the entire spline assumes the last value specified. Consequently, you cannot have one tolerance apply to some fit points and another apply to other fit points. AutoCAD retains the last tolerance specified and uses it as a default even when a new spline is started. If you exit the drawing, however, AutoCAD resets the default tolerance value to 0 when you re-open the drawing.

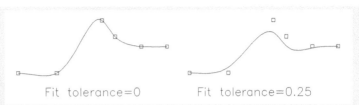

Fit tolerance=0          Fit tolerance=0.25

Notes:

- Because spline objects require much less computer computation and space in the drawing file's database, you should convert 2D and 3D polylines that have been fit to a spline curve to true splines whenever it is convenient.

- Splines made from 2D and 3D polylines do not have any fit points. Moreover, other splines lose their fit points when certain editing operations are performed on them.

- You also can set, as well as modify, the start and end tangents of an existing spline through the SPLINEDIT command. This command also can change the fit tolerance of a spline.

- In Release 13, spline-fit tolerance works in a different manner than in subsequent releases. In Release 13, gradually increasing the tolerance value of a spline does not cause the spline to gradually pull away from the fit points. Instead, there are threshold values at which the spline changes shape and pulls away from the fit points. That shape is maintained until some specific higher tolerance value is reached, at which it pulls farther from the fit points. These threshold values vary by spline size, shape, and end tangents.

Related system variables:

- **delobj**    When this system variable is set to 1, its default setting, 2D and 3D spline-fit polylines are deleted when they are converted to true splines. When **delobj** is set to 0, the original polyline is retained.

- **splframe**    This system variable can have a value of 0 or 1, with 0 being its default value. When it is set to 1, AutoCAD displays a set of lines (a frame) between the control points of a spline.

- **useacis**    Splines having a nonzero fit tolerance that were created in AutoCAD Release 13 might have a different shape in subsequent AutoCAD releases. You can retain the shape of the spline by using this system variable, which first appeared in AutoCAD Release 14.01. Set **useacis** to 1, open the file having a nonzero fit tolerance spline from Release 13, and use the SPLINEDIT command to purge the spline's fit data. The default value of **useacis** is 0.

## Creating Spline Curves

Although AutoCAD splines appear to be simple, smoothly curved objects, they have properties and characteristics that are significantly different from other AutoCAD object types. Probably the easiest way to explore these properties and characteristics is by drawing a simple 2D spline. Therefore, you should draw a spline using the command line sequence of prompts and input shown here. Although you can grasp how the SPLINE command works by merely reading through this sequence, you will find it more helpful to actually duplicate the input within AutoCAD, because you can see the spline's process and behavior as it is drawn. You will also find AutoCAD's LIST data for this spline interesting, and you can see how modifying its properties affects its shape. It will take you just a few seconds to draw this spline, and it does not require any special drawing setup. Integer coordinate values are used so that you can specify points readily from the keyboard, or by setting snap to 1, and using your pointing device.

```
Command:  SPLINE (Enter)
Specify first point or [Object]: 0,0 (Enter)
Specify next point: 1,0 (Enter)
Specify next point or [Close/Fit tolerance] <start tangent>: 1,1 (Enter)
Specify next point or [Close/Fit tolerance] <start tangent>: 2,0 (Enter)
Specify next point or [Close/Fit tolerance] <start tangent>: (Enter)
Specify start tangent: @1<180 (Enter)
Specify end tangent: @1<270 (Enter)
```

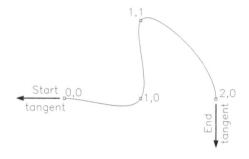

Your spline should look like the one shown in the accompanying figure.

Two things were especially noticeable as you drew this simple 2D spline. First, unlike the splines made from 2D and 3D polylines with the PEDIT command, the curve goes through each point you specified. As you will recall from the 3D Polylines section earlier in this chapter, splines made from 3D polylines through PEDIT use the original polyline vertices as control points. Consequently, except for their first and last points, those splines are not likely to go through any of the original vertices. (Splines made from 2D polylines, which are not discussed in this book, have basically the same properties as those made from 3D polylines.) Generally, this SPLINE command characteristic of drawing the curve through the selected points is popular because it is easier to control the shape and location of the curve.

You can, however, use the Fit Tolerance option (which is offered after the second spline point has been specified) to have the curve bypass the fit points. This option shows you the current fit tolerance value (it initially has a value of 0) and allows you to enter a new one. Then, the perpendicular distance from each fit point to the curve is proportional to the value assigned to fit tolerance. The net effect is that as you increase fit tolerance, the spline becomes straighter and less curvy. The endpoints of the spline, however, are always exactly on their fit points.

As Fit tolerance increases, the spline pulls further from the interior fit points.

Fit tolerance=0          Fit tolerance=0.05          Fit tolerance=0.15

Any one spline can have only one fit tolerance in effect, even though the option for setting it is offered each time a point is to be specified. If, for example, you set the fit tolerance to 0.15 just before specifying the fourth point on the demonstration spline, the spline moves away from the previous two fit points.

Most likely, you will seldom use the Fit Tolerance option as you create a spline. You also can set a fit tolerance value with the SPLINEDIT command (which is discussed shortly), and you might occasionally assign a fit tolerance in an attempt to improve the shape of a spline.

The second thing you probably noticed as you drew the spline was the effect that the start and end tangent directions have on the shape of the spline. As soon as you pressed the Enter key to signal an end to spline fit point input, AutoCAD anchored a rubber-band line on the spline's start point and prompted for the spline's start tangent direction. Although this input establishes a direction, you must specify a point; you cannot type in just an angle, such as 180. If you used your pointing device in specifying the start tangent, you could see the spline dynamically change shape as you moved your pointing device around, changing the tangent direction. The spline segment between the first and second fit points was affected the most, the change in the middle segment was not as pronounced, and there were very slight changes in the last segment. After you specified the start tangent to be in the minus X direction (180 degrees), AutoCAD prompted for the end tangent direction, and the spline changed shape again as you moved your pointing device about. You selected a tangent in the minus Y direction (270 degrees).

These tangents force the ends of the spline to point in the specified direction, and the spline assumes a shape to accommodate those directions while maintaining perfectly smooth curves. If you press the Enter key when prompted for a tangent rather than specify a point, AutoCAD allows the spline to swivel about the endpoint as it assumes its shape.

When you are trying to picture the shape of a spline, it helps to imagine the spline as a flexible steel rod and the fit points as round pins fixed in space. The flexible rod has a hole at each fit point location, through which one of the round pins is inserted. Thus, these points are fixed in space, but the flexible rod is free to swivel about the pins as it is bent. When you specify an end tangent, that end of the flexible rod is as if it were clamped and forced to point in the specified direction. If you do not specify an end tangent, the flexible rod is free to swivel about the endpoint.

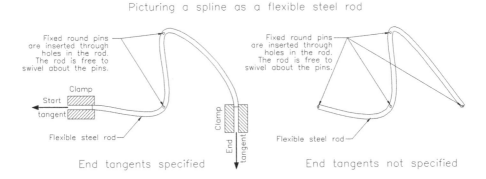

Picturing a spline as a flexible steel rod

Most of the time, you will want to specify the tangent of both ends, especially when the spline is to act as the continuation of, or be in line with, another object. As you would expect, you can use object snaps in specifying a tangent. You can even use the *Tangent* and *Perpendicular* object snaps. When the Tangent object snap is used in conjunction with an existing arc or circle, AutoCAD bases the tangent at a point on the arc or circle that is perpendicular to a line drawn from the end of the spline to the arc or circle. Consequently, your pick point on the arc or circle is not critical.

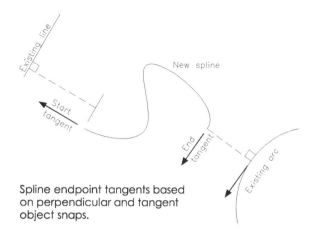

Spline endpoint tangents based on perpendicular and tangent object snaps.

## Spline Data

When you use the LIST command on the simple 2D spline drawn as a demonstration, you receive a surprisingly large amount of information, as shown in Table 5-1. In addition to listing the object type, its layer, and so forth, AutoCAD tells you the spline's length along the curve and that it is a fourth-order spline. Therefore, a third-degree (cubic) equation was used in drawing each segment of the spline. AutoCAD always makes fourth-order splines, although you can increase a spline's order (with SPLINEDIT) after it has been drawn.

### Table 5-1 LIST Command's Report for a Typical Spline

```
    SPLINE      Layer: OBJ01
                Space: Model space
    Handle = 10A
                Length: 3.6058
                Order: 4
    Properties: Planar, Non-Rational, Non-Periodic
    Parametric Range: Start    0.0000
                         End    3.4142
Number of control points: 6
Control Points: X = 0.0000   , Y = 0.0000   , Z = 0.0000
                X = 0.3333   , Y = 0.0000   , Z = 0.0000
                X = 1.3860   , Y = -0.4233  , Z = 0.0000
                X = 0.5472   , Y = 1.7444   , Z = 0.0000
                X = 2.0000   , Y = 0.4714   , Z = 0.0000
                X = 2.0000   , Y = 0.0000   , Z = 0.0000
```

## Table 5-1 LIST Command's Report for a Typical Spline (Continued)

```
Number of fit points: 4

    User Data: Fit Points
              X = 0.0000    , Y = 0.0000    , Z = 0.0000
              X = 1.0000    , Y = 0.0000    , Z = 0.0000
              X = 1.0000    , Y = 1.0000    , Z = 0.0000
              X = 2.0000    , Y = 0.0000    , Z = 0.0000


Fit point tolerance: 1.0000E-10


    Start Tangent
    X = 1.0000    , Y = 0.0000    , Z = 0.0000
    End Tangent
    X = 0.0000    , Y = -1.0000  , Z = 0.0000
```

Next, the LIST report shows the status of three properties of the spline. First it tells us that this spline is *planar*, which means that all its fit points lie on a plane. In Exercises One and Two of this chapter, you will draw splines that are not confined to a plane; AutoCAD lists those splines as being *non-planar*. The property list also shows that the spline in *non-rational*, which means that its control points all have equal weight. AutoCAD always assigns a weight of 1.0 to control points when a spline is drawn, but as you will see when SPLINEDIT is discussed later in this chapter, you can change the weight of individual control points, thus transforming the curve into a *rational* spline.

The last of the three spline properties shown by LIST tells you that the spline is *non-periodic*, which means it is an open spline. If the spline had been closed with the Close option of the SPLINE command, it would have been listed as a *periodic* spline. The terms *periodic* and *non-periodic* come from the Spatial Technology Inc. ACIS geo-

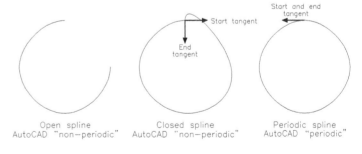

Open spline
AutoCAD "non—periodic"

Closed spline
AutoCAD "non—periodic"

Periodic spline
AutoCAD "periodic"

metric modeler that AutoCAD uses in making splines. Spatial Technology refers to splines that have their start points and endpoints in the same location as being *closed*. If, in addition to being closed, the spline's start points and endpoints have the same tangent, they say the spline is *periodic*. Because AutoCAD uses a single tangent for the endpoints of splines that have been completed with the Close option of the SPLINE command, those splines are always periodic. AutoCAD does not make the distinction between open and closed splines that Spatial Technology does.

Following the list of curve properties, AutoCAD shows the spline's *parametric range*. Splines are often classed as parametric curves, with the word *parametric* referring to variables (parameters) within equations, rather than to the interrelationship of dimensions and features as it does in a parametric modeler, such as Mechanical Desktop or Inventor. The LIST report for splines starts the parametric range at 0, and ends it with the cumulative straight line distance through the fit points. In the LIST report for the spline you've been looking at,

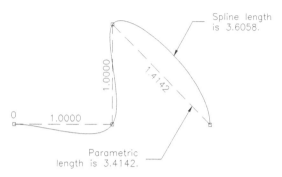

the length of the spline is longer than its parametric range, even though they both represent distances through the fit points. This is to be expected because a straight line is the shortest distance between two points.

Next, the LIST report shows the coordinates of each control point. There are six control points for the spline, including those on the start points and endpoints. Although AutoCAD does not normally display the control points, you can see them by setting the **splframe** system variable to 1. After a regen, AutoCAD displays the control points as the vertices of a framework of lines around the spline.

The coordinates of the fit points, which are the points selected while drawing the spline, are listed next. Not all splines have fit point data. Those made from spline-fit polylines have only control points. Also, splines that originally do have fit points can lose them when they undergo certain modifications (discussed later in this chapter). There are no surprises in the fit point data you have been examining.

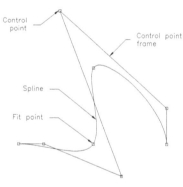

Spline when splframe
is set to 1 and
grips are activated

Then, the LIST report shows the fit-point tolerance used for the spline. Notice that, rather than the 0 that AutoCAD showed as the current tolerance while you were drawing the spline, the LIST report shows it as a very small number.

The last set of data shown are the coordinates of unit vectors (a unit vector is a 1-unit-long line used to indicate direction) for the start tangent and the end tangent, and there might be a surprise for you here. LIST shows the start tangent unit vector pointing in the positive-X direction, even though you specified a minus-X direction. This apparent discrepancy is because every spline has a specific direction, and AutoCAD points the tangent unit vectors in that direction. This spline was drawn from right to left (toward the positive-X direction), so that is the direction of the tangent unit vector.

## Modifying Splines

Although many of the general-purpose AutoCAD editing commands can be used to modify the shape of splines, the operations also can alter the spline's basic properties. You can BREAK and TRIM splines, for instance, but both of these operations cause the spline to lose its fit points. You cannot EXTEND, LENGTHEN, or EXPLODE splines.

The STRETCH command usually works well with splines. Normally, you must include a fit point in the crossing window used by STRETCH. You also can activate the spline's grips, which are on the fit points of the spline, and use them in modifying its shape. If you set the value of the system variable **splframe** to 1 (which causes the control points to be shown as the vertices of connected lines), you also can stretch the spline by its control points. The spline's fit points, however, are lost when you do this.

When a spline loses its fit-point data, it also loses its tangent and fit-tolerance data. You can identify a spline that no longer has fit data with the LIST command. Also, the spline's grips are on the control points rather than on the curve itself.

Grips when a spline has fit points

Grips when a spline does not have fit points

Although the PROPERTIES command shows you the spline's properties, such as start and end tangents and order (although it uses equation degree rather than order), it does not allow you to change some of them. You must use the SPLINEDIT command when you want to fine-tune a spline's shape or modify its basic structure. (Notice that there is only one E in the command's name). SPLINEDIT uses command line menus that have several levels of options in which it is easy to get lost. Probably your best strategy with this command is to remember what it can do and to review the explanation for making a particular change when you actually need to modify a spline.

Specifically, the SPLINEDIT command allows you to do the following:

- Operations on fit points:

    Open a closed spline, or close an open one, from fit point data.
    Add a fit point.
    Delete a fit point.
    Move a fit point.
    Remove (purge) all fit point data.
    Modify the end tangents.
    Modify the spline's fit tolerance.

- Operations on control points:

    Open a closed spline, or close an open one, from control-point data.
    Move a control point.
    Add a control point.

- Operations on spline properties:

    Elevate the spline's order.
    Modify the weight of a spline control point.
    Reverse the direction of a spline.

| | |
|---|---|
| Command: | SPLINEDIT |
| Purpose: | This command edits objects made by the SPLINE command. It can add fit points and control points, open and close splines, change fit tolerance, change the spline's order, change control point weights, and change endpoint tangents. |

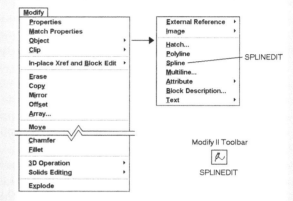

| | |
|---|---|
| Initiate with: | • From the command line, enter SPLINEDIT.<br>• From the Modify pull-down menu, select Spline.<br>• From the Modify II toolbar, pick the Edit Spline button. |
| Options: | The SPLINEDIT command prompts you to select a spline. When you have done so, the spline's control points are shown as grips, and the following command line menu is displayed: |

`Fit data/Close/Move vertex/Refine/ rEverse/Undo:`

If the spline is closed (periodic), the Close option is replaced by an Open option. If the spline has no fit points, the Fit Data option is not offered.

- Fit Data — This option, which can be started by entering either an F or a D, is for modifying a spline's fit points. The spline's control points are no longer shown, with the fit points shown instead. AutoCAD displays the following secondary menu on the command line:

    `Add/Close/Delete/Move/Purge/Tangents/toLerance/eXit <eXit>:`

    - Add — Fit points can be added to a spline with this option. They can be placed within the spline or beyond the spline's endpoints. When points are added beyond the endpoints, the original tangents are applied to the new endpoints. This option first asks you to pick an existing fit point on the spline. The prompts that follow depend upon the relative position of the selected point.

        - First Fit Point — If you select the first fit point of an open spline, the prompt displayed is

            `Specify new point or [After/Before] <exit>:`

If you press Enter, the option ends without adding a new point, and the Fit Data menu is redisplayed. If you specify a point, it becomes the first point in the spline. AutoCAD continues to prompt for points to serve as a new first point until you press Enter in response to the prompt. You can undo a point by entering the letter U.

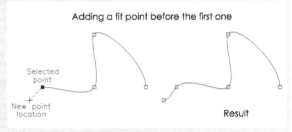

The Before option produces the same results. If you want the new fit point to be between the first and second points of the spline, select the After option. AutoCAD prompts for a point location and continues to prompts for points between the first and second fit points until you press Enter. Enter the letter U to undo a point.

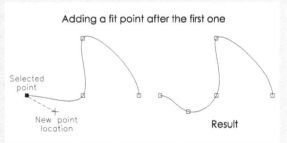

• Last Fit Point    If you select the last fit point of an open spline, AutoCAD highlights it and prompts for locations of new points until you press the Enter key. Entering the letter U will undo a point. You can add points only to the end of the spline. There is no option to add points between the last fit point and the next-to-last fit point.

Adding a fit point after the last fit point

Selected point

New point location

Result

- Interior Fit Points

If you choose an interior fit point in response to the option's original prompt to select a point, AutoCAD highlights the selected point and the next point and prompts for the location of a new point. You can add as many new fit points between the two highlighted points as you like. Press Enter when prompted for a new point to return to the main Fit Data menu. To undo a point, enter the U key.

Adding an interior fit point

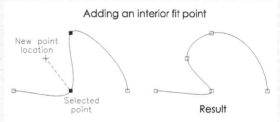

New point location

Selected point

Result

- Close

This option is available only if the spline is open (nonperiodic). If the start point and the endpoint of the spline are not in the same location, AutoCAD connects them with a new segment and sets the end tangent equal to the start tangent. If the start point and the endpoint are in the same location, AutoCAD sets the end tangent equal to the start tangent and reshapes the last segment of the spline. No additional prompts are used by this option.

Closing an open spline

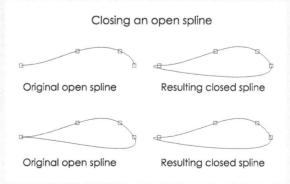

Original open spline          Resulting closed spline

Original open spline          Resulting closed spline

- Open

This option is offered only if the spline is closed. The last segment of the spline is always removed, even if the spline's start points and endpoints were originally in the same location. No additional prompts are used by this option.

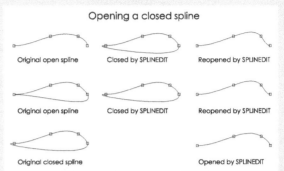

Opening a closed spline

Original open spline    Closed by SPLINEDIT    Reopened by SPLINEDIT

Original open spline    Closed by SPLINEDIT    Reopened by SPLINEDIT

Original closed spline    Opened by SPLINEDIT

- Delete

Fit points are removed by this option. You are prompted to select a point. It is deleted and the spline adjusts its shape to maintain smoothness through the remaining fit points. If you delete a start or end fit point, the tangent directions are moved to the new start or end fit points. You can delete points until you press the Enter key or until only two points remain.

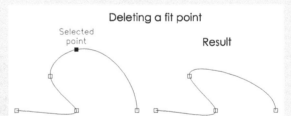

Deleting a fit point

Selected point    Result

- Move

You can move fit points with this option. The first fit point in the spline is highlighted and the following menu is displayed:

```
Specify new location or [Next/Previous/Select point/eXit]:
```

This menu is repeated until you select the eXit option to return to the main Fit Data menu. Use the Next, Previous, or Select Point options to highlight the fit point you want moved, and then specify a new location for the fit point. The Next option highlights the next fit point away from the spline's start point, and the Previous option highlights the next fit point toward the spline's start point. The Select Point option permits you to go directly to the fit point you want to move.

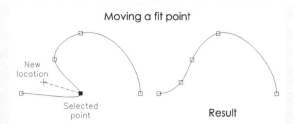

Moving a fit point

New location

Selected point

Result

- Purge

This option removes all fit-point data from the spline. After this data has been purged, it cannot be restored. This option has no prompts: it returns you to the main SPLINEDIT menu without the Fit Data option.

- Tangents

You can change the end tangents with this option. If the spline is open, it starts with the prompt:

`Specify start tangent or [System default]:`

As soon as you have finished editing the start tangent, the following prompt is displayed:

`Specify end tangent or [System default]:`

If you use the system default, in either of these prompts, the end of the spline swivels about the endpoint as necessary to obtain a continually smooth curve through the fit points. If you press the Enter key, the tangent remains as it is. If you specify a point, AutoCAD sets the tangent equal to the direction from the spline endpoint to the selected point. The end of the spline is then fixed to point in that direction, and the spline adjusts its shape to be continually smooth with that tangent and its fit points.

If the spline is closed (periodic), the Tangents option issues the prompt:

`Specify tangent or [System Default]:`

The direction (tangent) of the spline at its closing point equals the direction from the closing point to the specified point. If the system default is accepted, the spline treats the closing point the same as the interior fit points when it assumes its continually smooth shape.

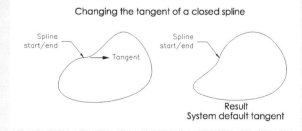

Changing the tangent of a closed spline

Spline start/end

Tangent

Spline start/end

Result
System default tangent

- toLerance

Notice that you select this option by entering the letter L. When tolerance is 0 (AutoCAD sometimes reports it as 1.0000E-10), the spline passes exactly through the fit points. When tolerance is given a value, the spline pulls away from the fit points in proportion to the specified tolerance value, thereby becoming straighter. The first and last fit points are always on the spline.

- eXit

This option exits the Fit Data menu and returns to the main SPLINEDIT menu. It is the default option.

- Close

This option in the main SPLINEDIT menu is available only for open (nonperiodic) splines. Although it performs the same function as the Close option in the Fit Data menu, it uses control points rather than fit points in closing a spline. Consequently, the shape of a spline closed through this option might be different than if it had been closed through its fit points. Also, this option causes the spline to lose its fit data.

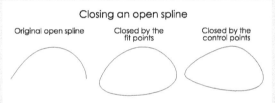

- Open

This option, which is offered only if the spline is closed (periodic), removes the last segment of a spline. Although it performs the same function as the Open option in the Fit Data menu, it uses control points rather than fit points in opening the spline. The Fit Data's Open option applies the spline's closing tangent to the new endpoints and adjusts the shape of the curve accordingly. This option, on the other hand, discards the closing tangent and keeps the spline's original shape in the remaining segments. This option causes the spline's fit data to be lost.

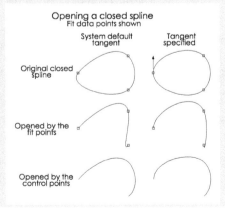

- Move Vertex

This option, which can be started by entering the letter M or the letter V, changes the location of control points (not fit points). It also destroys the spline's fit data. The spline's first control point is highlighted, and the following submenu is displayed:

Specify new location or [Next/Previous/Select Point/eXit] <N>:

Use the Next, Previous, or Select Point options to highlight the control point you want moved. Then, specify a new location for it, and enter an X (or the entire word exit) to fix its location and return to the main SPLINEDIT menu. The Next option highlights the next control point away from the spline's start point, and the Previous option highlights the next control point toward the spline's start point. The Select Point option permits you to go directly to the control point you want to move.

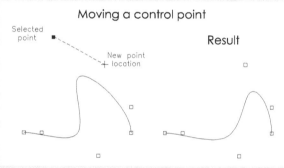

Moving a control point

- Refine

You can add control points, elevate the order of the spline's equation, and change the weight of control points with this option. All these modifications cause the spline to lose its fit point data. The option displays the following secondary menu:

Add control point/Elevate Order/Weight/eXit

- Add Control Point

This option adds a control point to the spline. The shape of the spline is not changed, and the locations of the other control points are changed as needed to maintain the original shape. The following prompt is issued:

Select a point on the spline: Select a point or press Enter.

This prompt is repeated until you press the Enter key to return to the Refine menu.

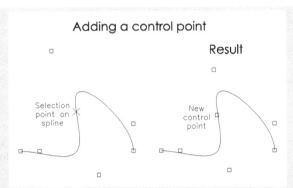

Adding a control point

Result

Selection point on spline

New control point

- Elevate Order

You can select this option by entering either E or O. It increases the order of the spline's equation. (When a spline is created, it always has an order of 4.) The option issues the following prompt:

```
Enter new order <current>:
```

Enter an integer number that is greater than the current order, or press Enter to accept the current order. The maximum order you can specify is 26. Additional control points are added to the spline, but the shape of the spline is not changed. After a spline's order has been increased, it cannot be reduced.

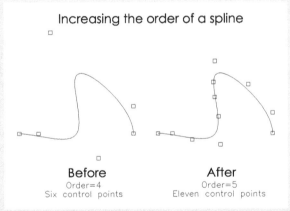

Increasing the order of a spline

Before
Order=4
Six control points

After
Order=5
Eleven control points

- Weight

When a spline is created, all control points have a weight of 1 and have an equal effect on the shape of the spline. This option enables you to change the weight of control points. When the weight of a control point is increased, the spline is pulled closer to it. When the weight of a control point is decreased, the spline moves away from it. This option highlights the spline's first control point and displays the following submenu:

```
Enter new weight (current = 1.0000) or [Next/Previous/Select Point/
    eXit] <N>:
```

Use the Next, Previous, or Select Point options to highlight the control point whose weight you want changed. AutoCAD displays its current weight, and you can enter a new value. The Next option highlights the next control point away from the spline's start point, and the Previous option highlights the next control point toward the spline's start point. The Select Point option permits you to go directly to the control point whose weight you want modified. The eXit option returns to the Refine option's menu.

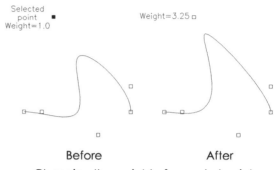

**Changing the weight of a control point**

| | |
|---|---|
| • eXit | This option exits the Refine menu and returns to the main SPLINEDIT menu. |
| • rEverse | By default, the order in which AutoCAD lists the fit points and control points is the same as the order in which the fit points were specified. This option of the main SPLINEDIT menu reverses the order — the last point becomes the first point, and the first point becomes the last point. |
| • Undo | This option cancels the last spline-editing operation. You can repeatedly use the option to undo all modifications made during a SPLINEDIT session. |
| • eXit | This option ends the SPLINEDIT command. |

### Exercise One

In this excercise you will finish the wire-frame model of an automobile oil pan that you started in Exercise Two of Chapter 4. You can use your model, or use the one in file f0438.dwg on the CD-ROM that accompanies this book. Your model should look similar to the one in Figure 1-1. In this exercise, you will use the SPLINE command to connect the two existing sections of the oil pan wireframe.

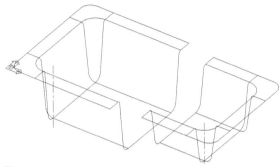

Figure 1-1

Zoom in for a closer look at the missing flange area near the X axis. You will recall that the oil pan flange is drawn on the WCS X-Y plane. Be certain that the WCS is in effect and draw a spline between the outside corners in the missing section of the flange. The command line sequence to draw this spline is

```
Command: SPLINE (Enter)
Specify first point or [Object]: (Pick point A in Figure 1-2.)
Specify next point: (Pick point B in Figure 1-2.)
Specify next point or [Close/Fit Tolerance] <start tangent>: (Enter)
Specify start tangent: @1<180 (Enter)
Specify end tangent: @1<0 (Enter)
```

It is important that you use these tangent directions. Otherwise, the spline will not be properly curved. Although relative coordinates are used to specify the tangents, object snaps or simply picking points somewhere along the flange outside edge would work equally well. Use the same steps to draw a spline on the other edge of the flange, or make a copy of the one you just drew. The copy would be located 1 inch in the WCS Y direction from the original.

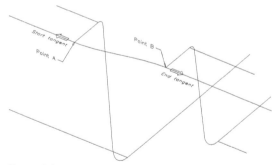

Figure 1-2

A 2D polyline could have been used to draw these curves because they are planar, but making them as splines requires less work. The next curve you will make, however, could not be made as a 2D polyline because it does not conveniently fit on a plane. The command line input to draw this curve is identical to that for the previous curve. Use endpoint object snaps in locating points A and B in Figure 1-3, and use typed-in relative coordinates to establish the tangent directions (because nothing is conveniently close to use as object snaps).

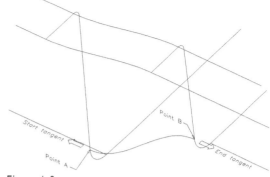

Figure 1-3

The curve connecting the other ends of the lower two arcs does not have the same shape as the one you just drew, so you have to again use the SPLINE command. This time, use the points and tangent directions given in Figure 1-4 as command line input in the SPLINE command. You can, however, use object midpoint snaps in establishing the spline's tangents.

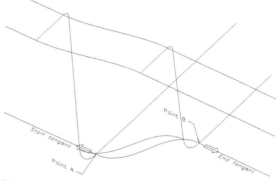

Figure 1-4

Now either make mirror-image copies (by using AutoCAD's MIRROR command) of these four splines for the other half of the oil pan, or use the SPLINE command to draw four new ones. Either way, your wireframe model should look like the one shown in Figure 1-5. On the CD-ROM that accompanies this book, the wireframe model is in file f0555.dwg. In Section 2 of this book, you will add surfaces to the wireframe.

### Exercise Two

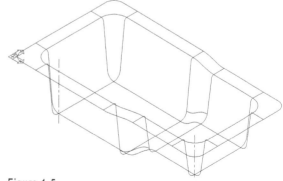

Figure 1-5

In this exercise, you will build the wireframe for a surface model airplane propeller. Start a new drawing, and set up some layers, having names such as WF01 and WF02, for the wireframe objects. You should also set up some layers having a CENTERLINE linetype and a layer for temporary construction lines.

You will make just one propeller blade. After the wireframe is given surfaces, you can then use the polar option of AutoCAD's ARRAY command to make as many blades as needed for the completed propeller. The axis of the propeller is in the Z direction, and the propeller blade extends in the X axis direction. You will make wireframes of the start and end cross-sections of the blade, and connect them with a spline to make the blade's leading and trailing edges.

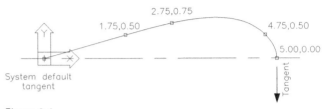

Figure 2-1

The start cross-section lays on the WCS Y-Z plane. Due to the requirements of the command you use to surface the propeller blade, you will make the cross-sections in two pieces — a top half and a bottom half. Make sure the WCS is in effect, and then use the following command line input to set up the UCS X-Y plane for the first cross-section:

```
Command: UCS (Enter)
Current UCS name: *WORLD*
Enter an option [New/Move/
   orthoGraphic/Prev/Restore/Save/
   Del/Apply/?/World] <World>: ZA
   (Enter)
Specify new origin point <0,0,0>:
   (Enter)
Specify point on positive portion of
   Z-axis <0.0000,0.0000,0.0000>:
   1,0,0 (Enter)
```

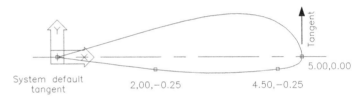

Figure 2-2

Because the orientation of the UCS relative to the WCS is not obvious in the first few figures for this exercise, the preceding command line input for the UCS command ensures that you start out with the X-Y plane in the same position. Switch to a plan view of the UCS and use the SPLINE command to draw the top half of the propeller blade cross-section. Use the coordinates given in Figure 2-1 as fit point locations for the spline. Use the default tangent on the left end of the spline, and a tangent in the minus-Y direction for the right end of the spline.

You might find it helpful to draw a line with a noncontinuous linetype (such as a CENTERLINE linetype) along the UCS X axis to help distinguish the division between the two halves of the cross-section. Now, use the SPLINE command to draw the bottom half of the propeller cross-section, with the coordinates in Figure 2-2 as the spline's fit-point locations. Use the default tangent on the left end of the spline, and a tangent in the positive-Y direction for the right end.

The cross-section for the other end of the propeller is 30 units in the WCS positive-X direction from the cross-section you just drew. Therefore, use the Origin option of the UCS command to move the X-Y plane 30 units in the current Z direction. Your current plan view will continue to be satisfactory, even though you have moved the X-Y plane. You will, however, want to turn off the layers used to draw the first cross-section (including the one for the center line) and use different layers for drawing the next one. Otherwise, the objects in the other plane will tend to clutter and confuse your view.

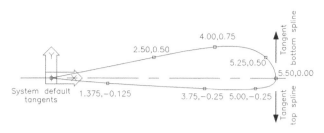

Note: These objects are on a plane 30 units in the WCS positive X direction from the other cross-section.

Figure 2-3

Just as with the previous cross-section, draw this one as two splines, using the coordinates in Figure 2-3 for their fit points. Accept the system default tangents for the left side of the splines, and use the tangents shown in the figure for the right side of the splines. You might also find it useful to draw a horizontal center line between the two splines.

Next, you draw the profile of the propeller's tip, which adjoins the cross-section you just drew. This is more complicated than you might think, because the AutoCAD command (EDGE-SURF) you will use to surface this section of the propeller requires four wireframe objects for a boundary. The objects can be in different planes (in fact, they do not

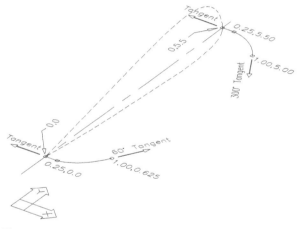

Figure 2-4

even have to be planar objects), but their endpoints must exactly touch. Each of the two cross-section halves you just drew will serve as one boundary, so you need to draw three more. Although arcs could be used to draw these three boundaries, use splines so you can easily control their end tangents.

Change from a plan view to an isometric-type view, and zoom in on the tip of the propeller blade. Twist the UCS so that it is on the WCS X-Y plane but its origin is unchanged (at the narrow end of the cross-section). You can do this in one step when you use the ZAxis option of the UCS command. Leave the origin as it is, and point in the current Y-axis direction for the new Z-axis direction.

Now use the SPLINE command to draw the two new curves shown in Figure 2-4. Use the given coordinates for fit-point locations, and use command line input to point the spline's end tangents as shown. As an example, the command line input for the lower curve is

```
Command: SPLINE (Enter)
Specify first point or [Object]: 0,0 (Enter)
Specify next point: .25,0 (Enter)
Specify next point or [Close/Fit tolerance]
    <start tangent>: 1,.625 (Enter)
Specify next point or [Close/Fit tolerance]
    <start tangent>: (Enter)
Specify start tangent: @1<180 (Enter)
Specify end tangent: @1<60 (Enter)
```

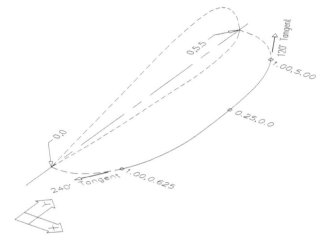

After you have drawn the two end curves, draw a spline between them, using the fit-point coordinates and end tangents shown in Figure 2-5. Notice that the tangents are 180 degrees from those of the adjacent splines — this makes the three curves appear to be a single, smoothly blended curve.

Figure 2-5

You want the surface of the propeller to twist through space, and you will accomplish that by rotating the five splines you have just drawn. This is most conveniently done, with the UCS in its current position, by the ROTATE3D command. After selecting the objects to be rotated (include the centerline if you drew it), pick a point 2.50 units in the Y direction from the UCS origin as the first point on the rotation axis, and a point to its right (having the same Y coordinate) as the second axis point. Enter 15 as the rotation angle. This operation is illustrated in Figure 2-6.

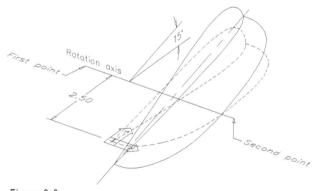

Figure 2-6

You will make the leading and trailing edge of the propeller blade by connecting the front and back ends of the two cross-sections with two splines. But first, because you want the surface of the propeller to be slightly wider in its middle than at its ends, you need to draw a construction line. Then, the spline for each edge of the propeller blade will have three fit points — one on each cross-section endpoint and one on the construction line endpoint.

Turn on the layers you used for the first cross-section, and Zoom back so that you can see the entire propeller blade. Draw a line 6.5 units long positioned as shown in Figure 2-7.

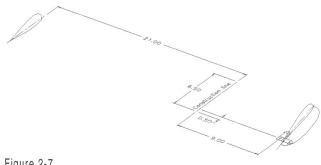

Figure 2-7

Use the ROTATE3D command to rotate the line you just drew 10 degrees about the rotation axis shown in Figure 2-8. (It is the same axis you used earlier to rotate the propeller end cross-section and tip.)

Finish the wireframe by drawing the leading and trailing edges of the propeller blade. Use the SPLINE command with the ends of the cross-sections as the ends of the splines and the endpoints of the construction line as their interior fit point. You can use object endpoint snaps to locate these points for the splines. You might find it helpful to have the graphics area divided into two viewports, with close-up views of the two cross-sections, when you draw the splines. On the left end of the splines, the end tangents should be in the WCS minus-X direction, and they should be in the positive-X direction on the right end. Your wireframe model should now look similar to the one shown in Figure 2-9.

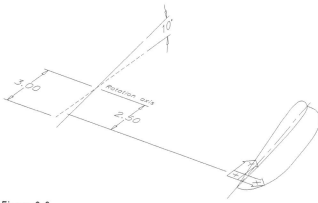

Figure 2-8

Adding surfaces to this wireframe is almost trivially easy, but you won't do that until Section 2 of this book. The completed wireframe propeller blade is in file mfe05209.dwg on the CD-ROM.

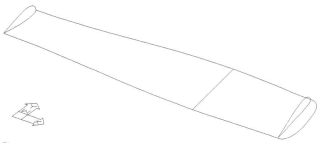

Figure 2-9

# Building Surface Models

# CHAPTER 6

# Extruded and Planar Surfaces

*Surface models are a step up in realism from wireframe models because their surfaces can hide objects, and they can assume material properties and reflect light in renderings. Your exploration of surfaces begins in this chapter as you concentrate on wireframe objects that have surface-like propeties, and on the AutoCAD commands that make flat surfaces. Even though these commands are limited in the shapes they can make, they are extremely important commands because so many objects and surfaces in the real world are flat.*

*This chapter*

- *describes the AutoCAD object types that can be used for surfaces;*

- *discusses the use of extrusion thickness as a surface;*

- *explains how to make three- and four-sided planar surfaces with the 3DFACE command;*

- *describes how to use the PFACE command to make surface models that have multiple planar surfaces;*

- *tells you how to convert 3D faces into a polyface mesh.*

3D wireframe models are often useful, but they are seldom realistic looking. You must imagine that surfaces exist between their edges, and there is no way to hide objects that you would not be able to see if the model was opaque. When you need a 3D model that is closer to reality, you make it as a surface model or as a solid model, rather than as a wireframe model. Either of those types of 3D models can be made to look reasonably realistic, especially when they are rendered.

Deciding whether a particular object should be built as a solid model or as a surface model depends on the geometry of the object as well as your intended use of the model. Objects based on fundamental geometric shapes — such as prisms, spheres, cones, and cylinders — are likely candidates for solid models. Also, most objects that are typically made in machine shops with lathes and milling machines are modeled as solids.

However, objects having sculpted, smooth, flowing surfaces are beyond the capabilities of AutoCAD's solid modeler. For instance, the automobile fender shown in the accompanying figure cannot be made in AutoCAD as a solid model. It is easily made as a surface model, however. In this figure, the surface model is shown in its wireframe mode in the three left-hand viewports, and is shown rendered in the large viewport on the right. The model of an oil pan that you started in Chapter 4 and the airplane propeller you started in Chapter 5 also have geometries that can be made only as surface models.

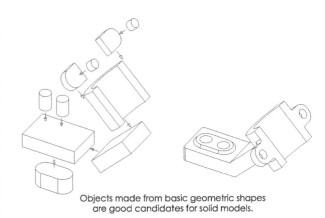

Objects made from basic geometric shapes are good candidates for solid models.

Although the 3D house that you started in Chapter 4 could be made as a solid model, it is better to make it as a surface model, because you will use it for renderings. Surface models usually give you more flexibility in setting and controlling surface appearance properties, such as color and texture, than solid models. For example, AutoCAD's renderer considers all six sides of a 3D solid cube to be a single object: You can attach only one material to the cube. A surface model cube, however, has six different surfaces, and you can treat each surface differently.

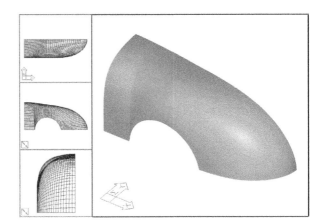

## AutoCAD Surface Object Types

An AutoCAD surface is an opaque object that has length and width but no thickness. Because it is opaque, it is able to hide objects that lie behind it relative to the current viewing direction (although a special command, such as HIDE, must be invoked before those objects are actually hidden). The object types that conform to this definition are listed in Table 6-1.

AutoCAD 3D solids are also opaque, and they have surfaces. But their surfaces represent the outside boundaries of 3D objects — the surface is not a separate object. Therefore, they are not listed in Table 6-1. I will discuss AutoCAD 3D solids extensively in Section 3 of this book.

2D solids (made with the SOLID command) and traces (made with the TRACE command) meet the definition of an AutoCAD surface and are therefore included in Table 6-1, but you are not likely to ever use them for surfaces. (AutoCAD, nevertheless, displays 2D solids in its Surfaces pull-down menu and on its Surfaces toolbar.) AutoCAD objects that are intended specifically to be used as surfaces can easily handle the geometry that these commands can make and give you more flexibility and control.

### Table 6-1 AutoCAD Object Types for Surfaces

| Object Type | Command | Remarks |
| --- | --- | --- |
| LWpolyline | PLINE | Lightweight polylines are surface objects only when they have width. |
| 3D face | 3DFACE | A fundamental AutoCAD object type, 3D faces always have either three or four edges. |
| Body | None | Bodies are nonplanar surfaces created when 3D solids are exploded. |
| Circle | CIRCLE | A fundamental AutoCAD object type. |
| Thickness | ELEV | Thickness is a property that imparts surface–like characteristics to certain wireframe objects. |
| Polygon mesh | Various | Polygon mesh surfaces are made through the 3DMESH, EDGESURF, REVSURF, TABSURF, and RULESURF commands. They are a special polyline form that can create a wide variety of surface shapes. |
| Polyface mesh | PFACE | A special polyline form, in which a set of three- and four-sided faces are united to make one object. |
| Region | REGION | A planar object that has no thickness yet has some properties similar to those of 3D solids. |
| 2D solid | SOLID | A 2D object that has width. |
| Trace | TRACE | A 2D object that has width. |

You will not often use LWpolylines that have width as surfaces, but because you can make some unusual planar shapes with them, you might occasionally make a surface using the PLINE command. When you do, you can turn off AutoCAD's **fillmode** system variable to avoid having the polyline being filled with its object color when it is seen from a plan view. Fill automatically goes away anytime you are looking at the polyline from a viewpoint that is not a plan view.

The inclusion of circle objects in Table 6-1 might surprise you. This common, often-used wireframe object is also a planar opaque surface — a disk — in many AutoCAD hidden line and rendered viewing modes. Sometimes, such as when you want to close the end of a tube, this property of circles is handy. At other times, such as when you need to use a circle as a surface boundary to create an open tube, it

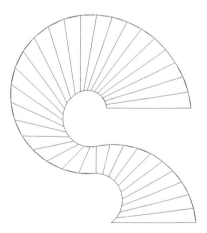

LWpolylines that have width can be used to make planar surfaces that have unusual shapes.

can be a nuisance. If you need a circular wireframe object that is not a surface, you can use two 180-degree arcs rather than one circle. In the hidden line and shaded viewing modes of the SHADEMODE command, however, circles are transparent. The SHADEMODE command is discussed in Chapter 7.

A region is a surface object type that acts like a 3D solid. It is created with the REGION command, or by exploding 3D solid objects that have flat sides. Because regions share properties with 3D solids, they are not described until Section 3 of this book. Nevertheless, you should keep them in mind because they can occasionally be useful as planar surfaces, especially when you need one that has interior holes or a curvy edge.

Bodies are object types that are created when a 3D solid is exploded. You cannot make them directly. The nonplanar surfaces of exploded 3D solids become bodies, while the flat surfaces become regions. Thus, if you use the EXPLODE command on a cylindrical 3D solid, the ends of the cylinder become regions, and the side of the cylinder becomes a body. You will seldom, if ever, need to deliberately make a body object.

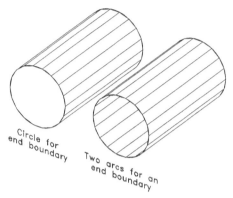

Circle for end boundary

Two arcs for an end boundary

Circles are disk-shaped planar surface objects.

## Using Thickness as a Surface

Table 6-1 includes one surface type — thickness — that is an object property rather than an object type. When a wireframe object has thickness, it is stretched in the Z direction, as if it were forced through a die, to form a wall-like surface. These surfaces are sometimes referred to as extruded surfaces, and the property is often called *extrusion thickness*.

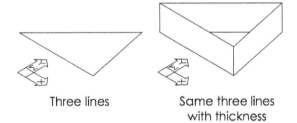

Three lines

Same three lines with thickness

The direction of the extrusion is always in the direction the Z axis was pointing when the object was created. AutoCAD keeps track of this direction, regardless of how the UCS is currently oriented, even if the object has an extrusion thickness of 0. The LIST command reports an object's extrusion direction.

Extrusion thickness is controlled by the **thickness** system variable. When **thickness** has a positive value, the extrusion direction is in the positive-Z direction; when it has a negative value, the extrusion direction is in the minus-Z direction. This system variable can be set directly or through the ELEV command. This command is described in Chapter 1.

When the value of **thickness** is changed, new objects are drawn with the new value, but the thickness of existing objects does not change. An existing object's extrusion thicknesses can be changed, however, through the CHANGE, CHPROP, and PROPERTIES commands. In fact, unless all your objects are to have the same thickness, a good practice is to leave **thickness** set to 0 and use one of these change property commands to assign a specific thickness to selected objects.

As you would expect, because they can twist and turn through space, and therefore might not have a constant Z direction, splines and 3D polylines cannot have thickness. On the other hand, most 2D wireframe objects can. Exceptions are dimensions, leaders, mlines, mtext, rays, viewports, and xlines. Moreover, spline-based ellipses cannot be given a thickness, although polyline-based ellipses can. (Polyline ellipses are made when the system variable **pellipse** is set to 1.)

A 3D face, which is discussed extensively later in this chapter, is another AutoCAD object type that does not accept thickness. If it could, the result would presumably be a hollow box-like object. However, AutoCAD does have a command, named AI_BOX, that makes such an object, so extruded 3D faces are not really needed. This command is described in Chapter 8.

Text based on any of the shape file fonts (which have an .SHX filename extension) cannot initially have thickness, but you can give it thickness through any of the commands previously listed for changing properties. AutoCAD accepts a thickness for TrueType fonts (which have a .TTF filename extension), but it does not use it; the text retains its 0 thickness.

Even point objects can have thickness. The result is a vertical line in the Z direction. Although you are not likely to ever have any reason to assign thickness to a point, in early versions of AutoCAD, this was the only way to draw a line that was perpendicular to the X-Y plane.

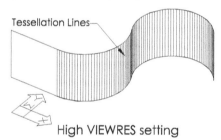

High VIEWRES setting

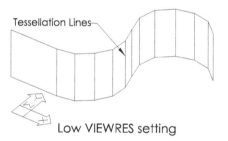

Low VIEWRES setting

Extruded arcs and circles have a set of evenly spaced and vertical parallel lines that are referred to as *tessellation* lines. The spacing of tessellation lines is controlled by the VIEWRES command, with the number and density of tessellation lines increasing as VIEWRES increases. These lines occur in printed output as well as on the computer display, and their relative density is seldom the same. The printed version usually has denser tessellation line spacing than the computer display.

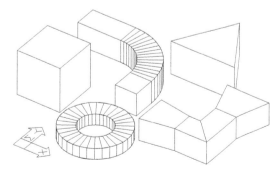

LWpolylines that have width and thickness

Objects that have width become 3D surface objects when they also have extrusion thickness. This enables you to quickly make 3D boxes, wedges, and duct-like objects from LWpolylines that have thickness as well as width. A disadvantage with this technique is that you cannot control individual surfaces, and the objects are always closed. You cannot, for instance, make a box with an open side. You can use the DONUT command (which makes specialized LWpolylines) to make 3D washers. And, because a circle is a surface-like disk, extruded circles become cylinders.

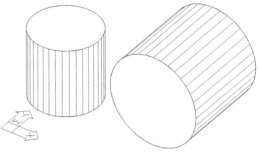

Circles that have thickness

When one end of a line has a different Z coordinate than the other end, the extruded surface shape is that of a rhomboid (a parallelogram with oblique corner angles) rather than a rectangle. An object can have only one thickness at a time. Consequently, you cannot have extruded lines in which the opposite sides have different lengths — their vertical shape is always a parallelogram. When grips are activated on an object that has thickness, grips are located on both edges of the extrusion surface. You can use these grips to move the object and to change its length (or radius for arcs and circles), but you cannot use grips to change its thickness.

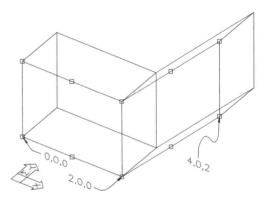

Grips on lines that have thickness

## Exercises in Using Thickness

These two exercises give you some experience in using thickness and point out some of its advantages and disadvantages. You don't need to keep these models, so the setup and the filenames you use for them are not important.

### Exercise One

On the X-Y plane of the WCS, draw the floor plan of a small house, similar to the one shown in Figure 1-1. This is strictly a 2D drawing, and you should leave **thickness** at 0. The hatches and dimensions are intended to help you draw the floor plan and should not be included in your drawing. This floor plan is simply a suggestion, and you can choose to draw one that has different dimensions, or a different arrangement and complexity.

When you have drawn your floor plan, switch to an SE isometric view, invoke one of the commands that change object property (such as PROPERTIES), select all, and set object thickness to 8 feet. The result, as shown in Figure 1-2 when the HIDE command has been invoked, is an almost instant 3D model from a 2D drawing. (Although the HIDE command has not been discussed, you only have to call it — by entering HIDE on the command line — to use it. REGEN restores the wireframe viewing mode.) But there are problems with the model. The door openings go completely up to the ceiling; furthermore, there is no good way to make openings for windows.

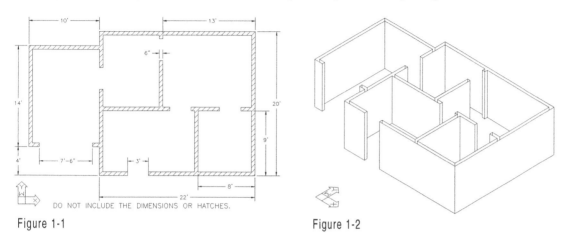

Figure 1-1

Figure 1-2

On the CD-ROM that accompanies this book, the file f0611.dwg contains this model.

### Exercise Two

In this second exercise you will build a half-round table that has three legs. Because you will be drawing some wide polylines within a plan view, you might want to turn object fill off by setting the system variable **fillmode** to 0. Leave the **thickness** system variable set to its default value of 0. You will add thickness to the objects after they have been drawn.

Use the following command line input to draw a LWpolyline 180-degree arc at an elevation of 3.0 units from the WCS X-Y plane that has a 2.0-unit width:

```
Command: PLINE (Enter)
Specify start point: 0,1,3 (Enter)
Specify next point or [Arc/Close/Halfwidth/Length/Undo/Width]: W (Enter)
Specify starting width <0.0000>: 2 (Enter)
Specify ending width <2.0000>: 2 (Enter)
Specify next point or [Arc/Close/Halfwidth/Length/Undo/Width]: A (Enter)
Specify endpoint of arc or [Angle/CEnter/Close/Direction/Halfwidth/Line/Radius/Second pt/Undo/Width]: CE
   (Enter)
Specify center point of arc: 0,2 (Enter)
Specify endpoint of arc or [Angle/Length]: 0,3 (Enter)
Specify endpoint of arc or [Angle/CEnter/Close/Direction/Halfwidth/Line/Radius/Second pt/Undo/Width]: (Enter)
```

Notice in this input, that the elevation of the polyline is established when you specify its start point. All subsequent point input is 2D. Switch to an SE isometric view and zoom back to give yourself working room. Use any of the property-editing commands to set the thickness of this 2D polyline to 0.1. Your table top should be similar to the one shown in Figure 2-1.

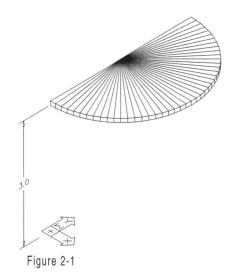

Figure 2-1

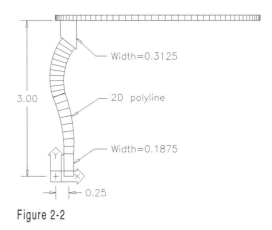

Width=0.3125

3.00

2D polyline

Width=0.1875

0.25

Figure 2-2

Now, rotate the UCS so that its X-Y plane is on the WCS Y-Z plane while leaving its origin location unchanged. An easy way to do this is with the ZAxis option of the UCS command — accept the default origin location and point in the X direction when you are prompted for the new Z-axis direction. You might also want to switch to a plan view of the new UCS.

Next, use a 2D polyline with a width varying from approximately 0.1875 to 0.3125 to draw a curved table leg similar to the one shown in Figure 2-2. This figure is only partially dimensioned because the 3.00-unit length is the only one that is important. You should start and stop with straight segments and have a couple of large radius curves in between. (A fairly low VIEWRES setting was used to make this figure. This is the reason for the apparent discontinuity near the top of the leg.)

When the table leg has been drawn, return to your SE isometric viewpoint. Then, assign a thickness of 0.125 units to the leg. Restore the WCS, and use a 180-degree polar array with a center at point 0.0625,2.0 to make a total of three legs. Your completed 3D model should look similar to the one in Figure 2-3. On the CD-ROM that accompanies this book, this model is in file f0614.dwg.

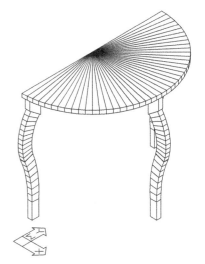

Figure 2-3

# Making 3DFACE Surfaces

3DFACE is one of the oldest AutoCAD commands for making surfaces, but it still cannot be beat for making three- and four-sided flat surfaces. Clean, unmeshed surfaces, along with invisible edges, give 3D faces a visual advantage over AutoCAD's newer surface object types, which generally have mesh lines running across their surfaces. If you are making 3D architectural models, you will use the 3DFACE command extensively as you make walls, roofs, floors, siding, and so forth. Even most furniture objects contain numerous flat areas that are conveniently made with 3DFACE.

3DFACE issues command line prompts for points to serve as the vertices of three- or four-sided 3D faces. The input, for example, to make one three-sided 3D face is

```
Command: 3DFACE (Enter)
Specify first point or [Invisible]: (Specify point 1.)
Specify second point or [Invisible]: (Specify point 2.)
Specify third point or [Invisible]<exit>: (Specify point 3.)
Specify fourth point or [Invisible]<create three-sided face>: (Enter)
Specify third point or [Invisible]<exit>: (Enter)
```

The input to make a 3D face with four edges is

```
Command: 3DFACE (Enter)
Specify first point or [Invisible]: (Specify point 1.)
Specify second point or [Invisible]: (Specify point 2.)
Specify third point or [Invisible]<exit>: (Specify point 3.)
Specify fourth point or [Invisible]<create three-sided face>: (Specify point 4.)
Specify third point or [Invisible]<exit>: (Enter)
```

The points for four-sided 3D faces must be entered in order, but the order can be either clockwise or counterclockwise. It is even possible to locate the corners of a four-sided 3D face so that its surface is folded diagonally. For example:

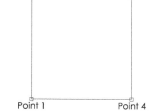

```
Command: 3DFACE (Enter)
Specify first point or [Invisible]: 0,0,1 (Enter)
Specify second point or [Invisible]: 1,0,0 (Enter)
Specify third point or [Invisible]<exit>: 1,1,1 (Enter)
Specify fourth point or [Invisible]<create three-sided face>: 0,1,0 (Enter)
Specify third point or [Invisible]<exit>: (Enter)
```

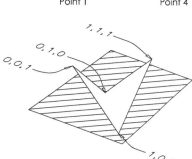

Folded 3D face

The adjacent corners have different elevations, which causes the 3D face to be folded across the second and fourth points. You are not likely to ever need to do this because you could make the same surface configuration more conventionally by using two 3D faces.

More than one 3D face can be made during a single call to the 3DFACE command, and the individual 3D faces can be in different planes. The following input, for example, makes three square 3D faces, each in a different plane:

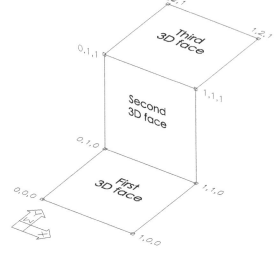

```
Command: 3DFACE (Enter)
Specify first point or [Invisible]: 0,0,0 (Enter)
Specify second point or [Invisible]: 1,0,0 (Enter)
Specify third point or [Invisible]<exit>: 1,1,0
    (Enter)
Specify fourth point or [Invisible]<create
    three-sided face>: 0,1,0 (Enter)      (This
    completes the first 3D face.)
Specify third point or [Invisible]<exit>: 0,1,1
    (Enter)
Specify fourth point or [Invisible]<create
    three-sided face>: 1,1,1 (Enter)      (This
    completes the second 3D face.)
Specify third point or [Invisible]<exit>: 1,2,1
    (Enter)
Specify fourth point or [Invisible]<create
    three-sided face>: 0,2,1 (Enter)      (This completes the third 3D face.)
Specify third point or [Invisible]<exit>: (Enter)
```

The resulting 3D faces are individual objects that can be moved, modified, or erased individually. Notice that the input direction for each 3D face alternated between counterclockwise and clockwise and that after the first 3D face was completed an edge was drawn from each new fourth point to the third point of the previous 3D face.

Edges are normally visible, being drawn in the current color, but you can make an edge invisible by entering the letter *i* prior to specifying the first point of the edge. This final example makes four four-sided faces around an interior hole. Each face has two invisible edges. The result is similar to a wall that has a cutout for a window.

```
Command: 3DFACE (Enter)
Specify first point or [Invisible]: I (Enter)
Specify first point or [Invisible]: (Specify Pt 1)
Specify second point or [Invisible]: (Specify Pt 2)
Specify third point or [Invisible]<exit>: I (Enter)
Specify third point or [Invisible]<exit>: (Specify Pt 3)
Specify fourth point or [Invisible]<create three-sided face>: (Specify Pt 4)
Specify third point or [Invisible]<exit>: I (Enter)
Specify third point or [Invisible]<exit>: (Specify Pt 3a)
Specify fourth point or [Invisible]<create three-sided face>: (Specify Pt 4a)
Specify third point or [Invisible]<exit>: I (Enter)
Specify third point or [Invisible]<exit>: (Specify Pt 3b)
Specify fourth point or [Invisible]<create three-sided face>: (Specify Pt 4b)
Specify third point or [Invisible]<exit>: I (Enter)
Specify third point or [Invisible]<exit>: (Specify Pt 3c)
Specify fourth point or [Invisible]<create three-sided face>: (Specify Pt 4c)
Specify third point or [Invisible]<exit>: (Enter)
```

In the accompanying diagram for these faces, the letter *i* within a circle indicates the start of an invisible edge, and the locations of invisible edges are indicated by dashed lines. Notice that the direction of the input alternates between clockwise and counterclockwise for each face. This example started with a counterclockwise direction, but a clockwise direction would have worked just as well.

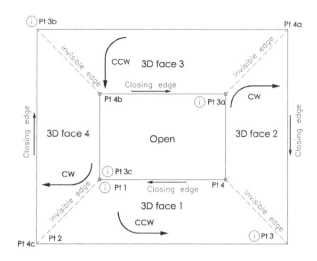

Even though these four 3D faces were made during the same session of the 3DFACE command, they are not connected, and they could have been made through four separate calls to 3DFACE. Generally, you are better off making one or two faces at a time than trying to make numerous faces during one session of 3DFACE.

There is no undo option for 3DFACE. If you specify the wrong location for a point, you either have to cancel the command or finish the face and modify it. If you cancel, the edges of the current 3D face are deleted, but the previous 3D faces are left as they are. 3D faces can be stretched through their grips, which appear on each vertex, or by the STRETCH command.

Creating invisible edges on 3D faces is not easy because you must act one step ahead of the edge that is to be invisible. AutoCAD comes with an AutoLISP program named EDGE.LSP that allows you to change visible edges into invisible edges, as well as invisible edges into visible edges. This program is automatically loaded and acts like a built-in AutoCAD command. It is so convenient to use that you might prefer to ignore invisible edges when you are creating 3D faces, and then use EDGE to change the edges you want to be invisible.

## Exercises in Using 3DFACE

To give you some practical experience in using the 3DFACE command, you will add 3D faces to the two models you constructed as wireframes in Chapter 4. You will continue to add features to these models in some of the following chapters, so you work through these exercises and save your work.

### Exercise Three

Open your drawing of the 3D wireframe house you began in Exercise 1 of Chapter 4. If you prefer, you can start with the model in file f0431.dwg on the CD-ROM that accompanies this book rather than the wireframe you constructed.

You will add 3D faces to the outside walls of the house, to its rooftop, to its roof ends, and to its eaves. Before you actually make any of these 3D faces, you should establish some layers for them. You should set up layers for surface models so you can selectively turn them off to get

| Command: | 3DFACE |
|---|---|
| Purpose: | The 3DFACE command makes planar surfaces that have either three or four edges. |
| Initiate with: | • On the command line, enter 3DFACE. |
| | • From the Draw pull-down menu, select Surfaces, and then 3D Face from the resulting flyout menu. |
| | • Select the 3DFACE button from the Surfaces toolbar. |
| Implementation: | 3DFACE operates from the command line using the following format: |

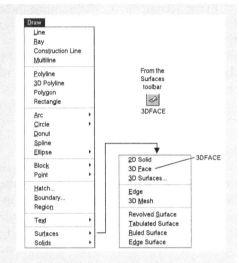

```
Specify first point or [Invisible]:
    (Enter an I or specify a point.)
```

```
Specify second point or [Invisible]: (Enter an I or specify a point.)
Specify third point or [Invisible]<exit>: (Enter an I or specify a point.)
Specify fourth point or [Invisible]<create three-sided face>: (Enter an I, specify a
    point, or press Enter.)
Specify third point or [Invisible]<exit>:
```

If you press the Enter key when prompted for a fourth point, AutoCAD draws an edge back to the first point to make a three-sided face and prompts for another third point. Pressing the Enter key at that point ends the command, leaving one three-sided 3D face. If you do specify a fourth point, AutoCAD draws an edge from it back to the first point and prompts for another third point. If you press Enter at that prompt, AutoCAD ends the command leaving a four-sided 3D face.

Point 2

Point 3

Point 1

**3D face with three sides**

Point 2

Point 3

Point 4

Point 1

**3D face with four sides**

When you add points after the fourth point, the prompts alternate between Third Point and Fourth Point, and AutoCAD draws an edge from each new fourth point back to the third point in the previous pair of prompts to make another 3D face. Pressing the Enter key when prompted for a point ends the command.

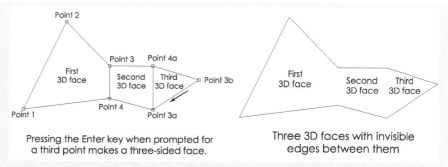

Pressing the Enter key when prompted for
a third point makes a three-sided face.

Three 3D faces with invisible
edges between them

If you press the Enter key in response to a new fourth point, AutoCAD draws an edge from the current third point back to the previous third point, making a three-sided face, and prompts for a new third point.

Edges are drawn in the current color. It is possible, however, to make an edge invisible by entering the letter *i*, or the entire word *invisible*, prior to specifying the first point for the edge.

Notes:

- Because each three- or four-sided 3D face is an individual object, there is seldom any advantage in making multiple faces with one call to the command. The results are the same, for instance, whether you use 3DFACE once to make five faces, or repeat 3DFACE five times in making them.

- Invisible edges cannot even be seen by AutoCAD. Consequently, if you need to select a 3D face, perhaps for moving or copying, you must include a visible edge in the selection set.

- An Autodesk-supplied AutoLISP program named EDGE.LSP can be used to permanently make visible edges invisible, as well as to make invisible edges visible.

Related system variables:

- **splframe**    Invisible edges of 3D faces are displayed when **splframe** is set to 1. When **splframe** is set to 0 (its default value), invisible edges are not displayed. A regen is required for a change in visibility to take effect.

objects out of the way and to improve visualization. An additional consideration for layers is that AutoCAD's renderer can attach materials by layer. Therefore, if you think that particular surfaces might be rendered in a specific color, or material type, you might want to have their objects reside in a specific layer. For example, you could use the names SID01, ROOF01, and EAVES for the layers that the 3D faces will be drawn in. Also, although you will probably want to use a different color for each of these layers, the actual colors you use is not important.

| | |
|---|---|
| Command: | EDGE |
| Purpose: | EDGE allows you to make selected visible edges of 3D faces become invisible, and selected invisible edges visible. |
| Initiate with: | • On the command line, enter EDGE. |
| | • From the Draw pull-down menu, select Surfaces, and then Edge from the resulting flyout menu. |
| | • Select the EDGE button from the Surfaces toolbar. |
| Options: | This command applies to any 3D face currently on the screen — you do not need to first specify a particular 3D face to modify the visibility of its edges. The following command line menu is displayed: |

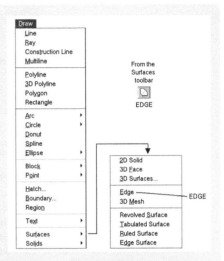

```
Specify edge of 3Dface to toggle visibility or [Display]: (Enter D, select a 3D face
    edge, or press Enter.)
```

- **Specify Edge**    This default causes the selected visible edge to become invisible. You must select an edge by picking a point on it — crossing and window selections are not allowed. AutoCAD automatically displays the midpoint object snap symbol when your pointing device is on an edge. If two edges are coincident (one edge is on top of another edge), they are both changed. As soon as an edge is picked, the main command line menu is repeated.

    When you select an edge, it is highlighted, and any invisible edges on the 3D face it belongs to are also highlighted. If you select one of those highlighted invisible edges, it becomes visible.

- **Display**    This option causes invisible edges to be displayed as highlighted lines. It brings up the secondary menu:

    ```
    Enter selection method for display of hidden edges [Select/All] <All>:
        (Enter an option, or press Enter.)
    ```

    - **All**    This option causes all invisible edges on all 3D faces currently on the screen to be visible and highlighted. The main EDGE menu is redisplayed.

    - **Select**    This option allows you to view the invisible edges on specific 3D faces rather than globally. It uses the prompt:

        ```
        Select objects: (Select one or more 3D faces.)
        ```

        You can use any object selection method in choosing the 3D faces. The invisible edges on those 3D faces are highlighted, and the main EDGE menu is redisplayed.

- Enter    When you press the Enter key in response to the main EDGE menu, the command ends, with the edge visibility changes taking effect.

Notes:

- You should leave the system variable **splframe** set to 0 when you are using EDGE because it is impossible to distinguish invisible edges from visible edges when **splframe** is set to 1.

- This is such an easy command to use, you might prefer to use it in making 3D face edges invisible, rather than directly through the 3DFACE command.

- EDGE is based on an Autodesk-supplied AutoLISP program. It is not a built-in AutoCAD command.

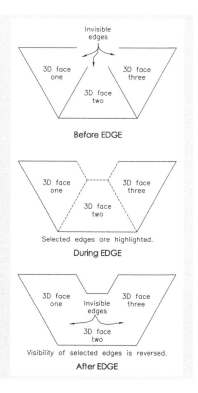

As you make the 3D faces for the walls, you will leave some openings for windows and doors that will be added in a later chapter. You should draw wireframe outlines of the doors and windows so that you can see their locations when you have the layer you use for the 3D faces turned off. You should create and use a layer for these door and window outlines that is different from the layers used to draw the wireframe objects of the house corners and roof.

Conceptually, there is nothing difficult in making the 3D faces for this house,

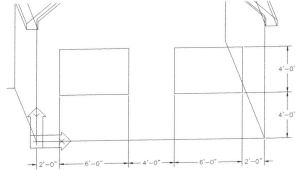

Figure 3-1

but you have to be systematic and careful. Otherwise, you might miss covering some areas or incorrectly position a 3D face. You probably will want your AutoCAD graphics area divided into several viewports as you work, even though the figures used for this exercise show only one view at a time.

Start on the right side of the house. Align the X-Y plane of the UCS on the right side of the house as shown in Figure 3-1. The viewpoint for this figure is 355 degrees (or minus 5 degrees) from the X axis in the WCS X-Y plane, and 12 degrees from the X-Y plane. Use a layer you have reserved for wireframe objects to draw the rectangular window borders shown in the figure. The dimensions are for your guidance and should not be added to your model.

Now, switch to the layer you intend to use for the side surfaces of the house (such as SIDE01) and make the six 3D faces shown in Figure 3-2. Do not bother to make any of the 3D face edges invisible. The faces numbered 1 through 4 in this figure can be easily made when you activate the snap mode, with the snap spacing set to 12 (1 foot). However, you have to use object endpoint snaps to establish the top corners for face number 5 and for each of the three corners of face number 6.

Figure 3-2 shows the right side of the house when the HIDE command has been invoked. To use this command, enter HIDE on the command line. Use the REGEN command to restore hidden lines. You also can enter SHADEMODE on the command line and select the Flat option to verify the 3D face

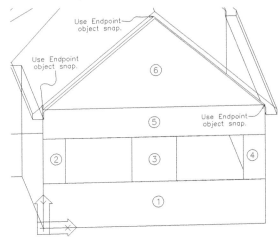

Figure 3-2

locations. This option, which fills the faces in with their object color, is useful when there is nothing behind a surface to be hidden. Although you can work in SHADEMODE's shaded views, the shaded faces occasionally get in the way, so you should again invoke SHADEMODE after you have verified your 3D face locations, and select the command's 2D wireframe option. (See Chapter 14 for a complete description of the SHADEMODE command.)

Move and reorient the UCS so that its X-Y plane is on the front of the house as shown in Figure 3-3. This figure shows the right half of the front of the house. Its view point is 280 degrees from the X axis in the X-Y plane, and 0 degrees from the X-Y plane. Then, in the layer you use for wireframe objects draw an outline of a garage door, a front door, and a window using the dimensions given in the figure.

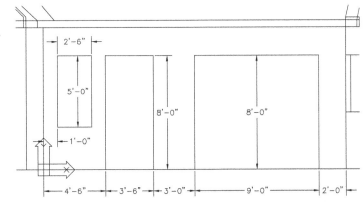

Figure 3-3

Change to the layer you use for the surface of the house siding, and make six four-sided 3D faces, as shown in Figure 3-4. Do not make any of the 3D face edges invisible. The numbers and notes in the figure are to help you in drawing the 3D faces. You can draw the lengths and widths of these faces easily in AutoCAD's snap mode with a snap spacing of 6 inches. The top edge of face 5 is 10 feet from the bottom of the wall. When you have drawn the six 3D faces, use the SHADEMODE command to verify they are correct.

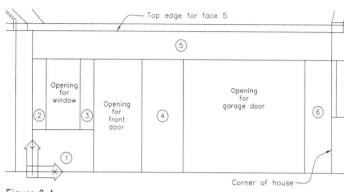

Figure 3-4

Move the UCS origin to the front extension of the house and draw (using a layer you've reserved for wireframe objects) the outline of the 8-by-6-foot window shown in Figure 3-5. You might recall from Chapter 4 that this section extends 7 feet from the main front of the house. The viewpoint for Figure 3-5 is 275 degrees from the X axis in the X-Y plane, and 2 degrees from the X-Y plane.

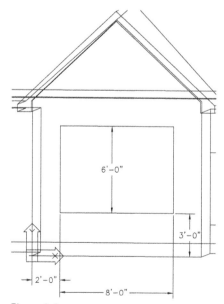

Figure 3-5

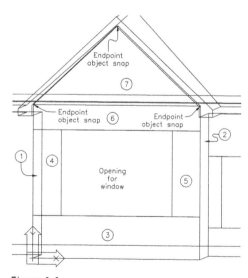

Figure 3-6

After switching back to the layer you have been using for the house siding, make the seven 3D faces shown in Figure 3-6. Notice that 3D faces 1 and 2 are perpendicular to the other five. To make them, you can either position the UCS X-Y plane on their plane, or use object endpoint snaps without changing the UCS. You should make those two faces first and use the SHADEMODE command to ensure that they are correct. Making the other five 3D faces is a straightforward process, although you have to use object endpoint snaps to locate the top edge of 3D face 6, and all three vertices of 3D face 7.

Finish covering the front of the house by moving the UCS to the left side of the house as shown in Figure 3-7. The viewpoint for Figure 3-7 is 260 degrees from the X axis in the X-Y plane, and 0 degrees from the X-Y plane. Draw the window outline using the dimensions given in the left side of Figure 3-7, and then make the four 3D faces shown in the right side of Figure 3-7. You can make the 3D faces most easily by using AutoCAD's snap mode with a snap spacing of 12 inches.

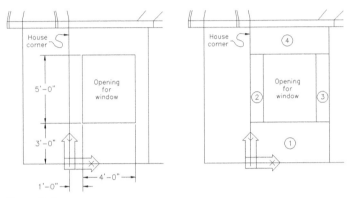

Figure 3-7

Cover the left side of the house with a copy of the six 3D faces and two window outlines you used for the right side of the house. After selecting those objects, use object endpoint snaps to establish the base and destination points for the copies. A quick check using the SHADEMODE command will help you verify that the copies were correctly made and positioned.

Now switch to a view of the back side of the house. Figure 3-8 shows the house from a viewpoint that is 70 degrees from the X axis in the X-Y plane, and 2 degrees from the X-Y plane. Set the UCS as shown in Figure 3-8. The 3point option of the UCS command works well for this.

The house is beginning to be cluttered, which makes it difficult to visualize its surfaces and select points. Because at this

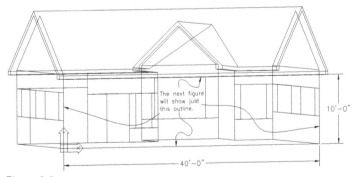

Figure 3-8

time you are only interested in the 40-by-10-foot rectangle that makes up the back wall of the house, make the 3D faces for it in an area that is in the same plane but is located away from the house. That will give you a clear, clean view of your work. When you are finished you will move the 3D faces onto the house.

Move the UCS origin 45 feet in the X direction. Then draw the outlines of one door and three windows using the dimensions given in Figure 3-9.

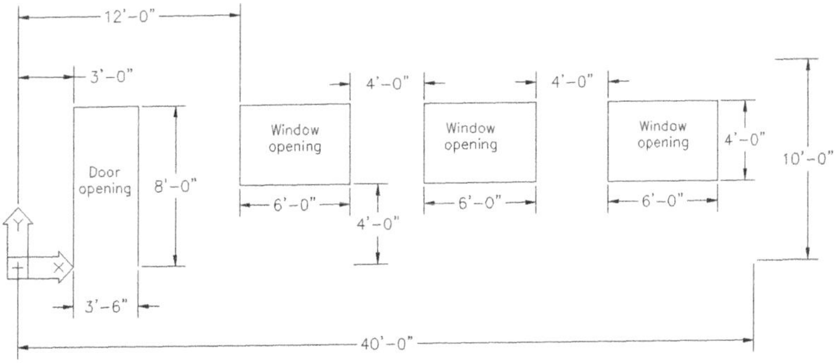

Make seven 3D faces similar to those shown in Figure 3-10. Other arrangements of these 3D faces would be equally satisfactory. Be sure to draw them in the layer you have been using for the house's siding.

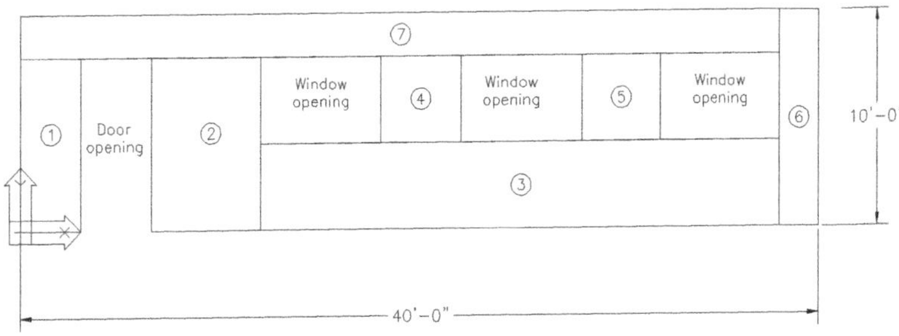

Figure 3-9

After checking the correct placement of your 3D faces with the SHADEMODE command, move them along with the wireframes for the door and windows 45 feet in the minus-X direction so that they are on the back of the house.

Figure 3-10

That finishes the surfaces for the sides of the house. Now, begin adding 3D faces to the eaves of the roof. Start on the right side of the house as shown in Figure 3-11. Turn off the layer you used to make the 3D faces for the siding as well as the layer used for the window and door outlines. Figure 3-11 uses a viewpoint rotated 315 degrees from the X axis in the X-Y plane and 55 degrees from the X-Y plane.

Make four 3D faces to cover the surfaces on the lower part of the roof overhang. The areas to be covered are shown hatched in Figure 3-11. Use a unique layer, having a name such as EAVES, for the 3D faces. Because you can use object endpoint snaps to locate the vertices of the 3D faces, the location and orientation of the UCS is not important.

Figure 3-11

Then, make four 3D faces on the outside edge of the roof end. The areas to be covered are shown hatched in Figure 3-12. Here also, you can use object endpoint snaps to locate the vertices of the 3D faces. Use the SHADEMODE command to verify that all eight 3D faces on this end of the roof are correctly positioned.

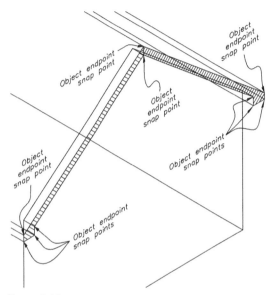

Figure 3-12

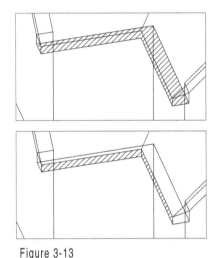

Figure 3-13

Use the same techniques to make 3D faces on the other end of the house (or else copy or mirror the ones you have just drawn) and on the front extension of the house. Then, cover the bottom of the eaves on the left-front side of the house. This area, which can be covered with two 3D faces, is shown hatched in the upper part of Figure 3-13. Also, cover the vertical sides of these eaves with two 3D faces, as shown (hatched) in the lower part of Figure 3-13.

After checking these 3D faces with the SHADEMODE command, cover the remaining eaves with 3D faces using the same techniques. You will probably want to use two view-

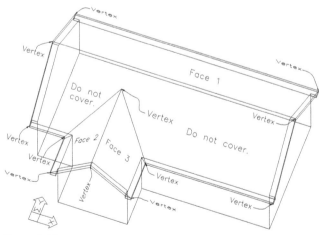

Figure 3-14

ports, zoomed in on opposite ends of the roof, to cover the 40-foot-long eaves on the back of the house. Check your 3D face locations with the SHADEMODE command.

Only the top of the roof remains to be covered. In this exercise, you will make only the three 3D faces shown in Figure 3-14. You will cover the remaining area of the roof later in this chapter in an exercise for the PFACE command. The viewpoint for Figure 3-14 is 290 degrees in the X-Y plane from the X axis, and 60 degrees from the X-Y plane. To reduce clutter in the model, you might want to turn off the layers you used for the windows, siding, and eaves. Switch to the layer you intend to use for the rooftop and make the three 3D faces, using object snaps at the vertex points shown in Figure 3-14. If you use object endpoint snaps, the orientation of the UCS is not important.

Your house is now fully covered, except for the doors, windows, and part of the roof. It should look similar to the one shown in Figure 3-15, when the viewpoint is 305 degrees in the X-Y plane from the X axis and 5 degrees from the X-Y plane. In this figure, the HIDE command is active. Even at this stage, the house doesn't look any better than the wireframe version but it is covered with surfaces that can make the house realistic looking when it is rendered.

Figure 3-15

Save the file of your 3D model because you will finish covering its roof in Exercise 6 of this chapter. This stage of the model is in the CD-ROM that accompanies this book as file f0641.dwg.

## Exercise Four

This next exercise in using the 3DFACE command is much less involved than the first one. You will add seven 3D faces to the oil pan you started as a wireframe model in Chapter 4 and added to in Chapter 5. The wireframe model is on the CD-ROM that accompanies this book as file

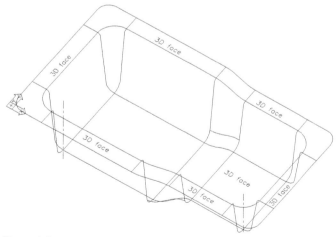

Figure 4-1

f0555.dwg. Figure 4-1 shows the model with the areas labeled in which you will add the 3D faces. Six of them are on the flange, and one is on the rectangular area of the raised bottom of the oil pan. Although there are other planar areas on the oil pan, those areas have curved rather than straight edges, so you will use other types of surfaces for them. Also, a dome-like surface will be created in the large rectangular area on the bottom of the oil pan.

Set up a layer for surfaces and use it to make all seven of the 3D faces. Because you are experienced in using the 3DFACE command, detailed instructions for creating the faces will not be provided. The areas are bounded by wireframe objects so you can use object endpoint snaps to locate the vertices of the 3D faces. There is no need to make any of the edges invisible. Your model with the 3D faces should look similar to the one in Figure 4-2 when the SHADEMODE command has been invoked. On the CD-ROM that comes with this book, the partially surfaced oil pan model is in file f0643.dwg.

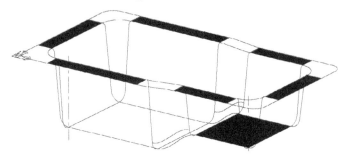

Figure 4-2

## Making Surfaces with the PFACE Command

The PFACE command is similar to the 3DFACE command in that it makes three- and four-sided planar surfaces. Another similarity with 3DFACE is that the PFACE command can make any number of faces each time it is used. The faces made with PFACE, however, are joined so that they form one object having multiple faces rather than a set of individual objects. Also, edges between the three- and four-sided faces are normally invisible.

Surfaces made by the PFACE command are called *polyface meshes*. This is a unique AutoCAD object type. Although it is a variation of the polyline object type, it's not recognized by the PEDIT command. AutoCAD has another object type for surfaces, which is described in Chapter 8, called a *polygon mesh*. The similarity in their names makes it easy to confuse these two object types, but they are different. Polygon meshes are a surface version of polylines that can be edited by PEDIT. To add to the possible confusion, when a polyface mesh is exploded, it turns into a set of 3D faces rather than a set of polylines.

Although both PFACE and 3DFACE make three- and four-sided faces, the input for PFACE is entirely different than it is for 3DFACE. In fact, the method is unlike the input for any other AutoCAD command. PFACE first asks you to pick points in space to serve as the vertices of the faces; as you pick those points, AutoCAD internally assigns a number to each vertex. When you have selected the locations of all the vertices, AutoCAD asks you to enter the vertex numbers that go with which face.

To get an idea as to how the PFACE command works, consider the six points shown on the left in the next figure. These points are all on the same plane. The input to make a polyface mesh having these points as its vertices is

```
Command: PFACE (Enter)
Specify location for vertex 1: 0,0,0 (Enter)
```

```
Specify location for vertex 2 or <define faces>: 0,2,0 (Enter)
Specify location for vertex 3 or <define faces>: 1,2,0 (Enter)
Specify location for vertex 4 or <define faces>: 1,1,0 (Enter)
Specify location for vertex 5 or <define faces>: 2,1,0 (Enter)
Specify location for vertex 6 or <define faces>: 2,0,0 (Enter)
Specify location for vertex 7 or <define faces>: (Enter)
Face 1, vertex 1: Enter a vertex number or [Color/Layer]: 1 (Enter)
Face 1, vertex 2: Enter a vertex number or [Color/Layer]<next face>: 2 (Enter)
Face 1, vertex 3: Enter a vertex number or [Color/Layer]<next face>: 3 (Enter)
Face 1, vertex 4: Enter a vertex number or [Color/Layer]<next face>: 4 (Enter)
Face 1, vertex 5: Enter a vertex number or [Color/Layer]<next face>: 5 (Enter)
Face 1, vertex 6: Enter a vertex number or [Color/Layer]<next face>: 6 (Enter)
Face 1, vertex 7: Enter a vertex number or [Color/Layer]<next face>: (Enter)
Face 2, vertex 1: Enter a vertex number or [Color/Layer]: (Enter)
```

The resulting polyface mesh is shown on the right in the figure. As is generally true with AutoCAD surfaces, only the edges of the surface show up in a wireframe view mode such as this. The vertex numbers are specified in the same order that was used to specify the point locations, but they did not have to be. The following input sequence during the second phase of the PFACE command would have worked equally well:

Coordinates of six points in space and the AutoCAD assigned vertex numbers

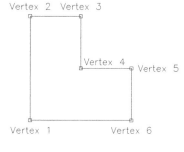

Polyface mesh using the points as vertices

```
Face 1, vertex 1: Enter a vertex number or [Color/Layer]: 4 (Enter)
Face 1, vertex 2: Enter a vertex number or [Color/Layer]<next face>: 3 (Enter)
Face 1, vertex 3: Enter a vertex number or [Color/Layer]<next face>: 2 (Enter)
Face 1, vertex 4: Enter a vertex number or [Color/Layer]<next face>: 1 (Enter)
Face 1, vertex 5: Enter a vertex number or [Color/Layer]<next face>: 6 (Enter)
Face 1, vertex 6: Enter a vertex number or [Color/Layer]<next face>: 5 (Enter)
Face 1, vertex 7: Enter a vertex number or [Color/Layer]<next face>: (Enter)
Face 2, vertex 1: Enter a vertex number or [Color/Layer]: (Enter)
```

Although outwardly these two different input sequences seem to produce the same results, the two polyface mesh surfaces are subtly different. If you were to turn on the **splframe** system variable (by setting it to a value of 1), the polyface mesh from the first vertex input order would look like the one on the left side of

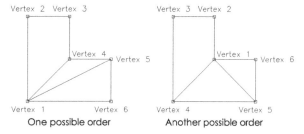

Same vertex locations, but entered in a different order. Splframe set to 1.

One possible order                    Another possible order the next figure, while the one using the second vertex input order would be like the one on the right.

Notice that both polyface meshes are internally composed of three subfaces, even though AutoCAD referred to this area as one face during the PFACE command. The first subface always has four edges, provided the entire face has at least four vertices, and the remaining subfaces always have just three edges. These subfaces are similar to those you might make with the 3DFACE command. Unlike 3D faces, however, these three subfaces are joined to form a single object — if you move one, they all move, and if you erase one they are all erased. Moreover, AutoCAD automatically makes the edges between the subfaces invisible.

Notice also in the preceding figure that one edge of each subface originates from the first vertex that was specified during the second phase of the PFACE command. As a result, the internal arrangement of the subfaces on these two polyface meshes is different, even though they appear to be identical when **splframe** is set to 0.

This means that the location of the vertex you specify for the first vertex is very important. The next figure shows a polyface mesh surface made using an improper input order for these same vertices — one that requires an edge from the first vertex to cut across the straight-line border between vertex points. The face vertex input was clockwise, starting with vertex 1.

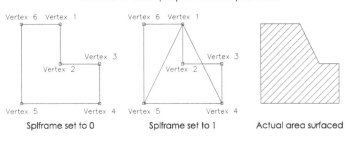

Results of an improper vertex input order

Splframe set to 0        Splframe set to 1        Actual area surfaced

In a wireframe mode, as shown on the left, the surface appears to be all right. If you were to set **splframe** to 1, however, you would see, as shown in the middle of the figure, that one subface edge extends beyond the apparent boundary of the surface. The actual area covered by the surface is shown hatched on the right in the figure. This area would be evident when you used the SHADE-MODE command to color the faces.

If you were to explode that polyface mesh, it would be transformed into three 3D faces as shown on the right in the next figure. In this figure, the 3D faces have been moved away from each other. Notice that one of these 3D faces,

Splframe set to 1

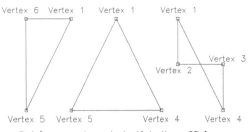

Polyface mesh exploded into three 3D faces

which has four vertices, crosses over itself. The edges of 3D faces created by exploding a polyface mesh retain the original subface edge visibility. As a result, all the edges on the 3D faces that originally represented interior edges of subfaces are invisible. In the figure, **splframe** has been set to 1, so all the edges on the 3D faces are shown.

Its cumbersome input has severely limited the popularity of PFACE, and Autodesk now even seems to be trying to ignore the command. Since Release 13, PFACE has not been included in any of the menus or toolbars, and the Command Reference manual, as well as on-screen help, suggests that you use 3DFACE or one of the commands that make polygon meshes instead of PFACE.

Nevertheless, it is a handy command for certain situations. You might prefer to use PFACE for making planar surfaces having five to seven sides instead of 3DFACE because you don't have to bother with making invisible edges. Furthermore, the interface isn't that bad when you get used to it. Most likely, however, you will need to make a diagram of the areas you want surfaced to ensure that the vertex numbers match the face input.

| Command: | PFACE |
|---|---|
| Purpose: | PFACE makes a single object consisting of multiple three- and four-sided planar surfaces. |
| Initiate with: | • On the command line, enter PFACE. |
| Implementation: | PFACE has two separate phases. First, the command prompts you for the vertices, the corners, of the surfaces you want to create. In this phase, you specify points in space, one at a time, to be surface vertices, and AutoCAD consecutively assigns a vertex number to each point. In the second phase of the command, AutoCAD creates surface faces as you enter the appropriate vertex numbers. |

The command line sequence of prompts and input for the first phase of PFACE is

```
Command: PFACE (Enter)
Specify location for vertex 1: Specify a point.
Specify location for vertex 2 or <define faces>: Specify a point.
Specify location for vertex 3 or <define faces>: Specify a point or press Enter.
Specify location for vertex n or <define faces>: Specify a point or press Enter.
```

You can specify as many points, using any input method, as you want. When you press the Enter key in response to a vertex point, AutoCAD moves to the second phase of the command:

```
Face 1, vertex 1: Enter a vertex number or [Color/
     Layer]: Enter the letter L or C, or a vertex
     number.
Face 1, vertex 2: Enter a vertex number or [Color/
     Layer]<next face>: Enter the letter L or C,
     or a vertex number.
Face 1, vertex n: Enter a vertex number or [Color/
     Layer]<next face>: Enter the letter L or C, a
     vertex number, or press Enter.
Face 2, vertex 1: Enter a vertex number or [Color/
     Layer]: Enter the letter L or C, a vertex
     number, or press Enter.
Face m, vertex n: Enter a vertex number or [Color/
     Layer]<next face>: Enter the letter L or C, a
     vertex number, or press Enter.
```

PFACE can make faces in different planes.

Whenever the Enter key is pressed, AutoCAD moves to the next face, prompting for the number of the first vertex on the face. These faces do not have to be in the same plane. Pressing the Enter key twice in succession ends the command.

Options:

Edges between faces are normally visible, but you can make them invisible if you enter the first vertex on the edge as a negative number.

If you enter the letter *c* or the word *color* when prompted for a vertex number, AutoCAD issues a prompt for a color. After you specify a color, either by number or name, AutoCAD resumes with a prompt for another vertex number.

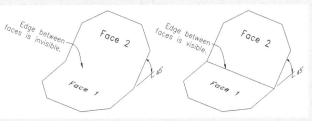

All edges of the current face, and of the faces that follow, are drawn in the specified color.

```
Face m, vertex n: Enter a vertex number or [Color/Layer]: color (Enter)
Enter a color number or a standard color name <CURRENT>: Enter a color number or
     name.
Face m, vertex n: Enter a vertex number or [Color/Name]:Enter a vertex number.
```

If you enter the letter *l* or the word *layer* when prompted for a vertex number, AutoCAD issues a prompt for a layer name. The current face, as well as the faces that follow, in the specified layer. After you specify a layer, AutoCAD resumes the prompts for vertex numbers.

```
Face m, vertex n: Enter a vertex number or [Color/Layer]:layer (Enter)
Enter a layer name<CURRENT>: Enter the name of a layer.
Face m, vertex n: Enter a vertex number or [Color/Layer]:Enter a vertex number.
```

Notes:

- If a face has more than four vertices, it is divided into subfaces having three or four vertices that are similar in shape to 3D faces. The edges between these subfaces are invisible.

- The type of object created by this command is a polyface mesh. Although this object type is within the polyline family, it cannot be edited by PEDIT. Moreover, when a polyface mesh is exploded, it becomes a set of individual 3D faces.

- AutoCAD does not draw any faces until you signal an end to the second phase of the command by pressing the Enter key twice in succession. If you cancel the command, no faces are drawn, even if their vertex numbers have already been entered.

Related system variables:

- **splframe**    If the system variable **splframe** is set to 1, invisible edges between faces and between subfaces are displayed. The default value of **splframe** is 0. A regen is required before changes in **splframe** have any effect.

- **pfacevmax**    This is a curious system variable that sets the maximum number of vertices per face. However, it is a read-only variable, so you cannot do anything with it. Its value is fixed at 4.

## Using AutoLISP to Make Polyface Meshes

Autodesk intended PFACE to be used primarily by applications, such as AutoLISP programs, and when PFACE first appeared in Release 11, Autodesk supplied an AutoLISP program as an example. This program, named MFACE.LSP, worked well in Release 11, but unfortunately, the Release 12 version of the program contained an error that prevented it from running, and subsequent releases of AutoCAD do not even include MFACE.LSP.

The CD-ROM that accompanies this book contains a corrected version of MFACE.LSP that works in AutoCAD 2000, 2000i, and 2002. After the program has been loaded, it uses the following command line input:

```
Command: MFACE (Enter)
Layer/Color/<Select vertex>: Enter an option or specify a point.
```

If you select the Layer option, the command prompts for a layer name to be used in drawing the face, with the current layer presented as a default. After a name is entered, or the Enter key is pressed to accept the default, the main menu is repeated.

If you select the Color option, the command prompts for a color name or number (with the current color offered as a default) to be used for drawing the face. After a color is specified, the main menu is repeated.

When you select a point in response to the main menu, it serves as the first vertex of a face, and the program prompts for additional vertex points:

```
Select vertex: Specify a point or press Enter.
```

This prompt is repeated until you press the Enter key. When you specify the fourth vertex, AutoCAD draws a highlighted line (representing the inside edge of the first subface) to it, and as each additional vertex is specified, AutoCAD draws a highlighted line (representing the edge of a three-cornered subface) to it.

Whenever you press the Enter key in response to a point, the current face is completed, and the original menu is repeated so that you can make another face:

```
Layer/Color/<Select vertex>: Enter an option, specify a point, or press Enter.
```

Pressing the Enter key terminates the command. The Layer and Color options allow the next face to be drawn in a different layer or with a different color than the previous face, and specifying a point establishes the first vertex of the next face.

The edges between the subfaces are always invisible (provided **splframe** is set to 0), while edges between faces are always visible — there is no provision for making invisible face edges, as there is in the PFACE command itself.

## Converting 3D Faces to Polyface Meshes

When you explode a polyface mesh, it is transformed into a set of individual 3D faces, with the invisible edges between faces remaining invisible. You can reverse the transformation, to make polyface meshes from 3D faces, although the process is not direct. You must first use AutoCAD's 3DSOUT command to export the 3D faces to a 3D Studio format file, and then import the 3D Studio file back into AutoCAD by way of the 3DSIN command. (3D Studio is a stand-alone rendering and animation program.)

The process is easy. When you invoke the 3DSOUT command, you are asked to select the objects to be exported and then for a name and location for the exported file. This is followed by a dialog box named 3D Studio File Export Options. You can safely accept the default options in this dialog box, and click its OK button to save the file. The original 3D faces remain as they were.

As soon as the file has been saved, you can start the 3DSIN command to import the 3D Studio version of the 3D faces. A standard file location dialog box is presented so that you can find and specify the 3D Studio file — it has a 3DS filename extension. As soon as you specify the file, a dialog box named 3D Studio File Import Options appears. A list of 3D Studio objects types available for import is shown in a list box located on the left side of this dialog box. Click the Add All button below this list box to select these object types, and move their names to a list box on the right side of the dialog box. Then click the OK button to import the objects into AutoCAD.

The imported objects, which are now a single polyface mesh, are inserted in the same spot as the original objects. This process can be useful when you want to join a set of 3D faces so that you can treat them as a single object. One drawback, however, is that edges on the original 3D faces that were originally invisible will be visible on the resulting polyface mesh. Actually, this transformation also works for other AutoCAD objects having surfaces, such as polygon meshes, regions, 3D solids, and even circles and extruded wireframe objects. You are not likely, however, to ever want to convert those objects to polyface meshes.

## Exercises in Using PFACE

The following two exercises give you experience using the PFACE command, help you understand how polyface meshes differ from 3D faces, and illustrate the usefulness of polyface meshes.

### Exercise Five

As an exercise in using PFACE, you will make the surface model of a sheet-metal air duct that has a 90-degree bend. You will not use this model in the future, so you might not want to keep it. Therefore, the setup for the drawing file and its name is not important. You will need at least two layers, however.

You will use a wireframe to establish the vertex points of the polyface mesh. Start by rotating the UCS about the X axis so that the UCS X-Y plane is on the WCS Z-X plane. Then, draw the seven lines that represent the edges of one side of the duct, using the dimensions given in Figure

5-1. When you have completed the one side, copy all seven lines 12 units in the WCS Y direction. Your finished wireframe should look similar to the one shown in Figure 5-1.

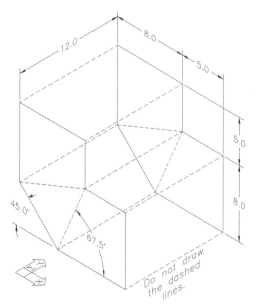

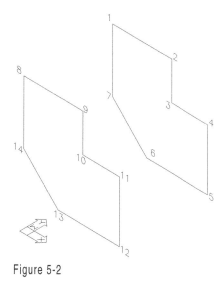

Figure 5-2

Figure 5-1

The dashed lines in Figure 5-1 are to give you an idea as to where the edges of the polyface mesh faces will be — you should not draw the dashed lines. You should now switch to a layer that is different from the one you used for the wireframe. Although you could do this during the PFACE command, it will be less confusing if you do it now.

Set up a running endpoint object snap through the OSNAP command, and then start the PFACE command. In the first phase of the command, pick the numbered line endpoints shown in Figure 5-2 in response to AutoCAD's prompts for Vertex 1, Vertex 2, Vertex 3, and so forth. When you have specified the location of 14 vertex points, press the Enter key when AutoCAD prompts for Vertex 15. Other equally suitable arrangements of the vertex numbers could be used, but this one is as good as any. You even could assign numbers randomly, as long as the numbers match the face vertices during the second phase of the command.

When you press the Enter key in response to a vertex point, AutoCAD moves to the second phase of the command in which you specify which vertex numbers correspond to which face. In this phase you will make a total of seven different faces on the duct. The top of the duct, represented by vertexes 1, 2, 9, and 8, is left open. The front of the duct — the space between vertexes 4, 5, 12, and 11 — will also be left open.

Enter vertexes 1, 7, 14, and 8 for the first face. Alternately, you could start with any of those vertex numbers, and traverse either clockwise or counterclockwise, but if you skip diagonally (such as 1, 14, 7, and 8), the face will cross over itself. Press the Enter key when you are prompted for Vertex 5 of Face 1. AutoCAD then asks for the vertexes that will define Face 2.

For Face 2, enter vertexes 6, 7, 14, and 13. Press the Enter key when AutoCAD prompts for Vertex 5 of Face 2, to move to the next face. Complete the PFACE command using the following vertex numbers for the remaining five faces:

Face 3    Vertex numbers 5, 6, 13, and 12

Face 4    Vertex numbers 2, 3, 10, and 9

Face 5    Vertex numbers 3, 4, 11, and 10

Face 6    Vertex numbers 3, 4, 5, 6, 7, 1, and 2

Face 7    Vertex numbers 10, 11, 12, 13, 14, 8, and 9

When AutoCAD prompts for Vertex 7 of Face 8, press the Enter key twice to finish PFACE. At this time, AutoCAD draws the seven faces. It is important that you start Face 6 with Vertex 3, and start Face 7 with Vertex 10. Otherwise, the surface might extend beyond the intended outline. Your completed surface model should look similar to the one in Figure 5-3. HIDE has been activated for this figure, and the viewpoint is 325 degrees from the X axis in the X-Y plane and 10 degrees from the X-Y plane. On the CD-ROM, this surface model is in the file f0652.dwg.

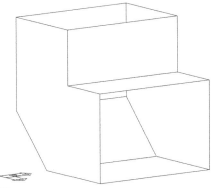

Figure 5-3

## Exercise Six

Finish the roof of your 3D surface model house with the PFACE command. The area you will cover has seven vertices. Although you could easily surface this area with three 3D faces, use a single polyface mesh instead. The reason for this is that when you set up material for a rendering of the house in Chapter 19, you will want that surface to be a single object rather than three separate objects.

Open your file of the surface model house, or retrieve and open file f0641.dwg on the CD-ROM that comes with this book. Set a viewpoint that is rotated approximately 300 degrees in the X-Y plane from the X axis and approximately 50 degrees from the X-Y plane. If your model is too cluttered, you can freeze the layers used for the house siding and windows. Your model should look similar to the one in Figure 6-1.

Switch to the same layer you used for the 3D face surfaces on the roof, and then start the PFACE command. When you are prompted in the first phase of PFACE to select vertex locations, pick the points labeled in Figure 6-1. If you

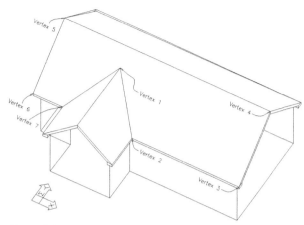

Figure 6-1

use a running object endpoint snap, you can do this without changing the UCS location or orientation. In the second phase of PFACE, specify the vertices in the same order that you entered them. After specifying Vertex 7, press the Enter key twice to end PFACE. That finishes the roof of the house. On the accompanying CD-ROM, the file f0653.dwg contains the house at this stage.

# CHAPTER 7

# Visualizing Surface Models

*Visualizing the 3D objects on your computer's 2D display can be a major problem as you build surface models. Fortunately, AutoCAD provides several commands that help, and this chapter shows you how to get the most from those commands.*

*This chapter*

- *discusses hidden-line removal with the HIDE command;*
- *describes the wireframe, hidden line, and shaded options of the SHADEMODE command;*
- *explains how to remove view-obstructing objects and how to make perspective views with DVIEW and with the commands related to 3DORBIT.*

Even though surface models are a step up in reality from wireframe models, their increased complexity can make them harder to visualize. This is especially true for models with polymesh surfaces, which are discussed in Chapter 8, but even models surfaced with 3D faces become cluttered with extra lines and edges, as you undoubtedly noticed in Chapter 6 when you added surfaces to your 3D house model. Furthermore, you can see completely through surfaces most of the time. This makes it difficult to tell where the surfaces are located, distinguish between surfaces, determine where a particular object is located on a model, and pick points on a model.

AutoCAD's HIDE, SHADEMODE, DVIEW, and 3DORBIT commands can help you obtain clearer, more understandable, and more realistic pictures of your 3D models. You will examine those commands in this chapter to see how they work, how they differ, and how you can best use them.

## Using the HIDE Command

Often, surface models (as well as solid models) are referred to as wireframes when they are displayed in a nonopaque form. This book, however, refers to the nonopaque form of surface models and solid models as their *wireframe mode* rather than as wireframes. This distinguishes them from models made solely from wireframe objects.

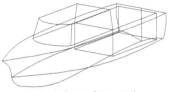

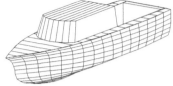

Wireframe 3D model            Surface model in wireframe mode            Surface model in hidden-line mode

The most frequently used method for making surfaces opaque is to invoke the HIDE command. HIDE requires no object selection and has no options. After performing some calculations, AutoCAD redraws the current viewport so that all objects, and parts of objects, that are behind surface objects are no longer shown. The result is often referred to as a *hidden-line image*, or as the *hidden-line mode*. The surfaces continue to be opaque until some operation causes a viewport screen regeneration. As you would presume, which objects are hidden is dependent upon the view direction. Objects can simultaneously be hidden in one viewport and visible in another.

If two objects are in the same plane, they will not hide each other. The accompanying figure shows the 3D model of a simple building made from 3D faces. The top edges of the walls show through the roof in hidden-line views because they are in the same plane as the roof, as can be seen on the right side of the figure. These edges will not show up in a rendering, so they might not really be a problem. If it is

Objects in the same plane do not hide one another.

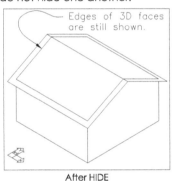

Before HIDE            After HIDE

important that the edges are not to appear in hidden-line views, however, you have two options. The best one is to make the edges invisible, perhaps with the EDGE command. A more complicated and possibly less desirable option (because it affects the accuracy and preciseness of your model), is to move, or remake, the objects so that they are no longer in the same plane.

As you can imagine, AutoCAD must perform extensive calculations to determine which objects are to be hidden. Normally, AutoCAD uses single-precision arithmetic to perform these calculations, and this can affect the accuracy of the hidden line removal. The left side of the next figure shows a circle that is 0.0005 units above a hatch pattern. With single precision arithmetic, AutoCAD has problems and the hatch is only partly hidden.

However, when AutoCAD uses double-precision arithmetic (which means that it uses more digits to the right of the decimal point), the HIDE command works properly in hiding the hatch, as shown in the upper-right figure. The system variable **hideprecision** controls whether AutoCAD uses single- or double-precision arithmetic. When **hideprecision** is set to 0, single-precision arithmetic is used; when it is set to 1, AutoCAD uses double-precision arithmetic. In practice, the

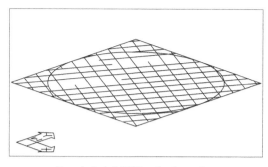

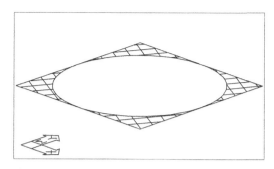

The circle is 0.0005 units above the hatch. HIDE does not work properly.

The circle is still 0.0005 units above the hatch, but **hideprecision** has been set to 1. HIDE now works properly.

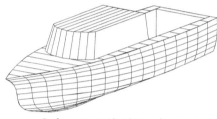

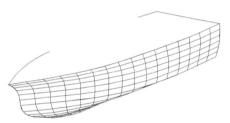

Surface model in hidden-line mode.
All layers for surfaces are ON.

Surface model in hidden-line mode.
Some layers for surfaces are OFF.

problem used as an example here seldom occurs, and you will seldom have any reason to change **hideprecision** from its default value of 0.

Surface objects in layers that have been turned off continue to hide objects that are behind them. In some cases, you can use this characteristic to obtain hidden-line views without the clutter of mesh lines. More likely, however, the result will be mysterious-looking gaps in your model. The left side of the figure of two boats shows the hidden-line view of a model in which all layers for surfaces are on. The right side of the figure shows a hidden-line view of the same model but with the layers for the deck and cabin surfaces turned off. This phenomenon does not occur with layers that have been frozen, and it does not affect plots.

| | |
|---|---|
| Command: | HIDE |
| Purpose: | This command causes all objects that have surfaces to be opaque in the current viewport. Objects, and parts of objects, that are behind surfaces relative to the current viewing direction are hidden from view. |
| Initiate with: | • On the command line, enter HIDE. |
| | • From the View pull-down menu, select Hide. |
| | • Select the HIDE button from the Render toolbar. |
| Implementation: | This command requires no input and has no options. As soon as it is invoked, it begins finding objects that are behind surfaces in the current viewport and removing them from the screen. The screen remains in its hidden-line mode until some operation — such as REGEN, ZOOM, or VPOINT — causes the screen to regenerate. The REDRAW command does not affect the hidden-line mode. |

Notes:

• Text is not hidden unless it has thickness.

• Objects in layers that are frozen are completely transparent, and therefore have no effect on hidden-line displays. However, surface objects in layers that are turned off are still considered to be opaque by the HIDE command, and consequently will hide objects that are behind them.

Before HIDE          After HIDE

• The HIDE command has no effect on hidden lines during plotting. That is handled by the Hide Lines option of the PLOT command, or (better) through paper space and the MVIEW command. (This command is discussed in Section 4.)

• The Advanced Modeling Extension (AME), an Autodesk solid modeling program that ran with AutoCAD Releases 11 and 12, required that a special AME command be used to create surface-like faces on solids before the HIDE command had any effect on them. Such a step is not necessary with AutoCAD's 3D solids. Whenever the HIDE command is invoked, all 3D solids currently on the screen are automatically changed into a faceted format that has opaque surfaces. (The details of hidden-line removal on 3D solids is discussed in Section 3.)

• Real-time zoom and pan is disabled when the hidden-line mode is in effect.

Related system variable:
• **hideprecision**

This system variable determines whether hide calculations are performed in single- or double-precision arithmetic. When **hideprecision** is set to 0, its default setting, hidden-line calculations, are performed in single precision, while double precision-arithmetic is used when **hideprecision** is set to 1.

Double-precision arithmetic requires more memory, and it can slow performance (especially when hiding 3D solids). Although double-precision calculation can result in more accurate hidden-line displays when objects are very close together, single- precision calculations generally yield satisfactory results, and you will probably never need to change **hideprecision** from its default value of 0.

# Creating Shaded Images

Surfaces shaded by the SHADEMODE command are colored in with their object color, and the relative brightness of each surface face depends on its orientation to the beam of a single light that is positioned over the left shoulder of the viewer and pointed toward the center of the viewport. Faces directly facing this incoming light are the brightest, and their relative brightness decreases as their angle to the light beam increases.

You have two reasons for shading surfaces as you construct surface models. The first is that shading can help you verify that a newly added surface is properly located and correctly shaped. The HIDE command also can be used to do this, but only if there is something behind the surface to hide. Shading, on the other hand, leaves no doubt as to the precise shape and location of a surface. You used the SHADEMODE command several times for this purpose in Chapter 6 as you added 3D faces to the 3D model house.

A second reason for using shaded images is that they often give you a clearer picture of your model's shape than hidden-line views. This can be especially useful as you set viewpoints with the 3DORBIT command, which are discussed later in this chapter.

The SHADEMODE command offers four different types of shading. Although Gouraud shading, which is named for the person who developed the computer technique for smoothly shading surfaces, creates the most realistic images, you are often more interested in the basic shape of a model than in having a realistic image of it. Also, there is no practical difference between flat shading and Gouraud shading for models that have no rounded or curved surfaces.

Wireframe

Hidden

Shaded

In addition to its shading modes, SHADEMODE has a hidden-line viewing mode. SHADE-MODE's hidden-line views differ from those of the HIDE command in that they are not affected by screen regenerations, they can be used for real-time zooms and pans, and circles are transparent.

SHADEMODE also has options for two wire-frame viewing modes. One of these, the 2D wireframe viewing mode, is AutoCAD's default viewing mode. You will select this option to return to your usual way of viewing objects. The most obvious difference between SHADEMODE's other wireframe viewing mode (3D wireframe) and the 2D wireframe mode is that the UCS icon consists of three mutually perpendicular, cone-shaped arrows on cylindrical shafts. Not so obvious differences are that raster, OLE, and line weights are not displayed in the 3D wireframe mode. Also, noncontinuous line types — such as center lines and dashed lines — are displayed as continuous.

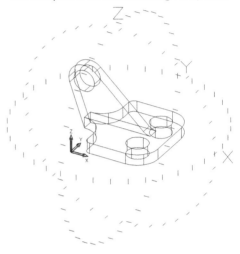

The compass is an aid for setting viewpoints.

An aid for setting viewpoints, called the compass, can be displayed in all viewing modes, except the 2D wireframe mode. The compass consists of three circular arrays of short lines representing the three principal UCS planes that are located in the center of the current viewport. Also, the positive X, Y, and Z directions are labeled. Similar to the UCS icon, the compass is invisible to object selection and cannot be printed. The compass is displayed when the system variable **compass** is set to a value of 1, and it is not displayed when **compass** is set to 0.

Unlike the views of the SHADE command that it replaced, you can freely work in any of SHADEMODE's viewing modes, even in shaded views. Generally, however, you will prefer to work in wireframe views because objects are not obscured, and therefore, more easily selected.

| | |
|---|---|
| Command: | SHADEMODE |
| Purpose: | SHADEMODE creates shaded images of solid and surface models, and sets special wireframe and hidden-line viewing modes. |
| Initiate with: | • On the command line, enter SHADEMODE. |
| | • From the View pull-down menu, select Shade, and then select an option. |
| | • Select a viewing mode from the Shade toolbar. |

Options:

- 2D Wireframe

This option restores the default AutoCAD 2D wireframe viewing mode. The UCS icon is displayed according to the settings of the UCSICON command, and all surface objects are transparent. The compass icon cannot be displayed.

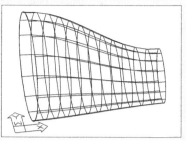

2D Wireframe

- 3D Wireframe

Just as in the 2D wire-frame viewing mode, all surface objects are trans-parent when this option is in effect. The UCS icon, however, appears as three mutually perpendicular cone-shaped arrows on round shafts. Raster and OLE objects are not dis-played. Lineweights, also, are not displayed, and noncontinuous linetypes are displayed as continuous. The compass is displayed when the system variable **compass** has a value of 1.

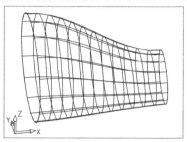

3D Wireframe

- Hidden

Surface objects are opaque, with the exception of cir-cles. Unlike the hid-den-line mode of the HIDE command, real-time pan and zoom can be used, and a screen regeneration does not cause the wireframe viewing mode to be restored.

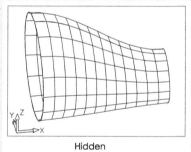

Hidden

- Flat Shaded

Surfaces are shaded according to their object color and their orientation with the viewport's line of sight. Rounded and curved surfaces are divided into distinct three- and four-sided facets.

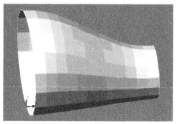

Flat shaded

- Gouraud Shaded

Surfaces are shaded according to their object color and their orientation with the viewport's line of sight. Rounded and curved surfaces are not divided into facets, and therefore, have a smooth appearance. This is true even for polygon mesh surfaces that have facets in wireframe and hidden-line viewing modes.

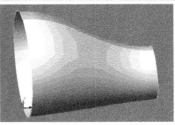

Gouraud shaded

- Flat Shaded Plus Edges

Surfaces are shaded, with rounded and curved surfaces being divided into facets as in flat shading. In addition, the edges of all visible faces are shown in their object color.

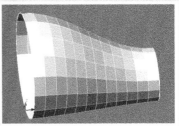

Flat shaded plus edges

- Gouraud Shaded Plus Edges

Surfaces are shaded without dividing rounded and curved surfaces into facets. Edges are shown in their object color, and the edges of facets on surfaces having a mesh are displayed in their object color, even though the surface is smooth and rounded.

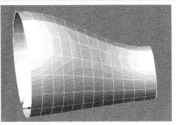

Gouraud shaded plus edges

Notes:

- SHADEMODE, which first appeared in AutoCAD 2000, replaced the SHADE command. Although the SHADE command is no longer documented, you can still invoke it from the command line. The resulting viewing mode will be one of the SHADEMODE viewing modes, as determined by the setting of the **shadedge** system variable.

- You also can initiate SHADEMODE and set its options through the right-click shortcut menus of PAN, ZOOM, and 3DORBIT.

- Circles are transparent in all SHADEMODE viewing modes.

Related system variables:

- **shadedge**

This system variable controls the shading mode used by the SHADE command. It can be set to an integer value of 0, 1, 2, or 3, with the following results:

| Value | Viewing Mode |
|-------|--------------|
| 0 | Gouraud Shading |
| 1 | Gouraud Shading Plus Edges |
| 2 | Hidden |
| 3 | Flat Shading Plus Edges |

- **shadedif**   This system variable controlled the contrast between the brightest and dimmest shaded faces for the SHADE command. It no longer has any effect.

- **compass**   When this system variable is set to 1, a visual aid named the compass that depicts the principal planes of the UCS is displayed in all SHADEMODE viewing modes, except 2D wireframe. When **compass** is set to 0, the compass is not displayed.

# Using the DVIEW Command

DVIEW, which stands for Dynamic VIEW, is a multipurpose viewing command that gives you a preview before you actually commit to its view parameters. For instance, when you set a view direction with DVIEW, you can rotate the line of sight in real time to see what your model looks like from various view angles until you find one that suits you. Its zooms and pans are also real-time operations.

DVIEW has 12 command line options, and many of those options have suboptions, which makes DVIEW one of AutoCAD's more complicated and involved commands. It is a powerful command that can create unique views, but it also can be a confusing and intimidating command. With DVIEW, you can

- Set viewpoints in 3D space. Although the DVIEW options produce the same results as the VPOINT command, they work in different ways.

- Set perspective views. Perspective views simulate those of the human eye and of photographs, in which objects appear to become smaller as their distance from the viewer, or camera, increases.

- Remove objects that obstruct or confuse your view of a model. If walls or ceilings prevent you from seeing inside a room, for instance, DVIEW can, in effect, slice through the walls and ceilings. It does this with a clipping plane that makes everything in front of the plane disappear. You also can install a clipping plane that removes everything behind the plane.

AutoCAD 2000, 2000i, and 2002 have a set of commands, including 3DORBIT, 3DCLIP and 3DDISTANCE, that can do everything that DVIEW can do. Nevertheless, you might still prefer to use DVIEW for setting clipping planes, and sometimes for establishing perspective views, because it allows you to easily enter specific point coordinates. Also, DVIEW's twist option is useful for

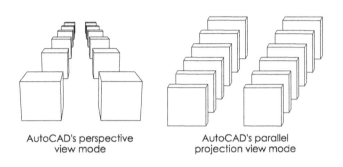

AutoCAD's perspective view mode

AutoCAD's parallel projection view mode

straightening views that have become tilted when view directions have been set in real time. The new commands for establishing view commands are discussed later in this chapter.

Because DVIEW uses previews to help set viewing parameters, it starts by prompting you to select the objects that are to be shown in the previews. All other objects then disappear from the screen for the duration of the command. When you exit DVIEW, all objects are restored and reflect the new view parameters.

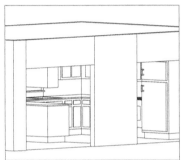

The room interior is obscured by walls.

Clipping planes allow you to see inside the room.

Your choice of preview objects is important. Too many objects can make the previews slow and confusing. On the other hand, you won't obtain a representative preview if you don't have enough objects, or you don't select the proper objects. If you don't select any objects at all, AutoCAD automatically creates a simple 3D surface model house for the previews. It is not a good choice for previews, however, because few of the parameters you establish with it are suitable for your model.

The DVIEW command often uses the words *target* and *camera* in its options. Target refers to the point in space in which the view direction, or line of sight, is pointing; camera refers to the point on the opposite end of the line of sight. For the DVIEW options that establish general view directions (the Camera, Target, and Point Selection options), these two points indicate only a viewing direction. Their actual location in space is not important, but the direction defined by a line drawn between them is important. However, for the DVIEW options related to perspective views (the Points and Distance options) and clipping planes (the Points and Clip options), the point locations of the target and camera are very important.

| Command: | DVIEW |
|---|---|
| Purpose: | DVIEW is a general-purpose viewing command. Within the current viewport, it can set 3D view directions, eliminate portions of 3D models from the view that are in front or in back of clipping planes, create perspective views, and rotate the view about the view's line of sight. |
| Initiate with: | • On the command line, enter DVIEW. |
| Options: | DVIEW starts with a prompt for you to select the objects that are to be viewed dynamically: |

`Select objects or <use DVIEWBLOCK>: Select objects or press the Enter key.`

Objects that are not included in the selection set disappear from the screen during the DVIEW command. Objects that are included are viewed in real time during the various options of DVIEW. Upon exiting DVIEW, all objects within the viewing area are restored with the selected DVIEW options in effect.

AutoCAD often uses the terms *camera* and *target* in DVIEW's options. Initially, the target is positioned approximately in the center of the viewport, and the camera is located somewhere along the line of sight.

If you press the Enter key when prompted to select objects, AutoCAD displays a 3D surface model house that you can view dynamically as you set various DVIEW options instead of objects from your own model.

The DVIEW preview house

After you specify the objects to be shown in the previews or press the Enter key to display the preview house, AutoCAD switches to the World Coordinate System (WCS) — provided the system variable **worldview** is set to its default value of 1 — and displays the following menu of DVIEW options on the command line:

`CAmera/TArget/Distance/POints/PAn/Zoom/TWist/CLip/Hide/Off/Undo: (Select an option,`
`    press Enter, or pick a point.)`

When you select an option, this menu is redisplayed when you have finished the option. Cancelling a partially completed option also returns control to this menu. Press the Enter key to end the command. The current viewport is redrawn to reflect the parameters established through DVIEW.

| • Point Selection | This option rotates the preview objects about the selected point. It takes effect when you pick a point with your pointing device in response to the main DVIEW menu. You cannot enter point coordinates on the command line, and you cannot use an object snap to specify the point. |
|---|---|

The option displays the prompt:

`Enter direction and magnitude angles: (Enter two angles, between 0`
`    and 360 degrees, separated by a comma, or specify a point`
`    with your pointing device.)`

The direction angle represents a rotation angle about an axis that is through the picked point and parallel with the horizontal sides of the viewport. The magnitude angle is a rotation angle about an axis that is through the picked point and parallel with the vertical sides of the viewport.

AutoCAD anchors a rubber-band line on the picked point and dynamically rotates the preview objects about the point as you move your pointing device. Horizontal movement of your pointing device rotates the view about a vertical axis, while vertical movement rotates the view about a horizontal axis.

• Camera

This option sets a view direction based on a horizontal angle in the X-Y plane from the WCS X axis and a vertical angle from the X-Y plane. It is basically the same as VPOINT's rotate option, even though its prompts and input sequence are entirely different. Despite its name, the Camera option does not set an exact camera location.

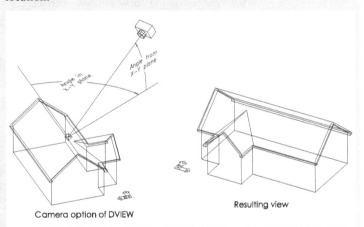

Camera option of DVIEW

Resulting view

You can specify the view-direction rotation angles by entering them on the command line or by picking a point as the preview objects appear to rotate on the screen. When you move your pointing device sideways, the screen cursor moves horizontally and the preview objects rotates in the X-Y plane. When you move the cursor vertically, the preview objects rotate from the X-Y plane.

- Target

Like the Camera option, the Target option sets a viewing direction through the input of two angles. The angle directions, however, are from the camera to the target, rather than from the target to the camera. Despite its name, this option does not set the target location. You can specify the view direction by entering the angles on the command line or

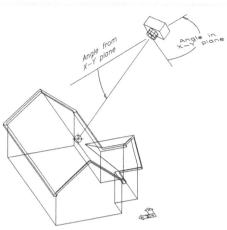

Target option of DVIEW

by picking a point as the preview objects appear to rotate on the screen. The preview objects will be a mirror image of those shown in the Camera option.

- Distance

This option performs two functions: It sets the camera's distance from the target, and changes the viewing mode from a parallel projection to a perspective view. The viewer's eye point for the perspective view is at the camera point. This option displays the command line prompt:

```
Specify new camera-target distance <current>: (Enter a distance or
    press Enter.)
```

The camera is located on the current line of sight (the viewing direction). A slider bar is positioned at the top of the screen and can be used to specify a distance. This slider bar is graduated from 0x to 16x, with 1x representing the current distance. You also can enter the distance from the camera to the target on the command line.

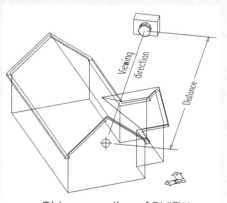

Distance option of DVIEW

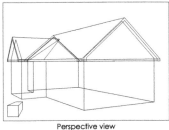

Parallel projection view | Perspective view

- **Points**

The target and camera points are set through this option. It first issues a command line prompt for the target location:

```
Specify target point <current>: (Specify a point or press Enter.)
```

AutoCAD anchors a rubber-band line on the new target point and prompts for a camera point:

```
Specify camera point <current>: (Specify a point or press Enter.)
```

If the perspective mode is active, AutoCAD temporarily turns it off as you specify the target and camera points. Any method can be used to specify the points. In the accompanying figure, the absolute coordinates shown are being used for the target's point, and relative polar coordinates are being

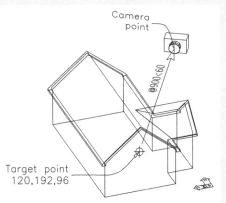

Setting a target and camera point

used to establish the camera's point. The parallel projection and perspective views shown in the previous figure are based on the target and camera points shown in this figure.

- **Pan**

This option shifts the view image without changing the viewing direction or zoom level. It performs a real-time pan, based on the command line prompts:

```
Specify displacement base point: (Specify a point.)
Specify second point: (Specify a point.)
```

- **Zoom**

DVIEW's Zoom option performs a real-time zoom. A slider bar, graduated from 0x to 16x, is displayed near the top of the viewport and can be used to set the zoom level. Pressing your pointing device's pick button selects the indicated zoom level. The current zoom level is 1x. A command line prompt is also shown. For parallel projection views, the command line prompt is

Specify zoom scale factor <1>: (Enter a value or press Enter.)

Values less than 1 zoom back, while values greater than 1 zoom in. You do not have to include an x with the value, as you do with AutoCAD's standard ZOOM command.

If the perspective mode is active, the command line prompt is

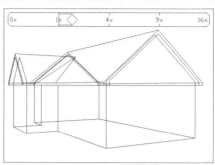

DVIEW's Zoom option

Specify lens length <current>: (Enter a value or press Enter.)

AutoCAD expresses lens length in millimeters. 50mm gives a view similar to a normal lens on a 35mm camera. Entering a value less than 50mm zooms in, acting like a wide-angle camera lens, while values greater than 50mm zooms back, similar to the telephoto lens of a camera.

- Twist  This option rotates the view about the line of sight. It issues the prompt

Specify view twist angle <current>: (Enter a value, specify a
    rotation angle, or press Enter.)

AutoCAD anchors a rubber-band line at the center of the viewport, and the view rotates about the viewport center as you move your pointing device. Picking a point fixes the view as it is shown. You also can enter an angle value, ranging from 0 to 360 degrees. This value is not a relative angle from the current one. A twist angle of 0 causes the vertical lines on the model to be vertical in the view, and a 90-degree twist angle causes the vertical lines on the model to be horizontal.

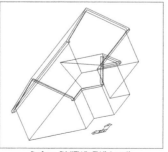
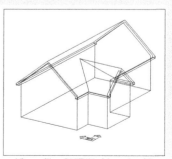

Before DVIEW's TWist option          View with a DVIEW twist angle of 0

• Clip

This option enables you to locate planes, called *clipping planes*, that hide sections of your model. These planes are invisible, have an infinite size, and are always perpendicular to the line of sight. There are two types of clipping planes — *front* clipping planes, which hide everything from the plane toward the camera, and *back* clipping planes, which hide everything from the plane away from the camera.

The option uses the following command line prompt:

```
Enter clipping option [Back/Front/Off] <Off>: (Enter an option or
    press Enter)
```

• Off

This option turns off all clipping planes. (When the perspective viewing mode is being used, AutoCAD automatically places a front clipping plane at the camera. This option has no effect on that clipping plane.)

• Back

This option establishes and controls back clipping planes. AutoCAD displays a nongraduated slider bar at the top of the viewport that can be used to set the clipping plane location. As you move the slider, the appearance of the DVIEW preview objects reflect the effect of the clipping plane. Pressing the pick button on your pointing device fixes the location of the clipping plane. The option also displays the command line prompt:

```
Specify distance from target or [ON/OFF] < <current>: (Enter an
    option, enter a distance, or press Enter)
```

The OFF option turns off the back clipping plane, but it remains in place. The ON option turns the back clipping plane on again, at the current location. Entering a distance specifies the location of the back clipping plane along the line of sight from the target. Positive values locate the plane toward the camera, while negative numbers locate it away from the camera (behind the target).

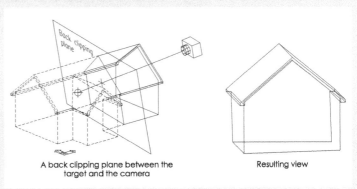

A back clipping plane between the
target and the camera

Resulting view

- Front

This option manages front clipping planes. A slider bar, with no graduations, is displayed at the top of the viewport. As you move your pointing device sideways, the slider moves and the display of the DVIEW preview objects indicate the location of the front clipping plane. Pressing your pointing device's pick button fixes the clipping-plane position. The option also displays the following command line prompt:

```
Specify distance from target or [set to Eye(camera)/ON/OFF]
    <current>: (Enter an option, enter a distance, or press
    Enter)
```

The Eye option places the front clipping plane at the camera point. OFF turns off the front clipping plane, and ON turns a previously turned off clipping plane on again. You cannot turn the front clipping plane off if the perspective view mode is active. Positive distance values place the front clipping plane toward the camera, and negative values place it behind the target (from the camera).

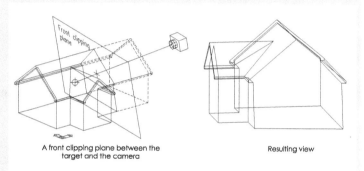

A front clipping plane between the target and the camera                    Resulting view

- Hide

This DVIEW option suppresses the view of objects behind opaque objects. Upon exiting the DVIEW command, or the implementation of another DVIEW option, hidden objects are restored.

- Off

The perspective view mode is turned off, and parallel projection is restored by this option.

- Undo

This option cancels the results of the last DVIEW option. You can repeatedly use Undo to step back through all the DVIEW operations to the start of the command.

Notes:

- The 3D surface model house that DVIEW displays when you press the Enter key in response to the Select Objects prompt is an internal block named DVIEWBLOCK. You can create your own DVIEWBLOCK block. If you do, it should fit in a 1x1x1-unit cube, and its insert point should be in its lower-left corner.

- Your selection set of preview objects is important. If you select too many objects, the dynamic previews of the DVIEW options and settings will be slow and might be confusing. On the other hand, if you do not select enough objects, or if you do not select representative objects, the previews might not display the information you need.

- Most of the time you will use DVIEW to set up perspective views and clipping planes, rather than to establish view directions. In the process of setting perspective views and clipping planes, however, you might need to set a view direction within DVIEW. Then, you will probably use the Camera option when you want to set specific viewpoint rotation angles, and the Point Selection option for dynamically setting a viewpoint. When you use the Point Selection option, you should pick a point near the geometric center of your preview objects to minimize skewing.

- The view-direction angles in the Camera and Target options are from opposite directions. Thus, the Camera view direction angles of 30 degrees from the X-Y plane and -55 degrees in the X-Y plane from the X axis result in the same view direction as the Target angles of -30 degrees from the X-Y plane and 125 degrees in the X-Y plane. You are not likely to find the Target option helpful.

- DVIEW's Twist option is useful for straightening out views that became skewed during the Camera, Target, or Point Selection options. It is also useful for setting up auxiliary views in paper space floating viewports. See Section 4 for a description of paper space floating viewports.

- The start and stop points for rendering fog are based on the distance from the camera to the back clipping plane. See Chapter 20 for a discussion of rendering fog.

| Related system variables: | | |
|---|---|---|
| | • **backz** | This read-only system variable stores the distance of the back clipping plane from the target. This distance is along the line of sight. |
| | • **frontz** | The distance from the front clipping plane to the target is stored in this read-only system variable. The distance is along the line of sight. |
| | • **lenslength** | The current zoom level for perspective views is stored in this read-only system variable. The units are in millimeters, with the effects similar to those of a camera lens. |
| | • **target** | This read-only system variable holds the 3D point location of the target. |
| | • **viewdir** | The view direction of the current viewport is stored in this read-only system variable. It is a 3D point location that represents an offset from the target point. |
| | • **viewmode** | The integer number in this read-only variable is the sum of the following bit values: |

| Bit Value | Condition |
|---|---|
| 1 | Perspective viewing mode is on. |
| 2 | Front clipping plane is on. |
| 4 | Back clipping plane is on. |
| 8 | UCS follow mode is on (**ucsfollow** is set to 1). |
| 16 | The front clipping plane is not at the camera (eye). |

- **viewtwist**    This read-only system variable stores the twist angle within the current viewport.
- **worldview**    When **worldview** is set to its default value of 1, the DVIEW command temporarily restores the WCS, and all view directions are based on WCS coordinates and directions. When **worldview** is set to 0, view directions are set according to the current UCS.

# Using the 3D Orbit Commands

Beginning with AutoCAD 2000, AutoCAD has a set of seven commands for dynamically establishing views in 3D space. They are 3DORBIT, 3DCORBIT, 3DSWIVEL, 3DDISTANCE, 3DCLIP, 3DPAN, and 3DZOOM. You can initiate any of them through the 3D Orbit toolbar, as well as by entering their name on the command line. Even though they are separate commands, you will often use them as if they were options of a single command because they are linked to 3DORBIT, they are often referred to as the 3D Orbit commands.

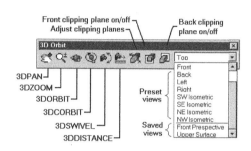

The 3D Orbit commands work in conjunction with the SHADEMODE viewing options. When any of SHADEMODE's shaded options or its hidden option is in effect, that viewing mode is retained during the 3D Orbit operations; if the 2D wireframe mode is in effect, the viewing mode automatically switches to SHADEMODE's 3D wireframe mode.

Parameters for the 3D Orbit commands are set dynamically in real time, even for shaded viewing modes. However, depending on the complexity of the model and your computer's speed and memory, images can degrade from shaded to wireframe to a bounding-box representation. If objects have been selected prior to initiating a 3D orbit operation, only the selected objects are displayed, which might improve dynamic viewing.

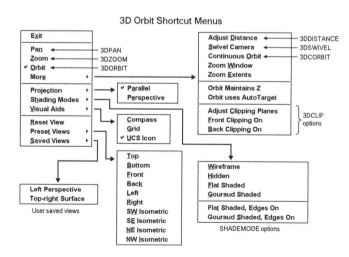

3D Orbit Shortcut Menus

You also can turn off degradation. To do this, start the OPTION command, select the Systems tab, and then click the Current 3D Graphics Display Properties button to open the 3D Graphics Display Properties Configuration. In this dialog box, clear the Adaptive Degradation checkbox.

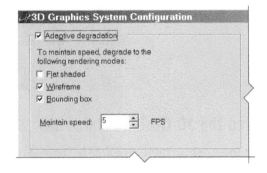

After any 3D Orbit command has been started, you can press the return button of your pointing device to display shortcut menus that allow you to invoke another view-related command or operation. With the options in these menus, you can do anything that the DVIEW command can do, except twist the view. Moreover, they are generally easier to work with than DVIEW.

The options in the 3D Orbit shortcut menu are described in the following paragraphs.

| | |
|---|---|
| Exit | Returns to the AutoCAD editing mode. |
| Pan | Initiates 3DPAN. |
| Zoom | Initiates 3DZOOM. |
| Orbit | Initiates 3DORBIT. |
| More | Opens a menu for initiating 3DDISTANCE, 3DSWIVEL, 3DCORBIT, Zoom Window, Zoom Extents, and specific options of 3DCLIP. The Orbit Maintains Z option locks the current orientation of the Z axis as you rotate the viewing direction with 3DORBIT. The AutoTarget option places the 3DORBIT view rotation center at the geometric center of the objects, rather than in the center of the viewport. |
| Projection | Opens a menu for toggling between the parallel and perspective viewing modes. A check mark indicates which mode is current. |
| Shading Modes | Opens a menu for setting all the SHADEMODE viewing modes, except 2D wireframe. |
| Visual Aids | Opens a menu for turning AutoCAD's compass, grid, and UCS icon on and off. The grid is displayed as a grid of lines, rather than dots. |
| Reset View | Restores the view that was current when the 3D Orbit operation started. |
| Preset Views | Opens a menu for setting one of the six orthographic views or one of the four isometric views that look down on the XY plane. The views are based on the WCS, and they do not affect the current UCS. |
| Saved Views | This option, which is available only if one or more user-saved views exist, opens a secondary menu that lists all user-saved views. Click a view name to restore the view. |

The CAMERA command is included in this discussion of the 3D Orbit commands, even though it does not appear on the 3D Orbit toolbar or in the 3D Orbit shortcut menus. Nevertheless, the CAMERA command is an important component of the 3D Orbit commands because it sets exact camera and target points — both of which are critical in setting perspective views and in positioning clipping planes.

| | |
|---|---|
| Command: | 3DORBIT |
| Purpose: | Dynamically sets viewpoints in 3D space. |
| Initiate with: | • On the command line, enter 3DORBIT. |
| | • From the View pull-down menu, select 3D Orbit. |
| | • Select Orbit from the 3D Orbit shortcut menu. |
| | • Select 3D Orbit from the 3D Orbit toolbar or the Standard toolbar. |
| | • Select 3D Orbit from the PAN or ZOOM shortcut menu. |
| Implementation: | When 3DORBIT starts, AutoCAD displays a large circle in the center of the current viewport. This circle is called the *arcball*, and small circles are centered on its quadrants. The compass, if it is displayed, coincides with the arcball. |

You set view directions in 3DORBIT by moving the screen cursor with your pointing device as you hold down its pick button. Your model will appear to revolve as you move the screen cursor, and when you have a view direction you like, release the pick button to set the view direction. To exit the command, select Exit from the 3D Orbit shortcut menu, or press the Enter or Esc keys.

The orientation of the axis about which your model appears to rotate depends on where the screen cursor is located when you press the pick button. Also, the form of the screen cursor changes to indicate the rotation-axis orientation. The screen cursor forms and orientations of the axis of rotation are described in the following paragraphs.

• When the cursor is within the arcball, its form is sphere encircled by a horizontal and a vertical circle. The viewpoint rotation angle axis is 90 degrees to the direction that the cursor is moved. For example, if you move the cursor down and to the right 45 degrees, the image rotates about an axis that passes through the center of the viewport (or, if AutoTarget is on, through the geometric center of the model) and is tilted 45 degrees from the edges of the viewport.

• When the cursor is outside the arcball, the screen cursor becomes a dot within a circular arrow, and the 3D model rotates about the viewport's line of sight.

• When the cursor is within either of the small circles at the top and bottom of the arcball, it assumes the form of a horizontal line that serves as an axis for a circular arrow. The view rotation axis is parallel with the horizontal sides of the viewport.

- When the cursor is within either of the small circles on the right and left quadrants of the arcball, it takes on the shape of a vertical line that serves as the axis of a circular arrow. The view then rotates about an axis that is parallel with the vertical sides of the viewport.

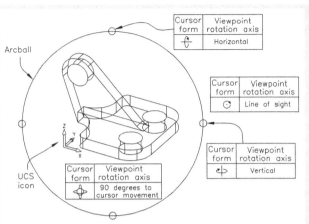

**Notes:**

- Unlike with the VPOINT and DVIEW commands, the X, Y, and Z axes orientation of the current UCS is used with 3DORBIT, rather than that of the WCS.
- The Orbit Maintains Z option in the 3D Orbit shortcut menu locks the current orientation of the Z axis as you rotate the viewing direction. This option, which first appeared in AutoCAD 2000i, is especially useful in architectural models to keep walls and such upright.
- The AutoTarget option in the 3D Orbit shortcut menu was introduced in AutoCAD 2002. It sets the point through which the orbit rotation axis passes through in the geometric center of the objects you are viewing, rather than in the center of the viewport. By default, this option is active.

| | |
|---|---|
| Command: | 3DCORBIT |
| Purpose: | Continually rotates the viewpoint in 3D space. |
| Initiate with: | • On the command line, enter 3DCORBIT. |
| | • From the 3D Orbit shortcut menu, select More, and then select Continuous Orbit. |
| | • From the 3D Orbit toolbar, select 3D Continuous Orbit. |
| Implementation: | The arcball disappears and the screen cursor changes to a sphere encircled by two arc-shaped arrows having axes that are 45 degrees to the edges of the viewport. Click the pick button of your pointing device, drag the cursor, and release the pick button. The model rotates about an axis that passes through the center of the viewport, or through the center of the model if AutoTarget is on, and is perpendicular to the direction that the cursor was moved. Moreover, the rate of rotation is proportional to the speed of the cursor movement. To stop the rotation, click the pointing device pick button again. Press Enter or Esc to end the command. |

| | |
|---|---|
| Command: | 3DSWIVEL |
| Purpose: | Sets a viewpoint by swiveling the camera about a fixed point. |
| Initiate with: | • On the command line, enter 3DSWIVEL. |
| | • From the 3D Orbit shortcut menu, select More, and then select Swivel Camera. |
| | • From the 3D Orbit toolbar, select 3D Swivel. |
| Implementation: | Unlike 3DORBIT, which sets a view direction by moving the camera about in 3D space as it is pointed toward a fixed target, 3DSWIVEL sets a view direction by locking the camera in a fixed location and swiveling it toward a movable target. The effect is as if you were looking through the viewfinder of a camera that is on a tripod; when you swivel the camera to the right, objects in the viewfinder shift to the left, and when you swivel the camera upward, objects appear to shift downward. Similarly, when you move the screen cursor to the left, objects on the screen move to the right; when you move the screen cursor up, the screen objects move down. Press Enter or Esc to end the command. |

| | |
|---|---|
| Command: | 3DZOOM |
| Purpose: | Dynamically increases or decreases the apparent size of objects in the current viewport. |
| Initiate with: | • On the command line, enter 3DZOOM. |
| | • From the 3D Orbit shortcut menu, select Zoom. |
| | • From the 3D Orbit toolbar, select 3D Zoom. |
| Implementation: | This command is similar to the real time option of the ZOOM command. The screen cursor changes to a magnifying glass with + and – signs. Press the pick button of your pointing device and drag the screen cursor up to magnify objects, and drag it down to make them smaller. Release the pick button to set the view, and press Enter or Esc to end the command. |
| | The most important difference between real time ZOOM and 3DZOOM is that 3DZOOM works in perspective views, while real time ZOOM, along with the other ZOOM options, does not. 3DZOOM differs from 3DDISTANCE in that it does not change the distance from the camera to the target. |

| | |
|---|---|
| Command: | 3DPAN |
| Purpose: | Dynamically moves objects in the current viewport without changing their apparent size. |
| Initiate with: | • On the command line, enter 3DPAN. |
| | • From the 3D Orbit shortcut menu, select Pan. |
| | • From the 3D Orbit toolbar, select 3D Pan. |

| | |
|---|---|
| Implementation: | Similar to the real-time version of PAN, the screen cursor assumes the shape of a hand. Press the pick button of your pointing device and drag the screen cursor in the direction that you want the objects in the current viewport to move. Release the pick button to set the view, and press Enter or Esc to end the command. |
| | The most important difference between real-time PAN and 3DPAN is that 3DPAN works in perspective views, while real-time PAN does not. In perspective views, the line of sight might appear to rotate as the view is panned. |

| | |
|---|---|
| Command: | CAMERA |
| Purpose: | Sets exact camera and target points. |
| Initiate with: | • On the command line, enter CAMERA. |
| | • From the View toolbar, select Camera. |
| Implementation: | This command is equivalent to the Points option of the DVIEW command. You are prompted from the command line to first specify a camera point, and then to specify a target point. |

| | |
|---|---|
| Command: | 3DDISTANCE |
| Purpose: | Dynamically moves the camera along the line of sight toward or away from the target. |
| Initiate with: | • On the command line, enter 3DDISTANCE. |
| | • From the 3D Orbit shortcut menu, select More, and then select Adjust Distance. |
| | • From the 3D Orbit toolbar, select 3D Adjust distance. |
| Implementation: | Although 3DDISTANCE dynamically changes the apparent size of the model in a manner that seems to be equivalent to 3DZOOM, it makes the size changes by moving the camera, rather than by using a zoom camera–like lens. When you drag the screen cursor up, the camera moves along the line of sight closer to the target; when you drag the cursor down, the camera moves away from the target. Release the pick button to set the distance, and press Enter or Esc to end the command. |

The distance between the camera and the target is important in perspective views. If the camera is too close to the target, the model will be overly

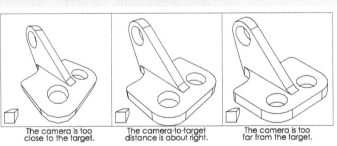

The camera is too close to the target.    The camera-to-target distance is about right.    The camera is too far from the target.

distorted; if it is too far from the target, the perspective mode will not be evident.

| Command: | 3DCLIP |
|---|---|
| Purpose: | 3DCLIP turns front and back clipping planes on and off, and moves their location along the line of sight. |
| Initiate with: | • On the command line, enter 3DCLIP. |
| | • From the 3D Orbit shortcut menu, select More, and then select Adjust Clipping Planes. |
| | • From the 3D Orbit toolbar, select Adjust Clipping Planes. |
| Options: | Clipping planes are two invisible, infinitely sized planes that are perpendicular to a viewport's line of sight. One of these planes is called the front clipping plane, and when it is activated everything from it to the camera is hidden. The other is called the back clipping plane, and it is able to hide everything that is from the plane away from the camera. You can independently move these planes along the line of sight, and you can individually turn them on and off. |

3DCLIP opens a small, square window titled Adjust Clipping Planes over the AutoCAD window. In this window, your 3D model will be shown from a view direction that is perpendicular to the view direction of the current AutoCAD

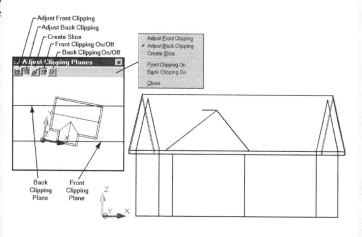

viewport. Two horizontal lines are also in the window that represent the edges of the clipping planes. The target is in the center of the viewport. Near the top of the window is a toolbar for selecting the options of 3DCLIP. You also can right-click anywhere within the window to bring up a shortcut menu that has these same 3DCLIP options.

• Adjust Front Clipping    Use this option to move the front clipping plane. Press the pick button of your pointing device, and move the screen cursor up or down to drag the front clipping along the line of sight. As you drag the clipping plane, the effect of the clipping plane location is dynamically shown in the current AutoCAD viewport.

- Adjust Back Clipping

  You move the back clipping plane with this option. Press the pick button of your pointing device, and drag the back clipping plane along the line of sight by moving the screen cursor up or down. The effect of the clipping plane location is dynamically shown in the current AutoCAD viewport as you drag the back clipping plane.

- Create Slice

  This option locks the current positions of the front and back clipping planes relative to each other, and allows you to drag them in tandem along the line of sight.

- Front Clipping On/Off

  This option activates or deactivates the front clipping plane.

- Back Clipping On/Off

  Use this option to activate or deactivate the back clipping plane.

Notes:

- The front and back clipping planes can be in the same location, but the front clipping plane cannot be further from the camera than the back clipping plane.

- When any of the toolbar buttons are active, its outline is drawn to give the button the appearance of being depressed. Moreover, the shortcut menu will have a check mark beside each active option.

- You also can turn the clipping planes on or off through options on the 3D orbit toolbar and in the More shortcut menu.

- When you start the 3DCLIP command, the front clipping plane is automatically turned on. Depending on the location of the front clipping plane, this can cause portions, or even all, of your model to disappear.

# Setting Up Perspective Views

Often, especially with models of structures and rooms, you will set up a perspective view as preparation for a rendering. AutoCAD perspective views are strictly for viewing because you cannot use your pointing device in them. If your model needs some editing or additions, you must do it in a viewport that shows the model in a parallel projection viewing mode. Also, you cannot use AutoCAD's ZOOM and PAN commands in viewports with perspective views — you must use DVIEW's versions of those operations or 3DZOOM and 3DPAN to adjust the view. And, you should not use VPOINT or PLAN for changing the view direction because these commands change the mode back to the parallel projection mode.

Creating a perspective view is not an especially complicated operation, but it does require some forethought, and you should expect to make changes and adjustments before you achieve the results you want. The parameters involved in setting up a perspective view are the view direction, the distance from the target to the camera, and the zoom level. The distance between the target and the camera is especially important. If it is too long, the perspective view will look like a parallel projection view, and if it is too close, the view will be grossly distorted. You can create perspective views with either DVIEW or the 3D Orbit options.

If they are not set up correctly, perspective views can be grossly distorted.

## Using DVIEW to Create Perspective Views

The steps you will most likely use in setting up a perspective view when you use DVIEW are as follows:

1. Establish the view direction. You can do this before you start DVIEW through the VPOINT or 3DORBIT commands, or within DVIEW with its Camera, Target, or Point Selection options.

2. Use DVIEW's Distance option to establish the initial zoom level and turn on the perspective viewing mode. You might possibly, or even probably, change the distance value after you see what your perspective view looks like, but a distance that is roughly equal to twice the width of the model section or side that will be shown is a good distance for the first try.

3. Use DVIEW's Zoom and Pan options to adjust the view, and use its Hide option for a clearer look at the model. If the model is severely distorted, go back to the Distance option and increase the distance between the target and the camera. If the model looks too much like it does in a parallel projection view, decrease the distance.

Differences in personal preferences means there are no right or wrong target-to-camera distances or zoom levels. Many people tend to favor a distance that gives a perspective zoom level of about 50mm (you will recall that AutoCAD uses the analogy of camera lens focal lengths, in units of millimeters, when referring to zoom levels for perspective views), but many people prefer a smaller one — perhaps even 35mm.

## Using 3DORBIT to Create Perspective Views

Setting up perspective views with the 3D Orbit commands and options is generally easier than with DVIEW. The steps in using them to create a perspective view are

1. Establish a view direction with 3DORBIT.

2. Use the Zoom and Pan options from 3DORBIT's shortcut menu to adjust the size and position of the model's image.

3. Open 3DORBIT's Projection shortcut menu and select Perspective. AutoCAD automatically sets an appropriate camera-to-target distance.

To increase or decrease the angle at which parallel edges on the model appear to converge, use the 3DDISTANCE command to move the camera toward or away from the target. Use 3DPAN and 3DZOOM to adjust the size and position of the model in the perspective view.

# Controlling Clipping Planes

Clipping planes are invisible walls of infinite size that are perpendicular to the view direction. The front clipping plane hides everything between the clipping plane and the camera. The back clipping plane hides everything from the clipping plane away from the camera. They are especially useful when you are setting up views of building interiors. Also, the back clipping plane is used as a reference location for fog, or depth cueing, in AutoCAD renderings. See Chapter 20 for information about fog within renderings.

You have full control over both clipping planes. They can be turned on and off independently so they can be used singly or together. You also can move each of them independently. You can't tilt the clipping planes; they are always perpendicular to the line of sight (the view direction).

Just as in setting up perspective views, setting up clipping planes requires some planning along with a knowledge of the dimensions and locations of key points on your model. The parameters to consider when setting up a clipping plane are the target location, the view direction, whether the plane is a front or back clipping plane, and the plane's distance from the target.

After a clipping plane has been turned on, it remains in effect even if the view direction changes. Clipping planes can be used in perspective views. In fact, AutoCAD automatically positions a front clipping plane at the camera when the perspective mode is active to prevent objects behind the camera from showing up when extremely close zooms are in effect.

### Establishing Clipping Planes with DVIEW

Although setting up clipping planes is easier with the 3D Orbit commands, you will still use DVIEW when you need to establish specific target and camera points and exact distances from the target to the clipping planes. The steps to set up clipping planes with the DVIEW command are as follows:

1. Establish the target point with DVIEW's Points option.

2. Establish the view direction. Within DVIEW this can be conveniently done at the same time you set the target location within the Points option, by using relative coordinates to set the camera point. Polar and cylindrical relative coordinates are especially convenient.

3. Use DVIEW's Clip option to select the type of clipping plane and set its distance from the target. In architectural models, you will use a front clipping plane to remove walls and other obstructions that are between the clipping plane and the camera.

4. If you want to create a perspective view, choose DVIEW's Distance option, and then zoom and pan until you achieve the view you desire.

## Establishing Clipping Planes with 3DCLIP

Use the following steps to set up clippling planes with 3DORBIT and the 3DCLIP options:

1. Use 3DORBIT to establish the view direction.

2. Select the More option from the 3DORBIT shortcut menu, and select Front Clipping On and/ or Back Clipping On. Front clipping removes obstructing objects that are between the front clipping plane and the camera, while back clipping removes objects that are behind the back clipping plane relative to the camera.

3. Select Adjust Clipping Planes form 3DORBIT's More menu to display the Adjust Clipping Planes window. In this window, use the cursor to move the clipping plane along the viewport's line of sight toward or away from the target. You also can move the target along the line of sight. As you move the clipping plane, the results are dynamically displayed in the current viewport. Working with a shaded viewing mode helps you visualize the effects of the clipping plane location better than a wireframe or hidden-line mode.

4. For a perspective view, select Perspective from the 3DORBIT shortcut menu, and use the Zoom, Pan, Adjust Distance, and Orbit options to achieve the view you desire.

## Exercises

The following two exercises give you some experience in setting up perspective views and clipping planes. The first exercise sets up a perspective view of the 3D surface model house you have been working with. The second exercise uses a 3D surface model kitchen to set up a cutting plane and a perspective view. Neither of these exercises requires you to draw anything.

### Exercise One

In this exercise, you will create a perspective view of the 3D house you started as a wireframe model in Chapter 4. You added surfaces to the walls and roof of the house in Chapter 6, but it still contained holes where the doors and windows were to be installed. A more complete version of the model is in file f0737.dwg on the CD-ROM, and you should retrieve and use that model for this perspective view exercise.

This version of the house, which is shown in Figure 1-1, has doors and windows. No object types or techniques that you are not familiar with were used in making the doors and windows. They are

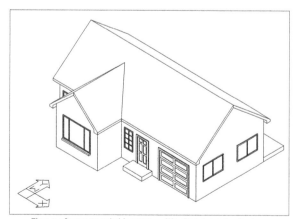

The surface model house, with doors and windows

Figure 1-1

made primarily from 3D faces, although a few polyface meshes and extrusions were also used.

You will first use DVIEW to set the per-spective view. After you have opened the file, start the DVIEW command. For pre-view objects, you can select just the roof and the siding, but selecting everything will not cause any problems, because most of the previews are for zooms and pans.

First, set the view direction. From the main DVIEW menu, choose the Camera option by entering the letters *ca* or the entire word *camera*. AutoCAD will first prompt for an angle from the X-Y plane and then for one in the X-Y plane (the reverse of the sequence used by the VPOINT command).

View of house after using DVIEW's camera option to set the view direction to 0 degrees from the X-Y plane, and -115 degrees in the X-Y plane from the X axis

Figure 1-2

```
Specify camera location, or enter angle from XY
    plane or [Toggle (angle in)] <35.2655>: 0
    (Enter)
Specify camera angle location, or enter angle in
    XY plane from X axis, or [Toggle (angle
    from)] <-45.0000>: -115 (Enter)
```

In VPOINT, you would most likely enter the angle in the X-Y plane as 245 degrees, but DVIEW does not permit horizontal angles greater than 180 degrees, so you must enter a negative number.

The view will change to look edge-on to the X-Y plane showing the front-left side of the house, as shown in Figure 1-2. The main DVIEW menu is displayed again. This time, select the Distance option by entering the letter *d* or the entire word *distance*. DVIEW prompts for a new tar-get-to-camera distance:

```
Specify new camera-target distance <0'-1 3/4">: 960 (Enter)
```

If you are using architectural units, you can enter 960 as 80' (do not overlook the apostrophe). Before you enter this value, you might want to observe the screen as you move the slider bar back and forth. However, your target-to-camera distance is probably so close that no meaningful image is displayed. Therefore, the command line numerical input is the best way to set the distance.

The image of the house will most likely recede into the distance. To bring it in closer, choose DVIEW's Zoom option. A slider bar appears at the top of the screen, and as you move the slider to the right, the house becomes larger. The zoom level, in millimeters, is updated on the status line as you move the slider bar. Also, the the zoom level currently in effect is displayed in a command line prompt, and you can enter a new lens length value.

```
Specify lens length <11.888>: 50 (Enter) (Or,
  move the slider until the house looks right
  to you.)
```

Lastly, use DVIEW's Pan option to center the house, and use Hide to make sure the house looks as you want it to look. When you are satisfied, exit the DVIEW command. Your house should look similar to the one in Figure 1-3 when HIDE is on.

Perspective view of the house, with a DVIEW zoom level of 50mm

Figure 1-3

Now use the following steps to use the 3D Orbit commands and options to set a perspective view.

1. Invoke VPOINT, and enter the view coordinates of 1,-1,1. In addition to establishing an SE isometric viewpoint, this turns off the perspective mode.

2. Invoke 3DORBIT. Starting from the small circle on the bottom quadrant of the arcball, rotate the view direction to about 0 degrees from the X-Y plane. Then, start from the small circle on the left quadrant of the arcball, and rotate the view direction to about minus 45 degrees from the X axis. Rotating the view direction with these two steps minimizes twist.

3. From 3DORBIT's shortcut menu, select Shading Modes, and then Flat Shaded.

4. From 3DORBIT's shortcut menu, turn on the perspective projection mode.

5. Use the Pan, Zoom, and Adjust Distance options from the shortcut menus until you are satisfied with the view. You will probably have to alternate several times between the Zoom and Adjust Distance options before you get the view you want.

### Exercise Two

In this exercise, you set up a perspective view of the 3D surface model kitchen shown in Figure 2-1. Because the kitchen has walls, you also need to set up a front clipping plane so you can see inside the kitchen. This model is on the CD-ROM that accompanies this book in a file named f0740.dwg. Architectural feet and inch units are in effect for this model.

The inside dimensions for this kitchen are 24 feet long (in the X direction), 16 feet wide (in the Y direction), and 9 feet high (in the Z direction). The walls are 6 inches thick. The WCS origin is on the inside lower-left corner of the kitchen. The left half of the kitchen, which is for dining, is not furnished in this model.

You will make a perspective view of the right half — the cooking half — of the kitchen. To do this you will position the target slightly outside the room, behind the sink and the window, at a height of 6 feet. Its coordinates will be 18',18',6'. The view direction will be rotated 15 degrees from the Y axis (equivalent to the view rotation angle of 105 degrees clockwise from the X axis), and you will place a front clipping plane 15 feet in front of the target. These locations are shown in Figure 2-2. The section of the room that you want to show is roughly 16 feet wide, so you will place the camera 32 feet from the target. (In Figure 2-2, the target-to-camera distance is not to scale.) It will be outside the room, but the front clipping plane allows you to see the kitchen interior.

First, use DVIEW to set up the front clipping plane. Open the file, invoke the DVIEW command, and select most of the objects on the right side of the room for preview objects. You can even select everything in the model. Then, choose DVIEW's Points option by entering the letters *po*, or the entire word *points*. AutoCAD issues prompts for the target point and the camera point:

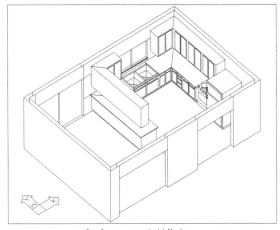

Surface model kitchen

Figure 2-1

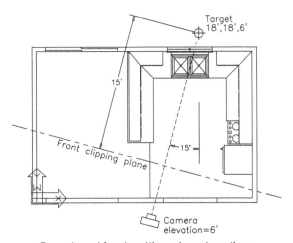

Target and front cutting plane locations

Figure 2-2

```
Specify target point <10'-0.0000", 8'-4.0000", 2'-11.0000">: 18',18',6' (Enter)
Specify camera point <9'-11.4375", 8'-3.3725", 2'-11.5736">: @32'<-105 (Enter)
```

Be certain to include the apostrophes, which signify that the input is in units of feet, when entering the coordinates. Notice that relative polar coordinates were used to specify the camera location. AutoCAD keeps the elevation of the resulting view direction at 6 feet. As soon as you enter the camera's location, AutoCAD switches to an edge-on view of the X-Y plane.

Choose DVIEW's Clip option next by entering the letters *cl*, or the entire word *clip*, on the command line. AutoCAD asks you what type of clipping plane you want and for its distance from the target.

```
Enter Clipping Option [Back/Front/Off] <Off>: F (Enter)
Specify distance from target or [set to [Eye (camera)/ON/OFF] <31'-11.9996">: 15' (Enter)
```

You can use the slider at the top of the viewport to set the clipping plane distance from the target, but with your viewpoint, you can't see where it actually is or its effects, so this command line input of 15 feet is the best way to locate the clipping plane.

Now choose DVIEW's Distance option to turn on the perspective viewing mode. Enter the letter *d*, or the entire word *distance*. AutoCAD prompts for a new camera-to-target distance.

```
Specify new camera-target distance <32'-0.0000">: (Enter)
```

Because you previously established the camera-to-target distance that you needed through the Points option, you accepted the default of 32 feet. AutoCAD zooms in and switches to the perspective viewing mode. You should not have to change the zoom level, but you probably will need to use DVIEW's Pan option to center the view, and its Hide option to ensure that your view is as you want it. Lastly, exit the DVIEW command. Your view should be similar to the one shown in Figure 2-3.

Next, you will use the 3D Orbit commands to set up a front clipping plane and a perspective view. Use the VPOINT coordinates of -1,-1,1 to set an SW isometric view of the room and simultaneously turn off the perspective mode. Then take the following steps to set up a front clipping plane and perspective view:

Perspective view with front clipping plane

Figure 2-3

1. Invoke the CAMERA command. In response to the command line prompt for a camera position, enter 10',-13',6'; in response to the prompt for a target position, enter 18',18',6'. Even though this command displays the current camera and target locations in inches, you can use feet when you enter the new values.

2. Invoke the 3DORBIT command. Select Zoom from its shortcut menu, and zoom back until the width of the model fills about one-half of the viewport length. This is to ensure that the entire model is shown in 3DCLIP's Adjust Clipping Planes window.

3. From 3DORBITs Shading Modes shortcut menu, select Hidden.

4. From 3DORBIT's More shortcut menu, select Adjust Clipping Planes.

5. By default, the front clipping plane is turned on, and the Adjust Front Clipping option is active. Drag the front clipping plane down in the Adjust Clipping Planes window until it is between the refrigerator and the front wall of the room. Close the Adjust Clipping Planes window.

6. From 3DORBIT's Projection shortcut menu, select Perspective.

7. Use the shortcut menu options of Zoom and Pan to size and position the image until the room looks similar to the one shown in Figure 2-3.

# CHAPTER 8

# 3D Polygon Mesh Surfaces

*This chapter discusses polygon mesh surfaces that, unlike the planar surfaces of 3DFACE and PFACE, can curve and twist through space, can be rounded, and can have irregular edges.*

*This chapter*

- *describes the characteristics and properties of polygon mesh surfaces;*

- *explains how each of the five AutoCAD commands that make polygon mesh surfaces work, what they can and cannot do, and how they differ from each other;*

- *describes AutoCAD's premade surface objects.*

## Properties of Polygon Mesh Surfaces

With a little ingenuity and imagination, you can use AutoCAD to make surfaces in a surprisingly wide variety of shapes, including shapes that cannot be made as solid models. Generally, these surfaces are made by the RULESURF, TABSURF, EDGESURF, REVSURF, or 3DMESH command.

Although these five commands have different requirements and use different input methods, they make the same type of AutoCAD object — a polygon mesh surface that has the following characteristics:

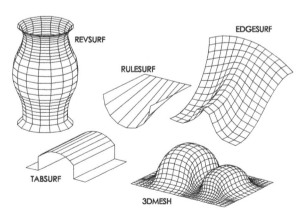

- The surface is generally composed of flat faces, although occasionally, depending on how the surface was created, some faces can be warped. Most of these faces have four sides, although a few have only three sides. Each face is not only similar to a 3D face object (made with the 3DFACE command) — if the surface mesh is exploded, it becomes a set of 3D faces.

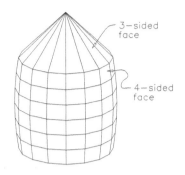

- The faces form a grid of rows and columns, although the rows and columns can bend and turn as they conform to the surface, and the faces are not necessarily uniform in size or shape. Moreover, some surface meshes have only a single row or a single column of faces.

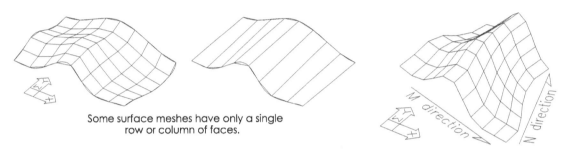

Some surface meshes have only a single row or column of faces.

- To identify the position of each face in the surface grid, AutoCAD establishes an origin on the surface and directions from this origin. AutoCAD calls one the *M direction* and the other the *N direction*. These directions have no relationship to the coordinate system directions, and often they are not even perpendicular to each other.

- Except for the 3DMESH command, AutoCAD controls the number of faces in the M and N directions through system variables **surftab1** and **surftab2**. With the 3DMESH command, the number of faces in both directions are specified as the command is implemented.

- When a surface mesh is wrapped around so that one edge is joined with its opposite edge, it is called a *closed mesh*. A mesh can be closed in the M direction or in the N direction, and if the surface forms a torus, it will be closed in both directions.

- Even though Autodesk's documentation often refers to ruled surfaces, tabulated surfaces, and revolved surfaces, all five commands make the same type of AutoCAD database

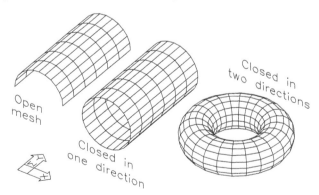

object. They are polygon mesh surfaces, which are a variation of 2D polylines. As a result, they can be edited on a basic level with the PEDIT command (which is discussed in the next chapter).

With the exception of those made through the 3DMESH command, polygon mesh surfaces are based on wireframe boundary objects. RULESURF, for example, makes a surface between two wireframe objects; EDGESURF makes a surface between four wireframe objects; TABSURF extrudes a wireframe object; and REVSURF revolves a wireframe object. When the 3DMESH command is used, the location of each vertex, or node, on the surface mesh must be specified.

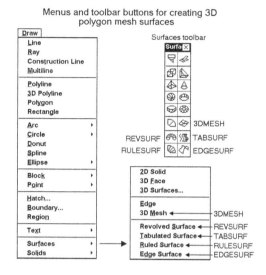

Polygon mesh surfaces are drawn using the current layer, and the boundary objects are retained. You should always use separate layers for surfaces and wireframe objects so you can get one or the other out of the way (by freezing or turning off its layer) as you work with the model.

Polygon mesh directions are potentially confusing because AutoCAD is not consistent with its names and labels. You would think, for instance, that the **surftab1** system variable would apply to either the M or N direction, while **surftab2** would apply to the other direction, but that isn't the case. **Surftab1** sets the number of faces in the M direction for REVSURF and EDGESURF, but it sets the number of faces in the N direction for RULESURF and TABSURF. **Surftab2**, on the other hand, sets the number of faces in the N direction for REVSURF and EDGESURF and has no effect on RULESURF and TABSURF (which have only one face in the M direction). You might find it less confusing when you ignore the M and N directions when setting mesh sizes and concentrate on the actual edges affected by **surftab1** and **surftab2** instead. You will, however, need to know which direction is which when you edit a mesh with PEDIT.

Now that you are familiar with the properties of polygon mesh surfaces, let's take a closer look at each of the five commands that create them. You will see how each command works, what it can and cannot do, and how it differs from the others. After looking at all five commands for making polygon mesh surfaces, you can work through some exercises in using the commands.

| Command: | RULESURF |
|---|---|
| Purpose: | Creates a polygon mesh surface between two wireframe boundaries. |
| Initiate with: | • On the command line, enter RULESURF. |
| | • From the Draw pull-down menu, select Surfaces, and then Ruled Surface from the resulting flyout menu. |
| | • Select the Ruled Surface button from the Surfaces toolbar. |

Implementation:   RULESURF reports the current value of **tabsurf1** and issues command line prompts for two boundary objects:

```
Current wireframe density: SURFTAB1=6
Specify first defining curve: (Select a wireframe object.)
Specify second defining curve: (Select a wireframe object.)
```

You must select the boundary objects by picking a point on them — window and crossing selection methods are not allowed. AutoCAD proceeds as soon as you pick an object — you do not have to press the Enter key. Despite the wording of the prompts, boundary objects do not have to be curved. Arcs, circles, 2D and 3D polylines, splines, lines, and even points can be used as boundaries. The boundaries can be open, such as those made with a line or an arc. or they can be closed, such as those made with a circle. Polylines are considered to be open boundaries even if their start points and endpoints are in the same location, unless they were closed with the Close option of their command or of the PEDIT command. Splines, on the other hand, are considered closed when the start points and endpoints are in the same location, even if the Close option of the SPLINE or SPLINEDIT command was not used.

You cannot mix open and closed boundaries — if one boundary is closed, the other boundary must be closed also. If a point is selected as a defining curve, the other curve cannot be a point. The other defining curve can be either open or closed.

As soon as the two defining curves are picked, AutoCAD constructs a polygon mesh surface between them. Each face on the surface has four sides, and the number of faces equal the value stored in the **surftab1** system variable. The N direction of the surface is along the boundary curves.

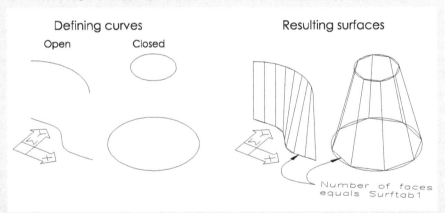

The pick point is important for open boundaries, because AutoCAD considers the end of the boundary closest to the pick point to be the leading edge of the polygon mesh surface. Therefore, you must pick corresponding ends to avoid making a surface that crosses itself.

Points picked on same ends

Curves                     Surface

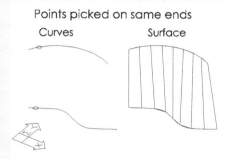

Points picked on opposite ends

Curves                     Surface

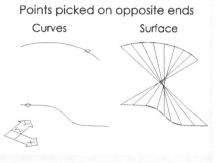

For closed boundaries, the location of the pick point is not important because AutoCAD starts the surface at a predetermined point. If the boundary is a circle, the edge of the first face starts at the first quadrant of the circle and the surface is built counterclockwise (as viewed from the positive Z direction). In most cases, therefore, the surface starts at the quadrant that has the largest X coordinate value, and proceeds counterclockwise. If, however, the **snapang** system variable contains a value other than 0, the start point will be different.

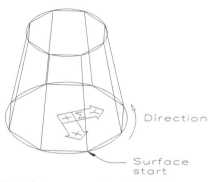

When circles are used as boundary curves, the surface starts at the first quadrant of the circles and is built counterclockwise.

For closed polylines, on the other hand, the surface starts at the last vertex and proceeds toward the first vertex. When a closed spline is used for a boundary curve, the surface begins at the first fit point of the spline and proceeds in the direction of the spline.

Notes:

- As a result of the differences in the surface start points and directions, the surface between a polyline and a circle is seldom satisfactory. In fact, boundaries made from closed polylines are often difficult to work with, and you are generally better off not closing polylines when they are to be used as RULESURF defining curves.

Related system variables:

- **surftab1**    The number of faces in a surface made by RULESURF is equal to the value of **surftab1**. Its initial value is 6.

- **snapang**    This system variable sets the snap/grid rotation angle, and along with that the orientation of the 0 quadrant of circles and arcs. Its default value is 0.0.

## Using RULESURF

The M direction of surfaces made with RULESURF is from one boundary curve to the other. In this direction, there is an edge at the beginning of the surface and another edge at its end. There are no further divisions or any mesh lines in the M direction. The N direction is along the boundary curves, with the number of mesh divisions being controlled by the **surftab1** system variable. Because the edges of each individual face on the surface are straight, the ends of the surface consist of short straight lines that deviate from the boundaries, unless the boundaries are straight. Because there is only one face in the M direction, the surface has straight sides in that direction.

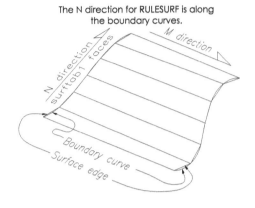

The N direction for RULESURF is along the boundary curves.

Use RULESURF any time one end of the surface is to have a different shape than the other end and the sides of the surface can be straight. Often, you can combine several surfaces, made with RULE-SURF or another surfacing command, to create a complex surface. The accompanying figure shows the steps to make a surface that changes from a round cross-section to a square cross-section. Four surfaces were used to make this surface. You might think that you could make the surface as a single surface using a circle for one boundary and a 2D polyline square for the other, but it is extremely difficult to match circle and polyline boundaries when you use RULESURF.

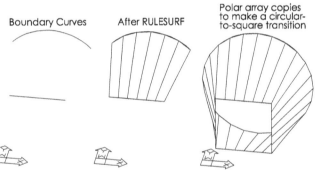

Boundary Curves    After RULESURF    Polar array copies to make a circular-to-square transition

| Command: | TABSURF |
|---|---|
| Purpose: | Creates a polygon mesh surface by extruding a wireframe boundary in a straight-line direction. |
| Initiate with: | • On the command line, enter TABSURF. |
| | • From the Draw pull-down menu, select Surfaces, and then Tabulated Surface from the resulting flyout menu. |
| | • Select the Tabulated Surface button from the Surfaces toolbar. |
| Implementation: | From the command line, TABSURF prompts you to select two wireframe objects: |
| | `Select object for path curve: (Select a wireframe object.)` |
| | `Select object for direction vector: (Select a line or an open polyline.)` |

You must pick a point on these objects to select them. The first object selected defines the shape of the surface. It can be any wireframe object, including 3D polylines and splines. Moreover, it can

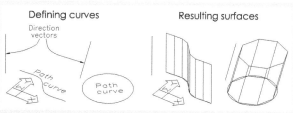

be either an open object, such a line or arc, or a closed object, such as a circle or closed polyline.

The second object selected, the direction vector, must be a line, an open 2D polyline, or a single segment 3D polyline. This direction vector determines both the length and the direction of the resulting surface. The surface starts at the path curve.

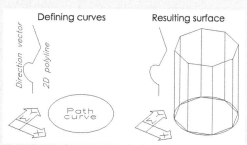

Interior vertices of a 2D polyline direction vector are ignored, with the length and direction of the surface being the same as that of a straight line drawn between the first and last vertices of the polyline. This is also true if the 2D polyline consists of a single arc-shaped segment. The direction vector's end closest to the object selection pick point is the starting direction of the surface.

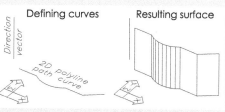

The N direction of the resulting surface is along the path curve, and the surface are always composed of four-sided faces of equal length. When the path curve is any object other than a 2D polyline that has not been spline fit, the faces on the surface are equal in size, and the number of faces are the same as the value of the **surftab1** system variable. If, on the other hand, the path curve is a 2D polyline that has not been spline fit, each straight segment of the polyline makes one face while each arc segment is divided into the number of faces that correspond to the value of **surftab1**. Thus, each polyline vertex marks the corner of a face on the surface.

| Notes: | • When you want to make a linear surface that closely fits its defining curve, TABSURF combined with a 2D polyline path curve is a good choice. |
| Related system variable: | • **surftab1**    This system variable determines the number of face divisions along the path curve on surfaces made with TABSURF. |

# Using TABSURF

TABSURF makes a surface by extruding a boundary curve, with both the direction and the length of the extrusion being controlled by a direction vector. Any existing line or open polyline can serve as a direction vector. AutoCAD calls the boundary curve the *path curve* in its command line prompts for TABSURF, which is potentially confusing because AutoCAD's prompts in the command for extruding solids — EXTRUDE — use the word "path" when referring to an object that sets the direction and length of solid extrusions. Thus, the word path has opposite meanings in TABSURF and EXTRUDE (extruded solids are discussed in Section 3).

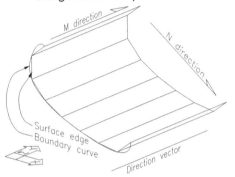

The N direction for TABSURF is along the boundary curve.

The M direction on surfaces made with TABSURF is in the direction of the direction vector, and the N direction is along the boundary curve. There is only one face in the M direction, and the number of faces in the N direction is equal to the value of the **surftab1** system variable.

The location of the direction vector is not important — it does not have to touch, or be centered with, the boundary curve.

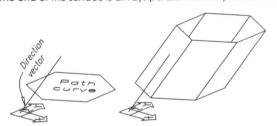

The end of the surface is always parallel with the path curve.

Also, the end of the surface is always parallel with the boundary curve, even if the direction vector is not perpendicular to the boundary curve.

TABSURF is similar to RULESURF in that it makes linear surfaces having straight sides and in that the number of faces on the surface is controlled by the **surftab1** system variable. The surface shown in the nearby figure, for instance, could have been made with either RULESURF or TABSURF. Without the defining curves, you cannot tell which command was used.

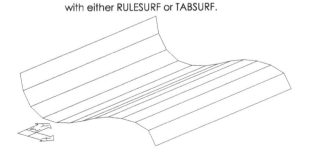

This surface could have been made with either RULESURF or TABSURF.

However, when 2D polylines are used as boundary curves, TABSURF's surfaces can track the boundary much closer than those of RULESURF. RULESURF always divides the surface along the boundary curve into faces having the same width; the number of faces is equal to the value of **surftab1**. On the other hand, when a 2D polyline is used as a TABSURF boundary, each straight segment of the polyline makes one face on the surface, while each arc segment of the polyline is divided into the same number of faces as the value of **surftab1**.

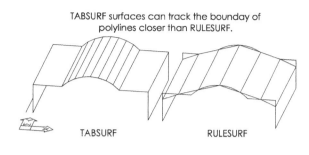

TABSURF surfaces can track the boundary of polylines closer than RULESURF.

TABSURF          RULESURF

The accompanying figure shows two surfaces made from the same 2D polyline boundary. The polyline has four straight segments and one arc segment, and **surftab1** was set to 8. Notice that the surface made by TABSURF fits the boundary curve much more closely than the surface made by RULESURF.

| | |
|---|---|
| Command: | REVSURF |
| Purpose: | Creates a polygon mesh surface by revolving a wireframe boundary about an axis. |
| Initiate with: | • On the command line, enter REVSURF. |
| | • From the Draw pull-down menu, select Surfaces, and then Revolved Surface from the resulting flyout menu. |
| | • Select the Revolved Surface button from the Surfaces toolbar. |
| Implementation: | REVSURF reports the current value of **surftab1** and **surftab2**, and issues command-line prompts for you to specify the boundary curve, the axis, the offset angle of the surface from the boundary curve, and the angle through which the boundary curve is to be rotated: |

```
Current wire frame density: SURFTAB1=6  SURFTAB2=6
Select object to revolve: (Select a wireframe object.)
Select object that defines the axis of revolution: (Select a line or an open
    polyline.)
Specify start angle <0>: (Enter an angle or press Enter.)
Specify included angle (+=ccs, -=cw) <360>: (Enter an angle or press Enter.)
```

The object to be revolved can be any open or closed wireframe object, even if it is a 3D polyline or a spline. As soon as you pick a point on it, AutoCAD prompts for the axis of revolution.

The axis of revolution must be a line, an open 2D polyline, or an open 3D polyline. You must select it by picking a point on it. If a polyline having multiple segments is selected as an axis, AutoCAD uses a straight line between the endpoints of the polyline as the rotation axis.

A 360 degree revolved surface

Object to revolve

Axis of revolution

Defining curves      Resulting surface

Revolved surface with specified start and included angles.

Object to revolve

Axis of revolution

Start angle    Included angle

Defining curves      Resulting surface

The start angle represents the angular offset from the object to be revolved at which the surface starts, while the included angle represents the number of degrees that the object is rotated.

Rotation direction follows the right-hand rule, with the positive direction of the axis being determined by the location of its object selection point. The positive direction of the axis is from the end closest to the pick point to the opposite end. You can reverse the normal rotation direction by preceding the angle with a minus sign (-).

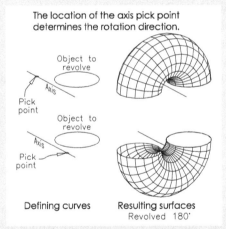

The location of the axis pick point determines the rotation direction.

Object to revolve

Axis

Pick point

Object to revolve

Axis

Pick point

Defining curves      Resulting surfaces
Revolved 180°

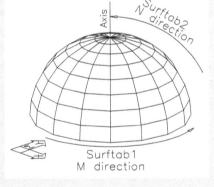

Axis

Surftab2 N direction

Surftab1 M direction

The number of surface faces around the axis (through the angle of revolution) is equal to the number of faces in the **surftab1** system variable, while the number of faces along the revolved object is controlled by the value in **surftab2**. If the revolved object is any object type other than a 2D polyline that has not been spline fit, the number of faces on the surface along the object will be equal to the value in **surftab2**.

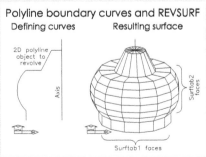

Polyline boundary curves and REVSURF

Defining curves      Resulting surface

2D polyline object to revolve

Axis

Surftab2 faces

Surftab1 faces

If, however, the revolved object is a 2D polyline that has not been spline fit, each line segment of the polyline constitutes one face while the number of faces of each arc segment of the polyline is equal to the value of **surftab2**.

| | |
|---|---|
| Notes: | • The manner in which REVSURF divides 2D polyline defining curves into polygon mesh faces is the same as TABSURF's. |
| | • When the wireframe boundary object is revolved a full 360 degrees, the direction of revolution and the start angle are not important. Consequently, the pick point location for the axis is not important. |
| Related system variables: | • **surftab1**  The number of polygon mesh faces through the angle of revolution is controlled by this system variable. |
| | • **surftab2**  The number of polygon mesh faces along the object that is revolved is controlled by **surftab2**. |

# Using REVSURF

REVSURF is a straightforward way to make a surface, especially if it is a full 360-degree surface of revolution. You simply pick a boundary curve (AutoCAD calls it the object to be revolved) and an axis, and AutoCAD generates the surface. The boundary curve can be any open or closed wireframe object, and while the axis is usually a line, it can be an open 2D or 3D polyline. Although you will generally have the axis either just touch the boundary curve, or be some distance from it, AutoCAD is not particular. It creates a surface even if the axis is in the middle of the boundary curve (which makes an impractical self-intersecting surface).

REVSURF shares some of TABSURF's characteristics. REVSURF uses the straight line direction between the endpoints of a crooked polyline (or one that has arc segments) for an axis, just as TABSURF does for a direction vector. Also in a manner similar to TABSURF, REVSURF makes a single face along flat segments of 2D polyline boundary curves, while the surface along the arc segments of a polyline is divided into the number of faces in one of the **surftab** system variables.

Unlike TABSURF, however, the number of faces along the boundary curve is controlled by the **surftab2** system variable, rather than by **surftab1**, even though this is the N direction of the surface in both instances. Around the axis of revolution, which is the M direction, the number of faces is equal to the value of **surftab1**.

Making a revolved surface is slightly more complicated if you revolve the surface only part way around the axis because the axis pick point determines the direction of revolution. The positive direction of the axis is from the end closest to the pick point to the other end. Rotation follows the right-hand rule, which is easily visualized by mentally grasping the axis with your right hand — your fingers will be curled in the positive rotation direction. You can reverse the direction by entering a negative angle value.

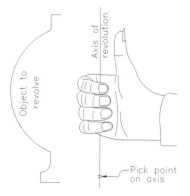

Normally, the surface starts at the boundary curve, but if you specify a start angle, the surface begins at the specified angle from the boundary curve. This angle also follows the right-hand rule.

| Command: | EDGESURF |
|---|---|
| Purpose: | Creates a polygon mesh surface between four wireframe boundary objects. |
| Initiate with: | • On the command line, enter EDGESURF. |
| | • From the Draw pull-down menu, select Surfaces, and then Edge Surface from the resulting flyout menu. |
| | • Select the Edge Surface button from the Surfaces toolbar. |
| Implementation: | EDGESURF reports the current values of the **surftab1** and **surftab2** system variables and issues four command line prompts for you to specify the four edges of the surface: |

```
Select object 1 for surface edge: (Select an open wireframe object.)
Select object 2 for surface edge: (Select an open wireframe object.)
Select object 3 for surface edge: (Select an open wireframe object.)
Select object 4 for surface edge: (Select an open wireframe object.)
```

Any mix-or-match combination of four open wireframe objects can be used as the surface boundary. A line, an arc, a 2D polyline, and a spline were used as edges in the accompanying figure. Their endpoints, however, must exactly touch. Not even

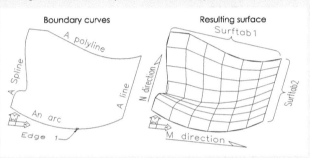

the smallest gap or overlap is allowed. If an edge does not touch an adjacent edge, EDGESURF fails and AutoCAD displays a command line message that reports which edge did not touch another edge.

You must select the edges by picking a point on them. The M direction of the surface is along the first edge that is selected, and the surface from that edge to the opposite edge has a polygon mesh face division equal to the value in the **surftab1** system variable. The N direction of the surface is along the edges adjacent to the first edge, and in that direction the number of polygon mesh faces is equal to the value of **surftab2**. After the first edge has been selected, the order in which the other three edges are selected is of no consequence.

| Notes: | • EDGESURF creates the surface by blending the opposite boundary edges as they sweep along the adjacent edges. |
|---|---|
| | • AutoCAD's documentation sometimes calls the surface created by the EDGESURF command a *Coons patch*. *Patch* refers to a specific surface area, while *Coons* refers to the person who developed the mathematics the surface is based on. The object created by EDGESURF is an AutoCAD polygon mesh. |
| Related system variables: | • **surftab1**   The number of polygon mesh faces along the first boundary edge selected is equal to the value in **surftab1**. |
| | • **surftab2**   The number of faces along the edges adjacent to the first boundary edge selected is equal to the value in this system variable. |

# Using EDGESURF

When you get used to it, EDGESURF might just be your favorite command for making polygon mesh surfaces. Using the command is easy: You pick four adjacent wireframe objects and AutoCAD generates the surface by sweeping and blending the boundary curves. The first edge you pick becomes the M-surface direction, and the number of faces along that edge to the opposite edge is equal to the value of **surftab1**. The order in which you pick the remaining three edges is of no consequence. The number of faces along the edges adjacent to the first edge is equal to the value of **surftab2**.

The key to mastering EDGESURF is in drawing the four wireframe boundary objects. First of all, their endpoints must exactly touch — absolutely no gaps or overlaps are allowed. Equally important in making the surface shape you want is your

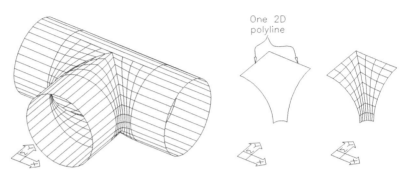

One 2D polyline

choice of the four boundary shapes and positions. Often you can use symmetry to make a complex surface that cannot be made in one piece. The tube intersection shown in the abore figure, for instance, is rather easily made with EDGESURF when it is divided into sections as shown in the figure.

| | |
|---|---|
| Command: | 3DMESH |
| Purpose: | A polygon mesh surface is created by specifying a point for each vertex of the mesh. |
| Initiate with: | • On the command line, enter 3DMESH. |
| | • From the Draw pull-down menu, select Surfaces, and then 3D Mesh from the resulting flyout menu. |
| | • Select the 3D Mesh button from the Surfaces toolbar. |
| Implementation: | AutoCAD first issues command line prompts for you to specify the number of surface mesh vertices, or nodes, in the M and N directions: |
| | Enter size of mesh in M direction: (Enter an integer number between 2 and 256.) |
| | Enter size of mesh in N direction: (Enter an integer number between 2 and 256.) |
| | The total number of vertices on the surface is equal to the M size multiplied by the N size, and the number of mesh faces in each direction is one less than the specified size. Next, AutoCAD issues a series of prompts for the location of each vertex in the surface mesh: |

```
Specify location for vertex (0, 0): (Specify a point.)
Specify location for vertex (0, 1): (Specify a point.)
Specify location for vertex (0, 2): (Specify a point.)
.
.
.
Specify location for vertex (0, n): (Specify a point.)
Specify location for vertex (1, 0): (Specify a point.)
Specify location for vertex (1, 1): (Specify a point.)
.
.
.
Specify location for vertex (1, n): (Specify a point.)
.
.
.
Specify location for vertex (m, 0): (Specify a point.)
.
.
.
Specify location for vertex (m, n): (Specify a point.)
```

Point locations can be specified by entering coordinates on the command line or by pointing. Each vertex is identified by two integers that are separated by a comma. The first integer is the vertex number in the M direction, and the second is the vertex number in the N direction. Numbering starts with 0. Notice that the input sequence is row by row down a column, with the N direction representing rows and the M direction representing columns. The M and N directions relative to the WCS depend entirely upon the user's input. The resulting surface is open (even if the surface wraps around so that one edge is adjacent to its opposite edge), and each face has four sides.

The accompanying figure shows a 4x3 polygon mesh surface. The numbers shown in this figure are vertex numbers, not point coordinates.
AutoCAD does not draw the surface until every vertex has been entered. There is no undo option, and if you cancel the command, nothing is drawn.

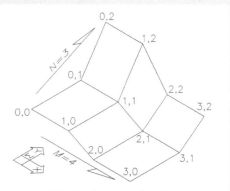

A 4-by-3 polygon mesh surface

Notes:     • This command is seldom used due to its tedious input. Autodesk originally intended the command to be used in applications, but only a few programs have been written. Some of the functions in 3d.lsp, which is the basis of the command named 3D, use 3DMESH.

# Using 3DMESH

3DMESH is a command for making surfaces that you will most likely use only as a last resort because you must specify the location of every vertex on the surface mesh. This can be extremely tedious and error prone. Nevertheless, 3DMESH can make some surfaces that no other AutoCAD command can make. The surface in the nearby figure, for example, could be made as a single surface only with 3DMESH.

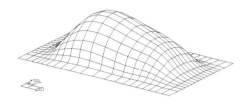

For a do-it-yourself demonstration of how 3DMESH works, start a new AutoCAD drawing and use the following command line input to draw a simple surface. The settings for this drawing are not important, and neither is your initial viewpoint. Also, you will probably not want to save the drawing when you are finished.

```
Command: 3DMESH (Enter)
Enter size of mesh in M direction: 4 (Enter)
Enter size of mesh in N direction: 3 (Enter)
Specify location for vertex (0, 0): 0,0 (Enter)
Specify location for vertex (0, 1): 1,0 (Enter)
Specify location for vertex (0, 2): 2,0 (Enter)
Specify location for vertex (1, 0): 0,1 (Enter)
Specify location for vertex (1, 1): 1,1,-1 (Enter)
Specify location for vertex (1, 2): 2,1 (Enter)
Specify location for vertex (2, 0): 0,2,1 (Enter)
Specify location for vertex (2, 1): 1,2,-1 (Enter)
Specify location for vertex (2, 2): 2,2 (Enter)
Specify location for vertex (3, 0): 0,3,1 (Enter)
Specify location for vertex (3, 1): 1,3 (Enter)
Specify location for vertex (3, 2): 2,3 (Enter)
```

Although the numbers in the prompts look like point coordinates in that there are two numbers separated by a comma, they are not. They are vertex identification numbers. You did not need to enter Z coordinates for the eight vertex points that were on the X-Y plane. From a plan view, the surface will look like six squares. For a better look at the surface, switch to an isometric-type viewpoint with the following command line input:

```
Command: VPOINT (Enter)
Current view direction: VIEWDIR=0.0000,0.0000,1.0000
Specify a view point or [Rotate] display compass and tripod: 2,-3,4 (Enter)
```

Your surface should look similar to the one shown in the figure to the right.

Although this is a simple surface, it illustrates many of the specific characteristics of 3DMESH surfaces, as well as some general characteristics of polygon mesh surfaces:

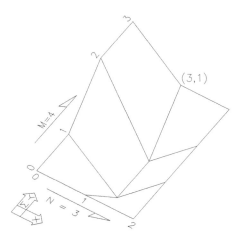

- Each vertex, or node, on the surface has an invisible two-digit identification number. The first number represents the vertex's position in the M direction on the surface, while the second number represents its position in the N direction. AutoCAD starts the numbers at 0, so vertex 3,1 is actually the fourth vertex in the M direction and the second vertex in the N direction.

- When 3DMESH starts, you must specify the number of vertices that the surface will have in both the M and N directions. The number of surface faces in these directions will be one less than the number of vertices.

- AutoCAD's command line prompts for 3DMESH vertex locations begin with vertex 0,0 and move in the N direction until the point of the last vertex is specified. Then, AutoCAD moves to the next vertex in the M direction (vertex 1,0) and again moves in the N direction. This is repeated until the location of the last vertex in the last row has been specified.

- Although the M direction of the demonstration surface you made is in the WCS Y-axis direction and the N direction is in the WCS X-axis direction, these directions could just as easily have been reversed. In fact, nothing prevents either of these directions from being in the Z-axis direction, or any angle in between. Furthermore, the M and N directions do not have to be mutually perpendicular.

- Every face on the surface mesh must have four sides. Often the faces are flat, but only one of the six faces in the surface you made is flat, and the corner faces are severely warped.

3DMESH doesn't draw the surface until the location of the last vertex has been specified. If you cancel the command, nothing is drawn. Not even the surface up to the last specified vertex. Also, there is no undo option — after the location of a point has been specified, it is fixed.

Even though its vertex-by-vertex input enables you to make unique shapes, 3DMESH is seldom a practical method of making surfaces when it is implemented from the command line. Script files can reduce, or even eliminate, input errors, but determining the coordinates of each point is no small task.

If you must use 3DMESH, you might find that drawing profiles can help you visualize the surface and also provide pick points for specifying vertices. The next figure shows the wireframe basis for the surface in the figure shown at the first of this section on using 3DMESH. The wireframe is made entirely of lines. Although this figure has tick marks to show the end of each line, the tick marks are not really needed to construct the surface. Object endpoint snaps were used in specifying points to create the surface shown on the right in this figure.

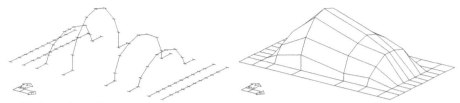

Wireframes for creating a surface with 3DMESH          The resulting polygon mesh surface

3DMESH surfaces can be made in a fairly crude, rough form, and then smoothed with the PEDIT command. The 3DMESH surface shown in the previous figure was smoothed with PEDIT to create the surface shown in the first figure of this section. Chapter 9 explains how to smooth polygon surface meshes with the PEDIT command.

Autodesk intended for 3DMESH to be used with applications, rather than by user input on the command line, and if you commonly make surfaces that can be defined by equations or formulas, you should consider making them through a program that uses 3DMESH.

The CD-ROM that comes with this book contains an AutoLISP program named fplot.lsp that can be used as a front end for 3DMESH or as an example of how to write a program of your own. This program, which was written by Autodesk and can be freely used and distributed, is no longer included with AutoCAD, but it still works well. Instructions for using and adapting the program are included as remarks within fplot.lsp.

This surface was made by fplot.lsp from a two variable equation.

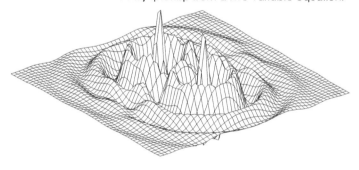

For an example of what can be done with fplot.lsp and 3DMESH, load the program (the AutoCAD APPLOAD command is the easiest way to do this) and enter DEMO on the command line. The result, which is shown in the figure, illustrates the interference pattern of two exponentially damped cosine waves. Two other demonstrations in the file, COSINE and EXPONENT, also plot mathematical equations having two variables. Because each of these plots is centered at the origin, you should erase one, or move it away from the origin, before making another.

## Exercises

In the following two exercises, you will try out each of the commands that make polygon mesh surfaces, except for 3DMESH. All the surfaces are based on wireframes that have already been constructed. Because making the wireframe boundary objects is the hardest and most time-consuming job in making surface models of polygon meshes, adding these surfaces will seem almost trivial.

### Exercise One

Retrieve file f0833.dwg from the CD-ROM that accompanies this book and open it. You started this model, which is of an automobile oil pan, as a wireframe in Chapter 4 and added seven 3D faces to it in Chapter 6. You should use the version of the model that is on the CD-ROM, however, because it includes some wireframe objects, which will be used for polygon mesh boundaries, that your model does not have. Also, the arc-line-arc objects at the corners

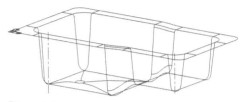

Figure 1-1

have been changed into 2D polylines with the PEDIT command so that they can be used to make one surface rather than three separate surfaces. This version of the model, which is shown in Figure 1-1, includes the 3D face surfaces that were added in Chapter 6.

You will use the RULESURF command to make surfaces that have straight sides and are between two boundaries that have different shapes. The six remaining planar areas on the flange of the oil pan meet this criteria. Change to the layer named Surf_Rule and set the **surftab1** system variable to 6. Start RULESURF, and pick two points on the wireframe corresponding to those labeled Pt1A and Pt1B in Figure 1-2. It does not matter which of the two points you pick first. However, each pick location should be near one end of the curve rather than near the middle, and you must pick the

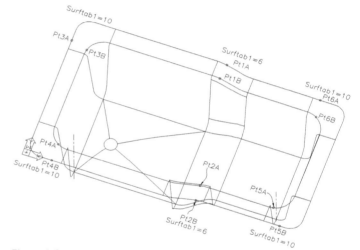

Figure 1-2

corresponding end of both curves. As soon as you pick the second point, AutoCAD draws the surface between the two curves.

Start RULESURF again, and pick points on your wireframe corresponding to those labeled Pt2A and Pt2B in Figure 1-2 to make the next surface. Then change the value of **surftab1** from 6 to 10, and use RULESURF four more times to add surfaces to the corners of the flange. Suggested pairs of point locations on the boundary curves are shown in Figure 1-2.

Use RULESURF to make three nonplanar surfaces near the middle of the oil pan. The boundary curve pick points are shown in Figure 1-3. VPOINT, with the rotation angles of 190 degrees in the X-Y plane from the X axis and 60 degrees from the X-Y plane, was used to set the viewpoint for this figure. Because the curvature of the boundary curves is relatively low, you can use a relatively low **surftab1** value. Therefore, set **surftab1** back to 6. Then invoke RULESURF three times, and pick the point pairs shown in Figure 1-3 for the boundary curves. If you happen to pick a pair of points such that the surface crosses over itself, use AutoCAD's UNDO command to back up, and then remake the surface.

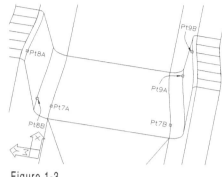

Figure 1-3

Use TABSURF to make the remaining sides of the oil pan. Switch to the layer named Surf_Tab and reduce the value of **surftab1** to 4. Start TABSURF and pick the curve labeled Path A in Figure 1-4 as the path curve for TABSURF, and the line labeled Direction Vector A as the direction vector of the surface. (Remember, in the prompts for TABSURF and REVSURF, AutoCAD refers to boundary curves as path curves.)

The viewpoint for Figure 1-4 is 305 degrees in the X-Y plane from the X axis and 15 degrees from the X-Y plane. Be certain that your pick point on the direction vector is in the half of the line that is closest to the path curve.

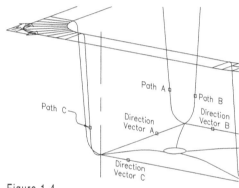

Figure 1-4

Repeat the TABSURF command and pick the curve labeled Path B in Figure 1-4 as the path curve, and the line labeled Direction Vector B as the direction vector. And, use TABSURF again with Path C and Direction Vector C to make a third surface.

Then move to the opposite end of the oil pan and use TABSURF three times to make similar surfaces. Because a 3D face lies on top of the wireframe in this section, you might have problems picking the direction vectors. If AutoCAD displays the message "Object not usable as direction vector," hold your keyboard's Ctrl key down as you pick the line. When the line, rather than the edges of the 3D face, is highlighted, press the

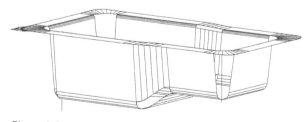

Figure 1-5

Enter key to signal acceptance. Your model should now look like the one in Figure 1-5 when HIDE is activated.

Next, use REVSURF to make the corners of the oil pan. Because the model is beginning to be cluttered with surface objects, you should switch to the layer named Surf_Rev and freeze the Surf_Face, Surf_Rule, and Surf_Tab layers. Set the **surftab1** system variable (which controls the number of faces around the axis of revolution) to 4, and set **surftab2** (which controls the number of faces along the boundary curve) also to 4.

Invoke REVSURF and pick the curve labeled Path A in Figure 1-6 as the object to be revolved. Pick a point on the lower end of the centerline to specify the axis of rotation. Accept AutoCAD's 0 degree start angle by pressing the Enter key and enter 90 as the included angle. Invoke REVSURF again, picking Path B as the object to be revolved, and pick the lower end of Axis B for the axis of revolution. Specify 0 degrees for the start angle and 90 degrees for the included angle.

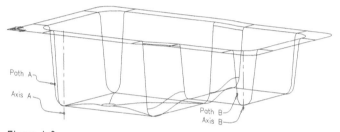

The corners on the opposite side of the oil pan model do not have an axis that can be used by REVSURF. You can either copy the existing center lines to those corners and use them with REVSURF to make the corner surfaces, or use MIRROR to make copies of the two surfaces you just made. Either way works well.

Figure 1-6

Use VPOINT or 3DORBIT to rotate the viewpoint 190 degrees in the X-Y plane from the X axis and 60 degrees from the X-Y plane. This viewpoint gives you an unobstructed view of the remaining eight areas that are to be surfaced. You will use EDGESURF to make the surfaces. Activate the layer named Edge_Surf. Leave **surftab1** set to 4, but change the value of **surftab2** from 4 to 6. Start the EDGESURF command; pick the point labeled A1 in Figure 1-7 as the first edge of the polygon mesh, and pick the objects labeled A for the other three edges of the mesh. The order in which you pick these three points as well as the location of the pick points on the curves is of no importance.

Repeat EDGESURF, selecting a point on the curve labeled B1 in Figure 1-7 as the first edge, and the three curves labeled B as the other edges of the surface. Make the two surfaces on the opposite side of the oil pan with two calls to EDGESURF, selecting the curve labeled C1 as the first edge of one surface, and curve D1 as the first edge of the other surface.

Set the value of **surftab1** to 6 and leave **surftab2** set to 6. Invoke EDGESURF four times, picking the curves labeled E in Figure 1-7 for one surface, those labeled F for the second surface, those labeled G for the third polygon mesh surface, and those labeled H for the remaining surface. Four of the curves serve as edges for two surfaces, and you might have to hold down the Ctrl key as you pick those curves so that AutoCAD cycles through the stacked objects until you find

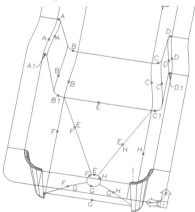

Figure 1-7

the one you want. For any one surface, the order in which you pick the curves and the pick point locations is not important.

You are now finished with the surface model oil pan. Thaw all the layers used for the surfaces (Surf_face, Surf_rule, Surf_tab, Surf_rev, and Surf_edge) and freeze the layers used for wireframe objects (Wf01 and CL). Your model should look like the one shown in Figure 1-8 when you view it from an angle 300 degrees in the X-Y plane from the X axis and -20 degrees from the X-Y plane to look up toward the bottom of the model. The completed version of this model is in file f0840.dwg on the CD-ROM that comes with this book.

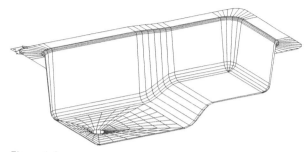

Figure 1-8

### Exercise Two

In this exercise you add surfaces to the wireframe airplane propeller you drew in Chapter 5. Open file f0841.dwg from the accompanying CD-ROM rather than the one you created. As you can see in Figure 2-1, the wireframe in this file contains some additions for making a hub on the propeller.

All the surfaces on this model are made with the EDGESURF command. Zoom in to the tip section of the wireframe. Set the **surftab1** system variable to 12, set **surftab2** to 4, and switch to the layer named Surf01. Start the EDGESURF command and follow the directions in Figure 2-2 when picking the surface edges. This figure uses tick marks to show where the three curves that make the propeller tip start and stop; the wireframe on your computer screen, however, will not have these tick marks. After you make the first surface, repeat EDGESURF and pick the points shown in Figure 2-2 for the surface edges. Three of the curves serve as edges for both surfaces.

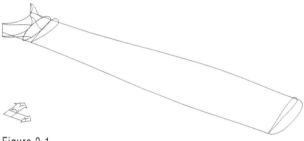

Figure 2-1

When HIDE is active, the tip of your propeller should look similar to the one in the Figure 2-3.

Change to the layer named Surf02 and freeze Surf01. (This makes picking edges easier.) Leave **surftab1** set to 12, but change **surftab2** from 4 to 16. Zoom out so that you can see the entire propeller. Start EDGESURF and pick the edges for the first (lower side) surface as shown in Figure 2-4. The first edge must be on one of the cross-sections of the propeller (so that the **surftab1** and **surftab2** face divisions will be as planned), but it does not matter which order you use in picking

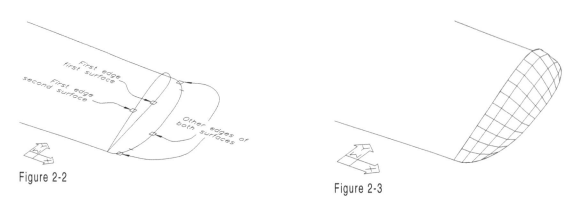

Figure 2-2

Figure 2-3

the other three edges. Repeat EDGESURF to make the second (upper side) surface on the propeller by picking the edges shown in Figure 2-4.

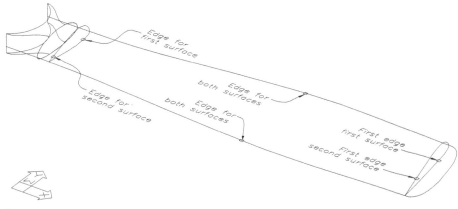

Figure 2-4

Zoom in close to the hub of the propeller as shown in Figure 2-5. Change to layer Surf03 and freeze layers Surf02 and WF03. The first two surfaces in this area, which make a cross-section transition from an airfoil to elliptical shape, are very short, so change **surftab2** from 16 to its minimum of 2. Leave **surftab1** at its current value of 12. Use EDGESURF and pick the points labeled Pt1, Pt2, Pt3, and Pt4 for the surface edges, with either Pt1 or Pt4 being picked first. Then repeat EDGESURF, using Pt2, Pt3, Pt5, and Pt6 as the edges, with Pt5 or Pt6 as the first edge.

The remaining six surfaces make the transition from an ellipse to one that will fit the side of a vertical cylinder. Change the layer of the two surfaces you just made from Surf03 to Surf02. (The PROPERTIES command, which can be initiated from the Standard toolbar, is a convenient way to do this.) Because Surf02 is frozen, the surface disappears. Freeze layers WF01 and WF02, and thaw layer OBJ03. When you zoom in close to the hub area of the propeller, you will see just the 18 wireframe objects that are in layer OBJ03, as shown in Figure 2-6.

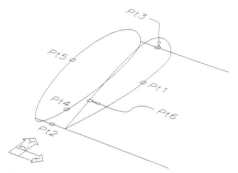

Figure 2-5

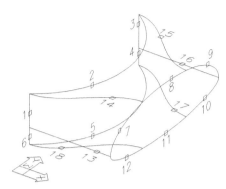

Figure 2-6

Set both **surftab1** and **surftab2** to 8. Verify that Surf03 is the current layer and invoke EDGE-SURF six times to make the six surfaces. Use the following table in conjunction with the numbers shown on the objects in Figure 2-6 as a guide in selecting the edges for EDGESURF. Because **surftab1** and **surftab2** are equal, it does not matter which edge you pick first.

| Surface | Edge Objects |
|---------|--------------|
| 1 | 4, 10, 16, 17 |
| 2 | 5, 11, 17, 18 |
| 3 | 6, 12, 13, 18 |
| 4 | 3, 9, 15, 16 |
| 5 | 2, 8, 14, 15 |
| 6 | 1, 7, 13, 14 |

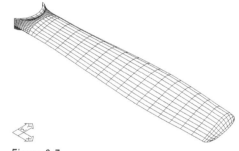

Figure 2-7

Notice that the sequence in creating the surfaces is to start in the back and work forward. This is to minimize visibility and selection problems. Because edges are on top of edges, you will probably have to hold down the Ctrl key as you pick the wireframe objects. When the wireframe object is highlighted rather than the adjoining surface, press the Enter key for AutoCAD to accept the edge. When you have finished making the six surfaces, thaw layers Surf01 and Surf02, and freeze layer WF03. Your fin-

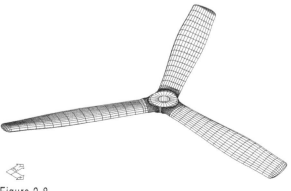

Figure 2-8

ished propeller blade should look like the one in Figure 2-7. The completed propeller blade is in file f0847.dwg on the CD-ROM that comes with this book.

You can make polar array copies of this blade to create propeller assemblies having up to three blades. You will have to add to the hub area, but you now have all the knowledge and skills to do this on your own. Figure 2-8 shows a three-bladed propeller. This surface model is on the CD-ROM in file f0848.dwg.

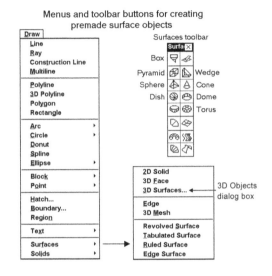

Menus and toolbar buttons for creating premade surface objects

## AutoCAD's Premade Surface Objects

AutoCAD has nine premade surface objects that can be used alone or in combination with other surface objects. They are comparable to the primitives in solid modeling (which are described in Chapter 11), but because surface objects are unable to interact in any way, they are not as useful. Nevertheless, they are handy when you need to make a basic geometric shape, such as a box or sphere.

The name of the command that makes these surface objects is simply 3D. If you invoke 3D from the command line, a command line menu is displayed for you to select the geometric shape you want. A more direct route to the object you want to make is to select its button on the Surfaces toolbar. A four-sided mesh is not available from the toolbar. You can, however, start that surface shape, as well as any of the other eight shapes, directly from the 3D Objects dialog box that opens when you select Surfaces from the Draw pull-down menu, and then select 3D Surfaces. This dialog box is an especially good way to start an object because it has image tiles that show an example of each object.

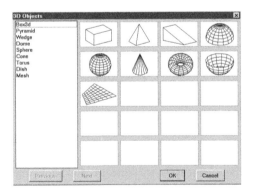

3D is not a built-in AutoCAD command — it is based on an AutoLISP program named 3d.lsp. The AutoCAD RULESURF, REVSURF, and 3DMESH command are used by this AutoLISP program to make the objects. Consequently, each object is a polygon mesh, and each object is a single entity. A box, for example, does not consist of six individual planar surface objects.

| Command: | 3D |
|---|---|
| Purpose: | This command creates a polygon mesh surface object in any of nine different basic geometric shapes. |
| Initiate with: | • On the command line, enter 3D. |
| | • From the Draw pull-down menu, select Surfaces, and then 3D Surfaces to bring up the 3D Objects dialog box. |
| | • Select the Box, Pyramid, Sphere, Dish, Wedge, Cone, Dome, or Torus button from the Surface toolbar. |
| Options: | When 3D is initiated from the command line, nine command line options are offered: |

`Box/Cone/DIsh/Dome/Mesh/Pyramid/Sphere/Torus/Wedge: Specify an option.`

If you start the command from the Draw pull-down menu, these options are shown in image tiles in the 3D Objects dialog box. You can select an object by double-clicking its image tile, or by highlighting it and then pressing the OK button.

The Surfaces toolbar has buttons for initiating any option directly, except for Mesh.

• Box    This option makes a rectangular parallelepiped or a cube on the X-Y plane of the UCS. From the command line, AutoCAD asks for the starting corner of the box, and then prompts for its length, width, and height. When the box is drawn, AutoCAD prompts for a rotation angle about the Z axis, based on the first corner of the box.

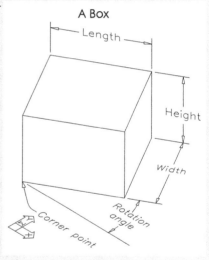

A Box

• Cone    You can make either a sharp-tipped cone or a truncated cone. AutoCAD first asks for the base center of the cone, and then for the radius or the diameter of the base. The next prompt is for the top radius or diameter of the cone, with a default response of 0 to make a sharp-tipped cone. The third prompt is for the height of the cone (in the Z direction), and the last is for the number of segments, or faces, the cone is to have.

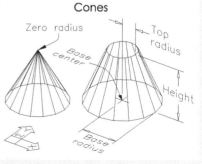

Cones

- Dish

This option makes a half-sphere that is open in the positive Z direction. AutoCAD issues command line prompts for the center of the dish, its diameter or radius, the number of longitudinal segments (around the edge of the dish), and the number of latitudinal segments (along the depth of the dish).

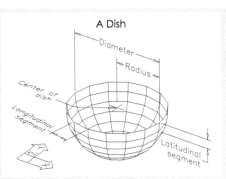

- Dome

A half-sphere that is open in the negative Z direction is made with this option. command line prompts are used to specify the center of the dome, its diameter or radius, the number of longitudinal segments (around the edge of the dome), and the number of latitudinal segments (along the height of the dome).

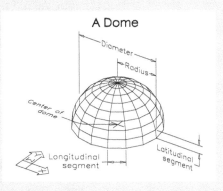

- Mesh

This option makes a four-sided mesh surface. AutoCAD issues command line prompts for the first, second, third, and fourth corners of the mesh. Although these corners do not have to be in the same plane, they must be specified in a clockwise or counterclockwise direction to prevent the mesh from crossing itself. As soon as the fourth corner is specified, AutoCAD highlights an edge in the M direction and prompt for the number of vertices in that direction; then AutoCAD prompts for the number of vertices in the N direction. The minimum allowable input for vertices is 2, and the maximum is 256. The number of faces in each direction is one less than the specified number of vertices.

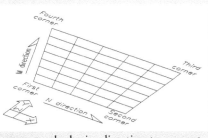

- Pyramid

You can make pyramids (five sides, including the base), tetrahedrons (four sides), and ridge-shaped objects with this option. Furthermore, the pyramids and tetrahedrons can be truncated. All these shapes are created through command line input.

Pyramids

- Sphere

This option makes a hollow ball that has an axis perpendicular to the UCS X-Y plane. command line prompts ask you to specify the center of the sphere, its radius or diameter, the number of faces around the axis (longitudinal segments), and the number of faces along the axis (latitudinal segments).

- Torus

A torus is the geometric shape obtained by revolving a circle about an axis that is in the plane of the circle and offset from its center line. The plane of the circle, and therefore the direction of the revolution axis, for tori made by 3D is always perpendicular to the UCS X-Y plane. The option uses command line prompts for you to specify the axis location, the distance to the center of

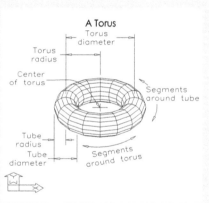

the circle (the torus radius or diameter), the circle's radius or diameter (the tube radius or diameter), the number of segments (faces) around the axis of revolution, and the number of segments around the circle (the tube).

• Wedge    A polygon mesh surface in the shape of a right-angle wedge is made by this option. Its first command line prompt is for a corner of the wedge on its high side. The next prompt is for the distance, or length, from the high side to the pointed side, a third prompt asks for the width of the wedge, and a fourth asks for the height of the high side of the wedge. The fifth, and last, prompt is for a rotation angle in the X-Y plane, with the first specified point as the rotation point.

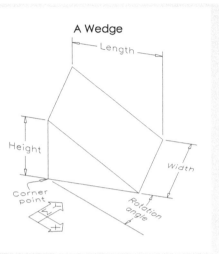

Notes:

• There is no toolbar button for the Mesh option.

• You can start each of the nine options directly from the command line by preceding its name with ai_. For example: ai_box starts the Box option, and ai_sphere starts the Sphere option.

• This command is based on an AutoLISP program named 3d.lsp, and each option is based on a function in this program. The program uses the 3DMESH command to make boxes, wedges, meshes, and pyramids; RULESURF to make cones; and REVSURF to make spheres, tori, domes, and dishes.

• Although the Pyramid option draws a variety of geometric shapes, its usefulness is impaired because you must supply points for the upper parts of the pyramids. You cannot simply specify their height. Therefore, you must know the point locations for the pyramid's peak, ridge, or upper corners of a truncated pyramid before you start the option.

# CHAPTER 9

# Modifying Polygon Mesh Surfaces

*After you have created a polygon mesh surface with the RULESURF, TABSURF, REVSURF, EDGESURF, or 3DMESH command, you will often need to modify it.*

*This chapter*

- *describes AutoCAD's capabilities and limitations in modifying polygon mesh surfaces;*
- *explains how to move surface mesh vertices;*
- *describes how to smooth polygon mesh surfaces by transforming them into B-spline and Bezier surfaces.*

## Polygon Mesh Modification Capabilities and Limitations

AutoCAD has respectable surface-modeling capabilities, as you have seen in the last three chapters, even though Autodesk has not added to those capabilities since Release 11. The main deficiencies in AutoCAD as a surface modeler are related more to its surface modification and editing capabilities than to its surface-creation capabilities.

You cannot trim two overlapping surfaces (or even find the curve where they intersect), you cannot fillet two adjacent surfaces, and you cannot join adjacent surfaces. Furthermore, for all practical purposes, you cannot break a surface into separate surfaces, you cannot make a hole in a surface, and you cannot make a surface longer or shorter. Actually, with a little ingenuity and a lot of time, you can do some of these modifications on a limited basis because you can work on individual nodes of a mesh. As a last resort (and certainly not recommended), you can even explode a polygon mesh surface down to its basic 3D faces and work on them one by one.

For the most part, modifications to polygon mesh surfaces — those surfaces made with RULE-SURF, TABSURF, REVSURF, EDGESURF, or 3DMESH — are limited to either moving vertices or fitting the mesh surface to a smooth curve. Because polygon mesh surfaces are a variation of 2D polylines, you can use the PEDIT command to do both of these operations.

## Moving Vertices

When a polygon mesh is selected as a PEDIT object, AutoCAD recognizes its object type and displays a special command line menu for modifying surface meshes. Similar to the PEDIT menu for polylines, this menu contains an Edit Vertex option, but unlike the Edit Vertex option for polylines, you cannot remove or add vertices to a polygon mesh. The only vertex editing you can do is to move them.

Moving vertices is sometimes useful when you need a specialized surface shape. You can, for instance, make a flat protrusion on a tube by moving vertices.

When you need to move vertices of a polygon mesh, you will most likely prefer the STRETCH command or the mesh's grips (there is one on every vertex) instead of the PEDIT command. PEDIT requires you to move a vertex marker from node to node on the surface until you reach the vertex you want moved. Then you specify a new location for that vertex. If you use grips, on the other hand, you can go directly to the vertex you are interested in, highlight it, and move it to a new location. If you need to move several vertices at one time, the STRETCH command is useful.

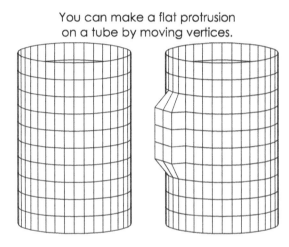

You can make a flat protrusion on a tube by moving vertices.

No matter what method you use, it helps to know exactly where you want a vertex to be before you move it, and often object snaps are useful in establishing destination points. The flat face on the tubular surface shown in the nearby figure, for example, was made by drawing a temporary rectangular-shaped wireframe in front of the tube so that object snaps could be used to pick the destination points of the vertices.

## Smoothing Surfaces

Probably, your main use of PEDIT will be to smooth polygon mesh surfaces. Before you smooth a surface, however, you will want to check, and most likely change, the values of three system variables.

One of these system variables, **surftype**, controls the type of equation used in shaping the smoothed surface. Your choices for equation types are quadratic B-spline, cubic B-spline, and Bezier, with cubic B-spline being the default. From the discussion of PEDIT and 3D polylines in Chapter 5, you are already familiar with the characteristics of quadratic and cubic B-splines. Bezier (pronounced BAY-zee-a — the name of the person who developed the equation) curves and surfaces are early versions of B-splines, which are easily implemented in computer applications.

As shown in the following table, surfaces must have at least three vertices in both directions to fit to a quadratic B-spline, and they must have at least four vertices in both directions to fit to a cubic B-spline. Therefore, you cannot use those equation types in smoothing polygon mesh surfaces made with RULESURF or TABSURF. They can, however, be fit to a Bezier surface. The vertices of the original surface mesh are used as control points for the smoothed surface. Consequently, the surface pulls away from its original vertices, except for those on the edges of the surface. Bezier surfaces deviate the most from the original surface, cubic B-spline surfaces come closer, and quadratic B-spline surfaces come the closest to matching the original surface.

| Surftype Value | Surface Shape | Minimum Number of Mesh Vertices in Either Direction | Maximum Number of Mesh Vertices in Either Direction |
|---|---|---|---|
| 5 | Quadratic B-spline | 3 | 0 |
| 6 | Cubic B-spline | 4 | 0 |
| 8 | Bezier | 2 | 11 |

One surface shape is not better than another — it just depends on what shape you are after. If you want the smoothest, least curving, and flattest surface, use the Bezier equation. If you want the surface to match the original surface as closely as possible, use a quadratic B-spline equation.

Despite the PEDIT option name of Smoothed Surface, the resulting surface is not perfectly smooth — it is still a mesh of generally flat faces. (Some faces, particularly those in corners, might be folded.) The number of faces on the smoothed surfaces is determined by **surfu** and **surfv**, which are the other two system variables you will want to set before you smooth a polygon mesh surface. **Surfu** sets the number of faces in the M direction on the surface, while **surfv** sets the number of faces in the N direction. The maximum value allowed for these system variables is 200, and the minimum is 2.

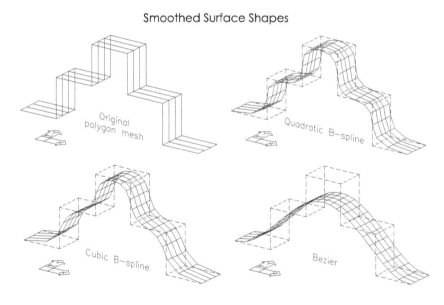

Smoothed Surface Shapes

Original polygon mesh

Quadratic B-spline

Cubic B-spline

Bezier

Just as it does for smoothed polylines, AutoCAD retains its information about the defining mesh of smoothed surfaces, and you can see the defining surface mesh by setting the **splframe** system variable to 1. A regen is required for the change to take effect. When **splframe** is set to 0, the default setting, only the smoothed surface is

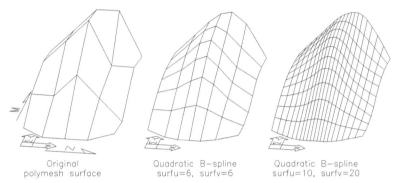

Surfu sets the number of faces in the M direction, and Surfv set the number of faces in the N direction.

Original polymesh surface

Quadratic B−spline surfu=6, surfv=6

Quadratic B−spline surfu=10, surfv=20

shown. When **splframe** is set to 1, the original surface is shown. The display would be too cluttered and confusing if both were shown simultaneously (as are smoothed polylines).

Furthermore, the original surface can be restored by selecting the Desmooth option from the PEDIT menu. This is a good feature — if you don't like the results of a smoothed surface, you can desmooth it and smooth it again with different parameters.

You can move the vertex location of smoothed surfaces with the Edit Vertex option of PEDIT, but it can be a daunting task because AutoCAD uses the vertices of the original surface rather than the smoothed surface. Even though the smoothed mesh is the one shown, the PEDIT vertex position marker is always located on one of the vertices of the invisible defining mesh. The marker appears to be jumping around in space, and it is difficult to tell where it actually is or what effect moving the vertex will have on the mesh. Using grips is slightly better. Although just the original vertex locations are shown as grips, all of them are shown, which gives you a better picture of the defining mesh.

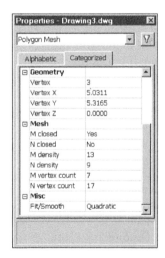

When a polygon mesh is selected, the dialog box of the PROPERTIES command contains information about vertices and meshes. Property names are listed in the left column of this dialog box and their values or settings are listed in the right column, as described in the following table.

| Property | Description |
| --- | --- |
| Vertex | An AutoCAD assigned number representing the current vertex. By clicking in the right-hand column, you can move to the next vertex or to the previous one. An X marker is displayed on the mesh to show the location of the vertex. |
| Vertex X | The X coordinate of the current vertex. You can edit the coordinate. |
| Vertex Y | The Y coordinate of the current vertex. You can edit the coordinate. |
| Vertex Z | The Z coordinate of the current vertex. You can edit the coordinate. |
| M closed | Indicates by a Yes or No whether the mesh is open or closed in the M direction. You can open a closed mesh, and close an open mesh. |
| N closed | Indicates by a Yes or No whether the mesh is open or closed in the N direction. You can open a closed mesh, and close an open mesh. |
| M density | Indicates the number of vertices in the M direction for smoothed meshes. The value represents the value of **surfu** plus one. You can edit the number. |
| N density | Indicates the number of vertices in the N direction for smoothed meshes. The value represents the value of **surfv** plus one. You can edit the number. |
| M vertex count | Indicates the number of vertices in the M direction for meshes that are not smoothed. The value represents the value of **surftab1** or **surftab2** plus one. This number cannot be edited. |
| N vertex count | Indicates the number of vertices in the N direction for meshes that are not smoothed. The value represents the value of **surftab1** or **surftab2** plus one. This number cannot be edited. |
| Fit/Smooth | Shows the type of surface curve fit: none, quadratic, cubic, or Bezier. You can change the curve fit type. |

Surface M and N directions, and consequently the **surfu** and **surfv** directions, can be confusing because AutoCAD is not consistent with M and N directions and **surftab1** and **surftab2** relationships. The accompanying figure shows the directions and controlling system variables for surfaces made with RULESURF, TABSURF, REVSURF, and EDGESURF. 3DMESH is not included because the M and N directions depend on user input.

M and N directions for  polygon mesh surfaces

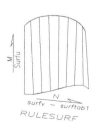
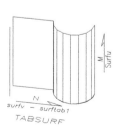
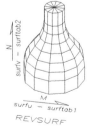
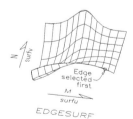

| | |
|---|---|
| Command: | PEDIT |
| Purpose: | PEDIT allows you to move individual vertex locations and to smooth the surface of polygon mesh surfaces, as well as to open a closed surface or close one that is open. |
| Initiate with: | • On the command line, enter PEDIT. |
| | • From the Modify pull-down menu, select Polyline. |
| | • Select the Edit Polyline button from the Modify II toolbar. |

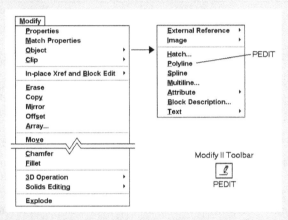

Options:

The PEDIT command asks you to select one object. If that object is a polygon mesh surface, AutoCAD displays the command line menu

```
Enter an option [Edit vertex/Smooth surface/Desmooth/Mclose/Nclose/Undo]:
```

If the surface is closed in the M direction, the Mclose option is replaced by the Mopen option; if the surface is closed in the N direction, the Nclose option is replaced by the Nopen option. This menu reappears after an option is completed. Press Enter to end the command.

• Edit Vertex

You can change the location of a vertex with this option. When it is selected, AutoCAD displays the following secondary menu on the command line:

```
Current vertex (M,N). Enter an option [Next/Previous/Left/Right/Up/
    Down/Move/REgen/eXit] <N>:
```

An X marker is positioned on a vertex of the polygon mesh, and the current M and N mesh position of the marker is shown on the left side of the menu. Most of the options in this secondary menu are for moving this marker. When the marker is on the vertex you want to move, select the Move option.

## PEDIT polygon mesh directions

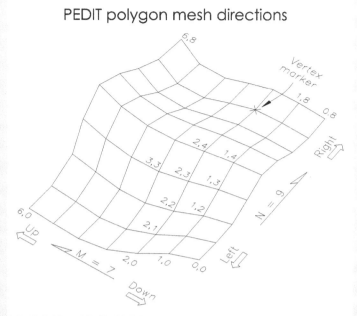

- **Next**

  This option moves the X marker to the next vertex in the N direction. Upon reaching the last vertex in the N direction, the M component of the vertex position number increments by 1, and the N component becomes 0. Using the mesh in the accompanying figure as an example, if the marker is on vertex (1,3), the next vertex is (1,4); if it is on (1,8), the next vertex is (2,0).

- **Previous**

  This option moves the X marker to the previous vertex in the N direction. Thus, if the marker is on vertex (1,3), the previous vertex is (1,2).

- **Left**

  The vertex marker is moved in the N direction to the previous vertex with this option. If, for example, the marker is on vertex (2,3), the Left vertex is (2,2). Unlike the marker movement of the Previous option, the marker stops when the first vertex in the N direction is reached.

- **Right**

  The N component of the X marker's vertex number is incremented by 1 when this option is selected. It is similar to the Next option, but movement stops when the last vertex in the N direction is reached. Thus, on the mesh in the previous figure, Right moves the marker from (1,3) to (1,4), but if the marker is on (1,8), Right has no effect.

- Up

This option moves the X marker one vertex in the positive M direction. For example, if the marker is on vertex (2,3), Up moves it to vertex (3,3). After the last vertex in the M direction is reached, Up has no effect.

- Down

The X marker is moved one vertex in the minus M direction with this option. If the marker is on vertex (2,4), for instance, Down moves it to (1,4). This option does not wrap the marker's movement.

- Move

Selecting this option signals that you want to move the vertex that the X marker is currently on. AutoCAD issues the prompt:

```
Enter new location: (Specify a point.)
```

You can use any AutoCAD method to specify a new location for the vertex.

- Regen

This option regenerates the polygon mesh.

- eXit

Select eXit to end the Edit Vertex option and return to the main PEDIT menu.

- Smooth Surface

This option changes the shape of the surface into that of a quadratic B-spline, a cubic B-spline, or a Bezier spline, depending the setting of the **surftype** system variable. The number of faces on the smoothed surface is controlled by the **surfu** and **surfv** system variables.

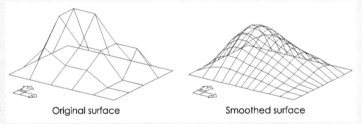

Original surface · · · Smoothed surface

- Desmooth

The original, unsmoothed version of the polygon mesh surface is restored with this option.

- Mclose/ Mopen

The Mclose option is offered if the polygon mesh surface is open in the M direction, and the Mopen option is offered if the surface is closed in the M direction. Mclose adds a row of faces between the first and last edges of the surface, while Mopen removes the last row of faces along the N edge of the surface.

### Closing an open surface

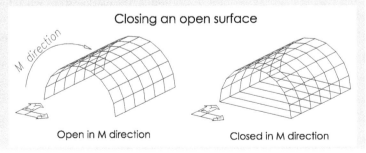

Open in M direction · · · Closed in M direction

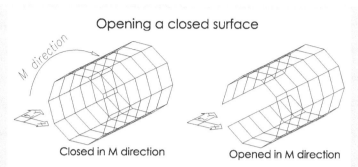

Opening a closed surface

Closed in M direction       Opened in M direction

- Nclose/ Nopen    If the polygon mesh surface is open in the N direction, the Nclose option is displayed; the Nopen option is displayed if the surface is closed in the N direction. When Nclose is selected, a row of faces is added between the surface's first and last edges in the N direction. When Nopen is selected, the last row of faces in the N direction is removed.

- Undo    This option reverses the last PEDIT operation.

Notes:

- Unlike the Edit Vertex options of PEDIT for polylines, you cannot remove or insert vertices in a polygon mesh and you cannot break the mesh. You only can move vertices. Because you also can move polygon mesh vertices by the STRETCH command, as well as with grips, you will seldom use the Edit Vertex option of PEDIT.

- Although you can move vertices of smoothed surfaces, this is not something you will want to do. First of all, you cannot move the vertices of the smoothed surface — you can move only the vertices of the original defining mesh. Second, AutoCAD moves the vertex marker from node to node on the original mesh, even though it is not visible. This makes the marker appear to be jumping about on invisible points in space.

- You can close an open polygon mesh even if the results are not logical. For instance, if you close a planar surface, a row of new faces is laid over the existing surface.

- If a mesh has more than 11 vertices in either its M or N direction, it cannot be smoothed to a Bezier surface.

- A mesh must have at least three vertices in both directions to be smoothed to a quadratic surface, and it must have at least four vertices in both directions to be smoothed to a cubic surface.

Related system variables:

- **surftype**    This system variable determines the equation type used by PEDIT in smoothing surfaces. It takes an integer value of 5, 6, or 8. A quadratic B-spline equation is used when **surftype** is set to 5, a cubic B-spline equation is used when it is set to 6, and a Bezier equation is used when it is set to 8. The initial setting is 6.

- **surfu**    This system variable controls the number of faces in the M direction of a smoothed polygon mesh surface. Its minimum value is 2, its maximum value is 200, and its initial setting is 6.

- **surfv**       The number of faces on a smoothed polygon mesh surface in the N direction is equal to the value in this system variable. Its initial value is 6, and it accepts any integer from 2 through 200.

- **splframe**    When **splframe** is set to its default value of 0, AutoCAD displays smoothed polygon mesh surfaces in their smoothed condition. When **splframe** is set to 1, the original unsmoothed form of the mesh is displayed. A regen is required to implement the change. This variable controls just the display of smoothed polygon meshes — if you want to permanently desmooth the mesh, you must use PEDIT.

## Exercises

These two exercises give you a feel for smoothing polygon mesh surfaces and demonstrate the effects of **surfu** and **surfv**. Feel free to perform additional experiments with the objects in these exercises on your own.

### Exercise One

Draw a 2D polyline on the X-Z plane of the WCS that has a shape similar to the one on the left side of Figure 1-1. The dimensions of this polyline are not important. Also, draw a center line that can be used as an axis of revolution. If you do not want to draw this 2D polyline and the axis, you can use those in file f0911.dwg on the CD-ROM that comes with this book.

Make a copy of the polyline and center line, and use REVSURF on one pair of the objects to make a surface model stemware glass, as shown on the right side of Figure 1-1. Use the default setting of 6 for both **surftab1** and **surftab2**.

Now, use the PEDIT or PROPERTIES command to fit the surface to various shapes by varying the surface type as well as the **surfu**

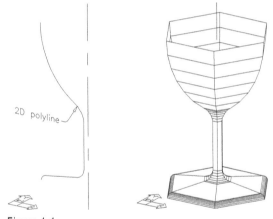

Figure 1-1

and **surfv** values. Because more vertices are in the N direction than permitted for Bezier surfaces, you can smooth the model only with quadratic and cubic equations. Figure 1-2 shows the model smoothed to a cubic B-spline with a **surfu** value of 20 and two different **surfv** values. Notice that smoothing the surface cancels the REVSURF characteristic of dividing polyline curved segments into **surftab2** faces and of not dividing straight segments at all.

Use REVSURF, combined with a **surftab1** value of 3 and a **surftab2** value of 6, with the other polyline and center line to make a surface model that has a triangular cross-section, as shown on the left side of Figure 1-3. Then use PEDIT or PROPERTIES to smooth the surface. A quadratic surface is your only choice, because there are too many vertices for a Bezier surface and not enough for a cubic B-spline. One example of the smoothed surface is shown on the right side of

Figure 1-3. Because the smoothed surface is based on the vertices of the original surface mesh, it is lobed rather than round in cross-section.

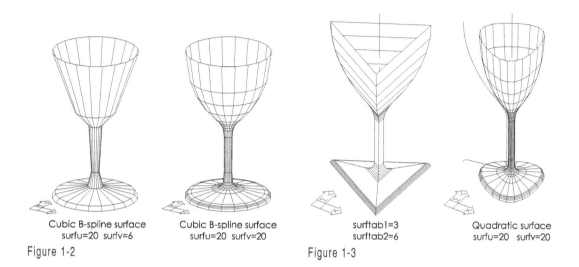

| Cubic B-spline surface<br>surfu=20 surfv=6 | Cubic B-spline surface<br>surfu=20 surfv=20 | surftab1=3<br>surftab2=6 | Quadratic surface<br>surfu=20 surfv=20 |

Figure 1-2                                                    Figure 1-3

### Exercise Two

Retrieve f0914.dwg from the CD-ROM that accompanies this book and open it. The surface model in this file, which is shown in Figure 2-1, was made with AutoCAD's 3DMESH command. It has eight vertices in the M direction and five in the N direction. The faces that appear to have only three sides (they are located on the corners of the model), were made by selecting the same point for two adjacent vertices, which makes one side of the face have a length of 0.

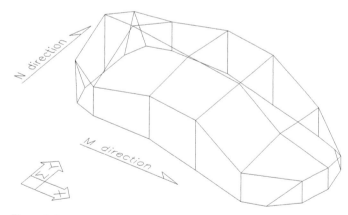

Figure 2-1

This is an open exercise in which you can modify the surface model in any way you want. You can move vertices with PEDIT, with STRETCH, or through the mesh's grips; and you can smooth the model using any of the three surface types. The model is complex enough to be interesting, but not so complex that it is difficult to work with. Figure 2-2 shows a hidden-line view of the model after it has been smoothed to a quadratic B-spline with **surfu** set to 32 and **surfv** set to 20.

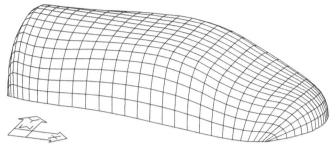

Figure 2-2

# Building Solid Models

# CHAPTER 10

# Getting Started in Solid Modeling

*Solids are the most realistic type of AutoCAD models because they have mass under their surfaces. Consequently, you can cut holes in them and add to them using techniques similar to those used in constructing real solid objects. This chapter starts by giving you an overall picture of solid-modeling processes, and then concentrates on some fundamental tools for creating 3D solid objects.*

*This chapter*

- *demonstrates the general techniques of solid modeling by leading you through the construction of a simple solid model;*

- *introduces you to the ACIS Geometric Modeler that AutoCAD solid models are based on;*

- *lists the uses and properties of regions, which are a 2D version of 3D solids, describes what their uses are, and how they are created;*

- *explains how to create 3D solid objects by extruding and revolving 2D cross sections.*

Solid modeling is not at all like surface modeling. The object types are different, the commands for making the objects are different, and even the approach and strategy for making models are different. Recall from Section 2 of this book that most surface models are constructed by drawing wireframe objects to represent edges and boundaries on the model, and then adding surfaces between those wireframe objects.

Solid models, on the other hand, start out as basic 3D geometric shapes, which can be joined or subtracted from one another to form complex models. Often, basic 3D geometric solids are referred to as *primitive* solids, and models made from combined primitives are referred to as *composite* solids.

In general, you will probably find solid modeling easier and more intuitive than surface modeling, and if you are designing objects that are typically made in a machine shop with tools such as lathes, milling machines, and drill presses, you will most likely model them as solids.

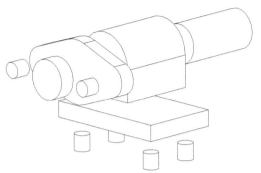

AutoCAD solid models start as basic geometric shapes.

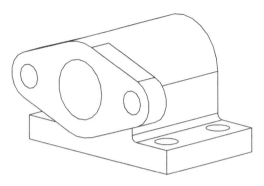

The basic geometric shapes are combined to make a complex solid model.

The commands for creating primitive solids can be conveniently divided into two categories. In one category, primitives are made from 2D profile objects. The commands in this category are EXTRUDE and REVOLVE, and this chapter concentrates on those two commands. In the other category, primitives are created directly in one of six basic geometric forms. The commands in this category are BOX, CONE, CYLINDER, SPHERE, TORUS, and WEDGE. Those commands are discussed in the next chapter. Then, you will know everything about creating primitives, and Chapter 12 will discuss the ways primitives can be combined to form composite solid models.

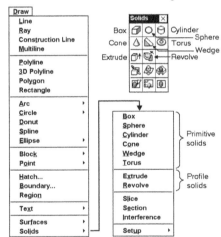

Menus and toolbar buttons for creating 3D solids

## Constructing a Simple 3D Solid Model

If you are not familiar with solid modeling, you should construct a simple 3D solid model by following the steps described in the next few pages. In building this model, you will be introduced to some of the fundamental concepts of solid modeling, as well as to some of the commonly used terms. The model gives you an overall picture of how solid objects are created and how they are combined to make a model having the geometry you want. You will use the command line to initiate all actions while building this model so you can concentrate on the actual commands rather than on menus and buttons.

You don't need to keep this demonstration 3D solid model. Start a new AutoCAD drawing using the AutoCAD English template, acad.dwt. You do not need to set up any layers in the file, but you will find it helpful to have the UCS icon located at the UCS origin and have snap spacing set to 1 unit.

## Extruded Solids

Start the model by using the PLINE command to draw the object shown in the adjacent figure, using the given dimensions. Make certain that its lower-left corner is on the WCS origin. Set an SE isometric viewpoint, and zoom and pan as necessary to give yourself working room.

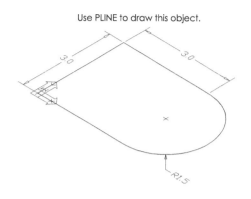

Use PLINE to draw this object.

Turn the 2D polyline into a 3D solid by using the following command line input:

```
Command: EXTRUDE (Enter)
Current wire frame density:  ISOLINES=4
Select objects: Select the 2D polyline, and press Enter.
Specify height of extrusion or [Path]: 1 (Enter)
Specify angle of taper for extrusion <0>: (Enter)
```

Your object should look similar to the one on the left side of the figure. Despite the similarity in names, the EXTRUDE command makes an object that is completely different from wireframe objects with an extrusion thickness. If you had given the polyline an extrusion thickness of 1 unit, it would have been like a 1-unit-high wall. This extruded solid, however, is a completely filled-in solid object. When HIDE is active, your model looks like the one on the right side of the figure. Notice that AutoCAD automatically adds facets to curved surfaces on a solid model during HIDE.

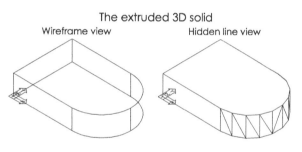

The extruded 3D solid
Wireframe view          Hidden line view

The object you created is often referred to as an extruded solid, due to the name of the command used to make it. Nevertheless, its AutoCAD database object type, which is 3D solid, is no different from those made by the other seven commands for creating solids.

AutoCAD first issued a message about the **isolines** system variable. (That system variable in is discussed Chapter 14.) Then, you were asked to select the objects to be extruded. Almost any closed wireframe object can be used to make an extruded solid — circles, splines, and polylines in any of their various forms. Any width that a polyline might have is ignored. You can select more than one object, although this doesn't mean that you can make an extruded solid from a set of connected lines and arcs, even if they form a closed path when combined. Each object selected must be closed. Objects used for making extruded solids are automatically deleted when the system variable **delobj** is set to 1, which is its default setting. If you want to retain objects used to make extruded solids, set **delobj** to 0.

After you selected the object to be extruded, the EXTRUDE command asked you to enter an extrusion height or to specify that the extrusion is to be based on a path. You respond by entering

1. This caused the profile to be extruded 1 unit in the polyline's extrusion direction, which is the positive Z direction. You could have specified the extrusion height by pointing on the X-Y plane, and the resulting extrusion would still have been made in the polyline's extrusion direction.

If you choose the Path option, you are prompted to select an object that establishes both the length and shape of the extruded solid. The profile object is swept along the path as it forms the solid, even if the path is curved. This is a powerful option — one that enables you to make unique, nonlinear 3D geometric shapes. Extrusions along a path at length are discussed later in this chapter.

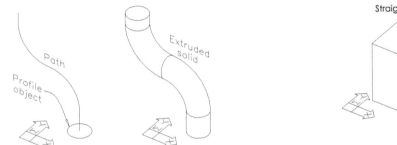 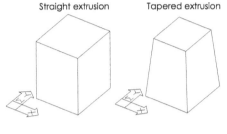

The final prompt for the EXTRUDE command is for an extrusion taper angle, with a default angle of 0 degrees. A positive taper angle causes the extrusion to taper inward (its cross-section area becomes smaller), while a negative taper angle causes the extruded solid to taper outward (its cross-section area becomes larger). Because you accepted the default taper angle of 0, the cross-section area of your solid remained the same through the extrusion length.

## Primitives

The second basic 3D geometric object for your model will be in the shape of a box. The command line sequence to make this box is

```
Command: BOX (Enter)
Specify corner of box or [CEnter] <0,0,0>: (Enter)
Specify corner or [Cube/Length]: 1,3,0 (Enter)
Specify height: 2 (Enter)
```

The prompts and options for the BOX command are similar to drawing a 2D rectangle and then specifying a height for the box. You accepted the default location, which is at the User Coordinate System origin, for the first corner of the box. Then you placed the opposite bottom corner of the box at the coordinates of 1,3,0 and you specified that the box was to be 2 units high. Your model should now look like the one shown in the figure below.

Even though the name of the command is BOX, the object you just created is more like a brick than an empty box — it is completely solid. In geometry books, this geometric shape is sometimes referred to as a rectangular parallelepiped and at other times as a rectangular prism; however, since both of those names are lengthy, we will follow Autodesk's lead and simply call them boxes.

You could have made this 3D solid by drawing a 2D polyline rectangle and extruding its units in the Z direction, but the BOX command is a shortcut method that creates a 3D solid without the need for a profile object. It is one of six commands for making basic, or primitive, 3D geometric shapes. The other five commands are CONE, CYLINDER, SPHERE, TORUS, and WEDGE.

You will notice that half of the box is inside the extruded solid. Soon, you will join the two solids, but first you make a cylinder-shaped primitive that is the basis of a hole in the extruded solid. The command line sequence of prompts and options to make this cylinder is

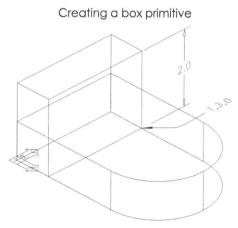

Creating a box primitive

```
Command: CYLINDER (Enter)
Current wire frame density:  ISOLINES=4
Specify center point for base of cylinder or [Elliptical] <0,0,0>: 3,1.5 (Enter)
Specify radius for base of cylinder or [Diameter]: .75 (Enter)
Specify height of cylinder or [Center of other end]: 1 (Enter)
```

Making a cylinder is similar to making a circle, and then specifying a height. Your circle is centered in the arc portion of the extruded solid, has a radius of 0.75 units, and a height of 1.0 units. You specify the height by entering a value, although you could have specified it by picking two points. Normally, the axis of the cylinder is in the Z-axis direction, but if you select the Center of Other End option, you can pick a point that establishes the end of the cylinder axis. The

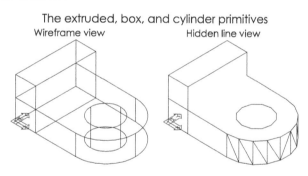

The extruded, box, and cylinder primitives
Wireframe view                    Hidden line view

cylinder starts at the initial center point and ends at the Center of Other End pick point. Notice also that you can even make cylinders that have an elliptical cross section.

Your three 3D solid objects should look similar to those on left side of the figure. In wireframe form, the model looks reasonably finished — the extruded solid and the box appear to be united, and you can imagine that the cylinder is a hole. However, when you invoke the HIDE command, as shown on the right side of the figure, there is no edge where the box intersects the extruded solid, and it becomes obvious that the cylinder is not a hole. You will have to join the box to the extruded solid, and you will have to subtract the cylinder's volume from the extruded solid.

## Boolean Operations

The three Boolean operations involve the interaction of two or more 3D solid objects. They are for shaping and transforming basic geometric shapes into complex solid models. (Their name is based on the name of mathematician George Boole who developed theories on logic and sets.) AutoCAD has three commands for performing Boolean operations. In accordance with the arithmetic of sets, the Boolean operations differ from one another in how they handle common (or shared) volumes. AutoCAD's Boolean operation commands are

| Command | Operation |
|---------|-----------|
| UNION | Joins two or more 3D solids into one solid. Volume common to the solids is absorbed into the united solid. |
| SUBTRACT | Subtracts the volume of one set of solids from the volume of a second set of solids. Volume of the first set that is not within the second set is automatically deleted. If there is no common volume, the first set of solids is simply deleted. |
| INTERSECT | Creates a solid from the volume shared by a set of solids. Volume that is not common disappears, and if there is no common volume, all the solids are deleted. |

You will use two of these commands on your solid model — UNION and SUBTRACT. First, subtract the cylinder's volume from the extruded solid's volume. The command line prompts and input to do this are

```
Command: SUBTRACT (Enter)
Select solids and regions to subtract from...
Select objects: (Select the extruded solid)
Select objects: (Enter)
Select solids and regions to subtract...
Select objects: (Select the cylinder)
Select objects: (Enter)
```

The model after subtracting the cylinder from the extrusion

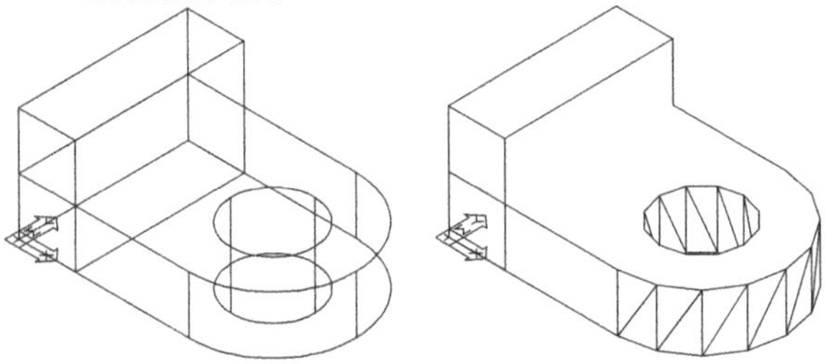

Wireframe view          Hidden line view

In wireframe form, as shown on the left side of the accompanying figure, nothing appears to be different in the model, but in the hidden-line mode, as shown on the right in the figure, you see that the cylinder has gone away, and in its place is a hole in the extruded solid.

The cylinder was the same height as the extruded solid, but even if it had been taller, the result would have been the same. The object that is subtracted always disappears at the end of the operation. Notice that the command first asks for the solids to subtract from, and then asks for the solids to be subtracted. Any of the standard AutoCAD selection methods can be used, and there is no limit to the number of solids in each selection set. The reference to regions is a reminder that Boolean operations also apply to regions, which are a 2D relative to 3D solids that are discussed later in this chapter.

Next, use the UNION command to join the box primitive and the extruded solid. (You could have performed this operation before the subtract operation just as well.)

The command line sequence to join the two solids is

```
Command: UNION (Enter)
Select objects: (Select the box and the extruded solid.)
Select objects: (Enter)
```

That's all there is to it. The two solids are now one solid. In the wireframe viewing mode, the edges of the box that were inside and on the surface of the extruded solid disappear, and a new edge is created where the two solids intersected. Even if the two solids had not touched each other, they would have been combined into one solid, although the gap between them would still exist. You can join as many 3D solids as you like, using any of the standard AutoCAD selection meth-

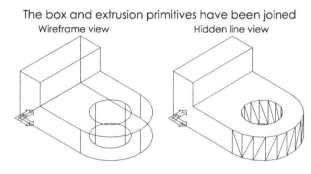

The box and extrusion primitives have been joined

Wireframe view            Hidden line view

ods to choose them. In wireframe mode, your model should now look like the one on the left in the figure, and it should look like the one on the right when HIDE is active.

## Modifications

Although AutoCAD's set of tools for modifying 3D solids is not as complete as you would like, it does have the capability to round (fillet) and bevel (chamfer) sharp edges of 3D solids. These operations are done through the same AutoCAD commands — FILLET and CHAMFER — used for comparable operations on wireframe objects. AutoCAD also has a command, named SLICE, that cuts a 3D solid into two pieces.

The commands for modifying 3D solids are discussed extensively in Chapter 13. To give you an idea of how the FILLET command works on 3D solids, however, you will round the sharp corner located at the intersection of the original box and extruded solid. The command line input to do this is

```
Command: FILLET (Enter)
Current settings: Mode = TRIM  Radius = 0.5000
Select first object or [Polyline/Radius/Trim]:
    (Pick the inside corner edge.)
Enter fillet radius <0.5000>: .25 (Enter)
Select an edge or [Chain/Radius]: (Enter)
```

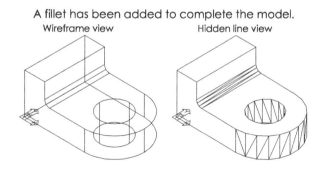

A fillet has been added to complete the model.

Wireframe view            Hidden line view

Unlike fillets on wireframe objects, in which you must select two objects for each fillet, you select an edge between two surfaces for fillets on 3D solids. When you pick the edge of a 3D solid in response to the FILLET command's "Select first object" prompt, AutoCAD recognizes the object type and issues command line prompts appropriate for rounding edges of 3D solids. The first of these prompts allows you to change the current fillet radius. You entered a radius value of 0.25. The second of the special prompts allows you to select additional edges on the 3D solid. To fillet just the one edge, you pressed the Enter key in response to this prompt. This ended the FILLET command, and AutoCAD rounded the initially specified inside corner.

In wireframe form, your completed model should now look like the one on the left side of the accompanying figure, and it should look like the one on the right when you invoke the HIDE command. You are finished with this model, and you do not need to save it. Before you abandon it, however, you might want to try SHADEMODE's hidden and shaded viewing modes on the model, and use 3DORBIT to view the model from a variety of viewpoints.

## The ACIS Geometric Modeler

AutoCAD's solid modeler is based on the ACIS Geometric Modeler from Spatial Technology, Inc. This is a widely used program (often referred to as the ACIS kernel) that contains functions and tools for creating and modifying 3D objects. Organizations throughout the world involved with 3D modeling license the ACIS kernel, incorporate it into their programs, and add their own interface to it.

Autodesk uses the ACIS kernel for 3D modeling in Mechanical Desktop and Inventor, as well as in AutoCAD. Although the ACIS kernel is normally invisible to AutoCAD users, you will sometimes see references to it in error messages, in some AutoCAD documentation, and even in the names of some AutoCAD commands. The ACISIN command, for instance, permits you to import ACIS-based objects into AutoCAD, and the ACISOUT command saves 3D solids in a file format usable by other programs that use the ACIS kernel. These files use SAT at their filename extension.

Like all computer programs, the ACIS Geometric Modeler undergoes periodic revisions. In most cases, the ACIS version is not important. You can though, control the ACIS version used by the ACISOUT command, by changing the default value, which is 40, of the **acisoutver** system variable. **Acisoutver** accepts values of 15, 16, 17, 18, 20, 21, 30, 31, and 40.

## Regions

When a 3D solid is exploded, its flat surfaces turn into an AutoCAD database object called **regions**, while its nonplanar surfaces turn into objects called **bodies**. Although they are a surface type of object (meaning they can hide objects, reflect light in renderings, and have no thickness), body database objects have no practical use. Moreover, the only way to create a body is to explode a 3D solid.

Regions, on the other hand, are an important object type. They are surface-type objects that respond to Boolean operations. You also can use the MASSPROP command on regions to find their area, their geometric center, and moments of inertia. (MASSPROP is discussed in Chapter 14.) Moreover, regions can be used as profile objects with the EXTRUDE and REVOLVE commands to make 3D solids. Because regions can have interior holes (made by subtracting one region from another), they sometimes have an advantage over other profile objects.

The capability of regions to have interior holes, and edges of virtually any shape, also makes them useful for covering planar areas in surface modeling. For example, surfacing the front of the model shown in the figure with polygon mesh objects is not only tedious, the resulting mesh lines tend to make the surface confusing. Covering this area with a region is much easier, and the surface is not cluttered.

Most of the time you will use the REGION command to make regions, but you also can make them with the BOUNDARY command. The BOUNDARY command is most useful when you want to make a region from an interior island, as shown in the following figure.

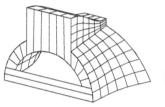

The front of this surface model consists of four ruled surfaces.

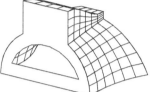

The front of this surface model is one region.

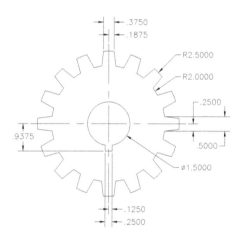

The BOUNDARY command is useful for making a region from this interior area.

## Exercise One

You will draw the cross section of s spur gear in this exercise, and turn it into a region. In subsequent exercies, you will create a solid model of the gear. Start a new AutoCAD drawing using the default English settings. Create a layer that has a name such as WF01, and make it the current layer.

Draw the cross-section of a spur gear on the X-Y plane of the WCS, using the dimensions given in Figure 1-1. The teeth on this gear, which have straight sides, are simplified because the exercise is in creating regions rather than in drawing gear teeth. Feel free to use involute teeth profiles and dimensions instead, if you have the knowledge and time to do so.

When you have finished your 2D drawing of the gear, invoke the REGION command and select all the objects. AutoCAD reports that out of a total of 68

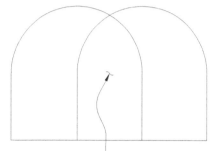

Figure 1-1

objects it found 2 loops, and that it created 2 regions. The center hole and keyway are in 1 region, and the teeth profiles are in the other region. Your gear profile, however, looks the same as when it was composed of individual lines and arcs. Later in this chapter, you will extrude these 2 regions to make 3D solids. These 2 regions are in the file f1015.dwg on the CD-ROM that accompanies this book.

| | |
|---|---|
| Command: | REGION |
| Purpose: | Transforms existing objects into region database objects. |
| Initiate with: | • On the command line, enter REGION. |
| | • From the Draw pull-down menu, select Region. |
| | • Select the Region button from the Draw toolbar. |
| Implementation: | A command line prompt asks you to select the objects that are to be transformed into regions. You can use any object selection method, and you cam select as many objects as you want. Press the Enter key to signal the end of the selection set. |

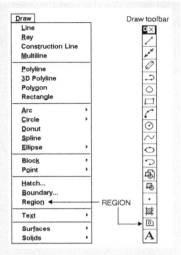

A region can be created from most single planar closed objects — a circle, a 3D face, an ellipse, a closed spline, and a closed 2D polyline (including any member of the 2D polyline family, such as a polygon or a donut). Polyline width is ignored. Splines and 2D polylines qualify when their first and last vertices are in the same location, even if they were not finished with the Close option. Splines and 2D polylines that cross over themselves (self-intersect), or have two vertices in the same location, are not accepted as regions. Nonplanar splines are rejected, and all 3D polylines are rejected, even if they are planar. Polygon and polyface meshes are not accepted.

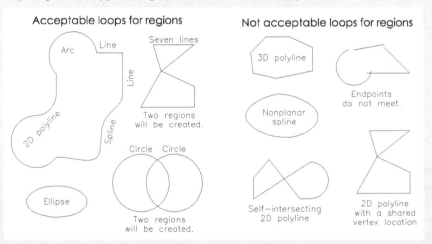

A region also can be created from a set of open wireframe objects that form a closed loop. The loop can be any combination of lines, arcs, 2D polylines, and splines. The objects must be end to end, with no gaps or noncoinciding endpoints, and they must all be in the same plane.

When you are creating a single region, whether it is based on a loop of open objects or on a single closed object, the orientation of the UCS with the plane of the object, or objects, is not important. Moreover, the orientation of multiple closed objects relative to each other and to the UCS is not important. However, multiple loops of open objects must be coplanar, although the orientation of their plane to the UCS is not important. Even if one out of several loops of open objects is not in the same plane as the other objects, no region is created.

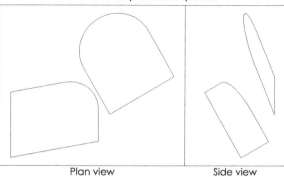

If both of these loops (each consisting of lines and an arc) are in the same selection set, no region is created, because they are not coplanar.

Plan view                    Side view

After you specify the objects that are to be transformed into a region, or regions, AutoCAD reports, on the command line, the number of loops it found in the selection set and the number of regions that were created. If some loops did not result in regions, AutoCAD briefly explains why they were rejected.

The newly created region, or regions, take on the current layer, color, and linetype properties. Thickness for region objects is always 0.

Notes:
  • Regions also can be created by the BOUNDARY command. Unlike the REGION command, BOUNDARY can make regions from planar 3D polylines. BOUNDARY also retains the original objects, placing the region over them.

Related system variable:
  • **delobj**   When **delobj** is set to 0, the object, or objects, used to create a region are retained. When **delobj** is set to 1, they are deleted when the region is created.

## Profile-Based 3D Solids

The eight commands for making 3D solids in basic shapes can be conveniently divided into two groups — those that make solids from profile objects and those that directly make solids having a fundamental geometric shape. The latter group of solids are generally referred to as primitives, although sometimes the word primitive is used for all the basic 3D solids. The AutoCAD database object type, which is 3D solid, is the same regardless of the command used to make them. The next chapter describes the commands for the six primitives and show how they can be used.

The two commands that base 3D solids on profile objects are EXTRUDE and REVOLVE. EXTRUDE makes a 3D solid by pushing the profile object linearly for a specific distance, or by pushing it along a path defined by a wireframe object. REVOLVE creates a 3D solid by revolving the profile object around an axis.

These two commands are even more fundamental than those that make the primitives because they can make any geometric shape that the commands for making primitives can. They also can make geometric shapes that the primitives cannot make. Any solid model that can be built with AutoCAD can be based on just these two commands. (Autodesk's other solid modeler — Mechanical Desktop — uses only profile-based solids and has no commands for making primitives.)

The EXTRUDE and REVOLVE commands have the same requirements for profile objects — each profile must be a single, closed, planar object. 2D polylines will be one of your most often used object types. Autodesk's documentation states that 2D polyline profiles cannot have more than 500 vertices, but they can. This is a moot point, however, because even 500 vertices in a profile will make a 3D solid that is unacceptably unwieldy.

Regions are especially useful as profile objects because they can have interior holes and can therefore create solids with interior holes. Although it is not essential that the holes be present when the solid is first created, because they can be added later, it is convenient.

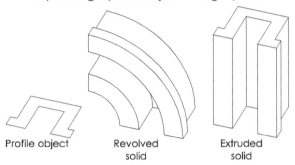

EXTRUDE and REVOLVE both create a solid by moving a profile object through space.

Profile object          Revolved          Extruded
                         solid             solid

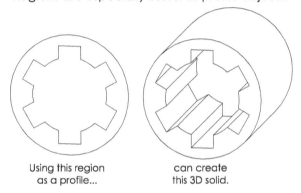

Regions are especially useful as profile objects.

Using this region          can create
as a profile...            this 3D solid.

## Making Extruded 3D Solids

EXTRUDE is the most versatile of the commands for making 3D solids, and will likely be the one you most often use. It can make solids having geometries that none of the other commands can make, and it can often make a geometric shape in one step that would require several steps if the commands for creating primitives were used.

The command gives you two distinct ways to extrude the profile — you can extrude it by specifying a height or by specifying a wireframe path for the extrusion to follow. Either way, you can extrude more than one profile with one call of the EXTRUDE command. Each extrusion, however, must have the same height or use the same path.

Extrusions based on height are so straightforward that little needs to be said about them. Notice, however, that the solid's extrusion direction is based on the profile object's extrusion direction. This is an object property representing the direction of the Z axis at the time the object was created. As a result, the extrusion is not necessarily in the current Z direction. AutoCAD's LIST command shows you an object's extrusion direction.

Extrusions based on paths, on the other hand, can be extremely complicated and can produce unexpected results. It is a powerful option, though — one that enables you to create unique geometries. The following rules will help you control your extrusions by path:

- Keep path shapes as simple as possible. Even when you are making a complex shape, it is often better to create the shape in several steps rather than in one step that requires a complicated path. The Boolean operations can be used to combine and join the extruded segments.

- Start the path in a direction that is perpendicular to the profile.

- Position the path midway between the ends of the profile. This is not necessarily at the weighted geometric center (the centroid) of the profile.

Arcs and 2D polylines are the most often used object types for planar paths. Splines can be tricky to use as path objects, because even a spline that appears to be relatively straight can contain small radius curves that would cause the surface of the solid to self-intersect. When this is the case, AutoCAD displays an error message and doesn't make the solid.

When you need a nonplanar path, 3D polylines are your only choice. Splines would be better, but AutoCAD doesn't accept nonplanar splines as paths.

Although circles can be used as paths, they must have a very large radius relative to the size of the profile. You might have more success with using a 2D polyline of two 180-degree arcs than using a circle. Furthermore, the REVOLVE command will probably create the solid shape you are after without the need for constructing a path.

## Exercise Two

This is the first of three simple exercises in creating extruded 3D solids to give you a feel for the EXTRUDE command. Chapter 12 has more complex exercises as you create 3D models rather than individual components.

Open your drawing of the spur gear profile you made as an exercise in using the REGION command. You also can use the file f1015.dwg on the CD-ROM that comes with this book. The spur gear profile consists of two regions — one for the gear teeth and one for the interior hole.

If you are using your drawing, create a layer named Sol01 and make it the current layer. If you are using the file from the CD-ROM, that layer already exists, and you need only to verify that it is the current layer. Set an SE isometric view point through one of AutoCAD's menus or tool-

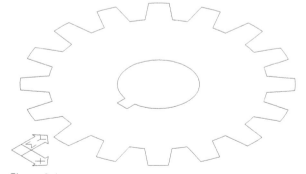

Figure 2-1

bars, or by using the VPOINT coordinates of 1,-1,1 and zoom back a little to give yourself working room. The spur gear profiles will look like the ones in Figure 2-1.

Then use the EXTRUDE command to turn both regions into 3D solids. On the command line, the prompts and input are

```
Command: EXTRUDE (Enter)
Current wire frame density: ISOLINES=4
Select objects: (Use any object-selection method to select both regions.)
Specify height of extrusion or [Path]: 1 (Enter)
Specify angle of taper for extrusion <0>: (Enter)
```

This extrudes both of the regions 1 unit in their extrusion direction, which was in the Z direction. Your model should look like the one in Figure 2-2 when HIDE is in effect. It consists of two separate 3D solid objects. In Chapter 12, you will finish the model by subtracting the solid that represents a hole from the gear blank solid. On the CD-ROM, this model is in file f1022.dwg.

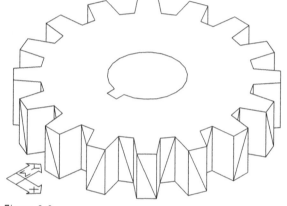

## Exercise Three

In this exercise, you will create a helix-shaped 3D solid that has a round cross-section. Start a new drawing using the default English setup. You will not use this drawing after the exercise is finished, so the setup of its layers and other parameters is not important.

Figure 2-2

The first step is to draw the helix path for the extrusion. Load the spiral.lsp program that is on the CD-ROM. (Probably the easiest way to do this is with the AutoCAD APPLOAD command. This command displays a dialog box you can use to browse for and load the AutoLISP program you want.)

After spiral.lsp has been loaded, use the following command line input to draw a helix.

```
Command: 3DSPIRAL (Enter)
Center point: 0,0,0 (Enter)
Number of rotations: 2 (Enter)
Starting Radius: 1.5 (Enter)
Horizontal growth per rotation: 0 (Enter)
Vertical growth per rotation: 1 (Enter)
Points per rotation <30>: 24 (Enter)
```

Switch the viewpoint to an SE isometric view. The VPOINT coordinates of 1,-1,1 will do this. Your next step is to set the UCS to be perpendicular to the first segment of the helix. This is not a straightforward step because 3DSPIRAL draws the first segment of the helix skewed to the principal planes. It does start on the X-Y plane, however. One of several ways to position and orient the

UCS to be perpendicular to the first segment is to use the 3point option of the UCS command with the point selections shown in Figure 3-1. Then rotate the UCS -90 degrees about its Y axis.

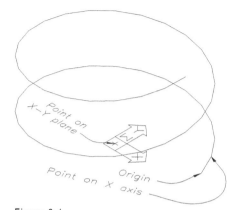

Figure 3-1

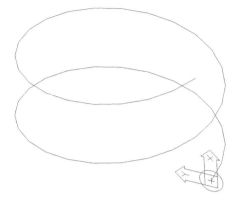

Figure 3-2

When the UCS is positioned, draw a circle centered on the UCS origin with a radius of 0.1875 units. This circle will be the profile for the 3D solid. Your circular profile and helix path should look like those in Figure 3-2.

Start the EXTRUDE command, pick the circle as the object that is to be extruded, choose the path option, and pick the 3D polyline for the path. The completed 3D solid is shown in Figure 3-3. The solid in this figure might not look like the one on your computer screen because the system variable **dispsilh** has been set to a value of 1. This suppresses the display of facets on curved and rounded surfaces of 3D solids when the HIDE command is active, which can result in a less cluttered display of the solid. The **dispsilh** system variable is discussed more extensively in Chapter 14. You should also invoke SHADEMODE to see the effects of its viewing modes.

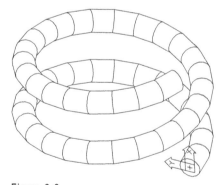

Figure 3-3

Notice that the 3D solid is composed of straight segments corresponding to the straight segments of the 3D polyline. A smooth helix curve made with the SPLINE command would be a much better path, but AutoCAD does not allow nonplanar splines, or even spline-fit 3D polylines, to be used as paths. Furthermore, you are basically restricted to using circular shaped profiles, because the profile tends to rotate as it is swept along the helix path.

The profile and path for this exercise, as well as the completed 3D solid, is in file f1025.dwg on the CD-ROM that comes with this book.

### Exercise Four

Start a new drawing using the English default settings. Create a layer, having a name such as WF01, for wireframe objects, and another, with a name such as CL and a CENTERLINE line type, for center lines. From the WCS, rotate the UCS 90 degrees about the X axis and switch the viewpoint to a plan view of the new UCS orientation. Make the CL layer current, and draw a straight line along the Y axis. This line serves as a location reference in this exercise and as a rotation axis in a later exercise. Then, change to the layer you are using for wireframe objects, and draw the profile shown in Figure 4-1. Do not include the dimensions or the hatch lines. Turn the profile objects into a 2D polyline or a region.

Restore the WCS and change the viewing direction to an SE isometric viewpoint. You will use the profile you just drew to make one side of a pan-shaped solid model. You will also use the profile to make a second side of the model. Therefore, use the polar option of the ARRAY command (or the 3DARRAY command) to make a copy of the profile that is rotated 90 degrees about the center line from the original. Your two profiles should look similar to those in Figure 4-2.

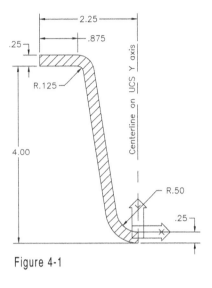

Figure 4-1

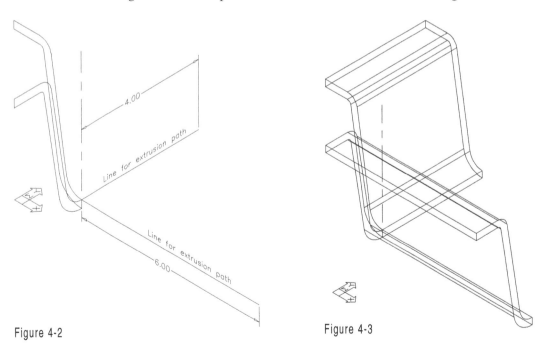

Figure 4-2

Figure 4-3

Because you will use this profile in Exercise 6 of this chapter to make a revolved solid, you should either make a copy of it or set the **delobj** system variable to 0 so it will not be deleted when it is used with the EXTRUDE command. Although you can use the Height option of the EXTRUDE command to make the solids, using a path for each extrusion reduces the uncertainty as to which direction EXTRUDE will push the profile. Therefore, draw a 6-unit-long line along the X axis, and a 4-unit-long line along the Y axis, as shown in Figure 4-2. These lines also are useful for making copies of the extruded solids.

Create a new layer, with a name such as SOL01, and make it the current layer. Start the EXTRUDE command, pick the profile that is in the WCS X-Z plane to be extruded, and pick the 4-unit-long line as its path. Start EXTRUDE again, this time picking the profile that is in the Y-Z plane to be extruded and the 6-unit-long line as its path. Your two extruded 3D solids should look similar to those in Figure 4-3.

Lastly, use the MIRROR command twice to make the opposite sides of the pan. Your model should look similar to the one in Figure 4-4. The model is shown in this figure with HIDE active and with the **dispsilh** system variable set to 1. If you activate SHADEMODE's Hidden option, facets are displayed on curved portions of the model, regardless of the **dispsilh** setting. You will

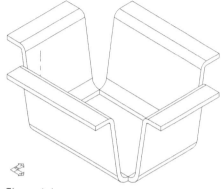

Figure 4-4

make the corners for this pan with the REVOLVE command in Exercise 6 of this chapter. The model, at this stage, is on the CD-ROM that comes with this book in file f1029.dwg.

| Command: | EXTRUDE |
|---|---|
| Purpose: | This command creates a 3D solid by extruding a profile object. The direction and length of the extrusion can be in accordance with the profile object's extrusion direction or in accordance with the direction and length of a wireframe object serving as a path. |
| Initiate with: | • On the command line, enter EXTRUDE. |
| | • From the Draw pull-down menu, select Solids, and then Extrude. |
| | • Select the Extrude button from the Solids toolbar. |
| Options: | • Select Objects | EXTRUDE first issues a command line prompt for you to select the profile objects that are to be extruded. You can select any number of profile objects, and you can use any AutoCAD selection method to choose them. Each profile must be a single closed planar object. Acceptable object types are circles, 2D polylines, and any member of the 2D polyline family, splines, ellipses, regions, and 3D faces. Splines and 2D polylines are considered closed as long as their start points and endpoints are in the same location. They cannot, however, self-intersect or have more than one vertex on a single point. Splines must be planar. 3D polylines are not accepted as profile objects, even if they are planar and closed. |

Thickness is ignored, as is 2D polyline width. Spline-fit 2D polylines are accepted as profiles, but they are a poor choice due to their large number of vertices. Traces and 2D solids (made with the SOLID command) also can be extruded. AutoCAD uses their outline for the extrusion boundary.

• Height of Extrusion

After the profile objects have been selected, you are given two choices for an extrusion method — by height or by a path. When you select the height method, you are asked to specify a height for the extruded solid. You can either enter a number or pick two points in specifying the height. When a positive number 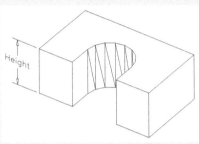 is entered for the height and when the height is specified by pointing, the extrusion is in the profile object's positive extrusion direction, which is the direction of the Z axis at the time the object was created. If you enter a negative number, the extrusion is in the profile object's negative extrusion direction.

• Extrusion Taper Angle

After you specify a height for the extrusion, you will be prompted to specify its taper angle. (This is sometimes, even by AutoCAD's on-screen messages, referred to as *draft angle*.) The angle's units (degrees, radians, and so forth) are determined by the **aunits** system variable. You can specify the angle by entering a number or by pointing. 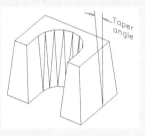 When a nonzero taper angle is entered, the sides of the extrusion are sloped rather than vertical.

The extrusion slopes inward when a positive taper angle is specified. That is, the cross-section area of the solid becomes smaller along the length of the extrusion. If you specify an angle that is so large 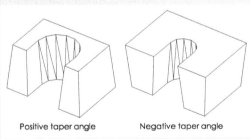 that the extrusion sides would intersect before the specified height is reached, AutoCAD displays an error message and no 3D solid is created. When you specify a negative taper angle, the cross-section area of the solid becomes larger along the length of the extrusion.

Positive taper angle          Negative taper angle

• Path

When the Path option is selected, you are prompted to select one object that determines the extrusion's length, direction, and shape. You can not, however, taper the extrusion. The path object can be either open or closed. Allowed object types are lines, arcs, circles, ellipses, 2D polylines and any member of the 2D polyline family, 3D polylines, and planar splines. Spline-fit 2D polylines can be used as paths, but spline-fit 3D polylines cannot. Nonplanar 3D polylines made of line segments can be used as paths. Nonplanar splines, however, are not accepted.

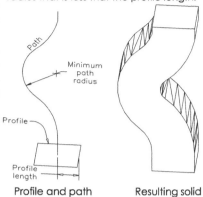

The path cannot have a curve having a radius that is less that the profile length.

Profile and path          Resulting solid

The path cannot be parallel to the plane of the profile object, and it cannot contain curves having a radius less than the profile length. Profile length is the distance from the path to the furthest edge of the profile.
On sharp corners and nontangent arc segment endpoints, the solid is mitered.

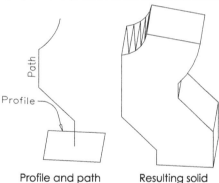

On path sharp corners, the solid is mitered.

Profile and path          Resulting solid

Unless the path is a spline, the extruded solid will start at the profile and its end plane will be perpendicular to the end of the path. This means that if the start of the path is not perpendicular to the profile, the cross-section area of the solid, perpendicular to the path, will be smaller than the profile's area.

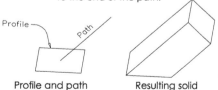

With non-spline paths, the extruded solid starts at the profile and its end plane is perpendicular to the end of the path.

Profile and path          Resulting solid

However, if the path is a spline that is not perpendicular to the profile, AutoCAD will rotate the profile so that it is perpendicular to the start of the path. The end plane of the solid will be perpendicular to the end of the path, the same as with paths of other object types.

The object used for a path does not have to touch the profile. AutoCAD projects the path to the geometric center of the profile, although the location of the object used for the path does not change. If the path object is perpendicular to the profile, this projection is of no consequence. However, if the path object is not perpendicular to the profile, its length and the radius of any arcs on it change according to the direction and distance of the projection.

With spline paths, the ends of the solid are always perpendicular to the path.

Spline path

Profile

Profile and path          Resulting solid

If the path is closed and has sharp corners, such as a hexagon, AutoCAD moves the path so that its closest corner to the profile is centered on the profile, and it rotates the profile to be in line with the mitered corner of the extruded 3D solid.

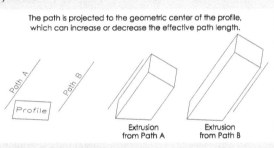

The path is projected to the geometric center of the profile, which can increase or decrease the effective path length.

Path A    Path B

Profile

Extrusion from Path A    Extrusion from Path B

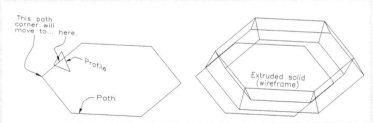

This path corner will move to... here.

Profile

Path

Extruded solid (wireframe)

Notes:   • Extruded 3D solids assume the current layer, linetype, and color properties.

• Regions are an especially useful profile object because they allow you to make extruded solids with interior holes.

Related system variables:

- **delobj**    When **delobj** is set to 0, profile objects are retained when 3D solids are created. When **delobj** is set to 1, its default setting, profile objects are deleted when 3D solids are created.

- **aunits**    This system variable controls the units for angles. Its default setting of 0 sets angle units to decimal degrees.

## Making Revolved Solids

AutoCAD's REVOLVE command transforms the path in space made by revolving a flat profile object about an axis into a 3D solid. Any real-world object machined by turning processes, such as with a lathe, is a likely candidate for a revolved solid. Pipe elbows, rounded corners of almost any object, as well as countersunk and counterbored holes, also can be easily made with REVOLVE.

Using REVOLVE is a three-step operation. First you select one or more profile objects, then you specify the axis of revolutionand lastly, you specify the angle through which the profile (or profiles) is to be revolved.

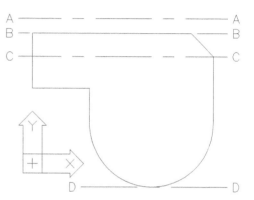

Defining the axis of revolution is a straightforward and flexible step. You can define the axis by picking two points in space, by selecting an existing linelike object, or by using the UCS X or UCS Y axis. The axis has a positive direction, which is important if you do not intend to revolve the profile in a complete circle. See the description of the REVOLVE command for details about the axis orientation.

Although the axis of revolution can touch the profile, no part of it is allowed to be inside the profile. The accompanying figure shows some examples of acceptable and unacceptable axes. You can revolve the profile about the UCS Y axis, but not about the X axis; and you can revolve it about the axes labeled A-A and B-B, but not about the axis labeled C-C.

You also can revolve the profile about the axis labeled D-D, although revolving it a full revolution results in an object that would be virtually impossible to manufacture.

### Exercise Five

This exercise demonstrates how one profile can create entirely different solid forms, depending upon the choice of an axis. Start a new drawing using the default English setup. The use of layers and so forth is not

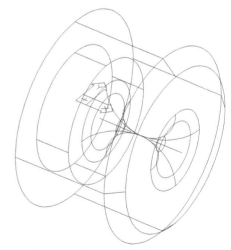

The resulting solid from using D-D as a rotation axis.

important because you will do nothing with the exercise when it is finished.

Rotate the UCS 90 degrees about the X axis and draw the profile shown in Figure 5-1 using the given dimensions. You do not need to include the dimensions or the hatch pattern. Either draw the profile as a 2D polyline, or turn it into one. (Turning it into a region will work just as well.)

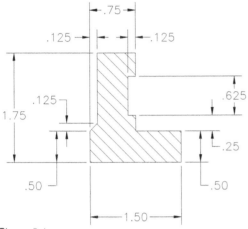

Figure 5-1

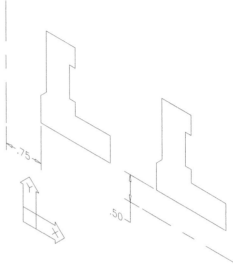

Figure 5-2

When you have finished the profile, make a copy of it located about three units from the original. Then, switch your viewpoint to that of an SE isometric view. (Using VPOINT with the coordinates of 1,-1,1 is one way to do this.) Next, draw the center lines shown in Figure 5-2 to serve as an axis of revolution for each profile. The length of the center lines is not important, nor is their line type.

Use the REVOLVE command twice to turn each profile into a revolved solid. Use the Object option to specify an axis of revolution and revolve both profiles full circle. Your two solids should look similar to those in Figure 5-3 when **dispsilh** has been set to 1 and HIDE is in effect. These two solids, along with copies of their profiles, are in file f1043.dwg on the CD-ROM that comes with this book.

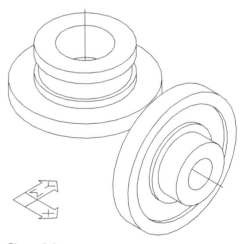

Figure 5-3

### Exercise Six

Open the drawing you used for Exercise 4 of this chapter, or file f1029.dwg on the accompanying CD-ROM. This file contains four extruded 3D solids that you will temporarily want out of the way. Therefore, you should freeze or turn off the layer they are in and create a new layer, having a name such as Sol02, for the revolved solids you are about to make.

Start the REVOLVE command and pick the profile that is in the X-Z plane as the object to be revolved. For an axis of revolution, choose REVOLVE's Object option and pick the vertical center line. Your object selection pick point should be in the lower half of the center line, as shown in Figure 6-1. (Alternately, you could select the other profile and pick the axis on its upper half.)

When the REVOLVE command asks for the angle of revolution, enter 90. Your revolved 3D solid should look like the one shown in Figure 6-2.

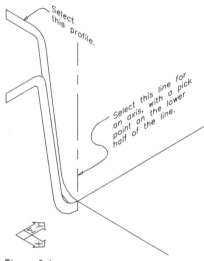

Figure 6-1

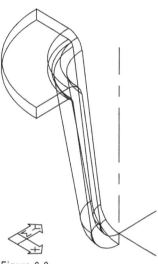

Figure 6-2

Make three copies of this solid, using any suitable sequence of AutoCAD commands you are familiar with (or make copies of the profile and use them in making revolved solids), at the other corners of the model. Then, your model should look like the one shown in Figure 6-3 after you thaw, or turn on, the layer containing the 3D solids you made in Exercise 4.

You will add more features, including a bottom, to this model in the next chapter. Therefore, you should save your file. On the accompanying CD-ROM, the model at this stage is in file f1046.dwg.

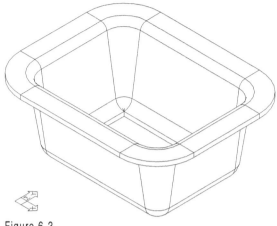

Figure 6-3

| Command: | REVOLVE |
|---|---|
| Purpose: | This command creates a 3D solid by revolving a profile object about an axis. |
| Initiate with: | • On the command line, enter REVOLVE. |
| | • From the Draw pull-down menu, select Solids, then Revolve. |
| | • Select the Revolve button from the Solids toolbar. |

| Options: | • Select Objects | You can use any AutoCAD selection method to choose one or more profile objects. A profile must be a single closed planar object that is one of the following object types: circle, 2D polyline or any member of the 2D polyline family, spline, ellipse, region, or 3D face. Splines and 2D polylines are considered closed, as long as their start points and endpoints are in the same location. They cannot, however, self-intersect or have more than one vertex on a single point. Splines must be planar. 3D polylines are not accepted as profile objects, even if they are planar and closed. |
|---|---|---|
| | | Thickness is ignored, as is 2D polyline width. Spline-fit 2D polylines are accepted as profiles, but they are a poor choice due to their large number of vertices. Traces and 2D solids (made with the SOLID command) also can be revolved. AutoCAD uses their outline to make the revolved solid's surface. |
| | • Axis of Revolution | When you have specified the profile object that is to be revolved, AutoCAD gives you four options for specifying the axis of revolution. This axis has a positive and negative end, and the angular direction of revolution of the profile follows the right-hand rule. The axis must be located so that the profile object does not cross it. |
| | | The command line menu to establish the axis of revolution is: |

```
Specify start point for axis of revolution or define axis by [Object/X
  (axis)/Y (axis)]: (Specify a point or choose an option.)
```

• Start
Point
of Axis

If you specify a point in response to the Axis of Revolution menu, AutoCAD accepts it as the starting point of the axis and prompts for its endpoint. The positive direction of the axis is from the first point to the second point.

Specifying two points as the rotation axis

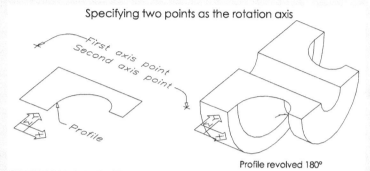

Profile revolved 180°

• Object

This option bases the axis on an existing line or a single-segment 2D or 3D polyline. The positive direction of the axis is from the end closest to the pick point to the opposite end.

Using an object as a rotation axis

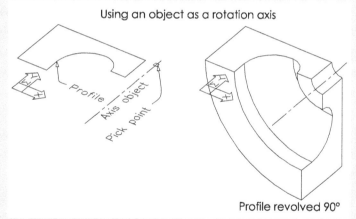

Profile revolved 90°

• X

The X option causes the current UCS X axis to be the axis of revolution. The positive direction of the axis of revolution is the same as the positive direction of the X axis.

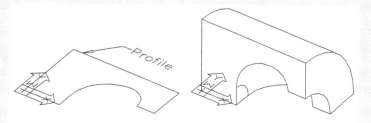

Profile revolved 90°

- Y
  The profile is revolved about the current UCS Y axis when this option is selected. The positive direction of the axis of revolution is in the positive direction of the Y axis.

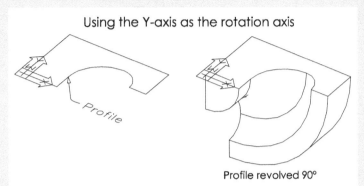

Using the Y-axis as the rotation axis

Profile revolved 90°

- Angle of Revolution
  After each option for specifying the axis of revolution, you will receive a command line prompt to enter the angle through which the profile is to be revolved. You can specify any angle up to a full circle. The units for angles are determined by the value of AutoCAD's **aunits** system variable. Rotation angles follow the right-hand rule, which is that positive rotation is counterclockwise when the axis is viewed from its positive end.

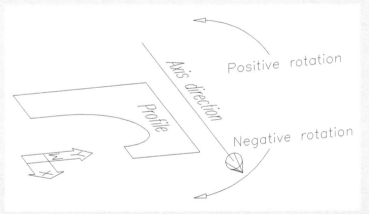

Notes:
- The solid always begins on the profile object and rotates through the specified angle of revolution.
- While the axis of revolution can touch the profile, it cannot cross it.

Related system variables:
- **delobj**
  When **delobj** is set to 0, the profile object is retained when the revolved 3D solid is created. When **delobj** is set to 1, its default setting, the profile object is deleted.
- **aunits**
  This system variable controls the units for the angle of revolution. Its default setting of 0 sets angle units to decimal degrees.

CHAPTER 11

# Primitive Solid Objects

*This chapter concentrates on AutoCAD's 3D solid primitives — those basic geometric shapes that can be used as building blocks to create complex solid models. For each of the six commands — BOX, CONE, CYLINDER, SPHERE, TORUS, and WEDGE — this chapter:*

- *describes how the primitive can be used;*
- *explains how the command for the primitive is implemented;*
- *demonstrates the use of each primitive.*

The word *primitive*, when used in conjunction with solid modeling, refers to fundamental geometric forms, rather than to crudeness or roughness. The primitive geometric shapes, along with the AutoCAD commands that make them, are

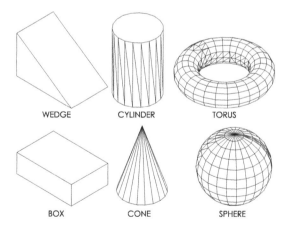

| Geometric Shape | Command |
|---|---|
| Right prism | BOX |
| Right wedge | WEDGE |
| Cylinder | CYLINDER |
| Cone | CONE |
| Sphere | SPHERE |
| Torus | TORUS |

Singly, the primitives are of little use, but they can make surprisingly complex solid models when they are combined and modified with the Boolean functions. Although the EXTRUDE and REVOLVE commands can make the geometric shape of any of the primitives, the commands for making primitives directly do not require profile objects, and they usually involve less manipulation of the UCS.

# The Box Primitive

You will probably use boxes (despite their name they are not hollow) most often because many of the objects you model will be comprised of boxlike shapes. The command is limited to drawing boxes that have their sides aligned with the principal coordinate system axes. If you need a box that is askew from the principal axes, you have to either reposition the UCS before you make the box or rotate the box after it is made.

When the BOX command is initiated, you are given the choice to base the box on a corner or on its center. The center option is useful when you want the box to be centered on a particular point in space, such as the center of gravity of an existing solid.

Most of the BOX command options involve picking a base corner for the box, drawing a rectangle to establish its length and width, and lastly, specifying a height. If you are making the box from a plan view, AutoCAD drags a rubberband rectangle from the base corner to help you locate the other corner. From all other viewpoints, and when the Center option is used, AutoCAD drags a single rubberband line rather than a rectangle.

Menus and toolbar buttons for creating primitive solid objects

## Exercise One

Open the file you used for Exercise 6 in Chapter 10. The same model is in the file f1046.dwg on the CD-ROM that accompanies this book. Recall that the sides of this model were made by extruding a profile and that the corners were made by revolving the same profile 90 degrees. In this exercise, you will make the bottom of the model.

Freeze the layer that the sides are on so that you gain a better view of the bottom part of the model. In the file on the CD-ROM, the layer to freeze is Sol01. Make certain that the layer you used for the corners is current, and invoke the BOX command.

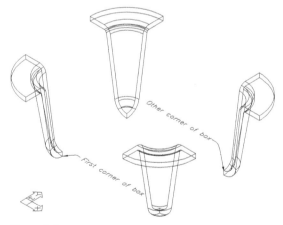

Figure 1-1

When you are prompted to specify a corner for the box, use an object endpoint snap to pick the point labeled "First corner of box" in Figure 1-1. And, when you are prompted to specify the other corner of the box, use an object endpoint snap to pick the point labeled "Other corner of box" in Figure1-1. Because these points have different elevations, AutoCAD makes the 3D solid without any additional prompts or input. Thaw the layer that the four sides of the model are in. When HIDE is in effect, and the system variable **dispsilh** is set to 1, your model should now look like the one in Figure 1-2. On the CD-ROM, this model is in file f1104.dwg. In other exercises in this chapter, you will join the componets of this model and make some bolt holes in its flange.

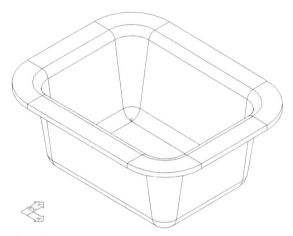

Figure 1-2

| Command: | BOX |
|---|---|
| Purpose: | BOX creates a 3D solid in the shape of a right prism. |
| Initiate with: | • On the command line, enter BOX. |
| | • From the Draw pull-down menu, select Solids, and then Box. |
| | • Select the Box button from the Solids toolbar. |
| Options: | When the BOX command is initiated, it displays the following command line menu: |

`Specify corner of box or [CEnter] <0,0,0>: Enter C, specify a point, or press Enter.`

Entering the letter C bases the box on its center point, while specifying a point or pressing Enter bases the box on a corner.

• Corner of Box — If you pressed the Enter key in response to the main menu, the first corner of the box will be on the UCS origin. If you specified a point, the first corner of the box will be on that point. In both cases, AutoCAD displays the following menu for establishing the other three key corners of the box.

`Specify corner or [Cube/Length]: Enter C or L, or specify a point.`

• Other Corner — Specifying a point establishes a second corner of the box. This point must have different X and Y coordinates than the initial corner. If the point has a different Z coordinate than the initial corner point, AutoCAD uses the point's X coordinate for the length of the box, the point's Y coordinate for its width, and the Z coordinate for its height.

If the other corner has the same Z coordinate as the first corner, AutoCAD uses it to set the box's length and width and prompts for the height of the box. Height is entered as a distance, rather than as a point. A positive distance value draws the box in the positive Z-axis direction, while a negative value draws the box on the negative Z-axis side of the X-Y plane.

The other corner sets the height of the box.

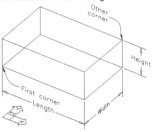

AutoCAD prompts for the box height.

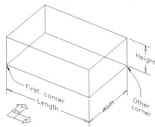

- Cube

This option makes a box that has equal-length sides. You will be prompted to specify a length by entering a number or by pointing. Pointing or entering a positive number causes the box to be positioned on the X-Y plane in the positive X and Y quadrant. Entering a negative number causes the box to be located below the X-Y plane in the negative X and Y quadrant.

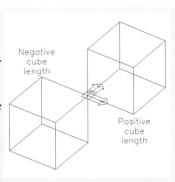

- Length

When this option is selected, AutoCAD issues command line prompts for the box's length, width, and height. Length represents the X dimension of the box, width is its Y dimension, and height is its Z dimension. Entering negative dimension values draws the box in the negative direction of the axis.

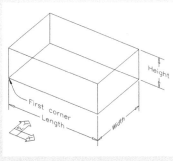

- Center of Box

Selecting the Center option from the main BOX menu bases the box on its geometric center rather than on a corner. AutoCAD issues command line prompts for you to specify the box's center and to establish its dimensions.

```
Specify center of box <0,0,0>: Specify a point or press Enter.
Specify corner or [Cube/Length]: Enter C or L, or specify a
    point.
```

- **Corner of Box**

Specifying the location of a point establishes a corner edge of the box. The point must have X and Y coordinates that are different from those of the box center. If you specify a point that has a different Z coordinate than the center of the box, AutoCAD uses it to establish the length, width, and height of the box. The length, width, and height dimensions of the box are twice the distances in the X, Y, and Z directions from the center of the box to the box corner.

If the specified point is at the same elevation as the box center point, AutoCAD uses it to set the length and width of the box and prompts for a distance to set the box's overall height. The resulting height is the same regardless of whether negative or positive distance values are entered.

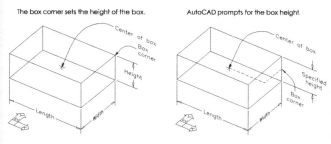

The box corner sets the height of the box.                AutoCAD prompts for the box height.

- **Cube**

The length, width, and height of the box will be equal when this option is selected. AutoCAD issues a command line prompt for the box's length. A negative length value produces the same results as a positive length value.

- **Length**

This option is for specifying the dimensions of the box with distance values, rather than with point locations. AutoCAD presents command line prompts for you to enter the length, width, and height

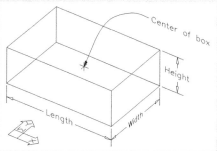

dimensions of the box. You can enter a numerical value or select two points to specify a dimension. Negative values produce the same results as positive values.

Notes:

- The sides of the 3D solid box are always aligned with the current UCS X, Y, and Z axes.

# The Wedge Primitive

Wedges are like boxes that have been sliced diagonally from opposite edges. Consequently, the prompts and input for the WEDGE command are similar to those of the BOX command. The sides of wedge primitives are always in the shape of a right triangle, and the slope of the wedge is always in the X-axis direction. You can, however, control whether the horizontal side of the wedge is on its top or on its bottom side, and whether the wedge's sharp end points in the positive or negative X direction by using positive and negative numbers when specifying the wedge's dimensions. Positive numbers for wedge length point the wedge in the positive X direction, while negative numbers point the wedge in the negative X direction. And, positive numbers for height input place the horizontal side of the wedge on the bottom, while negative numbers place it on the top.

## Exercise Two

Start a new drawing using the default English settings. You don't need to retain the model you make during this exercise, so the drawing setup is not important. Use VPOINT to set a viewpoint rotated 280 degrees in the X-Y plane from the X axis, and 10 degrees from the X-Y plane.

Use the following command line input to create a wedge that is based on its center point, fits in a 1-unit-sized cube, and is centered at the UCS origin:

```
Command: WEDGE (Enter)
Specify first corner of wedge or [CEnter] <0,0,0>: CE (Enter)
Specify center of wedge\<0,0,0>: (Enter)
Specify opposite corner or [Cube/Length]: C (Enter)
Specify length: 1 (Enter)
```

Your wedge should look similar to the one shown in Figure 2-1. Notice that what AutoCAD calls the center of the wedge is on the center of its slope, rather than at its center of gravity (the centroid). The coordinates for the center of this wedge are 0,0,0, while the coordinates for its center of gravity are -0.1667,0.0000,-0.1667. (The MASSPROP command, which is described in Chapter 14, reports the location of a 3D solid's center of gravity.) On the CD-ROM that accompanies this book, this wedge is in file f1110.dwg.

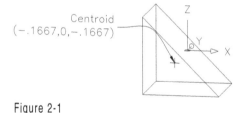

Figure 2-1

| Command: | WEDGE |
| --- | --- |
| Purpose: | WEDGE creates a 3D solid in the shape of a right-angle wedge. |
| Initiate with: | • On the command line, enter WEDGE. |
| | • From the Draw pull-down menu, select Solids, and then Wedge. |
| | • Select the Wedge button from the Solids toolbar. |

Options:

Wedges are similar to boxes that have been split diagonally from opposite edges. The flat side of the wedge is always parallel with the UCS X-Y plane, and its slope is in the X-axis direction. The WEDGE command begins by displaying the following command line menu:

```
Specify first corner of wedge or [CEnter]<0,0,0>: Enter C, specify a point, or press
    Enter.
```

Entering the letter C (Despite the capitalization in the prompt, you do not have to enter CE) bases the wedge on a point that is midway between its length, width, and height, while specifying a point or pressing Enter bases it on one corner of its high side.

- Corner of Wedge

If you pressed the Enter key in response to the main menu, the first corner of the wedge is on the UCS origin. If you specified a point, the first corner of the wedge is on that point. In both cases, AutoCAD displays the following menu for establishing the other three key corners of the wedge.

```
Specify corner or [Cube/Length]: Enter C or L, or specify a point.
```

- Other Corner

Specifying a point establishes an opposite corner of the wedge. This point must have X and Y coordinates that are different from those of the initial corner. If the point has a different Z coordinate than the initial corner point, AutoCAD uses the point's X coordinate for the length of the wedge, the point's Y coordinate for its width, and the Z coordinate for its height.

If the other corner has the same Z coordinate as the first corner, AutoCAD uses it to set the wedge's length and width and prompts for the length of the high side of the wedge. Height is entered as a distance, rather than as a point. A positive distance value locates the wedge in the positive Z-axis direction, while a negative value locates it on the negative Z-axis side of the X-Y plane.

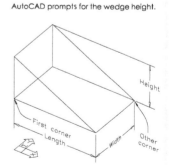

The other corner sets the wedge height.          AutoCAD prompts for the wedge height.

- Cube   This option makes the wedge's length, width, and height equal. You are prompted to specify the length by entering a number or by pointing. Pointing or entering a positive number causes the wedge to be positioned on the X-Y plane, in the positive X and Y quadrant, and pointed in the positive X direction. Entering a negative number causes the wedge to be located below the X-Y plane, in the negative X and Y quadrant, and pointed in the minus X direction.

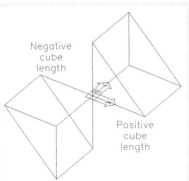

- Length   When this option is selected, AutoCAD issues command line prompts for the length, width, and height of the wedge. Length represents the X dimension of the wedge, width is its Y dimension, and height is its Z dimension. Entering negative dimension values draws the wedge in the negative direction of the axis.

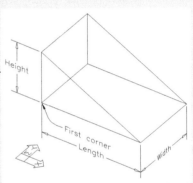

- Center of Wedge

  Selecting the Center option from the main WEDGE menu bases the wedge on a point midway between its length, width, and height, rather than on a corner. This point is on the slanted surface of the wedge. AutoCAD issues command line prompts for you to specify the center point of the wedge and to establish its dimensions.

  ```
  Specify center of wedge <0,0,0>: Specify a point or press Enter.
  Specify opposite corner or [Cube/Length]: Enter C or L, or specify a
      point.
  ```

- Corner of Wedge

  Specifying the location of a point establishes a corner on the high side of the wedge. The point must have X and Y coordinates that are different from those of the wedge center. If you specify a point that has a different Z coordinate than the center of the wedge, AutoCAD uses it to establish the length, width, and height of the wedge. The length, width, and height dimensions of the wedge are twice the distances in the X, Y, and Z directions from the center of the wedge to the selected corner.

  If the specified point is at the same elevation as the wedge center point, AutoCAD uses it to set the length and width of the wedge and prompts for a distance to set its height. If a negative height value is entered, the flat side of the wedge will be on its top side, rather than on its bottom side.

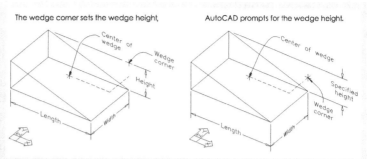

The wedge corner sets the wedge height,        AutoCAD prompts for the wedge height.

- Cube   The length, width, and height of the wedge are equal when this option is selected. AutoCAD issues a command line prompt for the wedge's length. When a positive length is used, the flat side of the wedge is on the bottom. When a negative length is entered the flat side of the wedge is on the top.

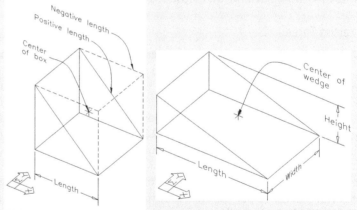

- Length   This option is for specifying the dimensions of the wedge with distance values, rather than with point locations. AutoCAD presents command line prompts for you to enter the length, width, and height dimensions of the wedge. You can enter a numerical value or select two points to specify a length. A negative length points the sharp edge of the wedge in the minus X direction, and a negative height places the flat side of the wedge on top. Negative width values have no effect.

Notes:   - The straight sides of the 3D solid wedge are always aligned with the current UCS X, Y, and Z axes, and the wedge always slopes in the X direction. Whether it slopes in the positive or negative X direction depends on input to the WEDGE command.

# The Cylinder Primitive

Cylinders, which are made with the CYLINDER command, are likely to be your second most often used primitive because they can be used to make round holes. In fact, if you routinely make holes in certain specific sizes, such as 7/16 of an inch or 10mm, you could benefit from a macro that implements the CYLINDER command with preset cylinder diameters.

The default input for establishing the length of the CYLINDER points the axis of the cylinder in the Z-axis direction. Positive height draws the cylinder in the positive Z direction, while entering a negative height draws it in the minus Z direction. You also can specify a point representing the center of the opposite end of the cylinder. Because this point sets both the orientation and length of the cylinder, you can use this option to make cylinders that point in any direction.

You will probably not use the option for drawing cylinders with an elliptical cross-section often, but it is available when you need it. Establishing the base dimensions of the elliptical cross-section is similar to drawing a 2D ellipse, but not as flexible. Although you can base the ellipse on its endpoints, or on its center, an ellipse rotation-angle option is not available, and AutoCAD does not drag an ellipse-shaped rubberband outline to help you draw the ellipse.

### Exercise Three

Open the solid model you used in Exercise 1 of this chapter to make a bottom for the 3D model of a thick-walled pan. On the CD-ROM that accompanies this book, the model is in file f1104.dwg. In this exercise, you will make some cylinders within the top flange of the part. In Chapter 12, you will use the Boolean subtract operation to turn these cylinders into holes.

Move the UCS to the top surface of the flange. Then, start the CYLINDER command to make one cylinder that has a radius of 0.25 units and a height of -0.25 units, located in the position shown in Figure 3-1. The negative height value places the cylinder inside the flange.

Place cylinders in the same position in the other three corners of the flange by copying the original cylinder or by implementing the CYLINDER command three more times. If you want to, you also can place cylinders at other locations of your choice on the flange. When you finish, your 3D model should look similar to the one in Figure 3-2 when HIDE is in effect and when the **dispsilh** system variable is set to 1.

The model looks complete, but its corners, sides, and bottom need to be joined, and the cylinders need to be turned into holes. You will do that in the next chapter. On the CD-ROM, the model at this stage is in file f1118.dwg.

# The Cone Primitive

The only difference between cone primitives and cylinder primitives is that cones taper to a point rather than keeping the same cross-section size throughout their length. Therefore, it is no surprise that the options and prompts for the CONE command are similar to those of the CYLINDER command.

After you specify the size of the cone base, which can be round or elliptical, the CONE command prompts for either the Apex or the Height of the cone. The Height option points the sharp

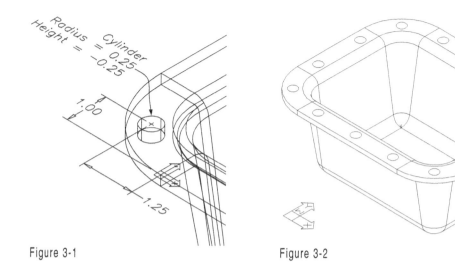

Figure 3-1                              Figure 3-2

tip of the cone in the Z direction, using the specified height as the base-to-tip length of the cone. The Apex option is equivalent to the Center of Other End option for cylinders. With it, you specify a point that serves as both direction and length to the tip of the cone. Cones always have sharp tips — there are no options for making truncated cones.

### Exercise Four

Start a new drawing using the default English setup. Because you will not use the model you will make in this exercise, the drawing's initial setup of layers and so forth is not important. Set the view direction to an SE isometric view.

Use the following command line input to make a cone that is 3 units long, has an elliptical base, and is pointed 45 degrees in the X-Y plane from the X axis and 45 degrees from the X-Y plane:

```
Command: CONE (Enter)
Current wire frame density: ISOLINES=4
Specify center point for base of cone or [Elliptical]
    <0,0,0>: e (Enter)
Center/<Axis endpoint>: (pick any point on the XY
    plane)
Specify second axis endpoint of ellipse for base of cone: @2<0 (Enter)
Specify length of other axis for base of cone: @.75<90 (Enter)
```

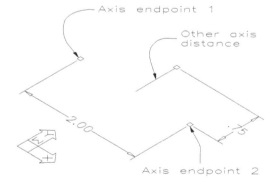

Figure 4-1

The preceding input, which is pictured in Figure 4-1, establishes the size and shape of the cone's base. The following input establishes the location of the cone's tip:

```
Specify height of cone or [Apex]: a (Enter)
Specify apex point: @3<45<45 (Enter)
```

Notice that relative spherical coordinates were used to set the apex point. Your cone should be similar to the one shown in Figure 4-2.

Figure 4-1 shows the model in its wireframe mode when AutoCAD's **isolines** system variable has been set to a value of 8. This variable sets the number of lines along the length of the cone. A regen is required before changes to **isolines** take effect. On the CD-ROM, you will find this model in file f1128.dwg.

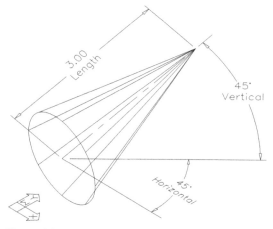

Figure 4-2

| | |
|---|---|
| Command: | CONE |
| Purpose: | CONE creates a 3D solid that tapers to a point from either a circular or elliptical base. |
| Initiate with: | • On the command line, enter CONE. |
| | • From the Draw pull-down menu, select Solids, and then Cone. |
| | • Select the Cone button from the Solids toolbar. |
| Options: | The cross-section perpendicular to the axis of cones can have either a circular or elliptical shape. CONE begins with the following command line menu: |

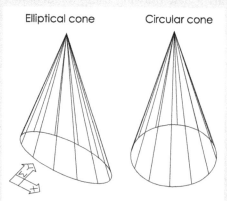

```
Specify center point for base of cone or
   [Elliptical] <0,0,0>: Enter an E,
   specify a point, or press Enter.
```

Specifying a point establishes the base of a cone having a circular cross-section, and pressing the Enter key results in a cone having a circular cross-section that is based at the UCS origin.

| | |
|---|---|
| • Center Point | After the base center point of a cone with a circular cross-section has been established (by picking a point or pressing the Enter key in response to the main CONE menu), AutoCAD anchors a rubberband line on the center point and issues the following prompt for you to specify the size of the base: |

```
Specify radius for base of  cone or [Diameter]: Specify a radius dis-
   tance or enter a D.
```

Responding to this prompt with a distance, by either pointing or entering a value, establishes the radius of the cone's base. Responding by entering a D (or by entering the entire word Diameter) brings up a prompt for you to specify the diameter of the cone's base. You can specify the diameter by entering a value or by picking a point.

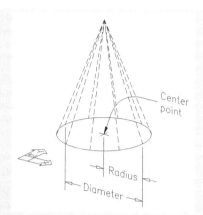

After you specify the size of the cone base, AutoCAD displays the submenu:

`Specify height of cone or [Apex]: Specify a distance or enter an A.`

- Height

When you respond to the submenu by specifying a distance, whether by entering a number or by picking two points, AutoCAD uses that distance as the height of the cone in the current Z-axis direction. Entering a negative number points the cone in the minus Z-axis direction.

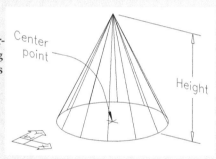

- Apex

When you enter an A, or the word apex, in response to the submenu, AutoCAD issues the prompt:

`Specify apex point: Specify a point.`

This point locates the cone's tip, and therefore sets both the length and the orientation of the cone.

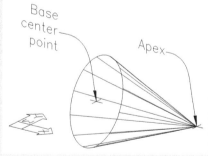

- Elliptical

Choosing the Elliptical option from the main CONE menu makes a cone that has an elliptical cross-section. AutoCAD displays the following menu for establishing the location and size of the base ellipse:

`<Specify axis endpoint of ellipse for base of cone or [Center]: Specify a point or enter a C.`

• Axis End-point

When a point is specified, by either entering its coordinates or by picking its location, AutoCAD uses it as one end of the elliptical cross-section axis and asks for the opposite end-point of this axis.

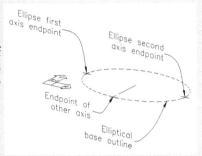

```
Specify second axis endpoint of
    ellipse for base of cone:
    Specify a point.
```

As soon as the second point is specified, AutoCAD anchors a rubber-band line midway between the two points and asks for the distance from this midpoint to one end of the other axis of the ellipse:

```
Specify length of other axis for base of cone: Specify a distance.
```

• Center

Entering the letter C brings up a series of prompts for basing the elliptical base of the cone on its center rather than on the endpoints of one axis:

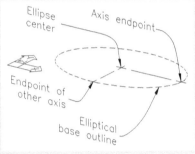

```
Specify center point of ellipse
    for base of cone <0,0,0>:
    Specify a point or press
    Enter.
Specify axis endpoint of
    ellipse for base of cone:
    Specify a point.
```

After you define the position and size of the elliptical cone base, AutoCAD displays the submenu:

```
Specify height of cone or [Apex]: Specify a distance or enter an A.
```

• Height

When you respond to this submenu by specifying a distance, either by entering a number or by picking two points, AutoCAD uses that distance as the cone's height in the current Z-axis direction. When a negative number is entered, the tip of the cone is pointed in the minus Z-axis direction.

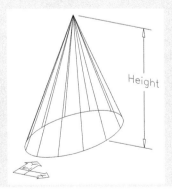

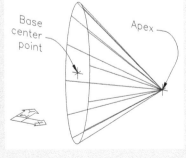

- Apex    When you enter an A, or the word Apex, in response to the submenu, AutoCAD issues the prompt:

  Specify apex point: Specify a point.

  The point you specify establishes the location of the cone's tip and, therefore, sets both the length and the orientation of the cone.

Notes:
- In wireframe viewing modes, the number of lines on the cone's surface from its base to its apex is controlled by the value of AutoCAD's **isolines** system variable.

# The Sphere Primitive

Making a sphere is the most straightforward operation of all the primitives. The SPHERE command prompts you to specify a center point, then it prompts for the size of the sphere. The only option of the command is whether the size of the sphere is to be based on its diameter or its radius.

The SPHERE command always bases spheres on their center points. Often, however, you need to make a sphere that it is on, or touches, a particular surface or object. Sometimes, it would also be nice if you could make a sphere by specifying two points that establish both the size and location of the sphere — similar to the two-point option of the CIRCLE command. The AutoLISP program globexyz.lsp on the CD-ROM that comes with this book solves both these problems.

One function in this program, SPHEREZ, makes a sphere that sits on top of (in the positive Z direction) a selected point. You merely specify a point and the radius of the sphere. The other function in this program, SPHERE_2P, allows you to make a sphere by specifying two points on its surface.

### Exercise Five

Start a new drawing using the default English setup for this exercise. You will not do anything with the objects you create in this drawing, so its initial setup of layers and so forth is not important. Set the view direction to an SE isometric view through the View pull-down menu, one of the two SE isometric toolbar buttons, or the VPOINT command. Then load the globexyz.lsp program. The APPLOAD command is a good way to do this.

Make a 3D solid sphere that sits on the X-Y plane and has a radius of 1 unit by using the following command line input:

```
Command: SPHEREZ (Enter)
Bottom of sphere: 1,1 (Enter)
Radius of sphere: 1 (Enter)
```

The sphere appears, sitting on the X-Y plane. Next, make a sphere by specifying two points:

```
Command: SPHERE 2PT
Specify a point on the sphere's surface: 3,3,0 (Enter)
Specify the opposite point: 3,3,-2 (Enter)
```

This sphere also has a radius of 1 unit and touches the X-Y plane, but it is below the plane, rather than above it. These two spheres are shown in Figure 5-1. This figure shows the spheres when AutoCAD's **isolines** system variable has been given a value of 8 to make the round shape of the spheres more apparent.

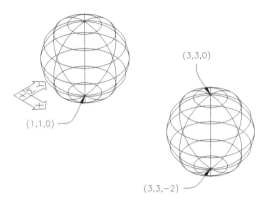

Figure 5-1

| Command: | SPHERE |
|---|---|
| Purpose: | SPHERE creates a 3D solid in the shape of a sphere. |
| Initiate with: | • On the command line, enter SPHERE. |
| | • From the Draw pull-down menu, select Solids, and then Sphere. |
| | • Select the Sphere button from the Solids toolbar. |
| Implementation: | The SPHERE command first asks for the center of the sphere: |

Specify center of sphere <0,0,0>: Specify a point or press Enter.

Then, AutoCAD anchors a rubberband line on the center point and prompts for the sphere's radius or diameter:

Specify radius of sphere or [Diameter]: Enter a D, or specify a distance.

- Radius        You can specify the radius of the sphere by entering a distance value or by picking a point.

- Diameter      If you enter a D at the Diameter/Radius prompt, AutoCAD leaves the rubberband line anchored to the center of the sphere and prompts for a diameter. If you pick a point for the diameter, the distance from the center of the sphere to the picked point represents the diameter rather than the radius of the sphere. You also can enter the diameter as a numerical value.

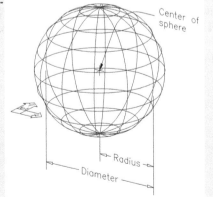

Notes:    • In its wireframe form, the number of latitude and longitude lines on spheres is controlled by AutoCAD's **isolines** system variable. If you have trouble visualizing spheres in their wireframe form, increase the value of **isolines** from its default of 4 to 12 or 16. A regen is required for the change

# The Torus Primitive

A torus is the geometric shape made when a circle is revolved about an axis located in the plane of the circle and (generally) outside the perimeter of the circle. A donut is an obvious example of a torus; an O-ring is another.

The command line prompts and input for the TORUS command reflect the geometric definition of a torus. First you specify the circle's distance from the axis (which AutoCAD calls the torus radius),

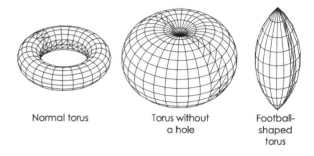

Normal torus      Torus without a hole      Football-shaped torus

and then you specify the size of the circle (which is referred to as the tube by AutoCAD). The axis of the torus is always perpendicular to the current X-Y plane. You are allowed to have a tube radius larger than the torus radius, which makes a torus that does not have a hole. Despite the use of the word tube, these tori are not hollow.

The TORUS command also allows you to make objects in the shape of a football. You do this by entering a negative number in response to the torus radius (or diameter) prompt. When you do this, you must specify a tube radius that is larger than the absolute value of the torus radius.

## Exercise Six

Start a new drawing using the default English settings for this exercise. The initial setup of drawing parameters is not important. Set the viewpoint to an SE isometric view. You will make three different tori. Use the following command line input to make the first one:

```
Command: TORUS (Enter)
Current wire frame density: ISOLINES=4
Specify center of torus <0,0,0>: (Enter)
Specify radius of torus or [Diameter]: 1.0 (Enter)
Specify radius of tube or [Diameter]: 0.5 (Enter)
```

The resulting torus is shaped like a donut and centered on the UCS origin. Next, you will make a torus that does not have a center hole:

```
Command: TORUS (Enter)
Current wire frame density: ISOLINES=4
Specify center of torus <0,0,0>: 3,3,0 (Enter)
Specify radius of torus or [Diameter]: .75 (Enter)
Specify radius of tube or [Diameter]: 1.0 (Enter)
```

Lastly, you will make a football-shaped torus:

```
Command: TORUS (Enter)
Current wire frame density: ISOLINES=4
Specify center of torus <0,0,0>: 5,5,0 (Enter)
Specify radius of torus or [Diameter]: -2.0
  (Enter)
Specify radius of tube or [Diameter]: 3.0
  (Enter)
```

Figure 6-1

These three tori are shown when HIDE is in effect in Figure 6-1.

| | |
|---|---|
| Command: | TORUS |
| Purpose: | TORUS creates a 3D solid in the shape of a circular ring or in the shape of a football. |
| Initiate with: | • On the command line, enter TORUS. |
| | • From the Draw pull-down menu, select Solids, and then Torus. |
| | • Select the Torus button from the Solids toolbar. |
| Options: | A torus is the geometric shape defined by revolving a circle about an axis that is in the plane of the circle. Usually the axis is outside the perimeter of the circle, but it doesn't have to be. The axis and the circle of tori made by the TORUS command are always perpendicular to the current UCS X-Y plane. |
| | The TORUS command first issues a command line prompt for you to specify the location of the axis: |
| | `Specify center of torus <0,0,0>: Specify a point or press Enter.` |
| | Then, AutoCAD prompts for the distance from the axis to the circle's center. You can express this distance as either a radius or a diameter: |
| | `Specify radius of torus or [Diameter]: Specify a distance or enter a D.` |
| | If you respond by entering a D (or the word diameter), AutoCAD prompts for the diameter of the torus. Negative radius and diameter values are permitted — they create a football-shaped solid. Lastly, AutoCAD prompts for the radius or the diameter of the circle that is to form the tube of the torus: |
| | `Specify radius of tube or [Diameter]: Specify a distance or enter a D.` |
| | If you enter the letter D, AutoCAD prompts for the diameter of the tube. The tube radius can be larger than the torus radius, which makes a torus without a center hole. |

## Standard torus

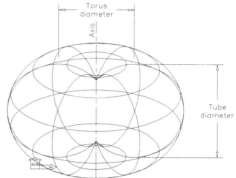

## Torus without a center hole

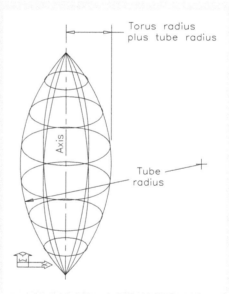

Torus diameter < Tube diameter

If a negative number was used to designate the radius or diameter of the torus, the tube must be larger than the absolute value of the torus. Thus, if you had entered a torus radius of -3, the tube radius must be larger than 3.

The radius of the thickest cross-section of a football-shaped torus (created by entering a negative torus radius or diameter) is equal to the torus radius plus the tube radius. For instance, if the torus radius is -3.0 and the tube radius is 4.0, the radius of the football will be 1.0 (-3.0 + 4.0). The radius of the arc-shaped profile of the football is equal to the tube radius.

# CHAPTER 12

# Using Boolean Operations

*In the previous two chapters, you learned how to create 3D solid objects in various shapes. Now you will learn how to use the interaction between two or more individual 3D solids to construct complex 3D solid models.*

*This chapter*

- *explains what Boolean operations are;*

- *describes how solids and regions can be joined with the Union Boolean operation;*

- *describes how one set of solids or regions can be subtracted from another set;*

- *describes how a new solid can be created from the intersecting volume of two or more solids, and a new region can be created from the intersecting area of two or more regions.*

## Boolean Operations

By themselves, 3D solids made as primitives or as extruded or revolved profiles are seldom useful, and generally, you must combine two or more 3D solid objects to make the geometry you need for a complete model. This is done through Boolean operations. (They are named after George Boole, the mathematician who developed theories on sets and logic that are used in computers and computer programs for switching and for filtering data.)

Most computer programs, including AutoLISP, have the three Boolean logical operators of AND, OR, and XOR. (In AutoLISP, a bit-wise form of these operators are in the BOOLE function.) AutoCAD has three operators, each implemented with its own command, for working with solids and regions that correspond to the logical operators for programming. The relationships between the logical operators, the Boolean operations in solid modeling, and the AutoCAD command for making them are shown in Table 12-1.

You can perform Boolean operations on 3D solids and on regions. You cannot, however, mix the two object types. Despite their close relationship to set theory and programming, you do not need to know anything about those subjects to perform Boolean operations on 3D solids and regions. The three commands are easy to grasp and straightforward to use.

## Table 12-1

| Boolean Logic Operator | AutoCAD Boolean Operator | AutoCAD Command |
|---|---|---|
| AND | Union | UNION |
| OR | Subtract | SUBTRACT |
| XOR | Intersection | INTERSECT |

UNION joins two or more 3D solids or regions. The individual solids, or regions, become a new single object even if they do not touch one another. If they have some volume, or area, in common (that is, if one solid, or region, is partly inside another), the common volume, or area, is absorbed into the new object. If one object is completely inside another, it is simply absorbed by the new object.

SUBTRACT removes the volume of one set of solids from another set, or the area of one set of regions from another. If they have no volume, or area, that is shared, the objects that are subtracted disappear. When the objects that are being subtracted are partly inside those that are to be subtracted from, their entire volume, or area, is deleted along with the common volume, or area. If the objects being subtracted enclose those that are being subtracted from, all the solids, or regions, are deleted.

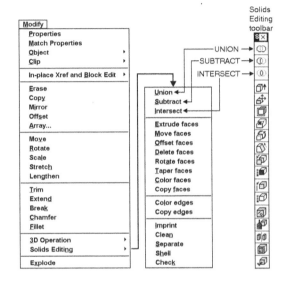

INTERSECT creates a new solid from the volume that two or more solids share, or a new region from the common area of two or more regions. If the objects have no volume or area in common, they are all deleted. If they have some volume (or area) in common, only that which is shared is retained — everything else disappears. If the solids or regions have the same shape and size and occupy the same space, they are all deleted.

These Boolean operations are summarized graphically in the following diagram. Although this diagram uses just two solids to demonstrate each of the Boolean operations, they work equally well on any number of solids. The Boolean operations work in the same way on regions.

Often, the solid that is obtained from a Boolean operation is referred to as a *composite solid*. Although some solid-modeling programs keep track of the primitives used to make up a composite solid, and can even restore them to their original form if necessary, AutoCAD does not retain data of the original components of Boolean operations, and there is no way to restore them. After a set of solids, or regions, has been modified by any of the Boolean operations, only the UNDO command can return them to their original state.

Because of this limitation, it is generally a good practice to postpone the Boolean operations as long as possible during the construction of a 3D solid model. This allows you to change individual components of the model before they are fused or subtracted from one another.

## Joining Solids and Regions

Very little needs to be said about the UNION command, especially when 3D solids are involved. You do not even need to be particular about the selection set when specifying the solids to be joined because AutoCAD automatically filters out objects not subject to the UNION command. The solids can be anywhere in 3D space. The only requirement of the command is that at least two 3D solids must be selected.

When regions are involved, the command is more restrictive, because all the regions must be in the same plane. The union operation will fail even if only one of several regions is not coplanar with the others. The current location of the UCS, however, has no bearing on the UNION command.

If the selected solids or regions are in a variety of layers, and you want the resulting solid or region to reside in a specific layer, you should make certain that the object you select first is in the layer you want. The layer that is current has no effect on the layer of the unioned objects.

The only aspect of the UNION command that might surprise you is that even solids and regions with a space between them can be unioned. AutoCAD does not, however, fill the space between them, and there is no change in their appearance (unless their layer changes). Nevertheless, AutoCAD treats them as one object, and you can move them or erase them by picking any one of them.

One use for unioning nonconnecting solids (or regions) is for making a modeling version of subassemblies. For example: If you regularly design pipe flanges that have different sets of hole sizes, shapes, and spacing, you could have several different sets of unioned cylinders (which can be

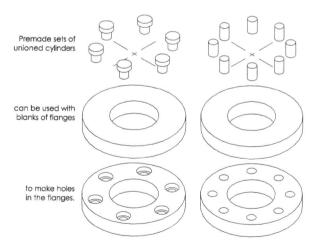

Premade sets of unioned cylinders

can be used with blanks of flanges

to make holes in the flanges.

unioned with other solids to make countersunk or counterbored holes) to be subtracted from the flanges. It is similar to using blocks in 2D drawings. Incidentally, although you can make blocks from solids, inserted blocks of those solids cannot be unioned. They can, however, be exploded (provided they have equal X and Y scales) and then unioned.

Unioning nonconnected solids is sometimes also useful when INTERSECT is to be used to create certain shapes. For example, if the two box-shaped solids shown on the left in the nearby figure are separate solids, INTERSECT between the three solids deletes all three because no common volume exists. On the other hand, if the two box-shaped solids are unioned, INTERSECT creates the

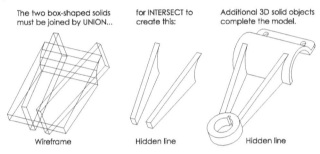

The two box-shaped solids must be joined by UNION...        for INTERSECT to create this:        Additional 3D solid objects complete the model.

Wireframe        Hidden line        Hidden line

solid shown in the middle of the figure. Additional solid objects and Boolean operations can then create the model shown on the right side of the figure.

## Exercise One

Open the file that holds the solid model you last used in Exercise 3 of Chapter 11. On the CD-ROM that comes with this book, the model is in file f1118.dwg. The model has all the components you intend for it to have; you just need to use Boolean operations to join individual components and make holes.

Recall that the corners of this model were made by revolving a profile, its sides were made by extruding the same profile, its bottom was made by the BOX command, and the cylinders in its flange were made by the CYLINDER command. You will first join the four corners, four sides, and one bottom into one object.

Start the UNION command and select everything except the cylinders. The seam on top of the flange separating the corners from the sides disappears, as shown in Figure 1-1. Otherwise, the model looks the same. If you miss selecting any of the eight objects, just repeat the UNION command to join the overlooked objects with those that are already joined.

That is all you will do with the UNION command on this model. You could use it to combine the cylinders so that they could be subtracted as a single object from the flange of the pan, but that provides no advantage. On the CD-ROM, the model at this stage is in file f1205.dwg. You will finish this model in Exercise 3 of this chapter.

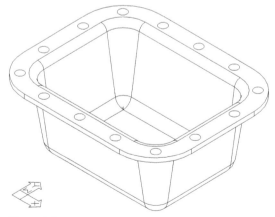

Figure 1-1

| | |
|---|---|
| Command: | UNION |
| Purpose: | This command performs the Boolean Union operation on two or more 3D solids, or on two or more regions. |
| Initiate with: | • On the command line, enter UNION. |
| | • From the Modify pull-down menu, select Solids Editing, and then Union. |
| | • Select the Union button from the Solids Editing toolbar. |
| Implementation: | When the UNION command is invoked, it issues a command line prompt for you to select the solids and regions that are to be joined. You can use any AutoCAD selection method for choosing the objects, but you must select at least two solids or two regions. AutoCAD filters out objects in the selection set that are not 3D solids or regions and joins the qualifying objects with no further prompts or options. |

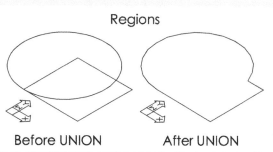

3D solid objects are unioned regardless of where they are located. They become a single 3D solid even if they do not touch, although the space between them remains open. Regions are unioned only if they are coplanar — that is they must be in the same plane. If any region in the selection set is not coplanar with the others, none of them are unioned.

If both 3D solids and regions are included in the selection set, the 3D solids are unioned to form one 3D solid, and the regions are unioned to form a single region, provided they are coplanar.

The new composite 3D solid, or region, takes the layer of the first solid, or region, selected, rather than the layer that is current.

# Subtracting Solids and Regions

Performing a Boolean subtract operation through the appropriately named SUBTRACT command is straightforward. First, you are prompted from the command line to select a set of objects that are to have other objects subtracted from them. If more than one object is selected, AutoCAD automatically performs a union operation to consolidate them into a single object. Next,

AutoCAD issues a command line prompt for you to select the objects that are to be subtracted from the first set. The volume, or area, that is shared by both selection sets is deleted as well as any volume, or area, that remains in the second selection set.

### Exercise Two

Retrieve and open the file containing the 3D solid spur gear you created by extruding a region in Exercise 2 of Chapter 10. On the CD-ROM that comes with this book, the model is in file f1015.dwg.

Recall that this model consists of two 3D solids — one is the main part of the gear, including the teeth, and the other is a solid that represents the center keyed hole of the gear. Use the following command line input to make a hole in the gear by subtracting the center solid from the gear blank:

```
Command: SUBTRACT (Enter)
Select solids and regions to subtract from...
Select objects: (Select the gear. Be certain that you do not include the center of the gear.)
1 found
Select objects: (Enter)
Select solids and regions to subtract...
Select objects: (Select the solid in the center of the gear.)
1 found
Select objects: (Enter)
```

In the wireframe viewing mode, the model appears to be unchanged. If you invoke the HIDE command, as shown in Figure 2-1, or use one of SHADEMODE's shaded modes, however, you can see that the gear does have a keyed hole in its center. You will not do anything further with this model. On the CD-ROM, the completed solid model gear is in file f1208.dwg.

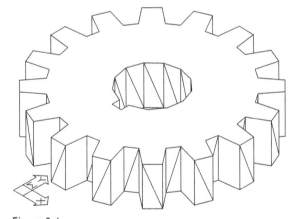

### Exercise Three

Open the file you used in Exercise 1 of this chapter. In this exercise, you will finish the model by making the bolt holes in the flange. On the CD-ROM, this model is in file f1205.dwg.

Figure 2-1

The hardest work in making the holes, that of making and positioning the cylinders for the holes, has been done. All you have to do now is subtract the cylinders from the flange.

Start the SUBTRACT command and select anywhere on the pan to specify the object that is to be subtracted from. Then, select the cylinders as the objects to subtract. You can use any object selection method to select them, including a crossing window. Your model should look similar to the one in Figure 3-1 when HIDE is active and the **dispsilh** system variable has been set to 1.

That completes this 3D model, although you might want to experiment with it yourself by adding more features and performing Boolean operations. On the CD-ROM, the completed model is in file f1209.dwg.

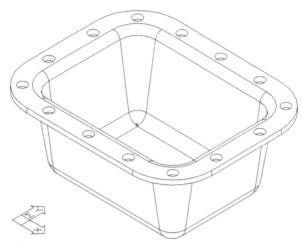

Figure 3-1

| Command: | SUBTRACT |
| --- | --- |
| Purpose: | This command performs the Boolean Subtract operation on two or more 3D solids or on two or more regions. |
| Initiate with: | • On the command line, enter SUBTRACT. |
| | • From the Modify pull-down menu, select Solids Editing, and then Subtract. |
| | • Select the Subtract button from the Solids Editing toolbar. |
| Implementation: | SUBTRACT issues two command line prompts for two sets of objects: |

```
Select solids and regions to subtract from...
Select objects: (Use any object-selection method.)
Select solids and regions to subtract...
Select objects: (Use any object-selection method.)
```

The objects in the second selection set are deleted, along with the volume, or area, that is common to the objects in both selection sets. You can include both 3D solids and regions in the selection sets, although there is no interaction between the two object types. Objects in either selection set that are not 3D solids or regions are ignored by the command.

If more than one solid or region is included in the first selection set, AutoCAD automatically unions them, and then proceeds with the subtraction operation. If you include an object in the second selection set that was part of the first selection set, AutoCAD proceeds with the subtraction as if the object had not been included in the second selection set.

If the object, or objects, in the second selection set do not have any volume or area in common with those in the first set, they disappear without any effect on the first set. If the objects in the second selection set completely enclose those in the first set, both sets of objects disappear, and AutoCAD reports that a null solid, or region, was created and was deleted.

The layer of the resulting solid is that of the objects in the first selection set. If more of the objects in the first selection set were in more than one layer, the resulting solid takes the layer of the object that was selected first.

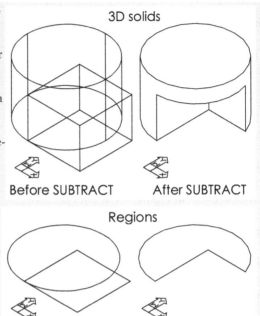

3D solids

Before SUBTRACT          After SUBTRACT

Regions

Before SUBTRACT          After SUBTRACT

## Using Intersect

The Boolean intersection operation is performed by the INTERSECT command. It creates a new object from the volume, or area, shared by two or more 3D solids or regions. In some respects, intersection is the reverse of the union operation. When overlapping objects are unioned, everything that is not shared is retained, with the shared volume, or area, being absorbed into the new object. When overlapping objects are intersected, everything that is not shared is deleted, with only the common volume, or area, being retained.

Similar to the UNION command, INTERSECT prompts for the objects to be operated on, and it filters out objects that are not 3D solids or coplanar regions. Although you will not use INTERSECT as much as UNION and SUBTRACT, it is a more interesting operation to experiment with, and it can make shapes that cannot be made by the other two Boolean operations. Using INTERSECT is comparable to cutting a shape out of a block by cutting along an outline traced on the sides of the block, such as cutting the general shape of a duck decoy from a block of wood with a band saw.

The INTERFERE command also performs an intersection-like operation on 3D solids and is a possible source of confusion. INTERFERE is not intended to be a command for modifying 3D solids — it is for checking for interference between two 3D solids in an assembly. Also, INTERFERE does not work on regions. The INTERFERE command is described in Chapter 14.

### Exercise Four

You will use INTERSECT to make a pyramid-shaped 3D solid. Start a new drawing using the default English setup. Because you will do nothing with the model when it is completed, layers and other drawing parameters are not important. Rotate the UCS 90 degrees about the X axis, and draw a triangle on the WCS Z-X plane using the dimensions shown in Figure 4-1.

Turn the triangle into a 2D polyline or a region, and place a copy that is rotated 90 degrees from the original, as shown in Figure 4-2. If you return to the WCS, the ordinary ARRAY command can easily make the copy.

Next, use the EXTRUDE command to make two wedge-shaped 3D solids from the triangles, as shown in Figure 4-3. Extrude each triangle at least 2 units. You will probably have to extrude the triangle on the WCS Z-X plane in its negative extrusion direction, although this depends on how the UCS was oriented when you drew its profile. If the bases of the two solids are not in the same location, as shown in Figure 4-4, use AutoCAD's MOVE command to place them in the same location.

Lastly, invoke the INTERSECT command, and select both wedges. Your resulting 3D-solid pyramid should look like the one in Figure 4-4 when HIDE is active. That finishes the exercise. On the CD-ROM that accompanies this book, the pyramid is in file f1215.dwg.

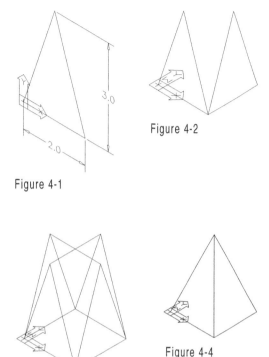

Figure 4-1

Figure 4-2

Figure 4-3

Figure 4-4

### Exercise Five

In this exercise, you will create a 3D solid model from a 2D drawing. Start a new drawing file using the default English setup. Your initial drawing setup of layers, linetypes, and so forth is not important.

Make a 2D drawing on the WCS X-Y plane using the dimensions given in Figure 5-1. You do not need to include the dimensions or anything drawn in centerline or hidden-line types. You should also leave out the horizontal line in the front view between the 0.25 radii. You need only the outline of each view and the circles in your drawing. On the CD-ROM that accompanies this book, the three outlines are in file f1216.eps.

Turn the three view outlines and three circles into regions, and subtract the circle-shaped regions from the outline they are in. Then, extrude the top view 2.5 units, the front view 1.5 units, and the side view 4.0 units. Do not taper the extrusions. Your three extrusions should be similar to those shown in Figure 5-2.

Next, rotate the 3D solids representing the front and side views 90 degrees so that they are oriented as shown in Figure 5-3. The ROTATE3D command is a good way to rotate these solids.

Move the three 3D solids so that they occupy the same space, as shown in Figure 5-4.

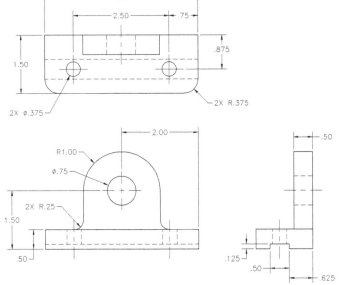

Figure 5-1

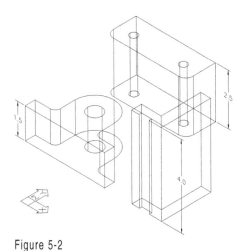

Figure 5-2

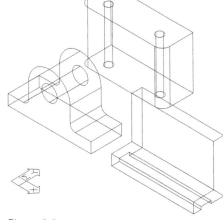

Figure 5-3

Lastly, invoke the INTERSECT command, and select all three solids. Your finished 3D model should look similar to the one in Figure 5-5 when HIDE is in effect. On the CD-ROM that comes with this book, this model is in file f1220.dwg.

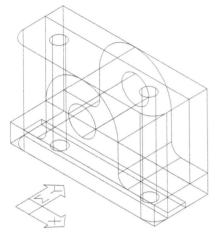

Figure 5-4

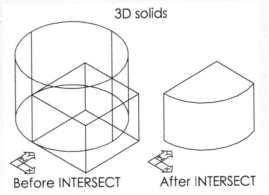

Figure 5-5

| Command: | INTERSECT |
|---|---|
| Purpose: | This command performs the Boolean Intersection operation on two or more 3D solids, or on two or more regions. |
| Initiate with: | • On the command line, enter INTERSECT.<br>• From the Modify pull-down menu, select Solids Editing, and then Intersect.<br>• Select the Intersect button from the Solids Editing toolbar. |
| Implementation: | The INTERSECT command issues a command line prompt for you to select objects. You can use any object-selection method, but you must select at least two suitable objects. Objects other than 3D solids and coplanar regions are filtered out of the selection set. That is the extent of command usage; there are no other prompts. |

3D solids

Before INTERSECT        After INTERSECT

A new 3D solid, or region, is created from the overlapping volume, or area, of the selected objects. The resulting object takes the layer of the first object in the selection set. Unshared volume or area disappears. If the objects do not share any volume, or area, they are all deleted, and AutoCAD reports that a null solid was created and then deleted.

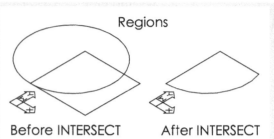

Notes:

• The INTERFERE command is easily confused with INTERSECT because of their similar names and because they both create a 3D solid from the intersecting volume of two solids. INTERFERE, however, does not delete the original solids, and it operates on one pair of solids at a time. It is for checking for interference between two solids.

## Exercise Six

In this exercise, you will build a 3D model using a variety of the commands for creating 3D solids and for performing Boolean operations that have been discussed in the last three chapters. In Chapter 13 of this book, you will round some of the sharp edges of this model, and in Section 4 you will make a 2D drawing from the model.

Start a new drawing using the default English setup, and establish layers for wireframe objects, center lines, and 3D solid objects. Use your layer for wireframe objects to draw two circles centered at the WCS origin having the diameters given in Figure 6-1. Turn the two circles into regions and subtract the inner one from the outer one to make a ring.

Rotate the UCS 90 degrees about the X axis, switch to your layer for center lines, and draw the center line that is also shown in Figure 6-1. This center line starts and ends with straight lines and has an arc in its middle. You will use this centerline as an extrusion path; therefore, turn the two lines and the arc into a 2D polyline. Change to the layer you have reserved for 3D solids, and use the path option of the EXTRUSION command to make a curved tube from the ring.

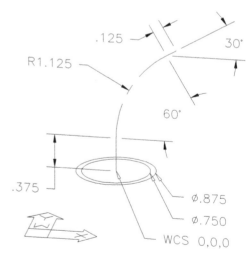

Figure 6-1

Switch back to the WCS and to your wireframe layer, and draw a 1.5x1.5 square centered on the WCS origin and having corners rounded with a radius of 0.25, as shown in Figure 6-2. Because you will use it to make an extruded 3D solid, turn it into a region. Also draw a circle having the same location and diameter as the inside of the tube. Turn the circle into a region, and subtract it from the square-shaped region that has rounded corners. Then extrude the region 0.25 units in the Z direction. Do not taper the extrusion. Activate a hidden-line or shaded-viewing mode and use 3DORBIT to look at your model to verify that the base you just created does not block the curved tube.

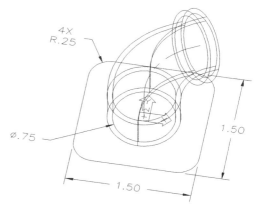

Figure 6-2

Move the UCS to the front side of the extruded base and rotate it 90 degrees about the X axis. Change back to your wireframe layer. Then, draw a D-shaped profile (with the arc in the WCS Z direction) as a 2D polyline, using the dimensions in Figure 6-3. Be certain you include a line segment along the bottom of the profile (on the edge of the base extrusion). Draw a circle within the polyline using the dimensions given in Figure 6-3.

Extrude the D-shaped profile 0.375 units in its minus Z direction (toward the tube). Then, union it with the tube extrusion and the base extrusion. Next, extrude the circle 0.50 units in its minus Z direction, and subtract the resulting 3D solid from the composite 3D solid. When the **dispsilh** system variable is set to 1, and HIDE is in effect, your model should now look similar to the one in Figure 6-4.

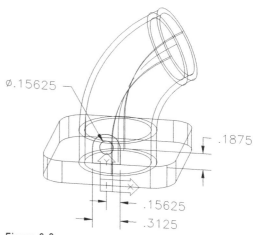

Figure 6-3

Restore the WCS, and then rotate the UCS 90 degrees about the X axis. Draw the profile for a counterbored screw hole in the WCS Z-X plane off to the side and out of the way from the model. Use the dimensions given in Figure 6-5 for the profile. Then, use the REVOLVE command to turn the profile into a 3D solid. The axis of revolution will be along the 0.25-long line on the profile. Your resulting 3D solid should look similar to the one in Figure 6-5.

Again restore the WCS, and move the revolved 3D solid into the base of the model as shown in Figure 6-6. Make three copies of the revolved 3D solid, positioned in the other three corners of the base as shown in Figure 6-6. Subtract the four revolved 3D solids from the main composite model.

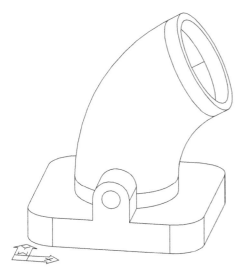

Figure 6-4

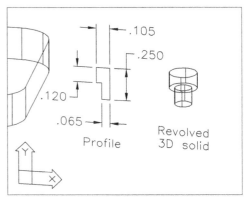

Figure 6-5

Position the UCS so that it is on the end of the extruded tube as shown in Figure 6-7. You can do this with the 3point option of the UCS command. Pick the end of the curved tube center line (or the center of the tube end) as the UCS origin, and use quadrant object snaps on the end of the tube to establish the X-and Y-axis directions. When the UCS is positioned, draw the profile shown to the right in Figure 6-7. Although the 3D solid is to be centered at the current UCS origin, it is easier to draw its profile away from the main model because the model is getting cluttered.

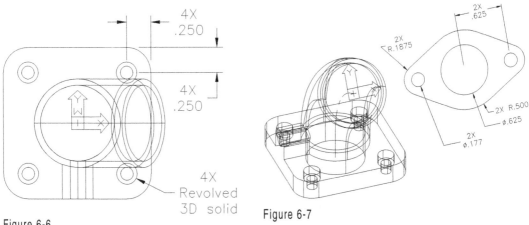

Figure 6-6

Figure 6-7

Turn the profile outline and the three circles into regions, and subtract the circle regions from the outline region. Then extrude the profile 0.1875 units in its positive Z direction. The 0.625-diameter hole in the 3D solid you just made is to be counterbored. Therefore, move the UCS origin to the end of this hole (a center object snap positions it), and draw a 0.75-diameter circle, as shown in Figure 6-8.

Extrude the circle 0.0625 units in its minus Z direction. Make the counterbore by subtracting the extruded circle from the diamond-shaped solid. Restore the previous UCS (at the end of the curved tube), and move the diamond-shaped solid to the end of the tube so that their center points are in the same location.

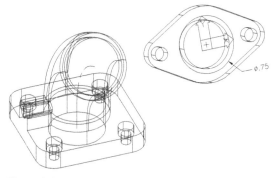

Figure 6-8

Figure 6-9

The last step is to use the UNION command to join the two solids. Your model should be similar to the one shown in Figure 6-9. On the CD-ROM that comes with this book, the model is in file f1231.dwg. You will add some fillets to this model in the next chapter.

## Exercise Seven

You will build the model of a sheet-metal part in this exercise. You will use the EXTRUSION command to make the 3D solid object, and SUBTRACT and UNION for Boolean operations. In the next chapter, you will use the FILLET command to round the folded edges of the model and use CHAMFER to bevel some of its sharp corners.

Begin a new drawing using the default English setup. Create layers having names such as WF01 and SOL01. Use your wireframe layer for drawing profile objects, and your solid layer when you create 3D solid objects. Draw five lines on the WCS X-Y plane, using the orientation and the dimensions given in Figure 7-1. Then, draw an oval (or an obround, as it is called in the sheet-metal industry) as shown in Figure 7-1. Do not include the dimensions or the center lines.

Turn the outline and the oval into 2D polylines or regions and use EXTRUDE to make two 3D solids. The height of the solids should be 0.10 units, and the taper angle should be 0. Eventually, the extruded oval will be subtracted from the main 3D solid, but you will postpone the Boolean operations until all the components of the model have been created. That allows you to more easily recover from mistakes.

Orient the UCS as shown in Figure 7-2. The viewpoint for this figure is 260 degrees in the X-Y plane from the X axis, and 20 degrees from the X-Y plane. The ZAxis option of the UCS command, followed by a rotation about the Z axis of 45 degrees, is a convenient way to position the UCS. Draw a rectangle according to the dimensions in Figure 7-2.

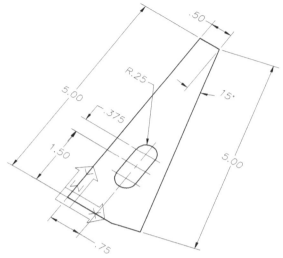

Figure 7-1

Turn the four lines into a 2D polyline or a region and extrude it to a height of 5.00 units, using no taper angle. Move and orient the UCS as shown in Figure 7-3. One way to do this is to use the 3point option of the UCS command along with object endpoint snaps. Make certain that all three of the picked points are on the same side of the extruded 3D solid. The viewpoint for Figure 7-3 is 335 degrees in the X-Y plane from the X axis, and 35 degrees from the X-Y plane. Draw a rectangle as a 2D polyline, along with two circles, using the dimensions shown in Figure 7-3, and extrude them to a height of 0.10 units, with no taper, into the previously extruded 3D solid. Whether you use a positive or negative extrusion direc-

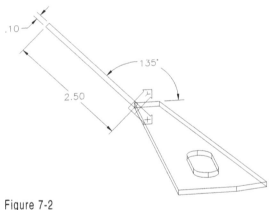

Figure 7-2

tion depends on which side of the previously extruded solid the profiles are on. The three new solids sould be within the previously extruded solid.

Next, position the UCS as shown in Figure 7-4. The ZAxis option of the UCS command coupled with object endpoint snaps is a convenient way to do this in one step. Using the dimensions given in the figure, draw six lines. Turn them into a 2D polyline or a region, and extrude it to a height of 5.0 units, with 0 taper.

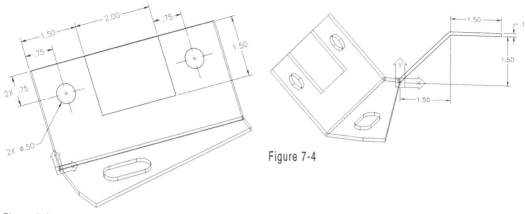

Figure 7-3

Figure 7-4

Leaving the UCS origin at its present location, rotate the UCS minus 90 degrees about the Y axis, and rotate it once more minus 45 degrees about the X axis. This positions the UCS on the lower side of the 45-degree slope on the most recently extruded solid. Then, draw three lines and one arc, using the dimensions shown in Figure 7-5. The viewpoint for this figure is 210 degrees in the X-Y plane from the X axis, and 45 degrees from the X-Y plane. The solid to be made from the outline will be subtracted from the main solid, and it deliberately extends beyond the 45-degree face on the solid to ensure that it removes all the material you want. Change the arc and the three lines into a 2D polyline or a region and extrude it to a height of 0.10 units, with no taper.

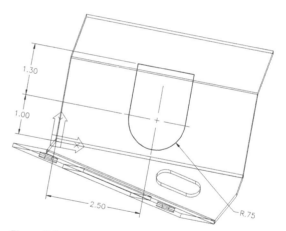

Figure 7-5

The last wireframe objects you need to draw are the two ovals and one square shown in Figure 7-6. Position the UCS on the bottom side of the upper horizontal 3D solid face, and use the dimensions given to draw the objects. Turn the wireframe objects into 2D polylines or regions, and extrude them with no taper to a height of 0.10.

Change to a viewpoint that allows you to clearly see all the 3D solids. The viewpoint for Figure 7-7 is 280 degrees from the X axis in the X-Y plane and 50 degrees from the X-Y plane.

When you are satisfied that the 3D solids are as you want them to be, union the three solid objects that were extruded to a height of 5.0 units, and subtract all the other solid objects from them. You can do this in one step with the SUBTRACT command by selecting the three 5.0-unit extruded objects as the solids to be subtracted from, and the remaining eight objects as the solids to be subtracted. Your model should look similar to the one in Figure 7-8. In the next chapter, you will finish this model by adding some fillets and chamfers. On the CD-ROM that comes with this book, the model at this stage is in file f1239.dwg.

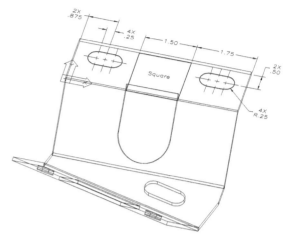

Figure 7-6

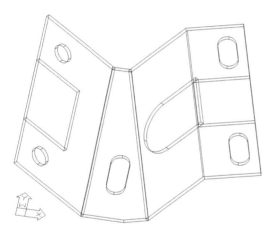

Figure 7-7

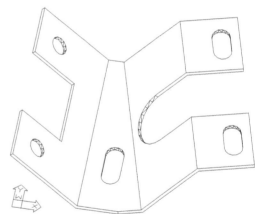

Figure 7-8

# CHAPTER 13

# Modifying 3D Solids

*Unlike the Boolean operations, the operations discussed in this chapter modify a single 3D solid object. You will use them to create and edit new features on your solid models.*

*This chapter*

- *explains how to round sharp edges and corners and how to blend surfaces of 3D solids with the FILLET command;*

- *shows you how the CHAMFER command is used to bevel sharp edges of 3D solids;*

- *describes how to cut a 3D solid into two separate pieces;*

- *explains how to edit 3D solids with AutoCAD 2000's SOLIDEDIT command.*

## Creating Fillets

For 3D solids, a fillet is, basically, a rounded surface between adjacent faces that has an arc-shaped cross-section and is tangent to each face. Fillets can be on inside edges, between two surfaces, or on outside edges; they can bend around cor-

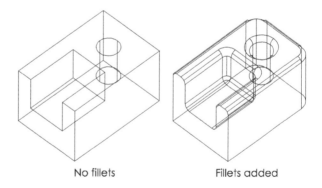

No fillets          Fillets added

ners, and they can blend multiple faces together at their intersection.

Sharp edges on 3D solids are changed into fillets through AutoCAD's FILLET command. You will recall that this command starts by asking you to select the first object to be filleted. When you pick a 3D solid in response to this prompt, AutoCAD recognizes it and displays a special command line menu for 3D solids rather than prompting for a second wireframe object. Through this menu, you can fillet any number of edges on the solid and you can specify various radii for the fillets. You can, however, fillet the edges of only one 3D solid with each call to the FILLET command — you cannot fillet two adjacent solids.

The fillets AutoCAD makes on 3D solids are sometimes referred to as rolling ball fillets because the tangent points of the fillet's arc (where it blends with the adjacent surfaces) can be mapped by rolling a ball along the intersection of two surfaces. And, sometimes imagining a ball rolling along the edge you want filleted can help you determine whether the edge will accept your fillet parameters. If the edge has curves that are smaller than the radius of your fillet, or if one surface adjacent to the fillet isn't as wide as your fillet radius, the fillet will fail.

## Exercise One

In this exercise, you will experiment with the FILLET command on a variety of 3D solids that you will find in the file f1305.dwg on the CD-ROM that accompanies this book. This file contains filleted and unfilleted versions of three different 3D solids. You will add fillets to the unfilleted version of each 3D solid and compare your results with the filleted version.

Find and zoom in close to the cube-shaped 3D solid shown if Figure 1-1. You will fillet three adjoining edges on this cube, assigning a different radius to each fillet. On the command line, the prompts and your input are

```
Command: FILLET (Enter)
Current settings: Mode=TRIM Radius = 0.5000
Select first object or [Polyline/Radius/Trim]: (Pick a point on a vertical edge.)

Enter fillet radius <0.5000>: .25 (Enter)

Select an edge or [Chain/Radius]: R (Enter)
Enter fillet radius <0.2500>: .125 (Enter)
Select an edge or [Chain/Radius]: (Pick a point on
    an adjacent horizontal edge.)
Select an edge or [Chain/Radius]: R (Enter)
Enter fillet radius <0.1250>: .375 (Enter)
Select an edge or [Chain/Radius]: (Pick a point on
    the other adjacent horizontal edge.)
Select an edge or [Chain/Radius]: (Enter)
3 edge(s) selected for fillet.
```

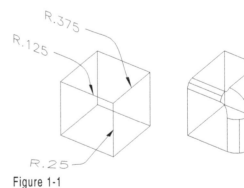

Figure 1-1

The first radius you specified was for the edge you initially selected, while the other radius inputs were for subsequent edge selections. Figure 1-1 shows the unfilleted and the filleted versions of the cube.

Next, locate and zoom in close to the 90-degree pipe bend that has a side outlet. Make three fillets that have a radius of 0.06. Notice that the ends of this bend are not identical — the bend's arc starts at the flange on the left, while there is a short straight segment between the arc's end and the flange on the right. AutoCAD, nevertheless, fillets both edges. AutoCAD also successfully fillets the saddle-shaped edge between the bend and the side outlet. See Figure 1-2 for the unfilleted and filleted versions of the pipe bend.

You might want to make copies of the unfilleted pipe bend so you can experiment with various fillet radii. You will find that because of the holes in the flange, you cannot have a fillet with a radius larger than 0.0938 on the pipe-to-flange edges.

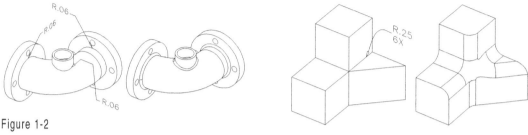

Figure 1-2

Figure 1-3

Lastly, find the 3D solid that looks like two blocks and a wedge that are fused together, shown in Figue 1-3, and zoom in close enough to work on it. Fillet the six edges that intersect, using a radius of 0.25. The result, which is shown on the right in Figure 1-3, is a complex blend among the six faces. You might want to make copies of the unfilleted version of this 3D solid, and try blending the surfaces using different fillet radii for different edges.

### Exercise Two

You will add fillets to the pipe fitting you created in Exercise 6 of Chapter 12. In this exercise, you will finish the model by using the FILLET command to round some of its sharp edges and corners. On the CD-ROM that accompanies this book, the model is in file f1231.dwg.

First, you will fillet the edges between the pipe, the square flange, and the side outlet. The model has so many edges that it is difficult to find and select edges, so you should zoom in close to the lower part of the model as shown in Figure 2-1. The viewpoint for this figure is 220 degrees from the X axis in the X-Y plane, and 20 degrees from the X-Y plane. Invoke the FILLET command, set the fillet radius to 0.06, and select the eight edges

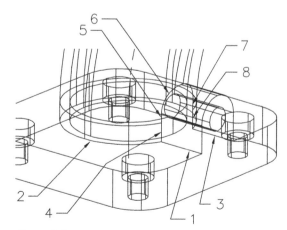

Figure 2-1

that are numbered in the figure. Notice that two edges are on each vertical side of the side outlet — edges 4 and 5, and edges 7 and 8 — even though they appear to form a straight line. The edges numbered 4 through 8 are most conveniently selected by the Chain option of the FILLET command.

When HIDE is in effect, and the system variable **dispsilh** has been set to 1, the rounded edges you made should look similar to those in Figure 2-2.

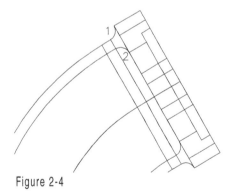

Figure 2-2

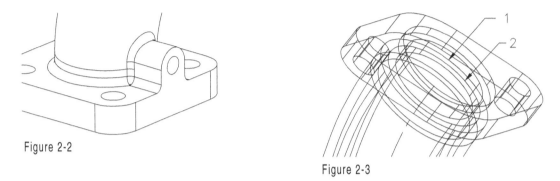

Figure 2-3

Pan to the upper flange area, start the FILLET command again, and use a radius of 0.06 to fillet the two edges marked 1 and 2 in Figure 2-3. Edge 1 is on the outside surface of the model; edge 2 is on the inside.

When you switch to a viewpoint having the coordinates of 0,-1,0 (a front view), your two newest fillets should look similar to the ones in Figure 2-4 when the wireframe viewing mode is in effect.

Figure 2-4

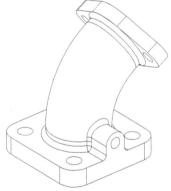

Figure 2-5

Those two fillets finish the construction of this model. Your model should look similar to the one in Figure 2-5 when it is viewed from a viewpoint that is rotated 230 degrees in the X-Y plane from the X axis and 30 degrees from the X-Y plane, with HIDE in effect and **dispsilh** set to 1. Retain your model because you will make a 2D multiview drawing of it in Section 4 of this book. On the accompanying CD-ROM, this model is in file f1310.dwg.

| Command: | FILLET |
|---|---|
| Purpose: | On 3D solids, the FILLET command rounds sharp edges and corners and makes transition blends between two or more surfaces. |
| Initiate with: | • On the command line, enter FILLET.<br>• From the Modify pull-down menu, select Fillet.<br>• Select the Fillet button from the Modify toolbar. |
| Options: | When you select a 3D solid in response to the FILLET command's prompt to select the first object to be filleted, AutoCAD issues a special set of prompts and options suitable for rounding sharp edges of 3D solids. Your pick point on the 3D solid can be on an edge or on an isoline. If it is on an edge, the edge is highlighted. |

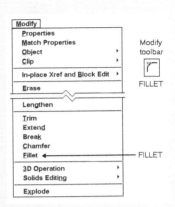

First, AutoCAD issues a prompt for a fillet radius. You must specify a radius greater than 0. Then, AutoCAD displays the following command line menu:

```
Select an edge or [Chain/Radius]: (Select an edge, enter C or R, or press Enter.)
```

When the Enter key is pressed, AutoCAD reports the number of edges that were selected, fillets them, and ends the command.

• Select Edge    An edge must be selected by picking a point on it. AutoCAD highlights the edge and redisplays the Select an edge [Chain/Radius] prompt.

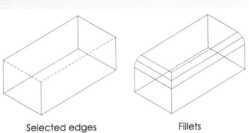

Selected edges          Fillets

After an edge has been selected, there is no way to deselect it.

• Chain    You can select several edges with one pick through this option. The edges, however, must be tangent to one another.

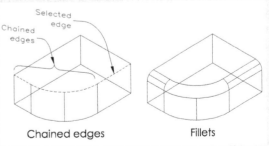

Selected edge
Chained edges
Chained edges          Fillets

The following submenu is displayed:

```
Select an edge chain or [Edge/Radius]: (Select an edge, enter E or
    R, or press Enter.)
```

Pressing the Enter key ends the command and fillets all selected edges on the 3D solid.

|  | |  |
|---|---|---|
| • Select Edge Chain | | When you select an edge, it and all edges tangent to it are highlighted for filleting, and the Chain option menu is redisplayed. Only the selected edge is highlighted if it is not tangent with its adjacent edges. |
| • Edge | | This option returns to the single edge mode. |
| • Radius | | When this option is selected, AutoCAD prompts for a new radius value to be applied to subsequently selected edges. The radii of previously selected edges doesn't change. |

• Radius     This option of the main FILLET menu for 3D solids allows you to have fillets of various radii. AutoCAD issues a command line prompt for a radius that will be applied to all subsequently selected edges. The radii of edges previously selected is not affected by the new value.

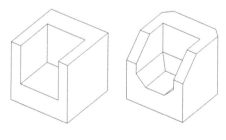

Fillets with different radii

Notes:     • You can fillet the edges of only one 3D solid with each implementation of the FILLET command. If, for instance, you want to round edges on two separate 3D solids, you must invoke the FILLET command twice.

Related system variable:     • **filletrad**     The current radius value used for fillets is stored in this system variable.

# Creating Chamfers

The CHAMFER command can turn the sharp edge of a 3D solid into a beveled surface. The command works equally well on inside and outside edges.

Unlike fillets, which require only one parameter (a radius), chamfers require two — a distance on one surface from the edge to the start of the chamfer, and a distance on the other surface from the edge to the start of the chamfer. These two distances can be different, and to keep track of them, AutoCAD refers to one of the surfaces adjacent to the edge that is to be filleted as the base surface. Consequently, the CHAMFER command requires that the base surface be identified, and it bevels only the edges of the base surface. To make the three sets of beveled edges on the model in the previous figure, the CHAMFER command was invoked three times.

Generally, you can chamfer any edge you need to chamfer, although there are some restrictions when curved edges are involved. If a curved edge is tangent with its adjacent edge, neither edge can be chamfered alone. For example, edges B and C in the adjacent figure are tangent, and therefore they cannot be chamfered by themselves, not even as a pair. On the other hand, edge A can be chamfered alone (as shown in the lower-right corner of the figure), because it is not tangent with either of its adjacent edges. Moreover, all three edges can be chamfered together, as shown in the upper-right corner of the figure.

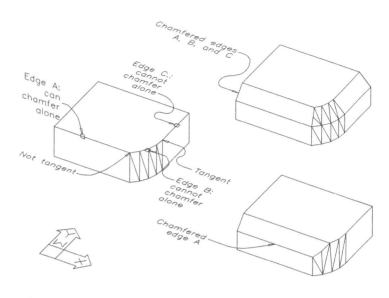

As you would expect, you cannot have a chamfer distance that exceeds the face width. However, if only part of an adjoining face is too narrow, the chamfer will succeed. Thus, you can chamfer any of the three edges of the triangle-shaped faces on a wedge.

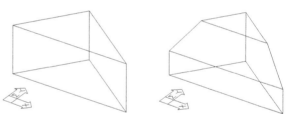

## Exercise Three

This exercise gives you more experience in using the FILLET command on solids and also demonstrates how the CHAMFER command can bevel corners, as you finish the sheet-metal part you built in Exercise 7 of Chapter 12. On the CD-ROM, this model is in file f1239.dwg.

First, you will round the edges of the fold lines of the part. There are four of them, and they are labeled in Figure 3-1. Start the FILLET command, and round the edge on the inside of each fold using a fillet radius of 0.10. Round the outside fold edges using a fillet radius of 0.20..

Next, pan to the side of the model that has the two round holes and zoom in, as shown in Figure 3-2, so that you can easily pick points on the 0.10-long edges. Round the six corner edges in this area of the model using a fillet radius of 0.75 for the outside corners and 0.25 for the inside corners, as shown in Figure 3-2. The 0.75-radius fillets completely round the ends of the two tabs containing the holes.

Now, pan to the other side of the model and zoom in to the horizontal flanges that contain an oval hole. You need to zoom in very close to the model so you can easily pick the 0.10-long edges. Start the CHAMFER command; pick an edge on the end of one of the two tabs and designate the

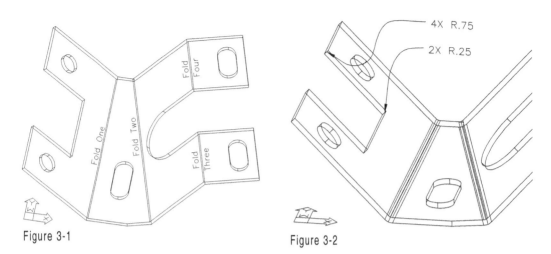

Figure 3-1

Figure 3-2

end surface of the tab (its dimensions are 0.10 by 1.75) as the base surface. Set both chamfer distances to 0.25 and pick the 0.10 edges, as shown in Figure 3-3, to be chamfered. Do the same with the other tab.

Set the view direction to 280 degrees from the X axis in the X-Y plane and 50 degrees from the X-Y plane. Activate HIDE, and your model should be similar to the one shown in Figure 3-4. This finishes the model. On the CD-ROM, the model is in file f1321.dwg.

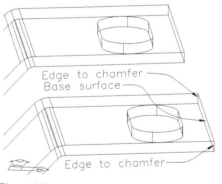

Figure 3-3

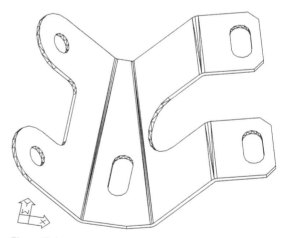

Figure 3-4

| Command: | CHAMFER |
| --- | --- |
| Purpose: | On 3D solids, the CHAMFER command bevels sharp edges. |
| Initiate with: | • On the command line, enter CHAMFER. |

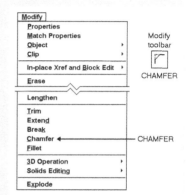

• From the Modify pull-down menu, select Chamfer.

• Select the Chamfer button from the Modify toolbar.

Implementation:
When a 3D solid is selected in response to the CHAMFER command's prompt for the first line to be chamfered, AutoCAD switches to a set of command line prompts suitable for solid, rather than wireframe, objects. If you picked an edge as the first line to be chamfered, AutoCAD highlights one of the two surfaces adjacent to that edge and issues the prompt

```
Base surface selection ...
Enter surface selection option [Next/OK (current)]<OK>: (Enter N or O, or press Enter.)
```

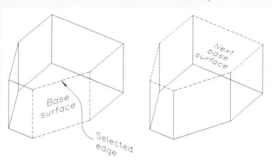

If the highlighted surface is the one you want as the base surface, choose the OK option. If you want the other surface adjacent to the selected edge to be the base surface, choose the Next option. AutoCAD will switch the highlights to the other surface and repeat the Next/OK prompt.

If an isoline or a mesh line was selected as the first line to be chamfered, AutoCAD will highlight its surface and skip the Next/OK prompt. Isolines and mesh lines, which are present only on curved surfaces, are discussed in Chapter 14.

After you have identified the base surface, AutoCAD will prompt for the chamfer distances on the base surface and on the surfaces adjacent to the base surface:

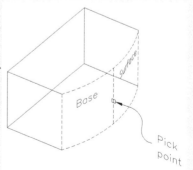

```
Specify base surface chamfer distance <current>:
    (Specify a distance or press Enter.)
Specify other surface chamfer distance <current>:
    (Specify a distance or press Enter.)
```

Press the Enter key to accept the current distance. Both chamfer distances must be greater than 0. Next, AutoCAD will prompt for the edges that are to be chamfered:

```
Select an edge or [Loop]:
  (Enter L, select an edge,
  or press Enter.)
```

This prompt is repeated until you press the Enter key, which ends the command.

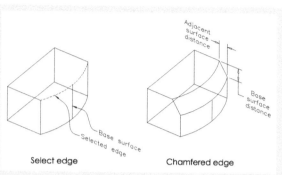

Select edge                 Chamfered edge

- Select
  Edge

  Use this option to select individual edges of the base surface. AutoCAD highlights the selected edges and chamfers them when the Enter key is pressed.

- Loop

  Use this option to chamfer all the edges of the base surface with a single pick. AutoCAD will display the submenu

```
Select an edge loop
  or [Edge]:
  (Enter E, select
  an edge, or
  press Enter.)
```

Selected edge loop          Chamfered edges

When an edge is selected, all edges of the base surface are highlighted, and the Edge/Select Edge loop menu is repeated. Press the Enter key to chamfer all edges that are highlighted and end the CHAMFER command. The Edge option returns you to the Loop/Select Edge menu.

**Notes:**

- You cannot set 3D solid chamfer sizes by distance and angle, as you can with wireframe objects.

- You can chamfer the edges of just one surface with the CHAMFER command. If you want to chamfer the edges of other surfaces on a 3D solid, you must invoke the CHAMFER command again.

**Related system variables:**

- **chamfera**    This system variable holds the distance from the edge to the start of the chamfer for the base surface.

- **chamferb**    This system variable holds the distance from the edge to the start of the chamfer for the surfaces adjacent to the base surface.

# Slicing 3D Solids

You can divide a 3D solid into two pieces with the SLICE command. The aptly named command uses a plane to slice through selected 3D solids. The slicing plane is infinitely large, so you cannot slice through just part of a solid. No volume is lost through the slice, and you can keep both portions of the solid, or just the portion on a selected side of the slicing plane. You can position the slicing plane in virtually any location and orientation you will ever need through the seven different options the command provides for defining the plane.

Most of the time, you will use SLICE as an editing command to reduce the length or height of some object. Occasionally, however, it's useful for creating a certain face or surface on a solid. Two brief exercises demonstrate each of these two uses.

### Exercise Four

Start a new drawing using the default English setup. You will not want to save the model you make, so the initial setup of the drawing file is not important. Use the BOX command to create a 1x1x1 cube, and set an isometric-type view point. (VPOINT with the coordinates of 0.4,-0.6,0.6 works well.)

Start the SLICE command, and select your cube as the 3D solid to be sliced. The command line prompts and your input for slicing the cube will be

```
Specify first point of slicing plane by [Object/Zaxis/View/XY/YZ/ZX/3points] <3points>: (Use an object
    mid-point snap to pick point 1.)
Specify second point on plane: (Use an object mid-point snap to pick point 2.)
Specify third point on plane: (Use an object mid-point snap to pick point 3.)
Specify point on the desired side of the plane or [keep Both sides]: (Use an object endpoint snap to pick point
    4.)
```

Your sliced cube should look like the one on the right side of Figure 4-1. Cutting the corner of this cube off as you just did is almost trivially easy with SLICE, but it would take a great deal of work to do it with the Boolean operations. Incidentally, the order in which you picked points 1, 2, and 3 was not important.

### Exercise Five

In this exercise, you will use SLICE to shorten a 3D solid. Retrieve and open the file f1328.dwg from the CD-ROM that comes with this book. The model is of the specialized metric wrench shown in Figure 5-1.

The wrench is too long, so you will use SLICE to make it 90 millimeters shorter. Slice it once, retaining both pieces; then, you slice it again 90 millimeters from the first slice, discarding the middle piece. Because the stem of the wrench is parallel to the X axis, you can use slicing planes that are parallel with the WCS Y-Z plane. Lastly, move the two end pieces together and join them with the UNION command. These steps are illustrated in Figure 5-2.

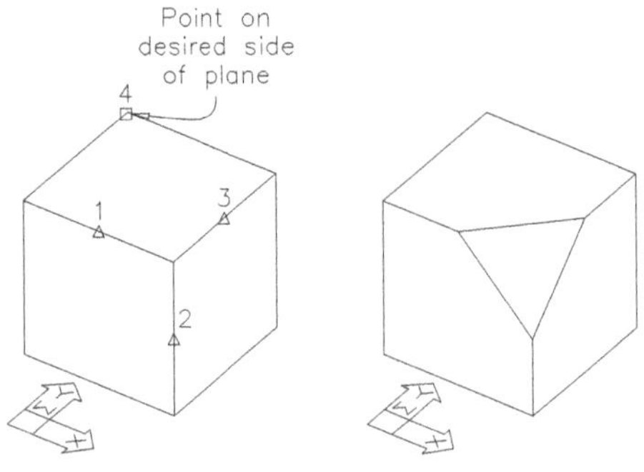

Point on
desired side
of plane

Figure 4-1

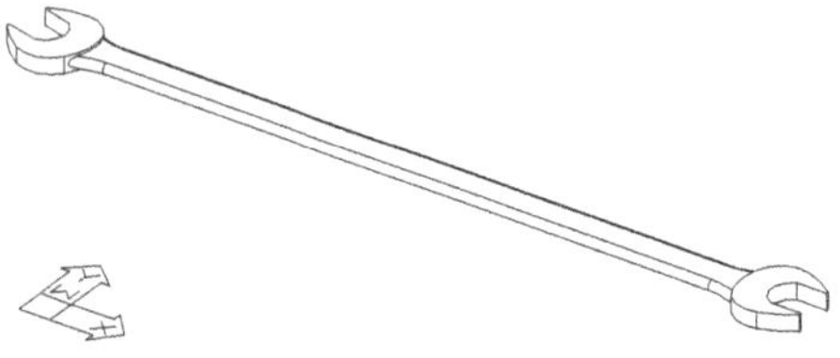

Figure 5-1

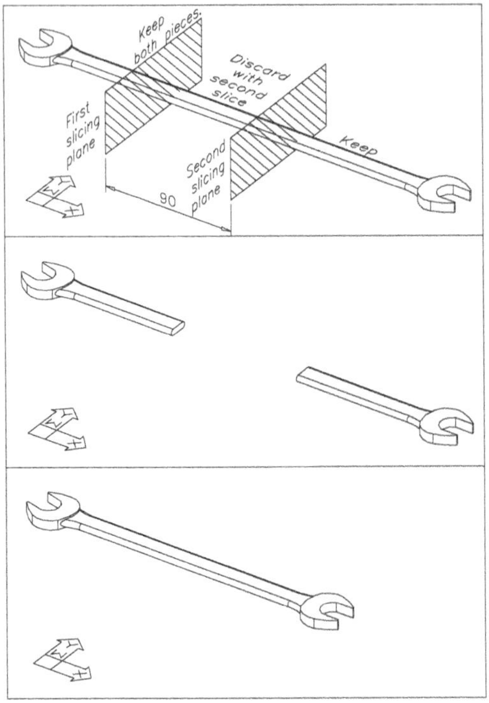

Figure 5-2

| Command: | SLICE |
|---|---|
| Purpose: | This command uses an infinite-sized plane to slice through one or more selected 3D solids. You can discard the sliced solids on a selected side of the plane or keep all the solids. |
| Initiate with: | • On the command line, enter SLICE. |
| | • From the Draw pull-down menu, select Solids, and then Slice. |
| | • Select the Slice button from the Solids toolbar. |
| Options: | The SLICE command first asks you to select the objects that are to be sliced. You can use any object-selection method to do this. AutoCAD filters out objects that are not 3D solids. Then SLICE displays a command line menu offering seven different methods for defining the slicing plane: |

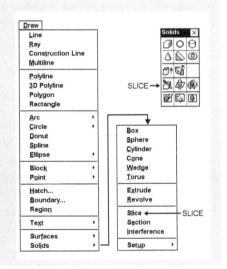

Specify first point on slicing plane by [Object/Zaxis/View/XY/YZ/ZX/3points] <3points>:
    (Specify a point, enter an option, or press Enter)

- 3points

This option is initiated by specifying a point in response to the SLICE main menu or by pressing the Enter key. If you specify a point, it serves as the first point of the plane, and AutoCAD issues prompts for the second and third points. If you press the Enter key, AutoCAD issues prompts for three points:

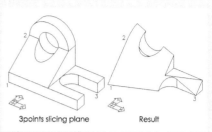

3points slicing plane            Result

Specify first point on plane: Specify a point.
Specify second point on plane:Specify a point.
Specify third point on plane: Specify a point.

A rubberband line, anchored at the first point, assists you in locating the second and third points of the slicing plane.

- Object

The plane of an existing object is used to define the slicing plane with this option. The object can be any member of the 2D polyline family, as well as an arc, circle, ellipse, or planar spline. Nonplanar splines, lines, and 3D polylines are not accepted. AutoCAD issues the command line prompt:

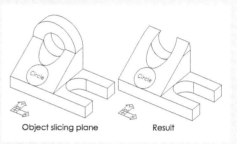

Object slicing plane            Result

Select a circle, ellipse, arc, 2D-spline, 2d-polyline: (Pick a point on
    one object.)

- Zaxis

This option uses two points to define the slicing plane. The plane is located on the first point and its orientation is normal (per-pendicular) to a line drawn from the first point to the second point. The option's prompts are

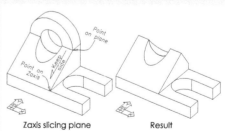

Zaxis slicing plane            Result

Specify a point on the section plane: (Specify a point.)
Point on Z-axis (normal) of the plane: (Specify a point.)

- View

The view option asks you to specify a point. The slicing plane is located at that point and is oriented so that it is perpendicular to the current viewing direction.

```
Specify a point on the
   current view plane
   <0,0,0>: (Specify a
   point or press Enter.)
```

View slicing plane          Result

If you press Enter, the slicing plane passes through the UCS origin.

- XY

This option orients the slicing plane so that it is parallel with the UCS X-Y plane. You are prompted to specify the plane's elevation.

```
Specify a point on the
   XY-plane <0,0,0>: (Spec-
   ify a point or press
   Enter.)
```

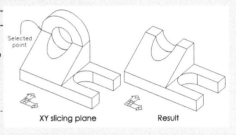

XY slicing plane          Result

This prompt is asking you to specify a point in the Z direction for the X-Y slicing plane rather than a point on the current X-Y drawing plane. If you press Enter, the slicing plane is on the current X-Y plane.

- YZ

The slicing plane is parallel with the UCS Y-Z plane when this option is selected. A follow-up prompt asks you to specify the slicing plane's distance from the current Y-Z plane.

```
Specify a point on the
   YZ-plane <0,0,0>: (Specify
   a point or press Enter.)
```

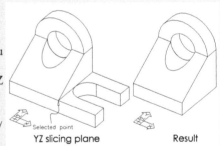

YZ slicing plane          Result

When Enter is pressed, the slicing plane and the Y-Z plane coincide.

- ZX

This option orients the slicing plane parallel with the UCS Z-X plane. You are asked to set the plane's distance from the UCS Z-X plane by specifying a point.

```
Specify a point on the
   ZX-plane <0,0,0>: (Spec-
   ify a point or press
   Enter.)
```

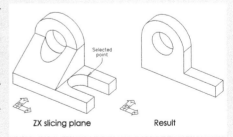

ZX slicing plane          Result

If Enter is pressed, the slicing plane will be on the Z-X plane.

After the slicing plane has been defined, AutoCAD displays a menu for you to specify which portion of the 3D solid iş to be retained.

```
Both sides/<Specify a point on desired side of the plane or [keep Both sides]: (Specify a
    point or enter B.)
```

- Point on desired side of the plane

  This point, which must be on one side or the other of the slicing plane, shows AutoCAD which portion of the sliced solid you want to retain. The portion of the solid that is on the other side of the slicing plane is deleted.

- Keep Both Sides

  When this option is selected, both portions of the sliced 3D solid will be retained as two separate 3D solids.

Notes:

- Because SLICE uses an infinitely large cutting plane, you cannot slice through only part of a 3D solid or have staggered sections through one.

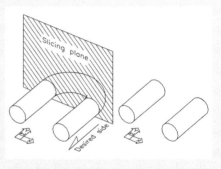

- The SLICE command divides a 3D solid into just two objects, even if the sliced solid is split into more than two pieces. For instance, two separate pieces remain after the 3D solid shown in the figure has been sliced. Even so, AutoCAD considers the two pieces to be one object.

Related command:

- SECTION

This command uses the same options for defining a plane that the SLICE command does in making a region from the cross-section of a 3D solid. The selected 3D solid is not affected by the command.

# Editing 3D Solids

AutoCAD 2000 contains a set of tools for editing 3D solids. Some of the operations you can perform with these tools are to

extend individual faces;

delete selected features;

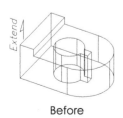
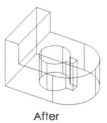
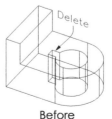

| Before | After | Before | After |

move a 3D solid's features;

add taper to selected faces;

rotate specific features;

hollow out a 3D solid.

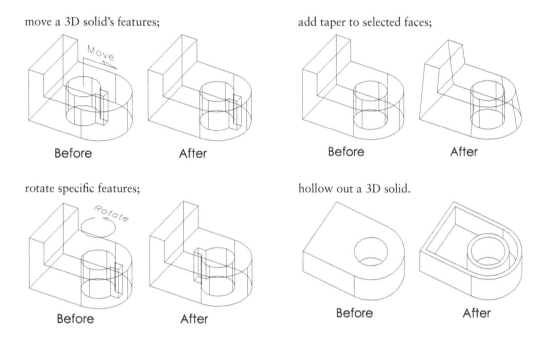

Before          After

Before          After

Before          After

Before          After

All the editing tools are accessed through one AutoCAD command — SOLIDEDIT. Within this command, the tools are separated into the categories of *face*, *edge*, and *body*; and options within these categories implement specific tools. You can select the options from the command line, from the Modify/Solids Editing pull-down menu, and from the Solids Editing toolbar.

## Editing 3D Solid Faces

The tools that you are likely to use most frequently are those for editing faces. A face is a surface area that has either a sharp edge with adjacent faces or is tangent to adjacent faces. A slot, for example, has four faces — two for the straight sides and two for the rounded ends. Examples of typical editing operations on faces are shown in the next figure.

Notice in this figure that SOLIDEDIT's face options of Move, Offset, and Extrude can all be used to change the length of the boss and the thickness of the base. The

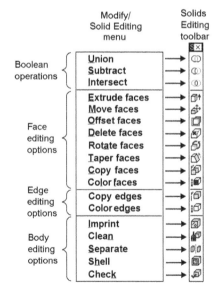

Extrude option offers more flexibility, though, because you can taper the extrusion or use a path to make it. However, if you wanted to change the length or width of the part's base, you could only

use the Move option because of the rounded corners. Extrude works only with planar faces, and offset changes the radius of the corners.

SOLIDEDIT's Move face option is useful for extending or contracting features, such as the thickness of the web on the part in the figure, or the length of one of its slots. You would also use the Move option to reposition the holes or slots that are in the part. A limitation of the Move option is that faces cannot be moved to another face. Thus, in the figure on the next page, you cannot move the slot from one flange to the other.

You will use SOLID-EDIT's Offset face option

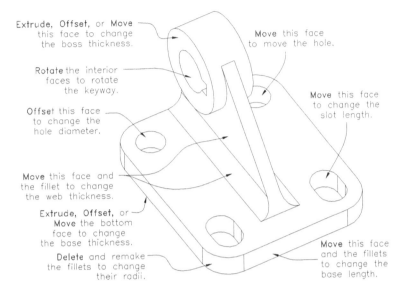

to change the diameter of holes and cylinders, and to extend planar faces that are skewed to the coordinate system axes. Although the Offset option does change the radii of fillets, the tangent between the fillet and its adjacent surfaces is not maintained. Therefore, you must delete and remake fillets to change their radii.

Uses for the Copy option in SOLIDEDIT's face category are limited because it only copies faces. You cannot, for instance, copy a round hole; you can only copy the sides of the hole.

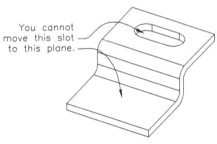

Probably the trickiest step in editing faces is selecting faces. You select faces by picking a point on an edge, an isoline, or on the surface of the face (even in wireframe views where the surface is invisible). Window and crossing selections are not allowed. When you pick a point on an edge, both faces adjacent to the edge are selected. When you pick a point on a surface, the foreground face is selected, and subsequent picks in the same point steps down through the layers of faces below. As a face is selected, AutoCAD highlights its edges.

Often, you end up having selected faces that you don't want, so you must use the Remove option to remove the faces you do not want edited from the selection set. You can minimize the selection of unwanted faces by using multiple viewports, with each viewport showing the model from a different viewpoint to give you an unobstructed view of every face you extend to edit.

## Editing 3D Solid Edges

Your options for editing edges are limited to making copies of them and adding color to them. With either option, you can select as may edges as you want by picking points on them. Similar to AutoCAD's COPY command, you can use either base and destination points or relative displacements to position copied edges. The AutoCAD object types of copied edges are lines, arcs, circles, or splines, depending on the shape of the edge.

## Editing 3D Solid Bodies

The name of this category is potentially confusing because its options edit 3D solid objects, rather than body objects. (A body is an AutoCAD database object type that is a meshless 3D surface. Bodies cannot be created directly. They are created when a 3D solid is exploded. Planar faces on an exploded solid become regions, while nonplanar faces become bodies. Bodies also are created when nonplanar faces are copied with SOLIDEDIT's face Copy option.)

The Imprint option of this category creates an edge on the surface of a 3D solid. Usually, you will have the imprint either extend completely across a face or be closed (although it does not have to be either). As a result, the face is divided into at least two faces, and you will probably then perform another editing operation — such as taper, extrude, offset, or move — on one, or both, of the faces.

The top frame of the imprint example in the figure shows a 3D solid that has recesses with tapered internal sides on its top and bottom halves. The editing objective is to split the part with horizontal edges and then taper its external sides. Each of the 8 external faces (4 are rectangular and 4 are arc-shaped) is divided by imprinting the intersecting region shown in the top frame onto the part. The second frame shows a hidden-line view of the part with the imprint. The region was deleted during the imprint operation. The third frame shows the part after each of the resulting 16 faces have been tapered by the face Taper option of SOLIDEDIT. This frame also shows a hidden-line view of the part.

The Separate option turns separated components of a 3D solid into individual 3D solids. The components must have empty space between them. As soon as you select a 3D solid, AutoCAD creates a separate 3D solid from each separate component without any additional user

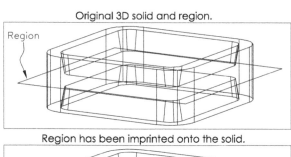

Original 3D solid and region.

Region

Region has been imprinted onto the solid.

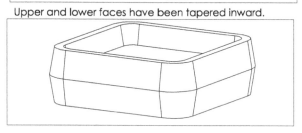

Upper and lower faces have been tapered inward.

input. The appearance of the solid objects will not change. This option does not decompose a 3D solid into its primitive, or more basic, components as the SOLSEP command of Autodesk's defunct AME (Advanced Modeling Extension) did.

You can visualize the results of the Shell option by mentally removing the mass from your 3D solid to leave just the faces, deleting the faces you do not want, offsetting the remaining faces by a specified distance (the shell thickness), and filling the space between the two sets of faces with mass. If you specify a positive shell thickness, the offset direction is toward the inside; if it is negative, the offset direction is toward the outside. The following figure shows a before and after example, in wireframe view, of a shell in which the top face of the 3D solid was removed and a positive shell thickness was used.

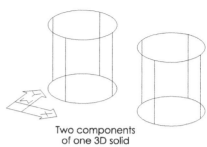

Two components
of one 3D solid

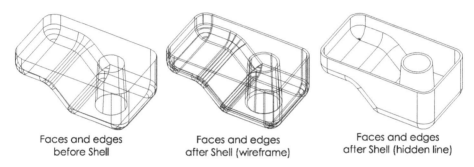

| Faces and edges before Shell | Faces and edges after Shell (wireframe) | Faces and edges after Shell (hidden line) |

| Command: | SOLIDEDIT |
|---|---|
| Purpose: | This command allows you to modify 3D solids by moving, rotating, extruding, offsetting, tapering, copying, and deleting specific faces. The command also can copy and create edges, and create shelled solids. |
| Initiate with: | • On the command line, enter SOLIDEDIT. |
| | • From the Modify pull-down menu, select Solids Editing, and then a specific option. |
| | • From the Solids Editing toolbar, select a specific option. |
| Options: | When you invoke SOLIDEDIT from the command line, a prompt listing three categories of editing options — face, edge, and body — is displayed. Upon selecting a category, a command line prompt for you to choose an option within that category is displayed. Alternatively, you can directly select a specific option within any category through the Solid Editing toolbar or pull-down menu. |

• Face Options    When you select this category of options from the command line, AutoCAD displays the following options:

Extrude/Move/Rotate/Offset/Taper/Delete/Copy/coLor/Undo/eXit

   • eXit         This is the default option. It returns to the main SOLIDEDIT prompt.

- Undo

Reverses the last face-editing operation.

- Extrude

This option uses the edges of a face as a profile that is extruded in the same way that AutoCAD's EXTRUDE command extrudes a wireframe profile. A command line prompt asks you to select the face that is be extruded. It must be flat. Then, the following command line prompt is displayed:

```
Specify height of extrusion or [Path]: (Specify a distance or enter a
    P.)
```

Positive extrusion distance values push the profile away from the existing solid, while negative values push the profile into the existing solid. After specifying a height, you are prompted to specify a taper angle. If you choose the Path option, you are prompted to select a path object. The requirements for a path object and the results of the path extrusion are the same as those of the EXTRUDE command.

### Extruded face, using the Path option

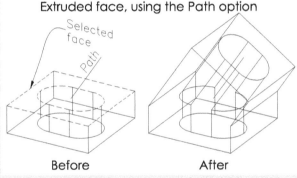

Before                     After

- Move

Use this option to move one or more faces. After selecting the face, or faces, to be moved, prompts similar to those of the MOVE command are displayed. As shown in the figure on the next page, you cannot move faces from one face to another.

### Moving Faces

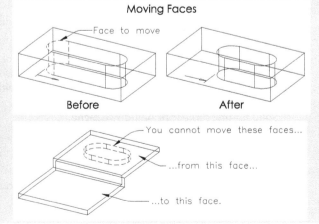

Before                     After

- Rotate

You can rotate one or more faces about an axis with this option. After selecting one or more faces, the following prompt is displayed for you to use in defining the rotation axis:

```
Specify an axis point or [Axis by object/View/Xaxis/Yaxis/
    Zaxis]<2points>: (Choose an option or specify a point.)
```

2points   Define the rotation axis by specifying two points that the axis is to pass through. You initiate this option by specifying the first point.

Axis by object   Define the axis by selecting an existing object. When a line, polyline, or spline is selected, the axis is through the object's startpoints and endpoints. When a circle, ellipse, or arc is selected, the axis is in the center of the object and is perpendicular to its plane.

View   Aligns the axis with the line of sight of the current viewport. You are prompted to select a point that the axis is to pass through.

Xaxis, Yaxis, Zaxis   The rotation axis is parallel to the specified UCS axis. You are prompted to select a point that the axis is to pass through.

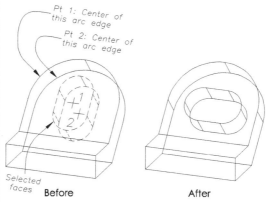

Rotating faces, with 2point axis

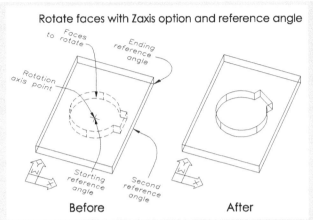

**Rotate faces with Zaxis option and reference angle**

Before                                                After

After specifying the rotation axis, you are prompted to specify the rotation angle. You can enter an absolute angle, or define a reference angle by selecting three points, as shown in the figure above.

- Offset

This option moves every point on a face in a direction that is perpendicular to the face. For flat faces, the result is as if the face was moved, but the radius of curved faces becomes larger or smaller as they are offset. After you select the faces that are to be offset, AutoCAD prompts for the offset distance. Positive distance values offset faces away from the solid, while negative values offset faces into the solid. In the figure below, the faces of the slot have been offset away from the solid to make the slot smaller.

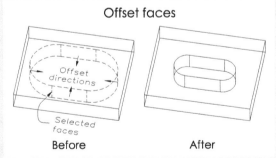

**Offset faces**

Before                                                After

- Taper

You can add a taper angle, which is often referred to as a draft angle, to individual faces with this option. After selecting the face, or faces, to be tapered, you are asked to specify a base point for the taper and then to specify the direction of the taper. The face, or faces, are rotated about an axis that is on the plane of the base point and is perpendicular to the direction from the base point to the second point. Lastly, you are prompted to specify the taper angle. This angle is added to any taper that the face currently has.

The figure below shows two examples of taper. In the first example, the selected base point is in the middle of an edge of the selected face, which causes the face to swivel. The second example shows how all four sides of the slot can be tapered.

## Taper

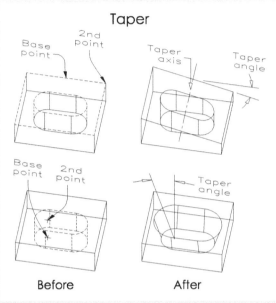

Base point

2nd Point

2nd Point

Base Point

Taper axis

Taper angle

Base point

Taper angle

**Before**                    **After**

- Delete    Use this option to remove features from your 3D solids that you no longer want. AutoCAD fills in the missing volume to match the adjacent faces. The selected faces must define a volume. In the figure below, for example, if only one face of the corner notch was selected, the delete operation would fail. Also, unless all four of the faces of the slot are selected, it could not be deleted.

### Deleting faces

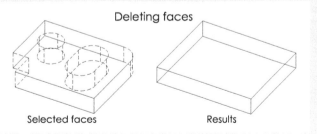

Selected faces                    Results

- Copy

This option makes copies of one or more faces. After you specify the faces that are to be copied, AutoCAD issues prompts similar to those of the COPY command for use in positioning the copy. Copies of planar faces are regions, while copies of nonplanar faces are bodies.

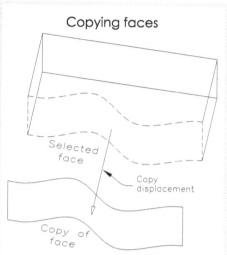

Copying faces

- coLor

This option allows you to assign a specific color to a specific face. After you have selected the face, or faces, AutoCAD displays the Select Color dialog box for you to choose one of the 255 AutoCAD colors.

- Selecting Faces

After you have selected an option from the main prompt in the face category, you are prompted to select one or more faces. All the options issue the same command line prompts. The first prompt is

Select faces or [Undo/Remove]: (Select a face.)

You must select a face by picking a point on it — window and crossing selections are not allowed. The point you pick can be on an edge, an isoline, or on the surface of the face (even in wireframe views, in which the surface is transparent). The edges of the face you select are highlighted, and AutoCAD issues the prompt

Select faces or [Undo/Remove/ALL]: (Enter an option, select a face, or press Enter.)

This prompt is repeated as each face is selected, until you press Enter to end the selection. When faces are behind other faces, a pick point on a surface selects the foreground face; and when you pick the same point again, the face behind the foreground face is selected; if you continue to pick the same point, the next face in the stack of faces is selected. The next figure shows the results of three picks in the same location.

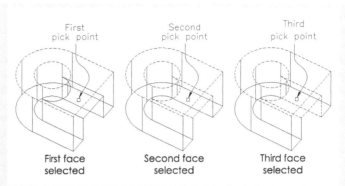

First          Second         Third
pick point     pick point     pick point

First face      Second face     Third face
selected        selected        selected

The ALL option selects all the faces on a 3D solid. The Remove option deselects faces. It displays the prompt

Remove faces or [Undo/Add/ALL]: (Enter an option, select a face, or press Enter.)

This prompt is repeated after each face is selected, until you press Enter to end the selection. Selecting faces to be removed from the selection set works the same as adding them. The ALL option deselects all faces, and the Add option returns to the Select Faces prompt.

- Edge
  Options

When you select Edge from the main SOLIDEDIT prompt, the following options are offered:

Copy/coLor/Undo/eXit

- eXit

This, the default option, returns to the main SOLIDEDIT prompt.

- Undo

Reverses the last edge-editing operation.

- Copy

This option makes copies of edges. After you select the edge, or edges, to copy, command line prompts similar to those of the COPY command are issued for you to specify the displacement position of the copy. Each copied edge is a separate line, circle, arc, or spline, depending on the shape of the edge.

- coLor

You can change the color of specific edges with this option. First you are prompted to select one or more edges, and then AutoCAD's Select Color dialog box is displayed for you to choose a color.

- Selecting
  Edges

When you choose either the Copy or coLor option, the following prompt is displayed:

```
Select edges or [Undo/Remove]: (Enter an option, select an edge, or
    press Enter.)
```

After an edge has been selected, this prompt is repeated. Press the Enter key to end the selection of edges. You must select an edge by picking a point on it — window and crossing selections are not allowed. Selected edges are highlighted. The Undo option cancels the last edge selection. The Remove option is for removing edges from the selection set. It displays the prompt

```
Remove edges or [Undo/Add]: (Enter an option, select an edge, or press
    Enter.)
```

When you select an edge by picking a point on it, this prompt is repeated. The Undo option reselects the last edge that was removed. Press the Enter key to end the selection process, or choose the Add option to return to the Select Edges prompt.

- Body
  Options

When you choose Body from the main SOLIDEDIT prompt, a command line prompt listing the following options is displayed:

```
Imprint/seParate solids/Shell/cLean/Check/Undo/eXit
```

- eXit

This option returns to the main SOLIDEDIT prompt.

- Undo

Reverses the last body-editing operation.

- Imprint

Use this option to divide a face into two or more faces. Often, you will then perform another editing operation on those faces. You might for instance, use Imprint to divide a face and then taper one of the resulting two faces, as shown in the figure.

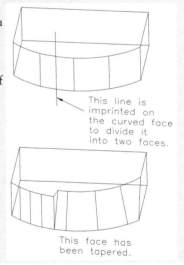

This line is imprinted on the curved face to divide it into two faces.

This face has been tapered.

You are first prompted to select a 3D solid. You must select it by picking a point on one of its edges or isoline. Then, you are asked to select the object that is to be used for the imprint. Valid objects for imprinting are lines, arcs, circles, splines, ellipses, 2D and 3D polylines, regions, bodies, and even 3D solids. You select the imprint object by picking a point on it. AutoCAD asks whether if you want to delete the imprint object, and then prompts for another imprint object. Press Enter to end the command. The imprint will be where each imprint object touches or intersects the selected 3D solid.

• seParate solids

This option creates separate 3D solids from a 3D solid that has empty space between two or more individual components. As soon as you select a 3D solid, AutoCAD creates separate 3D solids from each of the individual components without further user input. This option does not decompose a 3D solid into its internal primitives.

• Shell

Shell offsets the faces of a 3D solid and deletes the volume outside the faces to create a relatively thin-walled shell. You also can specify

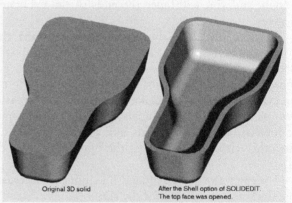

Original 3D solid    After the Shell option of SOLIDEDIT. The top face was opened.

that some faces will be deleted to make openings in the model. This option first prompts you to select the 3D solid that is to be shelled. Then, it prompts you to select the faces that are to be removed. This selection process works in the same way as selecting and deselecting faces for the Face options of SOLIDEDIT. Lastly, you are prompted to enter the shell offset distance. Positive values offset the faces inward, while negative values offset the faces outward.

• cLean

This is a utility option that removes imprints and any redundant edges and geometry that a 3D solid might have. You are prompted to select the 3D solid that is to be cleaned.

• Check

This option inspects a 3D solid for internal errors. You are prompted to select one 3D solid. AutoCAD then reports whether the 3D solid is valid or not. When the system variable **solidcheck** is set to 1, AutoCAD automatically implements this option after every SOLID-EDIT operation.

| Related system variable: | • solidcheck | When **solidcheck** is set to its default value of 1, AutoCAD automatically performs a validation check during each SOLIDEDIT operation. When **solidcheck** is set to 0, automatic solid validation is turned off. If SOLIDEDIT does not perform an operation and reports that the solid is not a valid ACIS solid, you can sometimes get SOLIDEDIT to work by first setting **solidcheck** to 0. Validity problems are most likely to occur with 3D Solids created in Release 13 and 14 versions of AutoCAD, and with those imported from other programs. |
|---|---|---|

## Exercise Six

You will try out some of the SOLIDEDIT options in this exercise as you modify the solid model shown in Figure 6-1. You will decrease the thickness of the rib by 12mm, and you will taper the ends of the cylinder 5 degrees.

Retrieve file f1364.dwg from the CD-ROM that comes with this book, and open it. You will first decrease the thickness of the rib. In doing this, you must select the outside surface of each side of the rib, and you can most easily make the selections by creating two tiled viewports. Set the viewpoint in one viewport to look at one side of the rib, and set the viewpoint in the other viewport to look at the opposite side of the rib.

Use the following command line input to decrease the thickness on one side of the rib:

```
Command: SOLIDEDIT (Enter)
Solids editing automatic checking: SOLIDCHECK=1
Enter a solids editing option [Face/Edge/Body/Undo/eXit]
    <eXit>: F (Enter)
Enter a face editing option
[Extrude/Move/Rotate/Offset/Taper/Delete/Copy/coLor/Undo/
    eXit] <eXit>: E (Enter)
Select faces or [Undo/Remove]: (Select either side surface
    of the rib as shown in Figure 6-2.)
Select faces or [Undo/Remove/ALL]: (Enter)
Specify height of extrusion or [Path]: -6 (Enter)
Specify angle of taper for extrusion <0>: (Enter)
```

Decrease the thickness of the rib by 12 mm

Taper the ends of the cylinder 5 degrees

Figure 6-1

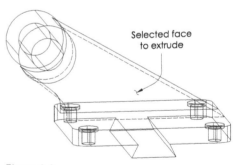

Selected face to extrude

Figure 6-2

AutoCAD issues two messages regarding its validation checks of the model, moves the face you specified 6mm inward, and redisplays the options for editing faces. Choose the Extrude option again, repeat your previous steps to move the surface of the opposite side of the rib 6mm inward, and exit the SOLIDEDIT command. The model now looks like the one in Figure 6-3. You could have used the Offset or the Move face options just as easily as Extrude to change the thickness of the rib.

Tapering the cylinder sides that protrude from the rib is more complex than decreasing the thickness of the rib, because you must first break the outside surface of the cylinder into three faces. Your first step is to move the UCS to either side face of the rib. The Face option of the UCS command is a good way to do this. Then, draw a circle on the face. The circle's diameter and centerpoint is not important, as long as it completely surrounds the cylinder. Turn the circle into a region object, and use any AutoCAD method to place a copy of the region on the opposite face of the rib. The model with these two regions is shown in Figure 6-4.

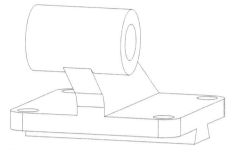

Figure 6-3

Use the regions to divide the side surface of the cylinder into three faces. The command line input to do this is:

```
Command: SOLIDEDIT (Enter)
Solids editing automatic checking: SOLIDCHECK=1
Enter a solids editing option [Face/Edge/Body/Undo/eXit]
    <eXit>: B (Enter)
Enter a body editing option
[Imprint/seParate solids/Shell/cLean/Check/Undo/eXit]
    <eXit>: I (Enter)
Select a 3D solid: (Pick a point anywhere on the model.)
Select an object to imprint: (Select either of the two
    regions.)
Delete the source object [Yes/No] <N>: Y (Enter)
Select an object to imprint: (Select the other region.)
Delete the source object [Yes/No] <Y>: (Enter)
Select an object to imprint: (Enter)
Enter a body editing option
[Imprint/seParate solids/Shell/cLean/Check/Undo/eXit] <eXit>: (Enter)
```

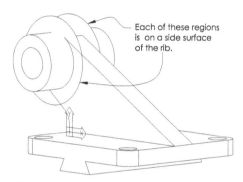

Each of these regions is on a side surface of the rib.

Figure 6-4

AutoCAD creates the imprints and displays the main SOLIDEDIT menu. On your model, the cylinder now has two bands on its surface, which indicates that it is divided into three separate faces. Continue with the SOLIDEDIT command as follows:

```
Enter a solids editing option [Face/Edge/Body/Undo/eXit]
    <eXit>: F (Enter)
Enter a face editing option
[Extrude/Move/Rotate/Offset/Taper/Delete/Copy/coLor/Undo/
    eXit] <eXit>: T (Enter>
Select faces or [Undo/Remove]: (Select the side surface of
    either outer cylinder.)
Select faces or [Undo/Remove/ALL]: (Enter)
Specify the base point: (Use a quadrant object to pick point
    A in Figure 6-5.)
Specify another point along the axis of tapering: (Use a
    quadrant object snap to pick point B in Figure 6-5.)
Specify the taper angle: 5 (Enter)
```

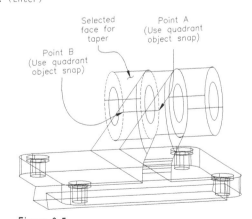

Selected face for taper

Point A (Use quadrant object snap)

Point B (Use quadrant object snap)

Figure 6-5

The cylinder you selected becomes tapered, and AutoCAD again displays the face-editing options. Select the Taper option again, and repeat your previous steps to taper the cylinder on the opposite side of the rib. Then, press the Enter key to return to the main SOLIDEDIT menu. You have probably noticed that when you imprinted the two regions to divide the cylinder, they also imprinted the sides of the rib. Use the following command line input to remove those two imprints:

```
Enter a solids editing option [Face/Edge/Body/Undo/eXit] <eXit>: B (Enter)
Enter a body editing option
[Imprint/seParate solids/Shell/cLean/Check/Undo/eXit] <eXit>: L (Enter)
Select a 3D solid: (Pick a point anywhere on the model.)
Enter a body editing option
[Imprint/seParate solids/Shell/cLean/Check/Undo/eXit] <eXit>: (Enter)
Enter a solids editing option [Face/Edge/Body/Undo/eXit] <eXit>: (Enter)
```

The arcs on the sides of the rib disappear. This completes the exercise. Your edited model should look like the one in Figure 6-6. On the CD-ROM that accompanies this book, the model is in file f1369.dwg.

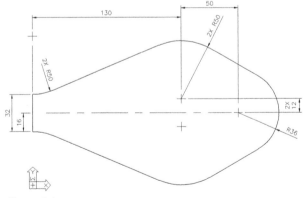

### Exercise Seven

You will use a variety of the commands and options you have learned in the last four chapters, including the Shell option of EDITSOLID, to construct a complex 3D solid model in this exercise. The part that this solid models could be used as the control arm in an automobile front suspension system.

Figure 6-6

Retrieve file f1370.dwg from the CD-ROM that accompanies this book, and open it. This file contains the first two profiles for constructing this model. If you would rather start from scratch and draw your own profiles, begin a new AutoCAD drawing using the acad-iso.dwt template, and draw the profile shown in Figure 7-1 on the WCS X-Y plane. Use the dimensions given in the figure for drawing your profile, but do not include them with your profile. When you have finished drawing the profile, turn the five arcs and five lines into a 2D polyline (with the PEDIT command) or a region (with the REGION command).

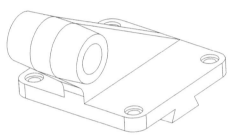

Figure 7-1

If you started this exercise by opening file f1370.dwg, you can ignore this paragraph and go directly to the next one. Otherwise, rotate the coordinate system X-Y plane 90 degrees about the X axis and position it next to the existing solid. Then draw the six lines and six arcs of the profile shown in Figure 7-2 according to the given dimensions. The arcs are tangent to each other as well as to their adjoining lines. Although this is a fairly complex profile, drawing it is strictly 2D work. The dimensions have been selected so that you can conveniently draw most of the lines and arcs using a snap-to-grid spacing of 2.0mm. Notice in Figure 7-2 that the two large radius arcs in the lower-left portion of the profile are created by offsetting (with the OFFSET command) the upper two arcs a distance of 32mm. After you have created the 10 profile objects, transform them into a 2D polyline or a region.

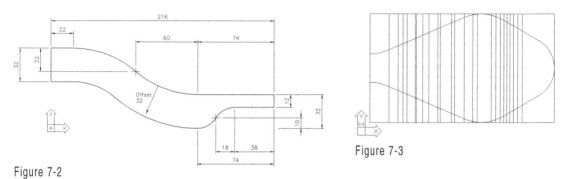

Figure 7-2

Figure 7-3

Use EXTRUDE to transform the profile that is on the WCS X-Y plane into a 3D solid. Specify an extrusion height of at least 76mm, and 0 as the extrusion taper angle. Next, extrude the second profile to a height of at least 124mm, with 0 as the extrusion taper angle. Move the two solids together as shown in Figure 7-3. This figure is a plan view of the WCS.

Start the INTERSECT command, and use any AutoCAD method to select the two solids when you are prompted to select objects. The resulting solid should look similar to the one shown in Figure 7-4. The viewpoint in Figure 7-4 looks up toward the

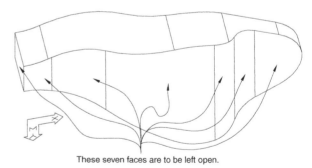

These seven faces are to be left open.

Figure 7-4

WCS X-Y plane from below the model, and hidden-line removal is on.

Start the SOLIDEDIT command, and select the Body option. Then, select the Shell option and pick an edge on your solid when you are prompted to select a 3D solid. The next prompt asks you to specify the faces that are to be open. Select the six bottom faces and the rear square face as shown in Figure 7-4 by picking a point anywhere on their surface. Press Enter to signify that you are finished designating the open faces, and then enter 3.0 as the shell offset thickness. Press Enter

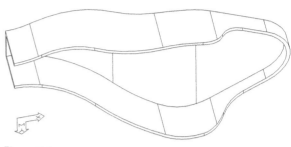

Figure 7-5

twice to exit the SOLIDEDIT command. Your 3D solid should now look similar to the one in Figure 7-5.

The profiles for the next solid you will create are also in file f1370.dwg. These profiles, which consist of three circles and one object made from three lines and five arcs, are to be used to cut the existing 3D solid. If you are drawing your own profiles for this model, verify that the WCS is in effect and then draw the objects shown in Figure 7-6. This figure also shows the existing 3D solid to help you visualize the cuts they will make. Transform the profile made from three lines and five arcs into a 2D polyline or a region.

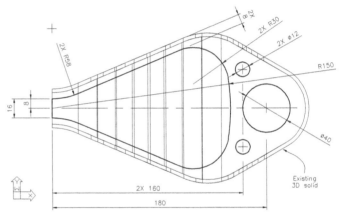

Figure 7-6

Start the EXTRUDE command, and select each of the four profiles when you are prompted to select the objects that are to be extruded. Specify an extrusion height of at least 76mm, and 0 as the taper angle. Move the solids, if necessary, to the positions shown in Figure 7-7.

Invoke SUBTRACT, and pick a point on the main 3D solid to specify the solid to subtract from. Then, select the four new 3D solids as the solids to subtract. Your model should now look similar to the one in Figure 7-8 when it is viewed from above and hidden-line removal is on.

Move the coordinate system origin to the center of the 40mm diameter hole in the model and rotate the Y-X axis 90 degrees about the X axis. Then, draw the profile shown in Figure 7-9. In this figure, the profile is shown with hatches to help you identify it, and it is placed out of its final position to make it easier to draw. Figure 7-9 also shows a centerline through the center of the 40mm hole to help you visualize the location of the profile, but you do not have to draw this centerline. After you have drawn the profile, turn its two lines and four arcs into a 2D polyline or a region, and move it down so that its top edge is aligned with the top edge of the 40mm diameter hole.

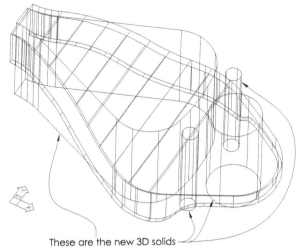

These are the new 3D solids

Figure 7-7

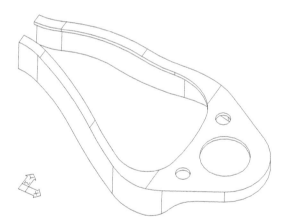

Figure 7-8

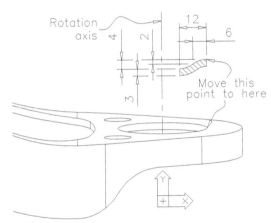

Figure 7-9

Start the REVOLVE command and select the profile as the object to revolve. When you are prompted to define the rotation axis, enter a Y (for Y axis). The last prompt is for you to specify the angle of revolution; press Enter to accept the default 360 degrees. Then, verify that the top edge of the revolved solid is even with the top rim of the 40mm hole, and use the UNION command to join the revolved solid with the main solid. Your model should now look similar to the one in Figure 7-10.

Move the UCS to the location shown in Figure 7-11, and draw the two profiles in the figure. One profile consists of three lines and one arc, while the other is simply a 16mm diameter circle.

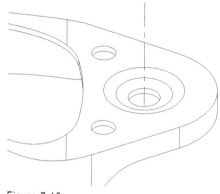

Figure 7-10

Use EXTRUDE, with an extrusion height of 3mm and no taper, to create a 3D solid from each profile. Copy both new solids using a displacement distance of 29mm in the WCS Y-axis direction. The original solids and their copies should look and be positioned the same as those in Figure 7-12.

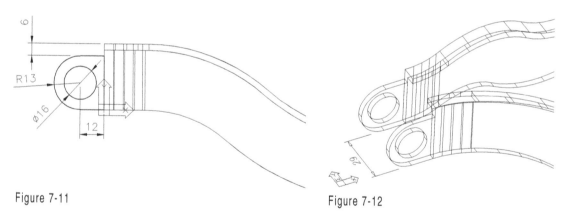

Figure 7-11                                        Figure 7-12

Use the UNION command to join the two D-shaped solids to the main 3D solid. Then, use SUBTRACT to remove the 16mm diameter disk-shaped solids from the main solid to create two round holes. You model should now look similar to the one in Figure 7-13.

You will finish this model by rounding some of its sharp edges and corners. Start the FILLET command, and pick a point on an edge of the inside corner of the 3D solid, as shown in Figure 7-13. Enter 3.0 when you are prompted for the fillet radius. The next prompt asks you to select another edge or an option. Enter C to choose the Chain option. Then, pick another point on the inside corner of the solid. All the edges on the inside corner are highlighted to indicate that they are selected. Press Enter for AutoCAD to create the inside fillets.

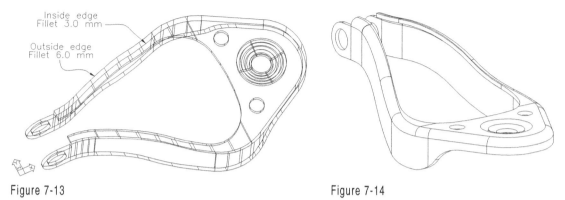

Figure 7-13                                     Figure 7-14

Repeat the FILLET command and select the outside corner of the solid as shown in Figure 7-13. Enter 6.0 as the fillet radius, and again choose the Chain option to select all the edges on the outside corner. These fillets complete your model, which should now look similar to the one in Figure 7-14. On the CD-ROM that comes with this book, the finished model is in file f1383.dwg.

# CHAPTER 14

# Visualizing and Using 3D Solid Models

*You now know how to use all the tools AutoCAD provides for constructing, modifying, and editing 3D solids. Now, you will learn how to control the appearance of 3D solids and how to extract useful objects and information from them.*

*This chapter*

- *describes how to use the system variables that control the appearance of 3D solids, whether they are in a wireframe mode or a hidden-line mode;*

- *tells how to set up shaded and semitransparent viewing modes for solids;*

- *explains how to check for interference between two mating 3D solids in an assembly;*

- *shows how to extract a region object from the cross-section of a 3D solid;*

- *describes the mass properties of regions and 3D solids.*

## Controlling the Appearance of 3D Solids

### The HIDE Command and 3D Solids

You have undoubtedly noticed during your use of the HIDE command in the previous four chapters that, by default, 3D solids automatically assume a faceted appearance in their hidden-line mode. Also in the previous four chapters, you have occasionally used, with virtually no explanation, the **dispsilh** system variable to turn off the faceted appearance during HIDE.

The **dispsilh** system variable is one of four system variables that give you some control over the appearance of 3D solids, whether they are in their wireframe or hidden-line viewing mode. The others are **isolines**, **facetres**, and **facetratio**.

You can set the value of **isolines**, **facetres**, and **dispsilh** through the Display tab of the OPTIONS command's dialog box. **Facetratio**, however, can be set only through the SETVAR command or by accessing it directly from the command line.

## The **Isolines** System Variable

Unlike the other three system variables affecting the appearance of 3D solids, **isolines** affects the appearance of solids only when they are in their wireframe viewing mode.

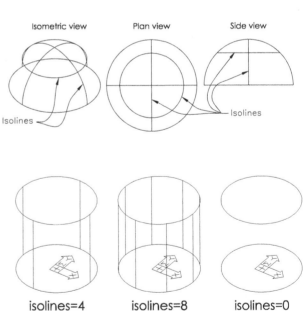

In their wireframe form, the edges of surfaces on 3D solids are indicated by lines or curves, depending upon the solid's shape. No lines are drawn across planar surfaces, but lines and curves are drawn across nonplanar surfaces. They are to help you identify and visualize the surfaces, and their quantity is controlled by the **isolines** system variable.

**Isolines**, which accepts an integer number from 0 to 2,047, represents the number of lines per 360 degrees on a curved surface. For example, when **isolines** is set to 4, a hemisphere-shaped solid that is resting on the X-Y plane will have one horizontal isoline (through 90 degrees) and four vertical isolines (through 360 degrees).

The figure to the right shows the effect of three different isolines values on the wireframe appearance of a cylinder. Notice that when **isolines** is set to 0, no lines are drawn along the side surface of the cylinder.

Only nonplanar surfaces are affected by **isolines**, and the system variable has no effect on the density of mesh lines and facets in hidden-line views. The current setting of **isolines** applies to all 3D solids — it is not possible for some 3D solids to have one **isolines** setting while others have another setting. A screen regeneration is required before any changes in **isolines** take effect.

Usually, you will keep **isolines** at its default setting of 4, but when a curved surface is difficult to visualize, you might want to increase its value. Increasing the **isolines** value can be especially useful when you are working with spherical surfaces. Conversely, you might occasionally want (at least temporarily) to decrease the value of **isolines** when you are working with a cluttered 3D solid.

## The **Dispsilh** System Variable

**Dispsilh**, which stands for **dis**play **sil**houette, affects 3D solids in both their wireframe and hidden-line viewing modes. It is a toggle-type system variable that can have a value of 0, which means it is turned off, or 1, which means it is turned on.

When **dispsilh** is set to its default value of 0, nonplanar surfaces on 3D solids in their wireframe mode are delineated solely by their isolines, as shown on the left in the top

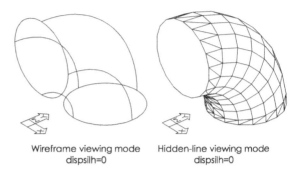

Wireframe viewing mode
dispsilh=0

Hidden-line viewing mode
dispsilh=0

figure. When HIDE is in use, curved surfaces on 3D solids are delineated by three- and four-sided facets, similar to those on polygon mesh surface models, as shown on the right in the top figure.

When **dispsilh** is set to 1, curves or lines delineate the profile, or silhouette, of non planar 3D solid surfaces in wireframe viewing modes. These are in addition to the isolines, and they are automatically adjusted to match the current view direction, as shown in the accompanying figure.

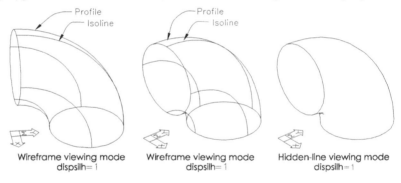

Wireframe viewing mode
dispsilh= 1

Wireframe viewing mode
dispsilh= 1

Hidden-line viewing mode
dispsilh= 1

Although these profile lines can help you visualize a surface's shape in wireframe viewing modes, **dispsilh**'s effect in the hidden-line viewing mode is even more pronounced. Only edges and the profiles of curved surfaces are shown. No facets are used to indicate curved surfaces when HIDE is in effect, which results in a clean, uncluttered appearance.

## The **Facetres** System Variable

The relative size of the facets that AutoCAD uses for curved and rounded surfaces on 3D solids when HIDE is in effect and **dispsilh** is set to 0 is controlled by the **facetres** system variable. **Facetres** (which stands for **facet res**olution) accepts any number from 0.01 to 10.00, with 0.50 being its initial value. The larger the number assigned to **facetres**, the smaller but more numerous are the facets.

**Facetres** also controls the apparent roundness of curved surfaces — such as the ends of cylinders, the edges of round holes, and the profile of spherical surfaces — during HIDE and RENDER, even when **dispsilh** is set to 1. AutoCAD approximates round edges and profiles of rounded surfaces with short straight lines during the HIDE and RENDER commands. When **facetres** has a low value, the lines are relatively long and are noticeable. When **facetres** has a high value, the lines are so short that they can scarcely be seen.

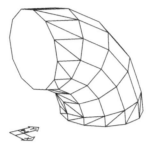
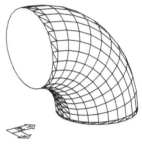

Hidden-line viewing mode
dispsilh=0
facetres=low value

Hidden-line viewing mode
dispsilh=0
facetres=high value

Even though the effects of **facetres** on the number and size of facets and on the length of lines approximating curved edges and profiles are relative to the magnitude of its value, you cannot directly control their number and size. In other words, doubling the value of **facetres** will increase the number of facets, but it will not necessarily double their number. Furthermore, the effect of **facetres** is different on the computer screen than it is for printed output. For a given **facetres** value, printed output of hidden-line views of 3D solids will have more facets than those of the same objects shown on the computer screen. Keep in mind, however, that **facetres** affects only the dis-

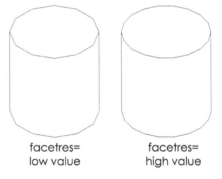

facetres=
low value

facetres=
high value

play and printed output of 3D solids, and it has no effect on wireframe view modes. Round 3D solids, for instance, are perfectly round even if they don't appear to be.

### The **Facetratio** System Variable

**Facetratio** controls the number of facets on cylindrical and conic 3D solids during HIDE when **dispsilh** is set to 0. It can have a value of either 0 — its default value — or 1. When **facetratio** is set to 0, it is off and has no effect. 3D solid cylinders and cones have facets on their round surfaces that extend for their entire length during hidden-line modes. Each facet, for instance, on the side of a cylinder extends from one end to the other.

When **facetratio** is set to 1, facets are added to the side surfaces of cylinders and cones by dividing each lengthwise facet into two or more facets. Although this system variable can make renderings and hidden-line views more accurate, you will seldom have a need to change **facetratio** from its default of 0 to 1.

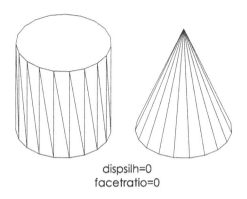

dispsilh=0
facetratio=0

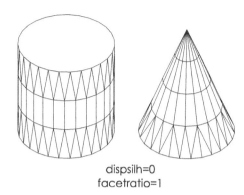

dispsilh=0
facetratio=1

## The SHADEMODE Command and 3D Solids

You will often use the various options of the SHADEMODE command as you construct 3D solid models. Its hidden-line mode has an advantage over the HIDE command in that you can perform real-time pans, zooms, and viewpoint rotations (with 3DORBIT). When SHADEMODE's 3D wireframe option is active, the HIDE command use the SHADEMODE version of hidden-line removal.

In AutoCAD 2002 and 2000i, SHADEMODE's Hidden option creates faceted images of 3D solids, similar to HIDE when **dispsilh** is set to 0. In AutoCAD 2000, however, the option creates non faceted images similar to HIDE when **dispsilh** is set to 1. However, AutoCAD 2000's hidden-line images are generally missing profile lines on curved surfaces. Also, the AutoCAD 2002 and 2000i versions of SHADEMODE's Hidden option revert to the AutoCAD 2000 version during real-time pans, zooms, and viewpoint rotations.

Often, you will work with SHADE-MODE's Gouraud Shading Plus Edges viewing mode. This mode helps you visualize your model even better than hidden-line modes, and you can easily select the model's edges because they are distinctly shown. A disadvantage with shaded viewing modes, as well as with hidden-line modes, is that you can neither see nor select edges on the far side of your model. You can, however, create a semitransparent shaded viewing mode by attaching material properties to a solid model. The slightly shaded surfaces help you visualize your

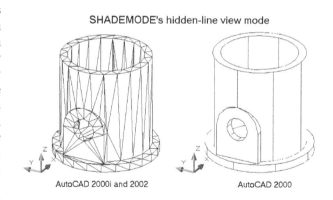

SHADEMODE's hidden-line view mode

AutoCAD 2000i and 2002          AutoCAD 2000

model's geometry, yet no section of the model is hidden, and you can see and select virtually any edge. Three steps are required to use a rendering material: you must enable material display, you must create a material, and you must apply that material.

To enable material display, invoke the OPTIONS command, select the System tab, and click the Current 3D Graphics Display Properties button. This button opens a dialog box titled 3D Graphics System Configuration.

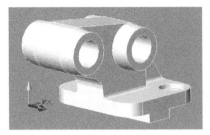

SHADEMODE's Gouraud Shading plus edges mode.

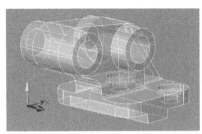

SHADEMODE's Gouraud Shading plus edges mode coupled with a semitransparent material.

Here you select Render options and then select Enable Materials. If you want to incorporate a bitmap pattern with the material, also select Enable Textures. Materials having bitmap patterns can simulate such things as wood grain, bricks, and floor tile, but you are not likely to use such a material when your objective is to improve 3D visualization while constructing a model, rather than to create a lifelike rendering of a finished model. See Chapter 19 for more information about textures and bitmap patterns.

To create a material, start the RMAT command to display the Materials dialog box. Make certain that Standard is displayed in the list box on the right side of the Materials dialog box, and click the New button to open the New Standard Material dialog box. Enter a name for the new material. On the left side of the dialog box is a list of material properties, or attributes, that you can control. For working with shaded viewing modes, you will probably need

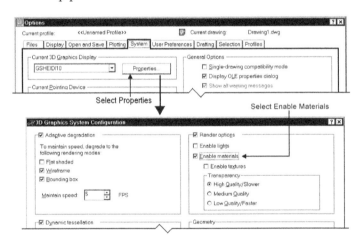

Select Properties

Select Enable Materials

to set only the Transparency attribute. Click the Transparency radio button and specify a transparency value. A value of 0 makes the material completely opaque, while a value of 1 makes the material completely transparent (and invisible). Generally, a transparency value between 0.50 and 0.75 gives good results. Chapter 19 contains detailed information about creating materials.

After you have set the material's properties, click the OK button of the New Standard Material dialog box to return to the Materials dialog box. Make certain that the name of your material is highlighted in the Materials list box, and then select the ByLayer button. A dialog box listing all the current drawing's layers is displayed for you to choose the layer your solid model uses. See Chapter 19 for more information about attaching materials to objects.

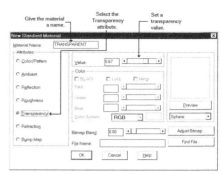

After you have enabled material display, created a semitransparent material, and attached that material to your solid model, activate SHADEMODE's Gouraud Shaded Plus Edges viewing mode. The shaded mode works during 3D orbit, as well as during real-time zooms and pans.

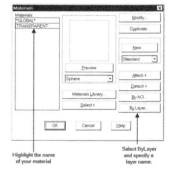

# Checking for Interference

Although the INTERFERE command resembles the INTERSECT command in that it can create a 3D solid from the intersecting volume of two or more solids, it is an inspection tool rather than a modification tool. It is for determining whether mating solids have clearance or whether they have an interference fit with each other. Consequently, when overlapping volume is found, creating a new 3D solid from it is optional. Moreover, unlike the INTERSECT command, the original 3D objects are not deleted when INTERFERE creates a solid from their common volume.

When interference is found, AutoCAD asks whether you want to create a solid from the overlapping volume or whether you just want the interfering solid objects highlighted. Usually, you will want to have the interference volume turned into a 3D solid because AutoCAD highlights just the solids that share the same volume — the interference volume is not highlighted by itself. This new solid not only allows you to see precisely where the interference is, but to measure it as well. These solids should be in a separate layer and have a distinct color so they will stand out and can be discarded when you are finished with them.

Although INTERFERE allows you to select as many solids as you want to be checked for interference, pinning down interference locations can be difficult and confusing even when as few as three or four solids are checked at once. Generally, you will find it best to select one key solid and compare it with its mating solids one by one, rather than all at the same time.

### Exercise One

Retrieve the file f1417.dwg from the CD-ROM that comes with this book and open it. Four separate 3D solids are in this file — a base part, a mating part, and two cylinders representing the bolts that will hold the two parts together. Figure 1-1 shows an exploded view of this assembly.

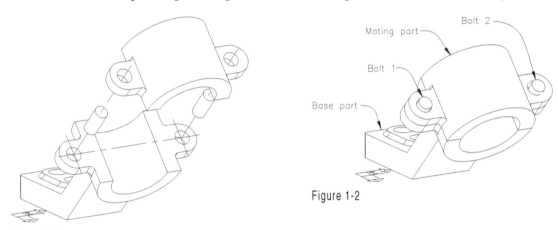

Figure 1-2

Figure 1-1

The model in the drawing file already has its four parts in position, as shown in Figure 1-2. Use the INTERFERE command to ensure that the bolt holes are properly located and that the bolts will pass through the holes without any interference.

Switch to the drawing file's layer named Sol_interfere. In the event that you do find interference, you will create an interference solid in that layer. Start the INTERFERE command and check Bolt 1 in Figure 1-2 with the base part and the mating part using the following command line input:

```
Command: INTERFERE (Enter)
Select first set of solids:
Select objects: (Use a crossing window to select the base part, the mating part, and Bolt 1.)
Select objects: (Enter)
Select second set of solids:
Select objects: (Enter)
Comparing 3 solids with each other.
Solids do not interfere.
```

Those three parts check out, so next determine whether the other bolt has no interference with the base part and the mating part:

```
Command: INTERFERE (Enter)
Select first set of solids:
Select objects: (Use a crossing window to select the base part, the
    mating part, and Bolt 2.)
Select objects: (Enter)
Select second set of solids:
Select objects: (Enter)
Comparing 3 solids with each other.
Interfering solids: 2
Interfering pairs: 1
Create interference solids? [Yes\No] <N>: Yes (Enter)
```

Figure 1-3

Figure 1-3 shows a close-up of the problem area, with the new solid moved up so that you can see the size and shape of the interfering volume. In your model, it is still down in the mating part and Bolt 2. The hole in the mating part needs to be moved with the face Move option of SOLID-EDIT. You can do that without a description of the necessary step because you have experience in editing solids.

| | |
|---|---|
| Command: | INTERFERE |
| Purpose: | INTERFERE identifies 3D solids that overlap. The common volume can be made into a new 3D solid. |
| Initiate with: | • On the command line, enter INTERFERE.<br>• From the Draw pull-down menu, select Solids, and then Interference.<br>• Select the Interfere button from the Solids toolbar. |
| Options: | The interfere command issues command line prompts for you to select two groups, or sets, of 3D solids:<br><br>Select first set of solids:<br>Select objects: (Use any object-selection method to select one or more 3D solids.)<br>Select second set of solids:<br>Select objects: (Use any object-selection method to select one or more 3D solids, or press Enter.)<br><br>AutoCAD automatically filters out objects in the selection sets that are not 3D solids. Specifying a second set of solids is optional and can be bypassed by pressing the Enter key in response to its prompt. If you have only one set of solids, each solid is checked for interference with the other solids. |

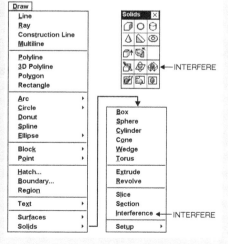

If you have two sets of solids, each solid in the first set is checked for interference with each solid in the second set, but solids within the same selection set are not checked for interference with each other. If a solid in the first set is also included in the second set, its inclusion in the second set is ignored.

As soon as the solids have been selected, AutoCAD reports the number of solids that were compared, the number of interfering solids, and the number of interfering pairs. AutoCAD also highlights all the interfering solids and asks if you want to create 3D solids from the volume they share.

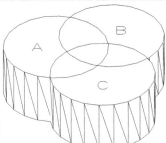

```
Create interference solids? [Yes/No] <N>: (Enter Y
    or N, or press Enter.)
```

If A, B, and C are in the same selection set:

    A will be compared with B.
    A will be compared with C.
    B will be compared with C.

If A and B are in one selection set, and C is in the other selection set:

    A will be compared with C.
    B will be compared with C.

If you enter the letter Y, AutoCAD creates new 3D solids from each of the interfering volumes. The new solids will be in the current layer, rather than in the layer of the original 3D solids. If you enter the letter N or press the Enter key, AutoCAD will not create any new 3D solids, but will highlight the interfering solids. When there are more than two interfering 3D solids, AutoCAD asks whether you want the individual pairs of interfering solids highlighted:

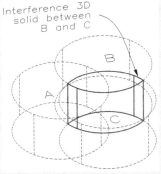

Interference 3D solid between B and C

```
Highlight pairs of interfering solids? [Yes/No] <N>:
    (Enter Y or N, or press Enter.)
```

If you press the Enter key or enter the letter N, the command ends. If you enter the letter Y (or the entire word yes), AutoCAD highlights one pair of interfering solids. Each entire solid is highlighted — not just the common volume. If there is more than one pair of interfering solids, AutoCAD displays the prompt

Highlighted pairs of interfering solids

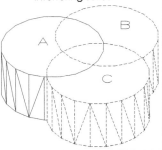

```
Enter an option [Next pair/eXit] <Next>: (Enter X
    or N, or press Enter.)
```

AutoCAD highlights the next pair of interfering 3D solids when the letter N is entered or the Enter key is pressed. Entering an X ends the command.

Notes:

    • The INTERFERE command does not accept regions. It works only with 3D solid objects.

- If you want to check only two solids for interference, it makes no difference if they are both in the first selection set or if one is in the first selection set and the other is in the second selection set.

Related command:    • INTERSECT    The Boolean intersect operation performed by INTERSECT also creates 3D solids from the common volume of two or more 3D solids. Unlike INTERFERE, however, the original solids are deleted, and the common volume is transformed into one 3D solid rather than into a 3D solid for each pair of intersecting solids.

# Extracting Cross-Sections from 3D Solids

Cross-sections of 3D solids can be created through the SECTION command. This command uses the same options for defining the cross-section's plane that the SLICE command uses for defining a slicing plane. Unlike the SLICE command, however, SECTION does not alter the selected 3D solid. Instead, it creates a new object, a region, from the outline of the 3D solid as it passes through the section plane.

Generally, you will make cross-sections from 3D solids for one of two reasons. One reason is to better examine the solid's shape, to ensure that it has the form and dimensions you intended. The other is to use the cross-section for stress and deflection analysis (More about this later in the discussion of mass properties of solids and regions). You do not need to make cross-sections for use in 2D drawings, because AutoCAD has special commands for doing just that. (Those commands are described Chapter 16.)

The SECTION command is straightforward to use. You select one or more 3D solids, and then define the cross-section plane. The resulting region takes the properties of the current layer, and it remains in the 3D solid. To examine the region, you can either move it out of the solid or freeze the solid's layer.

### Exercise Two

You will extract a cross-section from the 3D solid you used in Exercise 1. In Exercise 1, the INTERFERE command told you that some of the 3D solids in this model share the same volume. You will now use the SECTION command to examine the problem area.

Open the file f1417.dwg from the CD-ROM that comes with this book. Use this version of the model, rather than the one you ended up with at the conclusion of Exercise 1 (which created a 3D solid from the interfering volume).

Use the 3point or Face option of the UCS command to position the UCS as shown in Figure 2-1. The viewpoint for this figure is rotated 330 degrees in the X-Y plane from the X axis and minus 15 degrees from the X-Y plane. Notice in Figure 2-1 that the angled

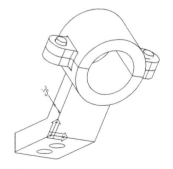

Figure 2-1

arm on the 3D solid is 0.75 units thick. Set the cross-section plane to be parallel with the UCS X-Y plane and in the middle of the angled arm (at an elevation of -0.375 units).

Switch to the drawing's layer named Section and use the following command line input to create the cross-sections:

```
Command: SECTION (Enter)
Select objects: (Use a crossing window to select all four 3D solids.)
Select objects: (Enter)
Specify first point on section plane by [Object/Zaxis/View/XY/YZ/3points]
    <3points>: XY (Enter)
Specify a point on the XY-plane <0,0,0>: 0,0,-.375 (Enter)
```

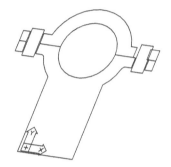

Because the newly created region of the cross-section is within the 3D solids, you probably will not be able to see it. When you freeze the layers of the 3D solids, however, the four regions appear as they do in Figure 2-2. The region representing the model's cap is one region, even though it is in three pieces. You can clearly see that one of its holes is incorrectly positioned, and you can take measurements from the regions to find its correct location.

Figure 2-2

| Command: | SECTION |
|---|---|
| Purpose: | The SECTION command creates a region from the cross-section of a 3D solid. Seven options exist for you to position th cross-section plane. |
| Initiate with: | • On the command line, enter SECTION.<br>• From the Draw pull-down menu, select Solids, and then Section.<br>• Select the Section button from the Solids toolbar. |

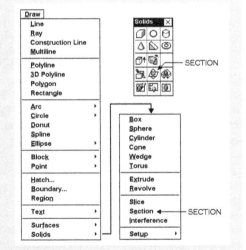

| Options: | The SECTION command issues a command line prompt for you to specify the 3D objects that are the basis for the cross-sections. If more than one solid is selected, a separate region is created for each solid. Then, AutoCAD displays a command line menu for you to choose a method for defining the cross-section plane: |
|---|---|

```
Specify first point on section plane by [Object/Zaxis/View/ XY/YZ/ZX/3points]
    <3points>: (Specify a point, enter an option, or press Enter.)
```

- **3points**

This option defines a section plane through the position of three points located on the plane. You can start the option by specifying a point from the main SECTION menu, by entering the number 3, or by pressing the Enter key. If you specify a point, it serves as the first point of the plane, and prompts for the second and third points are issued. If you enter the number 3 or press the Enter key in response to the main menu, AutoCAD prompts for three points:

```
Specify first point on plane: (Specify a point.)
Specify second point on plane: (Specify a point.)
Specify third point on plane: (Specify a point.)
```

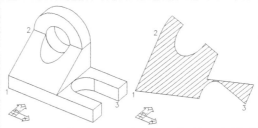

3points section plane   Resulting region (shown hatched)

- **Object**

The plane of an existing object is used to define the cross-section plane when this option is selected. An arc, circle, ellipse, any member of the 2D polyline family, or a planar spline can be used as the defining object. Nonplanar splines, lines, and 3D polylines cannot be used. The option displays the following command line prompt for an object:

```
Select a circle, ellipse, arc, 2D-spline, or 2D-polyline: (Pick a
    point on one object.)
```

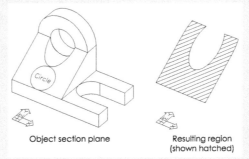

Object section plane   Resulting region
(shown hatched)

- **Zaxis**

This option uses two points to define the cross-section plane. The plane is located on the first point, and is normal (perpendicular) to a line drawn from the first point to the second point. The option's prompts are

```
Specify a point on the section plane: (Specify a point.)
Specify a point on the Z-axis (normal) of the plane: (Specify a
    point.)
```

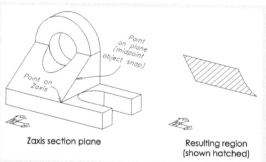

Zaxis section plane

Resulting region
(shown hatched)

- View

The View option uses a cross-section plane that is perpendicular to the current viewing direction and positioned at a specified point. Its command line prompt is

```
Specify a point on the current view plane <0,0,0>: (Specify a point or
    press Enter.)
```

The cross-section passes through the UCS origin if the Enter key is pressed.

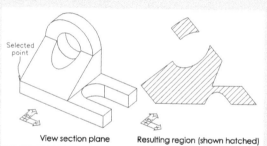

View section plane    Resulting region (shown hatched)

- XY

This option orients the cross-section so that it is parallel with the UCS X-Y plane. A prompt asks you to specify the elevation of the cross-section:

```
Specify a point on the X-Y plane <0,0,0>: (Specify a point or press
    Enter.)
```

If you press Enter, the cross-section is on the UCS X-Y plane.

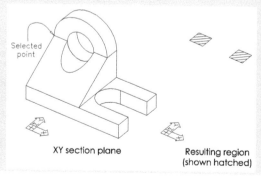

XY section plane

Resulting region
(shown hatched)

- YZ                The cross-section is parallel with the UCS Y-Z plane when this
option is selected. You are prompted to specify a point that the
cross-section will pass through.

```
Specify a point on the Y-Z plane <0,0,0>: (Specify a point or press
    Enter.)
```

The cross-section is on the UCS Y-Z plane if you press Enter.

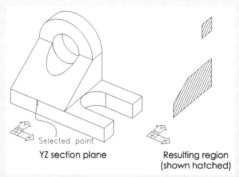

YZ section plane               Resulting region
(shown hatched)

- ZX                This option orients the cross-section parallel with the UCS Z-X
plane. You are asked to specify a point for the cross-section to pass
through.

```
Specify point on the Z-X plane <0,0,0>: (Specify a point or press
    Enter.)
```

If you press Enter, the cross-section is on the UCS Z-X plane.

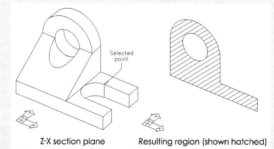

Z-X section plane         Resulting region (shown hatched)

Notes:
- The resulting regions reside in the current layer, rather than in the layer of the 3D solids they are based on.

- If the resulting region from one 3D solid is in two or more pieces, AutoCAD nevertheless considers it to be one region.

- The solid, or solids, selected for making cross-sections are not affected by the SECTION command.

Related
command:
- SLICE            The SLICE command cuts 3D solids into two pieces. It has the same options for defining a slicing plane that SECTION does for defining a cross-section plane.

## Analyzing 3D Solids and Regions

One of the advantages that solid models have over wireframe and surface models is that you can obtain data related to their geometric properties (such as surface area, volume, and center of gravity) and to their mass properties (such as weight and moments of inertia). The AREA command recognizes 3D solids and reports their surface area, while the MASSPROP command reports the other geometric and mass properties of 3D solids. AREA also recognizes regions, but it does not give any information beyond that supplied by the MASSPROP command.

### Mass Property Mathematics

While the properties for rectangular regions and box-shaped solids are relatively easy to compute, when you throw in some arcs, curves, spheres, hemispheres, and a few holes, the calculations can get involved quickly. For most objects, calculating mass property data — moments of inertia, centroids, and even area — requires complex mathematics.

The idea behind most of the mathematical techniques for computing property data is to divide the area (for regions), or the volume (for solids), into extremely small elements; calculate the property for each individual element; and then total the results. If you have ever estimated the size of an irregularly shaped object, such as an area on a map, by counting dots or squares on an overlaid grid, you have used a form of this same principle. The figure below and to the right shows a plane area, such as a region, divided into these small elemental areas.

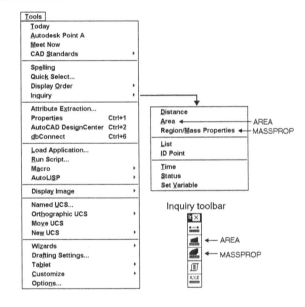

Inquiry toolbar

The mathematical convention is to use the symbols $dx$, $dy$, and $dz$ for the length, width, and height of these elements. These symbols are used in Tables 14-1 (page 366) and 14-2 (page 371) of this chapter, which show the equations behind the mass property data. Another symbol used in these tables is the uppercase sigma character, $\Sigma$, which signifies the summation of the results from operations on individual elements. For example, the equation used to find the area of a region is

$$A = \Sigma \, dxdy$$

This equation says that the length, $dx$, of each element is to be multiplied by its width, $dy$, to find an element's area. (The multiplication sign is implied.) Then, the areas of the individual elements are added together, as denoted by the $\Sigma$, to obtain the total area, A, of the region. Although the equations shown in the tables might appear at first to be abstract, they are much clearer and more concise than words and sentences in describing how a property is calculated.

For 3D objects, the elements are box-shaped, and the volume of a 3D object, such as a 3D solid, can be found by multiplying the length, width, and height of each elemental box, and then adding all the volumes together. Using equation notation, this operation can be written as

$$V = \Sigma\ dxdydz$$

In this equation, $dx$ represents the length of each elemental box, $dy$ is its width, and $dz$ is its height. Sometimes, as shown later, in Table 14-2, the volume of an elemental box is shown as simply $dv$, which is a shorthand version of $dxdydz$. Also, the mass (which is defined later when the mass property reports for 3D solids are described) of an elemental box is shown as $dm$ in Table 14-2.

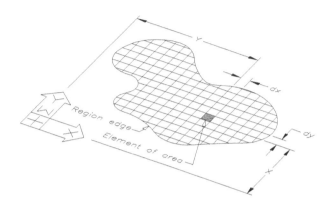

Although the principles for using elemental areas and boxes are simple, laying out the elements and computing the sums is tricky. It is part of a complex subject — numerical mathematics — that goes far beyond the comprehension of most. Fortunately, you do not have to understand the details to use the results, although it is helpful to know what is behind the data, as described previously and shown in Tables 14-1 and Table 14-2 (page 366 and page 371).

Integral calculus can be used when the object's shape can be defined by an equation, and this is the basis of the formulas found in mathematic and engineering handbooks for calculating the properties of various common shapes. Even with handbooks, however, the hand calculations are laborious and error prone and can be applied only to objects having standard shapes. Before AutoCAD had such objects as regions and solids, AutoLISP programs were sometimes used to calculate centroids and moments of inertia, but the results were approximations with often dubious accuracy.

Even Autodesk's Advanced Modeling Extension (AME) for AutoCAD Releases 11 and 12 used methods in calculating mass property data that sometimes gave obviously incorrect answers. It was possible to perform hand calculations that were more accurate than AME. This is not the case with AutoCAD's solid modeler based upon the ACIS kernel. The ACIS specification claims a maximum error of 1 percent for mass property data. Mass property data from regions and solids is not only easily and quickly obtained with AutoCAD, you can be confident of its accuracy.

As you would expect, because one is a 2D object while the other is a 3D object, AutoCAD reports different information for regions than it does for solids. Generally, the information for regions is easier to understand (and often more useful) than mass property data for solids.

## Mass Property Reports for Regions

Because regions are planar objects, and because AutoCAD combines all the regions selected into one report, their relationship to the coordinate system and to each other is important in both selecting objects for MASSPROP and in the extent of the information AutoCAD reports. First of all, AutoCAD ignores all regions that are not in the same plane as the first region selected. Second, AutoCAD gives more information for regions that are on the X-Y plane (coplanar) than for regions that are off the X-Y plane (noncoplanar).

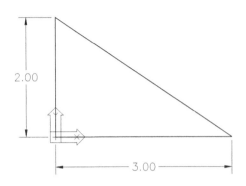

AutoCAD reports the area, perimeter, bounding box, centroid, moments of inertia, radius of gyration, and the principal moments of inertia for regions that are coplanar with the X-Y plane. Because the moments of inertia properties, as well as the radius of gyration, are always relative to an axis in the plane of the region, AutoCAD does not report them when the region is off of, or tilted to, the X-Y plane. Consequently, AutoCAD reports only the area, perimeter, bounding box, and centroid of noncoplanar regions.

An example of AutoCAD's mass property report for a region is shown in Listing 14-1. The region of this report has the shape of a right triangle 3 units long and 2 units high, lying on the X-Y plane. The 3-unit side lies on the X-axis, and the 2-unit side is on the Y-axis. The following paragraphs describe the data in this mass property report.

# Listing 14-1 Mass Property Report for a Coplanar Region

```
.............REGIONS...............
Area:                   3.0000
Perimeter:              8.6056
Bounding box:           X: 0.0000.....3.0000
                        Y: 0.0000.....2.0000
Centroid:               X: 1.0000
                        Y: 0.6667
Moments of inertia:     X: 2.0000Y: 4.5000
Product of inertia:     XY: 1.5000
Radii of gyration:      X: 0.8165 Y: 1.2247
Principal moments and X-Y directions about centroid:
                        I: 0.4325 along [0.9056 -0.4242]
                        J: 1.7342 along [0.4242 0.9056]
```

## Area

Area is the size of the region's surface, expressed in units of square length.

## Perimeter

Perimeter is the length of the region's boundary. If the region has one or more interior holes, the perimeter is the total length of both the inside and outside boundaries.

## Bounding Box

AutoCAD displays the coordinates for the corners of the smallest rectangular-shaped box the region will fit in. The sides of this box are always parallel to the coordinate system axes. Consequently, a long thin region will have a smaller bounding box when its sides are parallel to the coordinate system axes than it will when it is askew of them. If the region is on the X-Y plane, only the X and Y coordinates of the bounding box are given. If the region is off of, or is tilted to, the X-Y plane, the bounding box will have a Z coordinate also.

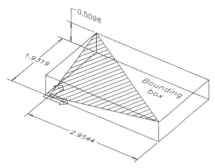

Bounding box for a noncoplanar region

## Centroid

The centroid is a point representing the geometric center of the region. For most regions it is the point at which the region could be balanced on the point of a pin. However, some regions, such as those shaped like the letter *L*, have their centroid outside the boundary of the region. If the region lays on the coordinate system X-Y plane, only the X and Y coordinates of the centroid are given. If the region is not on the X-Y plane, or is tilted to it, the centroid point will have a Z coordinate as well as X and Y coordinates.

## Moments of Inertia

Area moments of inertia are a more abstract property than area and centroids, and consequently they are not as easy to picture. Nevertheless, moments of inertia of areas are extremely important because they are used to calculate material-bending stresses and deformations (strains). Every region has two moments of inertia — one relative to the X axis, and a second relative to the Y axis. Because this property involves no mass, and hence no inertial forces, some prefer to call it the *second moment of area*, rather than *moment of inertia*.

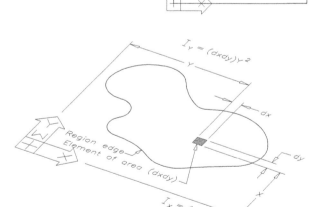

Area moments of inertia for a single element

## Product of Inertia

While area moment of inertia for an individual element is based upon the square of its distance from the X axis or the Y axis, product of inertia is based upon the product of the element's distance from the X axis and its distance from the Y axis. Consequently, a region has only one product of inertia, and its value can be either positive or negative, depending upon the location of the coordinate system. Product of inertia is used in computing the principal moments of inertia.

## Table 14-1 Region Properties — Basis Equations and Dimensions

| Property | Basis Equation | Dimensions |
|---|---|---|
| Area | $A = \sum dxdy$ | $L^2$ |
| Centroid | $\bar{x} = \dfrac{\sum (dxdy)x}{A}$ $\qquad \bar{y} = \dfrac{\sum (dxdy)y}{A}$ | x,y |
| Area Moments of Inertia | $I_{xx} = \sum (dxdy)^2$ | $L^4$ |
| | $I_{yy} = \sum (dxdy)y^2$ | $L^4$ |
| Product of Inertia | $I_{xy} = \sum (dxdy)xy$ | $L^4$ |
| Radius of Gyration | $K_x = \sqrt{\dfrac{I_{xx}}{A}}$ | L |
| | $K_y = \sqrt{\dfrac{I_{yy}}{A}}$ | L |
| Angle ($\theta$) of Principal Axis | $tan(2\theta) = \dfrac{2I_{xy}}{I_{xx} - I_{yy}}$ | Degrees |
| Principal Moments of Inertia | $I_{\substack{max \\ min}} = \left(\dfrac{I_{xx}+I_{yy}}{2}\right) \pm \sqrt{\left(\dfrac{I_{xx}+I_{yy}}{2}\right)^2 + (I_{xy})^2}$ | $L^4$ |

## Radius of Gyration

An area's radius of gyration is the distance from the reference axis at which the entire area could be considered as being concentrated without changing its moment of inertia. The property has such a catchy name that it is hard to forget, even if you never have any reason to use it. Similar to moments of inertia, every plane area always has one radius of gyration relative to the X axis and another relative to the Y axis. Radius of gyration is useful in the design of support columns because a column under a compression load tends to buckle in the direction of its least radius of gyration.

## Principal Moments of Inertia and X-Y Directions about Centroid

When the origin of the coordinate system is anchored on the centroid of a plane area, the X and Y axes can be rotated around the Z axis to an angle such that the area's maximum moment of inertia is about one axis, while its minimum moment of inertia is about the other axis. These two moments of inertia are called the *principal moments of inertia*, and the axes about which they are taken are called the *principal axes of inertia*. Product of inertia for the plane always has a value of 0 relative to the principal axes of inertia.

Principal moments of inertia as well as the orientation of the principal axes are based upon area moments of inertia and products of inertia, as shown in Table 14-1. In college classes covering engineering mechanics, a graphical technique called Mohr's circle is often used in finding the principal moments of inertia, as well as the orientation of the principal axes.

AutoCAD uses the letter *I* to indicate the principal moment of inertia about the principal axis corresponding to the X axis. Following this moment of inertia value are two numbers, enclosed within brackets, that are the coordinates of a point (relative to the current UCS) representing the end of a unit vector pointing in the direction of this principal axis. Thus, in Listing 14-1 the principal moment of inertia is 0.4325 about an axis pointed in the same direction as a line from 0,0 to 0.9056,-0.4242 (which is 25.1 degrees clockwise from the UCS X axis). AutoCAD uses the letter *J* for the other principal moment of inertia and indicates its axis direction also with a pair of point coordinates enclosed in brackets. As you would expect, these principal axes are always 90 degrees to one another.

If you were to rotate the UCS -25.1 degrees about the Z axis in the drawing for the region used for Listing 14-1, then move it to the region's centroid, the moments of inertia for the region would be 0.4325 units to the fourth power about the X axis, and 1.7342 units to the fourth power about the Y axis. Also, the product of inertia would be 0.

You will notice there is no mention of mass in Table 14-1. None of the properties for regions have mass — they are based solely upon length. Actually, this is to be expected because regions, by definition, are infinitely thin. They have no thickness, no volume, and no mass. The units of length in the mass property report for regions are based upon the measurement unit you are working with. For instance, if millimeters have been used to draw the region, area is in square millimeters, moments of inertia is in millimeters to the fourth power, and so forth.

## Mass Property Reports for 3D Solids

Listing 14-2 shows the mass property report of a wedge-shaped 3D solid that was made by extruding the triangle-shaped region used a few pages ago for illustrating AutoCAD's mass property report for a region to a height of 1 unit.

Unlike the mass property report for regions, AutoCAD does not report the surface area of 3D solids. You can find that property, however, by using the AREA command. The following paragraphs describe the data in the mass property report for solids.

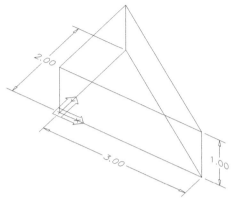

## Listing 14-2  AutoCAD Mass Property Report for a 3D Solid

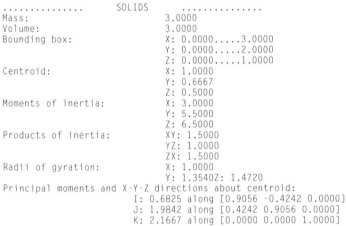

```
. . . . . . . . . . . . .      SOLIDS      . . . . . . . . . . . . .
Mass:                          3.0000
Volume:                        3.0000
Bounding box:                  X: 0.0000.....3.0000
                               Y: 0.0000.....2.0000
                               Z: 0.0000.....1.0000
Centroid:                      X: 1.0000
                               Y: 0.6667
                               Z: 0.5000
Moments of inertia:            X: 3.0000
                               Y: 5.5000
                               Z: 6.5000
Products of inertia:           XY: 1.5000
                               YZ: 1.0000
                               ZX: 1.5000
Radii of gyration:             X: 1.0000
                               Y: 1.3540Z: 1.4720
Principal moments and X-Y-Z directions about centroid:
                               I: 0.6825 along [0.9056 -0.4242 0.0000]
                               J: 1.9842 along [0.4242 0.9056 0.0000]
                               K: 2.1667 along [0.0000 0.0000 1.0000]
```

## Mass

Although most people generally use the words *mass* and *weight* interchangeably, there is a subtle difference between them. Mass is one of the three fundamental physical dimensions (length and time are the other two), while weight is an expression of force — it is mass multiplied by an acceleration due to gravity factor. Mass is independent of gravity. Weight, on the other hand, is dependent upon the strength of a gravitational field. Consequently, you would weigh less on the moon than you do on Earth, but your mass would remain the same. Nevertheless, weight is usually the way in which we relate to mass, and it is also a convenient way to obtain an object's mass.

Because computer programs have no means to weigh 3D models, most solid-modeling programs determine mass indirectly by multiplying the model's volume by a per-unit weight — the material's density. Density, which is designated by a lowercase Greek rho ($\rho$) in Table 14-2, is mass divided by volume. It is a material property.

AutoCAD, unfortunately, always uses a density of 1, and does not allow you to change it. Therefore, AutoCAD always reports the same value for mass as it does for volume. If you need to know the mass or weight of an AutoCAD 3D solid, you must do the calculations yourself.

## Volume

Volume is the amount of space within the solid, expressed in units of length raised to the third power.

## Bounding Box

These numbers are the diagonally opposite corner coordinates for the smallest box in which the solid would fit. The sides of the bounding box are always parallel to the coordinate system axes. Therefore, this box is not necessarily the smallest box into which the solid will fit.

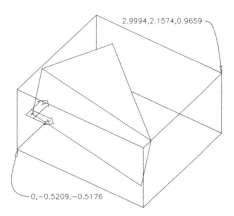

If a 3D solid is skewed to the principal planes, its bounding box will be larger than if it was aligned to the planes.

## Centroid

A solid's centroid is a 3D point representing its geometric center. If the density of the solid's material is homogeneous (which is usually the case), the centroid is also the solid's center of gravity — the point at which all the solid's weight appears to be concentrated.

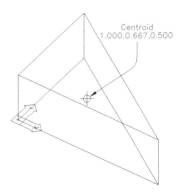

## Moments of Inertia

The moment of inertia of a box element about an axis is defined as the element's mass multiplied by the square of its distance from the axis. Notice that unlike moments of inertia for a region, the calculation for solids really does involve mass.

Because the mass of an object is equal to its density multiplied by its volume, an element's moment of inertia can also be found by multiplying its volume by the square of its distance from the axis and by its density. AutoCAD uses this approach, but it uses a density of 1. Thus, to obtain the correct moments of inertia of your solid, you have to multiply AutoCAD's values by the solid's material density. Mass moments of inertia are used principally in calculations of forces and motions of rotating objects.

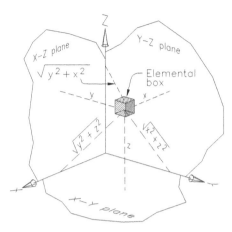

Moments of inertia for a single element

## Products of Inertia

The product of inertia for an elemental box is defined with respect to two planes that are perpendicular to one another (orthogonal) as the product of the element's mass and the perpendicular distances from each of the planes to the element (see the accompanying figure). For example, the XY product of inertia is calculated by multiplying the elemental box's mass by its distance in the Y direction from the X axis and by its distance in the X direction from the Y axis. In other words, the box's mass is multiplied by its X and Y coordinates. Although there are six products of inertia, only three of them are independent, as shown in Table 14-2.

Mass products of inertia can be calculated alternately by multiplying the element's volume, density, X coordinate, and Y coordinate together. AutoCAD uses this alternate calculation method, and as it does for moments of inertia, it uses a material density of 1. Therefore, you have to multiply the reported values by the solid's material density to obtain the true products of inertia.

## Radii of Gyration

Radius of gyration is the distance from the axis of rotation at which the entire weight of a body can be assumed to be concentrated, without changing its moment of inertia. It is sometimes used in the design of rotating parts, such as flywheels and governors. Every solid has three radii of gyration — one for each axis of the coordinate system. Each is found by dividing the body's moment of inertia about the axis by its mass and taking the square root of the result. Because density was used in calculating both moments of inertia and mass, the radii of gyration reported by AutoCAD is correct.

## Principal Moments and X-Y-Z Directions about Centroid

If the coordinate system origin is moved to the solid's centroid, it can be twisted to an orientation resulting in a maximum moment of inertia about one axis and a minimum moment of inertia about a second axis. The moment of inertia about the third axis will, of course, have a value somewhere between the maximum and minimum. These three moments of inertia are referred to as the principal moments of inertia, and the axes they are about are called the principal axes. The products of inertia is 0 when the coordinate system is aligned with the principal axes.

## Table 14-2 3D Solid Mass Properties — Basis Equations and Dimensions

| Property | Basis Equation | Dimensions |
|---|---|---|
| Mass | | |
| General: | $M = \rho V$ | |
| Element: | $dm = \rho(dxdydz) = \rho dv$ | $M$ |
| Volume | $V = \sum(dxdydz) = \sum dv$ | $L^3$ |
| Density | | |
| General: | $\rho = \dfrac{M}{V}$     (Always equals 1 in AutoCAD) | |
| Element: | $\rho = \dfrac{dm}{dv}$ | $\dfrac{M}{L^3}$ |
| Centroid | $\bar{x} = \dfrac{\sum xdv}{V} \quad \bar{y} = \dfrac{\sum ydv}{V} \quad \bar{z} = \dfrac{\sum zdv}{V}$ | $x, y, z$ |
| Moments of Inertia | $I_{xx} = \sum(y^2+z^2)dm \quad I_{xx} = \rho\sum(y^2+z^2)dv$ | $ML^2$ |
| | $I_{yy} = \rho\sum(x^2+z^2)dv$ | $ML^2$ |
| | $I_{zz} = \rho\sum(x^2+y^2)dv$ | $ML^2$ |
| Products of Inertia | $I_{xy} = I_{yx} = \sum xydm \quad I_{xy} = I_{yx} = \rho\sum xydv$ | $ML^2$ |
| | $I_{xz} = I_{zx} = \rho\sum xzdv$ | $ML^2$ |
| | $I_{yz} = I_{zy} = \rho\sum yzdv$ | $ML^2$ |
| Radius of Gyration | $K_x = \sqrt{\dfrac{I_{xx}}{M}}$ | $L$ |
| | $K_y = \sqrt{\dfrac{I_{yy}}{M}}$ | $L$ |
| | $K_z = \sqrt{\dfrac{I_{zz}}{M}}$ | $L$ |

---

### Table 14-2 3D Solid Mass Properties — Basis Equations and Dimensions (Continued)

Principal
Moments
of Inertia

$$\begin{bmatrix} I_{xx} & I_{xy} & I_{xz} \\ I_{yx} & I_{yy} & I_{yz} \\ I_{xz} & I_{zy} & I_{zz} \end{bmatrix}$$

The moments and
products of inertia
are arranged in a matrix

$$\begin{bmatrix} I_1 & 0 & 0 \\ 0 & I_2 & 0 \\ 0 & 0 & I_3 \end{bmatrix}$$

which is diagonalized
to find the principal
moments of inertia

$ML^2$

---

The principal axes are important in the design of rotating equipment, because parts rotating about a principal axis draw minimum power during speed changes. A rotating device, such as a shaft or propeller, is said to be *dynamically balanced* when its center of mass lies on the axis of rotation and it is rotating about a principal axis.

In AutoCAD's mass property report, the three principal moments of inertia are designated as I, J, and K, with the orientation of each corresponding principal axis shown within brackets. These numbers within brackets are the endpoint coordinates, relative to the current coordinate system, of a unit direction vector.

For example: If the UCS for the model used for the mass property report shown in Listing 14-2 is twisted so that the X axis is pointing in the same direction as a line from 0,0,0 to 0.9025, -0.4242,0; while the Y axis is pointing in the same direction as a line from 0,0,0 to 0.4242,0.9056,0; then the UCS origin is moved to the solid's centroid, and the mass moments of inertia will be 0.6825 about the X axis, 1.9842 about the Y axis, and 2.1667 about the Z axis. Also, all the products of inertia will be 0. You have to multiply AutoCAD's principal moments of inertia by density to obtain their correct values.

| | |
|---|---|
| Command: | MASSPROP |
| Purpose: | MASSPROP reports the mass properties of 3D solids and the area properties of regions. |
| Initiate with: | • On the command line, enter MASSPROP. |
| | • From the Tools pull-down menu, select Inquiry, and then Mass Properties. |
| | • Select the Mass Properties button from the Inquiry toolbar. |
| Implementation: | The MASSPROP command asks you to select the objects to be included in its mass properties report. You can select as many objects as you want. AutoCAD ignores objects that are not 3D solids. |
| | When more than one 3D solid is selected, AutoCAD issues a single report, as if the solids were a single, unified object. AutoCAD also combines regions when more than one is selected, provided that they are coplanar. If they are not, AutoCAD issues a report only for the first region selected. If a mixture of 3D solids and regions are selected, AutoCAD issues separate reports for each object type. |

The properties listed here appear in a text window.

| Properties of 3D Solids: | Properties of Regions: |
|---|---|
| Mass | Area |
| Volume | Perimeter |
| Bounding box | Bounding box |
| Centroid | Centroid |
| Moments of inertia | Moments of inertia |
| Products of inertia | Products of inertia |
| Radii of gyration | Radii of gyration |
| Principal moments and | Principal moments and |
| X-Y-Z direction about centroid | X-Y directions about centroid |

AutoCAD asks whether you want the data written to a file. The resulting file will be in ASCII text format, with a default filename the same as the current drawing file and with the file extension of .mpr.

Notes:

- If a region is not on the UCS X-Y plane, AutoCAD reports only its area, perimeter, bounding box, and centroid.

- AutoCAD always uses a density of 1 when it computes the mass of a 3D solid. Consequently, the reported values for mass and volume are always equal.

- The data for 3D solids is given in units of volume and mass, while the data for regions is in units of area.

- Mass property data is always relative to the current UCS origin.

| | |
|---|---|
| Command: | AREA |
| Purpose: | AREA reports the surface area of 3D solids and the area and perimeter of regions. |
| Initiate with: | • On the command line, enter AREA. |
| | • From the Tools pull-down menu, select Inquiry, and then Area. |
| | • Select the Area button from the Inquiry toolbar. |
| Implementation: | Choose the AREA command's Object option and select a 3D solid in response to its prompt to select objects. You can select only one object (despite the prompt's plural use of the word object), and you must do so by picking a point on the object. AutoCAD reports the surface area of a 3D solid. It also reports the solid's perimeter, but because perimeter has no meaning for a 3D solid, the perimeter value is always listed as 0. |

The AREA command also recognizes regions and reports their area and perimeter length.

# 2D Output and Paper Space

# CHAPTER 15

# Paper Space and Floating Viewports

*Sometimes, you need to create dimensioned, multiview 2D drawings, as well as isometric-type drawings, of your 3D models. You work in AutoCAD's paper space mode, rather than in model space mode, to do this. Paper space uses layouts to establish paper and plotting parameters for drawings, and uses floating viewports to establish drawing views in those layouts.*

*This chapter*

- *explains the role of paper space and describes its properties;*

- *describes how to set up layouts;*

- *tells you how to create floating viewports and how to set them up for making multiview orthographic 2D drawings;*

- *explains the techniques for controlling the appearance and visibility of objects within floating viewports;*

- *tells you how to dimension, annotate, and plot 2D paper space drawings of 3D models.*

In the not too distant future, it will be common to send digital data from 3D computer models directly to the machine shop. Then, multiview 2D drawings, with their elaborate dimensions and symbols, will no longer be needed. Now, however, they are still a necessity.

Actually, some paper-based 2D form of mechanical part models will probably always be needed for reviews and documentation. Furthermore, at this time, it is difficult to conceive of any technique that will transform 3D models of buildings and structures into real objects. Controlling the motions of milling machines and lathes is one thing; controlling the placement of two-by-fours and pouring concrete footings is altogether different. Therefore, paper drawings, along with other media forms for 2D representations, are going to be around for many, many years; in this book section, you will explore the AutoCAD tools and techniques for converting 3D models to 2D drawings.

# The Role of Paper Space

Up to this point, everything discussed in this book has pertained to model space — that fully 3D world where you can set viewpoints that look in any direction you choose, and where you can divide the AutoCAD graphics area into multiple tiled viewports to simultaneously view a 3D model from different view directions. Although model space is well suited for creating 3D models, it is not suitable for making 2D drawings of those models. Among its problems:

- Only the contents of the current viewport can be printed. This makes the printing of multiview drawings that show aligned top, front, and side views of a 3D model virtually impossible.

- Prints with an accurate scale from any viewpoint other than plan views are difficult to set up.

- Drawing views with a scale different from that used for other views is not practical.

- Controlling which objects are to be shown and which are not to be shown (such as interior and back-face edges) is awkward, as is the drafting practice of showing hidden edges with dashed lines.

These problems are largely solved through paper space. Paper space is a 2D world that acts as a screen placed over model space. You can make multiple viewports in this screen that look into model space, and you can establish different view directions in different viewports, just as you can in model space. Unlike model space, however, paper space allows you to simultaneously print all viewports — not just the current one.

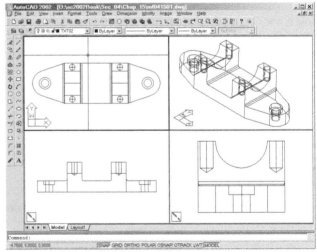

Model space tiled viewports

Paper space's purpose is to make 2D drawings from 3D models. It is a space comparable to a sheet of paper attached to a drafting board. If you intend a drawing to be on paper that is 22x17 inches, for instance, you set the extents of your paper space drawing to those dimensions. And, if you intend the printed text height of the notes to be 0.125 inches, that is the paper space text height you use.

Drawing scale is handled by adjusting the apparent size of the model in the paper space viewports. Moreover, because you can accurately scale the apparent size of the model viewport by viewport, you can have some views that have a different scale than the others. This enables you to conveniently have enlarged views showing details of your model.

# Floating Viewports

The key feature of paper space is *floating viewports*. They are similar to the *tiled viewports* of model space in that multiple viewports can coexist and each viewport can have a different 3D view direction, a different UCS, and different snap, grid, and UCS icon settings. Unlike tiled viewports, though, the floating viewports of paper space:

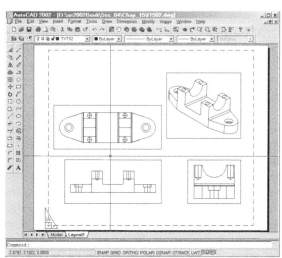

Paper space floating viewports

- Do not need to be side by side, or fill the entire graphics area. There can be gaps between the viewports, and the viewports can overlap and even be on top of each other.

- Can be erased, moved, stretched, copied, and scaled.

- Reside in a layer. Their borders take the color of the layer. If you turn off or freeze the viewport's layer, its borders disappear while its contents remain visible.

- Allow you to control which objects are visible in a viewport by freezing layers on a viewport-by-viewport basis.

- Can precisely set the scale of the 3D model. Moreover, the scale can vary between viewports.

- Permit hidden-line removal during plotting to be controlled on a viewport-by-viewport basis.

- Can have a border with any shape that can be drawn as a spline or a 2D polyline.

# The Properties of Paper Space

Despite the word space in its name, it is helpful to consider paper space more as an operational mode than as a location. In fact, even Autodesk uses the terms *drawing mode* and *model mode*, rather than paper space and model space in its Mechanical Desktop parametric 3D modeling program. Moreover, AutoCAD often uses the word *layout* when referring to paper space.

Controlling whether model space or paper space is active is done by the **tilemode** system variable. AutoCAD operates in model space when **tilemode** is set to 1, and it operates in paper space when **tilemode** is set to 0. The system variable's name is a reference to the tiled viewports used in model space — when **tilemode** is on (that is, when it is set to 1), tiled viewports are used; when **tilemode** is off (set to 0), floating viewports are used.

Beginning with AutoCAD 2000 you seldom set **tilemode** directly. Instead, you click one of the tabs that are located below the AutoCAD graphics window. Tabs having names such as Layout1 open paper space, while the tab labeled Model opens model space. You also can open model space from paper space with the MODEL command. This command, which can only be invoked from the command line, simply sets **tilemode** to 0.

As described shortly, you can have multiple paper space layouts so that you can make multiple 2D drawings of one 3D model. For example, one layout could be for a multiview orthographic drawing and another layout could be for an isometric drawing.

You can freely switch between the paper space and model space modes. Thus, you can return to model space if you discover your 3D model needs more work. When you are finished, you can switch back to paper space, with your paper space objects and environment as it was when you were last there, and the changes you made to your model are shown in the floating viewports. You even can change view directions and zoom levels in space without affecting the view directions and zoom levels in the other paper space floating viewports. If you change the size

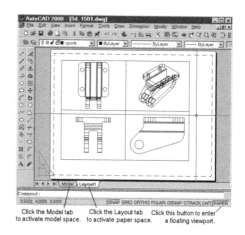

Click the Model tab       Click the Layout tab     Click this button to enter
to activate model space.  to activate paper space.     a floating viewport.

or location of your model in model space, however, it might affect the contents of the paper space floating viewports.

You also can go into model space through the paper space floating viewports, as described later in this chapter. Changes in view direction and zoom levels affect the appearance and contents of floating viewports when you enter model space through floating viewports.

The UCS icon has a different form in paper space — it is shaped like a 30- to 60-degree drafting triangle. The icon has a small x on the short side of the triangle to indicate the direction of the X axis. Other than its different form, however, the icon behaves the same as the model space UCS icon. The UCS command also works the same in paper space as it does in model space, although you are not likely to ever move the UCS X-Y plane away from the WCS X-Y plane or tilt it so that it is not parallel with the WCS X-Y plane. The color and size of the paper space UCS icon, is controlled by the UCSICON command.

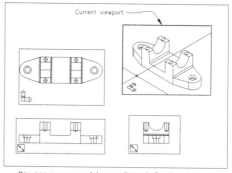

You can access model space through floating viewports.

The UCS icon is displayed only in the main paper space viewport, which is always viewport 1 (the value in the system variable **cvport**). Individual floating viewports do not contain a UCS icon. An exception occurs when you enter model space through a floating viewport. Then, each floating viewport will have the model space version of the UCS icon, and the paper space UCS icon will not be displayed.

Paper space is intended to be strictly a 2D world. Although you can draw 3D objects in paper space, you cannot easily work with them because only views that look straight down on the WCS

X-Y plane are allowed. You cannot use the VPOINT, 3DORBIT, or DVIEW commands in paper space. Again, exceptions occur when you enter model space through a floating viewport.

Paper space and model space share the same layers, text styles, and dimension styles. Nevertheless, they are two distinct spaces, and from paper space AutoCAD only partially recognizes the model space objects that are within floating viewports. Although object snaps on model space objects work from paper space, you cannot erase, move, stretch, or copy model space objects from paper space. There is also no straightforward way to transfer objects from one space to another, but it can be done.

One way to change the space of objects is to use the AutoLISP program ps2ms.lsp on the CD-ROM that comes with this book. This program moves one object at a time from paper space to model space, or from model space to paper space. Thus, if you inadvertently write some text within model space when it should be in paper space, you can load ps2ms.lsp, enter PS2MS on the command line, and pick a point on the text. It will be moved to paper space at the same coordinates it had in model space. This program works by changing the object's database group code 67. An object's 67 group code is 0 when it is in model space and 1 when it is in paper space.

Another way to move objects from one space to another is to use the Window's Clipboard. Press the Ctrl+X keys, and then select the object, or objects, to be moved. This removes the objects from the file and places them in the Clipboard. Switch to the other space, and press the Ctrl+V keys to retrieve the objects from the Clipboard and paste them in a location you specify. Also, you can use the Ctrl+C keys to copy, rather than cut, objects to the clipboard.

## Layouts

Relationships between paper space and plotting are maintained through specific, named combinations of plotting and paper space parameters that are called *layouts*. At a minimum, a layout designates the printing device and its settings, including the paper size and orientation. Typically, however, a layout also includes floating viewport configurations and a title block. You can have several layouts in a drawing file, which enables you to have layouts for different paper sizes, view arrangements, and even printers. By default, AutoCAD drawing files start with two identical paper space layouts that have one floating viewport and page settings based on the default printer.

The names of layouts appear on tabs on the lower edge of AutoCAD's graphics window. The names of the default paper space layouts are Layout1 and Layout2. To activate any layout, click its tab. The Model tab also that activates model space. With the exception of the model layout, you can change layout names, delete layouts, change the order of layout tabs, copy layouts, and import and export layouts.

## Creating and Managing Layouts

The basic command for establishing and working with paper space layouts is LAYOUT. It displays the following options on the command line:

`Copy/Delete/New/Template/Rename/SAveas/Set/?`

The question mark option displays a list of all existing layouts, and Set activates a specified layout. You must enter the layout name on the command line. The SAveas option exports a layout as a drawing template (DWT) file so that it can be used in other drawings, while the Template option imports an existing template or drawing (DWG) file. Only layout geometry and page settings are exported or imported. Importing a template is especially useful for adding borders and a title block to a layout. When you import a template or drawing file, AutoCAD automatically creates a new layout, rather than inserting the geometry in the current layout. AutoCAD has a collection of pre-made templates in both inch and metric formats in the Template folder. The New option creates a basic layout that uses the default printer and, by default, has one floating viewport. You use this option when you want to start from scratch in creating a new layout.

Most of the LAYOUT command's options are also available from the shortcut menu displayed when you right-click a layout tab, and you will probably use the shortcut menu more often than the LAYOUT command. Normally, the layout tabs are arranged from left to right in the order that they were created, but you can rearrange them with the Move option of the shortcut menu. You can select several layouts at once by holding the Shift key down as you pick their tabs. Then you can use the shortcut menu to move or delete the selected layouts. The shortcut menu also has an option that will select all the layouts except Model.

## Setting Page Parameters

After a layout has been created, you use the PAGESETUP command to establish page and printing parameters for it. By default, this command is automatically invoked when you activate a new layout. It displays a dialog box titled Page Setup that is similar to the one used by the PLOT command. You are probably familiar with this dialog box from your work in 2D, so just the options that are particularly applicable to paper space layouts are described here.

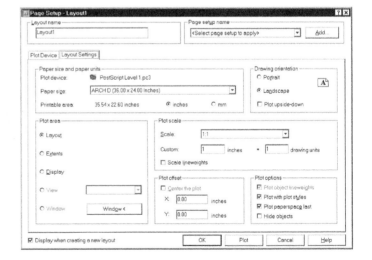

The options in the "Paper Size and Paper Units" section are based on the plotting device you selected from the Plot Device tab of the dialog box. The paper size of the layout is controlled by your selection of a paper size from the Paper Size drop-down list.

Only those paper sizes that can be handled by the selected plotting device are available. Because virtually all plotting devices reserve a paper margin for handling the paper, the printable area is always less than the paper size. The inches and mm buttons toggle the paper size dimensions between inches and millimeters.

In the Plot Area section, you will usually select Layout as the area to plot. The Plot Scale options pertain to paper space, rather than model space objects. Drawing scale is controlled within floating viewports, using methods described later in this chapter. Therefore, except in special situations (such as when plotting a C-sized drawing on A-sized paper), you will always use a plot scale of 1-to-1.

The Page Setup Name list box in the upper-right corner of the dialog box is for exporting and importing the page settings of a layout. To export the current settings, click the Add button and enter a name for the setup in the drop-down edit box. The page setup is saved when you choose the OK button of the dialog box. To import a saved page setup into the current drawing, invoke PSETUPIN from the command line. (No toolbar buttons or menu options are available for this command.) The Select File dialog box is displayed for you to locate and specify the drawing file that contains the page setup you want. Then, the Import User Defined Page Setup(s) dialog box is displayed that lists the name of all saved page setups in the selected drawing file. Select the one you want, and click OK. When you start the PAGESETUP command, the specified page setup will be listed in the Page Setup Name list box. If you select it, all the layout parameters assume the values of the imported page setup.

## Using the Layout Wizard

An easy way to create and set up a paper space layout is with the LAYOUTWIZARD command. This starts the Layout Wizard, which leads you through a series of dialog box–based steps to establish layout parameters. These steps are

- Assign a name to the layout.

- Select a printer from a list of those currently configured for your computer.

- Choose the paper size from a list of sizes available for the selected printer, and specify whether the units used in constructing the model represent inches or millimeters.

- Specify whether the orientation of the paper is to be portrait or landscape.

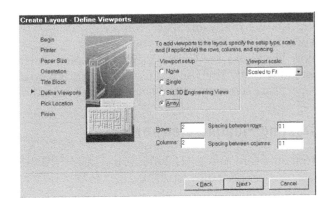

- Select a drawing border and title block for the layout. You are offered 25 choices in both metric and inch formats, and they can be inserted as a block or as an Xref. You also can choose to not have a border or title block inserted.

- Define the floating viewports that the layout is to have. You are given the options of having no viewports, a single viewport, a rectangular array of viewports, or a 3D engineering set of viewports. If you select Array, you are prompted to specify the number of rows and columns for the array, and for the gap between the viewports. The 3D engineering set of viewports consists of four viewports, arranged in two rows and two columns, showing top, front, side, and isometric views of the model. You also can specify a scale to be used for displaying the model within the viewports. Scaled to Fit is the default scale.

- Specify the location of the floating viewport, or viewports. The wizard dialog box is temporally dismissed to give you full access to the AutoCAD graphics area. The paper extents and margins, as well as the drawing border and title block are displayed, and you are prompted to specify the opposite corners of a rectangle that the viewports are to fit in.

## Controlling the Display of Layout Elements

By default, AutoCAD displays a sheet of paper, as well as its margins, on a gray background for each layout. Also, one floating viewport is automatically created and the Plot Setup dialog box is displayed for every new layout. You can change these defaults, however, through the Display tab of the Options dialog box that is opened when the OPTIONS command is invoked. Choose the check boxes in the Layout Elements cluster to specify the elements you want. When you are working with 3D models, you will

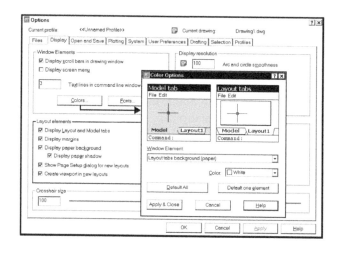

most likely turn the Create Viewport in New Layout option off, and leave the others in their default settings. You also can use this dialog box to change the color used for the paper, or for the paper space screen if paper display has been turned off.

## Creating Floating Viewports

Beginning with AutoCAD 2000, you can use either the MVIEW or VPORTS command to make viewports. MVIEW always uses command line prompts and input, while VPORTS generally uses a dialog box. However, if you start VPORTS in paper space from the command

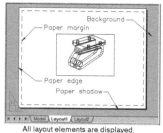

All layout elements are displayed.

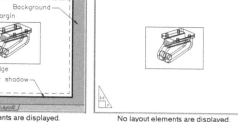

No layout elements are displayed.

line and precede its name with a hyphen, command line prompts and options identical to those of MVIEW are displayed. In addition to making rectangular viewports, these commands can make viewports in any shape that can be drawn as a polyline, circle, spline, ellipse, or region. Furthermore, viewports based on regions can even have internal islands. In making drawings of 3D models, however, you will seldom need viewports in any shape other than rectangular.

Making rectangular floating viewports is a straightforward process. You can pick a point and drag the rubber-band rectangle anchored at that point to set the viewport's opposite diagonal corner. Your model, as it appeared in the last current model space tiled viewport, is displayed in the new floating viewport. The initial size and location of the floating viewport is not especially important, because you can stretch and scale the viewport to change its size and you can move it to another position. These operations do not change the floating viewport contents. If you change the size of a viewport, the relative size of the model within it stays the same; if you move a viewport, its contents move with it.

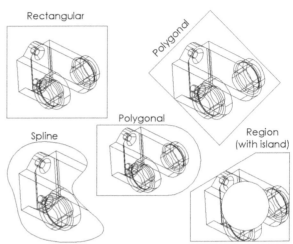

Floating viewports can have a variety of shapes

You also can copy floating viewports, with the contents of the original viewport remaining within the copies. If you want to get rid of a viewport, you erase it. You cannot rotate rectangular floating viewports so that their edges are oblique to the WCS X and Y axes. You can, however, freely rotate nonrectangular viewports. Only their borders rotate; not their contents. You also can mirror viewports, and you even can make polar array copies of floating viewports. The contents of the viewports are not, however, affected by either operation.

By default, AutoCAD scales the image of the model as necessary to fit within a new viewport. You can, however, set a specific scale in viewports as they are created by assigning a positive value to the **psvpscale** system variable. For instance: If you intend all the viewports of a layout to have a scale relative to a paper space of one-half, you can set **psvpscale** to 0.5. After you have the scale of a viewport set, you can maintain that scale with the Lock option of the MVIEW and VPORTS commands. The ZOOM command is disabled in viewports that are locked, which prevents you from inadvertently changing the scale of the viewport. The PAN, DVIEW, and VPOINT commands are also disabled in locked viewports. 3DORBIT, however, is not disabled.

Floating viewports are special AutoCAD entities that reside in layers just as other entities do. Their borders take the color of their layer, but they are always drawn in a continuous linetype, even if a noncontinuous linetype has been assigned to their layer. Grips are located at their vertexes, and object snaps work on viewport vertexes, the midpoints of straight edges, and the center point of arc and circular edges. If you freeze or turn off the layer that a viewport resides in, the borders of the viewport disappear, but its contents remaining visible. Because you will often do this to get rid of floating viewport borders, it is a good practice to place viewports in their own unique layer.

Although there is no limit to the maximum number of floating viewports you can create, there is a maximum number that can be active. If more than the allowed number of active viewports are created, no objects will be displayed in the extra viewports. You should not confuse the terms *active viewport* and *current viewport*. An active viewport is visible and contains an image, while the current viewport contains the crosshair screen cursor. Many active viewports can exist simultaneously, but only one can be the current viewport.

The maximum number of active viewports is determined by the value in the **maxactvp** system variable, and in turn, the maximum value you can assign to **maxactvp** depends upon your computer system. However, even modest computer systems support up to 48 active viewports, so you are not likely to ever be concerned about exceeding the maximum allowed number of floating viewports. Furthermore, the contents of inactive floating viewports are plotted even though you cannot see their contents, and the MVIEW and VPORTS commands allow you to switch active viewports by turning some off and others on.

The MVIEW and VPORTS commands also allows you to specify which floating viewports are to have hidden lines removed during plotting. In fact, this is the only way to have hidden lines removed during plotting — the Hide Lines option of the PLOT command has no effect on objects within paper space floating viewports. The characteristics of hidden-line views in plots are similar to those of the HIDE command, rather than to those of SHADEMODE's hidden-line option.

### Exercise One

You will begin a paper space drawing of the surface model of the automobile oil pan you last worked on in Chapter 8. Open your file of the model, or else retrieve file f0840.dwg from the CD-ROM that comes with this book and open it. The model is shown in Figure 1-1, as it is seen in model space with hidden lines removed from a viewpoint that looks upward toward the bottom of the oil plan.

As is often the case with surface models, this model has no thickness. But, because the drawing of the model is intended for making a die to be used for manufacturing the oil plan, rather than the oil pan itself, a single surface is what you want. There is no need to simulate the material thickness. Your 2D paper space drawing of the oil pan die will have three views: one each for showing its top, front, and right sides. In this exercise, you will create three floating viewports for those views.

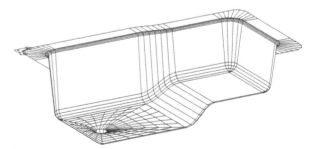

Figure 1-1

Initiate the OPTIONS command to open the Options dialog box and select the Display tab. Clear the Create Viewport in New Layouts check box, and click the OK button to exit the dialog box.

Now, activate paper space by selecting the Layout1 tab that is located below the graphics area. The Page Setup - Layout1 dialog box should automatically appear. (If it doesn't, enter PAGESETUP on the command line.) In this dialog box, select the Plot Device tab, and from the drop-down list box of plotters that are configured for your computer, select one that can handle ANSI D-sized paper (34x22-inches). Return to the Layout Settings tab of the dialog box. Select an ANSI-D size paper from the Paper Size list box, verify that the plot area is set to Layout and that the plot Scale is 1:1, and then click OK. AutoCAD displays a 34x22-inch sheet of paper over a gray background and indicates the printer margins with dashed lines.

Switch to the layer named Vports, and make three floating viewports. Two of the viewports are to be 12x6 inches and one is to be 6x6 inches, and they are to be located approximately as shown in Figure 1-2. You can do this with the either the MVIEW or VPORTS command, using any of three different approaches:

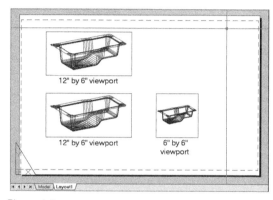

Figure 1-2

1. You can simultaneously make the two large viewports with the 2 option of MVIEW or VPORTS to make two horizontal viewports that fit in a square that is approximately 12x12 inches, and move the two viewports apart. Then make the third, smaller, viewport.

2. You can make just one 12x6-inch viewport, and copy it for the second viewport. Then, make the third viewport.

3. You can invoke MVIEW or VPORTS three times, drawing a single viewport each time.

Do not be concerned if your viewports are of a different size, shape, or location because it is virtually a given that viewports will need to be moved and resized after the viewpoints and model scales have been fixed. Their initial size, location, and contents are not critical.

That completes this exercise. Save your drawing file because you will set the view direction in each viewport, adjust the scale of the model, and align the views in Exercise 2 of this chapter.

| Command: | MVIEW |
|---|---|
| Purpose: | MVIEW creates the floating viewports of paper space. It also can turn floating viewports on and off, remove hidden lines in selected viewports during plotting, and lock the zoom level within selected viewports. |
| Initiate with: | • On the command line, enter MVIEW. |

Options:      On the command line, MVIEW displays the following menu for selecting an option:

```
Specify corner of viewport or [ON/OFF/Fit/Hideplot/Lock/Object/Polygon/Restore/2/3/4]/
    <Fit>: (Enter an option, specify a point, or press Enter.)
```

- Corner of viewport    When you specify a point, AutoCAD uses it as one corner of a new floating viewport and issues a command line prompt for the opposite diagonal corner of the viewport. A rubberband rectangle anchored at the first point will help you judge the size and location of the viewport.

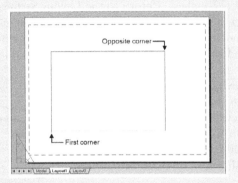

- ON    This option turns on previously turned off viewports. Their model space contents will again be visible. A follow-up prompt asks you to select the objects (the floating viewports) that are to be turned on.

- OFF    The OFF option turns off active viewports. Their model space contents will no longer be visible. AutoCAD issues a command line prompt for you to select the objects (the floating viewports) that are to be turned off.

- Fit    One floating viewport with its edges corresponding to the paper's print margins is created by this option. If paper display has been turned off, the viewport will fill the current graphics area. No additional input is called for. This is the default MVIEW option.

- Hideplot    This option controls the plotting of hidden lines in selected viewports. It does not control the display of hidden lines on the computer screen. The option uses the following command line prompts:

```
Hidden line removal for plotting [ON/OFF]: (Enter ON or OFF)
Select objects: (Select one or more floating viewports.)
```

Entering ON turns on hidden-line removal during plotting in the selected viewports — hidden lines are not plotted. Entering OFF turns off hidden-line removal during plotting — hidden lines are plotted.

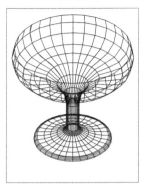
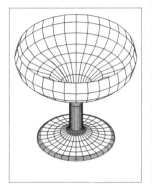

Hidden line removal OFF          Hidden line removal ON

- Lock

Locking the view of a viewport preserves its scale, or zoom level, relative to paper space. When the ZOOM command is invoked within a locked viewport, the cursor automatically returns to paper space so that the zoom occurs in paper space rather than model space. The following command line prompt is displayed for you to select the viewports that are to be locked, or unlocked:

```
Viewport View Locking [ON/OFF]: (Enter ON or OFF.)
Select objects: (Select one or more floating viewports.)
```

- Object

This option uses an existing closed wireframe object to define a new floating viewport. The object can be a spline, 3D or 2D polyline, circle, ellipse, or region. Even splines and polylines that cross over themselves are acceptable objects. You are prompted to select one object:

```
Select object to clip viewport: (Select a closed wireframe object.)
```

- Polygonal

You can create a viewport that has arcs and straight segments as in a 2D polyline with this option. command line prompts similar to those of the PLINE command are issued.

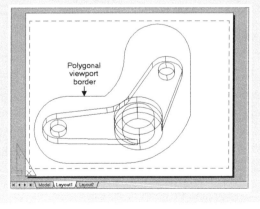

• Restore

When this option is selected, the number of viewports, their arrangement, and the view directions within them correspond to an existing configuration of tiled viewports. AutoCAD first displays a menu for you to use in specifying a particular viewport configuration:

```
Enter viewport configuration name or [?] <*Active>:
(Enter a ?, a viewport configuration name, or press Enter.)
```

The tiled viewport configuration that is currently in use in model space is used when the *ACTIVE option is selected. When a question mark is entered, AutoCAD displays a list of all tiled viewport configurations that have been saved through the VPORTS command. Entering the name of a saved viewport configuration bases the number, arrangement, and view directions of the floating viewports on that configuration.

Next, AutoCAD prompts for the rectangle that the floating viewports are to fit within:

```
Specify first corner or [Fit] <Fit>: (Press Enter, enter F, or specify a
    point.)
```

The Fit option fits the floating viewports within the margins of the paper, or within the edges of the graphics area if the paper is not displayed. If you specify a point, AutoCAD uses it as one corner of a rectangle and prompts for its opposite diagonal corner. Floating viewports corresponding to the tiled viewports are fit within this rectangle. If the rectangle used to define the boundaries of the floating viewports has different proportions than those of the tiled viewport configuration, AutoCAD adjusts the proportions of the individual floating viewports to fit the specified area.

The Restore option fits a tiled viewport configuration
into a specified paper space area.

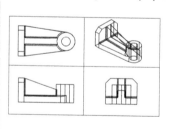 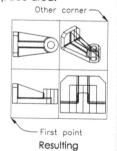

Tiled viewport configuration

Resulting
floating viewports

• 2

This option creates two floating viewports. It issues the following command line prompts for you to specify the orientation, size, and location of the two viewports:

```
Enter viewport arrangement [Horizontal/Vertical] <Vertical>: (Enter H or
    V, or press Enter.)
Specify first corner or [Fit] <Fit>: (Press Enter, enter F, or specify a
    point.)
```

If you specify a point, AutoCAD uses it for one corner of the two viewports and prompts for the opposite diagonal corner. Both viewports will fit within the specified rectangle. The Fit

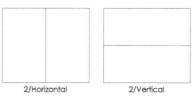

option fits the two viewports within the drawing margins, or within the extents of the graphics area if paper display has been turned off.

- 3    Three viewports within a specified area are created by this option. AutoCAD displays command line menus and prompts for you to specify the arrangement of the viewports and their size, orientation, and location:

```
Enter viewport arrangement
[Horizontal/Vertical/Above/Below/Left/Right] <Right>:
(Enter an option or press Enter.)
Specify first corner or [Fit] <Fit>: (Press Enter, enter F, or specify a
    point.)
```

The Fit option fits the three viewports within the paper margins, or within the current view if paper display is turned off. When you specify a point, AutoCAD uses it as one corner of a rectangle that the three viewports will fit in and prompts for the other corner of the rectangle.

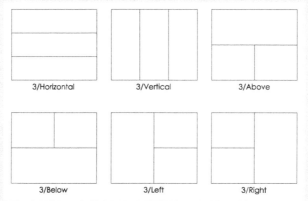

- 4    This option creates four equal-sized viewports, arranged in quadrants within a specified rectangular area. command line prompts ask you to specify the size and location of the rectangle that the viewports are to fit within.

```
Specify first corner or [Fit] <Fit>: (Press
    Enter, enter F, or specify a point.)
```

Choose the Fit option to have the four viewports fit within a rectangle corresponding to the current paper margins, or to the current extents of the graphics area if paper display is turned off. If you specify a point, it serves as one corner of the rectangle, and AutoCAD asks you to specify its opposite diagonal corner.

Notes:

- AutoCAD displays absolute coordinates on the status line when you are dragging the rubberband rectangle to establish the opposite diagonal corner of a viewport. This might make it difficult for you to judge the size of the viewport. You can, however, enter relative coordinates on the command line to establish the opposite corner of a viewport.

- The LIST command reports if hidden-line removal during plotting has been turned on for a particular viewport, and if view scale locking is in effect.

- If **psvpscale** is set to 0, AutoCAD does a zoom-all on the view within floating viewports when they are created. Otherwise, the zoom level (or scale) of the viewport is equal to the value in **psvpscale**.

- All the options for creating multiple viewports place the viewports so that their sides exactly touch. There are no gaps between the viewports, but you can easily move them apart after they have been created.

- The VPORTS command also can be used to create floating viewports. The command line version of VPORTS, which is invoked by preceeding the command's name with a dash, has prompts and options identical to those of MVIEW. The dialog box version of VPORTS graphically offers the MVIEW options of single, 2, 3, and 4.

- The Lock option disables the ZOOM and PAN commands, but you can still use the 3DORBIT command, as well as its zoom and pan options, in a locked viewport.

Related system variables:

- **cvport**       The number of the current viewport is stored in this system variable. The main paper space viewport is always viewport 1.

- **maxactvp**   This system variable controls the maximum allowed number of active viewports. Because the main paper space viewport is considered to be a viewport, the number of floating viewports is 1 less than the value in **maxactvp**.

- **psvpscale**   When this system variable is set to its default value of 0, AutoCAD performs a zoom-all in new viewports. If you assign a positive value to **psvpscale**, that value is used as a zoom scale factor relative to paper space in new viewports.

- **tilemode**    When **tilemode** is set to 1, only tiled viewports can be created. When **tilemode** is set to 0, only floating viewports can be created.

| | |
|---|---|
| Command: | VPORTS |
| Purpose: | VPORTS creates both model space tiled viewports and paper space floating viewports. |
| Initiate with: | • On the command line, enter VPORTS |

- From the View pull-down menu, select Viewports, and then an option of your choice.
- Select an option from the Viewports toolbar.

Options:

When this command is started by entering -VPORTS on the command line, the same options offered by MVIEW are displayed in a command line prompt. Otherwise, VPORTS displays the New Viewports tab of the Viewports dialog box. The available viewport arrangements displayed in the Standard Viewports list box are the same as those for MVIEW and the command

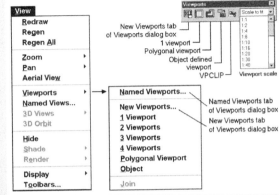

line version of VPORTS. When you select one, its viewport arrangement and the viewpoint within each viewport is displayed in the Preview window. If you select 3D from the Setup list box, you can set the viewpoint in each viewport to one of the six orthographic views or to one of the four isometric views that look down on the X-Y plane. These viewpoints are preset in each viewport by AutoCAD, but you can change the viewpoint in any viewport with the Change View To list box. You also can specify a gap between the viewports by entering or selecting a number in the Viewport Spacing edit box.

When you select the OK button in the Viewports dialog box, AutoCAD issues a command line prompt for you to draw a rectangle that the viewports are to fit in, or to specify that the viewports are to fit within the paper margins or within the view border if paper display is disabled.

You also can access the Named Viewports tab of the Viewports dialog box. This tab lists any named and saved tiled viewport

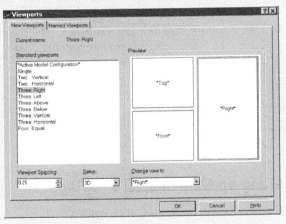

configurations available for defining floating viewports. You cannot, however, name and save floating viewport configurations.

| | |
|---|---|
| Command: | VPCLIP |
| Purpose: | VPCLIP changes the shape and size of an existing floating viewport. The new boundary can be defined by an existing wireframe object or by a user-drawn polyline-type window. |
| Initiate with: | • On the command line, enter VPCLIP. |
| | • Select Clip Existing Viewport from the Viewports toolbar. |
| Options: | From the command line, VPCLIP first asks you to select a viewport. Then, it issues the prompt: |

```
Select clipping object or [Polygonal/Delete] <Polygonal>: (Select an object, press
    Enter, or enter an option.)
```

- Object   An existing object is used to define the new viewport boundary. Valid objects are closed polylines and splines, circles, ellipses, and regions. You are prompted to select one object.

- Polygonal   When you select this option, you draw a polyline-type object to serve as the new viewport boundary. Prompts similar to those for 2D polylines are displayed on the command lines as you draw the line and arc segments of the boundary.

Before VPCLIP     After VPCLIP

Viewport edge     Object for clip boundry     Viewport edge

- Delete   This option is only displayed if the viewport has already been clipped. It restores the original viewport boundary.

Notes:   • You also can start VPCLIP by selecting a floating viewport boundary, pressing the return button of your pointing device, and selecting Viewport Clip from the shortcut menu.

• Despite the name of this command, the view within the viewport, depending upon the size and shape of the new boundary, is not necessarily clipped.

• The scale of the model within the viewport does not change when its boundary is changed.

• The LIST command reports that clipping is on for viewports that have been clipped.

# Setting Up Multiview 2D Drawings

When you are making a 2D multiview drawing of a 3D model, you will need to

- Make one floating viewport for each view

- Set a view direction within each viewport that corresponds to the desired orthographic view

- Set the scale of the model in each viewport

- Align the views with each other.

AutoCAD has some special commands, which are described in the next chapter, for completing these steps when you are working with solid models. These commands work well and make the process of transforming 3D solid models into 2D drawings almost automatic, except for dimensions.

When you are working with wireframe and surface models, however, you have to manually make the floating viewports, set the viewpoints within them, set their scale, and align the views. These last three steps are done through the familiar AutoCAD commands of PLAN, DVIEW, VPOINT, ZOOM, and MOVE. AutoCAD, though, does have some shortcuts. Its **psvpscale** system variable allows you to set the scale of viewports as they are created, and you can set their view directions as they are created through the New Viewports dialog box of VPORTS.

To set view directions and scale within floating viewports, you use the MSPACE command or double-click within a viewport to access model space through a floating viewport. After you are within a viewport, you can switch to another one by moving the cursor to the new viewport and pressing the pick button on your pointing device, just as you do with tiled viewports. You also can change viewports by pressing Ctrl+R. When you are finished working in model space, either use the PSPACE command or double-click outside a floating viewport to return to paper space.

After a floating viewport has been created, you need to set a view direction within that viewport corresponding to the view that the viewport represents. If the viewport represents the top view, for instance, you use the VPOINT coordinates of 0,0,1 or else use the PLAN command. If the viewport represents the front view, you use the VPOINT coordinates of 0,-1,0. You use the coordinates 1,0,0 for a right-side view.

An auxiliary view of a surface that is not aligned with any of the principal planes requires a viewing direction that looks straight down on the surface. After you set the view direction, you can use the Twist option of the DVIEW command to rotate the image in the auxiliary viewport so that it matches the inclined plane.

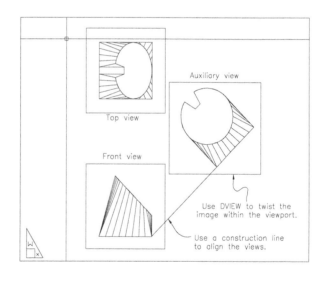

After you set the view direction in each floating viewport, you set each viewport's scale relative to paper space by using an XP scale factor with the ZOOM options of Scale, Center, and Left. (Beginning with AutoCAD 2000, the command line menu for ZOOM does not list the Left option, but it still accepts it.) A scale factor of 1XP zooms the view so that it is the same as paper space dimensions, while a scale factor of 0.5XP scales the view so that it is one-half paper space sizes, and 2.0XP scales the view to twice paper space sizes. Because you always treat paper space as a one-to-one space, the ZOOM

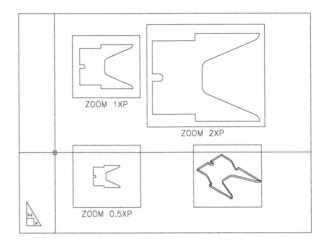

XP scale factor of a viewport is also the scale at which its image is printed. The LIST command shows a floating viewport's scale relative to paper space. After you set the scale of a viewport, you might want to use the Lock option of MVIEW and VPORTS to ensure that it is not inadvertently changed.

After you set the view direction and the scale of each viewport for your multiview drawing, you need to align the views so that corresponding points in the top and front view match vertically, corresponding points in the front and side views match horizontally, and so forth. One method for doing this involves moving viewports.

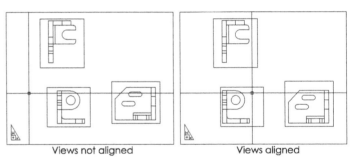

After selecting the viewport that will be moved, use an object snap on an object within the viewport as the base point and use a point filter, a snap to grid, an object snap on the corresponding point in another viewport, or typed-in coordinates as the destination point. Also, the MVSETUP command has an option for aligning orthographic viewports that works well. Aligning auxiliary views with orthographic views might require that you draw a temporary construction line or rotate the paper space UCS. When the views are aligned, the floating viewport borders are likely to not be aligned, but that is of no consequence because you will almost always hide the viewport borders before printing the drawing.

## Exercise Two

In Exercise 1 of this chapter, you created three floating viewports to serve as the basis of a 2D multiview drawing of an automobile oil pan. In this exercise, you will set the appropriate view direction within each viewport, set their scale, and align the views.

Open the file you saved at the conclusion of Exercise 1. Then, use the MSPACE command, its status line button equivalent, or double-click in a floating viewport to go into model space. In the top viewport, use VPOINT to set the view direction coordinates of 0,0,1 (or invoke the PLAN command). In the viewport below the top one, use VPOINT with the view direction coordinates of 0,-1,0. This is generally referred to as the front view, even though the name has more to do with the view direction than to the orientation of the model. In the small viewport to the right, use VPOINT with the view direction coordinates of 1,0,0. This will be the right-side view. Your paper space drawing should now look similar to the one in Figure 2-1.

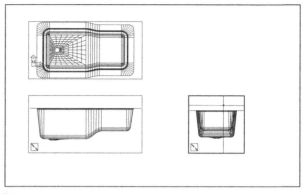

Figure 2-1

Now that the view directions have been established, you set the scale in each viewport. The drawing scale will be half-size, so you will set each viewport's zoom level to one-half of the paper space sizes. With MSPACE still in effect, go into each viewport, invoke ZOOM, and enter a zoom scale of 0.5XP. Use the Lock option of MVIEW or VPORTS to fix the scale of the three viewports.

That finishes your work in model space. Use the PSPACE command, its status line button equivalent, or double-click outside a floating viewport to return to paper space. Before you align the views with each other, you should

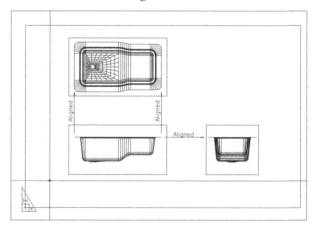

Figure 2-2

enlarge any floating viewport in which the model is partly hidden. You can do this with the STRETCH command or by pulling the grips on the viewport borders. Stretching a viewport does not affect the zoom level or view direction of the viewport's contents.

To align the views, turn on AutoCAD's grid snap mode and set a snap spacing of 0.5. Then, move the viewports one at a time, using an object snap on the model to set the base point (such as an endpoint near one end of the oil pan's flange), and use a grid snap point in paper space as the destination point. Figure 2-2 shows the layout with the views aligned.

Your last step in this exercise is to add a border and title block. If you have a D-size title block and border, use it in this exercise. Otherwise, start the INSERT command and click the Browse button. Find and open the folder named Template, and select the file named ANSI D title block.dwg. AutoCAD returns to the Insert dialog box. Specify 0,0,0 as the insert point for the block, 1.0 as its scale, and 0 as its rotation angle. Then, select the OK button to insert the title block. You might need to explode the block and then stretch or move some of its objects so that they will fit within the margins of your paper.

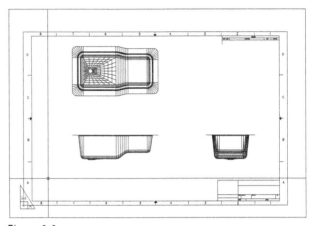

Figure 2-3

That finishes this exercise. When you freeze or turn off the layer that your floating viewports are in, your paper space drawing should look similar to the one shown in Figure 2-3. Save your drawing so that you can add dimensions to it in Exercise 3 of this chapter.

| Command: | MSPACE |
| --- | --- |
| Purpose: | MSPACE switches from the main paper space viewport to the last current floating viewport. |
| Initiate with: | • On the command line, enter MSPACE. |
| | • On the status bar, click the PAPER button. |
| Implementation: | This command enters model space from the main paper space viewport through a floating viewport. The paper space UCS icon disappears, the PAPER button on the status bar is replaced by the MODEL button, and model space UCS icons appears in all the active floating viewports (provided the UCS icon is turned on). The screen crosshair cursor is in the last current floating viewport. |
| Notes: | • Beginning with AutoCAD 2000, you also can enter a floating viewport by double-clicking inside its borders. |
| | • If you need a close look at your model, zoom in while you are in paper space and then use MSPACE. Model space zooms change the scale of the model relative to paper space and also can upset view alignments. Moreover, if the viewport is small, you might not get the model space magnification you want. |
| | • This command does not change the value of the **tilemode** system variable. |

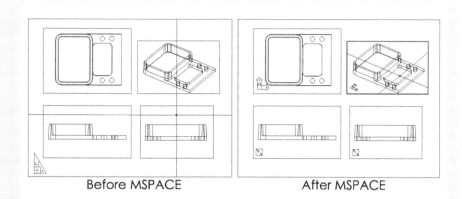

Before MSPACE                    After MSPACE

| Command: | PSPACE |
|---|---|
| Purpose: | PSPACE switches from the current floating viewport to the main paper space viewport. |
| Initiate with: | • On the command line, enter PSPACE. |
| | • On the status bar, click the MODEL button. |
| Implementation: | PSPACE returns to paper space from the current model space floating viewport. The model space UCS icons disappears from the floating viewports, the paper space UCS icon reappears, and the MODEL button on the status bar is replaced by the PAPER button. |
| Notes: | • Beginning with AutoCAD 2000, you also can return to paper space by double-clicking outside a floating viewport border. |
| | • The value of **tilemode** is not affected by this command. |

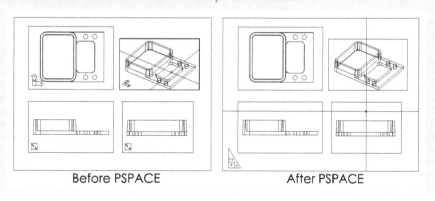

Before PSPACE                    After PSPACE

| | |
|---|---|
| Command: | MVSETUP |
| Purpose: | MVSETUP is a utility command for creating, scaling, and aligning space viewports, and for inserting premade drawing borders and title blocks. |
| Initiate with: | • On the command line, enter MVSETUP. |
| Options: | If **tilemode** is set to 0, MVSETUP displays the following command line options: |

`Align/Create/Scale viewports/Options/Title block/Undo:`

If **tilemode** is not set to 0, MVSETUP asks whether you want to enable paper space. A negative answer brings up a series of prompts for establishing the parameters of a drawing in model space — these parameters are not suitable for creating a drawing of a 3D model. If you give a positive answer, AutoCAD sets **tilemode** to 0 and displays the menu shown previously.

• Align    This option is for aligning the contents of one viewport with those of another. AutoCAD asks you to specify a base point in one viewport, and a point in another viewport corresponding to the base point. AutoCAD then pans the image in the second viewport until the two points are aligned. A menu is displayed offering options for aligning the viewports vertically, horizontally, or at a specified angle, plus an option for rotating the image in a viewport by a specified angle. If viewport scale locking is on, this option will not work properly.

• Create    Floating viewports are created through this option. Create also allows you to delete an existing viewport. Secondary menus are displayed for creating a single viewport, a rectangular array of viewports, or an arrangement of viewports called Standard Engineering in which four viewports are created. These four viewports show the top, front, and right side of the model, plus an SE isometric view of it. None of the other options for creating viewports set view directions.

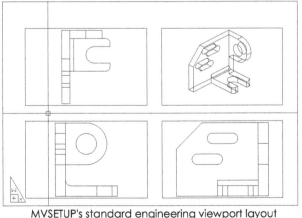

MVSETUP's standard engineering viewport layout

- Scale Viewports

  You can set the scale of the model as it appears in selected floating viewports with this option. It does this by asking you to specify a number for the paper space units and then a number for the model space units. The resulting scale is the paper space units divided by the model space units. If, for example, you specified 1.0 for the paper space units and 2.0 for the model space units, the resulting scale is one-half.

- Options

  Preferences for the title block and for paper space units are set through this option. You can specify a layer for the title block, whether the paper space limits are to be adjusted to match the title block size, and whether the title block is to be inserted as an externally referenced object. Paper space units can be feet, inches, meters, or millimeters.

- Title block

  This option inserts a border and title block at the paper space origin. Five premade borders and title blocks for ISO (metric) sizes are offered, as are six for ANSI (inch) sizes, and two for general inch sizes. You can add others to this list.

Notes:

- MVSETUP, which is based on an AutoLISP program named mvsetup.lsp, is intended to serve as a front end for the MVIEW and VPORTS commands. However, you will probably find that it is more convenient to use the MVIEW and VPORTS commands directly. With the exception of the Standard Engineering option for creating viewports, you must still use VPOINT to set view directions in each floating viewport. Its options for aligning viewports vertically and horizontally can be useful, however.

- When you select one of MVSETUP's 12 title blocks, it looks for a matching drawing and inserts it. If a drawing is not found, MVSETUP uses data in a file named mvsetup.dfs to draw the border and title block. For example: If you select an ISO A2 title block, MVSETUP looks for a file named iso_a2.dwg and inserts it. If it cannot find iso_a2.dwg, it uses data in mvsetup.dfs to draw the border and title block. It will be a set of individual entities rather than a block.

- The data in mvsetup.dfs draws the title blocks exactly according to the ANSI (American National Standards Institute.) 14.1 specification.

- AutoCAD includes title block drawings for German (DIN) and Japanese (JIS) standards, as well as for American (ANSI) and international (ISO) standards. You can directly insert any of these drawings as a block in paper space — you do not need to use MVSETUP. If you used the default directory names when you installed AutoCAD, these title blocks are in the Template folder. This folder also contains DWT files of the title blocks that can be inserted in a layout as a template.

# Controlling the Appearance of Objects in Viewports

## Object Visibility Control

Because the view direction in each floating viewport of a multiview paper space drawing is generally aimed toward the same location in 3D space, all the objects in that location are seen in all the

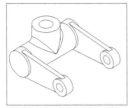

All objects are visible.

Only objects in layer Sol01 are visible.

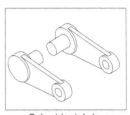

Only objects in layer Sol02 are visible.

viewports. Indeed, looking at the same 3D model from different viewpoints is one of the advantages of paper space viewports and drawings because any changes that are made in the model are instantly reflected in all the viewports. You don't have to go from view to view making changes manually as you do in pure 2D drawings.

Sometimes, however, it is desirable for an object to be visible in one viewport, but not in another. For instance, if you were working on a model that has separate but mating parts, you would likely find it useful to be able to look at the individual parts by themselves without moving them. AutoCAD allows you to do this through an object's layer — you can freeze selected layers within selected viewports. Therefore, you can have the different parts reside in different layers, and freeze certain layers in certain viewports.

The AutoCAD command that selectively freezes layers on a viewport-by-viewport basis is VPLAYER (*ViewPort LAYER*). Freezing layers with VPLAYER is subtly different from freez-

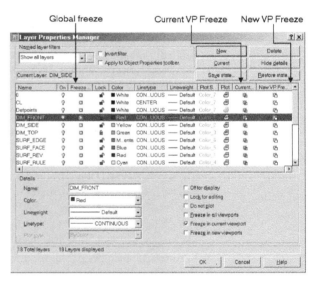

ing them globally with the LAYER command, and a layer must be both thawed and on globally before it can be frozen in specific viewports by VPLAYER. Moreover, VPLAYER only works with the floating viewports of paper space. The command is disabled in model space.

You also can use the Layer Properties Manager dialog box of the LAYER command, when it is accessed from paper space, to selectively freeze layers in floating viewports. Click the icon in the Current VP Freeze column  to selectively freeze a layer or thaw a previously frozen layer, and click the icon in the New VP Freeze column to have the layer frozen or thawed in floating viewports that are to be created. Check boxes corresponding to these two options are in the Details area of the dialog box. In AutoCAD 2000, but not in AutoCAD 2000i and 2002, this dialog box inappropriately refers to the current viewport as the active viewport, rather than as the current viewport.

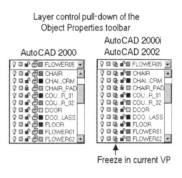

Layer control pull-down of the
Object Properties toolbar

AutoCAD 2000        AutoCAD 2000i
                    AutoCAD 2002

Freeze in current VP

Also, in AutoCAD 2000i and 2002, the layer control pulldown of the Object Properties toolbar has an icon for each layer for freezing and thawing the layer in the current viewport. This column of icons is not in AutoCAD 2000's layer control pull-down.

| Command: | VPLAYER |
|---|---|
| Purpose: | VPLAYER prevents objects from being displayed in specified viewports by freezing their layers in those viewports. They continue to appear in viewports in which their layer is not frozen. |
| Initiate with: | • On the command line, enter VPLAYER. You cannot invoke this command from model space. |
| Options: | The VPLAYER command displays the following menu on the command line: |

```
Enter an option [?/Freeze/Thaw/Reset/Newfrz/Vpvisdflt]: (Enter an option or press
    Enter.)
```

  This menu is redisplayed after each option is completed. Press Enter to end the command and trigger the changes.

- ?

    The question mark option reports the names of the layers that are frozen in a selected floating viewport. A follow-up prompt asks you to select one viewport.

- Freeze

    This option freezes specific layers in specific viewports. It displays the follow-up prompts:

```
Enter layer name(s) to freeze: (Enter a list of layer names.)
Enter an option [All/Select/Current] <Current>: (Enter an option
    or press Enter.)
```

    You can specify as many layers to be frozen as you like by separating their names with commas and by using the standard wildcard characters of ? and *.

The All option in the second prompt freezes the specified layer, or layers, in all viewports, including the main paper space viewport. If PSPACE is in effect, the Current option freezes the specified layer, or layers, in the main paper space viewport. If MSPACE is in effect, the Current option freezes the specified layer, or layers, in the current floating viewport (the one that has the screen cursor). The Select option brings up a prompt asking you to select specific viewports in which the specified layer, or layers, are to be frozen. If MSPACE is active, AutoCAD temporarily switches to PSPACE to enable you to select the viewports.

- Thaw

This option thaws one or more layers in specified viewports. Layers frozen globally through the LAYER command cannot be thawed by this option. Its follow-up prompts are

```
Enter layer name(s) to thaw: (Enter a list of layer names.)
Enter an option [All/Select/Current] <Current>: (Enter an option
    or press Enter.)
```

Your input for these prompts is the same as those for the Freeze option.

- Reset

Use this option to reset specified layers in specified viewports to the default frozen or thawed condition established by VPLAYER's Vpvisdflt option. It uses the follow-up prompts of:

```
Enter layer name(s) to reset: (Enter a list of layer names.)
Enter an option [All/Select/Current] <Current>: (Enter an option
    or press Enter.)
```

Your input for these prompts is the same as those for the Freeze option.

- Newfrz
  (New Freeze)

New layers can be created through this option. The layers, however, are automatically frozen in all viewports — those that currently exist and those that will be created in the future — with the exception of the main paper space viewport. Its follow-up prompt is

```
Enter name(s) of new layers frozen in all viewports: (Enter a list
    of layer names.)
```

You can enter several names by separating them with commas.

- Vpvisdflt
  (Viewport
  Visibility
  Default)

Whether specified layers are to be frozen or thawed by default in subsequently created viewports is controlled by this option. It uses the following command line prompts:

```
Enter layer name(s) to change viewport visibility: (Enter a list
    of layer names.)
Enter a viewport visibility option of [Frozen/Thawed] <Thawed>:
    (Enter F or T, or press Enter.)
```

You can name as many layers as you like by separating their names with a comma and by using the wildcard characters of ? and *. If you choose the Frozen option of the second prompt, the specified layers are automatically frozen in subsequently created viewports. The Thawed option of the second prompt causes the specified layers to be thawed in subsequently created viewports. It overrides the effects of the Newfrz option of VPLAYER.

## Linetype Scale

A potentially undesirable side effect of having viewports with different zoom levels, and hence different scales, is that noncontinuous linetypes — such as center, dashed, and hidden — have different appearances in different viewports. The lengths of their line segments are longer in some viewports than in others, including the main paper space viewport (unless the scale of a viewport is 1XP). This is illustrated on the left side of the following figure, in which the lengths of the center linetype segments are different in the half-scale views, the one-fourth scale view, and the main paper space viewport.

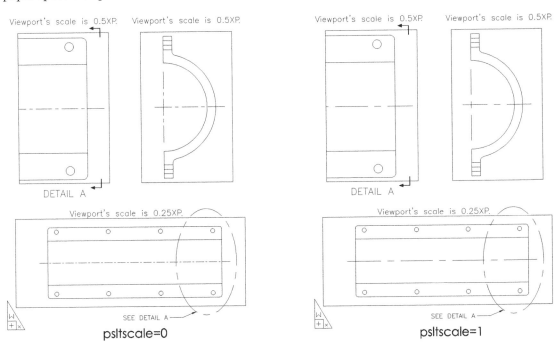

To prevent that from happening, you can set the value of the system variable **psltscale** (*Paper Space LineType SCALE*) to 1. Then, in each floating viewport, the current global linetype scale is multiplied by the viewport's scale relative to paper space. The line segment length of noncontinuous linetypes will be the same throughout the drawing, as shown on the right side of the figure. The initial setting of **psltscale** in AutoCAD's template drawings is 1.

# Dimensioning, Annotating, and Plotting Paper Space Drawings

## Dimensioning in AutoCAD 2000 and 2000i

AutoCAD 2000 and 2000i do not fully recognize model space objects from paper space when you are adding dimensions. For example, lines can be dimensioned only by picking their endpoints, and because arcs and circles are not recognized, radius and diameter dimensions cannot be added directly. Moreover, because the dimensions and the model are in different spaces, associative dimensions are not connected to the feature they represent. Therefore, you must go into model space through floating viewports to add dimensions in model space.

If all the dimensions are in the same layer, all of them appear in every viewport. They might be backward or even on edge, but they are visible. Consequently, when you add dimensions to a 3D model, you use as many layers for the dimensions as you have viewports, and the layer for dimensions in a specific viewport is frozen in all the other viewports. For example, in a drawing that has a top, front, and right-side view, you would use a layer having a name such as dim_top for the dimensions in the top view, and you would freeze that layer in the viewports for the front and right-side views.

The sizes of dimension features — arrowheads, text, and so forth — must be

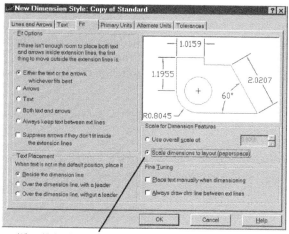

When this box is checked, dimscale is set to 0.

adjusted in viewports that do not have a 1:1 scale with paper space. Otherwise, they will have different sizes in different viewports, and they will be too large in some viewports and too small in others. Therefore, if you want dimension text to be printed at a height of 0.125 inches, the actual height of the text has to be 0.25 inches in viewports that are half-scale, and 0.0625 inches in viewports that have a 2:1 scale with paper space.

Although you can manually change the sizes of dimension features to adjust for a viewport's scale, a much better way is to use the **dimscale** system variable. AutoCAD multiplies the size of dimension features by the value in **dimscale**. Thus, if **dimscale** has an assigned value of 2.0, dimension text will be twice its specified height; if it has an assigned value of 0.5, dimension text will be one-half its specified height.

An even better way to manage the size of dimension features is to set **dimscale** to a value of 0. Then, AutoCAD automatically multiplies the size of dimension features by the scale factor of the current floating viewport. You can set **dimscale** to 0 directly or by selecting the Scale Dimensions to Layout (Paper Space) check box in the Fit tab of the DDIM command's dialog box.

The figure to the right shows an example of the effects of **dimscale**. The paper space drawing has three floating viewports (their borders are turned off). Two of the viewports show the model at one-half scale and the other viewport shows the model at one-fourth scale. Nevertheless, the size of the dimension features are the same in all three viewports.

If you were to turn on **tilemode** and look at this dimensioned model from an isometric-type viewpoint, you would see that there are two sizes of dimension features — one twice as large as the paper space size and the other half as large.

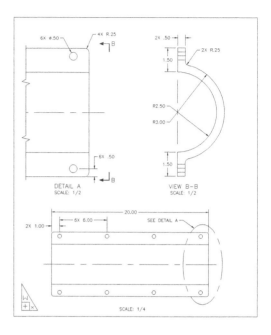

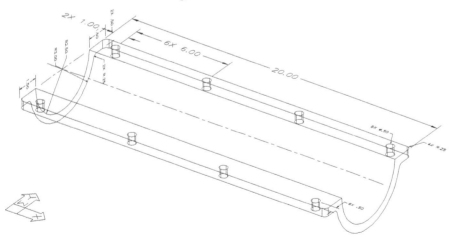

If you add dimensions from paper space rather than model space, leave the **dimscale** system variable set to 1.0, and instead adjust the value of the **dimlfac** system variable to fit the scale of the viewport used for the dimension. Although **dimlfac** has no effect on the size of dimension features, such as text height, it does multiply measured dimension lengths by the value it contains. For example, if **dimlfac** is set to 2.0, a line that is 2.50 inches long would be given a dimension length of 5.00 inches; if **dimlfac** was set to 0.5, that same line would be given a dimension length of 1.25

inches. Because model space objects in a floating viewport that has a scale relative to paper space that is not 1:1 are not their true size, you must use **dimlfac** to correct their dimension lengths.

AutoCAD sets a value of **dimlfac** for you that is appropriate for the viewport you are going to dimension, if you use AutoCAD's dimension mode. This must be done from the command line as follows:

```
Command: DIM (Enter)
Dim: dimlfac (Enter)
Enter new value for dimension variable or Viewport <1.0000>: V (Enter)
Select viewport to set scale: (Pick the edge of a floating viewport.)
DIMLFAC set to -4.0000
```

The actual value of **dimlfac** varies according to the scale of the viewport you selected, although it will always be a negative number to signify it is based on a floating viewport. You must then use object snaps on the model space objects to create dimensions for it. No good way exists for creating radius, diameter, and angular dimensions on model space objects from paper space.

## Dimensioning in AutoCAD 2002

AutoCAD 2002 is able to fully recognize model space objects from paper space when you are adding dimensions, which greatly simplifies dimensioning. You do not have to go into model space to add dimensions, you do not have to use a unique layer for the dimensions in each view, and you do not have to concern yourself with scale factors for arrowhead and text sizes. Furthermore, model space changes in the size of objects are recognized by their dimensions, and the dimensions automatically change to reflect the new sizes.

The association between dimensions and objects is controlled by AutoCAD 2002's **dimassoc** system variable. (This system variable replaces the **dimaso** system variable used in previous AutoCAD releases.) **Dimassoc** accepts a value of 0, 1, or 2, with the results shown in the following table.

| Dimassoc Value | Association Level |
|---|---|
| 0 | There is no association between dimensions and model objects, and AutoCAD's dimensioning commands do not recognize model space objects from paper space. Also, each dimension is a collection of individual objects — lines, arcs, text, and so forth. |
| 1 | There is no association between dimensions and model objects. However, the components of each dimension are interrelated and comprise a single AutoCAD object. If you stretch a dimension line, for example, the dimension value changes to reflect the new dimension line length. Although AutoCAD's dimensioning commands do recognize model space objects from paper space, they do not compensate for viewport zoom levels. Thus, the dimension values of objects in a viewport having a zoom level of 0.5xp are one-half the correct value. |
| 2 | Dimensions are associated with model objects. Therefore, if you modify the length of a line or the radius of an arc, the dimension components and the dimension value automatically change to match the modification. Also, AutoCAD's dimensioning commands fully recognize model space objects from paper space and they automatically compensate for differences in viewport zoom levels to assign correct values to dimensions. |

As with all system variables, you can set the value of **dimassoc** from the command line. You also can set **dimassoc** to a value of 2 with the OPTIONS command. Select the User Preferences tab from the Options dialog box, and then click the Make New Dimensions Associative check box.

Existing dimensions are not affected by changes to **dimassoc,** so it is possible to have both associated and nonassociated dimensions in a drawing. The LIST command reports whether a dimension is associated or not. You can make a dimension associative with the DIMREASSOCIATE command. This command prompts you to select the dimensions to be associated, and to then identify the dimensioned object of each dimension by either reselecting it or by specifying extension line origins. If a dimensioned object is erased and redrawn, you must use DIMREASSOCIATE to update its dimension. You can disassociate dimensions with the DIMDISASSOCIATE command.

After you set **dimassoc** to 2, you can proceed to dimension the orthographic views of a 3D model from paper space just as if it were a 2D drawing. If you move a viewport that has associative dimensions, the dimensions move as well, even if they are not included in the move selection set.

## Dimensions and 3D Objects

Even on 3D models, dimensioning is a 2D operation that occurs on the current UCS X-Y plane, whether it is in model space or paper space. Horizontal dimensions are parallel with the X axis and vertical dimensions are parallel to the Y axis. Therefore, objects that are askew of the X-Y plane are foreshortened, and their dimensioned length is not correct. This is illustrated in the following figure. The UCS X-Y plane is not parallel with the sides of the 1x1x1 cube on the left, and as a result, the horizontal dimension for it is incorrect. The UCS X-Y plane, however, is parallel with one side of the left-hand cube, so both its horizontal and vertical dimensions are correct. Notice, in both cases, how the dimensions have been projected onto the X-Y plane, regardless of the selected object's location.

Creating views and dimensions of 3D surface models presents a few unique problems. Their surface mesh lines tend to make the drawing cluttered and confusing, and no satisfactory method exists for removing them. In AutoCAD 2000 and 2000i, because you generally place dimensions in model space, surfaces also are likely to hide the extension lines of dimen-

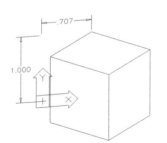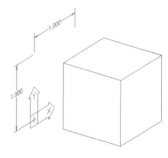

sions, so you must make certain that the UCS X-Y plane is in front of the model when you add dimensions. Furthermore, in all AutoCAD versions, hidden edges that you want shown in dashed linetypes are either completely hidden (when hidden-line removal is on) or completely visible (when hidden-line removal is off). There is no in-between. Even the selection of objects to be dimensioned can be uncertain in orthographic views, because objects are stacked on top of each other.

Furthermore, the spline curves that commonly occur on surface models cannot be dimensioned completely. This is not due to a shortcoming of AutoCAD — rather it is a characteristic of splines. Even planar splines have curves with continually changing radii, which means that radius dimensions do not apply, and the radius and diameter dimensions used for arcs and circles have no meaning in nonplanar splines. In earlier times, plaster or wood models were used as masters for objects having spline curves and surfaces. Both machining and inspection were based on the physical model. Now, organizations working with such objects often use a computer model as the master for manufacturing and inspection. Their 2D drawings, which merely show the object's general shape and size, are used to document part numbers, specify materials, and provide other necessary information for manufacturing.

You always locate a drawing's title block, borders, general notes, and other annotation in paper space using a 1:1 scale. Occasionally, you also need to draw some objects in paper space, perhaps to make an end line or a break line for a partial view or a broken view. When your drawing is dimensioned, viewports are in their correct locations, and (if needed) hidden-line removal during plotting has been specified in selected viewports, turn off or freeze the layer you have used for the floating viewports. This causes the viewport borders to disappear, while their contents remain visible.

## Plotting

Plots are made using a 1:1 scale. You do not need to specify in the Plot Settings tab of the Plot dialog box that hidden objects are to be removed (in fact, that parameter has no effect in paper space floating viewports). If you are using a pen plotter, you will probably want to eliminate the plotting of overlapping lines. To do this, select the Plotting tab from the Options dialog box, and click the Add or Configure Plotters button. From the list of currently configured plotters, select the plotter you are using. Select the Device and Document Settings tab and then select Pen Configuration from the outline-like list of parameters. In the Pen Optimization Level drop-down list box select Adds Elimination of Overlapping Diagonal Vectors."

### Exercise Three

In this exercise, you will finish the paper space drawing of a die for manufacturing an automobile oil pan.
In Exercise 2, you set up the orthographic views for the drawing and inserted a D-sized border and title block. In this exercise, you will add dimensions and general notes, and fill in the title block. If you are using AutoCAD 2002, your steps in dimensioning the drawing will be different than the steps in AutoCAD 2000 or 2000i.

## Dimensioning the Drawing in AutoCAD 2000 or 2000i

Open your drawing file of the oil pan. If the floating viewport borders are not visible, the layer they are in is either frozen or turned off. Because you need to work with the viewports, they must be thawed and turned on. Increase the size of the three viewports so that there is space in them for the dimensions you are going to add. You can do this without affecting the viewport's contents through the STRETCH command or through the viewport's grips.

This particular 3D surface model is well defined by its wireframe objects, and the surfaces only add clutter to the 2D drawing. Therefore, globally freeze all the layers that the surfaces are in.

Create three new layers that have names such as Dim-top, Dim-front, and Dim-side to be used for the dimensions. Use the Freeze option of VPLAYER to have only one of these new layers appear in each floating viewport. For example: Dim-top should be thawed only in the viewport showing the top view, and the layers Dim-front and Dim-side should be frozen in the top view.

Set the dimension style parameters to conform to your methods and work standards for making 2D drawings. The only parameter that will be different from those of a D-sized 2D drawing will be that **dimscale** is set to 0 (by either setting it directly, or by checking the Scale Dimension to Layout (Paperspace) check box in the Fit dialog box of the DDIM command).

Now, you are ready to add the dimensions. The general steps you will take are

1. Choose a particular view to work in, such as the top view, and zoom in until you can see the 3D objects clearly. Zooms and pans should be done only in paper space because zooms and pans within a model space viewport affect the view alignment and scale of the orthographic views. You might want to turn on scale locking in all the floating viewports to ensure that you do not inadvertently change their scale.

2. Use MSPACE, or one of its equivalents, to go into model space. Make the viewport you have chosen to work in be the current viewport.

3. Adjust the UCS so that its X-Y plane is perpendicular to the viewport's line of sight. The View option of the UCS command is a convenient way to do this.

4. Switch to the layer you intend to use for the dimensions in the chosen viewport. Then, dimension the view's objects as you would in any 2D drawing.

5. When you have finished dimensioning objects in that viewport, use PSPACE or any of its equivalents to return to paper space. Zoom back so that you can see your entire drawing.

6. Repeat steps 1 through 5 until the model is completely dimensioned.

## Dimensioning the Drawing in AutoCAD 2002

Open your drawing of the oil pan model. The model's surfaces tend to confuse, rather than clarify, the drawing, so you should globally freeze their layers. If the model is only partially shown in any viewport, thaw the layer the viewports are in, stretch the viewport borders as necessary to completely show the model, and turn off or freeze the layer of the viewports.

Set the dimension style parameters to conform to your methods and work standards for making D-sized 2D drawings. Also, assign a value of 2 to the **dimassoc** system variable. Create a layer, having a name such as Dim, for the dimensions. Activate that layer, and dimension the drawing views just as you would any 2D drawing.

**Finishing the Drawing**

When you have finished dimensioning the drawing (or even as you are adding dimensions) you will often need to reposition the viewports to increase or decrease the gap between them or to move them away from the drawing's borders. You can freely move the viewports, but you must take care that their alignment and zoom levels are preserved. When the dimensions and viewport positions are as you want them, freeze or turn off the layer that the viewports are in.

Add the drawing's general notes to the main paper space viewport and fill in the title block as you would with a pure 2D drawing. Because the drawing will be plotted using a 1:1 scale, the height of this text will be its true height.

A version of the finished 2D drawing is shown in Figure 3-1. Your choices for dimension arrangement and for annotation, however, might be different. Notice that the spline curves on the model have not been dimensioned. Also, the views have been cleaned up by selectively freezing some wireframe layers, and some lines and arcs have been added to the model to delineate the edges of fillets and rounds on the model. The AutoCAD 2000 and 2000i version of the model and drawing is in file f1542.dwg on the CD-ROM that accompanies this book, and the 2002 version is in file f1542a.dwg.

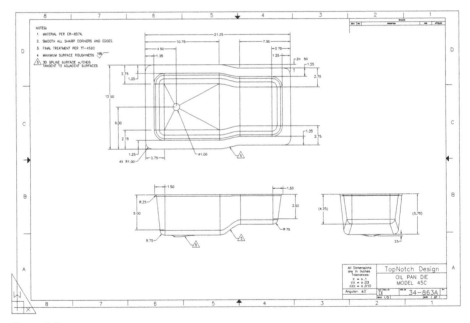

Figure 3-1

# CHAPTER 16

# 2D Drawings from 3D Solid Models

*AutoCAD has three special commands for making 2D drawings from solid models. With these commands, you can create both isometric-type drawings and multiview, orthographic, dimensioned drawings. They do not work with wireframe or surface models.*

*This chapter*

- *describes how to make 2D isometric-type drawings of 3D solid models with the SOLPROF command;*

- *explains how to use the SOLVIEW command to set up views for multiview orthographic 2D drawings based on a 3D solid model;*

- *tells you how to use SOLDRAW to create 2D objects that represent the solid model in the views set up by SOLVIEW;*

- *explains how to dimension and annotate multiview drawings of 3D solid models.*

## 2D Objects from 3D Solids

Although you can use the techniques described in Chapter 15 to make 2D drawings directly from 3D solid models, there are problems with this approach:

- Although you can set the system variable **dispsilh** to a value of 1 to eliminate facets on 3D solids and thereby obtain a clean, uncluttered look when HIDE is on, you cannot show hidden edges.

- When **dispsilh** is set to 1, visible tangential edges — the boundary along the tangent between two curved surfaces or between a curved surface and a plane — are always shown. Thus, all fillets will have lines where they blend with their adjacent surfaces. Sometimes, you will want these tangential lines to be shown, but not always.

- Section views can be made only indirectly.

- Two or more edges are almost always on top of one another in orthographic views, which can make the process of selecting objects to be dimensioned uncertain. Also, if you are using a pen plotter, you must change the plotting optimization parameters to prevent overlapping lines from being retraced.

A better way to make a 2D drawing from a 3D solid is to project the solid's edges and profile onto a plane where they are drawn as 2D objects. The problems of dimensioning 3D objects are eliminated, hidden edges can be shown as dashed lines, and section views are made conveniently.

This is the approach taken by three AutoCAD commands for making 2D drawings from 3D solid models — SOLPROF, SOLVIEW, and SOLDRAW. These commands are in an external program named acsolids.arx, which is automatically loaded whenever any of the three commands are called. They work only on 3D solid objects — not on wireframe or surface models.

SOLVIEW and SOLDRAW are for making multiview, orthographic 2D drawings from 3D solid models. These two commands must be used in tandem. SOLVIEW is used first to set up drawing views, and SOLDRAW is used to create 2D objects that are suitable for dimensioning in those views. The third command, SOLPROF, is for making general-purpose, isometric-type drawings from 3D solids.

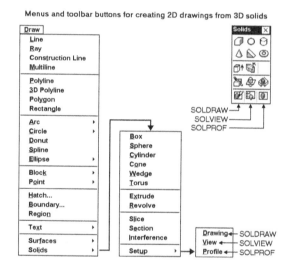

Menus and toolbar buttons for creating 2D drawings from 3D solids

## Making 2D Isometric-Type Drawings from 3D Solids

SOLPROF projects the edges and profiles of selected 3D solids onto a plane that is perpendicular to the viewing direction. Although it can be used to make any of the six principal orthographic views, SOLPROF is especially useful for making 2D isometric-type drawings that can be used for presentations, assembly drawings, and catalog illustrations. The results can be virtually identical to those drawn within AutoCAD's isometric snap mode. You don't, however, have to manipulate isoplanes or use ellipses for making arcs and circles as you draw objects. In fact, even if your objective is to make just an isometric 2D drawing, you might find it easier to make it as a 3D solid and convert it to 2D with SOLPROF.

SOLPROF is especially useful for making drawings that have *isometric projection views*. These are a special form of axonometric views in which the viewing plane is tilted to have equal angles (hence the name, isometric) with the three cardinal planes. Because all lines in the cardinal directions are inclined relative to the line of sight, they are not seen in their true length — they are foreshortened 81.65 percent. Also, horizontal angles are shown sloped 30 degrees.

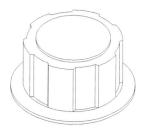

This isometric drawing of an instrument knob is easier to make as a 3D solid that is converted to 2D than as a 2D drawing from AutoCAD's isometric snap mode.

To make isometric projection views in AutoCAD, first choose the corner of the 3D model you want the view to look toward, and use the X, Y, Z coordinates of +/-1,+/-1,+/-1 with the VPOINT command. The signs of the coordinates depend upon which corner of the object you are focusing on. For instance, to set up a view looking at the front-right upper corner of a 3D model, use the VPOINT coordinates of 1,-1,1. This often-used viewpoint is listed as an SE Isometric in AutoCAD's View menu and View toolbar.

The foreshortened lines cause isometric projection drawings to be difficult to make with hand-drafting techniques, and consequently they were seldom used when most drawings were done on drafting boards. Isometric drawings were much more common. They have their viewing plane positioned exactly as those for isometric projection drawings, but their lengths in the cardinal directions are drawn full size. This makes them much easier to draw and scale, although it does make objects larger than their actual size. Isometric drawings are what you get with AutoCAD when the isometric snap mode is in use. To convert the isometric projection drawings you get from SOLPROF to true isometric drawings, scale them 1.2247 times.

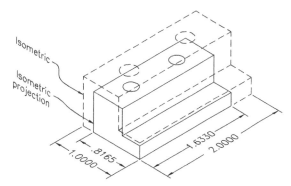

The length of lines in isometric projection views are 81.65 percent of the length of lines in true isometric views.

SOLPROF is easy to use and versatile. You set a viewpoint that shows the solid, or solids, as you want it to appear, invoke the command, and enter yes or no responses to three command line prompts for options. You must do this from the paper space side of AutoCAD through a floating viewport, even though the results are in model space.

The wireframe objects are placed in blocks and in unique layers for easy management and transfer to other programs. You have a choice of placing hidden lines in their own layer and block or having them included with the layer and blocks used for visible lines. Most of the time, you will choose to have hidden lines in their own block. Then, you can use a linetype that is different from that used for the visible lines, and you can freeze their layer or erase their block to eliminate them altogether. SOLPROF also can make 3D wireframe models from the edges of 3D solids. You are not likely to use this capability often, but it does provide you with one more conversion tool.

The blocks created by SOLPROF are anonymous blocks. Consequently, they have no name and cannot be inserted. If you want to use them in another drawing, however, you can make a named block from them with either the BLOCK or WBLOCK command. If the block is 2D, be certain to first set the UCS X-Y plane on the plane of the block. Because the block is on a plane that passes through the UCS origin and is perpendicular to the line of sight, you can do this with the View option of the UCS command, provided you have not changed the UCS or viewpoint after the block was created. If you have, you can use the 3point option of the UCS command, coupled with object snaps on the block.

SOLPROF also gives you the option of including tangential edges, which mark the transition between flat and curved surfaces and between two adjacent curved surfaces, on the profiles. Orthographic drawings seldom show tangential edges, but you will generally want them included when you are making isometric-type drawings.

### Exercise One

In this exercise, you will create a 2D isometric drawing from the 3D solid model of a pipe fitting, which shown in Figure 1-1, you created in Section Three. On the CD-ROM that accompanies this book, the completed model is in file f1310.dwg. Retrieve that file, open it, and immediately save it under another name of your choice. Later in this chapter, you will make a multiview drawing of the same model.

Set the layer named Vports as the current layer. You should also load AutoCAD's HIDDEN linetype so that SOLPROF uses it for the layer it makes for hidden objects.

Select the Layout1 tab to go into paper space. Start the PAGESETUP command if it doesn't automatically start, and select a paper size of about 11.0x8.5 inches. Set the plot area to Layout and the plot scale to 1:1. Exit the Page Layout dialog box. If a viewport is already in Layout1, stretch it until it is about 5x5 units in size, and change its layer to Vports. Otherwise, use VPORTS or MVIEW to make one floating viewport approximately centered in the graphics area that is roughly 5x5 units in size in the Vports layer.

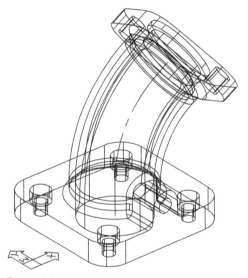

Figure 1-1

The 3D solid model appears in the floating viewport, looking as it did in model space. Use the MSPACE command, or its equivalent, to go into model space through the floating viewport. Then, set an SE isometric view of the model, and zoom and pan as needed for the model to completely fill the viewport, as shown in Figure 1-2. The zoom level of the viewport relative to paper space is not important.

While you are still within the floating viewport, use the following command line input to create a 2D isometric projection drawing of the model:

```
Command: SOLPROF (Enter)
Select objects: (Select the 3D solid.)
Display hidden profile lines on separate layer? [Yes/No] <Y>:
    (Enter)
Project profile lines onto a plane? [Yes/No] <Y>: (Enter)
Delete tangential edges? [Yes/No] <Y>: N (Enter)
```

Because AutoCAD must perform intensive calculations to project the 3D objects onto a plane, your computer might appear to be inactive for a few seconds. When the operation is complete, there is no discernable differences within the viewport, but when you look through the list of layers in the drawing, you will notice that AutoCAD created two new ones having names such as Ph-2d6 and Pv-2d6.

The characters to the right of the hyphen in these names represent the handle of the floating viewport,

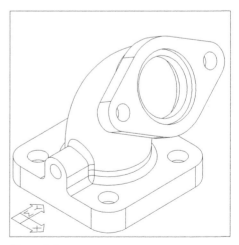

Figure 1-2

and those in your drawing might be different. That is not important. What is important is that the hidden objects in the model are in the layer that has a name beginning with Ph and that the visible objects are in the layer whose name begins with Pv. Assign the HIDDEN linetype to the layer for hidden objects, if AutoCAD has not done so. When you freeze the layer that the solid model is in — Sol01 — the image in your floating viewport should be similar to the one in Figure 1-3.

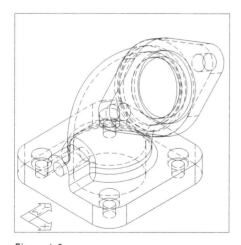

Figure 1-3

Figure 1-4

Because the numerous hidden lines tend to clutter and confuse the drawing rather than clarify it, you might want to freeze their layer also. Then, the drawing will look similar to the one in Figure 1-4.

On your computer screen, you are now viewing a 2D isometric projection drawing on a plane that is perpendicular to the line of sight and that passes through the UCS origin. If you want to export it to another drawing, use the View option of the UCS command so that the drawing is on the UCS X-Y plane, and use the WBLOCK command to save it in a new file. If you want the drawing to be a true isometric drawing, increase its size 1.277 times with AutoCAD's SCALE command.

On the CD-ROM that accompanies this book, the 3D model and the 2D isometric drawing of it — both within a floating viewport — are in the file f1607.dwg.

| | |
|---|---|
| Command: | SOLPROF |
| Purpose: | SOLPROF creates blocks made of wireframe objects that are derived from the profile and edges of one or more 3D solids. |
| Initiate with: | • On the command line, enter SOLPROF. |
| | • From the Draw pull-down menu, select Solids, then Setup, and finally Profile. |
| | • Select the Setup Profile button from the Solids toolbar. |
| Options: | SOLPROF must be initiated within a paper space floating viewport. The wireframe objects that are created are in anonymous blocks within model space, and they are in either one or two layers (depending upon the command options you select) that AutoCAD automatically creates if they do not exist. One of these layers is for visible edges and profiles, while the other is for hidden edges and profiles (provided you specify that visible and hidden edges and profiles are to be in separate layers). Also, AutoCAD's HIDDEN linetype is used for the layer for hidden objects, if that linetype is loaded. |

An example of SOLPROF

Two 3D solids
Hidden-line viewing mode

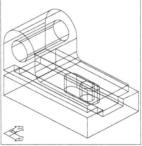

Two 3D solids
Wireframe viewing mode

Two 2D blocks created by SOLPROF
Visible edges are in one layer,
and hidden edges are in another.

The command first asks you to select the 3D solids that the wireframe objects are to be based on. You can select as many as you like, using any AutoCAD selection method, with objects that are not 3D solids — including regions and blocks of 3D solids — being filtered out. Then, three options in the form of command line prompts for yes or no responses are offered:

```
Display hidden profile lines on a separate layer? [Yes/No] <Y>: (Enter Y or N, or
    press Enter.)
Project profile lines onto a plane? [Yes/No] <Y>: (Enter Y or N, or press Enter.)
Delete tangential edges? [Yes/No] <Y>: (Enter Y or N, or press Enter.)
```

- Display hidden profile lines on a separate layer?

    When a positive response is given to this prompt, AutoCAD places the objects derived from hidden edges and profiles of the 3D solid, or solids, in a different layer than the one the visible edges and profiles are in. All of the visible edges and profiles are in one block, regardless of how many 3D solids were in the selection set, while the hidden edges and profiles (including those hidden by other solids in the selection set) are in a second block.

    If you give a negative response, objects made from visible and hidden edges and profiles of the 3D solid, or solids, are placed in the same layer used for visible objects. One block is created for each 3D solid in the selection set. All edges, even those that are hidden, are included in the block, or blocks.

Results from the "Display hidden lines on a separate layer?" option

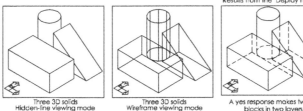

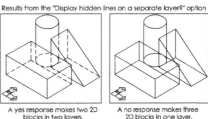

| Three 3D solids Hidden-line viewing mode | Three 3D solids Wireframe viewing mode | A yes response makes two 2D blocks in two layers. | A no response makes three 2D blocks in one layer. |

- Project profile lines onto a plane?

    If your answer to this prompt is yes, the 3D solid's edges are projected onto a plane that passes through the UCS origin and is perpendicular to the floating viewport's line of sight. The resulting block, or blocks, are 2D.

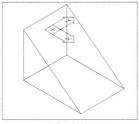

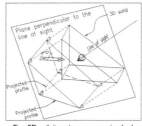

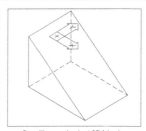

| 3D solid in wireframe viewing mode | The 3D solid's edges are projected onto a plane passing through the origin and perpendicular to the viewport's line of sight. | Resulting projected 2D blocks |

If your answer to the prompt is no, wireframe 3D blocks that are derived from the edges and profiles of the 3D solids in the selection set are made. Because the 3D blocks are based on the edges and profiles as they are seen, they might not be complete. For example, spherical solids produce a block that is simply a circle, and if a 3D solid wedge is seen from a plan view, only the edges of its slanted surface are included in the 3D block.

When a 3D wireframe block is created, only the edges visible in the current viewport are included in the block.

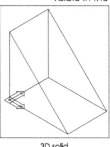
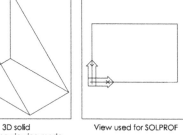
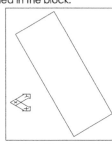

3D solid
Wireframe viewing mode
SE isometric view

View used for SOLPROF

Resulting 3D wireframe block
SE isometric view

- Delete tangential edges?

A tangential edge is the boundary between two curved surfaces, or between a curved surface and a planar surface. It represents the points of tangency between the two surfaces. If you give a positive answer to this prompt, tangential edges are not shown, while a negative answer causes the tangential edges to be included in the blocks made by SOLPROF.

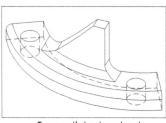
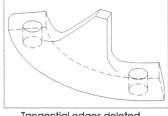

Tangential edges kept

Tangential edges deleted

Notes:

- Wireframe objects created from visible edges and profiles of the selected 3D solid, or solids, are placed in a layer named PV-handle. Objects created from hidden edges and profiles are also placed in that layer, unless you specify that hidden profile objects are to be placed in a separate layer. Then, they are placed in a layer named PH-handle. Handle in these layer names is the handle of the current floating viewport. For example, if the handle of the viewport used for SOLPROF is 8D7, the layer names are PV-8D7 and PH-8D7. If these layers do not exist, AutoCAD creates them.

- The handle of an object is a hexadecimal number that serves as a name for the object. All AutoCAD objects, including floating viewports, have a unique handle that is assigned by AutoCAD. No two objects have the same handle, and as long as an object exists, it retains the same handle. The LIST command displays an object's handle.

- The blocks created by SOLPROF are anonymous blocks. Their names are not displayed by the BLOCK, INSERT, or DDINSERT commands, and they cannot be inserted or written to a file.

# Making Multiview 2D Drawings from 3D Solids

## The Roles of SOLVIEW and SOLDRAW

Although you could use SOLPROF to make multiview 2D drawings from 3D solids, SOLVIEW and SOLDRAW are intended exclusively for that purpose and require much less work on your part. SOLVIEW sets up views of the solid model in paper space floating viewports, and SOLDRAW draws 2D objects that are suitable for dimensions in those viewports. These two commands also tie the 2D drawing closer to the 3D model than SOLPROF. After making a drawing with SOLVIEW and SOLDRAW, you can change the 3D model, rerun SOLDRAW, and the changes are reflected in the 2D drawing.

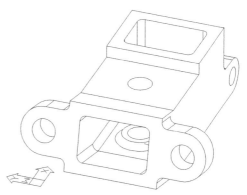

SOLPROF is best used for creating isometric-type 2D drawings.

Through SOLVIEW, you specify the basic scale of the drawing, its views, and the locations of those views. Typically, multiview 2D drawings have at least two principal views (such as a top, front, and perhaps a side view) that are orthogonal to one another, plus any auxiliary and section views needed to fully define the part. SOLVIEW does a good job of setting up these fundamental views.

In using SOLVIEW, you specify the drawing's views one at a time. SOLVIEW makes a paper space rectangular floating viewport for each view, sets the view's 3D viewing direction and zoom level according to your input, and aligns the views with each other. Although SOLVIEW doesn't draw anything other than floating viewport borders, it does create special layers that are used by SOLDRAW for drawing objects in the viewports. These special layers are for visible objects, hidden objects, and hatches (for section views only). The layers for hidden objects use AutoCAD's HIDDEN linetype, if it is loaded. SOLVIEW also creates, as a convenience for the user, a layer for the dimensions of each viewport. All these layers are selectively frozen so that objects appear only in the proper viewport.

When you have your drawing views established, you will exit SOLVIEW and move on to SOLDRAW. SOLDRAW is a command that requires little user input, but does a great deal of work. You pick the paper space floating viewports that were made by SOLVIEW, and then sit back and

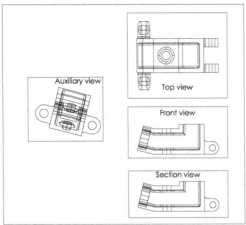

Viewports for a 2D drawing made by SOLVIEW.

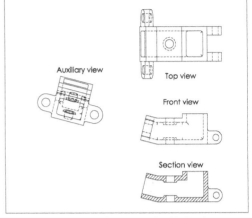

2D drawing views made by SOLDRAW

watch as SOLDRAW goes about drawing objects in those viewports. When it is finished, the 3D solid model is no longer shown. In its place in each viewport is a 2D drawing of the appropriate view of the model. If there are section views, the sliced areas are hatched. However, tangent lines are not drawn, which sometimes leaves blank areas in the model's image. To prevent objects from appearing in the wrong viewport, they are placed in a layer that is thawed only in the proper viewport.

## Using SOLVIEW and SOLDRAW

Your preliminary steps in creating a 2D drawing from a 3D solid model are:

1. Decide on the views that your drawing will have, the size of paper it will be printed on, and the scale the views will have. This is a step you would do in setting up any 2D drawing, whether it is done directly on paper or with a computer.

2. Open the drawing file containing the 3D solid model. Load the HIDDEN line type so that AutoCAD uses it for the layers it makes for hidden objects.

3. Select a Layout tab to activate paper space. Invoke PAGESETUP and specify a printer and the paper size of the drawing. If AutoCAD includes a floating viewport in the layout, erase it.

4. Insert a border and title block in the layout. This helps you judge the locations of the viewports, although some prefer to postpone inserting the border and title block until after the views, and perhaps even after the dimensions, have been created.

When these initial steps are finished, you use the SOLVIEW command to create drawing views in the layout. You first use SOLVIEW's UCS option to make the base view of the drawing. Often, this is the top view, but it doesn't have to be. The UCS option creates a floating viewport with a view direction that looks straight toward the X-Y plane of the UCS (or the WCS if you prefer).

When you create this base view, you specify its scale, its location, and the extent of its viewport borders; then, you assign a name to the view.

After the base view is in place, you can use SOLVIEW's Ortho option to create views that are orthogonal to it. You establish the view direction of an orthogonal view by selecting the side of the base view's border that the view is to look toward. AutoCAD then switches to its ortho mode and fixes a rubberband line on the base viewport's border; and, you drag the cursor

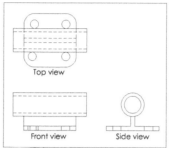

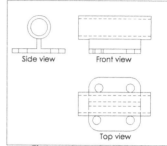

to set the location of the orthogonal view. If you are creating drawing views that conform to the Third Angle Projection standard, drag the cursor *away from* the base viewport to position the orthogonal view. If, on the other hand, you are using the First Angle Projection standard, drag the cursor *back through* the base viewport and past its opposite side to position the orthogonal view. Typically, most drawings made in North America use Third Angle Projection, while most drawings made in the rest of the world use First Angle Projection.

If your model has a face that is inclined or askew to a principle plane, use SOLVIEW's Auxiliary option to create a view that shows the face in its true size and shape. This option issues command line prompts for you to specify the edge of the face. Then, AutoCAD anchors a rubberband line on the edge of the face and perpendicuar to it for you to specify the location of the auxiliary view.

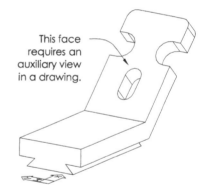

This face requires an auxiliary view in a drawing.

Use SOLVIEW's Section option when your model has interior faces and edges. You are prompted to select the location of the section view's cutting plane. You must make this selection in an existing view that has a line of sight perpendicular to the cutting plane. The section view can have a scale that is different than its parent view. SOLVIEW can make full section views only.

Detail views are magnified areas of other views for showing and dimensioning small or crowded features. Although SOLVIEW does not have an option for creating detail views, you can use its UCS option and specify a scale that is larger than the one used for the base view. You will specify corners of the view's border that uncover only the detail area of the model.

You can make all of a drawing's views during one call to SOLVIEW, or you can invoke the command several times. As you create each view, SOLVIEW creates three layers for it — one layer is for visible edges, one is for hidden edges, and one is for dimensions. The names of these layers correspond to the name you assigned to the view when you created it, and to the purpose of the layer. For example, if you assigned the name FRONT to a view, its layers would be FRONT-VIS, FRONT-HID, and FRONT-DIM. Section views have a fourth layer, with a name such as SECTION-HAT, for the crosshatching in the view. These layers are thawed, and visible, only in the proper viewport. Except for the layers for dimensions, you should not use the layers SOLVIEW creates, because SOLDRAW might delete them as it draws objects in the viewports.

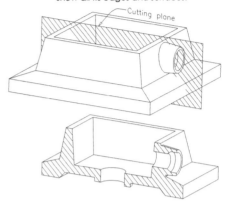

This model requires a section view to clearly show all its edges and surfaces.

SOLVIEW also creates a layer named VPORTS for the viewport borders. All the layers created by SOLVIEW are assiged Black as a color, so you should change their colors to match your standards.

When you have created the drawing views, save your drawing file, start the SOLDRAW command and select the floating viewports created by SOLVIEW as the viewports to be drawn. SOLDRAW draws 2D objects in model space that represent the model's edges as they are seen in each viewport. It also crosshatches section views and freezes the 3D solid's layer in all the floating viewports.

You can modify your 3D model even after drawing views have been created. After making the model modifications, rerun SOLDRAW. The old objects are erased and new ones representing the current geometry of the model are drawn. After SOLDRAW has drawn 2D objects in the drawing views, you add dimensions and annotation to the views and drawing.

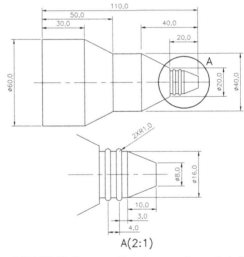

Use SOLVIEW's Base option to create a detail view.

## Dimensions and Annotation

### Adding Dimensions with AutoCAD 2000 and 2000i

Before you create any dimensions, set the dimension style parameters to your standards. The dimension parameters are the same as for any 2D drawing, except for **dimscale**. You should set **dimscale** to 0, either directly or by checking the Scale to Dimensions to Layout (Paper Space) option in DDIM's Fit dialog box. When **dimscale** is set to 0, AutoCAD automatically uses a value that is appropriate for the viewport in which dimensions are being added.

You will add dimensions within model space, working in one floating viewport at a time, using the following procedure:

- Zoom in to get a good view of the viewport you are going to work in. Use the MSPACE command (in any of its several forms described in the previous chapter) to switch from paper space to model space and make the viewport you intend to work in the current viewport.

- Use the View option of the UCS command to orient the X and Y axes to match the view. Follow this with the Origin option of the UCS command, and use an object snap on some object within the viewport. This ensures that the dimensions are on the same plane as the objects being dimensioned.

- Set the layer for the dimensions to the one that matches the view. For example, if the view in the viewport you are working in is named Top, use the layer named Dim-top. This causes dimensions to appear only in the proper viewport.

- Add the dimensions as you would in any 2D drawing. If the viewport is too small to accommodate some dimensions, temporarily switch back to paper space and stretch the viewport's border. Do not zoom or pan within a floating viewport.

### Adding Dimensions with AutoCAD 2002

Dimensioning drawing views is considerably easier in AutoCAD 2002 than in earlier releases because you can add the dimensions in paper space, rather than in model space, and you can use just one layer for all the dimensions. Also, all dimension size parameters are 1:1 because dimensions are in paper space.

You will most likely ignore the layers that SOLVIEW created for dimensions, and instead set up a new layer for all the drawing's dimensions. Your dimensioning techniques are exactly the same as if you were working with a pure 2D drawing.

After setting the dimension style parameters to match your standards, assign a value of 2 to the system variable **dimassoc**. When **dimassoc** is set to 2, the AutoCAD dimensioning commands recognize model space objects from paper space. The dimensioning commands also recognize the scale of a viewport and automatically compensate for viewport scale differences. For example, if a drawing has some views in half-scale and other views in full-scale, the dimensioning commands use the correct dimension values for the objects in each viewport, regardless of its scale. To find out more about **dimassoc**, read the "Dimensioning in AutoCAD 2002" section in Chapter 15.

Moreover, when **dimassoc** is set to 2, dimensions are associated with their objects, even though they are in different spaces, and when you make any changes to the objects, you can update the dimensions to reflect the changes. This means that you can fully dimension the SOLVIEW/SOLDRAW views of a 3D solid model, modify the 3D solid, rerun SOLDRAW, and then update the dimensions to reflect the modifications.

Because SOLDRAW erases and redraws the edges and profiles of the model in the drawing views, dimensions lose their association with the model space objects. Dimensions for unmodified portions of the model will be correct, even though they are no longer associative. You can choose to either associate those dimensions to the new objects, or leave them as they are. Dimensions for model geometry that has changed in size or location will have incorrect values or positions. You need to associate those dimensions with the new objects through the DIMREASSOCIATE command, or else erase the existing dimensions and then add new ones.

From the command line, DIMREASSOCIATE prompts you to select the dimensions that are to be updated. Then, it steps through all the selected dimensions, issuing command line prompts for you to respecify points for the extension lines or to select an object — such as a line or arc — for each dimension. As soon as you specify the parameters for a dimension, its extension and dimension lines move and its dimension value changes to accommodate the geometry.

## Adding Annotation

You add general notes, centerlines, and other annotation to your drawing using the same techniques you would use in any 2D drawing. Because scale in paper space is 1:1, all objects in paper space are entered in their true size.

If necessary, you can move the views to better fit the paper and borders you are using. Although you can freely move viewports and change their border size, you must make certain that you do not alter their scale or alignment. When the views are as you want them, turn off or freeze the layer named Vports.

## Exercise Two

In this exercise, you will make a 2D multiview drawing from the same 3D model you used in making an isometric drawing in Exercise 1 of this chapter. The model, which represents a pipe fitting, is in file f1310.dwg on the CD-ROM that comes with this book. Find that file and open it.

Your drawing needs four views to completely define the part. One view will look straight down toward the square base of the part, and another will be perpendicular to the part's bend radius. The drawing also needs an auxiliary view for showing the true size and form of the diamond-shaped face, and lastly, it needs a section view through the plane of the part's bend. You will use C-size paper (22x17 inches), and some back-of-the-envelope calculations based on the overall size of the part indicate that the four views will fit nicely on C-size paper when a 2:1 scale is used.

Select the Layout1 tab to activate paper space. Use the PAGESETUP command (it might automaically start) to set the plot device to one that can handle C-sized paper, set the paper size to 22x17 inches, the plot area to Layout, and the scale to 1:1. (Remember that this scale pertains to the layout scale, rather than the drawing scale.) Exit the Page Setup dialog box. If AutoCAD has created a floating viewport, erase it. This is also a good time to ensure that AutoCAD's HIDDEN linetype is loaded. Often, you will insert a border and title block to the layout at this time, but for this particular exercise, you will insert them as a last step instead of a first step.

Now, you are ready to use SOLVIEW to make the four views you've decided on. You will create the top view first. The command line sequence of prompts and input to do this is

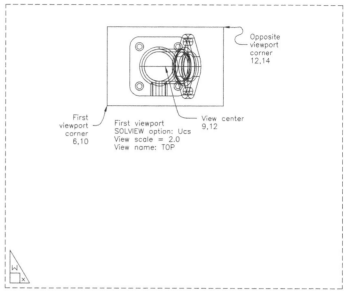

```
Command: SOLVIEW (Enter)
Enter an option [Ucs/Ortho/Auxiliary/
    Section]: U (Enter)
Enter an option [Named/World/?/
    Current] <Current>: W (Enter)
Enter view scale <1.0000>: 2 (Enter)
Specify view center: 9,12 (Enter)
Specify view center <specify
    viewport>: (Enter)
Specify first corner of viewport:
    6,10 (Enter)
Specify opposite corner of viewport:
    12,14 (Enter)
Enter view name: TOP (Enter)
```

Figure 2-1

This viewport is shown in Figure 2-1. The Ucs option of the main SOLVIEW menu, which is the only option you can select when no viewports exist, creates a view that looks straight down on an X-Y plane. You specified that the X-Y plane of the WCS be used because the square base of the part sits on the WCS X-Y plane. Your responses to the prompts for viewport location and size are not especially important because the viewport can be easily moved and resized later. You named the view in the viewport TOP.

Next, you will make the model's front view by using SOLVIEW's Ortho option. The command line input is

```
Enter an option [Ucs/Ortho/Auxiliary/Section]: O (Enter)
Specify side of viewport to project: (Pick the bottom edge of the top viewport.)
Specify view center: 9,7 (Enter)
Specify view center <specify viewport>: (Enter)
Specify first corner of viewport: 6,5 (Enter)
Specify opposite corner of viewport: 12,9 (Enter)
View name: FRONT (Enter)
```

Figure 2-2 shows the new viewport. The Ortho option makes a view that is folded 90 degrees from an existing one. From the top view that you created first, you can make a front view, a right-side view, a left-side view, or a back view by picking the appropriate edge of the viewport. Because you want a front view, you picked its bottom edge.

AutoCAD displays an image of the model's front view and locks into the ortho mode to keep the image aligned with the top view as you drag it down to a convenient location. The Y location of the viewport's center is not critical, nor are the viewport's corners. You assigned the name FRONT to the view in this viewport.

View names for mechanical parts such as this are rather arbitrary, having more to do with the interrelationship of the views than the real-life orientation of the part. Some would correctly call the view you just established a side view.

Your third view will be an auxiliary view that looks directly toward the diamond-shaped plane on the model. The command line input to create this view is

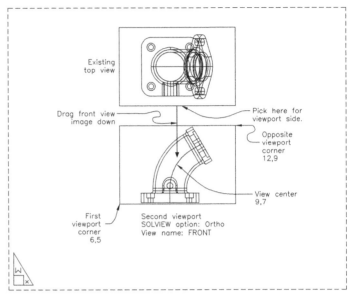

Figure 2-2

```
Enter an option [Ucs/Ortho/Auxiliary/Section]: A (Enter)
Specify first point of inclined plane: (Use a quadrant object snap to pick point 1 in Figure 2-3.)
Specify second point of inclined plane: (Use a quadrant object snap to pick point 2 in Figure 2-3.)
Specify side to view from: (Pick point 3 in Figure 2-3.)
Specify view center: 5<90 (Enter)
Specify view center <specify viewport>: (Enter)
Specify first corner of viewport: 13,7 (Enter)
Specify opposite corner of viewport: 18,12 (Enter)
Enter view name: AUX (Enter)
```

SOLVIEW's Auxiliary option creates a view that is perpendicular to a plane seen edge-on in the parent viewport. It is useful for showing true sizes on a plane that is askew to the principal planes. SOLVIEW asks you to specify the plane by picking two points that are on its edge. These points must be in a viewport that shows an edge-on view of the plane. Generally, you use object snaps to specify the points. You used quadrant object snaps for this particular plane, but an endpoint object snap would have worked equally well. After the plane is identified, SOLVIEW prompts for a point to indicate which side of the plane the viewpoint is to look toward.

AutoCAD then rotates the paper space UCS around the Z axis to match the slope of the plane, locks into the ortho mode, and prompts for the auxiliary viewport's center location and its corners. After positioning the viewport, you named its view AUX.

The fourth, and final, viewport will be for a section view that slices the part in the plane of the curvature of its bend. The sequence of prompts and input to make this viewport are

```
Ucs/Ortho/Auxiliary/Section/<eXit>: S (Enter)
Specify first point of cutting plane: (Use a midpoint object snap to pick point 1 in Figure 2-4.)
Specify second point of cutting plane: (Use a quadrant object snap to pick point 2 in Figure 2-4.)
Specify side to view from: (Pick point 3 in Figure 2-5.)
Enter view scale<2.0000>: 2 (Enter)
Specify view center: 9.5<270 (Enter)
Specify view center: (Enter)
Specify first corner of viewport: 6,.25 (Enter)
Specify opposite corner of viewport: 12,4.5(Enter)
Enter view name: SEC (Enter)
```

Specifying a cutting plane is similar to specifying an auxiliary plane — you pick two points to identify the edge of the plane and a third point to indicate the view direction. The cutting plane is perpendicular to the first two points. You used a midpoint object snap to specify the first point and a quadrant object snap for the second. You use a 2:1 scale, just as in the top view. Then, you showed AutoCAD the center and the corners of the section view, and named its view SEC. Although this section view appears to be identical to the front view, SOL-DRAW treats it differently.

You are now finished with SOLVIEW. If you look through the list of layers, you will see

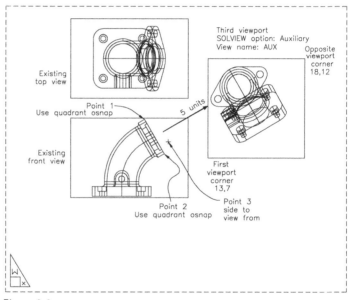

Figure 2-3

that SOLVIEW has created 13 new ones that have names such as SEC-HAT, TOP-VIS, TOP-HID, AUX-DIM, and FRONT-VIS. The first part of these layer names consists of the view names you assigned to the viewports, while the second part indicates the purpose of the layer. SOLDRAW uses the layers whose names end with VIS for drawing visible lines, and those having names ending with HID for drawing hidden lines. The layer named SEC-HAT is used for hatches in the section view. Because these layers are for SOLDRAW, you should not use them. On the other hand, the layers with names ending with dim are for your use in adding dimensions. A layer named Vports also was created, and the borders of the four viewports are in this layer.

The four floating paper space viewports now contain just the 3D solid model. It is difficult to dimension such a model, and you have limited control over the display of hidden lines and edges. Therefore, use SOLDRAW to draw a 2D version of the 3D model in each viewport. The command line input for SOLDRAW is

```
Command: SOLDRAW (Enter)
Select viewports to draw...
Select objects: (Pick the borders
    of the four viewports.)
```

AutoCAD's initial response to the command is a message reminding you of the type of object to select rather than a prompt for input. As soon as you pick the borders of the four viewports that were created with SOLVIEW, SOLDRAW goes to work. When SOLDRAW is finished, as shown in Figure 2-5, the layer that the original 3D solid model is in is frozen in all the viewports, and in its place are 2D versions of the model made from lines, arcs, and circles. Furthermore, the section view now shows the part's cross-section, and it is also hatched. All these 2D objects are thawed, and therefore visible, only in the appropriate viewport. For instance, the TOP-VIS and TOP-HID layers are frozen in all viewports except the one for the top view. Moreover, while the viewport for the section view does have objects in the SEC-HID

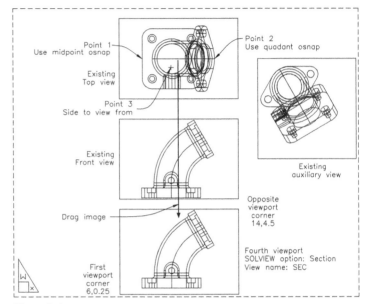

Figure 2-4

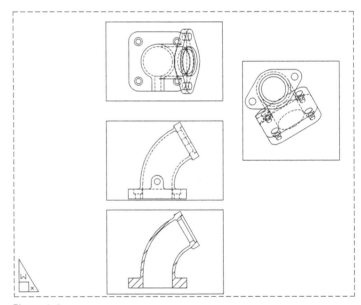

Figure 2-5

layer, that layer is frozen because most drafting practices do not show hidden lines in section views.

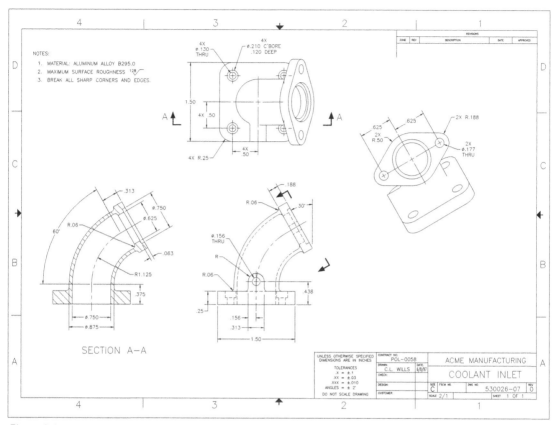

Figure 2-6

Follow the instructions given earlier in this chapter to add dimensions to the 2D objects that SOLDRAW has drawn in the floating viewports. In AutoCAD 2000 and 2000i, you will probably need to enlarge the floating viewports to accommodate the dimensions, and you might even want to move the viewports further apart or closer together. Be certain, however, that you do not change their zoom level or their alignment. Also, in all AutoCAD versions, you might want to move the section view so that it fits better on the paper.

Your completed drawing, with the Vports layer frozen, should look similar to the one in Figure 2-6. The title block and border in this figure is based on one from AutoCAD's MVSETUP command. One based on ANSI C title block.dwg in the Templates folder, or one that you have on hand, will work equally well.

In the file Figure 2-6 is based on, the section view has been moved and the hatch pattern has been modified. The layer for the center line that is shown in the front and section views is thawed only in those viewports. Other center marks are in the appropriate dimension layer. Because SOLDRAW does not draw tangential edges, the auxiliary view has some empty spots.

On the CD-ROM that accompanies this book, the AutoCAD 2000 and 2000i version of the completed drawing and model are in file f1625.dwg, and the AutoCAD 2002 version is in file f1625a.dwg.

| | |
|---|---|
| Command: | SOLVIEW |
| Purpose: | SOLVIEW creates and sets up floating viewports to be used for orthographic, section, and auxiliary views of a 2D multiview drawing of a 3D solid model. SOLVIEW must be followed by the SOLDRAW command to have 2D objects, which represent the model's edges and profiles, drawn in the viewports. |
| Initiate with: | • On the command line, enter SOLVIEW.<br>• From the Draw pull-down menu, select Solids, Setup, and View.<br>• Select the Setup View button from the Solids toolbar. |
| Options: | SOLVIEW sets up the views of a multiview 2D drawing based on a 3D solid model. It is an interactive command in which you specify, one at a time, the views that the drawing is to have, their scale (for some viewports only), and their relative location. SOLVIEW makes a paper space floating viewport for each view, sets the viewport's view direction and zoom level, and aligns the views with each other. SOLVIEW also creates special layers to be used for drawing visible objects, hidden objects, dimensions, and hatches within the floating viewports. |

Although SOLVIEW creates viewports for orthographic, auxiliary, and section views, it does not draw anything in those viewports. When you are finished with SOLVIEW, you must use the SOLDRAW command to have objects drawn within the floating viewports.

SOLVIEW sets the **tilemode** system variable to 0 if it currently has a value of 1 and displays the command line menu:

```
Enter an option [Ucs/Ortho/Auxiliary/Section]: (Enter an option or press Enter.)
```

AutoCAD returns to this menu when work within an option is completed. Press the Enter key to end the command. If no floating viewports exist, you must use the Ucs option to create one. The Ortho, Auxiliary, and Section options can be used only if at least one floating viewport exits.

- Ucs    A viewport in which the view direction looks straight down on an X-Y plane — a plan view — is created with this option. It often is used for showing the top view of the 3D model. The following submenu is displayed for you to specify whether the plan view is based on the WCS, the current UCS, or a named UCS:

```
Enter an option [Named/World/?/Current] <Current>: (Enter an option or
    press Enter.)
```

The question mark suboption displays a list of existing UCSs that have been saved by the UCS command. After you specify which coordinate system you want the plan view based on, AutoCAD prompts for the viewport's scale relative to paper space:

```
Enter view scale<1.0000>: (Enter a number or press Enter.)
```

Next, AutoCAD prompts for the paper space location of the viewport's center:

```
Specify view center: (Specify a point.)
Specify view center <specify viewport>: (Specify a point or press
    Enter.)
```

As soon as you specify a point for the viewport, AutoCAD displays the model centered at that point in the specified scale and allows you to select a different point if your original location does not suit you. You can continue to move the center point until you find the location you want and press the Enter key to accept it.

Then, AutoCAD asks you to specify the size of the viewport by picking two points representing its opposite diagonal corners:

```
Specify first corner of viewport: (Specify a point.)
Specify opposite corner of viewport: (Specify a point.)
```

A rubberband rectangle, anchored at the first corner, helps you specify the opposite corner. Lastly, AutoCAD prompts for the name of the view:

```
Enter view name: (Enter a valid view name.)
```

• Ortho

This option creates a viewport with a view that is folded 90 degrees from the view in an existing viewport. You are first prompted to select one side of the base viewport:

```
Specify side of
    viewport to
    project: (Pick a
    point on the
    edge of a view-
    port.)
```

The next prompt is for the location of the new viewport:

```
Specify view center:
    (Specify a
    point.)
Specify view center
    <specify
    viewport>: (Spec-
    ify a point or
    press Enter.)
```

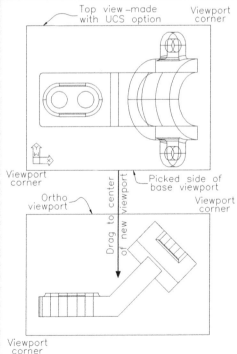

AutoCAD turns on the ortho mode and extends a rubberband line from the midpoint of the base viewport's border. When you pick a point for the viewport center, AutoCAD displays the model centered at that point, as seen from a viewpoint that is 90 degrees from that of the base viewport, and in the same scale as the base viewport. You can pick any number of view center locations until you signal acceptance of a point by pressing the Enter key.

As soon as the viewport center has been established, AutoCAD prompts for the viewport's opposite diagonal corners:

```
Specify first corner of viewport: (Specify a point.)
Specify opposite corner of viewport: (Specify a point.)
```

A rubberband rectangle, anchored at the first corner, helps you locate the opposite corner. The last prompt by the Ortho option is for the name of the view:

```
Enter view name: (Enter a valid view name.)
```

- Auxiliary

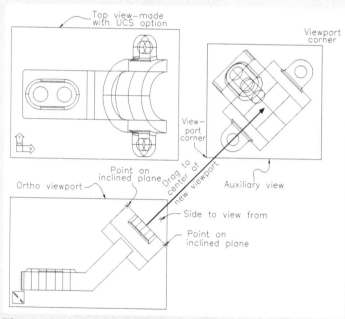

The Auxiliary option creates a view that is perpendicular to a plane seen edge-on in a base viewport. It is useful for showing true sizes and shapes on a plane that is not aligned with any of the principal planes. AutoCAD asks you to specify the angle of the auxiliary plane by picking two points on an edge view of it and asks you to specify the side from which the plane is to be seen.

```
Specify first point of inclined plane: (Specify a point.)
Specify second point of inclined plane: (Specify a point.)
Side to view from: (Specify a point.)
```

Typically, you will use object snaps to specify the two points on the plane. The side to view from point must be in the same viewport and off the line between the first two points. AutoCAD then rotates the paper space UCS so that the X axis is perpendicular to the inclined plane, anchors a rubberband line on the plane, locks into the ortho mode, and prompts for a view center:

```
Specify view center: (Specify a point.)
Specify view center <specify viewport>: (Specify a point or press
    Enter.)
```

As soon as you pick a center location, AutoCAD displays the model as it will appear in the auxiliary view, and repeats the View Center prompt so that you can specify a location closer or further from the base viewport. When you have the location you want, press the Enter key. After the viewport center has been established, AutoCAD prompts for the viewport's opposite diagonal corners and the name of the view:

```
Specify first corner of viewport: (Specify a point.)
Specify opposite corner of viewport: (Specify a point.)
Enter view name: (Enter a valid view name.)
```

A rubberband rectangle, anchored at the first viewport corner, helps you specify the opposite corner.

• Section    This option sets up a cross-section view through the model. The section slices completely through the model — partial sections and off-set sections are not possible. You are prompted to specify two points that establish the edge of the cutting plane and to specify a third point indicating the side from which the section is to be seen. All three points must be in the same viewport.

```
Specify first point of cutting plane: (Specify a point.)
Specify second point of cutting plane: (Specify a point.)
Specify side to view from: (Specify a point.)
```

Next, AutoCAD asks for the scale of the section view.

```
Enter view scale<1.0000>: (Enter a number or press Enter.)
```

AutoCAD then anchors a rubberband line on, and perpendicular to, the cutting plane, turns on the ortho mode, and prompts for the paper space location of the viewport's center:

```
Specify view center: (Specify a location.)
Specify view center <specify viewport>: (Specify a location or
    press Enter.)
```

As soon as you specify a point for the viewport, AutoCAD displays the model centered at that point, in the specified scale. You can try different points until you are satisfied with the view location and press the Enter key. When the viewport's center has been established, AutoCAD prompts for its opposite diagonal corners and for the name of the view:

```
Specify first corner of viewport: (Specify a point.)
Specify opposite corner of viewport: (Specify a point.)
Enter view name: (Enter a valid view name.)
```

A rubberband rectangle, anchored at the first viewport corner, helps you specify the opposite viewport corner.

Notes:

• AutoCAD places all the floating viewports in a layer named Vports. If that layer does not exist, SOLVIEW creates it.

• The names of the layers created by SOLVIEW for visible and hidden lines, dimensions, and hatches are based on the names assigned to the views by the user. The names begin with the view name and conclude with the extension of -vis, -hid, -dim, and -hat. For example, if the view within a viewport is named Top, AutoCAD creates layers having the names Top-vis, Top-hid, and Top-dim. Layers using the -hat name extension are created only if a section view has been created.

• Layers are thawed only in the applicable viewport. Continuing with the previous example, the layers Top-vis, Top-hid, and Top-dim are thawed in the viewport showing the top view and are frozen in all other viewports.

• The layers AutoCAD creates for hidden lines take on the HIDDEN linetype, provided that linetype has been loaded.

• The names assigned to the views become standard AutoCAD view names, so they must follow the VIEW command's rules for naming views and they cannot be the name of an existing view.

• SOLDRAW deletes and redraws objects in the layers SOLVIEW creates for visible objects, hidden objects, and hatches. Therefore, you should not use those layers.

• Section views do not look like section views until SOLDRAW is used. Although viewports for section views must initially be located at a point perpendicular to the cutting plane, they can be moved later.

• In creating orthogonal views, drag the cursor directly away from the parent viewport when creating views in accordance with Third Angle Projection, and drag the cursor through and then away from the parent viewport when creating views in accordance with First Angle Projection.

| | |
|---|---|
| Command: | SOLDRAW |
| Purpose: | SOLDRAW draws 2D objects that are suitable for dimensioning in viewports set up by the SOLVIEW command. |
| Initiate with: | • On the command line, enter SOLDRAW. |
| | • From the Draw pull-down menu, select Solids, Setup, and Drawing. |
| | • Select the Setup Drawing button from the Solids toolbar. |
| Implementation: | SOLDRAW draws 2D objects in floating viewports that have been set up by SOLVIEW for orthographic, auxiliary, and section views. The command has no options. It issues a command line prompt for you to select the viewports that it is to work in, and then draws objects within those viewports. The selected viewports must have been created by the SOLVIEW command, and the object in them must be a 3D solid that is not a block. |

Within each viewport SOLDRAW draws the visible edges, the hidden edges, and the profiles of the 3D solid as seen within the viewport. Cross-section areas within section views are hatched using the current settings of the **hpname**, **hpscale**, and **hpang** system variables.

| | |
|---|---|
| Notes: | • The objects are drawn using the appropriate layer for visible objects, hidden objects, and hatch patterns (these layers were created by SOLVIEW). Any existing objects that are in those layers within the viewports are erased. |

• Tangent lines, which delineate the transition between flat and curved surfaces or between two adjacent curved surfaces, are not drawn.

• Typically, the layers for hidden objects use the HIDDEN linetype. In each viewport, layers not needed to draw the objects specific to that viewport are frozen, and the layer of the 3D solid is frozen in all the viewports. The layer for hidden objects is frozen in viewports for section views, because most drafting practices do not show hidden lines in section views.

• Objects within the orthographic views are drawn on the principal planes, while objects or auxiliary and section views are drawn on the planes selected during SOLVIEW.

# Renderings from 3D Models

# CHAPTER 17

# Renderings

*So far in this book, you have worked with wireframe, hidden-line, and shaded viewing modes. Now, you will begin to work with renderings, which are shaded, realistic images of 3D objects. In creating renderings, you can simulate the effects of both natural and artificial lighting, and you can transform surfaces into bricks, tile, and other patterned material, as well as create transparent and reflective surfaces.*

*This chapter*

- *gives you an overview of rendering — what it is, what you can do with it, and what its limitations are;*

- *describes bitmap files, the various formats they come in, and their relationships to renderings;*

- *introduces you to the steps and processes in making renderings.*

## An Overview of Rendering

Rendering in AutoCAD is handled by render.arx, an external program that is automatically activated the first time a command related to rendering is called. Rendering is a model space operation. None of the rendering commands are allowed in paper space, although you can render within a floating viewport. Also, rendering works only on surface and solid models — wireframe objects vanish during a rendering.

Although the Gouraud Shading option of the SHADEMODE command can make rendering-like images in that surfaces become smooth and shaded and mesh lines disappear, the rendering commands go far beyond making smooth surfaces. Here is a list of some of their capabilities:

- A variety of light types for obtaining different effects are supported. You can control the position, intensity, and color of these lights, and they also can cast shadows.

- You can enhance the realism of 3D models by attaching texture and pattern images from bitmap files to their surfaces.

- AutoCAD can simulate materials that are transparent and materials that have reflective surfaces.

- You can use images from bitmap files in the backgrounds of renderings, and you can add images of trees, shrubs, and other landscape objects to renderings.

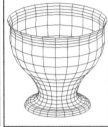

Wireframe      Hidden lines removed

Rendering has two basic components — lights and materials. AutoCAD supports the four different types of lights shown in Table 17-1.

Lights also can be given a specific color, and, with the exception of ambient light, can cast shadows. You can turn shadows on or off for each light you install. You will most likely install several lights to fully bring out the features of your 3D model. Lights for rendering are described in more detail in Chapter 18.

Shaded      Rendered

You can install a variety of light types that cast shadows, and you can attach patterned materials to 3D objects.

AutoCAD can simulate materials that are transparent and materials that have reflective surfaces.

Materials, the second major component of renderings, control the appearance of specific surface objects of a 3D model. You can make surfaces appear to be shiny or dull, opaque or transparent; you can control their overall color as well as the color of their highlights; and you can make them reflective. To simulate objects that have patterns and textures — such

A rendering without a background image, or landscape objects

A rendering with a background image and landscape objects

as wood, brick, wallpaper, and marble — you can attach images from bitmap files to surface objects. Chapter 19 contains an extensive discussion of rendering materials.

Rendering is a more subjective process than most AutoCAD operations. There is seldom a right or wrong selection of lights and their placement, and choices for materials vary widely between individuals. You should, however, keep renderings as simple as you can. An abundance of lights and complicated materials does not necessarily make a better rendering.

## Table 17-1 AutoCAD Rendering Light Types

| Light Type | Purpose | Characteristics |
|---|---|---|
| Distant | General illumination | Parallel light beams and constant intensity. |
| Spot | Brightens specific areas | Light beams radiate in a cone-like pattern from the source. The relative brightness of the light can be set to diminish as distance from the source increases. |
| Point | Brightens specific areas | Light beams radiate in all directions from the source. Their intensity can be set to diminish at rates proportional to distance from the light. |
| Ambient | Relative brightness of shaded areas | No specific light source. |

# Bitmaps

Most AutoCAD objects are based on *vector graphics*, in which a few key points are used as anchors, with equations being used to define the object between the points. Although vector graphics work well for depicting wireframe objects, as well as the edges and profiles of surface and 3D solid objects, they are not suitable for working with the broad colored and shaded areas of renderings. Consequently, renderings are based on *bitmap graphics*. Not only are renderings saved in bitmap files, images in bitmap files are used for material patterns and textures, as well as in backgrounds and as landscape objects. When you work with renderings, you work with bitmaps.

In bitmap graphics, the color of each dot on the computer screen (and on the printed output) is specified. In the word *bitmap*, *bit* refers to the binary digits used to specify the color of the dot, while *map* refers to the system for keeping track of each dot's location on the computer screen or printed output. Usually the dots on a computer screen are called *pixels*, which stands for picture element. Sometimes bitmap graphics are also called *raster graphics*.

Because binary numbers are used to specify a particular color, the number of colors a pixel can have is 2 raised to the power of the number of bits available per pixel. In turn, the number of bits available for each pixel is dependent upon how much memory a computer's video system has and how many pixels are being used (the resolution of the screen or printed picture). Computer video systems often use the term *N-bit* in their specifications, where $N$ is the number of bits per pixel that they support at a given resolution. This is often called *color depth*.

| | |
|---|---|
| 8-bit | Maximum of 256 colors |
| 16-bit | Maximum of 65,536 colors |
| 24-bit | More than 16 million colors |

Some commonly encountered color depths are

| 8-bit | Maximum of 256 colors |
|-------|----------------------|
| 16-bit | Maximum of 65,536 colors |
| 24-bit | More than 16 million colors |

Occasionally, you even will see references to 32-bit systems. However, in most cases, differences between similar colors are not significant when you use more than 65,000 colors. Some of AutoCAD's dialog boxes for rendering give you options related to color depth.

Bitmaps are usually generated on a horizontal, row-by-row basis. Often a bitmap file is able to reduce the overall number of bytes needed to store an image, especially if large areas in the bitmap have the same color. Rather than specifying the color of each pixel, the file can contain signals indicating that the next so-many pixels have color number such-and-such. This is called *compression*.

Unfortunately, no standard format exists for bitmap files. Many different formats exist; you will probably work with several as you use them in renderings and as you export your renderings to output devices and to other programs. Commonly, each bitmap file format type has a distinctive filename extension. The filename extensions of the formats, along with some information about the format, that AutoCAD's renderer is able to work with are as follows:

| TIF | They are often called TIFF files, which stands for Tagged Image File Format. The format was developed to be portable across different computer platforms. Variations, however, exist within the format, and the variants are not necessarily compatible with each other. |
|-----|---|
| GIF | GIF, which stands for Graphics Interchange Format, was developed by the Compuserve Information Network for exchanging graphic files electronically between different computer platforms and operating systems. For a given image, its file size tends to be small. It is, however, generally limited to 256 colors. |
| PCX | This format originated with an early personal computer paint program. It is a widely accepted format that has been kept updated and can be read by many modern paint programs, including the Windows Paint accessory program. |
| BMP | Microsoft created this format for use in its Windows operating systems and accessories. Its images are stored uncompressed, which typically makes them fast to load, but large in size. |
| TGA | The TGA format was developed by Targa Truevision, a manufacturer of high-end computer graphics hardware. The files handle large numbers of colors well, but their file sizes tend to be large, even when they are compressed. Most of the files AutoCAD uses for materials, backgrounds, and landscape objects are in this format. |
| JPG | This format comes from an international standards committee — the Joint Photographic Experts Group (JPEG) — for digitizing photographs. It handles images having a large number of colors in relatively small file sizes. |

# Making Renderings

Although invoking the RENDER command is always the last step you take in making a rendering, this book will discuss that command — and those associated with it — first. Actually, RENDER is the only essential command in making a rendering. If you do not install a light, AutoCAD automatically installs one that has its light beams pointed in the current view direction. And, if you do not create or attach materials to your objects, AutoCAD uses its default global material characteristics.

The RENDER command gives you a choice of three different types of rendering. The most elementary type, called *Render*, supports the four types of lights mentioned earlier, can do smooth shading, and can have materials with colors and various degrees of shininess. However, the lights cannot have shadows, and bitmaps are supported only for background images. The second rendering type is *Photo Real*. It supports all the basic rendering features, plus shadows, transparent materials, bitmaps for materials, and bitmap landscape objects. The third rendering type, *Photo Raytrace*, supports everything that Photo Real does, plus reflective materials and light refraction (the bending of light beams as they pass through a transparent material).

Menus and toolbar buttons for RENDER and its related commands

Render is the fastest of the three rendering types, and you can sometimes use it for preliminary renderings or when you want to quickly obtain a smoothly shaded view of your 3D model. It is not, however, capable of making serious renderings. Most of the time, you will use Photo Real rendering. You will probably use Photo Raytrace rendering only when you need its unique features, because it is usually (but not always) the slowest of the rendering types.

Your first step in making a rendering will be to set up a view of the 3D model. The viewing direction and the zoom level will depend on the shape of the model and on the features you want to show. When you are working with large objects, especially buildings and structures, you will use a perspective view. Nothing prevents you from creating several different renderings of a model, each having a different view and combinations of lights. In fact, AutoCAD has a command, SCENE, that allows you to save and render specific combinations of views and lights.

Your second step will be to install lights, and your third will be to create materials and attach them to surface objects. Within each of these steps, you will make numerous preliminary renderings. The sequence of these steps, however, is not absolute, and you will often change the lighting after you see its effects on materials. You might even tweak the view a little to improve the rendering.

As you try out combinations of lights and materials, your rendering destination is the current viewport, and you will often use the rendering options that speed the rendering process — such as Query for Selections, Crop Window, and Sub Sampling. Also, because rendering speed is related to the number of pixels in the rendering, dividing AutoCAD's graphics area into multiple viewports significantly reduces rendering times. This also allows you to compare rendering results when you make changes in materials and lights.

When you have all the parameters set to your liking, you will send the rendering to a file or to the render window, because within the RENDER command, there is no provision for directly printing a rendering. Either of these two destinations work well for exporting the rendering to another file or document. Although the render window is a more direct method for printing the rendering with the system printer, the file destination gives you more choices for file type, color depth, and resolution. Renderings also can be saved to a file with the SAVEIMG command, but this command has no advantage over saving the rendering to a file.

## Exercise

This exercise will give you an overall view of rendering — it uses shadows, bitmaps, transparent materials, and reflections. Start a new drawing. It does not need any special setup, and you will not need to retain it. Before you start this exercise, you should read through the descriptions of the RENDER and BACKGROUND commands in this chapter. You should also have the Render toolbar displayed on the screen for easy access when initiating rendering commands.

Before you can make a rendering, you need to create one or more objects that can be rendered. This exercise uses a round ball that is sitting on a flat surface. Switch to a layer that has a red color, or set object color to red, and then use the following command line input to make a surface model sphere that sits on the WCS X-Y plane:

```
Command: AI_SPHERE (Enter)
Specify center point of sphere: 0,0,1 (Enter)
Specify radius or [Diameter]: 1 (Enter)
Enter number of longitudinal segments for surface of sphere<16>: 24 (Enter)
Enter number of latitudinal segments for surface of sphere<16>: 24 (Enter)
```

A solid model sphere in the same location with the same radius works equally well. If you use a 3D solid sphere, however, you should set the system variable **facetres** to a value of 1.0. After the sphere is drawn, change to an object color of white and draw a 3D face under the sphere by using the following command line input:

```
Command: 3DFACE (Enter)
Specify first point or [Invisible]: -2,-2 (Enter)
Specify second point or [Invisible]: 2,-2 (Enter)
Specify third point or [Invisible] <exit>: 2,2 (Enter)
Specify fourth point or [Invisible] <create three-sided face>: -2,2 (Enter)
Specify third point or [Invisible] <exit>: (Enter)
```

After drawing the 3D face, switch to an SE isometric view. Even though the sphere and 3D face look the same from any of three other viewpoints, this particular one is important because you will set the direction of your rendering light to match it. After setting the viewpoint, zoom in closer to the sphere and 3D face. It's allright if the corners of the 3D face are even clipped a little. Your objects from this viewpoint should look similar to those in Figure 1-1.

You might also want to divide the AutoCAD graphics area into multiple viewports. This speeds up rendering slightly, and enables you to compare the effects of different rendering settings. To divide the graphics area into four viewports, enter the word -VPORTS (be certain to precede the name with a hyphen) on the command line, and then enter 4 in response to the list of options.

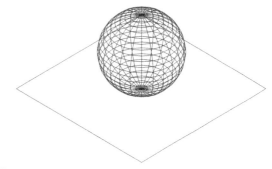

You will now use the LIGHT command to set up a light for the rendering. You can start this command in any of three different ways. You can enter the word *light* on the command

Figure 1-1

line, select Render and then Light from the View pull-down menu, or click the Light button on the Render toolbar. Any of these actions brings up the Lights dialog box. On the left side of this dialog box is a pull-down list of light types. Highlight Distant Light in this list, and then click the New button.

This brings up a dialog box titled New Distant Light. In this dialog box, which is shown in Figure 1-2, give the light a name that has no more than eight characters, check the Shadow On check box, set Azimuth to 45, and set Altitude to 45. These last two parameters, which can be set by entering a value in their edit boxes or by moving their slider bar, aim the light. Azimuth is the light's angle in the X-Y plane from the Y axis, while Altitude is its direction from the X-Y plane. Then click the OK button to leave the New Distant Light dialog box, and click the OK button in the Lights dialog box to leave the LIGHT command.

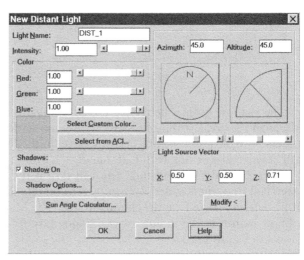

The distant light appears in your drawing as a block containing the name you assigned to the light. It may be

Figure 1-2

located almost inside your sphere, but that is of no consequence, because direction, not location, is what's important in installing distant lights.

Start the RENDER command. You will use a neutral gray color for the rendering background, both to make the rendered objects stand out better and to be free from dependence on the current AutoCAD screen color. Click the Background button in the Render dialog box to display the Background dialog box. Select Solid from the row of radio buttons at the top of that dialog box, and then clear the AutoCAD Background check box. This activates the Colors section of the dialog box. Set each of the three colors — red, green, and blue — to a value of 0.30, and then click the OK button to return to the Render dialog box.

In the Render dialog box, select Render as the rendering type. Make certain that Viewport is set as the rendering destinations and that Smooth Shade is on. Then, click the Render button. Your rendering will look something like the one shown in grayscale in Figure 1-3.

You are not likely to be impressed with the rendering. Although the sphere does look round, there is nothing to indicate that it is sitting on the 3D face. Therefore, start the RENDER command again. This time, select Photo Real as the rendering type. Then click the Shadows check box, and lastly click the Render button to render the current view. Your rendering should look like the one shown in Figure 1-4.

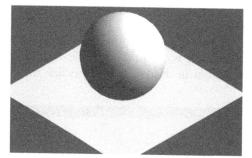

Figure 1-3

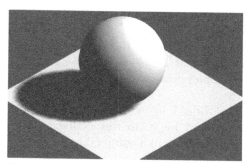

Figure 1-4

The shadow gives a better picture of the relative positions of the sphere and planar surface. Although the areas within the shadows are too dark now, they will become lighter when you add material properties to the objects. You have finished installing the lights for the rendering, and you will now begin working with materials.

Start the RMAT command. You can do this by selecting the button with a paint brush and green ball from the Render toolbar, by selecting Render/Materials from the View pull-down menu, or by entering RMAT on the command line. The Materials dialog box appears. Click the Material Library button in the middle of this dialog box to display the Material's Library dialog box, as shown in Figure 1-5.

On the right side of the Materials Library dialog box, the names of some ready-made materials you can use with your surface objects appear in a large list box. This list box might contain only four names, or it might contain about 150 names, depending on how you installed AutoCAD. In any case, you'll see a material named CHECKER TEXTURE in the list. Find that material (they are arranged alphabetically), and click it so that it is highlighted. (If you want to see what the material looks like, click the Preview button.) Then, click the Import button. The name of the material appears in the list box on the left side of the dialog box. Click the OK button to return to the Materials dialog box, which is shown in Figure 1-6.

You now need to attach the material to a surface. The name CHECKER TEXTURE is displayed in the list box on the left side of the Materials dialog box. This name should be highlighted, but if it isn't, click on the name to highlight it. Then, click the Attach button. The dialog box disappears to give you access to the entire AutoCAD graphics area. Pick an edge on the 3D face, and

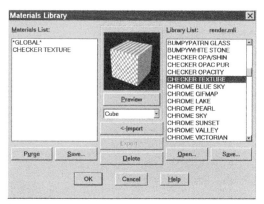

Figure 1-5

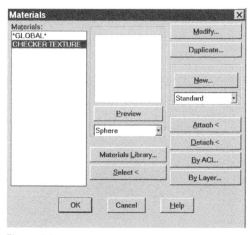

Figure 1-6

press the Enter key. This restores the Materials dialog box. Click the OK button to end the RMAT command.

Invoke the RENDER command again. Make certain that the Apply Materials option is on, and click the Render button. Your rendering should look similar to the one in Figure 1-7. The blue-and-white tile-like pattern on the 3D face surface is from a bitmap file named checkers.tga. If you were to view that file with AutoCAD's REPLAY command, or with an external graphics program, you would see that it looks exactly like the image on the 3D face in your rendering. AutoCD automatically scales bitmap images to fit the size and shape of the surface they are attached to.

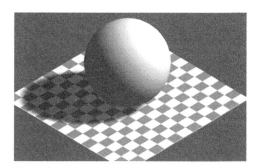

Figure 1-7

Next, you will add material properties to the sphere. Invoke the RMAT command again. When the Materials dialog box is displayed, notice that on its right side is a New button. Make certain that the word *Standard* is shown in the list box directly below the New button, and then click the New button. A dialog box titled New Standard Material appears.

Enter any name you like in the Material Name edit box, as shown in Figure 1-8, as long as it has 16 or fewer characters and spaces. On the left side of the dialog box is a cluster of radio buttons for setting material attribute parameters. Check the Transparency attribute and go to the Value edit box. For transparency, value represents the fraction of light that passes through material. When transparency is 0, no light passes through the material — it is completely opaque. Conversely, when transparency is 1, all light passes through the material — it is completely clear. Set a value of about 0.50 by entering it directly in the edit box or by using the slider bar. Then, click the OK button to leave the dialog box.

When you are back in the Materials dialog box, highlight the name of your new material if it is not already highlighted and click the Attach button. When the dialog box temporarily disappears, pick a point on the sphere and press the Enter key to bring back the dialog box. Lastly, click the OK button to end the RMAT command.

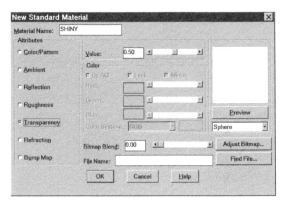

Figure 1-8

Figure 1-9

When you render the current viewport this time, your rendering with the transparent sphere should look similar to the one in Figure 1-9. You might notice that as you add features to the rendering, rendering times take progressively longer. You can use the STATS command to see exactly how long each rendering takes, as well as other details about the rendering and the current rendering settings.

The last changes you will make in material attributes will cause the sphere to be reflective as well as transparent. Start RMAT. In the Materials dialog box, highlight the name you assigned to your transparent material and click the Modify button. This brings up a dialog box identical to the New Standard Material dialog box you used before, but titled Modify Standard Material. Activate the Reflection attribute radio button, and set the value of reflection to 1.00. Below the slider bar for value is a Mirror check box that was grayed-out until you selected the Reflection attribute. Click this check box, click the OK button to return to the Materials dialog box, and click its OK button to exit the RMAT command.

Figure 1-10

Start the RENDER command. This time, set Rendering Type to Photo Raytrace, and then click the Render button to render the view in the current viewport. The rendering takes a relatively long time, perhaps even two minutes, depending upon your computer and the number of pixels involved in the rendering. Your rendering should be similar to the one shown in grayscale in Figure 1-10.

That finishes this exercise. On the CD-ROM that accompanies this book, the 3D model and the rendering parameters associated with it are in the file f1715.dwg. You will not use this model in the future, so you do not need to keep it. Before you discard it, however, you might want to try out some of the other options of the RENDER command — such as Query for Selection, Crop Window, and Sub Sampling.

| | |
|---|---|
| Command: | RENDER |
| Purpose: | Rendering operations for making shaded images of 3D models are implemented through this command. |
| Initiate with: | • On the command line, enter RENDER. |
| | • From the View pull-down menu, select Render, and from the resulting flyout menu, select Render. |
| | • Select the Render button from the Render toolbar. |

Options: This command displays the Render dialog box, unless rendering preferences have been set to not display it, for you to select rendering options and to initiate the rendering operation. Changes made to the settings in this dialog box remain in effect until they are specifically changed. The rendering parameters also remain in the drawing file's data base.

   • Rendering Type    Select one of the three rendering types from this drop-down list box.

     • Render    Only basic shading, lights, and materials are supported by this rendering type. It does not support shadows, transparent or reflective materials, or materials with bitmaps. It

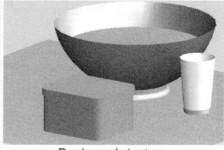

Render rendering type

is, however, considerably faster than the other two rendering types.

- Photo Real | This rendering type has all the features of the Render type, plus it supports shadows, transparent materials, bitmap-based materials, and landscape objects.

Photo Real rendering type

- Photo Raytrace | In addition to the features of Photo Real rendering, Photo Raytrace rendering supports reflective materials and refracted light beams.

Photo Raytrace rendering type

- Scene to Render | All existing scenes are displayed in this list box. The current viewport's view and light installations are listed as *current view* in this list box. Highlight the name of the scene you want to render.

- Rendering Procedure

  - Query for Selections | When this toggle is checked, you are prompted to select objects after you click the Render button. Only the selected objects are rendered, and the other objects disappear during the rendering.

  - Crop Window | When this check box is selected, AutoCAD clears the screen after you click the Render button and asks you to draw a rectangular window. Only objects within the window are rendered. This option is available only when the rendering destination is the current viewport.

  - Skip Render Dialog | In subsequent calls to the RENDER command, the Render dialog box is not displayed when this toggle is checked. The current render settings are used for the rendering. After this toggle is set, you must use the RPREF command to turn it off.

- Light Icon Scale | Use this edit box to change the relative size of the blocks AutoCAD uses to mark the locations of distant, spot, and point lights.

- Smoothing Angle

The value in this edit box tells the renderer the size of the angle between faces on polygon mesh surfaces at which their common edge is to be interpreted as a sharp edge. If the angle between two faces is equal or less than this value, their edge will be smoothed. If the angle is greater than this value, their common edge will be kept sharp. This value has an effect only if the Smooth Shade rendering option is on. Also, it has no effect on objects other than polygon mesh surfaces. Its default setting is 45 degrees.

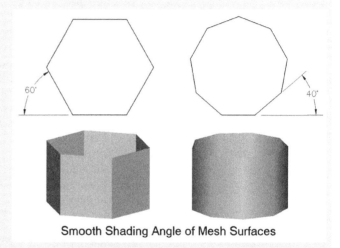

Smooth Shading Angle of Mesh Surfaces

- Rendering Options
  - Smooth Shade

When this check box is selected, rendered edges between faces on polygon mesh surfaces are smoothed, pro-

Faceted Shading        Smooth Shading

vided the angle between the faces is equal or less than the current smoothing angle. When this check box is off, each face on a polygon mesh appears as a distinct facet.

  - Apply Materials

Unless this toggle is turned on, materials that have been created and attached to objects through the RMAT command have no effect. All objects are rendered using AutoCAD's default material properties.

- Shadows

Shadows are generated in the rendering when this box is checked, provided shadows have been specified

Shadows Off          Shadows On

within one or more installed lights within the scene to be rendered. This option is available only for Photo Real and Photo Raytrace rendering.

- Render Cache

When this option is selected, AutoCAD writes some of the information it needs for renderings in a cache file on the computer's hard disk. This can save time in subsequent renderings, especially when 3D solids are involved. The cache file is rewritten whenever changes in the view or object geometry have been made.

- More Options

Clicking on this button brings up one of three dialog boxes having options appropriate

Backfaces Rendered     Backfaces Discarded     Backfaces Reversed and Discarded

to the rendering type. All these boxes have an option to discard backfaces and an option to reverse backfaces. Only surface objects have backfaces. By default they are rendered, and you will probably never need to discard them during renderings, or switch backfaces with frontfaces.

Photo Real and Photo Raytrace renderings also have the following options:

*Anti-aliasing.* This sets the level of control for smoothing jagged diagonal lines in renderings. You can choose between Minimal, Low, Medium, and High, with Minimal being the default setting. Setting Anti-aliasing to High results in the smoothest lines, but rendering times increase.

*Texture Map Sampling.* This option lets you choose the sampling method for bitmap images used in materials when the view is very close or very distant. You will probably always use the default method.

*Shadow Map Controls.* This option allows you to set the minimum and maximum bias levels for shadow maps. The default values generally work satisfactorily.

In addition to these options, Photo Raytrace rendering also has the following two options:

*Adaptive Sampling.* Photo Raytrace rendering can use a special sampling technique to accelerate the anti-aliasing process when anti-aliasing is set above the minimal level. You can enable or disable this method, and you also can set its sampling sensitivity. Most likely, you will always accept the default settings.

*Ray Tree Depth.* This option has two controls that affect the ray tree. You are not likely to ever change the default settings.

| | |
|---|---|
| • Destination | The pull-down list box offers three different output options. |
| • Viewport | This output option renders the selected scene in the current viewport. The dimensions of the viewport, in pixels, are listed below the list box, along with the bitmap color depth. |
| • Render Window | The rendering is sent to an operating system window titled Render, where it is displayed using the pixel resolution and color depth listed below the Destination list box. From the Render window, you can print the rendering, save it in a BMP bitmap file format, or save it in the Windows Clipboard. AutoCAD automatically opens the Render window when you send your rendering to it. You also can open it yourself by clicking the Render button on the Windows taskbar. |
| • File | This option saves the rendering in a bitmap file. The default resolution of the file, in pixels, and its color depth are displayed below the Destination list box. The More Options button is activated, and from there you can choose to save the rendering as a BMP, PCX, Postscript, TGA, or TIFF file. Additional options allow you to control the file's resolution and color depth. You even can set the rendering's resolution and color depth to values that exceed those of your computer system. |
| • Sub Sampling | This option allows you to reduce rendering time while retaining such features as shadows and reflections by combining rows of pixels in the rendering. It is useful when you are establishing parameters in a preliminary rendering. |

Sub Sampling combines rows of pixels. It is sometimes useful when you are making preliminary renderings.

Select a ratio from the drop-down list box to set the number of rows that are to be combined. These ratios range from 1:1 (which renders every row) to 8:1 (which combines eight rows in one).

|   |   |
|---|---|
| • Background | Clicking this button brings up the same dialog box used by the BACKGROUND command. |
| • Fog/Depth Cue | When this button is clicked, the same dialog box used by the FOG command is displayed. |
| • Render | Click this button to start the rendering process and end the RENDER command. AutoCAD reports the progress of the rendering on the command line as it performs its calculations, and you can stop the rendering at any time by pressing the Esc key. |
|   | If you are rendering to the current viewport, the rendered scene remains until a redraw or screen regen takes place. If the rendering destination is a file, AutoCAD displays a file dialog box for you to specify the name and location of the file. If the destination is the Render Window, that window is displayed in front of the AutoCAD graphics screen. |

| | |
|---|---|
| Command: | RPREF |
| Purpose: | The RPREF command allows you to establish rendering parameters without performing a rendering operation. |
| Initiate with: | • On the command line, enter RPREF. |
| | • From the View pull-down menu, select Render, and from the resulting flyout menu, select Preferences. |
| | • Select the Rendering Preferences button from the Render toolbar. |
| Options: | This command uses a dialog box that is the same as the one used by the RENDER command, except for its title (Rendering Preferences rather than Render), and that it has an OK button instead of a Render button. (See the discussion on the RENDER command for a description of the dialog box and the options it contains.) |
| Notes: | • You might occasionally use the RPREF command to establish rendering parameters when you do not want to perform a rendering. You have to use RPREF when the Skip Render Dialog toggle is on and you want to change the current rendering parameters. |

| Command: | BACKGROUND |
|---|---|
| Purpose: | This command controls the appearance of areas within the rendering that are not filled with objects. |
| Initiate with: | • On the command line, enter BACKGROUND. |
| | • From the View pull-down menu, select Render, and from the resulting flyout menu, select Background. |
| | • Select the Background button from the Render toolbar. |
| Options: | The BACK-GROUND command uses a dialog box, titled Background, for you to specify how areas within the rendering that are not filled with objects are to appear. You also can access this dialog box from the RENDER command. |

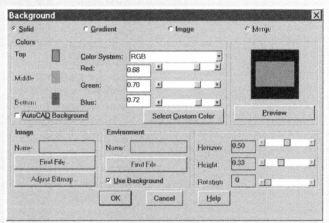

The dialog box gives you three options for controlling the background, plus one for controlling whether the render buffer is cleared before rendering and one that affects the relationship between objects with reflective (mirror-like) materials and the background. The first four options — solid, gradient, image, and merge — are selected through four radio buttons at the top of the dialog box. When you select the solid, gradient, or image options, appropriate clusters of buttons and edit boxes in the Background dialog box are activated. Clicking the Preview button of the dialog box shows the effects of the current background settings. The option affecting objects with mirror-like finishes is accessed through the buttons in the Environment section of the dialog box.

When you specify a color within the Background dialog box, you can use the edit boxes and slider bars for either the RGB (Red, Green, Blue) or the HLS (Hue, Lightness, Saturation) color systems. You also can click the Select Custom Color button to bring up the Color dialog box. Within this dialog box, you can choose from 48 basic colors that are shown in image tiles or you can specify a color by picking a point within a large image tile showing blended bands of colors.

- Solid

This, the default option, assigns one color to the background. If the AutoCAD Background check box is on, the current color of the AutoCAD

Solid background

graphics window is used for the rendering background. If this check box is cleared, the Colors section of the Background dialog box is activated for you to specify a color. The color you choose is reflected in the Top color tile, as well as in the preview panel when you click the Preview button.

- Gradient

This background option uses two or three colors in bands that blend together. To select the color of a particular band, click the color tile

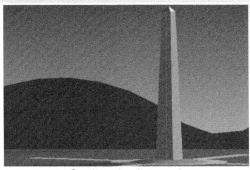

Gradient background

labeled Top, Middle, or Bottom, and then specify a color. The color tile changes in accordance with your selected color. Use just the top and bottom colors for a two-color gradient.

The relative location, width, and orientation of the color bands are controlled through the three edit boxes, and their corresponding sliders, located in the lower-right corner of the Background dialog box.

- Horizon establishes the center of the color band gradient. It represents the percent of viewport height.

- Height, which also represents a percent of screen height, determines where the second color of a three-color gradient begins. To use a two-color gradient, set Height to 0 and ignore the middle color.

- Rotation allows you to slant the color bands. You can specify any angle value between 90 degrees and -90 degrees. Positive angle values place the top color to the left, while negative angle values place it to the right.

- Image

Select this option to use the image in a bitmap file for the rendering background. The buttons in the Image section are activated for you to

Image background

specify the bitmap file. You can enter the bitmap file's name directly in the Name edit box  or click the Find File button to search for the file you want. The types of bitmap file formats you can use for background images are BMP, TGA, TIF, GIF, JPG, and PCX.

When you click the Adjust Bitmap button, AutoCAD displays the Adjust Background Bitmap Placement dialog box. The default setting in this dialog box is to fit the image to the screen. If the Fit to Screen check box is cleared, you can adjust the relative size of the image through the Scale edit boxes and sliders, and you can establish its

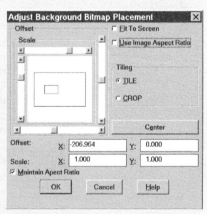

relative location through the Offset edit boxes and sliders. Scale values greater than 1 reduce the image size, while values less than 1 increase the image size.

When the Use Image Aspect Ratio check box is on, the proportions of the image are maintained. When this check box as well as the Maintain Aspect Ratio check box are cleared, you can distort the image by using different scales in the X and Y directions. You can center the image by setting the X and Y offsets to 0 or by clicking the Center button.

When scale values are greater than 1 (thus reducing the relative image size), the image is repeated to fill the entire background when the TILE radio button is selected. When the CROP radio button is selected, the image appears just one time, and does not completely fill the background if the image scale is greater than 1.

• Merge

Normally, AutoCAD clears the render buffer at the beginning of each rendering and repaints the entire viewport. If the Merge radio button is selected, however, the current render buffer is retained, and any differences in the new rendering are combined with the existing rendering. This can be useful when you are working with complicated renderings. Merge, however, does not work well when the Crop Window option of the RENDER command is in effect, because AutoCAD clears the screen before it prompts you to specify the crop window.

• Environment

When either Photo Real or Photo Raytrace rendering is used, objects that have a mirror-like material attached reflect the background (see the discussion of the RMAT command in Chapter 19 for information about mirror-like materials). This occurs when colors,

Object with a mirror-like surface reflecting the background image's checkerboard pattern

Same object reflecting an environment map image rather than the background image

either solid or gradient, and bitmap images are used for the background.

You can, however, have the mirror-like object reflect the image within a bitmap file rather than the rendering background. To do this, clear the Use Background check box. The Name edit box and the Find File button are then activated for you to specify a file to be reflected from the mirror-like objects in the rendering. The same bitmap file formats that can be used for background images can be used for environment maps.

As long as the Use Background check box is cleared and a file for the environment map has been specified, AutoCAD automatically attaches the file's image to all objects in the rendering that have mirror-like surfaces — you do not need to explicitly attach the image to objects.

Notes:

- The dialog boxes that AutoCAD uses to find bitmap files for background images and environment maps are initially set to display only BMP files. Use the drop-down list box to specify bitmap files having other formats.

Command:      SAVEIMG

Purpose:      SAVEIMG saves the image within the current viewport to a bitmap file.

Initiate with:

- On the command line, enter SAVEIMG.

- From the Tools pull-down menu, select Display Image, and from the resulting fly-out menu, select Save.

Options:      SAVEIMG displays the Save Image dialog box that allows you to save the image within the current viewport in any of three bitmap formats: BMP, TGA, or TIF. Options for the TGA and TIF formats also allow you to compress the files. By default, the entire viewport is saved, but you can specify an area within it to be saved by picking two points in the image tile labeled Active Viewport. AutoCAD draws a box representing the viewport area to be saved and displays the coordinates, in pixels, in edit boxes. You also can specify the area by entering numbers in the edit boxes. When the OK button is clicked, AutoCAD displays a dialog box for you to specify a name and location for the bitmap file.

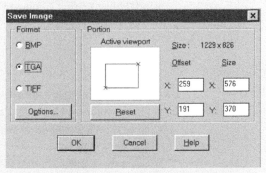

Notes:

- In Release 13 and earlier versions of AutoCAD, SAVEIMG has an option for saving the contents of the current viewport, the contents of all viewports in the graphics area, or of the entire screen, including the menus. Beginning with Release 14, however, SAVEIMG can save the contents of only the current viewport.

- SAVEIMG is probably more useful for saving wireframe, outline, or shaded images than for saving rendered images, because the RENDER command offers more options for file type, resolution, and color depth.

| | |
|---|---|
| Command: | REPLAY |
| Purpose: | REPLAY displays the image within a bitmap file in the current viewport. |
| Initiate with: | • On the command line, enter REPLAY. |
| | • From the Tools pull-down menu, select Display Image, and from the resulting fly-out menu, select View. |
| Options: | REPLAY is strictly for viewing the image in a bitmap file. You cannot use the image in any way, and it disappears when the viewport is redrawn. The bitmap file formats that can be displayed are BMP, TGA, and TIF. Each pixel of the bitmap file is mapped to a pixel in the current viewport — there is no provision for enlarging or reducing the image. You can, however, specify the location of the image within the viewport, and you also can clip part of the image. If the image is larger than the size of the current viewport, the image is clipped at the viewport borders. |
| Notes: | • REPLAY is a convenient way to view the contents of a bitmap file, especially if you do not have a graphics file viewing program. |
| | • You also can view the contents of bitmap files through AutoCAD's IMAGE command. However, that command is for inserting bitmaps in a drawing, not just for viewing them. Consequently, it is more involved to use. |

| | |
|---|---|
| Command: | STATS |
| Purpose: | This command displays information and data about the last rendering. |
| Initiate with: | • On the command line, enter STATS. |
| | • From the View pull-down menu, select Render, and from the resulting flyout menu, select Statistics. |
| | • Select the Statistics button from the Render toolbar. |
| Implementation: | The information about the last rendering is displayed in a read-only list box within the Statistics dialog box. You can save this information by selecting the Save Statistics to File check box and entering a filename. You must supply the extension to the file-name. If the file exists, AutoCAD adds the data from the most recent rendering to the end of the file. The file is in ASCII format, which can be read and edited by Windows' Notepad text editor. |

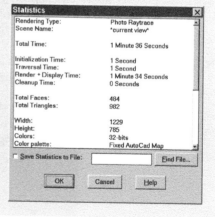

# CHAPTER 18

# Lights in Renderings

*Lights are an essential component of renderings, and you will install a variety of lights in each of your renderings to obtain a realistic representation of your model.*

*This chapter*

- *describes the properties of rendering lighting;*

- *discusses the four types of AutoCAD rendering lights — ambient lights, distant lights, point lights, and spotlights;*

- *explains how to cast shadows with rendering lights;*

- *tells you how to use the numerous dialog boxes of the LIGHT command;*

- *tells you what scenes are, how to use them, and how to create them.*

Most of this chapter is devoted to the one AutoCAD command — LIGHT — that both creates rendering lights and modifies them after they have been installed. In addition to lighting, the parameters for viewing the objects that are to be rendered is also very important. Because lights and views are such important components of a rendering, AutoCAD has a special command — SCENE — for combining and managing them.

Menus and toolbar buttons for lights and scenes

## Properties of Rendering Lighting

A key characteristic in AutoCAD lighting, as well as in real-world lighting, is that surfaces directly facing a light are brighter than surfaces that are inclined to the light. This is illustrated by the 16-sided extruded polygon in the following figure. The face on the polygon that directly faces the incoming light beams, which are traveling in the same direction as the view's line of sight, is the brightest, and the brightness of the other faces is directly proportional to their angle with the light beams. The more a face is inclined to the light beams, the dimmer it is. This characteristic is what shading is all about, and you place your lights to take advantage of it.

The 3D cube on the left side of the next figure is illuminated by a single light whose beams are at the same angle to the three visible surfaces of the cube. The rendering of the cube is simply a blob, with no evidence that it is a 3D object. In the rendering on the right side of the figure, however, the light has been rotated so that its light beams strike the three visible surfaces at different angles. In this rendering, there is no doubt that the object is a cube, even though the viewpoint is the same as in the other rendering.

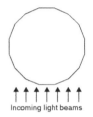

Incoming light beams

Although AutoCAD's lights are able to simulate this property of real lights, as well as some others that will be mentioned shortly, they are unlike real lights in other ways. For one thing, you cannot see an AutoCAD light. You can see the results of the light as it shines on objects, but you cannot see the light itself, as you can a glowing light bulb or the sun.

Also, AutoCAD lights pass completely through objects to illuminate other objects. This is shown on the left in the next figure, where the same sixteen-sided polygon solid shown earlier now has a round hole through it. An AutoCAD light aimed directly at the side of this object illuminates the

The brightness of a face depends on its angle with incoming light beams.

outside faces of the solid as you would expect, but it also illuminates the inside hole in the solid. This characteristic can be annoying at times and beneficial at other times. When you add shadows to lights, this effect is diminished, as shown in the rendering on the right in the same figure.

Although AutoCAD's rendering lights are white by default, they can be given color. However, colored lights significantly add to the complexity of renderings, and the results do not necessarily follow the standard rules for mixing colors. A blue light shining on a yellow surface, for instance, will not make the surface green, or even blue. Furthermore, because you cannot see rendering lights, the effects are not the same as those of colored lights in a theater or on an electrical panel. For example, you cannot simulate a warning light by placing a red point light on the surface of a model. You must instead reflect a light from an object that represents the warning light, and the results are the same regardless of whether a white light is reflected from a red surface or a red light is reflected from a white surface. As you will see in the next chapter, you can use rendering materials to assign colors to specific surface objects, and in almost all cases it is better to handle color through material than through lights. Generally, you will leave rendering lights white.

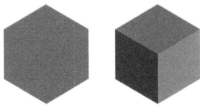

The faces on this cube are not evident when the light beams have the same angle as the view.

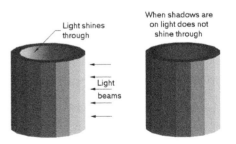

Light shines through

When shadows are on light does not shine through

Light beams

AutoCAD's rendering lights can vary in brightness, or intensity, just as real lights do. Each light is assigned an intensity value that has no units. Its effect is on the relative brightness of the objects illuminated by the light. Thus, surfaces reflecting a light that has an intensity of 0.5 will be darker than those reflecting a light that has an intensity of 1.0. The maximum intensity value that you can assign to a light depends on the light's type and sometimes on the extent of the AutoCAD drawing area. For many types of rendering lights, intensity can range from 0 to 1, but a point light for the model of a large structure can have an intensity of several hundred thousand. You can assign an intensity value of 0 to a light, which has the effect of turning the light off. The specifics of intensity values are discussed later in this chapter during the descriptions of AutoCAD light types.

All real light becomes dimmer as distance from the light source increases. This is true even for the sun, although it is not apparent because of the great initial intensity of the sun's light. Similar to real lights, AutoCAD point lights and spotlights can be set to become dimmer with distance. AutoCAD refers to this falloff of intensity as *attenuation*. AutoCAD distant lights, which imitate sunlight, cannot be attenuated.

Attenuation in point lights and spotlights can be set to have one of two falloff rates:

- *Inverse linear attenuation*. The light's intensity is inversely proportional to distance from the light. For instance, an object twice as far from the light source as another object is one-half as bright.

- *Inverse square attenuation*. The light's intensity decreases in inverse proportion to the square of the distance from the light. Thus, an object twice as far from the light source as another object is one-fourth as bright.

Attenuation causes lights to become dimmer as distance from the light source increases.

You also can turn off attenuation in point lights and spotlights so that objects far from the light are just as bright as objects close to the light.

## AutoCAD Light Types

AutoCAD supports four different types of rendering lights, each with characteristics that make them suitable for specific rendering lighting tasks. With the exception of ambient light, each light is given a unique name, and you can install as many lights in as many combinations as you like. Only one ambient light can exist, and it does not have a name. You can use the SCENE command to associate particular lights with particular views of a 3D model.

AutoCAD inserts a block at the location of each light (again, with the exception of ambient light). The type of block inserted indicates the type of light installed, and the name assigned to a light is shown as a visible attribute of the block. Other information AutoCAD needs about the light's parameters is stored as invisible attributes. You can adjust the scale of these blocks through the Light Icon Scale edit box used by the RENDER and RPREF commands.

## Ambient Light

Ambient light sets the overall level of illumination in a rendering. It has no particular source, no light beams, and cannot cast shadows. Even though ambient light can not shade objects or produce realistic renderings by itself, it does give you some control over the relative brightness of shaded areas.

Ambient light, which is set from the main Lights dialog box of the LIGHT command, applies to the entire rendering. Its intensity can range from 0 to 1, with 0.30 as its default intensity. Generally, you will initially leave ambient light set to its default value until you set the other lights, and then increase its value if your rendering has areas that are too dark, or decrease its value if your rendering is overly bight. You can assign a color to ambient light. Ambient light is not assigned a name.

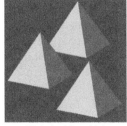

High Ambient Light          Low Ambient Light

## Distant Lights

A distant light is comparable to light from the sun as it strikes the Earth. Its light beams are all traveling in the same direction, and the light source seems far away. Although each distant light has a specific location, the direction in which the light is pointing is the important parameter. Location is of no consequence because, as shown in the accompanying figure, even objects that are behind a distant light are illuminated by it.

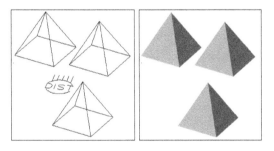

AutoCAD places a block named DIRECT at the installed location of a distant light. This block is in the form of a circle with five parallel lines, indicating the light's direction, on one side of the circle and the assigned name of the light in the middle of the circle. Initially, AutoCAD aims a new distant light in the current view direction, and it inserts the block in the center of the viewport. You can move and rotate the block to move and re-aim the distant light, and you can reposition or re-aim the light through several options in the LIGHT command's dialog box for distant lights.

The intensity of distant lights can be set to any value between 0 and 1. Their light intensity cannot be attenuated. Distant lights can cast shadows, and you can give them a color.

Distant light is useful for providing general illumination in a rendering, and generally each of your renderings will have at least one distant light. In renderings of exterior scenes, sunlight is generally simulated with a distant light. Because distant lights are so often used for sunlight, AutoCAD's LIGHT command uses the terms azimuth and altitude in aiming distant lights, and it provides a special sun angle calculator for aiming them according to the position of the sun at a specific time and date for various geographic locations.

## Point Lights

Light beams from a point light radiate in all directions from a point in 3D space. The lights are similar to a candle or to a bare incandescent light bulb. When installing a point light, you specify its location — you do not aim it.

AutoCAD inserts a block, named OVERHEAD, at the point light's location. This block looks like a circle with short lines, representing light beams, pointing in all directions from its perimeter. The name of the light is shown in the middle of the circle. AutoCAD locates a new point light in the center of the current viewport. You can move it by moving its block or by specifying a point through an option in the LIGHT command's dialog box for point lights.

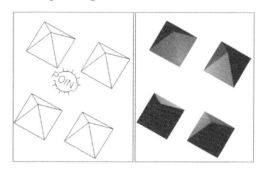

The intensity of point lights can be attenuated, using either inverse linear or inverse square falloff rates. Maximum allowed intensity varies according to the extent of the drawing area and to the falloff rate used. When attenuation is set to 0, intensity can range from 0 to 1.

Point lights are useful for emphasizing local areas of a model and for simulating street lamps and ceiling lights. Point lights can cast shadows, and they can be given a color.

## Spotlights

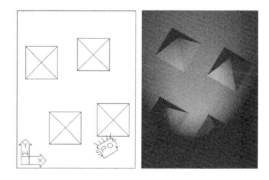

An AutoCAD spotlight sends out light in the shape of a cone, similar to a desk lamp or a theater spotlight. You must specify both a target point and a light point when you install a spotlight. By default, AutoCAD places the target for a new spotlight in the center of the current viewport and the light about 1 unit from the target toward the viewer.

A block, named SH_SPOT, is inserted by AutoCAD at the spotlight's location. It is in the form of a square, with five short lines pointing toward the target and with the name of the light in the center of the square. You can move the block to move the light, and you can rotate it to re-aim the light. The target moves as the block is moved or rotated. You also can specify point location coordinates for the target and light through the dialog box that the LIGHT command uses for creating and modifying spotlights.

Spotlights send out two concentric cones of light. The inner cone is called the hotspot cone, and the outer one is called the falloff cone. The intensity of light in the hotspot cone is constant throughout the disk of the cone, while the intensity of light in the falloff cone diminishes from the center of the cone to its edges.

The angle of the hotspot cone can equal that of the falloff cone, but it cannot exceed it. When the two cones have the same angle, the edge of the spotlight is sharp. When the hotspot cone is smaller than the falloff cone, the edge of the light gradually fades away, producing a soft edge. You must use Photo Real or Photo Raytrace rendering for these effects to be evident. The cone angles, which are specified through the LIGHT command, can range from 0 to 160 degrees.

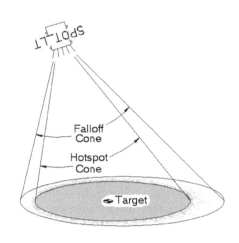

This fading in light intensity across the falloff cone is not the same as attenuation, which is the loss of intensity as distance from the light source increases. You can, however, specify either inverse linear or inverse square attenuation for spotlights. Their maximum allowed intensity varies according to the extent of the drawing area and the falloff rate used. When attenuation is set to 0, spotlight intensity can range from 0 to 1.

Spotlights are useful for brightening specific areas of a 3D model and for simulating the effects of artificial lighting. They can cast shadows, and they can be colored.

Installing a spotlight is more involved than installing a distant light or a point light because more parameters must be specified. You must locate the light and its target, set its cone angles, and set its intensity. Furthermore, the size of the area illuminated by a point light depends upon its distance from the surface and the size of the cone angles. One good technique for positioning a spotlight is to place the target in a spot that will be approximately in the center of the light beams and on the surface you want to illuminate. Then, use relative spherical coordinates to specify the light's location. This can be done through the Modify button of the New/Modify Spotlight dialog box.

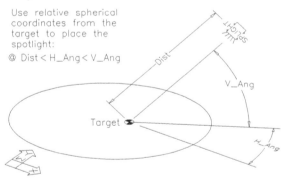

## Shadows

Both Photo Real and Photo Raytrace rendering allow you to have one of two types of shadows. In Photo Real rendering, AutoCAD's lights can cast shadows by either generating volumetric shadows or by using *shadow maps*. Photo Raytrace rendering can also use shadow maps to generate shadows, but the other choice for shadow type is *ray traced shadows* rather than volumetric shadows.

You make your choice for a shadow type within the LIGHT command by picking the Shadow Options button in the New/Modify dialog box for the light type you are working with. This will bring up the Shadow Options dialog box. If you want volumetric or ray traced shadows, click the Shadow Volumes/Ray Traced Shadows check box. If you want the shadows generated from shadow maps, clear the Shadow Volumes/Ray Traced Shadows check box.

Visually, the difference between the shadow types is that volumetric and ray traced shadows have sharp edges, while shadow map shadows have soft, or blurred, edges. Volumetric and ray traced shadows also can transmit color from transparent and translucent objects. Shadow map shadows can be more accurate than volumetric shadows, but they tend to pull away from the object casting the shadow, and they sometimes affect the appear-

Volumetric shadows and ray traced shadows

Shadow map shadows

ance of objects outside the shadows. Furthermore, shadow map shadows slow rendering speeds significantly. Ray traced shadows have the same appearance as volumetric shadows, but they are more accurate, and in complex renderings, they can even be faster.

The Shadow Options dialog box contains several options that apply only to shadow map shadows. The Shadow Map Size option gives you some control over the accuracy of the shadows. You can pick the shadow map size from a list of set values ranging from 64 to 4,096 pixels through a pull-down list box. The larger the shadow map, the greater its accuracy and the slower its rendering. You also can control the softness of the shadow edges. And, for point and distant lights, you can pick specific objects that are to cast shadows. This option is not available for spotlights. Additional controls for shadow maps can be accessed through the More Options button in the Render and Render Preferences dialog boxes.

To have shadows in renderings, Photo Real or Photo Raytrace rendering must be used, and shadows must be enabled in the Render or Render Preferences dialog box as well as in the dialog box for the lights that are to make the shadows.

Click here to use volumetric shadows or ray traced shadows. Otherwise, shadow map shadows will be used.

Increasing this number increases the accuracy of shadow map shadows and rendering times.

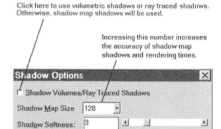

Controls the fuzziness of shadow map shadow edges.

This option is available only for shadow map shadows. It allows you to specify the objects that are to cast shadows.

# Installing Lights

Although it is not inherently difficult to install rendering lights, it is almost a trial-and-error process that can be tedious. Typically, while installing a light, you go through several cycles of adjusting its properties, and then rendering the scene to view the results. Furthermore, there is an infinite combination of light types and properties, and many combinations are equally satisfactory. Installing lights, like most rendering steps, is a subjective process.

The best strategy for lighting a rendering is to first install a key light that will provide general illumination. Often, this is a distant light, and you should aim it so that as many surfaces and edges as possible in the rendering stand out. If you want this light to cast shadows, you need to also consider which direction the shadows are to be in. When the parameters of this key light are as you want them, look the rendering over closely to determine which areas need further illumination — perhaps to make a surface brighter or to make edges stand out. Then, if needed, take care of one of these areas by installing a second light, using a light type suitable for the area and what you want to accomplish. When the lighting for that area is as you want it, you can install a third light, perhaps a fourth one, and maybe even a fifth one. Too many lights, however, can make the rendering overly complicated, and the lights will begin to cancel each other's effects.

Using multiple small viewports helps reduce rendering times as you adjust lights, and they also help you compare results when you add or change lights. If you are rendering a perspective view, you will find it helpful to have at least one viewport that has a non-perspective view so you can use your pointing device when setting light and target locations.

### Exercise One

This simple exercise demonstrates some important principles that you should consider when you install rendering lights. Locate and open file f1814.dwg on the CD-ROM that accompanies this book. This file contains the 3D solid model of a small mechanical part that is lying on the WCS X-Y plane as shown in Figure 1-1.

Use AutoCAD's VIEW command to switch to the view named ISO_SE _50. Then, you might want to use the 4 option of the command line version of VPORTS to divide the AutoCAD graphics area into four viewports. This step is optional, but it helps you compare the effects of various lighting parameters.

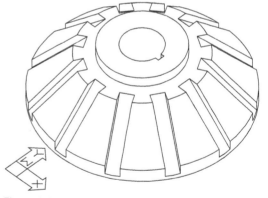

Figure 1-1

First, make a rendering without any installed lights. Just invoke the RENDER command and render the current viewport. AutoCAD makes the rendering using a single distant light pointed in the view direction. The results are not bad, but the rendering has little contrast between surfaces on the model, and some of the model's edges do not show up.

Start the LIGHT command, select Distant Light from the pull-down list box, and click the New button. Enter DIST_1 in the Name edit box, and set the light's parameters as follows:

| | |
|---|---|
| Intensity: | 1.0 |
| Azimuth: | 90 degrees |
| Altitude: | 45 degrees |
| Shadows: | On |
| Shadow Options: | Shadow Volumes/Ray Traced Shadows |
| Color: | White |

Leave ambient light set to its default value of 0.30. Render the current viewport. Make certain that rendering type is set to Photo Real and that Shadows are activated. Set the rendering background to any solid color of your choice. Your rendering of the current viewport should resemble the one shown in Figure 1-2.

Having shadows and shining the light from the right side improves the rendering, but there are still some edges that are not distinct, and the left side of the model is a little dark. Therefore, you will install another distant light. Name this second distant light DIST_2 and assign the following parameters to it:

Figure 1-2

| | |
|---|---|
| Intensity: | 0.33 |
| Azimuth: | 180 degrees |
| Altitude: | 25 degrees |
| Shadows: | On |
| Shadow Options: | Shadow Volumes/Ray Traced Shadows |
| Color: | White |

Your rendering should now look like the one in Figure 1-3. The shadows of the second light help delineate the upper round edges on the model, and they brighten up its left side. This model with the lights installed is in file f1816.dwg on the CD-ROM that comes with this book. These two lights represent just one of an infinite combination of lights and viewpoints that could be used in a rendering of this model; you might want to experiment further on your own.

Figure 1-3

### Exercise Two

This second exercise in installing lights is more complicated. You will install some lights in the surface model of a kitchen and dining room that was used in Exercise 2 of Chapter 7. This exercise uses a different version of the model, so find and open the file f1817.dwg on the CD-ROM. This model has a table, some chairs, a floor lamp, and a ceiling light in the dining area. Also, the color of all the layers has been set to white. You will install the lights in the dining area.

Use the VIEW command to restore the view named DINING_ROOM, which is pictured in Figure 2-1. This is a perspective view of the dining room as seen from the kitchen. Because it is a perspective view, you have to specify point coordinates from the keyboard. The drawing uses architectural units, so coordinates can be entered either as feet (which are used in this example) or as inches. Also, you might want to divide the graphics area into four viewports, so you can see the effect that each light has.

Install one distant light, one point light, and two spotlights using the following parameters. Leave ambient light set to its default of 0.30. To better see the effects of each light, you

Figure 2-1

should render the current viewport after installing each light. Use Photo Real rendering, and make certain that shadows are activated in the Render dialog box.

| Light type: | **Distant** |
| --- | --- |
| Name: | FILL |
| Intensity: | 0.45 |
| Azimuth: | 105.0 |
| Altitude: | -20.0 |
| Shadows: | None |
| Color: | White |
| Remarks: | Notice that this light points up. |

| Light type: | **Point** |
| --- | --- |
| Name: | CEILING |
| Intensity: | 75.0 |
| Attenuation: | Inverse Linear |
| Position: | 8',8',8.5' |
| Shadows: | On |
| Shadow Options: | Shadow Volumes/Ray Traced Shadows |
| Color: | White |

| Light type: | **Spotlight** |
| --- | --- |
| Name: | LMP_TOP |
| Intensity: | 13.0 |
| Attenuation: | Inverse Linear |
| Target Position: | 2',9',9' |
| Light Postion: | 2',9',5.5' |
| Hotspot cone: | 150 |
| Falloff cone: | 160 |
| Shadows: | None |
| Color: | White |
| Remarks: | Simulates light from the top of the floor lamp. |

| Light type: | **Spotlight** |
| --- | --- |
| Name: | LMP_BTM |
| Intensity: | 50.0 |
| Attenuation: | Inverse Linear |
| Target Position: | 2',9',0 |
| Light Position: | 2',9',5.5' |
| Hotspot cone: | 125 |
| Falloff cone: | 160 |
| Shadows: | On |
| Shadow Options: | Shadow Volumes/Ray Traced Shadows |
| Color: | White |
| Remarks: | Simulates light from the bottom of the floor lamp. |

With all four lights installed, your rendering should resemble Figure 2-2. On the CD-ROM, the model with the installed lights is in file f1818.dwg.

### Exercise Three

In this exercise, you will install some lights for a rendering of the 3D house you built as a surface model in Section 2. Find the file f1819.dwg on the CD-ROM. This version of the model has some 3D surfaces that will serve as backgrounds for the rendering. Open the file and restore the view named DIST_80. (This is the perspective view you set up during an exercise in Chapter 7.) The model as seen in this view is shown in Figure 3-1. Because this is a perspective view, you will not be able to use your pointing device.

Figure 2-2

Install three distant lights and one point light, using the following parameters. Leave ambient light set to its default value of 0.30. To see the effects of the lights, you should render the current viewport after installing each light. You might also want to divide the AutoCAD graphics area into four viewports so you can better compare the effects of the lights.

Figure 3-1

| Light type: | Distant |
| --- | --- |
| Name: | SUN |
| Intensity: | 1.00 |
| Azimuth: | 136.0 |
| Altitude: | 45.0 |
| Shadows: | On |
| Shadow Options: | Shadow Volumes/Ray Traced Shadows |
| Color: | White |

| Light type: | Distant |
| --- | --- |
| Name: | FILL |
| Intensity: | 0.20 |
| Azimuth: | -90.0 |
| Altitude: | 21.0 |
| Shadows: | Off |
| Color: | White |
| Light type: | Distant |
| Name: | FRONT |
| Intensity: | 0.33 |
| Azimuth: | -155.0 |
| Altitude: | 0 |
| Shadows: | Off |
| Color: | White |
| Light type: | Point |
| Name: | POINT_1 |
| Intensity: | 15.0 |
| Attenuation: | Inverse Linear |
| Position: | 25',4',7' |
| Shadows: | Off |
| Color: | White |

Your final rendering will look similar to the one in Figure 3-2. At this stage, the rendering is not especially impressive. It will look more realistic when you add some materials and landscape objects to it. On the CD-ROM, the model with the three distant lights and one point light is in file f1820.dwg.

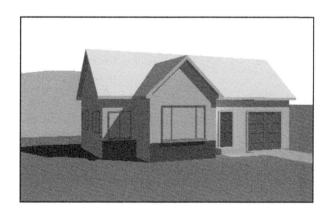

Figure 3-2

| | |
|---|---|
| Command: | LIGHT |
| Purpose: | All three different types of AutoCAD lights are installed and modified through this command. It also controls the intensity and color of ambient light. |
| Initiate with: | • On the command line, enter LIGHT. |
| | • From the View pull-down menu, select Render, and then Light. |
| | • Select the Lights button from the Render toolbar. |
| Options: | Dialog boxes are used in establishing all light parameters. When the LIGHT command is initiated, the Lights dialog box is displayed, and as you select options from that dialog box, appropriate secondary dialog boxes appear. The names of all lights currently installed in the drawing are displayed in a list box in the upper-left corner of this dialog box. A specific light in this list can be selected for modification or deletion by clicking on its name or by using the Select button. |

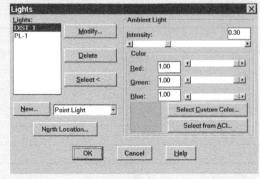

| | |
|---|---|
| • Modify | This button brings up a dialog box for modifying the selected light. Double-clicking the name of the light has the same effect as selecting the Modify button. |
| • Delete | Clicking this button deletes the selected light. An alert box asks you to confirm the action. |
| • Select | When you click this button, AutoCAD temporarily dismisses the Lights dialog box and issues a command line prompt asking you to select a light. Select one light by picking a point on the block AutoCAD has inserted at its location. The Lights dialog box reappears with the name of the light in the list box highlighted. |
| • New | Click this button to create a new point, spot, or distant light. AutoCAD replaces the Lights dialog box with one appropriate for the type of light specified in the drop-down list box to the right of the New button. |

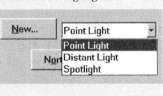

| | |
|---|---|
| • North Location | AutoCAD uses the metaphor of compass directions when aiming distant lights, and, by default, north points in the WCS Y-axis direction. You can change that by clicking this button. AutoCAD will display a dialog box named North Location, in which you can specify another direction on the X-Y plane as north, or specify that the Y axis of a saved UCS will be used rather than the Y axis of the WCS. |

- Ambient Light

This cluster of buttons, edit boxes, and sliders is for controlling the intensity and color of ambient light. Use the Intensity edit box, or the slider just below the edit box, to set the intensity of ambient light. Its minimum allowed value is 0, its maximum value is 1, and its default value is 0.30.

You can use any one of three methods to set the color of ambient light. One method is to specify values, ranging from 0 to 1, for the red, green, and blue color components either by entering them in the edit boxes or by using the sliders. Another 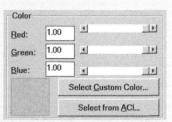 method is to click the Select Custom Color button. This brings up a dialog box titled Color that has 48 basic colors shown in image tiles for you to choose from, along with a large image tile showing blended bands of colors from which you can pick a point to specify a color. The third way to specify ambient light color is to click the Select from ACI button. This causes the same dialog box used by the DDCOLOR command, titled Select Color, to be displayed for you to specify one of the 255 colors in the AutoCAD Color Index (ACI). The default color of ambient light is white.

Point Light

AutoCAD displays the New Point Light dialog box when you create a point light, and it displays the Modify Point Light dialog box when you modify an existing point light. These two dialog boxes are the same, except for their title.

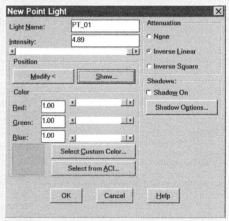

- Light Name

Use this edit box to enter the name of the new light or change the name of an existing light. Each light must have a name that has no more than eight characters. Spaces, asterisks, and question marks are not allowed in names.

- Intensity

The relative brightness of the point light is controlled through this edit box. You can enter values directly or with the slider below the edit box. The maximum intensity allowed depends on the light's attenuation and on the drawing extents.

- When attenuation is none, maximum intensity is 1.

- When attenuation is Inverse Linear, maximum intensity is equal to one-half the distance between the coordinates in the **extmin** and **extmax** system variables.

- When attenuation is Inverse Square, maximum intensity is equal to one-fourth the square of the distance between the coordinates in the **extmin** and **extmax** system variables.

- Position

  The two buttons in this cluster are related to the point coordinates of the light's location. When you click the Show button, AutoCAD displays the coordinates of the light's location in an information box. You can change the location of the point light by clicking the Modify button. AutoCAD temporarily dismisses the dialog box and issues a command line prompt for you to specify a new location. You can use any point selection method. Initially, AutoCAD places the point light in the center of the viewport.

- Color

  This cluster of buttons and sliders for setting the color of the point light is the same as the one in the main Lights dialog box for setting the color of ambient light. The default color of point lights is white.

- Attenuation

  These three radio buttons control the type of attenuation — the light intensity falloff rate — for the point light.

- Shadows

  The check box and button in this cluster control whether the light casts shadows, as well as its parameters for casting shadows. To enable shadows, click the Shadows On check box. When you click the Shadows Options button, AutoCAD displays the Shadows Options dialog box.

  When the Shadow Volumes/Ray Traced Shadows box is checked, AutoCAD uses volumetric shadows when Photo Real rendering is in effect and ray traced shadows when Photo Raytrace rendering is in effect. Both of these shadow types make sharp-edged shadows. When that check box is cleared, AutoCAD uses shadow maps, which make shadows having blurred edges. You can control the accuracy of the shadows through the Shadow Map Size pull-down list box, and you can control the relative fuzziness of their edges through the Shadow Softness edit box and slider. Generally, the default settings give satisfactory results.

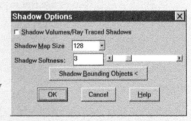

The Shadow Bounding Objects button is available only when shadow maps are being used. When you click this button, AutoCAD temporarily dismisses the dialog boxes and issues a command line prompt for you to select the objects that are to cast shadows. The light will not cast shadows for objects that are not selected.

**Distant Light**

When you install a new distant light, AutoCAD displays the New Distant Light dialog box, and when you modify an existing distant light, AutoCAD displays the Modify Distant Light dialog box. Except for their titles, these two dialog boxes are the same.

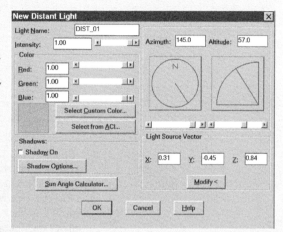

- **Light Name**    Use this edit box to enter the name of the new light or to change the name of an existing light. Names cannot have more than eight characters and cannot contain spaces, asterisks, or question marks.

- **Intensity**    Set the intensity of the distant light with the slider or by entering a value in the edit box. The maximum intensity allowed is 1. Distant light intensity cannot be attenuated.

- **Color**    Set the color of the distant light through the buttons, edit boxes, and sliders in this cluster. See the discussion for setting the color of ambient light in the main Lights dialog box for a description of this cluster. The default light color is white.

- **Shadows**    See the discussion of point lights for a description of the options available in this cluster.

- **Azimuth/Altitude**    These two parameters are used to aim the distant light. Azimuth is the light's horizontal angle from north, while altitude is its vertical angle from the X-Y plane. By default, north is in the direction of the WCS Y axis, but you can change it through the North Location dialog box accessed through the Lights dialog box. You can set azimuth and altitude by entering values in their edit boxes, by picking a point within the image tiles, or by moving the sliders located below the image tiles. A negative altitude is allowed, but you must enter it in the edit box. Initially, AutoCAD aims the light in the current viewing direction.

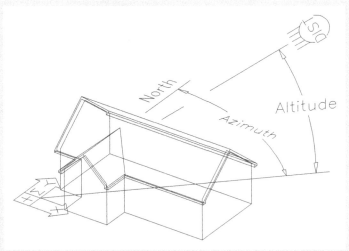

- Light
  Source Vector

The values in these three edit boxes are the coordinates of a direction vector. The distant light points in the same direction as that of a line drawn from the direction vector coordinates to the UCS origin. If you click the Modify button, AutoCAD temporarily dismisses the dialog box and issues command line prompts for two points:

```
Enter light direction TO <current>: (Specify a point.)
Enter light direction FROM <current>: (Specify a point.)
```

The light points in the direction from the second point to the first point. In these prompts, current is the actual word used — AutoCAD does not display the current target and direction vector points. You can use any method to specify the points. Relative coordinates are often useful for specifying the location of the second point.

- Sun Angle
  Calculator

When you click this button, AutoCAD displays the Sun Angle Calculator dialog box for you to find the angle of the sun for a specific date, time, latitude, and longitude. The azimuth and altitude of the distant light are set to correspond to the sun's angle.

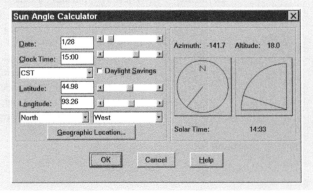

The Geographic Location button in this dialog box brings up a dialog box that enables you to set the latitude and longitude by selecting the name of a city from a list or by picking a point on a map in an image tile. Most regions of the world are included.

**Spotlight**

AutoCAD displays the New Spotlight dialog box when you install a new spotlight, and it displays the Modify Spotlight dialog box when you modify an existing one. Except for their titles, these two dialog boxes are the same.

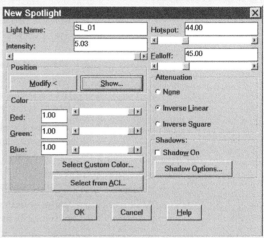

- **Light Name**  Enter the name of the new light or change the name of an existing light through this edit box. Light names can have up to eight characters. Spaces, asterisks and question marks are not allowed in light names.

- **Intensity**  This parameter controls the relative brightness of the spotlight. You can specify intensity by entering a value in the edit box or by moving the slider below the edit box. The maximum intensity allowed is dependent on the light's attenuation and on the drawing extents.

  - When attenuation is none, maximum intensity is 1.

  - When attenuation is Inverse Linear, maximum intensity is equal to one-half the distance between the coordinates in the **extmin** and **extmax** system variables.

  - When attenuation is Inverse Square, maximum intensity is equal to one-fourth the square of the distance between the coordinates in the **extmin** and **extmax** system variables.

- **Position**  Two points are required for positioning spotlights. One is the location of the spotlight, and the other is the location of its target. When you click the Show button, AutoCAD displays the coordinates of the light and of its target in a read-only dialog box.

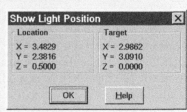

You can change these points by clicking the Modify button. AutoCAD temporarily dismisses the dialog box and issues command line prompts for you to specify two points:

```
Enter light target <current>: (Specify a point.)
Enter light location <current>: (Specify a point.)
```

In these prompts, current is the actual word used — AutoCAD does not display the current light target and location points. You can use any method to specify the points. Relative coordinates are often useful for specifying the location of the second point. Initially, AutoCAD places the target on the X-Y plane in the center of the current viewport and places the light about 1 unit away on the line of sight toward the viewer.

- Color

This cluster of buttons and sliders for setting the color of the spotlight is the same as the one in the main Lights dialog box for setting the color of ambient light. The default color of spotlights is white.

- Hotspot

Set the edge-to-edge taper angle of the spotlight's interior cone of uniform light by entering an angle value within this edit box or by moving the associated slider. The angle can range from 0 to 160 degrees, but it cannot exceed the falloff cone angle.

- Falloff

Specify the edge-to-edge taper angle of the spotlight's full cone of light by entering the value of an angle in this edit box or by moving the slider below the edit box. The angle can range from 0 (which effectively turns the light off) to 160 degrees. If the angle of the hotspot cone equals the angle of the falloff cone, the edge of the light beam is sharp.

- Attenuation

The three radio buttons in this cluster control the type of attenuation — the light intensity falloff rate — for the spotlight.

- Shadows

The controls for spotlight shadows work the same as those for point lights, except that the Shadow Casting Option is not available for spotlights.

Notes:

- After a light has been installed in a drawing, AutoCAD's HIDE command no longer works.

# Using Scenes

A scene is the association of a view with one or more lights. If you create a scene when no named views exist and no lights are installed, the scene consists of the current view and all the lights (even if none exist). However, to obtain any benefit from scenes, at least one named view should exist and at least one light should be installed. Views for scenes are created through AutoCAD's VIEW command. (Because VIEW is a 2D command that has long been part of AutoCAD, it is not described here.)

After a scene has been created, its name is shown in the Scenes to Render list box in the dialog box used by the RENDER command. You can render a scene — using the current viewport, the render window, or a file as a destination — even if the view for the scene is not currently displayed.

Command:          SCENE

Purpose:          This command associates a view with one or more lights. Scenes are named, and you can render a specific scene even if the view for the scene is not currently displayed.

Initiate with:      • On the command line, enter SCENE.

                • From the View pull-down menu, select Render, and then Scene.

                • Select the Scene button from the Render toolbar.

Options:          The initial dialog box used by the SCENE command displays the names of existing scenes in a list box. A scene named *NONE* is always included. This scene consists of the current view and all the existing lights. If no light has been installed, AutoCAD uses a single distant light pointed in the viewport's view direction during renderings.

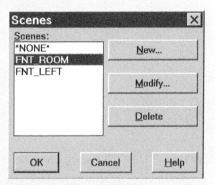

Click the New button to create a new scene. To modify an existing scene, click its name in the list box, and then click the Modify button. To delete a scene, click its name, and then click the Delete button.

The New and Modify buttons lead to dialog boxes that are identical except for their titles. Use the edit box in the upper-right corner of this dialog box to enter or modify the name of the scene. Scene names must be eight or fewer characters long. They cannot contain spaces, question marks, slashes, or asterisks.

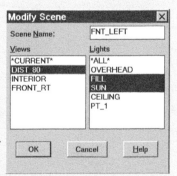

The names of all existing views are displayed in the left-hand list box. A view named *CUR-RENT*, representing the view in the current viewport, is always included. The names of all installed lights are shown in the right-hand list box. This list includes the name *ALL*, which represents all the installed lights, or the default distant light if none have been installed.

You can select only one view from the left-hand list box for each scene, but you can have any number of lights from the right-hand list box as part of the scene. To select multiple lights, hold down the Control key as you pick light names. Renderings of the scene will use the scene's view and only those lights that have been specified for the scene.

# CHAPTER 19

# Rendering Materials

*An AutoCAD rendering material is a set of properties that controls the appearance of a surface object during a rendering. For example, you can create a material that is shiny and red, and attach that material to one or more surface objects — such as a polygon mesh, a 3D face, or a 3D solid — to have those surfaces appear to be shiny and red when they are rendered.*

*This chapter*

- *describes the properties, or attributes as they are generally called, that can be assigned to a material;*

- *explains how bitmap images can be incorporated into rendering materials to simulate bricks, floor tile, and other pattered material;*

- *tells you how to adjust the scale and location of bitmap images to accommodate various surface shapes and orientations;*

- *discusses the mechanics of attaching and managing materials;*

- *describes how to assemble and save a collection of rendering materials.*

Materials are created through the RMAT command. Similar to the LIGHT command discussed in the previous chapter, RMAT is a flexible command that uses numerous dialog boxes to define a material. Because creating a material can be an involved process, each material is given a unique name, and you can save a material in a file so that it can be retrieved and used in other drawings. AutoCAD refers to these files of saved materials as *material libraries* and has a command, MATLIB, for managing them.

For simulating objects that have texture or patterns — such as wooden boards, brick walls, shingled roofs,

Menus and toolbar buttons for materials

galvanized steel, and tiled floors — you can include images from bitmap files in the properties of a material. Because bitmapped images are basically 2D rectangles, you often need to adjust them to fit surfaces that are cylindrical or spherical and to fit planar surfaces that are not aligned with the coordinate system axes. These adjustments are made through the SETUV command.

## Material Attributes

Every material is created by assigning values to certain properties, or attributes. Attributes affecting colors allow you to specify their color as well as their value. Descriptions of these attributes, along with the meaning of their values, are given in the following paragraphs.

### Color

Although all objects in the real world, except for those that are completely transparent, have color, their color is seldom uniform, especially if they are not planar. Their main color is darkened on surfaces that are inclined to incoming light beams, and surfaces directly facing incoming light beams may reflect the color of the light source. Because of these surface color variations, AutoCAD has three different attributes for controlling material color:

- *Color.* In the dialog boxes for setting material attributes, the name of the main color of the material is called simply Color. You can assign virtually any color you want to this attribute. The finish of the color is diffuse, or matte, similar to that of a flat wall paint. The relative brightness of surfaces having this base color depends on the value assigned to color, as well as the surface's angle to incoming light beams. (This phenomenon is described in the previous chapter in the discussion on the properties of rendering lighting.) You can assign color a value ranging from 0 to 1.

- *Ambient.* This is the base color of shaded areas. You can use an ambient color that is different from the material's main color. You also can control its relative brightness by assigning it a value between 0 and 1.

- *Reflection.* When you look directly into the light beams that are reflected from a surface, you indirectly see the color of the light source, as shown in the diagram to the right. As a result, areas of reflected light on a surface can have a different color than the object's main color. To simulate this, you can assign a color to areas of reflection on a surface that correspond to the light's color. Because most light is white, you will often use white as a reflection color. This attribute is most noticeable on rounded and curved surfaces. If, on 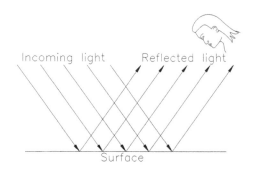 the other hand, you want a surface to have a diffuse, matte finish, you generally use the same color, or a similar color, for the reflected light that you use for the material's main color.

The reflection attribute also enables you to give a mirror-like finish to a surface. This is handled through an on-off toggle in the dialog boxes that create and modify materials. When the mirror toggle is checked, the material causes surfaces to which it is attached to reflect other objects in a rendering. Ray-traced rendering must be used to enable mirror-like reflections. Similar to the other two attributes for color, you can assign reflection a value ranging from 0 to 1.

## Roughness

If a surface is perfectly smooth, all light beams are reflected from the surface at the same angle at which they struck the surface, as illustrated in the accompanying figure. Consequently, from a cylinder that is highly reflective, you will see just a narrow band of light reflecting; and from a highly reflective round surface, you will see just a small spot of reflected light. The highlights caused by reflected light are small but

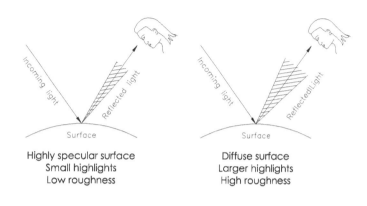

Highly specular surface
Small highlights
Low roughness

Diffuse surface
Larger highlights
High roughness

intense on highly reflective surfaces. Such extremely smooth, reflective surfaces are called specular surfaces. Few surfaces, however, are perfect reflectors, and some of the reflected light from them will be scattered. Therefore, their highlights are larger, but less intense than those from highly specular surfaces.

AutoCAD lets you control the relative degree of specular reflection through an attribute called roughness. You can assign a value ranging from 0 to 1 to the roughness attribute. Low roughness values result in small, bright highlights that make the surface look shiny. High roughness values result in large highlights that blend with the surface's main color, and the surface appears to have a matte finish.

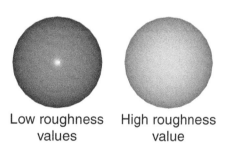

Low roughness
values

High roughness
value

## Transparency

When light beams pass through an object, rather than reflect from its surface, the object is transparent. Many objects are semitransparent — some light beams pass through the object, while others are reflected from its surface. AutoCAD allows you to set the transparency of a material to a value between 0 and 1. Objects assigned a transparency of 0 are opaque, while objects having a transparency of 1 are completely transparent; they are not even visible in a rendering.

### Refraction

Light beams bend when they enter a transparent material, and they return to their original direction when they exit on its far side. This phenomenon, which is called *refraction*, causes objects viewed through a transparent material to be offset or distorted. The degree to which the light beams bend is a material property called *refraction index*.

You can set the degree of refraction for a rendering material by giving the refraction attribute a value other than 1. When a material has a refraction of 1.0, the light beams do not bend as they pass through a transparent material. Refraction values greater or less than 1 cause objects on the opposite side of a transparent material to be shifted, and the degree to which they are shifted increases as the deviation of refraction from 1.0 increases. Raytraced rendering must be used for the refraction attribute to have an effect.

## Mapping

The material attributes just described work great for materials that have uniform surfaces and color, but they cannot simulate wood, marble, wallpaper, or other materials that have texture or patterns. Therefore, AutoCAD's renderer lets you supplement a material's attributes with bitmap images. This use of bitmap images is often referred to as *mapping*, and the images themselves are called maps. Photo Real or Photo Raytrace rendering must be used to enable mapping. Some sophisticated rendering and animation programs, such as 3D Studio, also support bitmaps, and AutoCAD's maps can be exported to some of them.

AutoCAD comes with a good supply of bitmap files that you can use to render materials. They are all in the TGA bitmap file format, although you also can use images in the bitmap file formats of GIF, PCX, BMP, TIF, GIF, and JPG.

If you used the default AutoCAD installation folder names, all the bitmap files for mapping are in the AutoCAD Textures folder. Depending on the AutoCAD version you are using, and on the type of installation you used, there might be only three files in that folder. If that is the case in your system, you should copy all the files that are in the Acad\Textures folder on the AutoCAD CD-ROM to the AutoCAD textures folder in your computer. This gives you more than 140 bitmap files to work with. Many of the files in this folder — such as the ones of a TV set, an aquarium, and the face of a chimpanzee — will be of little value to you. Others, however, will be useful for materials and backgrounds. The names of the files you are most likely to use are listed in Table 19-1 at the end of this chapter.

You should also find the file render.mli in your AutoCAD Support folder. If that file is only about 2KB in size, replace it with the one on the AutoCAD CD-ROM that is about 47KB. This file is in the Acad\Support folder on the CD-ROM. It contains about 150 ready-made materials in a materials library that you can use for your models. This materials library is referred to later in this chapter in the discussion of the MATLIB command.

## Types of Mapping

AutoCAD supports four different types of mapping. Each type serves a specific purpose, and the interface of each type is through a specific material attribute.

### Texture Maps

Texture maps make surfaces appear to have patterns or texture. Wood, concrete, tile floors, shingled roofs, rusted or oxidized metal, and furniture fabric are just a few of the materials that can be simulated by texture maps. You do, of course, need to have a bitmap file with a suitable image. Texture maps are connected to a material through the color attribute, and because texture maps are so often used, AutoCAD has added the word pattern to the color attribute in its dialog boxes for creating and modifying materials.

### Reflection Maps

Reflection maps simulate mirror-like reflections on shiny surfaces, such as the reflection of clouds on a polished automobile hood. They are not the same as the mirror reflections you can have in ray-traced renderings. Their interface with the material is through the reflection attribute. Three conditions are necessary for reflection maps to render well. First, the surface must be curved; second, the material's roughness attribute must be set to a low value; and third, the bitmap used must have a relatively high resolution.

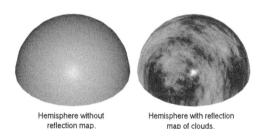

Hemisphere without          Hemisphere with reflection
reflection map.               map of clouds.

### Opacity Maps

Opacity maps are for making transparent areas on surfaces. When rendered, pure white areas of an opacity map become completely opaque, black areas are completely transparent, and the transparency of gray shades is proportional to their darkness. Colors take on their equivalent grayscale values.

   The figure on the right shows the image of a typical opacity map. It is simply six black squares on a white rectangle, but when it is projected onto a 3D face, it makes

holes in the face, as illustrated in the rendering in the next figure. The image seen through this window is from another bitmap file that is used as a rendering background.

Although AutoCAD supplies almost no bitmap files that are suitable for opacity maps, it is not difficult to custom make your own for simulating the panes of a window or a hole through a surface. One way to make them is to use a white AutoCAD background and black as an object color as you make planar surface objects in the shape of the holes you want. Circles make good round holes, 3D faces work well as rectangular holes, and regions can be used for more complex shapes. When the objects have been drawn and arranged as you want them, invoke the SHADE-MODE command so that the surfaces become black objects on a white background, and then save the viewport image with the SAVEIMG command. A paint program can be helpful in touching up and cropping the image, but it is not necessary. The opacity file for the image and rendering shown here was made using this method.

## Bump Maps

AutoCAD uses the brightness values of pixels in bump map images to create the illusion of a slight change in height; as if the surface were embossed. A bump map is always used in conjunction with a texture map.

Sometimes, the same bitmap file is even used for both the texture map and the bump map. By themselves, bump map images are rendered black and white, even if the image in the bitmap file has colors. Consequently, the bitmap blend of the bump map is always set to a low value — usually to 0.10 or less. In the rendering in the figure to the right, the material for the bottom half of the brick wall uses a straight texture map, while the material for the top half of the wall uses the same texture map plus a bump map. The added realism is noticeable, even in this grayscale illustration.

## Tiling and Cropping

By default, when a bitmap image is projected onto a surface, it will, by default, adjust its size and shape to completely fill the surface. In the figure to the right, for instance, the bitmap image attached to the cylinder on the left is stretched so that it completely wraps around the cylinder. As a result, the image is distorted. You can, however, adjust the scale and the insert point of the bitmap image so that it fits

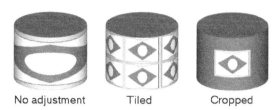

No adjustment        Tiled        Cropped

the surface better, as shown on the other two cylinders. When the image is reduced in size, as it is on these two other cylinders, you can have the image either repeated as many times as necessary to completely fill the surface, as shown on the middle cylinder, or you can have the image displayed just once, as shown on the right-hand cylinder. The repeated image effect is called *tiling*, while the single image effect is called *cropping*.

## Mapping Projection and Scale

Bitmap images are 2D rectangular objects, yet in a rendering they are often projected onto surfaces that are curved and rounded, and surfaces that are triangular-shaped or have wavy edges. Moreover, they are often projected onto surfaces that are oriented at odd angles to the principal planes of the WCS. You also must set the size, or scale, of a bitmap image to one that is appropriate for the size of your model and the intended use of the material. For instance, the relative scale of a black-and-white check pattern bitmap is smaller when it is used to simulate a tablecloth than when it is used as a floor covering.

Mapping projection and scale is handled by AutoCAD's RMAT and SETUV commands. Basic planar projection and scale is set by options of RMAT, while more complex projection and scale is set by SETUV. SETUV also allows you to rotate an image and move its insert point. The letters U and V in the name of thess command refer to the labels used for the mapping coordinates. These coordinates are roughly comparable to the X and Y coordinates of the World Coordinate System (WCS) and User Coordinate System (UCS), but their orientation is independent of them. Furthermore, because the U and V directions correspond to the edges of the surface being mapped, they are not necessarily perpendicular to one another, or even straight.

The SETUV command has provisions for three projection types: planar, cylindrical, and spherical. When the surface you are mapping does not match any of these basic geometric shapes, you must pick the projection type that comes closest to the shape of your surface. An idiosyncrasy of AutoCAD's renderer is that you must select Crop as the mapping type in the RMAT command (even when you intend to tile the bitmap) to enable SETUV to set projection orientation and scale.

### Planar Projection

A default setting of the RMAT command automatically correctly maps bitmaps on any plane that is parallel with one of the three principal WCS planes — the X-Y, Y-Z, and Z-X planes. On the other hand, if you are applying the bitmap to a planar surface that is not parallel with one of the

WCS principal planes, you have to use the SETUV command to tell AutoCAD what the orientation of the surface is by selecting three points on the surface of the plane.

Notice in the figure to the right that no adjustments are needed when the bitmap image of a checkerboard pattern is projected onto a 3D face that is lying on the WCS X-Y plane or to a face that is parallel with the WCS Z-X

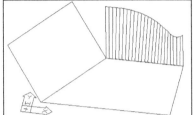

plane. However, when that same image is projected onto the rectangular 3D face that is askew to the three principal planes, the image is askew to the surface. You must use SETUV to tell AutoCAD what the orientation of the surface is. Notice, also, in this figure, that the image is simply clipped at the curved edge of the polygon mesh rather than being distorted to conform to it.

## Cylindrical Projection

When a bitmap is projected onto a cylinder, the image is wrapped around the cylinder. You do, however, have to tell AutoCAD, through the SETUV command, that the surface is cylindrical. Furthermore, if the axis of the cylinder is not pointing in the Z-axis direction, you also must tell AutoCAD how the cylinder is oriented.

The figure on the right shows a rendering of four different cylinders, each with the same square bitmap image attached as a texture map. The cylinders are all surface models, with the texture map attached to sides of the cylinder, but not to the cyl-

inder ends. Notice the following about the cylinders in this figure:

- AutoCAD was not told that the cylinder in the upper-right corner is a cylinder. Consequently, the image that is projected on it is distorted beyond recognition.

- The scale of the image projected onto the cylinder in the upper-left corner was not changed from its 1:1 correspondence, and therefore, the image is elongated as it wraps around the circumference of the cylinder.

- The scale of the image projected onto the cylinder in the lower-left corner, however, was set so that its size around the cylinder is about one-third its size along the cylinder. As a result, the image comes closer to matching its original square shape.

- The scale of the image on the cylinder in the lower-right corner was adjusted in both directions to achieve an even different effect. Moreover, because the axis of this cylinder is not parallel with the Z axis, its orientation had to be specified as well.

- Although the object in the center is not a true cylinder, that is its closest geometric shape. The image is distorted, and there isn't anything you can really do about it. This has more to do with conflicting geometries than limitations of AutoCAD's renderer.

### Spherical Projection

If you do not tell AutoCAD that an image is attached to a sphere, the image will be projected onto the top and bottom halves of the sphere, as shown on the left-most sphere in the figure to the right. When you specify through SETUV that the surface is a sphere, however, the image is compressed to a point at the poles of the sphere, and at the same time it is stretched to fit around the sphere's equator, as shown on the right-most sphere in the figure. Images mapped onto spheres generally look better when they are scaled down in relative size, as shown on the other two spheres — one has been tiled, while the other has been cropped.

When images are mapped onto a sphere, AutoCAD assumes by default that the pole of the sphere is parallel with the Z axis, but you can specify another direction.

### Bitmap Scale

You can independently set the scale of a bitmap image in the U and V directions, to have the scale in the U direction be different than the scale in the V direction. Also, AutoCAD's renderer has two different meanings for scale value. In the SETUV command, scale value always represents the number of times the bitmap is repeated on the surface object in the specified direction.

Scale in the SETUV command represents the number of times the bitmap is repeated in the specified direction.

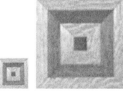  

Bitmap

Scale U: 1.0
Scale V: 1.0

Scale U: 2.0
Scale V: 2.0

Scale U: 1.0
Scale V: 2.0

For example, when scale is equal to 1.0, the image is shown one time in the indicated direction; and, when scale equals 2.0, the image is shown two times in the indicated direction.

In the RMAT command, scale value is, by default, a size magnification factor of the bitmap image for the specified direction. For example, when scale is equal to 1.0, the bitmap image is shown in its actual size and is repeated as necessary to fill the surface. (Provided tiling is on.) And, when scale is set to 2.0, the image is magnified to twice its original size in the indicated direction.

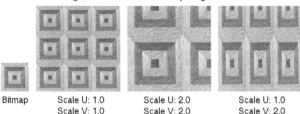

By default, scale in the RMAT command represents a size magnification factor of the bitmap image.

Bitmap   Scale U: 1.0   Scale U: 2.0   Scale U: 1.0
         Scale V: 1.0   Scale V: 2.0   Scale V: 2.0

However, in the RMAT command you can, have scale value represent the number of times the bitmap is repeated on the surface object, just as in the SETUV command. Which scale representation method is in effect is controlled by the Map Style option within the Adjust Material Bitmap Placement dialog box of the RMAT command. When Map Style is set to Fixed Scale, scale value represents a maginification factor; and when Map Style is set to Fit to Object, scale value represents an image repeat quantity.

## Template Materials

Bitmap images do not work well on 3D solid objects. AutoCAD considers the entire surface of the 3D solid to be a single surface object and attempts to map the image on all sides of the solid. Consequently, while the image is satisfactory on one face of the 3D solid, it is severely distorted on most of its other faces.

AutoCAD, however, does support three special rendering materials that work well on 3D solids. They are generally called *template* materials, although AutoCAD sometimes refers to them as *solid* materials. The three materials simulate wood, granite, and marble. The figure to the right shows an example of a material based on the wood template when it is applied to a 3D solid.

Although these template materials look much like bitmap images, their patterns are generated at the time of rendering — they are not based on bitmap files. One consequence of this is that template

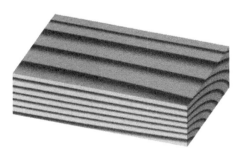

Example of the wood template material

materials cannot be exported to other programs. Materials using these templates are created through an option of the RMAT command.

# Creating Materials

If no material is attached to an object, AutoCAD uses one that is named *GLOBAL*, which has its attributes set as follows:

| Attribute | Value | Color |
|---|---|---|
| Color | 0.70 | By ACI |
| Ambient | 0.10 | Same as that for Color |
| Reflection | 0.20 | Same as that for Color |
| Roughness | 0.50 | |
| Transparency | 0.00 | |
| Refraction | 1.00 | |

No bitmaps are used with the *GLOBAL* material. When the color attribute is set to By ACI (which stands for AutoCAD Color Index), the rendering material takes the color of the surface object's AutoCAD color. This default material is opaque and has a slightly glossy appearance.

Actually, the number values for the color, ambient, and reflection attributes have little effect on the material's appearance, and you can generally set all three of them to 1.00. If you want the material to have a matte finish, set roughness to a high value, such as 1.00, and set the color of the reflection attribute to one that is either similar to that of the color attribute or one that has a dull, gray-like hue. If, on the other hand, you want the material to be shiny, set roughness to a value below 0.50 and set the color of the reflection attribute to white, or another bright color.

To create a transparent material, set the value of transparency somewhere between 0.50 and 0.80, depending upon how transparent you want the surface to be. If transparency is set to 1.00, you will not be able to see the object that the material is attached to.

You will use the refraction attribute only in special circumstances. Although you can set refraction to any value between 0 and 100, those that are very close to 1.00 produce the best results, and you might find that values less than 1.00 (in the 0.80 to 0.90 range) work better than values greater than 1.00. When refraction is set to 1.00 (its default value), no light refraction occurs. You must use Photo Raytraced rendering for the refraction attribute to have any effect.

You also will use the mirror toggle only in special circumstances. When you want the material to reflect other objects, click the Mirror check box. This check box is available only through the reflection attribute. Furthermore, Photo Raytraced rendering must be used for the objects to actually have mirror-like reflections. If an object does have a mirror-like material attached, it will not reflect other objects when Photo Real rendering is being used. It will, however, reflect the color of the background, which can be undesirable.

The vast majority of your maps will be texture maps. Texture maps are incorporated into a material through the Color/Pattern attribute. If the texture map is the only thing that is important for the material, you can leave the settings of the other attributes at their defaults. Occasionally, however, you might want to have some color show through the bitmap image. You will then assign a color to the color attribute, and perhaps to the reflection attribute as well, and make the image (not the material) somewhat transparent by reducing its bitmap blend value from its default setting of 1.00. You will also want to give the material some color if you are going to crop the texture map. Otherwise, the unmapped areas on the surface are rendered in the object's color.

Bump maps add realism to materials for stones, bricks, and embossed metal. You use them in conjunction with a texture map from the same bitmap file, or from a companion file. The bitmap blend for the texture map 1.00, while the bitmap blend for the bump map is 0.10, or even less. See Table 19-1 at the end of this chapter for a list of files supplied by AutoCAD that are suitable for bump maps.

Only rarely will you use reflection maps. Nevertheless, you should keep them in mind for the time when you do need one to simulate a reflection on a rounded surface. If you want to use an image to simulate a reflection on a planar surface, such as a mirror or a window, use a texture map rather than a reflection map.

You will not use opacity maps often either, and when you do need to use one (to make a hole in a surface), you generally have to make your own bitmap file (using the method described earlier) for the opacity map.

Most problems in mapping are related to having the image conform to the shape and size of the surface. To solve these problems, you will use the SETUV command extensively.

3D solid objects do not work well with bitmaps. AutoCAD considers their surface to be a single object, and the bitmap image is projected onto all sides of the solid. The image may be recognizable on some faces of the solid, but on many faces it will be just a blur. You can, however, use the template materials to add patterns to 3D solids during renderings. These are truly 3D images, but you are restricted to only three different materials — granite, marble, and wood. Also, they are not as realistic looking as are bitmap images based on photographs of real materials.

Although nothing is inherently difficult in the individual steps for creating materials and attaching them to objects, the number of materials and the number of objects involved can make the process complicated. You should keep your rendering materials as simple as possible, and match them to the scale of your renderings. For instance, there is no point in creating a complicated material, complete with a reflection map, for the knob of a door handle that will be seen 40 feet away. Also, you must be organized when you work with materials, and keep track of which materials are attached to which objects.

## Exercise One

This exercise will show you how to project a bitmap image onto a cylindrical surface and how to create tiled and cropped images. Start a new drawing. Its initial setup is not important, and you are not likely to save the drawing file when you have finished the exercise.

You will first create a surface model cylinder to be used for the rendering. Draw a circle with a radius of 1 unit, and place a copy of that circle 1.50 units in the positive Z direction. Then, use any method you like to set an SE isometric view. Set the value of the **surftab1** system variable to 18, and finally, use the RULESURF command to create a surface between the two circles.

You might want to divide the AutoCAD graphics area into four viewports so you can compare the results from different material settings.

Start the RMAT command and begin a new standard material. Assign any name you like to the material. Make sure the Color/Pattern attribute is checked and click the Find File button to locate the file named 3d.tga. It probably will be the very first file in the Textures folder within your AutoCAD folder.

When you locate this file, double-click on it to associate the file with your material and restore the New Standard Material dialog box. If you use the preview panel with a cube, you will see that the image in this file is simply the characters 3D on a red background. Click the Adjust Bitmap button to bring up the Adjust Material Bitmap Placement dialog box. In that dialog box, select Fit to Object as the Map Style, and clear the Use Auto Axis check box. Leave the other parameters at their default settings, and click the OK button to return to the New Standard Material dialog box.

Click the OK button to return to the Materials dialog box. If the name of your new material is not highlighted in the Materials list box, highlight it by clicking once on its name. Click the Attach button, and pick one of the vertical surface mesh lines when AutoCAD asks you to select objects to attach your material to. Be certain that you do not include either of the circles in your selection set. Press the Enter key to return to the Materials dialog box and press the OK button to end the RMAT command.

Start the RENDER command. Be certain that Photo Real is the rendering type, and render the current view. Your rendering is likely to resemble the one shown in Figure 1-1. The image is not at all evident in the rendering.

To fix the image, start the SETUV command. Select the tube surface when you are prompted to select objects, and press the Enter key. When the Mapping dialog box appears, notice that the bitmap projection is planar, which does not match the shape of your surface. Click the Cylindrical radio button, and then click the OK button to exit the SETUV command. When you render the scene this time, your model should look similar to the one shown in Figure 1-2. The characters in the image are now evident, although they are distorted.

Figure 1-1

Start the SETUV command, and again pick the surface mesh when you are prompted to select objects. This time, click the Adjust Coordinates button in the Mapping dialog box. (Notice that the dialog box now reports that the projection is cylindrical.) The Adjust Cylindrical Projection dialog box appears. If the axis of this tube was not pointed in the Z direction, you would use this dialog box to make some changes, but you are just passing through now, so you don't need to change anything. Therefore, click the Adjust Bitmap button to move to the Adjust Object Bitmap Placement dialogbox.

Figure 1-2

This dialog box is similar to the Adjust Material Bitmap Placement dialog box of the RMAT command, and it performs the same basic functions. The difference is that one controls the global parameters of a material, while the other controls the bitmap image parameters for specific objects.

Set the bitmap Scale in the U direction to a value of 6.0 and the Scale in the V direction to 2.0. This causes the image to be repeated six times around the tube and two times along its length. Also, set the Offset in the V direction to a value of 0.25. Because AutoCAD starts the bitmap in the middle of the tube's length, this offset in the V direction prevents the image from being clipped at the ends of the tube. Click three OK buttons to exit the SETUV command. Your rendered tube should now look like the one in Figure 1-3.

Figure 1-3

The image in this rendering is tiled; that is, it is repeated as often as necessary to completely fill the surface. For the last rendering of this cylinder, you will crop the image so that it appears just once. Start the SETUV command, pick the tube, click the Adjust Coordinates button, and click the Adjust Bitmap button to bring up the Adjust Object Bitmap Placement dialog box. Do not change the U and V scales, but return the V Offset to 0 so that the image is centered along the length of the tube. Finally, click the Crop radio button, and then click three OK buttons to leave the SETUV command. This time, your rendering should be similar to the one shown in Figure 1-4.

Figure 1-4

The bitmap image looks as if it were a label on a can. Autodesk sometimes refers to cropped images as the *decal effect*. The rest of the surfaces are rendered in their object color, which on your model is white.

That finishes your work in this exercise. You might, however, want to further experiment with the model and the material on your own. One thing that you might try is to rotate the cropped image. This is done through the SETUV command's Adjust Cylindrical Coordinates dialog box, and it moves the image around the circumference of the cylinder. Rotating it -45 degrees, for instance, makes the image face the SE isometric view direction.

## Exercise Two

In this exercise, you will experiment with one of AutoCAD's template materials. These are useful for adding patterns to materials for 3D solid objects. Start a new drawing. You do not need to keep this drawing, so its initial setup is not important.

The model will be that of a short wooden beam, and the easiest way to make it is with the following command line-input:

```
Command: BOX (Enter)
Specify corner of box or [CEnter]: (Enter)
Specify corner or [Cube/Length]: 6,24,4 (Enter)
```

That's all there is to making the beam. Now switch to a SE isometric viewpoint. In the wireframe viewing mode, your model should look like the one in Figure 2-1.

Start the RMAT command. In the Materials dialog box, highlight Wood in the list box below the New button and click the New button. A dialog box titled New Wood Material is displayed. Give the new material any name you like. The attributes of the material are in a column of radio buttons on the left side of the dialog box. You will change only the Scale attribute, leaving the others at their default settings. Click the Scale button, and enter 0.50 in the Value edit box.

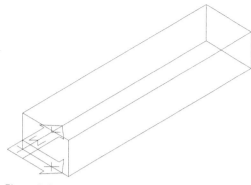

Figure 2-1

Click the OK button to return to the main Materials dialog box.

Make certain that the name of your material is highlighted in the Materials list box, and click the Attach button. When AutoCAD asks you to select objects to attach your material to, pick an edge of the 3D solid and press the Enter key. When the Materials dialog box reappears, press the OK button to end the RMAT command.

Begin the RENDER command. Set the rendering type to Photo Real, and render the current viewport. Your rendering of the wooden beam should look like the one in Figure 2-2. It is highly unlikely that a 24x6x4-inch wooden beam would ever be like this one. In real lumber, the grain of the wood invariably lies along the length of the beam or board, and the circular growth rings are on the ends of the beam or board.

The problem in this rendering occurs because of the directions AutoCAD uses in mapping the wood pattern on the model. AutoCAD always places the end view of the

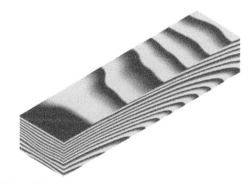

Figure 2-2

growth rings in its wood template material on a plane that is parallel with the V-W plane of the bitmap projection coordinate system, and the grain of the wood extends in the U direction. By default on wood material, the U projection direction is in the WCS X direction, V is in the WCS Y direction, and W is in the WCS Z direction. You just need to change the U and V directions relative to the WCS.

Start the SETUV command, and pick the 3D solid when you are prompted to select an object. When the Mapping dialog box appears, click the Projection radio button that is labeled Solid, and then click the Adjust Coordinates button.

The Adjust UVW Coordinates dialog box is displayed. In this dialog box, turn the Maintain Aspect Ratio check box off, and then click the Pick Points button. The dialog box disappears, and on the command line you are prompted to specify three points and a distance. Using the points shown in Figure 2-3, respond to these prompts as follows:

```
Place the origin of the mapper: (Specify point 1)
Place the U axis of the mapper: (Specify point 2)
Place the V axis of the mapper: (Specify point 3)
Length of W axis: 4 (Enter)
```

The Adjust UVW Coordinates dialog box reappears. Click its OK button, and click the OK button in the Mapping dialog box to end the SETUV command. When you render the current viewport this time, your wooden beam should look similar to the one shown in Figure 2-4. The grain in the wooden beam is now aligned as you would expect it to be.

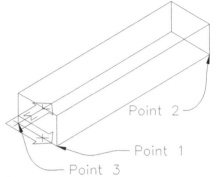

Figure 2-3

This finishes the exercise. You might, however, want to experiment further with the model and its material on your own by changing the values of the wood material's attributes to see how they affect the appearance of the rendering.

## Exercise Three

In this exercise, you will add materials to the 3D model house you have been working on throughout this book. You last worked on this model in Chapter 18, when you installed some rendering lights. This exercise in adding materials to the house is divided into three parts. The

Figure 2-4

first part will consist of creating and attaching some standard materials that have only color. In the second part, you will create and attach a material that includes a bump map for making a brick wall. And, in the third part, you will create and attach a material with a texture map simulating roofing shingles.

### Part One of Exercise Three

Retrieve file f1820.dwg from the CD-ROM that accompanies this book and open it. You will create five standard materials and assign them to layers in the drawing. None of these materials will have bitmap files associated with them. In each material, set the values of the color, ambient, reflection, and roughness attributes to 1.00. Also have the color of the ambient and reflection attributes locked to that of the color attribute. The only differences between these materials will be their color. To establish the color of the color attribute in each material, set its red, green, and blue color components to the values shown next:

| Material | Red | Green | Blue |
|----------|-----|-------|------|
| BACKDROP | 0.0 | 0.25 | 0.0 |
| TRIM | 0.35 | 0.20 | 0.10 |
| GARAGE_DR | 0.55 | 0.30 | 0.20 |
| GLASS | 0.10 | 0.10 | 0.10 |
| SIDING | 0.75 | 0.50 | 0.40 |

When you have created these materials, click the By Layer button in the Materials dialog box to bring up the Attach by Layer dialog box. In this dialog box, attach the materials to the layers as follows:

| Material Name | Layer(s) |
|---------------|----------|
| BACKDROP | BACKDROP |
| TRIM | FRAME_SIL, FRAME_WIN, FRAME_DOOR, FRAME_GAR_DOOR, EAVES |
| GARAGE_DR | DOOR_GAR |
| GLASS | GLASS |
| SIDING | SID01 |

The procedure to attach a material to a layer, or to several layers, is to highlight one material in the left-hand list box of the Attach by Layer dialog box, and then highlight the layers in the right-hand list box you want to attach the material to. Then, click the Attach button.

After the materials have been attached, exit the RMAT command, and start the RENDER command. You will use a bitmap image for the background from now on, so click the Background button in the Render dialog box to bring up the Background dialog box. Click the Image radio button, and then click the Find File button. The file you want is named cloud.tga. After you find it, double-click its name to bring it into the Background dialog box. Then, click the OK button to restore the Render dialog box. Make certain that Photo Real rendering is in effect and click the Render

Figure 3-1

button to render the current viewport. A grayscale version of the rendering is shown in Figure 3-1.

**Part Two of Exercise Three**

In this part of Exercise 3, you will create a brick material that you will attach to the surfaces below two windows on the front of the house. Start by invoking the VPOINT command with the view rotation angles of 245 degrees from the X axis and 10 degrees from the X-Y plane. In addition to establishing a convenient view direction, this action turns the perspective viewing mode off, which allows you to use your pointing device. It leaves you far from the house, however, so you need to zoom in until the house looks similar to the one in Figure 3-2.

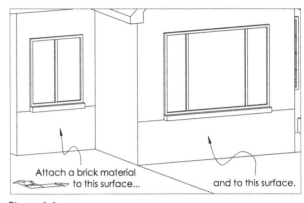

Figure 3-2

As soon as you have established a good view of this part of the house, you might want to freeze all the layers in the drawing except for the one named Brick. Two 3D faces are then the only objects visible.

Start the RMAT command and begin a new standard material. Name the material BRICK_WALL. With the Color/Pattern attribute's radio button checked, click the Find File button. The file you want is named bmbrick.tga. When you find it, double-click its name to bring it into the New Standard Material dialog box. Leave the Bitmap Blend value for this file set to its default of 1.00.

Next, turn on the Bump Map attribute's radio button. The name of the file you want to associate with this attribute is bmbricb.tga. After you have brought this file into the dialog box, set the value of Bitmap Blend to 0.10.

Click the Color/Pattern attribute radio button again, and then click the Adjust Bitmap button to bring up the Adjust Material Bitmap Placement dialog box. Specify the following parameters in this dialog box:

| Tiling type: | Tile |
| --- | --- |
| Map Style: | Fixed Scale |
| Use Auto Axis: | On |
| Scale U: | 18.0 |
| Scale V: | 18.0 |
| Offset U: | 0.0 |
| Offset V: | 0.0 |

AutoCAD correctly renders bitmaps on planes that are parallel with one of the WCS principal planes when Use Auto Axis is active. Click the OK button to return to the New Standard Material dialog box, and click its OK button to return to the main Materials dialog box. Attach this new material to the two 3D faces.

You do not need to use the SETUV command with this material because both faces are parallel with the WCS Z-X plane. Figure 3-3 shows a grayscale rendering of the small 3D face. Notice how the bump map adds depth and realism to the brick material. You are now finished with the brick facing, so you can thaw all the drawing's layers.

### Part Three of Exercise Three

Your last task in creating, attaching, and adjusting materials for the house will be to add a material that has a texture map of wooden shingles to its roof. Although AutoCAD supplies one bitmap file

Figure 3-3

of roof shingles (file ishingl2.tga), it is a small image that does not work well when it must cover a large surface. Therefore, you will use shing1.tga from the CD-ROM that accompanies this book. See Appendix A for help locating this file. When you find it, copy it to the folder on your computer that contains your rendering texture files.

Before you begin working on the roof, you might want to freeze all the layers in the drawing except for ROOF01. Figure 3-4 shows a plan view of the roof. Surfaces one, three, and four of the roof are 3D face objects, while surface two is a polyface mesh object (made with the PFACE command).

Use the RMAT command to create a new standard material. Name the material SHINGLES. The only attribute you will use in this material is Color/Pattern. Be certain that its radio button is on, and then locate and bring the file shing1.tga into the material as a texture map. Click the Adjust Bitmap button to display the Adjust Material Bitmap Placement dialog box. Verify

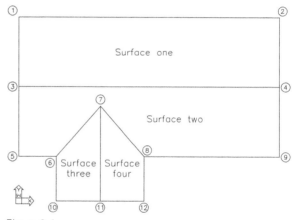

Figure 3-4

that Scale is 1.0 and Offset is 0.0 in both the U and V directions. Because the faces of the roof are all askew to the principal planes, you have to use SETUV to establish the orientaion of the bitmap. Therefore, select Fit to Object as the Map Style.

Return to the Standard Material dialog box, and then to the main Materials dialog box. Attach the SHINGLES material to the four objects that make up the roof of the house, and exit the RMAT command.

You must use the SETUV command four times to set the orientation and scale of the texture map on each surface. Because none of these surfaces are parallel with the WCS principal planes, you will have to use the Picked Plane option to specify the lower-left, lower-right, and upper-left corners of each plane to establish their orientation. You will also set the U and V scale, and the V offset, for each surface.

Use the values given in following table as a guide in setting the SETUV parameters. The surface identification numbers and the numbers for the corners of the surfaces correspond to those shown in Figure 3-4.

| Surface | Lower Left | Lower Right | Upper Left | ScaleU | ScaleV | OffsetU | OffsetV |
|---------|-----------|-------------|------------|--------|--------|---------|---------|
| One | 2 | 1 | 4 | 5.00 | 2.74 | 0 | 0.40 |
| Two | 5 | 9 | 3 | 5.00 | 2.74 | 0 | 0.40 |
| Three | 6 | 10 | 7 | 1.00 | 2.25 | 0 | 0.10 |
| Four | 12 | 8 | 11 | 1.00 | 2.25 | 0 | 0.10 |

When you thaw all the layers in the drawing, your rendering of the house should resemble the one shown in grayscale in Figure 3-5. Rendering might take several minutes.

That finishes this exercise. On the CD-ROM that comes with this book, the surface model house with the bitmaps and materials attached is in file f1929.dwg. It was saved in AutoCAD 2002 format. Therefore, if you are opening it in AutoCAD 2000 or 2000i, you need to modify the BRICK_WALL and SHINGLES materials by changing the path for their Color/Pattern maps, and for the bump map of BRICK_WALL, from Program Files\AutoCAD 2002\Textures to Program Files \Acad2000\Textures or Program Files\Acad2000i\Textures (or where ever your material texture files are stored). You also need to update the path to the the image (cloud.tga) used for a rendering background.

Figure 3-5

In the next chapter, you will add some landscape items to the rendering so that the house does not look quite so barren. If you do not like the colors or the bitmap images selected for the rendering, don't hesitate to change them. You have all the knowledge and experience you need to make any modifications you like — both to the rendering and to the 3D model.

| | |
|---|---|
| Command: | RMAT |
| Purpose: | Rendering materials are created, attached to objects, and modified through this command. |
| Initiate with: | • On the command line, enter RMAT. |
| | • From the View pull-down menu, select Render, and then Materials. |
| | • Select the Materials button from the Render toolbar. |

Options:    The RMAT command starts and ends through a dialog box titled Materials. When options in this dialog box are selected, dialog boxes appropriate for the option are displayed.

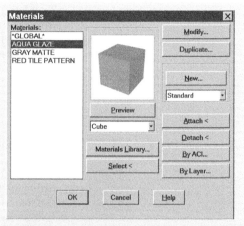

The names of all existing materials are displayed in a list box. A material named *GLOBAL* is always included, and all surface objects in a rendering assume the properties of that material, unless another material is specifically attached to it. The *GLOBAL* material has the default standard material attribute settings.

To perform an action on a material, click on its name to highlight it, and then select the action by clicking the appropriate button. Material names also can be selected through the Select button. You can select only one material in the list at a time. Double-clicking a name is equivalent to highlighting a name and clicking the Modify button.

- Preview    When the Preview button is clicked, the highlighted material is displayed as it would appear on a 3D solid sphere or cube. Every one of the dialog boxes used by the RMAT command has a similar preview panel for the material.

- Materials Library    This button displays the Materials Library dialog box. See the discussion later in this chapter of the MATLIB command for a description of this dialog box.

- Select    When the Select button is clicked, the Materials dialog box is dismissed, and AutoCAD issues a prompt for you to select one object. You must select the object by picking a point on it. When you do, AutoCAD restores the Materials dialog box with the name of the material highlighted in the list box. The material's name is also displayed in the lower-left corner of the dialog box, along with the method that was used to attach it.

- Modify    Clicking this button brings up a dialog box appropriate for the type of material selected. All the material's properties are displayed in the dialog box, and they can be modified. Double-clicking the name of a material in the list box is equivalent to highlighting it and clicking the Modify button.

- Duplicate    Click this button to create a new material based on the properties of the highlighted material. A dialog box for a new material is displayed. Except for the new material's name, all the properties of the highlighted material are preset in the dialog box.

- New

To create a new material, select a material type from the pull-down list box, and then click the New button. A dialog box appropriate for the type of material will be displayed.

- Attach

When this button is clicked, AutoCAD dismisses the Materials dialog box and issues a command line prompt to select the objects that are to receive the properties of the material specified in the Materials list box. You can use any object selection method, and objects are highlighted as they are selected. Objects that already have the specified material attached are also highlighted. Press the Enter key to restore the Materials dialog box.

- Detach

This option detaches an object from its material. The Materials dialog box temporarily disappears, and AutoCAD displays a command line prompt for you to select objects. Use any object selection method, and press the Enter key to return to the Materials dialog box. All objects selected have their material detached, even if the name of their material was not specified.

- By ACI

You can attach a material to all objects of a specific color through this button. The Attach by AutoCAD Color Index dialog box is displayed. On the left side of this dialog box is a list of all materials in the drawing, while the 255

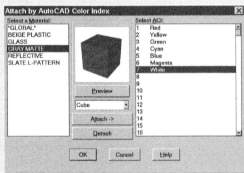

AutoCAD color numbers are displayed on the right side of the dialog box. You can select as many colors as you like by clicking their name or number as you hold down the Ctrl key, but you can select only one material at a time. Click the Attach button to assign the selected material to AutoCAD objects that have the specified colors. You can remove the association between a material and an ACI color by clicking the Detach button. Objects drawn in that color will no longer have any material attached.

- By Layer

Clicking this button brings up the Attach by Layer dialog box. On the left side of this dialog box is a list of materials, and on the right side is a list of the layers in the drawing.

Although you can select just one material at a time, you can select as many layers as you want. Click the Attach button to associate the selected material with the selected layers. All objects within the selected layers are attached to the selected materials. Clicking the Detach button detaches any material currently attached to objects in the selected layers.

- New/Modify Standard Material

The same dialog box used for creating a new standard material is used for modifying an existing standard material. Only the titles of the dialog boxes are different.

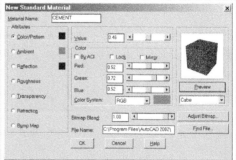

- Material Name

Enter the name of a new material in this edit box or modify the name of an existing one. Names can have up to 16 characters and can contain spaces.

- Attributes

Select an attribute from this column of radio buttons. Then set the properties of that attribute. Properties that are not appropriate for the selected attribute are grayed out.

- Color/Pattern
  - Set a Value from 0 to 1. The default value is 0.70.
  - The default color is By ACI — the material uses the color of the AutoCAD object it is attached to. Clear the By ACI check box to specify a color.
  - A texture map can be specified through the File Name edit box.

- Ambient
  - Set a Value from 0 to 1. The default value is 0.10.
  - By default, ambient color is locked to that of the Color attribute. To assign a color to ambient, clear the Lock check box. To specify a particular color, clear the By ACI check box.

- Reflection
  - Set a Value from 0 to 1. The default value is 0.20.
  - By default, reflection color is locked to that of the Color attribute. To assign a color to reflection, clear the Lock check box, and to specify a particular color, clear the By ACI check box.
  - Check the Mirror check box to give the material a mirror-like finish. Ray-traced rendering must be used to obtain mirror images.
  - A reflection map can be specified within the File Name edit box.

- Roughness
  - Set a Value from 0 to 1. The default value is 0.50. Smaller values result in smaller reflection highlights.

- Transparency
  - Set a Value from 0 to 1. The default value is 0. When the value is 0, the material is completely opaque; when the value is 1, the material is completely transparent.
  - An opacity map can be specified by entering a filename in the File Name edit box.

- Refraction
  - Set a Value from 0 to 100. With the default value of 1.0, no refraction occurs. Ray-traced rendering must be used for this attribute to have an effect.

- Bump Map
  - Specify the name of the bump map in the File Name edit box.

- Value

  The meaning of the number in this edit box varies by attribute. Value can be entered directly, or with the slider.

- Color

  This cluster of check boxes, edit boxes, and sliders controls the color of the color, ambient, and reflection attributes. When the By ACI check box is turned on, the attribute's color is the same as the color of the AutoCAD object that the material is attached to. The Lock check box applies only to the ambient and reflection attributes. When it is turned on, the attribute has the same color as the color attribute. The Mirror check box is enabled only for the reflection attribute. When it is checked, the material has a mirror-like reflection (when ray-traced rendering is used).

If the By ACI check box is cleared, you can specify a color for the attribute through the three edit boxes and sliders for color. When the RGB color system is in effect, the three color parameters are red, green, and blue. When the HLS color system is used, the three color parameters are hue, lightness, and saturation. If you click within the color swatch, the Color dialog box is displayed and can be used to specify a color.

- Bitmap Blend

This edit box and slider controls the extent to which the attribute's color shows through the bitmap image of texture maps and reflection maps. For opacity maps, bitmap blend controls their transparency; for bump maps, it controls the degree of bumpiness. Values can range from 0 to 1; the higher the value, the greater the effect of the bitmap. Bump maps generally work best with bitmap blends of 0.10 or less.

- File Name and Find File

Enter the name of a bitmap file for a texture, reflection, opacity, or bump map in the File Name edit box, or initiate a search for a file by clicking the Find File button.

- Adjust Bitmap

Click this button to adjust the scale and insert point of the bitmap image of texture, opacity, and bump maps. The Adjust Material Bitmap Placement dialog box is displayed.

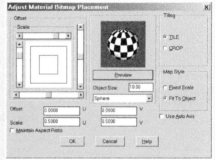

The Map Style options in this dialog box determine how the renderer interprets bitmap scale. When Fixed Scale is selected, the bitmap image size is multiplied by the scale value. For example, the image is three times its 1:1 scale when a scale of 3.0 is in effect, and is one-half its 1:1 size when a scale of 0.5 is used.

On the other hand, when Fit to Object is selected, scale represents the number of times the bitmap image is displayed

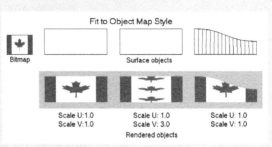

on surface objects in the specified direction. Thus, if the scale in the U direction is 3.0, the image is shown three times in that direction; and if scale is 0.5, only half of the image is displayed in that direction. If the proportions of the surface do not match those of the bitmap, the image becomes distorted; and, if the shape of the surface does not match that of the bitmap, the image is clipped.

You can set the scale in the U and V directions with the slider bars that are above and to the left of the image tile or by entering a value in the edit boxes. If the Maintain Aspect Ratio toggle is checked, changing the scale in one direction changes it in the other direction as well.

Offset is the displacement of the insert point of the image in the specified direction. For instance, if the offset in the V direction is 0.25, the image is shifted in the V direction by a distance that is one-fourth its projected size. You can set the offsets with the slider bars that are below and to the right of the image tile or by entering numbers in the Offset edit boxes.

When the Tile radio button is checked, the image is repeated as many times as necessary to fill a surface. When Crop is checked, the image is shown just once. Surface areas outside the image is rendered in the material's color.

When Use Auto Axis is selected, images on surfaces that are parallel with the WCS X-Y, Z-X, and Y-Z planes are mapped correctly. If this option is cleared, only surfaces that are parallel with the WCS X-Y plane are correctly mapped.

Click the Preview button to display the effects of the parameters you have selected on a sphere or cube in an image window. Values in the Object Size edit box change the apparent size of the image in this window. For best results, enter a value that is approximately the same as the bitmap scale. This edit box is disabled when Fit to Object has been selected.

If you intend to use the SETUV command, you must either select CROP as the tiling method (even if you are going to tile the image), or you must set Map Style to Fit to Object.

- New/Modify Granite Material

Granite is one of the three template materials that generates bitmap images during rendering. The New Granite Material dialog box is displayed when a new granite material is being defined, while

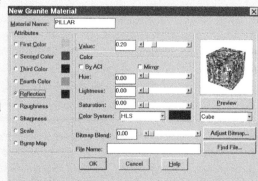

the Modify Granite Material dialog box is displayed when an existing granite material is being changed. Both dialog boxes are the same, except for their titles.

- Material Name

Enter the name of a new granite material in this edit box, or modify the name of an existing one. Names can have up to 16 characters, and they can contain spaces.

- Attributes

Select an attribute from this column of radio buttons. Then, set the features of that attribute. Features that are not appropriate for an attribute are grayed out.

- First, Second, Third, and Fourth Color

The image for granite material has random shaped patches of four colors, as shown highly magnified in the

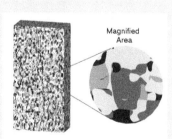

figure. Click the radio button for a color, and use the same procedure used for a standard material to give it a value and a color. The By ACI toggle is grayed out. To use fewer than four colors, set the value of the unwanted colors to 0, or set their color to be the same as another's.

- Reflection

This attribute is the same as the reflection attribute for standard materials. You can assign a value and a color to reflection, and you can have the material reflect other objects by checking Mirror. Photo Raytraced rendering must be used to enable mirror-image reflections.

- Roughness

  This attribute accepts a value from 0 to 1 for controlling the size of reflected light highlights, just as the roughness attribute of standard materials does.

- Sharpness

  This attribute can be assigned a value ranging from 0 to 1. When sharpness equals 1, the edges between the granite grains is sharp, as shown in the previous figure. At the other extreme, when sharpness is set to 0, the edges between grains are blended together.

- Scale

  The relative size of the grains, or color patches, in the granite is controlled by this attribute. You can assign it any value from 0 to 100, with larger values resulting in larger grain sizes.

- Bump Map

  This attribute allows you to use a bump map with the granite material. The controls for the bump map are the same as those for standard materials.

- New/Modify Marble Material

  Marble is a template material that simulates marble. The New Marble Material dialog box is used when a new marble material is being defined, and the Modify Marble Material dialog box is used when an existing marble material is being modified. Both dialog boxes are the same, except for their titles.

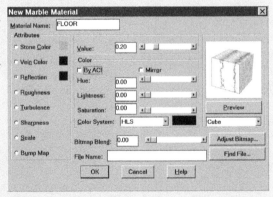

- Material Name

  Enter the name of the marble material, or edit the name of an existing material, through this edit box. The name can have up to 16 characters, including spaces.

- Attributes

  Materials are defined through these eight attributes. When an attribute is selected, appropriate edit boxes, sliders, and toggles for setting its parameters are available.

- Stone Color and Vein Color

The Stone Color attribute controls the overall color of the marble, while the Vein Color attribute controls the color of the marble's veins. Only the edit boxes and sliders in the Color section of the dialog box are available. The By ACI button and the edit box and slider for Value are disabled. The default stone color is white, and the default vein color is black.

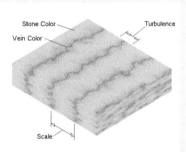

- Reflection

Just as with standard materials, you can set both the value and color of reflected light. If the By ACI toggle is selected, the color of reflected light is the same as the object's color. You also can give the marble material a mirror-like finish, and you can use a reflection map with it.

- Roughness

The relative size of reflected light highlights is controlled by this attribute. Only the Value edit box and slider are available.

- Turbulence

This attribute controls the relative distance between the peaks of the squiggly, wave-like veins in the marble. Although it accepts any value between 0 and 100, values between 1 and 10 generally give the best results. The veins are straight lines when turbulence is set to 0.

- Sharpness

When sharpness is set to its maximum value of 1, the veins in the marble consist of distinct squiggly lines that blend into the surrounding stone color. When sharpness is set to its minimum value of 0, the lines are not distinct and the blend area of the veins dominate. The default sharpness is 1.

- Scale

This attribute sets the overall size of the marble-like features and the relative distance between the veins. You can specify any value between 0 and 100.

- Bump Map — Through this attribute, you can assign a bump map to the marble material.

- New/Modify Wood Material

This template material simulates the annual growth ring patterns of wood. The New Wood Material dialog box is used for creating a new material, and the Modify Wood Material dialog box is used for

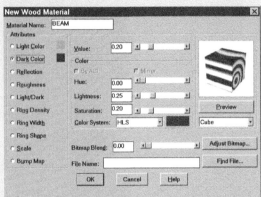

modifying existing materials. Both dialog boxes are the same, except for their titles.

- Material Name — Enter the name of the wood material in this edit box, or change the name of the existing material. Names can have up to 16 characters, including spaces.

- Attribute — To establish the characteristics of the wood material, set the parameters of each of these 10 attributes. When the radio button for an attribute is selected, the parameters appropriate for it are available, while the others are grayed out.

  - Light Color and Dark Color — Dark Color controls the color of the dark rings of summer wood in the material, while the Light Color attribute controls the color of the spring wood rings. The Value and By ACI parameters are not available.

  - Reflection — This attribute is the same as the reflection attribute for standard materials. You can assign both a value and a color to reflection, and you can have the material reflect other objects when Photo Raytraced rendering is used by checking the Mirror check box.

  - Roughness — This attribute accepts a value from 0 to 1 for controlling the size of reflected light highlights, just as the roughness attribute of standard materials does.

- Light/Dark

This attribute, which takes a value between 0 and 1, controls the relative width of the rings of dark wood and light wood. When low values are used, the dark wood bands are wider than the light wood bands. When high values are used, the dark wood bands are narrower than the light wood bands. The default value is 0.50.

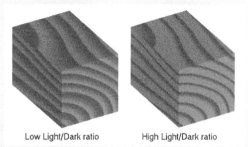

Low Light/Dark ratio          High Light/Dark ratio

- Ring Density

The number of annual growth rings for a set scale is controlled by this attribute. You can assign it any value between 0 and 100, with larger values resulting in more rings.

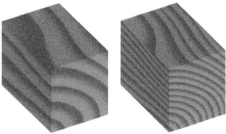

Low Ring Density value          High Ring Density value

- Ring Width

This attribute controls the variation in the distance between the growth rings. It accepts any value from 0 to 1. When Ring Width is set to 0, the distance between each ring is the same. As higher ring width values are assigned, the spacing between the rings becomes increasingly varied. The greatest variation occurs when Ring Width is set to 1. The default setting is 0.40.

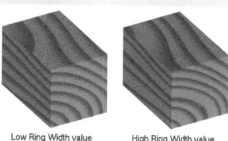

Low Ring Width value · High Ring Width value

- Ring Shape

By default, the wood's growth rings are almost perfect circles or arcs. You can, however, make them irregular by increasing the value of this attribute. Ring Shape accepts any value from 0 to 1, and its default value is 0.20. Higher values result in more irregular rings.

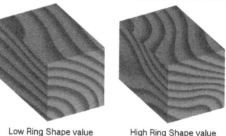

Low Ring Shape value · High Ring Shape value

- Scale

The overall scale of the wood's pattern is controlled by this attribute. You can assign it any value between 0 and 100, with larger values resulting in relatively larger growth ring patterns. The default scale is 6.25.

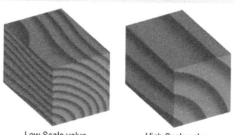

Low Scale value · High Scale value

- Bump Map

A bump map can be assigned to the wood material through this attribute.

Notes:

- You must use the Materials Library dialog box to delete a material. See the discussion of the MATLIB command for details.

- Material attachment to objects by ACI takes precedence over attachment by layer, and a material explicitly attached to an object through the Attach button takes precedence over both ACI and layer attachments.

- You can detach an object from a material through the Attach button of the Materials dialog box. When you click the Attach button, the AutoCAD objects that are already attached to the specified material are highlighted as AutoCAD asks you to identify objects for a selection set. Any object you remove from the selection set is detached from the material.

- Selecting Fixed Scale as the Map Style in the Adjust Material Bitmap Placement dialog box disables the Adjust Coordinates options of the SETUV command.

| | |
|---|---|
| Command: | SHOWMAT |
| Purpose: | This command shows the name of the material attached to an object and the method used to attach it. |
| Initiate with: | • On the command line, enter SHOWMAT. |
| Implementation: | This command performs the same function as the Select button in the Materials dialog box. You are prompted from the command line to pick one object. AutoCAD then displays one of the following responses on the command line: |

```
Material <material name> is explicitly attached to the object.
Material <material name> is attached by ACI to ACI <color number>.
Material <material name> is attached by layer to layer <layer name>.
Material *GLOBAL* is attached by default or by block.
```

| Command: | SETUV |
| --- | --- |
| Purpose: | This command controls the mapping of texture maps, opacity maps, bump maps, and template materials on specific objects. |
| Initiate with: | • On the command line, enter SETUV. |
| | • From the View pull-down menu, select Render, and then Mapping. |
| | • Select the Mapping button from the Render toolbar. |

Options:     The SETUV command starts with a command line prompt for you to select the AutoCAD objects that are to be mapped. Although you can freely select as many objects as you like, the objects should have similar geometric properties and similar orientation in 3D space. The objects selected do not need to have a material attached — you can establish the mapping properties of an object and attach a material to it later. The objects selected retain the mapping properties if they are moved, and copies of them will have the mapping properties also. See the note at the end of this command description for a method to detach mapping properties from an object.

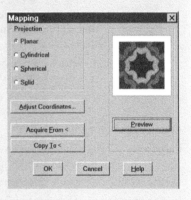

When you press the Enter key to signal completion of the object-selection process, AutoCAD displays a dialog box titled Mapping.

- Projection  From this set of four radio buttons, select the geometry — planar, cylindrical, spherical, or solid — that comes closest to matching the geometry of the selected objects. Solid is for objects having one of the three template materials.

- Preview  Unlike the preview panels of the other rendering dialog boxes, those of the SETUV command show the selected object rather than a solid cube or sphere.

- Acquire From  This option allows you to assign the mapping properties of another object to the currently selected objects. The Mapping dialog box temporarily disappears, and AutoCAD issues a command line prompt for you to select objects. You should select only one object, even though AutoCAD permits you to select as many as you want. Press the Enter key to restore the Mapping dialog box. The newly acquired properties can be modified or accepted as they are.

- Copy To  You can assign the mapping properties of the current selection set to other objects through this option. AutoCAD hides the Mapping dialog box and asks you from the command line to select the objects that are to acquire the current mapping properties. Press the Enter key to end the selection process and return to the Mapping dialog box.

- Adjust Coordinates

Clicking this button brings up one of four dialog boxes appropriate for the specified projection type. Through it, you can orient the map's projection, shift and rotate the image, and adjust the scale of the image.

Note: You can adjust the coordinates of a surface only if Crop has been selected in the Adjust Material Bitmap Placement dialog box of the RMAT command.

- Adjust Planar Coordinates

When the Planar projection radio button in the Mapping dialog box is selected, clicking the Adjust Coordinates button brings up a dialog box titled Adjust Planar Coordinates.

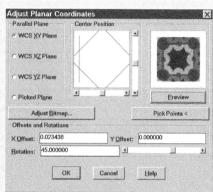

- Parallel Plane

Specify the orientation of the plane by selecting one of these four radio buttons. The default orientation is that the plane is parallel with the WCS X-Y plane. If the plane is not parallel with any of the principal WCS planes, select the Picked Plane button. AutoCAD hides the dialog box and prompts for the lower-left, lower-right, and upper-left corners of the plane. The angle between the upper-left, lower-left, and lower-right corners does not have to be 90 degrees.

- Center Position

The center of the bitmap's projection is shown as a dot in this image tile, and you can move it with the sliders that are beside the image tile. The outline of the projected image is also shown.

- Preview

The bitmap image with the current settings is displayed in this image tile. It is not updated automatically, so you must click the Preview button to view the effects of current settings.

- Pick Points

Use this button to change the orientation of a plane that is not parallel with any of the three principal planes of the WCS. AutoCAD temporarily dismisses the dialog box and issues command line prompts for the lower-left, lower-right, and upper-left corners of the plane.

- Offsets and Rotations

You can move the center of the bitmap by entering values in the X Offset and Y Offset edit boxes. Moreover, you can rotate the bitmap by entering an angle in the Rotation edit box or by moving the slider. The rotation angle limits are 180 degrees and -180 degrees. The Center Position image tile is updated when you change the center offsets and rotation angle.

- Adjust Bitmap

Clicking this button brings up the Adjust Object Bitmap Placement dialog box.

This dialog box is similar to the Adjust Material Bitmap Placement dialog box used by the RMAT command. It has an additional radio button, labeled DEFAULT, for tiling. When DEFAULT is selected, the image is either tiled or cropped,

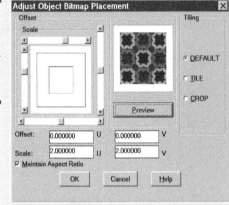

depending on the setting for the material as a whole. You can override the material's setting by specifying that the image on the selected object will be tiled or that it will be cropped.

The offsets specified in this dialog box are added to the offsets for the material, while the scales specified in this dialog box are multiplied with those of the material. Thus, if the U scale for a material is 2.0 and the U scale for the object is 3.0, the scale of the image is 6.0 when it is rendered.

- Adjust Cylindrical Coordinates

When the Cylindrical projection radio button in the Mapping dialog box is selected, clicking the Adjust Coordinates button brings up the Adjust Cylindrical Coordinates dialog box.

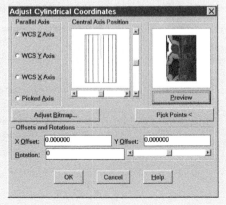

| | |
|---|---|
| • Parallel Axis | Select one of these radio buttons to specify the direction of the cylindrical surface's axis direction. The default direction is that of the WCS Z axis. If the axis is not parallel with any of the three cardinal axes, select the Picked Axis button. AutoCAD hides the dialog box and prompts for two points to define the direction of the axis and a third point to specify the seam of the bitmap (the point at which the image wrapped around the cylinder begins and ends). |
| • Central Axis Position | This image tile shows the cylinder projected onto a plane parallel with the cylinder's axis, as well as a cross-section of the cylinder. You can use the two sliders next to the image to move the axis. A line from the center of the cylinder indicates the image seam line. The seam is in the minus Y direction when the cylinder's axis is in the Z direction, and the minus Z direction when the axis is in either the X or Y directions. |
| • Preview | The bitmap image, based on the current projection settings, is displayed in this panel. |
| • Adjust Bitmap | Clicking this button brings up the Adjust Object Bitmap Placement dialog box. See the earlier description for adjusting planar coordinates for a description of this dialog box. The U direction of the bitmap is around the circumference of the cylinder, while the V direction is in the direction of the cylinder's axis. |
| • Pick Points | You can respecify the direction of the cylinder's axis and wrap line by clicking this button. AutoCAD hides the dialog box and issues prompts for points to specify the bottom of the axis, the top of the axis, and the direction of the seam line. |
| • Offsets and Rotation | You can move the projection axis by entering values for the X Offset and Y Offset in the edit boxes. Rotation refers to the direction of the seam line. You can change it by entering a value in the edit box or by moving the slider. The rotation limits are -180 degrees and 180 degrees. |
| • Adjust Spherical Coordinates | When the Spherical projection radio button in the Mapping dialog box is selected, clicking the Adjust Coordinates button brings up the Adjust Spherical Coordinates dialog box. |

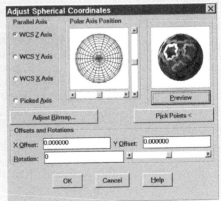

| • Parallel Axis | Specify the direction of the sphere's axis by picking one of these radio buttons. When Picked Axis is selected, AutoCAD temporarily dismisses the dialog box and issues command line prompts for three points. The first point is for the center of the sphere, the second is for the sphere's north pole, and the third is for the image seam line. |
|---|---|
| • Polar Axis Position | The projection of the image onto the sphere is shown in this panel, and the seam line is indicated by a line from the center of the sphere. You can move the image insert point by moving the sliders beside the panel. |
| • Preview | This panel displays the sphere with the current mapping settings. |
| • Adjust Bitmap | When this button is clicked, the Adjust Object Bitmap Placement dialog box is displayed. See the earlier description of adjusting planar coordinates for a description of this dialog box. The U direction of the bitmap is around the equator of the sphere, while the V direction is in the direction of the sphere's axis. |
| • Pick Points | This button enables you to respecify the axis and the seam line of the sphere. The dialog box is hidden while AutoCAD prompts for three points from the command line. The first point is for the center of the sphere, the second is for the sphere's north pole, and the third is for the direction of the image wrap line. |
| • Offsets and Rotation | You can move the projection center by entering values for the X Offset and Y Offset in the edit boxes. Rotation refers to the direction of the seam line. You can change it by entering a value in the edit box or by moving the slider. The rotation limits are -180 degrees and 180 degrees. |

• Adjust UVW Coordinates

When the Solid projection radio button in the Mapping dialog box is selected, clicking the Adjust Coordinates button brings up the Adjust UVW Coordinates dialog box. This dialog box is for adjusting the coordinate scales and the orientation of the image for the three template materials — granite, marble, and wood.

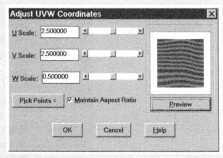

| • U Scale, V Scale, and W Scale | Use the edit boxes or the sliders to change the scale of the pattern in the specified direction. |
|---|---|

• Pick Points

By default, the U direction is in the WCS X direction, V is in the WCS Y direction, and W is in the WCS Z direction. You can change those directions, however, with this option. AutoCAD hides the dialog box and prompts you from the command line to enter three points and a distance:

```
Place the origin of the mapper: (Specify a point.)
Place the U axis of the mapper: (Specify a point.)
Place the V axis of the mapper: (Specify a point.)
Length of W axis: (Specify a distance.)
```

The three points control the orientation of the plane as well as the direction of its axes and the scale in the U and V directions, while the distance sets the scale in the W direction.

The accompanying figure shows two identical 3D solid objects that have the same wood template–based material attached. The mapping axes have been twisted, however, on the solid on the right so that they no longer match the edges of  the solid. This skews its pattern and gives the material a different appearance.

• Maintain Aspect Ratio

When this check box is cleared, you can change the scale independently in the three directions. When it is checked, the scales of the three directions are linked together so that if one is changed, the scales in the other two directions also change to maintain their original proportions.

Notes:

• To remove mapping properties from an object, enter the following AutoLISP function on the command line:

```
(c:setuv "D" (ssget))
```

A command line prompt is displayed asking you to select objects. Mapping properties are deleted from the objects you select.

• You can set the mapping parameters of a surface with SETUV before you attach a material to the surface.

• The Adjust Coordinate options of SETUP have no effect unless one of the following options of RMAT's Adjust Material Bitmap Placement dialog box is in effect:

• Tiling method is CROP;

• Map Style is Fit to Object.

# A Materials Library

Because the creation of a material can be an involved process — one that you do not want to repeat unnecessarily — AutoCAD allows you to save materials in a file so that they can be used in other drawings. MATLIB is the command that manages such a file. With it, you can save a newly created material, import a material from the file into your current drawing, and remove unwanted materials from your current drawing or from the file.

You can have any number of different material files — each having a filename extension of .mli — to make a library of material files. You can, for example, have your materials for building interiors in one file, materials for exteriors in another, materials for metals in another, and so forth. You create and manage the files in this library also through the MATLIB command.

AutoCAD comes with a ready-made collection of about 150 materials in the file render.mli. If the version of render.mli in your computer has only about 4 materials, read the instructions at the beginning of the mapping section for loading the larger version of render.mli from the AutoCAD CD-ROM. As you have time, you will want to look at the materials in this file. The file encompasses a wide range of material types, and you are likely to find that some are useful but, many are not. As you find materials that are useful, transfer them into your own files so the materials are better organized and easier to find.

| Command: | MATLIB |
|---|---|
| Purpose: | This command enables you to create, manage, and use a collection of rendering materials. |
| Initiate with: | • On the command line, enter MATLIB. |
| | • From the View pull-down menu, select Render, and then Materials Library. |
| | • Select the Materials Library button from the Render toolbar. |
| | • Click the Materials Library button in the Materials dialog box of the RMAT command. |
| Options: | The MATLIB command uses the Materials Library dialog box. You also can access this dialog box through the RMAT command, and you are likely to often use that approach because it allows you to both retrieve materials and attach them to objects. It also allows you to delete unwanted materials from your drawing file. |

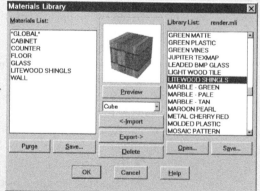

All the materials in the current drawing are shown in a list on the left side of the dialog box, while a list of the materials in the library file are shown on the right side of the dialog box. You can select any number of items in either list (to make multiple selections, hold down the Control key as you click item names), but you can work in only one list at a time. After materials have been selected, they are highlighted, and buttons for appropriate options are available.

The following options are available for items in the materials list:

- Purge       When you click this button, all unattached materials in the materials list are deleted, even if they are not highlighted.

- Save        All materials in the material list, whether they are highlighted or not, are saved in a file having an .mli filename extension when this button is clicked. AutoCAD prompts for the name and the location of the file.

- Export      When this button is clicked, the highlighted materials are added to the library list. If the exported material has the same name as a material in the library list, AutoCAD displays a dialog box for you to use in reconciling the duplication.

The following options are available for items in the library list:

- Open        You can switch to another material file by clicking this button. A dialog box for finding and specifying the file will be displayed.

- Save        Click this button to save the materials in the library list in a new materials file. The file will have an .mli extension, and AutoCAD displays a dialog box for you to use to specify a name and location for the file.

- Import      Highlighted materials in the library list are added to the materials list when this button is clicked. If a name conflict occurs, AutoCAD displays a dialog box to help you resolve it.

The following options are available for items in either list:

- Preview     This panel gives you an idea of what the selected material looks like when it is attached to a solid sphere or a cube.

- Delete      The selected items are deleted when this button is clicked. If the material is attached, AutoCAD displays a warning and asks you to confirm the deletion.

## Exercise Four

Open the file f1955.dwg from the CD-ROM that accompanies this book. The model in this file is a one-room café or coffee shop that contains some chairs, tables, and other furnishings. A plan view diagram of the model is shown in Figure 4-1.

The first step in creating a rendering of this room is to establish a perspective view and set up a clipping plane to see inside the room. Here are the DVIEW command options and parameters that position the target, camera, and front clipping plane to do that:

```
Points option:
Target point: 0,4',5'
Camera point: @32'<10<10
Distance option:
Distance: 32'
Clip option:
Front clip plane location: 23'
```

```
Zoom option:
Zoom level: 40
Pan option:
Pan the view as needed to center the objects
Exit DVIEW
```

Be certain that you include the apostrophes, which incate feet, in the distance and coordinate point input. Notice that a relative spherical coordinate was used to specify the camera location. Your view of the room should be similar to the one in Figure 4-2, when hidden-line removal is on.

If you prefer, you can use the options of 3DORBIT to set up a view and clipping plane similar to this one without entering data from the keyboard. If you have problems establishing the view, initiate the VIEW command and select the view named PER_40 to be the current view.

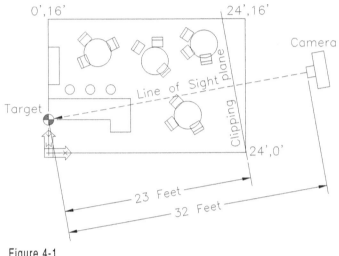

Figure 4-1

The lights for rendering this model have been installed for you. There are three of them — two distant lights and one spot light. You can use the LIGHT command to review the settings of these lights. One distant light, named D_TOP, simulates sunlight shining through the skylights of the room. The other distant light, D_FRONT, is aimed approximately in the same direction as the view's line of sight, and adds overall brightness to the room. The spotlight, SPOT_1, illuminates the back wall of the room.

Ten different materials have been created for the room. Of these materials, CHAIR_PAD, DARK_WOOD, LIGHT_WOOD, PILLAR, POT_BLUE, POT_RED, and WALLS do not use bitmaps. The material named FLOOR uses checkop.tga as a bitmap to create black and white floor tiles. The PICTURE material uses earthmap.tga to create the picture on the left wall of the room. Marbpale.tga is used as the bitmap for the TABLE_TOP material, which is attached to the round table tops and the top of the counter.

Cloud.tga is used as a rendering background to simulate the sky as seen through the room's skylights. This file, along with those used in materials, are supplied by AutoCAD. F1955.dwg was saved within AutoCAD 2002, and as a result the path of the bitmap files is

```
C:\Program Files\AutoCAD 2002\Textures
```

Figure 4-2

Figure 4-3

If you are using AutoCAD 2000 or 2000i, or if you have used other than the default AutoCAD installion folders, you will have to correct the path in the three materials that use bitmaps and in the background image file.

A grayscale rendering of the room is shown in Figure 4-3, and a color rendering is shown on the cover of this book. You might now want to modify the rendering materials and lights, reposition the objects in the room, or even add new objects to it.

### Table 19-1 AutoCAD Supplied Bitmap Files That Are Useful in Renderings

| File | Size in Pixels | Description |
|------|----------------|-------------|
| **Wood:** | | |
| ashsen.tga | 320 x 200 | light-colored wood pattern |
| bubinga.tga | 320 x 200 | dark wood pattern |
| oak_bed1.tga | 256 x 131 | light-colored wood veneer |
| oak_bed2.tga | 310 x 135 | light-colored wood veneer |
| teak.tga | 320 x 200 | dark wood pattern |
| whiteash.tga | 320 x 200 | light-colored wood pattern |
| **Brick and concrete:** | | |
| cement.tga | 125 x 100 | gray finished cement |
| grybrick.tga | 128 x 78 | gray brick with white mortar |
| **Stone and marble:** | | |
| benediti.tga | 320 x 200 | light-gray mottled compound marble |
| granite.tga | 73 x 65 | polished gray granite |
| gravel1.tga | 64 x 64 | polished pink-and-blue gray granite |
| graymarb.tga | 320 x 200 | gray marble with black-and-white veins |
| marbpale.tga | 320 x 200 | light-gray polished marble with pink veins |
| marbteal.tg | 320 x 200 | blue-green marble with white veins |
| pinkmarb.tga | 178 x 146 | bright pink marble in four squares |
| **Tile and patterns:** | | |
| bmmarop.tga | 99 x 81 | four square gray tiles |
| brwmmarb.tga | 101 x 83 | four square brown tiles with marble pattern |
| checker.tga | 161 x 153 | four squares — two black and two white |
| checkers.tga | 394 x 319 | 16x13 set of light blue-and-white squares |
| checkop.tga | 391 x 390 | 16x16 set of black-and-white squares |
| conctile.tga | 93 x 69 | single light-gray tile with darker-gray border |
| idkwood.tga | 32 x 32 | light and dark square wood tiles |
| inlay3.tga | 103 x 108 | wood inlay pattern |

### Table 19-1 AutoCAD Supplied Bitmap Files That Are Useful in Renderings (Continued)

| | | |
|---|---|---|
| inlay4.tga | 103 x 108 | wood inlay pattern |
| tile*.tga | 106 x 106 | single floor tile with black border |
| pat*.tga | various | various geometric patterns for tile or wallpaper |
| **Miscellaneous:** | | |
| lattic1.tga | 40 x 40 | single white X on black background |
| lattic2.tga | 40 x 40 | single white X, shaded, on black background |
| bluchina.tga | 258 x 194 | random white patterns on a dark-blue background |
| fence.tga | 320 x 200 | chain-link fence |
| **Bump maps:** | | |
| bmbricb.tga | 128 x 78 | bump map for bmbrick.tga |
| bmbrick.tga | 128 x 78 | texture map, dark red/brown brick |
| camoflab.tga | 140 x 114 | bump map for camofla.tga |
| camoflag.tga | 138 x 112 | texture map, green camouflage pattern |
| imarble1.tga | 64 x 64 | light brown and white — no distinct veins |
| istone2.tga | 64 x 64 | light-gray rounded stone |
| imetalb.tg | 64 x 64 | bump map for imetal.tga |
| imetal.tga | 64 x 64 | texture map, metal tread plate |
| iltwood1.tga | 86 x 88 | light-colored wood pattern |
| ishingl2.tga | 64 x 64 | reddish-brown cedar shingles |
| ipavers.tga | 64 x 64 | dark-gray brick with white mortar |
| ivines.tga | 66 x 65 | green foliage |
| **Backgrounds:** | | |
| biglake.tga | 20 x 200 | lake and snow-covered mountain |
| cloud.tga | 320 x 200 | deep-blue sky with white, lacy clouds |
| house.tga | 512 x 241 | Victorian house, front view |
| sky.tga | 320 x 200 | blue sky with fluffy clouds |
| sunset.tga | 320 x 200 | stratus clouds at sunset |
| valley_l.tga | 512 x 480 | yellow tree, sagebrush, and mountains |

# CHAPTER 20

# Landscape Objects and Depth Perception

*AutoCAD has a set of tools for improving the realism of renderings. These tools include objects that you can add to renderings for representing such things as trees and shrubs, which enable you to emphasize distance by making far objects hazy.*

*This chapter*

- *explains how to insert realistic bitmap images of trees, shrubs, people, and so forth in renderings;*

- *tells you how to enhance the illusion of distance in renderings by making far objects hazy.*

In addition to tools for incorporating lights and materials in renderings, AutoCAD's Renderer contains tools for adding external objects to renderings. If, for instance, you want to have a tree within a rendering, you don't need to construct a 3D tree; instead, you can insert an external object that looks like a tree.

Often, these external objects represent trees and shrubs, and therefore, they are generally referred to as *landscape objects*. Despite the name, however, the objects also can represent people, automobiles, signs, and so forth. They are based on bitmap images from photographs of real objects. All you need is a suitable pair of images. (As explained later in this chapter, two bitmap images are needed for each object.)

These landscape objects are comparable to cardboard cutouts used in a department store window or as scenery in a stage play in that they are 2D surfaces with an image that resembles a 3D object. Nevertheless, they are able to cast shadows, just as if they were 3D objects. Furthermore, you can have them always face the current viewing direction. Thus, when you switch from a front view of a house to a side view, the landscape objects automatically rotate to face the new view direction.

AutoCAD has three commands relating to landscape objects. LSNEW is for installing a landscape object, LSEDIT is for modifying the features of an installed object, and LSLIB is for managing the bitmap files used as landscape objects.

AutoCAD's renderer also has a tool for simulating the visual effects of distance. Just as real objects, such as hills and city skylines, become hazy and dim when they are far away, you can have objects in a rendering become hazy and dim. The AutoCAD command that manages this effect is FOG.

As you would expect, Photo Real or Photo Ray-traced rendering must be used for the landscape and fog features to have an effect. In this chapter, you will first explore landscape objects, and then see how the tools for creating distant effects work.

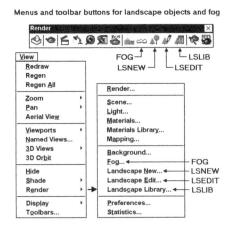

Menus and toolbar buttons for landscape objects and fog

## Landscape Objects

Installing landscape objects is a straightforward process that you will have little or no trouble with. You install them one at a time with the LSNEW command. This command uses a dialog box, through which you specify the following parameters:

- *The landscape object.* Although landscape objects are based on bitmap files that often have cryptic names, such as 8tree44l.tga, they go by names that are reasonably descriptive, such as Quaking Aspen. The names of available objects are shown in a list box, and you click the name of the object you want. Moreover, you can use a preview panel to see what an object looks like.

- *Geometry style.* The landscape object is projected onto a planar object that AutoCAD creates. As an alternative, you can have the image projected onto two planes that intersect at right angles. This can enhance the realism of some objects, such as a tree. If your landscape object is a sign, however, stick with a single plane.

- *View Aligned.* You can choose whether you want the landscape object to always face the same direction or to automatically rotate to match the current view direction. Generally, you will have 3D objects, such as trees and shrubs, be view-aligned. However, if the object represents a 2D object, such as a stop sign, you might want its orientation to be fixed. If you ever want to change the orientation of a nonview-aligned object, you can rotate it with the AutoCAD ROTATE command.

- *Height.* You specify a height for the landscape object, using the current drawing units. The height of a tree, for example, might be 240 inches (20 feet), and the height of a bush might be 48 inches (4 feet). Height, as you would expect, is in the Z-axis direction. Unfortunately, AutoCAD does not permit you to specify a height that is greater than 100 units. As a result, the tallest tree you can insert is only 8'-4" high, when your model is based on architectural units.

- *Position.* By default, AutoCAD inserts landscape objects at the UCS origin. You can, however, specify any base point you want. You also can move objects, through the Move command or through their grips, after they have been inserted.

Landscape objects are able to cast shadows when Photo Raytrace rendering is in effect. After a landscape object has been inserted, you can use AutoCAD commands and grips to erase it, move it, make copies of it, and change its height. You also can rotate it, provided it is not a view-aligned object. You can modify the landscape object through the LSEDIT command. This command uses a dialog box that is identical to that used by the LSNEW command. You cannot, however, change the image of an inserted landscape object.

Every landscape object is based on two bitmap files. One, called the image file, contains the image you will see in the rendering on a black background. The other, called the opacity file, has the area of the image filled with white. It too has a black background. See the figure in the discussion of the LSLIB command in this chapter for an example.

This image file and opacity map combination is similar to a texture and opacity map combination in a rendering material. In fact, you can use the bitmap file pairs intended for landscape objects in a material and attach it to a 3D face plane to create your own landscape object. There is no reason to do this, however, because it involves more work than the renderer's landscape objects, and the results are not as good.

The image file and its companion opacity file are linked together with the LSLIB command. This command also allows you to assign a meaningful name, such as Quaking Aspen, to the pair of files. Similar to the material libraries, you can group any number of landscape objects together and save them in a landscape library file. They always have a filename extension of LLI.

When you begin the LSNEW command, the landscape objects it lists as being available for installation are those in the current landscape library. If the landscape object you want is not in the list, you have to exit the LSNEW command and use the LSLIB command to open the landscape library file that contains the object you want. Then, that landscape library is the current one, and the LSNEW command's list of landscape objects include the object you want to install. This is somewhat awkward, but it's not really a problem because AutoCAD supplies the files for only 11 landscape objects, and they conveniently fit in one library.

The CD-ROM supplied with this book contains the files for 11 more landscape objects for trees. (See Appendix A for information about the files and for locating the files you are interested in.)

The default current landscape library is render.lli, and if you used the typical AutoCAD installation, there may be only one landscape object in it. If this is the case, you should replace your abbreviated render.lli file with the one on the AutoCAD CD-ROM. This gives you access to all 11 landscape objects. On the CD-ROM, render.lli is in folder \Acad\Support. The render.lli file it should replace in your computer is in the AutoCAD 200X\Support folder. The bitmap files (which all have a tga filename extension) needed for the landscape objects are already in your computer, provided you followed the instructions for loading all AutoCAD's bitmap files in your computer that were in the section on mapping in Chapter 19.

## Exercise One

You will add some trees and shrubs to the rendering of the 3D surface model house that you have been working with throughout this book. Open your file of the model, or else retrieve file f1929.dwg from the CD-ROM that comes with this book, and open it. File f1929.dwg was saved in AutoCAD 2002. Therefore, if you are opening it in AutoCAD 2000 or 2000i, you need to modify the BRICK_WALL and SHINGLES materials by changing the path for their Color/Pattern maps, and for the bump map of BRICK_WALL, to indicate the location where your texture files are stored. You also need to update the path to the the image (cloud.tga) used for a rendering background.

Use AutoCAD's VIEW command to make the view named DIST_80 the current one, or use an equivalent view if you are working with the file you created. Use the VPORTS command to divide the AutoCAD graphics area into four equal-sized, two up and two down, viewports. In one of these viewports, invoke the PLAN command so that the viewing direction is straight down on the WCS X-Y plane. This allows you to use your pointing device to position the landscape objects in one viewport and to make renderings in the other viewports.

Start the LSNEW command. If the list box of the Landscape New dialog box does not contain the names of 11 landscape objects, stop and replace your render.lli file with the one on the AutoCAD CD-ROM. The instructions for doing this were given a few paragraphs ago.

In the Landscape New dialog box, select the landscape object named Wandering Yew by clicking on its name. Click the Crossing Faces radio button and the View Aligned check box. Set the object's height to 48 (4 feet). Click the Position button, and place the base of the object at the WCS coordinates of 5'-0",5'-0",0'-0". Then, click the OK button. Two intersecting triangles appear in the perspective views. You want two of these plants, so use the AutoCAD COPY command to make a duplicate of the one you just created. Locate the copy at the WCS coordinates of 8'-0",5'-0",0'-0".

Rendering times for this model are becoming increasingly longer. If you want to see how these two landscape objects look when they are rendered, use the Crop Window option of the RENDER command to render just the area around the two plants. You should also use Photo Raytrace rendering. This actually speeds up rendering times a little, but more importantly it enables the landscape object to cast shadows.

Invoke the LSNEW command again. This time, select Bush #1 as the landscape object. Click the Crossing Faces geometry radio button and the View Aligned check box. Although there isn't much difference in the appearance of crossing faces and a single face with this bush, crossing faces casts better shadows. Set its height to 36, position its base at the WCS coordinates of 30'-0",-1'-0",0'-0", and click the OK button of the Landscape New dialog box. Then, make two copies of the plant — one placed at the WCS coordinates of 30'-0",-7'-0",0'-0" and the other at the WCS coordinates of 30'-0",-13'-0",0'-0".

The next landscape object you will install is a person, rather than a plant. Start LSNEW, and select People #2 as the landscape object. Set Geometry to Single Face, click View Aligned, and set Height to 70 (5'-10"). Position the base of the object at the WCS coordinates of 29'-0",6'-0",1'-0". (Do not overlook the 1'-0" Z coordinate.)

Next, place a tree in the rendering. Select Sweetgum, Summer, from the list of objects in the Landscape New dialog box. Set its geometry to Crossing Faces and View Aligned. Give it a height of 36, and position it at the WCS coordinates of 25'-0",-21'0",0'-0". Invoke the SCALE command. Select the sweetgum tree landscape object, specify the WCS coordinates of 25'-0",-21'0",0'-0" as the base point, and 10 as the scale factor. The tree is now 30 feet tall.

Lastly, place a tree in back of the house. Start LSNEW, and select Quaking Aspen from the Landscape New dialog box's list of landscape objects. Use a Single Face (this makes the tree broader than crossing faces), and set it to View Aligned. Set its height to 36, and place it at the WCS coordinates of 3'-0",43'-0",0'-0". Then, use the SCALE command with a scale factor of 10 to make the tree 30 feet tall.

Your rendering of the model should now resemble the one shown in grayscale in Figure 1-1. On the CD-ROM that accompanies this book, the model and the

Figure 1-1

landscape objects are in file f2002.dwg. This file also has been saved in AutoCAD 2002, so you will need to modify the file's paths to the bitmaps and landscape objects as described at the beginning of this exercise.

| | |
|---|---|
| Command: | LSNEW |
| Purpose: | This command installs new rendering landscape objects in a drawing. |

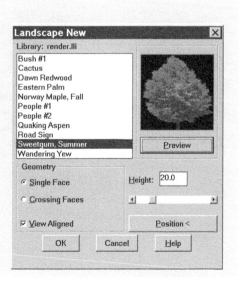

Initiate with:
- On the command line, enter LSNEW.
- From the View pull-down menu, select Render, and then Landscape New.
- Select the Landscape New button from the Render toolbar.

Options:

LSNEW uses a dialog box titled Landscape New. Objects in the current landscape library file are shown in a list box in the upper-left corner of this dialog box. (See the upcoming description of the LSLIB command for instructions in establishing the current landscape library file.) Select the object in this list box that you want installed in the drawing by clicking once on its name.

In nonrendered views, landscape objects have either a triangular or a rectangular shape, depending upon the installation options selected. The name of the landscape object is displayed on the object.

- Preview

When you click this button, an image of the selected landscape object appears in the panel.

- Single Face/
Crossing Faces

You must select one or the other of these two radio buttons. When Single Face is selected, the image is projected onto a single planar face. When Crossing Faces is selected, the image is projected onto two planar faces that intersect at a 90 degree angle. The intersecting faces are usually slanted to the view line of sight, which causes the rendered object to be thinner that that of a single face object.

Single Face     Crossing Faces

In nonrendered views, single face landscape objects appear as a single triangle or as a rectangle, depending on whether or not the object is view-aligned. Crossing faced objects appear as two triangles that intersect at right angles.

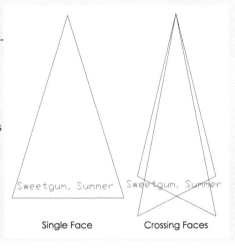

Sweetgum, Summer     Sweetgum, Summer

Single Face          Crossing Faces

- View Aligned

When this toggle is on, the landscape object always faces the current horizontal view direction. Whenever the view point is changed, the landscape object automatically rotates to face the new view. When the toggle is off, the orientation of the landscape object is fixed in a plane that is parallel with the WCS Z-X plane.

In nonrendered views, single-faced fixed landscape objects appear as rectangles. You can rotate these objects. Single-faced view-aligned objects, on the other hand, are triangular, and cannot be rotated manually.

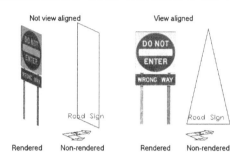

Crossing-faced objects are always shown in nonrendered views as two triangles. The triangles of a view-aligned object are always 45 degrees to the current view direction's horizontal angle from the X axis, while those of fixed objects are parallel with the WCS Z-X and Y-Z planes. You can rotate fixed crossing-faced objects.

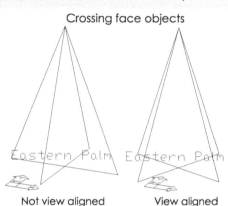

- Height

Specify the height of the landscape object with the slider or by entering a value in the edit box. The maximum value you can specify is 100. The default height is 20. The units of height are those of the current AutoCAD drawing file. Height is always in the positive Z-axis direction of the UCS.

- Position

You can specify the base location of the landscape object when you click this button. AutoCAD hides the dialog box and issues a command line prompt for you to specify the base of the landscape object. The default location is the UCS origin.

Notes:

- Use Photo Raytrace rendering to enable shadow casting by landscape objects.

| | |
|---|---|
| Command: | LSEDIT |
| Purpose: | This command modifies rendering landscape objects that are in a drawing. |
| Initiate with: | • On the command line, enter LSEDIT. |
| | • From the View pull-down menu, select Render, and then Landscape Edit. |
| | • Select the Landscape Edit button from the Render toolbar. |

Options: This command starts with a command line prompt for you to select a landscape object. You can select only one object, and you must do so by picking a point on it. As soon as you pick a landscape object, AutoCAD displays the Landscape Edit dialog box.

The type of object you selected is highlighted in the landscape object list box. The other landscape object types in the current landscape library are also listed, but they are grayed-out and cannot be accessed. You can edit only the object you selected, and you cannot change its landscape object type.

The options in the Landscape Edit dialog box are the same as those in the Landscape New dialog box of the LSNEW command.

| | |
|---|---|
| Command: | LSLIB |
| Purpose: | This command creates and manages files containing landscape objects. |
| Initiate with: | • On the command line, enter LSLIB. |
| | • From the View pull-down menu, select Render, and then Landscape Library. |
| | • Select the Landscape Library button from the Render toolbar. |

Options: The LSLIB command displays the Landscape Library dialog box. The name of the current landscape library file is shown in the upper-left corner of the dialog box, and the names of the objects in that file are shown below it in a list box. You can highlight a name in this list box by clicking on it. The highlighted object can then be modified or deleted.

- Modify/New

The Modify option is for changing the parameters of the landscape object highlighted in the landscape objects list box. The New option is for defining a new landscape object that will be added to the contents of the list box. Both of these options use a dialog box that is the same except for its title. Modify uses a dialog box titled Landscape Library Edit, while New uses one titled Landscape Library New.

**Landscape Library Edit**

Default Geometry
- ⦿ Single Face
- ○ Crossing Faces
- ☑ View Aligned

Preview

Name: Norway Maple, Fall

Image File: maple.tga    Find File...

Opacity Map File: maple_op.tga    Find File...

OK    Cancel    Help

- Default Geometry

These two radio buttons and one check box determine the default settings for the landscape object's geometry options in the Landscape New dialog box of the LSNEW command. See the discussion of that command for their descriptions.

- Name

Enter a descriptive name for a new landscape object, or modify the name of an existing one, in this edit box. The name can have up to 17 characters, including spaces. This name appears in the Landscape Library list box, as well as the Landscape New list box of the LSNEW command.

- Image File

Two bitmap files are needed for every landscape object. One contains a full color image of the landscape object on a black background — this is the image file. In the other file, the area of the landscape object is pure white, while the rest of the file image is pure black — this is the opacity map file. In a rendering, the image is projected onto the white area of the opacity map file, and the black area of both images is completely transparent. Enter the names of the two files for the landscape object you are creating in the appropriate edit box, or click the Find File button to browse for the files. The files AutoCAD supplies for landscape objects all have .tga filename extensions, but BMP, GIF, TIF, JPG, and PCX files are also accepted.

Image    Opacity map

- Preview     When you click this button, the image in the specified files is displayed in the panel.

- Delete     When you click this button of the Landscape Library dialog box, the highlighted landscape object will be removed from the current landscape library file.

- Open     Use this option to change from the current landscape library file to another. A folder and file dialog box is displayed to help you locate the file you want. All landscape library files have an .lli filename extension.

- Save     This option saves the contents of the current landscape library file. A dialog box is displayed to help you specify the location and name of the library file. The filename extension of the file is .lli.

# Fog and Depth Cueing

If you anticipate that the FOG command will produce an effect in your renderings similar to that of mist rising from the ground, you will be disappointed. Much like real fog, it results in an overall coloration of the rendering. You can make the fog white to produce a hazy effect, you can make it black to darken the rendering (when black is used, AutoCAD refers to the results as *depth cueing*), and you can use any color between these two extremes. You can have rose-colored fog if you like. The purpose of fog is to create an illusion of distance. Just as distant hills and buildings often appear hazy, you can make distant objects in renderings appear hazy.

AutoCAD bases distances at which fog takes effect on the back cutting plane of a view. Recall from Chapter 7 that cutting planes are established as an option of the DVIEW command, or with the 3DCLIP command. They are perpendicular to the line of sight, and they are located relative to the target point, which is set by either the DVIEW or CAMERA commands. The purpose of a back cutting plane is to hide everything that is behind it. After a cutting plane has been set up, it can be turned on and off. For the FOG command, you will want a back cutting plane established and turned on; but, you want it positioned so that it does not hide objects you want rendered.

### Exercise Two

Find the file named f2013.dwg on the CD-ROM that comes with this book, and open it. The model in this file, which is shown in Figure 2-1, is the downtown buildings of a city beside a large lake bisected by a river. You might create a model such as this for an urban design project.

The view for rendering this model is named PERS_01. It looks in the X-axis direction toward the tall buildings of the model. The rendering setup for this model is relatively simple. No bitmaps have been used in the materials, and only two lights have been installed. One distant light, with shadows turned on, simulates sunlight, and a second distant light, pointed approximately in the view's line of sight, adds general brightness to the rendering. A blue-to-white gradient has been established as the rendering background.

Make PERS_01 the current view. Start 3DORBIT and open its shortcut menu without changing the viewpoint. Select the More option, and select Back Clipping On. If this causes part of the model to disappear, open the More menu again and select Adjust Clipping Planes to move the back clipping plane behind the tall buildings. Then, exit 3DORBIT without changing the viewpoint.

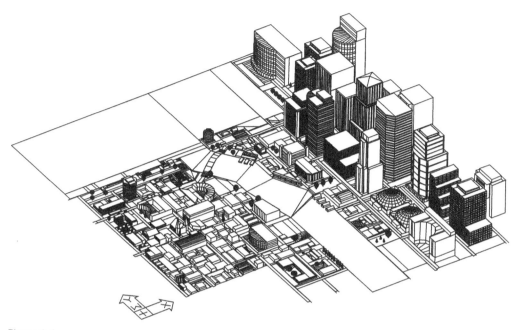

Figure 2-1

To compare the effects of various fog settings, use the the VPORTS command to divide the graphics area into four equal sized viewports — two above and two below. Start the RENDER command, set the rendering type to Photo Raytrace, and render one of the viewports without any fog effects. This rendering, which is shown in grayscale in Figure 2-2, serves as a comparison base.

Figure 2-2

Move to another viewport, and start the RENDER command again. Click the Fog/Depth Cue button to bring up the Fog dialog box. In this dialog box, click the Enable Fog toggle. Also click the Fog Background toggle. Set the fog color to white by moving the Red, Green, and Blue color sliders all the way to the right, or else enter 1.0 in their edit boxes.

Leave the Near Distance set to its default of 0.00 and Far Distance to its default of 1.00. Also, leave the Near and Far Fog Percentage setting at their default setting of 0.00 and 1.00. Then, click the OK button to return to the Render dialog box and render the viewport. The rendering will have a decidedly foggy appearance, with the fog density increasing with distance. The most distant buildings are barely visible, and the background is completely white.

Move to a third viewport. Start the RENDER command, and again go into the Fog dialog box. Change the Near Distance from 0.00 to about 0.50, and leave all the other settings as they are. The rendering will be similar to the previous one, except that the buildings on the near side of the river are in the clear. This is because the fog begins at about the river.

For the ren-
dering in the
fourth view-
port, reduce the
Far Fog Per-
centage to
about 0.80,
clear the Fog
Background
check box, and
leave all the
other fog set-
tings as they
are. In this ren-
dering, the sky
background is
completely
clear and the
tall buildings
are less hazy.

Figure 2-3

Figure 2-3 is a grayscale version of this rendering.

You should experiment on your own to see the results from various settings of fog distance and percentages. You should also see the effects of using black as a fog color. The results are comparable to those when white is used, except that distant objects in the rendering become darker rather than whiter.

Command:         FOG

Purpose:         During renderings, this command enables you to add color to objects that are beyond a specified distance from the back clipping plane. This color can enhance the illusion of distance.

Initiate with:   • On the command line, enter FOG.

                      • From the View pull-down menu, select Render, and then Fog.

                      • Select the Fog button from the Render toolbar.

                      • Click the Fog/Depth Cue button in the Render or Render Preferences dialog boxes, used by the RENDER and RPREF commands.

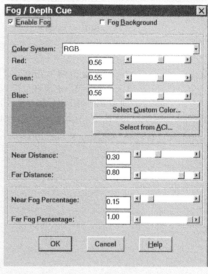

Options:         The FOG command uses a dialog box titled Fog/Depth Cue for setting its options.

                      • Enable Fog           This toggle button turns fog on and off. Although all other sections of the dialog box are grayed out when it is turned off, their current settings are retained and will be in effect when the Enable Fog toggle is turned back on.

                      • Fog Background      When this toggle is on, the fog settings also apply to the rendering background.

                      • Color Controls       Use the buttons and sliders in this section of the dialog box to set the color of the fog. You can choose between the RGB (Red — Green — Blue) and the HLS (Hue — Lightness — Saturation) color systems, and you can set the individual color components by entering values in the edit boxes or by moving the sliders. If you click the Select Custom Color button, a dialog box with panels showing a wide range of colors is displayed for you to choose a color. If you click the Select from ACI button, a dialog box showing the 255 standard AutoCAD Color Index colors is displayed. This is the same dialog box displayed by the DDCOLOR command.

| | |
|---|---|
| • Near Distance/Far Distance | These two distances represent the percent of the distance from the camera point to the back clipping plane. The higher the value, the closer the distance to the clipping plane. Near Distance is the distance at which the band of fog begins, and Far Distance is the distance at which it ends. |
| • Near Fog Percentage/Far Fog Percentage | The relative effect of the fog at the near and far distances is controlled by these two values. Their value can range from 0 to 1. The higher the value, the more the fog color hides objects. |

Notes:

- The camera point and the location of the back clipping plane are established through the DVIEW or 3DCLIP commands. The back clipping plane is perpendicular to the line of sight and is located relative to the target point, which is also established by the DVIEW command or by the CAMERA command.

- The back clipping plane must be turned on for the fog effects to work properly.

# Inside the Book's ZIP Files

There are three zip files availible for downlload:

| | |
|---|---|
| 3Dmodeling-utilities.zip | AutoLISP programs and script files referred to in the book |
| 3Dmodeling-exercises.zip | AutoCAD drawing files for the book's exercises |
| 3Dmodeling-images | Bitmap files that are useful in renderings |

You can download the files using CMP Books FTP site at: `ftp://ftp.cmpbooks.com/pub`

The files all have their read-only attribute set. You can not edit or modify the files in AutoCAD unless you clear the read-only file attribute.

To clear the read-only attribute of a file, highlight the name of the file in Windows Explorer. Then, press the right-hand button of your pointing device to bring up a shortcut menu. Select Properties from that menu to bring up the Properties dialog box. The attributes of the file are shown near the bottom of the General tab in this dialog box. Click the read-only attribute check box to clear it.

Also, you can use this same technique to clear file read-only attributes within AutoCAD's Select File dialog box, and you can clear the read-only attribute of multiple files by using any of the Windows file-selection methods to highlight them.

The layers in most of the AutoCAD files for the exercises use black as the object color. For many files, you will want to change the layer colors so they are appropriate to your computer's screen color.

**Utility folder file contents**

| File | Chapter | Description |
|------|---------|-------------|
| 4_lgr.lsp | 4 | Makes four model space viewports with preset view directions. |
| helix_01.scr | 5 | Script file to draw a simple 3D helix wireframe curve. |
| helix_02.scr | 5 | Script file to draw a complicated 3D helix wireframe curve. |
| helix_02.xls | 5 | Excel spreadsheet file that Helix_02.scr is based on. |
| spiral.lsp | 5 | Draws 3D wireframe helixes and spirals as 3D polylines. |
| join3dpl.lsp | 5 | Joins two 3D polylines. |
| mface.lsp | 6 | A front end for PFACE. |
| fplot.lsp | 8 | Uses 3DMESH to map mathematical functions. |
| globexyz.lsp | 11 | Additional location and size parameters for the SOLID command. |
| ps2ms.lsp | 15 | Moves objects from paper space to model space and vice versa. |

**Exercises folder file contents**

| File | Chapter | Description |
|------|---------|-------------|
| f0232.dwg | 2 | Completed wireframe exercise. |
| f0245.dwg | 2 | Completed 3D wireframe of a sheet metal part. |
| f0431.dwg | 4 | 3D wireframe for a house. |
| f0458.dwg | 4 | 3D wireframe for an automobile oil pan. |
| f0555.dwg | 5 | 3D wireframe for an automobile oil pan with splines. |
| f0564.dwg | 5 | 3D wireframe for an airplane propeller blade. |
| f0611.dwg | 6 | Walls made from extruded lines. |
| f0614.dwg | 6 | Three legged table made from extruded polylines. |
| f0641.dwg | 6 | 3D model house partially surfaced with 3D faces. |
| f0643.dwg | 6 | Oil pan partially surfaced with 3D faces. |
| f0652.dwg | 6 | Surface model of an air duct made with PFACE. |
| f0653.dwg | 6 | 3D model house with roof surfaced by PFACE. |
| f0737.dwg | 7 | 3D house with doors and windows for setting up perspective views. |
| f0740.dwg | 7 | A 3D kitchen and dining area for setting up perspective views and clipping planes. |
| af0833.dwg | 8 | Oil pan with 3D faces and extra wireframe curves, ready to be completely surfaced. |
| f0840.dwg | 8 | Completely surfaced oil pan. |
| f0841.dwg | 8 | Airplane propeller ready for surfacing. Has wireframes for hub. |
| f0847.dwg | 8 | Airplane propeller blade completely surfaced. |
| f0848.dwg | 8 | Three-blade airplane propeller surface model, with center hub. |

**Exercises folder file contents (Continued)**

| File | Chapter | Description |
|------|---------|-------------|
| f0911.dwg | 9 | 2D polyline and axis for exercise. |
| f0914.dwg | 9 | 3D mesh for 3D mesh-editing experiments. |
| f1015.dwg | 10 | Profile of a spur gear as a region. |
| f1022.dwg | 10 | Spur gear extruded into a 3D solid. |
| f1025.dwg | 10 | Extrusion along a helix-shaped path. |
| f1029.dwg | 10 | Sides of a thick-walled pan from extruded profiles. |
| f1043.dwg | 10 | Two similar profiles revolved about different axes. |
| f1046.dwg | 10 | Thick-walled pan with corners from revolved solids. |
| f1104.dwg | 11 | Thick-walled pan with bottom added. |
| f1110.dwg | 11 | Exercise in making a wedge primitive. |
| f1118.dwg | 11 | Thick-walled pan with cylinders added flange for holes. |
| f1128.dwg | 11 | Exercise in making a cone primitive. |
| f1205.dwg | 12 | Thick-walled pan with pieces unioned. |
| f1208.dwg | 12 | Spur gear solid model with center hole subtracted. |
| f1209.dwg | 12 | Thick-walled pan with holes in flange. Completed model. |
| f1215.dwg | 12 | Pyramid made with the INTERSECT command. |
| f1216.dwg | 12 | 2D drawing outlines to be extruded. |
| f1220.dwg | 12 | Outline extrusions transformed into a 3D solid model with INTERSECT. |
| f1231.dwg | 12 | Flanged pipe elbow solid model. |
| f1239.dwg | 12 | Sheet metal part with complex bends. Solid model. |
| f1305.dwg | 13 | Three solid models for practicing fillets. |
| f1310.dwg | 13 | Flanged pipe elbow solid model. Completed. |
| f1321.dwg | 13 | Sheet metal part with fillets and chamfers. Completed. |
| f1328.dwg | 13 | Solid model of a wrench that is to be shortened. |
| f1364.dwg | 13 | Solid model to modify with SOLIDEDIT. |
| f1369.dwg | 13 | Modified solid model. |
| f1370.dwg | 13 | Profiles for creating a complex solid model. |
| f1383.dwg | 13 | Completed complex solid model. |
| f1417.dwg | 14 | Model for exercises with INTERFERE and SECTION. |
| f1542.dwg | 15 | Dimensioned, multiview paper space drawing of the oil pan. AutoCAD 2000 and 2000i version. |
| f1542a.dwg | 15 | Dimensioned, multiview paper space drawing of the oil pan. AutoCAD 2002 version. |

**Exercises folder file contents (Continued)**

| File | Chapter | Description |
|------|---------|-------------|
| f1607.dwg | 16 | Isometric drawing made from the flanged pipe elbow. |
| f1625.dwg | 16 | Dimensioned, multiview drawing of the pipe elbow. AutoCAD 2000 and 2000i version. |
| f1625a.dwg | 16 | Dimensioned, multiview drawing of the pipe elbow. AutoCAD 2002 version. |
| f1715.dwg | 17 | Demonstration of rendering features. |
| f1814.dwg | 18 | Solid model for light installion exercise. |
| f1816.dwg | 18 | Solid model with lights installed. |
| f1817.dwg | 18 | 3D surface model kitchen and dining area for light-installation exercise. |
| f1818.dwg | 18 | Kitchen and dining area with lights installed. |
| f1819.dwg | 18 | 3D surface model house for light-installation exercise. |
| f1820.dwg | 18 | 3D house with rendering lights installed. |
| f1929.dwg | 19 | 3D house with materials attached. |
| f1955.dwg | 19 | 3D café with lights and materials. |
| f2002.dwg | 20 | 3D house with landscape objects installed. |
| f2013.dwg | 20 | 3D surface model city for an exercise with FOG. |

**Image folder file contents**

The Image folder contains files of bitmap images that are useful in creatings backgrounds, materials, and landscape objects for renderings. See the file readme.txt for the contents and description of the files in this folder.

# Index